Approaches to
Social Research

Approaches to Social Research

Royce Singleton, Jr.
Holy Cross College

Bruce C. Straits and Margaret M. Straits
University of California, Santa Barbara

Ronald J. McAllister
Northeastern University

New York   Oxford
OXFORD UNIVERSITY PRESS
1988

Oxford University Press

Oxford   New York   Toronto
Delhi   Bombay   Calcutta   Madras   Karachi
Petaling Jaya   Singapore   Hong Kong   Tokyo
Nairobi   Dar es Saalam   Cape Town
Melbourne   Auckland

and associated companies in
Beirut   Berlin   Ibadan   Nicosia

Library of Congress Cataloging-in-Publication Data

Approaches to social research.

Bibliography: p.
Includes index.
1. Social sciences—Research.   2. Social sciences—
Methodology.   I. Singleton, Royce.
H62.A628   1988   300′.72   87-12187
ISBN 0-19-504469-X

2 4 6 8 9 7 5 3 1

Printed in the United States of America
on acid-free paper

Preface

To the Student

Of all the courses we teach, none is more important than research methods. First of all, methodology is the heart of the social sciences; more than anything else, it is what distinguishes social science from journalism and social commentary, from the humanities and natural sciences. Understanding social research methods, therefore, should give you a better sense of sociology and related disciplines and of exactly what it is that social scientists do. To facilitate such understanding, in this book we have introduced an abundance of actual research studies that cover the full range of social science disciplines.

Second, the methods and findings of social research influence us in so many ways that a knowledge of social research is essential for making informed decisions about our daily lives. Many government social programs are shaped and evaluated by social research; businesses constantly rely on consumer research for key marketing and management decisions; the popular press daily reports research findings on the most personal aspects of peoples' lives—from altruism to zero population growth. One of the goals of this book is to help you understand the logic and limitations of social research so that you can evaluate it effectively.

Finally, the study of social research methods should sharpen your powers of critical thinking and evaluation and enable you to become a more intelligent gatherer of information. Social research consists of activities and ways of thinking in which everyone frequently and profitably can engage. Realizing that most readers will not become social scientists, we have linked many topics to familiar subjects and frames of reference so that you can see how broadly social research may be applied.

The book is organized into four sections. Section I, on the scientific and logical foundations of research, describes the general process of scientific inquiry (chapter 2) and the role of logical reasoning in this process (chapter 3). Section II, on research design, first introduces the basic terminology of social research (chapter 4) and then examines two key considerations in the planning or design of a study: the measurement of variables (chapter 5) and the sampling of units of analysis (chapter 6). Section III, on data collection, examines the four basic approaches to social research: experiments, surveys, field research, and research using available data. The four main chapters (7, 9, 11, and 12) describe the distinctive process of executing a study that characterizes each approach; two other chapters (8 and 10) discuss technical features of experiments and surveys; and the final chapter in this section (chapter 13) presents strategies for using a combination of methods and approaches. Section IV deals broadly with the interpretation phase of research. Here we discuss data processing and elementary data analysis (chapter 14), more advanced, multivariate analysis (chapter 15), as well as research ethics (chapter 16) and the writing of research reports (chapter 17).

The book has several special features. Key terms are italicized when they first appear in the text and are also listed at the end of each chapter. If you are unsure of the meaning of a term introduced earlier in the text, you can always refer to the comprehensive glossary at the end of the book. Each chapter also contains an integrative summary of main points as well as review questions and problems to help test your memory and mastery of material. Finally, boxes are inserted in each of the main chapters to complement and expand the text; these present interesting research examples, provide additional aids to learning, or discuss the historical, social, and political contexts of research.

To the Instructor

Research methods texts differ in various ways. Some books, emphasizing the "how to" aspect of the subject, try to provide students with the skills necessary to conduct their own research; others, emphasizing the "wherefore," try to make students more intelligent consumers of research findings. Still other texts, like this one, try to achieve a balance between the "how to" and "wherefore" of research. Some books simplify or ignore the complexities and contradictions of research; some are filled with hypothetical examples that idealize research procedures and outcomes. By contrast, this book discusses hundreds of actual studies drawn from sociology, social psychology, demography, history, education, and political science. Whereas some books present simpler, outmoded techniques of data processing and analysis, this book presents the latest data processing methods and goes beyond the dated discussion of three-variable "elaboration" in order to introduce students to the terminology and journal presentation formats of contemporary statistical modeling.

What primarily distinguishes this book from others, however, is the way that we choose to focus on the four most basic approaches to social research: experimentation, survey research, field research, and the use of available data. We discuss the advantages and disadvantages of each, while treating the approaches as complementary rather than mutually exclusive, ultimately advocating a multiple methods strategy (chapter 13). The decision to focus on overall approaches to conducting social research has several pedagogical advantages. First, it enables the reader to see each approach not as a method of data collection per se, divorced from research design and analysis, but as a fundamental choice that affects the entire research process. Other books tend to separate issues of design and data collection, or discuss certain design issues only in relation to specific approaches; for example, sampling techniques are described as survey methods, or measurement is described merely in terms of self-report questionnaire items. However, because measurement and sampling must be addressed in all research, we discuss these issues in relation to each basic approach. Second, the reader's sense of both the logic and the mechanics of doing research is enhanced by understanding the unique process of executing a study that distinguishes each approach (chapters 7, 9, 11, and 12). Unlike the present text, other methods texts disregard the field administration phase of survey research, limiting the discussion to sampling and/or questionnaire design. Similarly, other texts discuss experiments merely in terms of experimental design, without describing the basic parts or staging of experiments. A focus on the basic approaches, we believe, gives the reader a better sense of the integrity of social research and a greater appreciation both for its power and its limitations.

We feel strongly that social research methods is the most challenging and important course we teach. The challenges lie in doing justice to the complexities of research, in going beyond the simplest techniques to provide enough information for readers to become intelligent consumers of research, in developing an understanding not only of each individual stage of research but of the interrelatedness of all phases, and in presenting information about the "nuts and bolts" of research (e.g., how to draw a sample and how to code data for computer analysis) while not losing sight of the logic of inquiry or the overall research process. Much of what researchers do is informed by their understanding of the entire research process, so that elements of research design are dictated by a knowledge of the means of data collection and analysis. Thus, we precode questionnaires to facilitate data processing, and in anticipation of multivariate statistical analysis, we include seemingly irrelevant background items in a questionnaire. Getting students to comprehend this overall process is perhaps our greatest challenge, and we believe that this challenge is best met by focusing on the basic approaches to social research.

Aside from our emphasis on the four major approaches, we cover essentially the same topics found in most other methods texts in approximately the same sequence. We tell the student what makes social research scientific, discuss the relation between theory and research, introduce basic terminology, and then provide chapters on measurement, sampling, the major methods of data collection (i.e., the four approaches), data analysis, and ethics. Unlike most other texts, we also provide extended treatments of logical reasoning in social science, multiple methods (triangulation), and report writing.

Because we subsume methods of data collection under the four approaches, we do not have separate chapters on evaluation research, which we discuss in relation to experimental design (chapter 8), and on observational methods, which we cover in our discussion of field research (chapter 11). Rather than presenting largely outdated material, we have chosen not to devote a full chapter to index and scale construction. Instead, we discuss this topic relatively briefly in connection with multiple methods (chapter 13).

More advanced chapters have been included, but they may be skipped without any loss of continuity. This provides considerable flexibility in using the text, allowing instructors to adopt it either for a one- or two-term course, for a low-level undergraduate or more advanced graduate-level course. One can skip chapter 3, or both chapters 2 and 3, and go directly from chapter 1 to chapter 4. Other advanced chapters are 8 and 10, in which we discuss technical design issues related to experimentation and survey research, respectively. For instructors who want to examine the logic of experimental design, chapter 8 introduces sources of invalidity and basic true, factorial, and quasi-experimental designs. For instructors who emphasize survey research and want to engage students in collecting data, we have found chapter 10 on survey instrumentation very effective in preparing students to design their own questionnaires. Chapter 13, on multiple methods, and especially chapter 15, on multivariate analysis, also are advanced. Instructors teaching one-term courses may easily skip all or portions of the more advanced chapters.

In Appreciation

Various manuscript drafts of this book have been class tested several times with students at Holy Cross College and at the University of California, Santa Barbara. We owe a special debt to these students, especially those whose feedback helped to make this a better book. We also thank Victoria Swigert of Holy Cross for using the manuscript in several classes, even when it was in the very early stages of development. It was the faith in the project and constant support of colleagues like Victoria Swigert that were most instrumental in our seeing the book through to completion.

Several individuals read and helped us to improve specific chapters. We thank Bob Garvey, Dave Hummon, and Rogers Johnson of Holy Cross College, Ken Kerber of Data General, Don Zimmerman of the University of California, Santa Barbara, and Arnold Arluke, Morris Freilich, and Jack Levin of Northeastern University. Peter Callero of Western Oregon State College, Pam Oliver of the University of Wisconsin, and Paul Wiener of Western Michigan University reviewed the entire manuscript. We were very impressed by their professional competence and hope that they will appreciate, as much as we do, the improvements in the manuscript that were made as a result of their careful reviews.

Two individuals helped to prepare a comprehensive instructor's manual. Josephine Ruggiero of Providence College coauthored the manual and is responsible for the detailed chapter outlines and many of the objective questions. Lynne Forcier, Holy Cross '88, produced an excellent draft of answers for the manual by painstakingly answering every review question and problem in the text. We also wish to thank Siu Zimmerman for compiling the index.

Finally, Royce Singleton thanks Holy Cross College for its generous support. Much of his contribution to the manuscript was completed during a sabbatical year and with the support of a faculty fellowship provided by the college.

Contents

Chapter 1   Introduction   3

Why Study Research Methods?   3
   Consuming Research Evidence   4
   Producing Research Evidence   5
Topics for Research   6
Methodological Approaches to the Social World   7
   Some Preliminary Research Questions   8
   An Experimental Answer   9
   An Answer from Survey Research   10
   An Answer from Field Research   11
   An Answer from Available Data   12
Conclusions   13

**SECTION I   SCIENTIFIC AND LOGICAL FOUNDATIONS
OF SOCIAL RESEARCH   15**

Chapter 2   The Nature of Science   17

The Aim of Science   17
Science as Product   18
   Scientific versus Nonscientific Questions   18
   Knowledge as Description   21
   Knowledge as Explanation and Prediction   22
   Knowledge as Understanding   25
   Tentative Knowledge   27
Science as Process   28
   Empiricism   31
   Objectivity   32
   Control   33
Science: Ideal versus Reality   35
Summary   37

Chapter 3   The Logic of Scientific Reasoning   40

Logic and Reasoning   40
Elements of Logical Analysis   41
   Terms   41

Propositions   41
Arguments   42
Validity and Truth: Logic and Science   43
Deduction and Induction   44
Deductive Reasoning in Science   45
    Argument Forms   45
    The Deductive Pattern of Scientific Explanation   48
Inductive Reasoning in Science   50
    Inductive Generalization   52
    Testing Hypotheses: The Hypothetico-Deductive Method   54
Summary   60

SECTION II   RESEARCH DESIGN   65

Chapter 4   Elements of Research Design   67

Selecting Topics for Research   67
Units of Analysis   69
Variables   72
    Types of Variables   72
Relationships   74
    Relationships among Qualitative Variables   75
    Relationships among Quantitative Variables   76
    Relationships between a Qualitative and a Quantitative Variable   78
    The Nature of Causal Relationships   79
Stating Problems and Hypotheses   85
Research Purposes and Research Design   89
Stages of Social Research   91
Summary   93

Chapter 5   Measurement   97

The Measurement Process   97
    Conceptualization   98
    Specification of Variables and Indicators   98
    Operationalization   100
Operational Definitions in Social Research   100
    Verbal Reports   101
    Observation   104
    Archival Records   105
    Selection of Operational Definitions   105
Levels of Measurement   106
    Nominal Measurement   107
    Ordinal Measurement   108
    Interval Measurement   109
    Ratio Measurement   109
Reliability and Validity   110
    Sources of Error   112

Reliability Assessment   114
  Test–Retest Reliability   114
  Parallel Forms, Split-Half, and Internal Consistency Reliability   115
  Intercoder Reliability   116
  Improving Reliability   116
Validity Assessment   117
  Subjective Validation   118
  Criterion-Related Validation   119
  Construct Validation   120
A Final Note on Reliability and Validity   124
Summary   124

Chapter 6   Sampling   130

Why Sample?   131
Population Definition   134
Sampling Designs   136
Probability Sampling   137
  Random Selection   137
  Simple Random Sampling   140
  Stratified Random Sampling   145
  Cluster Sampling   147
  Systematic Sampling   151
Nonprobability Sampling   152
  Convenience Sampling   153
  Purposive Sampling   153
  Quota Sampling   154
Combined Probability and Nonprobability Sampling   155
Factors Affecting Choice of Sampling Design   156
  Stage of Research and Data Use   156
  Available Resources   157
  Method of Data Collection   157
Factors Determining Sample Size   158
  Population Heterogeneity   158
  Desired Precision   159
  Sampling Design   160
  Available Resources   161
  Number of Breakdowns Planned   161
Other Considerations   162
Summary   163

SECTION III   METHODS OF DATA COLLECTION   169

Chapter 7   Experimentation   171

The Logic of Experimentation   171
  Testing Causal Relations   172
  Matching and Random Assignment   174

Internal and External Validity   175
Sampling in Experiments   176
Staging Experiments   177
    An Example: Who Will Intervene?   178
    Introduction to the Experiment   179
    The Experimental Manipulation   181
    Manipulation Checks   182
    Measurement of the Dependent Variable   183
    Debriefing   183
    Pretesting   184
    Experimental and Mundane Realism   184
The Experiment as a Social Occasion   185
    Demand Characteristics   186
    Evaluation Apprehension   187
    Other Motives of Experimental Subjects   188
    Experimenter Effects   189
    Minimizing Bias Due to the Social Nature of Experimentation   190
Experimentation outside the Laboratory   192
    Field Experiments   192
    Experimental Designs in Survey Research   195
    Units of Analysis Other than Individuals   196
Summary   197

Chapter 8   Experimental Designs   201

Threats to Internal Validity   201
Pre-Experimental Designs   205
    Design 1: The One-Shot Case Study   205
    Design 2: The One-Group Pretest–Posttest Design   206
    Design 3: The Static-Group Comparison   207
True Experimental Designs   208
    Design 4: The Pretest–Posttest Control Group Design   208
    Design 5: The Posttest-Only Control Group Design   210
    Design 6: The Solomon Four-Group Design   210
    Overview of True Experimental Designs   211
Factorial Experimental Designs   212
    Interaction Effects   214
Quasi-Experimental Designs   217
    An Example: Interracial Attitudes and Behavior at a Summer Camp   219
Evaluation Research   225
    Internal Validity   225
    External Validity   227
Summary   228

Chapter 9   Survey Research   233

General Features of Survey Research   233
    Large-Scale Probability Sampling   233
    Systematic Procedures: Interviews and Questionnaires   235
    Sophisticated Data Analysis   236

Survey Research Designs   237
Advantages and Disadvantages of Surveys   239
Steps in Survey Research: Planning   240
    Constructing the Instrument   241
    Developing the Sampling Plan   243
Face-to-Face and Telephone Interviewing   243
    Face-to-Face Interviewing   244
    Telephone Interviewing   245
Self-Administered Questionnaires   247
A Final Note on Planning   248
Field Administration   251
    Interviewer Selection   251
    Interviewer Training   252
    Pretesting   253
    Gaining Access   253
    Interviewing   254
    Supervision and Quality Control   258
    Follow-up Efforts   259
Summary   260

Chapter 10   Survey Instrumentation   264

Materials Available to the Survey Designer   265
    Open and Closed Questions   265
    Direct and Indirect Questions   270
    Response Formats   271
    Visual Aids   274
    Existing Questions   274
"Sketches" or Preliminaries   275
    The Opening   275
    The Placement of Sensitive and Routine Questions   276
    Order, Flow, and Transition   276
Filling in the Sketch: Writing the Items   278
    Using Language Effectively   278
    The "Frame of Reference" Problem   281
    Reason Analysis   282
    Memory Problems   285
    Response Bias Problems   286
    Format Considerations   288
The Final Product   290
    Pretesting   290
Summary   291

Chapter 11   Field Research   296

When to Adopt Field Methods   297
Field Observation   299
    Nonparticipant Observation   300
    Participant Observation   302

Research Design and Sampling   304
    Sampling in Field Research   305
Stages of Field Research   306
    Selecting a Research Setting   307
    Gaining Access   309
    Presenting Oneself   311
    Gathering Information   314
    Analyzing the Data and Formulating Theory   317
The Anthropological Study of Brady's Bar   319
The Products of Field Research   320
Summary   322

Chapter 12   Research Using Available Data   326

Sources of Available Data   326
    Public Documents and Official Records   326
    Private Documents   331
    Mass Media   332
    Physical, Nonverbal Evidence   333
    Social Science Data Archives   334
Advantages of Research Using Available Data   335
    Understanding the Past   335
    Understanding Social Change   336
    Studying Problems Cross-Culturally   336
    Improving Knowledge through Replication and Increased Sample Size   336
    Savings on Research Costs   337
    Nonreactive Measurement   337
Obtaining and Sampling Available Data   338
Measurement Issues in Available Data Research   340
    Inadequate and Insufficient Measurement   340
    Indirect Measurement   342
    Reliability and Validity: Authenticity and Accuracy   342
Data Analysis and Interpretation   345
    Historical Interpretation   345
    Content Analysis   347
    Cohort Analysis   353
Summary   356

Chapter 13   Multiple Methods   360

Triangulation   360
Multiple Measures of Concepts within the Same Study   362
    Composite Measures: Indexes and Scales   363
    Structural Equation Modeling   367
Multiple Tests of Hypotheses across Different Studies   369
    Replications Using the Same Research Strategy: Compliance without Pressure   369
    Replications Using Different Research Strategies: Interpersonal Influence   371
Summary   374

SECTION IV DATA PROCESSING, ANALYSIS, AND INTERPRETATION 377

Chapter 14 Data Processing and Elementary Data Analysis 379

Beginning the Analysis 380
Data Processing 380
  Coding 381
  Editing 385
  Entering the Data 385
  Cleaning 386
  Data Modification 388
The Functions of Statistics in Social Research 388
Univariate Analysis 390
Bivariate Analysis 397
  Relationships Involving Nominal-Scale Variables 397
  Relationships between Two Ordinal-Scale Variables 401
  Relationships between a Nominal/Ordinal and an Interval/Ratio Variable 403
  Relationships between Two Interval/Ratio Scale Variables 405
Summary 408

Chapter 15 Multivariate Analysis 414

Modeling Relationships 415
Elaboration 417
Multiple-Regression Analysis 419
  A Three-Variable Example 419
  Use of Dummy Variables 424
  Other Linear Techniques 429
Log-Linear Modeling 430
  Using Odds to Describe Relationships 430
  Modeling Cell Frequencies 430
  Model Testing 432
  "Logit" Modeling 433
Summary 436
Appendix: Log-Linear Model Estimation 440
  Polytomous Variables 441

Chapter 16 Research Ethics 444

Treatment of Human Subjects 445
  Harm 446
  Informed Consent 448
  Deception 451
  Privacy 453
  Making Ethical Decisions 456
The Uses of Research: Science and Society 457
Summary 464

Chapter 17 Writing Research Reports   467

Using the Library for Research   467
Outlining and Preparing to Write   472
Major Headings   474
   The Abstract   474
   Introduction   475
   Literature Review   475
   Methods   476
   Findings   477
   Discussion   477
   References   478
Other Considerations   478
   The Writing–Reading Interface   478
   Revisions   479
   Length   479
Summary   480

Glossary   481
References   497
Name Index   517
Subject Index   523

Approaches to
Social Research

1

Introduction

People by nature are curious about the world around them. All you need to do is spend time with a 5-year-old child, and you will see this curiosity in flower. Why is the sky blue? How far is the moon? Where is California? When is Christmas? How much is 47 + 4? Often as people get older, they lose some of this spirit of inquiry; they stop asking the questions that curiosity encourages. But this is not true of everyone. Sometimes people who maintain their curiosity about the world become researchers—people whose vocation (or avocation) is to ask the why, how, where, when, and under-what-circumstances questions. This book is about how social science researchers operate. You will see, however, that the research process is not limited to the world of the professional researcher. The research process is made up of a series of steps, techniques, exercises, and events that can be applied to every sphere of life. The methods of research can be applied to investigate any curiosity— from such mundane issues as where to select a residence or a school, to such life-shaking questions as how to prevent disease or nuclear accidents.

The world lies waiting for the curious to observe, manipulate, make judgments about, and understand. The fundamental question is how this will be done. There are many ways of observing the world: up close through a microscope, with the naked eye, from far away through a telescope. The approach we take will depend in large part on the kind of question we want to ask and the tools at our disposal. Learning which questions to ask and which tools to use is essentially the business of research methods.

"Research methods" is the study of ways of understanding the world. It is an absolutely essential set of skills, insights, and tools needed to answer intelligently any but the simplest questions. If you are curious about the social world *or* plan to have such curiosity *or* had it once and would like to get it back, then you are a good candidate for studying research methods. Without such skills, insights, and tools you can easily be a foolish consumer, a misinformed voter, a poorer student than need be; the world may seem to be in a state of chaos to you. It is the job of the well-informed researcher to reveal the order in the chaos we call the world. It is the job of research methods to facilitate such a revelation of order.

Why Study Research Methods?

You may have pondered the question of why one should study research methods. Indeed, this question may be asked more often about research methods than about

3

any other area of study in the social sciences. Often we have heard students say: "I don't intend to go to graduate school. And I don't intend to do research. Why do I need to study ('suffer through') methods?" The irony in such a statement is that, beyond providing a foundation of knowledge for those who do go on to become social scientists, the study of research methods may provide more immediate and useful information than any other single course of study. A knowledge of methods can benefit you as both a consumer and producer of research evidence.

Consuming Research Evidence

You may be a consumer of research in several positions: as a student reading research reports and journal articles to satisfy your curiosity or to meet course requirements and write term papers; as a social worker, educator, librarian, journalist, manager, or other professional keeping up to date in your field and acquiring knowledge to guide you in making decisions; or as an average citizen attempting to deal with the varied claims that are purported to be based upon research. To make intelligent decisions about much day-to-day information you must be able to understand and evaluate it. It is unfortunately true that much research evidence reported in professional journals as well as in newspapers and on television either is itself in error or is misinterpreted. Let us consider some of the kinds of misinformation to which you are likely to be exposed.

A few years ago the Riverside, California *Press-Enterprise* contained an article with the following headline: "Beware Crosswalk Safety Lines—They're Dangerous." The article reported a study on safety in crosswalks which showed that more pedestrian accidents occur in marked crosswalks than in unmarked crosswalks by a ratio of six to one. Marked crosswalks refer to painted crosswalks without a guard, stop sign, or traffic light. Unmarked crosswalks refer to intersections with no painted crosswalk, no stop sign, traffic light, or other controlling device. The article went on to point out how shocked traffic engineers had been by this finding, to speculate about factors that might contribute to a pedestrian's apparent false sense of security and carelessness in marked crosswalks, and to mention the major policy implication of phasing out unnecessary crosswalks. Very interesting—yet are these conclusions warranted? A knowledge of social research methods will sensitize you to a major problem with this type of study that casts serious doubt on the conclusions. The problem is that statistical associations, such as that between marked crosswalks and pedestrian accidents, do not always imply that one factor has caused the other. Marking crosswalks, in other words, may not cause more accidents. In fact, a more plausible interpretation for the reported six to one accident ratio is that more accidents occur in marked crosswalks because pedestrians use them much more often and because they appear at intersections where the traffic is heaviest. If this is the reason for the greater number of accidents in marked crosswalks, then of course it makes no sense to consider phasing out "unnecessary crosswalks" or to speculate about pedestrians' lack of vigilance.

A knowledge of research methods also can make you aware of the mischievous use of research evidence by television advertisers. For example, how seriously should we take the TV pitch that "75 percent of doctors interviewed prescribed drug

X for relief of arthritic pain?" Among the questions that a careful researcher could raise about this "fact" are these:

1. How many doctors were interviewed? (The 75 percent statistic could be based on as few as four interviews.)
2. What were the doctors asked about their prescription of drug X? (If they were asked, "Have you ever prescribed drug X?" then they may be just as likely to prescribe drugs A, B, C, and D, as well as X.)
3. Who interviewed the doctors? (If the manufacturers of drug X did the interviewing, then they may have influenced, wittingly or unwittingly, the doctors to favor their product.)

Politicians also like to cite research when they believe that it supports their cause. Consider the 1978 gubernatorial campaign in Massachusetts. Most states, including Massachusetts, prohibit capital punishment. Yet one of the candidates chose to make this a campaign issue, claiming studies showed that capital punishment is a deterrent to crime. His opponent disagreed, suggesting that research findings do not support this conclusion. Although many people oppose capital punishment on moral grounds, the majority of people in the United States favor capital punishment, apparently because they believe it is a crime deterrent. It is important, therefore, to know something about the research evidence on this issue. How many studies have been conducted? What is the nature of the evidence? How consistent are the findings? A skeptical attitude such as this is one of the basic tenets of scientific inquiry. Scientists never accept a statement as true because someone, however authoritative he or she may be, says it is true. Conclusions are accepted because they are supported by evidence, and then only after the evidence has been examined thoroughly. [For the record, available evidence indicates that capital punishment may have a very brief deterrent effect on homicides but no net long-term effect (see D. P. Phillips, 1980).]

As every good social scientist knows, research findings must be interpreted and applied with great care. Whether your position requires that you know the policy implications of research findings or whether you are simply an ordinary citizen wanting to be better informed about such findings, the study of research methods can help you develop the ability to understand and evaluate the limits of social scientific knowledge.

Producing Research Evidence

In addition to being consumers, we also are gatherers and producers of research evidence. We manufacture evidence every time we seek out the opinions of others about some issue, attempt to estimate the prevailing opinion within a particular group, or draw conclusions about persons and events on the basis of our own observations. As a producer of information, you will find in this introduction to social research some principles and techniques that can be applied at levels of sophistication ranging from casual observation to the conduct of small-scale research projects.

Suppose you are trying to decide whether to take a certain course from professor X or professor Y. You have not taken courses from either professor before, but past experience tells you that the choice of professors is important. To gather information on which to base your decision, you may seek out opinions about the professors in question from fellow students. A knowledge of research principles could not only increase your awareness of the limitations in this approach but could also facilitate the collection of more trustworthy information. For example, research principles suggest that you can be more confident about your information if you have gotten opinions about both professors rather than just one. The reason is that a comparison case enables you to examine explanations that exist for findings about only one case. For instance, a generally negative or positive opinion about professor X may be due to the subject matter rather than to the professor; but this explanation could be eliminated if you discover a different opinion about another professor who teaches the same course. Following other principles, it could be shown that the trustworthiness of your information will also depend on (a) the number of opinions you have solicited, (b) the consistency of those opinions, (c) whether your informants' opinions have been formed and have been solicited independently of one another, and (d) how you have posed the question when asking for opinions about professors X and Y.

At a slightly less mundane level, a knowledge of research techniques is essential for the nonscientist who needs to acquire reliable information about a particular group. This occurs more often than you might think. For example, politicians often need to find out what their constituents think about an important legislative issue; corporate executives may need information about their clients' or employees' reactions to proposed policy changes; journalists may want to know something about the makeup of their newspaper's or magazine's readership or may want to determine a community's attitude toward certain services or policies as part of a story they are preparing; and students may want to collect data about student body behaviors or opinions as part of a term project or student newspaper article. None of these endeavors appears to entail the kind of massive research effort that would require expert researchers and statisticians. Yet each endeavor calls for the systematic collection of information, which is precisely what research methods is all about.

Topics for Research

The topics of research in the social sciences range broadly, from juvenile crime to political leadership and from organized religion to family violence. With such a wide range of topics it is reasonable to ask: "Is there anything that cannot be studied?" The answer, of course, is "yes." In fact, whether a topic is amenable to social science research hinges on two obvious criteria.

First, social scientific research is *social*. By this is meant that the research subject involves people, how they act, think, and feel, and how they interact with one another. It looks also at the groups that people form, from bowling clubs to leagues of nations, at relations within and among such groups, and at how they adapt to changes in society. Second, because of its *scientific* nature this type of

FIGURE 1.1. The world of social inquiry.

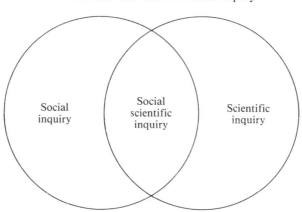

research is "empirical," that is, it is derived from observation. Of course, not all research (scholarly inquiry) is scientific per se, and not all scientific topics are within the purview of social science. Figure 1.1 depicts the possible combinations. As the figure shows, some scholarly inquiry is social without being scientific (such as philosophical studies on values and social ethics), while other types of inquiry may be scientific without being social (such as the research astronomers do on distant stars). The kind of scholarly inquiry addressed in this book is that which is both social *and* scientific. As we show in chapter 2, there are similarities among all types of scientific research. Many of the methods and techniques discussed here are not unique to the social sciences. Still, our concern is with research as it is practiced in such fields as anthropology, economics, history, political science, psychology, and sociology.

Methodological Approaches to the Social World

Among the social sciences there are four principal research strategies for under-standing the world: experiments, surveys, field research, and the use of available data. Each discipline tends to favor one particular strategy; for example, psycholo-gists typically conduct experiments, sociologists most often do survey research, anthropologists characteristically conduct field research, and historians tend to make use of available data. However, all four strategies are important to the world of social research, because any of the four can be used to study most social science topics. In fact, one of the early tasks of researchers is to decide which approach or approaches to take.

A discussion of the four basic strategies or approaches to social research com-prises the central core of this book (see chapters 7–12). As each strategy is dis-cussed, it will be seen that each has certain strengths and weaknesses that make the researcher favor one or another in different situations. Sometimes one strategy may not be feasible for ethical reasons (see chapter 16). Sometimes an approach will be ruled out because of constraints of time, personnel, space, or some other resource.

Furthermore, many researchers argue, as we do in chapter 13, that it is best, whenever feasible, to study a given problem with a variety of methods so that the weaknesses of one strategy may be cancelled out by the strengths of another. But it is often feasible to study a social science topic using any one of the four basic research strategies. To demonstrate this we will consider the topic of altruism.

Some Preliminary Research Questions

The subject of altruism has been investigated by social scientists for a number of years. It also has been the focus of some speculative philosophy as well, but this has not been scientific. Let us suppose that you as a social science researcher are interested in the subject of altruism. Where should you begin?

First of all, you will need to have some understanding of the concept. What do people mean by the word altruism? A quick library search would at least turn up a dictionary definition:

> **al·tru·ism** ('al-troo-iz m) *n*: Concern for the welfare of others, as opposed to egoism; selflessness (*The American Heritage Dictionary of the English Language*, 1976).

This gives you one meaning, but scientists like to be even more precise in defining their concepts. In particular, they would want to distinguish between altruism and similar concepts such as "helping" or "aiding." For this kind of conceptual clarification, dictionaries are not very helpful. Instead, you would need to conduct a search and review of the relevant social science literature. In fact, this is where most social research begins. Now suppose that your review turned up the following reference:

Midlarsky, Elizabeth. 1968. Aiding responses: An analysis and review. *Merrill-Palmer Quarterly of Behavior and Development* 14 (No. 3, July):229–260.

Reading this journal article, you would find that Midlarsky defines altruism "as a subcategory of aiding, referring to helpful actions which incur some cost to the individual but bring either very little or nothing by way of gain, relative to the magnitude of the investment." Notice how much more precise this definition is than the dictionary definition.

Through your literature review, you can begin to understand how other researchers have identified altruism and how you can recognize it should you encounter it in the empirical world. Altruism is not a commodity sold in packages at a hardware store or mined as a natural resource in remote places. One of the first tasks in research, therefore, is to decide how to define the phenomenon of interest not with words but with observable (*empirical*) characteristics. To do this is to *operationalize* the concept. Operationalizing concepts is a very critical step in the research process. Without going into the principles too deeply here, let us simply say that we decide we are observing altruism whenever we see someone pick up a hitchhiker. This operational definition (one of the very many possible operationalizations) corresponds to Midlarsky's conceptual definition above, yet it is empirical.

Giving a hitchhiker a ride is

1. "a helpful action" (since the person apparently needs a ride),
2. "which costs the individual something" (the time and effort to stop),
3. "but which brings nothing by way of gain" (the driver does not charge the rider, for example).

There are problems with this operational definition (e.g., the driver may gain in that he or she receives companionship which may be very important to him or her at the time), as there are whenever we operationalize concepts. But this example should give you a sense of how the researcher moves from abstract definitions to specific, concrete observations, a process that will be considered in detail in chapter 5.

As we begin to think about how to conduct a scientific study of altruism, we must not only consider ways of observing the phenomenon but also decide more specifically what questions we want to ask. Such questions may derive from a review of current literature on altruism. They may derive from the researcher's personal biases and goals, and may develop out of intuition or plain curiosity. Regardless of the basis for the decision, however, it is necessary to formulate questions that narrow the topic, reducing the original grand question to one of manageable proportions. For example, instead of asking "what is altruism?" or even "what explains it?" suppose we ask: What social norms motivate altruism? What situational features determine whether one person will help another? Will familiarity with the setting increase the likelihood that someone will help another in an emergency? How does a person's emotional mood influence his or her willingness to help? What is the family background of committed altruists? These are narrow, specific, and consequently *answerable* research questions. There are, of course, a limitless variety of interesting and worthwhile questions that might be investigated. In chapters 2 and 4 we will consider the form these questions should take to make them scientifically meaningful.

Having posed a researchable (i.e., answerable) question, we are in a position to decide which strategy might be used to uncover an answer. Remember, however, that while any social science topic is researchable, not every approach is reasonable or feasible in every situation. It is only by considering such things as available resources and the kind of information sought that a decision can be reached on which methods to use. Putting such considerations aside, let us consider how we might investigate altruism using each of the four data collection methods highlighted in this book: experiments, surveys, field research, and available data research. Each of these, it will be seen, can be used to investigate the topic of altruism and to answer the general question "what explains altruism?" Which alternative is considered most reasonable is up to you, the researcher, to determine for yourself.

An Experimental Answer

For several reasons that we will discuss in chapter 7, *experiments* frequently offer the best approach for investigating the causes of phenomena. In an experiment the researcher manipulates systematically some feature of the environment and then observes whether a systematic change follows in the behavior under study. Suppose that we are interested in determining if "mood" affects altruism. More specifially, will the experience of success or good fortune increase a person's willingness to help others? To study this question experimentally, we must create a situation wherein some persons will experience good fortune and others will not, after which, all persons are presented with the opportunity to help someone else. If those who experienced good fortune are more likely to help than those who did not, the "hypothesis" that good mood promotes altruism will be supported. In fact, this hypothesis has been supported in several experimental studies. Let us consider one such study by social psychologists Alice Isen and Paula Levin (1972).

To induce a good mood or feeling, Isen and Levin set up public telephone booths so that users would find "lost" change unexpectedly in the coin return slot. To do this, one of the experimenters entered the booth, made an incomplete call, ostensibly took her dime from the return slot, and then left. In actuality, the dime was left for half of the experimental trials. In this way half of the persons using the booth afterward received an unexpected dime when they checked the coin return, while half did not.

After the telephone booth had been "stocked" and subjects had made their calls, subjects were presented with the opportunity to help someone in the following manner. As the subject left the booth, an accomplice of the experimenter, who had stationed herself nearby, started walking in the same direction as the subject and, while walking slightly ahead of him or her, dropped a manila folder full of papers in the subject's path. "Helping" occurred if the subject helped pick up the papers. The results of the experiment supported clearly the hypothesis that feeling good leads to helping. Subjects who found a dime helped in 14 of 16 cases, whereas only 1 subject in 25 who did not find a dime stopped to help.

The essential feature of the Isen and Levin study that illustrates the experimental approach is that a potential influence on altruism—mood—was isolated and systematically varied from subject to subject while all other factors that might influence altruism were "held constant," or remained the same for all subjects. For example, the same experimenter used the same telephone booth with the same accomplice and the same procedures. But what purpose does it serve to hold these features of the experiment constant? Why was it necessary to include a comparison group of subjects who did not receive a dime? How did the experimenters decide which subjects to let find the dime, and why is this such an essential part of the experiment? More generally, why go to the trouble of contriving and conducting an experiment when there are lots of naturally occurring acts of altruism that can be studied? In chapter 7 we examine the logic of the experimental approach and various mechanisms for staging experiments, as well as the advantages and disadvantages of this form of research. In chapter 8 we look at different types of experimental designs.

An Answer from Survey Research

A second approach to studying altruism that might be taken is the *survey*. Survey research involves the application of questionnaires or interviews to relatively large groups of people. One purpose of surveys is to identify the presence of certain characteristics among groups. For example, a survey might tell you how many people at your college, or in your organization, have voluntarily given blood, have done volunteer work for a charitable organization, or have contributed money to charities. Such information can be related to various other characteristics of respondents, such as their gender, age, marital status, religion, and occupation, thereby enabling the survey researcher to understand as well as describe the incidence of altruism among particular groups.

Richard Titmuss's (1971) cross-national study of blood donating provides one example of the use of survey research in the study of altruism. As part of this study, Titmuss collected information via a questionnaire from over 3800 blood donors in England and Wales. Britain offers an excellent milieu for studying blood donating as an altruistic act since, unlike the United States at the time of this study—where donors often were paid or insured for their blood needs in return for their blood— donors in Britain are prohibited by law from receiving any tangible reward. In order to study the characteristics and motives of blood donors, Titmuss asked donors at several collection points to fill out a two-page questionnaire as they waited to give blood. The questionnaire requested information on the respondent's age, gender, marital status, family size, occupation, income, number of blood donations given, whether the respondent and close relatives had received a blood transfusion, and the respondent's reasons for giving blood. One of the findings was that the donor population closely resembled the general population in terms of age, sex, and marital status when age-related incapacity and childbearing were taken into account. This is a particularly interesting finding when compared with the United States, where those under the age of 30, singles, and males are vastly overrepresented among donors.

While questionnaires and interviews often are used in conjunction with other forms of research, a key feature of survey studies is that information is collected from part of a group (e.g., 3800 actual donors) in order to make generalizations about the whole group (all donors in England and Wales). However, such generalizations are hazardous unless careful procedures are followed in deciding who is to be included in the study. Furthermore, collecting data from very many people may exceed the budgets for most research. In chapter 6 we discuss sampling techniques for choosing respondents that are designed to increase accuracy and reduce costs.

Many questions can be raised about survey research in general and the Titmuss study in particular. Why did Titmuss choose to use written questionnaires rather than face-to-face interviews? How did he decide which questions to ask, how best to word the questions, and in what order to ask them? These are the kinds of issues we address in chapters 9 and 10.

An Answer from Field Research

Field research is essentially a matter of immersing oneself in a naturally occurring (rather than a "staged") set of events in order to gain firsthand knowledge of the situation. Anthropologists who live in remote communities for long periods to study the culture of the inhabitants are engaged in this form of research, as are other social scientists who voluntarily become members of organizations and groups or take jobs for the sake of conducting social research. In such settings, the field researcher seeks to understand the world as his or her subjects see it and to collect information without unduly influencing its shape and content.

Field research on altruism seldom has been conducted, although there are numerous settings where this approach could be applied. For example, one could work in a blood donor center, or join the Red Cross, Salvation Army, or some other emergency relief organization. One also might observe altruistic actions in the wake of a community disaster, as Louis Zurcher (1968) did when he joined a volunteer work crew after a tornado ripped through Topeka, Kansas in June of 1966. While not focusing directly on helping, Zurcher's field study provides interesting insights into why people help others.

Thirty-six hours after the tornado struck, Zurcher became a member of a spontaneously formed work crew that spent 3 days removing fallen tree limbs and trees from houses. Crew members were Topeka residents who lived outside of the tornado's direct path and whose homes had not been seriously damaged. According to Zurcher, his own and others' attraction to the crew came from an urge to do something to fight back at the tornado's destructive force. Unlike other crew members, however, Zurcher decided to use the occasion for data-gathering purposes—to observe and record the group processes. He was particularly interested in how the crew created a set of temporary disaster roles that offset the role "voids" experienced when the usual work and community activities were disrupted by the calamity. His account describes the development of the crew from a bunch of co-acting individuals to a cohesive group with a well-defined division of labor and "a sense of group history, loyalty, and humor."

To analyze this setting Zurcher relied heavily on his direct observations as a participant in the work crew and to a lesser extent on interviews with crew members after the group dissolved. The crucial feature of his research was a running log of observations recorded at the end of each day. But how did Zurcher decide what aspects of the extraordinarily complex range of stimuli to record? Deciding what to record and when and how to record one's observations are basic problems for field researchers. While Zurcher's study was impromptu, most field researchers also face problems of selecting an appropriate setting or group for study and then of gaining entry to and getting along with others in the setting. In chapter 11 we discuss such issues in detail; we also consider the special techniques that field researchers have developed for entering the field of observation and for handling, organizing, and analyzing their observations.

An Answer from Available Data

The final approach to studying the social world discussed in this volume is the use of *available data*—that is, data that have been generated for purposes other than those for which you as the researcher are using them. Prominent among these would be records, letters, autobiographies, diaries, and other documents, whether written, oral, or produced by some other means. Even tombstones could be considered data in this sense, since they are created for one purpose (to mark graves) but could be used for others (e.g., to study the diffusion of sculptural styles over several generations). How might altruism be studied with this approach?

In one of the earliest empirical studies of altruism, sociologist Pitirim Sorokin (1950) used two interesting data sources. The first consisted of 500 letters describing individuals who had performed good deeds. The letters were recommendations that had been sent to a 1940s radio program that rewarded "good neighbors" with an orchid and a citation on the program. The second data source consisted of biographies of Catholic saints as compiled in Thurston's twelve-volume *The Lives of the Saints*.

Sorokin's analysis of these letters and biographies revealed the kinds of acts regarded as altruistic as well as numerous characteristics of people who had acted altruistically. Among other things, he found that the "good neighbors" and saints often were societal deviants whose level of moral conduct rose above or conflicted with the official law and government, that a catastrophic event frequently precipitated their altruism, and that they usually had experienced happy childhoods in strong, well-integrated families.

Obviously, it requires a great deal of imagination and ingenuity just to think of and uncover the kinds of information analyzed by Sorokin. Simply finding appropriate available data is a major problem encountered with this approach. But once the data are in hand, still other problems arise. The most fundamental of these is how to codify the data in a systematic fashion; other issues include what to do when there is insufficient information about cases or when information is not comparable from one case to another. Then there is the issue of the authenticity of the information. How accurate is the biographer's information? How much has the biographer embellished and glorified the life of his or her subject? These and other issues raised by the use of available data are discussed in chapter 12.

Conclusions

What we have seen in this brief chapter are some very important points that the remaining chapters will help to make clear. The basic lessons are fourfold:

1. Research is both a pervasive pastime and an important vocation. As a set of skills, research methods can be applied to help answer the most mundane or the most complex and sophisticated problem.

2. Everyone has the opportunity to utilize the skills of research methods on a regular basis either as a consumer of someone else's research or as a producer of research themselves.

3. Any social science topic is amenable to research provided that the phenomenon studied is empirical (observable).

4. Most social science topics may be studied using any of the four data collection methods discussed here. This is not to say that there is no one best way. Very likely there is, but the definition of the best way is something that can be determined only in light of the researcher's resources, purposes, and goals.

Keeping these points in mind should help to provide some perspective on the detailed descriptions that follow. These four points provide a framework within which to understand the strengths and weaknesses, advantages and disadvantages of the various methods of social research. Two other frameworks are also important for understanding social research: science and logic. In chapters 2 and 3 we will examine the nature and relevance of these.

Key Terms

social scientific research	*experiment*
empirical	*survey*
operationalization	*field research*
	available data

Review Questions and Problems

1. From the standpoint of the consumer of research evidence, why is it important to study research methods?

2. Briefly describe and contrast each of the four major research strategies for understanding the social world: experiments, surveys, field research, and the use of available data.

3. Find an example in the media (e.g., newspaper, magazine, television) of a report of a study involving social research or of a contention (e.g., an advertising claim) purportedly based upon empirical evidence.

I

SCIENTIFIC AND LOGICAL FOUNDATIONS OF SOCIAL RESEARCH

Social research is fundamentally a scientific enterprise. As such, we believe that it is important to understand what unites sociology and other social sciences with the natural sciences. Obviously, it is not the subject matter. Nor is it the specific research techniques; a book on chemical analysis would be of no practical value to someone doing sociological research. Perhaps it is for this reason that most books on methods of social research either say very little about the nature of science or, to the extent that they do, choose not to give examples from non-social scientific disciplines. By contrast, in the following two chapters, we say quite a bit about science and we draw as much upon examples from the natural sciences as from the social sciences.

What unites science is its objectives, its presuppositions, its general methodology, and its logic. That is what we focus on in these two chapters—the philosophical and logical foundations of science that transcend specific subject matters, guiding the efforts of researchers in many different disciplines. Chapter 2 describes the general process of scientific inquiry, and chapter 3 examines the role of logical reasoning in this process. Together these chapters constitute a philosophical position that has informed social scientific inquiry for many years. This position has not gone unchallenged by some philosophers, who note its inconsistencies with how scientists actually work, and by some social scientists, who argue that a general scientific method is inapplicable to the study of human interaction. But the latter voices represent minority positions; most social research is guided by a belief in the generality and unity of science.

2

The Nature of Science

To appreciate and understand research methods it is important to have a clear understanding of the nature of science, for the procedures surveyed in this book are guided above all else by scientific principles. That sociology (as well as the other social sciences—anthropology, economics, political science, and psychology) claims to be scientific will not come as news to most students of research methods. Yet, many students reject this claim altogether, while others believe that regardless of how scientific sociology may be, it differs substantially from other "true" sciences. After all, their image of sociology simply does not fit their recollections of high school science courses in biology, chemistry, or physics. Nor does it seem consistent with what they know about the theoretical genius of such well-known scientists as Albert Einstein and Sir Isaac Newton or about important scientific discoveries with great practical significance like the Salk vaccine or laser beam. Such impressions, however, rest not only upon a misconception of the discipline of sociology but also upon a distorted image of science.

In this chapter we will examine the most fundamental characteristics of science. "Fundamental" is the key word here, for any attempt to define the nature of science in a few brief pages cannot give a complete picture. Our aim is to present science at its best, in terms of its ideal goals and practices. In later chapters we can then compare the ideal with actual practice and consider the human side of science as well. Like all intellectual endeavors, science has its human limitations, as attempts to be totally rational and purely objective are seldom, if ever, completely successful.

The Aim of Science

Science in Latin means knowledge. Contemporary science has been characterized falsely by some as a *profound* body of knowledge, profound in that it is not trivial and not comprehensible to the average person (Mazur, 1968). What is profound, however, is a matter of perspective and judgment. Today's seemingly trivial finding may be tomorrow's major scientific breakthrough. Research that the layperson sees as trifling and irrelevant, which the scientist may pursue purely from intellectual curiosity, may help to solve important practical problems. Who would have thought, for example, that discoveries about the mating behavior of certain insects

17

would provide a basis for pest control? That learning principles derived from study-ing the bar-pressing behavior of animals in boxes could be used to help the mentally retarded? Or that research on ant "trails" would provide clues to the chemistry of communication? The practical implications of scientific knowledge, as these exam-ples suggest, often are difficult to foresee. It is clear, therefore, that qualities like profundity, relevance, and significance are of little use in differentiating science from nonscience. (See Box 2.1 for a discussion of the importance of understanding the nature of science.)

The aim of science is to produce knowledge, to understand and explain some aspect of the world around us. But accumulated knowledge per se does not distin-guish science from mythology. What, then, makes an endeavor scientific? Basi-cally, it is a matter of *how* and *why* knowledge is accepted by the scientific com-munity. Two interrelated sets of criteria determine acceptance or rejection. One set of criteria pertains to the form or logical structure of knowledge, the other to the evidence upon which it is based. In discussing the nature of science, therefore, we distinguish among the laws, principles, and theories that constitute the *product* of science and the methods and logic of inquiry that comprise the *process* through which scientific knowledge is created, tested, and refined.

Although the analogy is imperfect, it may help in following our discussion to think of a factory or industrial plant in which certain raw materials are processed to create a finished product. One of the differences between industry and science lies in what is processed: industries manufacture material things, but science processes *ideas*. Of course, science has made possible innumerable technological advances, whose material fruits, perhaps because of their visibility, are often seen as the essential end-product of science. But these practical results are mere by-products of scientific inquiry. The real goal of science is to achieve understanding; the basic product is ideas.[1] We will see the form that these ideas take as we first consider science as a product. Then we will turn our attention to the science process.

Science as Product

Scientific disciplines differ in terms of their objects of study. Physics is concerned with matter and energy, biology with the life processes of plants and animals, psychology with human and animal behavior, sociology with properties and pro-cesses of social groupings. As a consequence, each of these disciplines has devel-oped its own unique concepts, laws, and theories. Yet, in spite of such differences, all scientific knowledge, regardless of the field of study, shares certain defining characteristics, the first of which is the type of questions that may be addressed.

Scientific versus Nonscientific Questions

Whether a question can be approached scientifically depends on whether it can be subjected to verifiable observations. That is, it must be possible for the scientist to make observations, which others also are capable of making, that can answer the question. This means that philosophical questions about essence, existence, or

BOX 2.1

Senator William Proxmire and the Golden Fleece:
On Misunderstanding the Nature of Science

Judging the value of scientific work by everyday standards of relevance and significance is not only unsound but also an injustice to the scientists who devote their
professional careers to research. This is why scientists have been so rankled by Senator
William Proxmire's infamous "Golden Fleece of the Month Awards." The "awards"
are press releases that Proxmire began in 1975 allegedly to draw public attention to the
"biggest or most ridiculous or most ironic example of government waste" his staff
could locate. Now publicizing wasteful government spending is a worthy cause. But
some people wonder whether Proxmire might be more interested in publicity than in
rooting out the evils of waste. He often has singled out federally funded social scientific research for ridicule. And in casting the awards with some very colorful charges,
he has leveled inaccurate criticisms, misrepresented and distorted research projects,
and shown little appreciation for the general purpose of scientific inquiry.

Consider, for example, Proxmire's comments about an $84,000 National Science
Foundation grant to professors Ellen Berscheid and Elaine Walster to continue their
study of romantic love:

> I object to this not only because no one—not even the National Science Founda-
> tion—can argue that falling in love is a science; not only because I'm sure that
> even if they spend $84 million or $84 billion they wouldn't get an answer that
> anyone would believe. I'm also against it because I don't want the answer. I
> believe that 200 million other Americans want to leave some things in life a
> mystery, and right at the top of things we don't want to know is why a man falls
> in love with a woman and vice versa. . . .

Proxmire's "ignorance is bliss" position takes aim at the value of doing research
on romantic love. His remarks can be countered in one way by pointing out the
potential application of Berscheid and Walster's research for solving problems of
marital discord and divorce. However, Proxmire's position is more broadly threatening. As Charles Kiesler (1980:689), former executive officer of the American Psychological Association, notes, "Proxmire has presumed to dictate which human behaviors
are open to legitimate scientific investigation and which are not." And "limiting the
nature or scope of scientific inquiry is antithetical to the core of scientific thought."

The problem is not that scientists believe they should be immune to criticism.
Critically evaluating one another's work is understood by the scientific community to
be an integral part of the scientific process (see text discussion of objectivity below).
Furthermore, in this day of nuclear technology and recombinant DNA, it is important
that scientists share the public's concern about the political and moral consequences of
their work. However, judgments on the value of research are difficult even when one
has a firm grasp of the field; such judgments at least should be informed by a basic
understanding of the nature of science—of its goals, potentialities, and limitations.
Proxmire's criticisms of the romantic love research revealed not only an ignorance of
the field but also a basic misunderstanding of science.

At a time when many people entertain the view of science as destroyer, it is

Box 2.1 (*continued*)

important, as Isaac Asimov (1980) points out, that the public's concerns and reactions toward science "not be based on ignorant emotion alone."

> Of the millions who watch sports events, a vanishingly small percentage can play any of the games they watch with anything approaching professional skill, yet virtually all understand the rules well enough to appreciate what they see. The public must then, in the same way, understand science if it is to react intelligently. They must at least be capable of following the game, even if they can't play it.

morality are beyond the realm of science. Answers to some questions raised by philosophers do become the fundamental postulates, or assumptions, of science, but these cannot be investigated scientifically. Thus, scientists can only assume that the world exists, that empirically verifiable knowledge is possible, that we can know the world through our senses, and that there is an order to the world.[2] Having made such assumptions, what scientists try to do is discover the order that they assume to exist and discover the "laws" that describe that order.

It would be proper for a social scientist to ask such questions as: Why do some persons read pornographic literature or view pornographic films? Why is one type of organization more efficient than another? How are patterns of communication in the family related to childhood schizophrenia? But it would *not* be within the realm of science to ask: Is pornography morally wrong? Should efficiency be valued over morale? Should there be families? The difference between these two sets of questions is that the former deal with how and why regular patterns of events occur, whereas the latter ask what is desirable. Questions of morality, existence, or ultimate causality are certainly worth asking and speculating about, but they fall within the purview of philosophy and religion. They are not scientific because they cannot be framed in such a way that *observations* can be made to answer them.

Both philosophers and scientists ask about the "why" of things. But to the scientist, as psychologists Doherty and Shemberg (1978:6) note, "the 'why' is just shorthand for, What is the relationship between . . . or, Under what conditions . . . ." When we can use these phrases, "then the question could be a legitimate scientific question, provided the other terms in the question meet the test of observability." Thus, we can observe whether people read pornographic literature or view pornographic films, and we can try to determine, through observation, the "conditions" (e.g., personal characteristics, relationships with parents and others, occupation) under which this is likely to occur. Alternately, we can determine what the relationship is between type of organization and efficiency, assuming we can decide how to distinguish different forms of organization and can decide on the pattern of observations that represents "efficiency." No such appeals to objective evidence, however, will enable us to decide if purveyors of pornography should be legally prosecuted or left alone, or to decide the relative importance of efficiency and morale.[3]

In short, scientific questions are questions that can be answered by identifying observable events that are thought to result in the situation or pattern of interest.

Still, to qualify as scientific knowledge, the *answers* to such questions must take a particular form, a form that meets the requirements of description, explanation, prediction, and understanding.

Knowledge as Description

Scientific knowledge is by definition verifiable. For verification to be possible, explanations and findings must be communicated clearly to others. Consequently, scientists make a great fuss about language: observations must be precisely and reliably reported; terms must be carefully defined, with clear referents; and the phenomena to which each scientific discipline addresses itself must be organized and classified in a meaningful way. Thus, description is the first step in producing scientific knowledge. We must describe objects and events before we can understand and explain the relationships among them. In order to describe, each discipline develops its own special language or set of concepts.

Concepts are abstractions communicated by words or other signs that refer to common properties among phenomena. The term "weight," for example, symbolizes a conception of a property of all physical objects. Likewise, the sociological term "status" is an abstraction that points to a property of a social structure or group. The first rule about the scientific use of concepts is one word, one concept. Sociologist George Zito (1975:21) notes that in everyday language one word may stand for many different things; "mass," for example, may mean the quality of size and weight, the main part, a Christian religious ceremony, and the like. To the physicist, however, "it means only the quantity of matter in a body as measured in relation to its inertia." Because everyday language is so full of vagueness and multiple meanings, scientists find it necessary to restrict or redefine the meaning of common words or to invent new terms (sometimes called constructs), thereby creating highly technical vocabularies.

Scientists' second rule about concepts is that there must be agreed-on ways of tying concepts to tangible objects and events. This extends the first rule by stating that concepts must be defined directly or indirectly in terms of precise, reliable observations. It would be scientifically unacceptable to describe something as "heavy," not only because this term has many different connotations (i.e., refers to more than one concept), but also because as a symbol for any single concept its referent is imprecise. Suppose by "heavy" you meant the weight of a certain object. Some people may agree with your description but others may not—an intolerable situation for science. But if you use a scale and describe the weight as 50 pounds, then others can more readily agree on the accuracy of your description. By the same token, many concepts (e.g., "energy," "electron," "wavelength") that are not simply and directly observable in the sense of "weight" are scientifically acceptable because they imply characteristics that are observable. For example, physicists cannot directly observe or measure the movement of molecules postulated by the kinetic theory of gases; however, by using a pressure gauge they can measure the pressure that this movement implies. Linking concepts to observable events, called measurement, is something about which we will have a great deal more to say in chapter 5.

One additional feature of language, in both conventional and scientific usage, is that it tends to determine what we see in the world. Since what we know about objective reality is represented and communicated with words, words make some distinctions more salient than others. Furthermore, implicit in the use of all concepts are assumptions about their relative importance for describing and explaining the world around us. For example, Eskimos have several distinctive terms for different kinds of snow and ice, distinctions that are important for their survival but that are not likely to be noticed by inhabitants of temperate regions. Similarly, scientists develop special concepts because they are useful for understanding. For instance, the existence of the term "social class" reflects its utility for explaining sociological concerns like social order and social change. This implies a third rule about language usage in science: concepts are judged by their usefulness. Scientists are not dogmatic about concepts. Once a concept has outlived its usefulness, or the explanation in which it is embedded has been superseded by a better explanation, it is discarded. Thus, the history of science, to paraphrase an unknown philosopher, is a graveyard of concepts.

Knowledge as Explanation and Prediction

Explanations, according to sociologist Gwynn Nettler (1970), are attempts to satisfy curiosity. Depending on the type of question and the needs of the interrogator, curiosity may be satisfied in several ways: by labeling (as when the appropriate term is given in response to a child's question about what something is), by defining or giving examples (as when new terms are clarified with familiar terms and images), by evoking empathy (as when people offer motives or other "good reasons" for their conduct), by appealing to authority (as, for example, when something is attributed to "God's will"), or by citing a general empirical rule (as, for example, when we say that this book falls when dropped because it is denser than air, and all objects denser than air fall when dropped). Only this last form of explanation is capable of meeting the twin objectives of scientific knowledge—to *explain* the past and present and to *predict* the future.

The "empirical rules" with which scientific explanations are built consist of abstract statements, or propositions, that relate changes in one general class of events to changes in another class of events under certain conditions. Consider, for example, the following two propositions, the first Boyle's law from chemistry, the second a generalization from social psychology known as the social facilitation or "audience" effect:

   1. If the volume of a gas is constant, then an increase in temperature will be followed by an increase in pressure (Reynolds, 1971:5).
   2. If a task is simple or well learned, then an individual will perform it better in the presence of others than in isolation.

According to each of these propositions, a change in one set of events (temperature of a gas, absence or presence of others) is followed by a change in another set of events (pressure of the gas, performance of an individual) under specified conditions (constant volume, simple or well-learned task). The propositions are abstract in two senses. First, since they may refer to past, present, or future changes, they make no reference to historical time. Second, each proposition pertains to a *general* class of events: gases of a constant volume in one instance and individuals performing simple tasks in the other. The second proposition would be less abstract if it made reference only to males, and still less abstract if it applied only to males with high self-esteem. Level of abstractness is important because the ideal in science is to develop the most general understanding: to search out generalizations capable of explaining and predicting the widest range of events possible.

But how does citing an empirical rule satisfy the scientist's curiosity and his or her needs to explain and predict? To answer this question, we must further examine the form that scientific explanations take.

Philosophers of science (e.g., Hempel, 1965, 1967; Beckner, 1967) generally agree that scientific explanations can be expressed in a particular form adopted from deductive logic. In this form the event to be explained or predicted consists of a conclusion that logically follows from a set of statements, one of which is a general empirical proposition like the ones cited above. We will discuss logical argument forms at length in chapter 3. For now, consider the following two examples:

1a. If the volume of a gas is constant, and the temperature increases, the pressure of the gas increases.
1b. In situation A the volume of gas G is constant, and the temperature increased.
1c. Therefore, the pressure of gas G increased in situation A (Reynolds, 1971:6).

2a. If an individual performs a simple task, then his or her performance will be better in the presence of others than in isolation.
2b. In situation B an individual will perform simple task S in isolation; in situation C the individual will perform task S in the presence of others.
2c. Therefore, the individual's level of performance on task S will be greater in situation C than in situation B.

Notice that, as stated, the first logically deduced consequence (1c) refers to a past event (the pressure of gas G *increased*), whereas the second (2c) refers to a future event (the level of performance *will be greater*). By constructing the explanations in this way—with different time frames—we intend to convey the idea that scientific explanations, assuming the above form, may be applied to the past, present, or future. One thus can see that the process of *prediction* is logically equivalent to the process of *explanation*; prediction is carried out before the event occurs and explanation afterward. Any valid scientific explanation, therefore, is at once a prediction of the future.

It will simplify our discussion if we now introduce a few of the terms associated with scientific explanations. First, several terms denote the abstract propositions (1a, 2a above) from which observed or observable events are logically deduced. Propositions of this sort are called *hypotheses* when their observable predictions have not yet been tested. Hypotheses derived directly from observation are sometimes referred to as *empirical generalizations*, and to the extent that they have been repeatedly verified and are widely accepted, they may become scientific *laws*. Once observed and recorded, the specific events (1b, 1c, 2b, 2c above) become facts and are admissible as scientific evidence, or data. Finally, the terms contained within these scientific explanations are the concepts that describe—organize and classify—the phenomena to be explained. Boyle's law classifies gases according to their volume, temperature, and pressure; the audience effect generalization organizes individual behavior in terms of the concepts of task simplicity, presence or absence of others, and level of performance.

Putting all of these terms together, we can say that scientific explanations describe the world by classifying phenomena according to concepts; they explain and predict by showing how facts and predictions logically follow from empirical generalizations or laws. Scientific explanation does not end here, however. Indeed, what has been said thus far merely presents the foundation upon which scientific knowledge is constructed. For although specific events are "explained" by empirical laws, the regularities expressed by these laws themselves require explanation. Boyle's law raises the question of *why* increases in temperature invariably increase the pressure of gases under constant volume. Similarly, in the case of the audience effect, why should the presence of others facilitate one's performance of simple tasks?

To answer such questions, and generally to explain empirical generalizations or laws, science introduces theories. "Theory" is one of the most elusive and misunderstood terms in science. It does not mean, as it is popularly understood, idle speculation or conjecture. In fact, for an explanation to be called a theory in science usually implies considerable supporting evidence (McCain and Segal, 1977:98). The complete, formal presentation of a theory includes definitions of concepts and a set of assumptions describing the circumstances under which it applies; its central feature, though, is a set of interconnected, abstract principles, or propositions, that have the same basic form as laws but are more general.

Theories explain laws deductively in the same manner that laws explain facts. The following set of propositions (adapted from Reynolds, 1971:8), for example, shows how Boyle's law is a logical consequence of the kinetic theory of gases.

> As the temperature increases, the kinetic energy of the gas molecules increases.
> As the kinetic energy increases, there is an increase in the velocity of the motion of the molecules.
> As the molecules travel faster, but are prevented from traveling further by a vessel of constant volume, they strike the inside surface of the vessel more often and with more force.
> As the molecules strike the sides of the vessel more frequently, the pressure on the walls of the vessel increases.
> Therefore, assuming a constant volume, as the temperature increases, the pressure increases.

By following the rules of logic we can move from propositions to hypotheses and laws, as above, to the prediction and explanation of observable events. In this way, theoretical concepts that may not be directly observable or measurable (e.g., the velocity and energy of molecules) are linked to phenomena that are measurable (e.g., the pressure and temperature of a gas).

The confirmation of a particular prediction, however, is not enough to confirm a theory, as it is possible to have several theories that explain a given empirical regularity and that make the same or similar predictions. This is true of the audience effect, for which no established theoretical explanation exists, even though several theories have been proposed. One theory holds that an audience enhances performance on simple tasks because the mere physical presence of others increases one's physiological arousal. According to another theory, enhanced performance occurs when persons believe that the other persons present are judging or evaluating their behavior. Scientific research often is directed toward testing such alternative theories, but ultimately one theory should be judged superior to other competing theories to the extent that (1) it involves the fewest number of statements and assumptions, (2) it explains the broadest range of phenomena, and (3) its predictions are more accurate.

By explaining more with greater accuracy, theories offer a more general understanding than laws. A sound theoretical explanation can *broaden* our understanding by accounting for a wider range of phenomena than can the established laws that the theory explains and can *deepen* our understanding by reducing the laws to a common set of principles as well as showing how accepted laws are only approximate (Hempel, 1967). Philosopher of science Carl Hempel (1967:83) illustrates this point with Newton's theory of motion and gravitation.

From Newton's theory it is possible to explain (or deduce) Kepler's laws describing the motion of the planets, Galileo's law of free fall, and the law of the tides, in addition to the motion of numerous objects that these laws cannot explain. Furthermore, Newton's theory improves upon the laws it explains. For example, it implies certain deviations in the elliptic orbits of planets because they are subjected to gravitational pull not only from the sun, as predicted by Kepler, but also from the other planets; moreover, it shows how the acceleration of free fall near the earth's surface "is not strictly a constant, as asserted by Galileo, but changes with the distance of the falling body from the earth's center of gravity." And so, once constructed, Newton's theory covered more ground and was more accurate than the existing laws that it explained. Later Einstein formulated his general theory of relativity, which explained and improved upon Newton's theory and also made new predictions about the motion of light near massive objects. The progress and ultimate structure of scientific theory thus reveals a hierarchy of explanations, where facts are explained by laws that are explained by theories, which are explained in turn by theories at a higher level of abstraction.

Knowledge as Understanding

Now that we have outlined the essential ingredients of scientific explanations, we must introduce two complications. First, many scientists maintain that, in addition to explanation and prediction, scientific laws and theories must provide a sense of understanding, a criterion that deductive explanations do not always meet. Second, while empirical generalizations are necessary for explanation and prediction, not all such generalizations are sufficient for these tasks; in short, they do not always predict nor do they always explain. Neither of these complications, or issues, is simply resolved. In fact, those who study science do not agree themselves about the meaning or necessity of the "understanding" criterion or about the characteristics of scientifically adequate generalizations.

Nevertheless, social scientists generally agree that a sense of understanding is provided by describing the causal process that connects events (Reynolds, 1971). Very often a theory will furnish this understanding for a law or empirical generalization. The connection between temperature and pressure in Boyle's law, for example, seems more understandable when we know the underlying process, described by the kinetic theory, by which temperature causes an increase in kinetic energy, which causes an increase in the velocity of molecules, and so on. Similarly, a generalization is thought to be scientifically meaningful when it describes a *causal relationship*—that is, a relationship in which a change in one event forces, produces, or brings about a change in another. In fact, unless a true causal relationship is identified, empirical generalizations cannot meet the dual requirement of explanation and prediction. We can see this by examining some empirical generalizations considered inadequate for scientific purposes.

Many "scientific" generalizations purport to explain but have no readily observable consequences and hence cannot predict. Standard examples abound in Freudian psychology. For instance, Freud suggested that all dreams represent the fulfillment or attempted fulfillment of a wish, and that all persons have a death wish (Hall and Lindzey, 1970). The problem with these generalizations is that they too readily "explain" things after the fact. We can always find some wish with which to interpret or explain a dream, once it has occurred. Similarly, every suicide or accident can be attributed to a death wish. This is like placing your bet after the race is over. Once an event has occurred, any number of plausible, intuitively appealing explanations can be offered. The trick is also to indicate what to expect under given conditions. Without this kind of objective testability, it is impossible to tell if one event has caused the other; such post hoc generalizations thus give us a false sense of understanding.

It is also possible to predict an event on the basis of empirical generalizations without understanding the connection between generalization and prediction. Astronomical predictions of the movement of the stars were quite accurate long before satisfactory explanations for the movement existed. Today, the healing powers of aspirin are put to use even though the reason for its effectiveness is not well understood; election outcomes can be predicted accurately while their explanation remains unsatisfactory; and, more mundanely, people continue to use a variety of time-tested, reliable, yet seemingly inexplicable predictors of weather changes. It is a folk wisdom, for example, that the leaves of trees show their light green undersides when a storm is imminent. Generalizations such as these, unlike those that "explain" but do not predict, can be tested and are useful in certain contexts. However, their utility is limited. Once we have an adequate theory, which describes the causal process connecting events, we get not only a better sense of understanding but more accurate and more useful predictions.

There are many examples in the history of science of how the utility of knowledge has been enhanced by identifying causal processes. One of the more interesting cases is the discovery of the cause and cure of rickets (Loomis, 1970). Rickets is a disease resulting in the softening and bending of growing bones. It is caused by a deficiency of solar ultraviolet radiation, which is necessary for synthesis of a calcifying hormone released into the bloodstream by the skin. Without this hormone (calciferol), an insufficient amount of calcium is deposited in growing bones, causing the crippling deformities of rickets. Either adequate sunlight or the ingestion of minute amounts of calciferol will prevent and cure rickets. Before the causal process underlying rickets was understood, however, scientists could, in a sense, predict its occurrence. They noted, for example, seasonal variations in rickets—that is, its rise during the "darker" winter months. They observed its greater prevalence in cities than in rural districts and in northern industrial nations as opposed to northern nonindustrialized nations. Identifying such patterns eventually led to the conclusion that sunlight had the power to prevent and cure rickets. But it was not until the sun's role in the production of calciferol was understood—until the complete causal process was identified—that rickets could be eradicated completely, even in areas where the sun's ultraviolet radiation is absent.

Thus, explanation in social science generally boils down to a search for causes. Knowing when and how to infer causality is a prerequisite for most social research. One of our goals, therefore, is to enhance this ability, which we will begin to do in chapter 4, when we discuss criteria used to establish causality.

Tentative Knowledge

Psychologist B. F. Skinner (1953:11) has argued that "science is unique in showing a cumulative progress," which enables each succeeding generation of scientists to begin a little further along. Thus, "our contemporary writers, artists, and philosophers are not appreciably more effective than those of the golden age of Greece, yet the average high school student understands much more of nature than the greatest of Greek scientists."

To the extent that this is true, it is due largely to the *tentative* nature of scientific knowledge. Scientists never achieve complete understanding. One reason is that every answer leads to new questions, every new fact, law, or theory presents new problems, so that no matter what the present state of scientific knowledge, there is always more to know. When or where this progression ends is impossible to tell; however, it is clear that science has barely scratched a very large surface.

Aside from the vast amount that there is to know, however, the primitive scientific knowledge that we now possess is assumed to be tentative and uncertain for another, more definitive reason. Unlike mathematics or logic, where the "truth" of statements is either assumed or rests upon other statements that are assumed to be true, science bases the "truth" of its statements upon observable evidence. And such evidence is always open to change through reinterpretation or to possible contradiction by new evidence. In other words, at some point scientific propositions are accepted because they describe or interpret a recurring, observable event. But just because an event has occurred on several occasions is no guarantee that it will continue to occur. This can be seen from the following parable from McCain and Segal (1977:70):

> Once upon a time there lived a very intelligent turkey. He lived in a pen and was attended by a kind and thoughtful master. All of his desires were taken care of and he had nothing to do but think of the wonders and regularities of the world. He noticed some regularities—for example, that mornings always began with the sky getting light, followed by the clop, clop, clop of his master's friendly footsteps. These in turn were always followed by the appearance of delicious food and water within his pen. Other things varied: sometimes it rained and sometimes it snowed; sometimes it was warm and sometimes cold; but amid the variability footsteps were always followed by food. This sequence was so consistent it became the basis of his philosophy concerning the goodness of the world. One day, after more than 100 confirmations of the turkey's theories, he listened for the clop, clop, clop, heard it, and had his head chopped off.

Thus, since it is apparent that regularity does not guarantee certainty, scientific propositions, which are based upon such regularity, cannot be proven. Theories are therefore accepted as more or less reasonable and credible according to the accuracy of their predictions and the frequency with which they have been supported by empirical evidence. Let us now examine how such evidence is processed.

Science as Process

The word process means a series of operations or actions that bring about an end result. In industry the longer phrase, manufacturing process, describes the sequence of steps through which raw materials are transformed into a finished product. Of course, this process differs according to what is manufactured; furthermore, technological advances, shifting consumer demands, and the like, lead to periodic changes in the sequence and in its products. But in a given industry for long periods of time the process is repeated over and over again along the same line from beginning to end. In science, by contrast, change is built into the process. The product itself—knowledge—is never "finished," but is constantly remodeled to fit the facts. Furthermore, the sequence of steps followed in one scientific investigation is seldom repeated precisely in another, and the end of one investigation often marks the beginning of another. In short, while the industrial process typically follows a linear progression from raw materials to completed goods, the most characteristic feature of the scientific process is its cyclical nature.

According to Kemeny (1959:85), the great physicist Albert Einstein, whose own scientific contributions were theoretical, repeatedly emphasized that science "must start with facts and end with facts, no matter what theoretical structures it builds in between." In other words, at some point scientists are observers recording facts; next they try to describe and explain what they see; then they make predictions on

FIGURE 2.1. The scientific process.

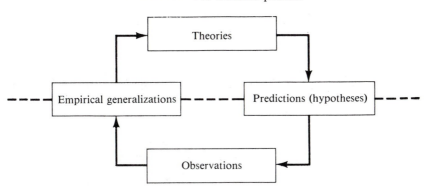

the basis of their theories, which they check against their observations (i.e., the facts) again. This chain of events is diagrammed in Figure 2.1. Where we begin in this chain is arbitrary. But at some point, theories generate predictions or hypotheses, hypotheses are checked against observations, the observations produce generalizations, and the generalizations support, contradict, or suggest modifications in the theory.

The horizontal line in the diagram bisecting empirical generalizations and predictions separates the world of theory from the world of research. The development of theory, as we have seen, is the goal of science. Research supports this goal through systematic observation that generates the facts from which theories are inferred and tested. In the next chapter we discuss some of the logical foundations of theory and the connection between theory and research. Then, in the remainder of the text, we are concerned almost exclusively with the research side of science. The important point to remember, however, is that science is a process involving the continuous interaction of theory and research. (To see the interesting turns that scientific inquiry can take, read Box 2.2.)

Still, this depiction of the science process is not complete, for there is also a characteristic mode of inquiry that distinguishes scientific research from other forms of research. Some people refer to this as "the scientific method." But this unfortunate phrase implies a definitive, orderly procedure that simply does not exist in science. Also, each scientific discipline has its own distinctive tools, procedures, and techniques, which are not readily interchangeable. Questionnaires, one-way mirrors, and videotape, for example, are as useless to the biochemist as microscopes, test tubes, and centrifuge are to the sociologist. Indeed, that is why this book deals with *social* research rather than general scientific research. Yet in spite of such differences there is a common process of justification and a common set of standards that all scientists follow in generating and assessing the evidence upon which their theories are based. The three key principles underlying this process are (1) empiricism, (2) objectivity, and (3) control. To the extent that there is a single agreed-on "method" in science, it is captured in these three key principles, which we will now discuss.

BOX 2.2

The Serendipity Pattern in Science

Scientific inquiry, for the most part, works within the framework of a theory. Hypotheses are derived, researches are planned, and observations are made and interpreted in order to test and elaborate theories. Occasionally, however, unanticipated findings occur that cannot be interpreted meaningfully in terms of prevailing theories and that give rise to new theories. Robert Merton (1957) refers to such discoveries as the *serendipity pattern*. In the history of science, there are many cases of scientific discoveries in which chance, or serendipity, played a part. One of these is Pasteur's discovery of immunization.

> Pasteur's researches on fowl cholera were interrupted by the vacation, and when he resumed he encountered an unexpected obstacle. Nearly all the cultures had become sterile. He attempted to revive them by sub-inoculation into broth and injection into fowls. Most of the sub-cultures failed to grow and the birds were not affected, so he was about to discard everything and start afresh when he had the inspiration of re-inoculating the same fowls with a fresh culture. His colleague Duclaux relates: "To the surprise of all, and perhaps even of Pasteur, who was not expecting such success, nearly all these fowls withstood the inoculation, although fresh fowls succumbed after the usual incubation period." This resulted in the recognition of the principle of immunization with attenuated pathogens (Beveridge, 1957:27).

Social science has had its share of serendipitous findings also. The well-known "Hawthorne effect," which refers to the effect that a worker's awareness of being under study has on his or her performance, was an unanticipated finding of a series of studies carried out between 1927 and 1932 at the Western Electric Hawthorne plant in Chicago (Roethlisberger and Dickson, 1939). In one of the studies six women with the task of assembling telephone relays were placed in a special test room for observation. The idea of the study was to determine the effects of various changes in working conditions (e.g., method of payment, number and length of rest pauses, length of working day) on productivity, as measured by the number of relays completed. Over an extended period of time, numerous changes, each lasting several weeks, were introduced while the women's output was recorded. To the researchers' surprise, however, the changes were not related systematically to output. Instead, the women's output rate rose slowly and steadily throughout the study, even when working conditions introduced early in the study were reintroduced later. As the women were questioned it became evident that their increased productivity was a response to the special attention given to them as participants in what was considered an important experiment. The fun of the test room and the interest of management simply had made it easier to produce at a higher rate. This was an important finding in the history of social research, for it indicated that subjects' awareness of being under study could affect the very actions that an investigator wishes to observe. Experiments, in particular, must take into account such effects, as we discuss in chapter 7.

Empiricism

The foremost characteristic of scientific inquiry is that it is based upon *empiricism*. Empiricism is a way of knowing or understanding the world that relies directly or indirectly on what we experience through our senses: sight, hearing, taste, smell, and touch. In other words, information or data are acceptable in science only insofar as they can be observed or "sensed" in some way under specifiable conditions by people possessing the normal sensory apparatus, intelligence, and skills. Selltiz, Wrightsman, and Cook (1976:22), for example, point out that whereas people can see a baseball, they cannot see a neutron. "But people can see neutrons indirectly, by observing photographic representations of paths neutrons leave. Under no normal conditions can people regularly observe ghosts. Nor do ghosts leave any other observable or tangible manifestations. Thus, we can have scientific theories about baseballs and neutrons but not about ghosts." In the same sense, exobiology (the study of extraterrestrial life) could not be considered a science, as some now claim, until observations or data exist that can test its speculations. Thus, to say that science is based upon empiricism is to say that the only admissible evidence for or against a scientific hypothesis or theory must be observable, directly or indirectly, through some tangible manifestation.

This statement has several implications. Most broadly, it means that appeals to authority, tradition, revelation, intuition, or other nonempirical ways of knowing, which may be acceptable in other endeavors (such as theology and philosophy), cannot be used as scientific evidence. Scientists do not accept a statement or generalization about the world because an authority or expert says it is true, or because tradition and common sense say it is so, or because it seems intuitively plausible. As Katzer, Cook, and Crouch (1978:14) say:

> Evidence is paramount. If the results of well-conducted studies disagree with the authorities, then the authorities may very well be wrong. The proper method for an expert to appeal this verdict is to conduct another study. Or, if two research reports disagree, then additional studies need to be conducted to resolve the issue. The point is that knowledge about the world is best obtained by carefully looking at the world, not by looking at someone's idea of the world.

Empiricism in science also means that scientists limit themselves to problems and issues that can be resolved by making observations of some kind. To determine the appropriateness of a scientific inquiry, one need only ask: Is this an empirically resolvable issue? If it *is not*, then it is beyond the realm of science. If it *is*, then the scientist can proceed to design research to investigate it. In the same fashion, scientific theories must be empirically testable. That is, it must be possible to specify the observable events the theory predicts and the observable conditions under which it applies.

Finally, it should be noted that the terms observable and empirical have broader meaning in science than in philosophy. To the philosopher, "observable" applies to properties like "red," "round," "hot," which can be perceived directly by the senses. To the scientist, observables are anything that can be related to the results of perceived measurements. For example, a temperature of 98.6 degrees Fahrenheit is considered observable to the scientist because it can be related to the height of a column of mercury in a thermometer. It is not an observable to the philosopher, however, because there is no direct sensory perception of such a magnitude. One cannot feel or "see" temperature directly; one can only see a pointer reading on a thermometer (Carnap, 1966). Thus, empiricism in science often takes the form of *indirect* observation, whereby instruments are employed that aid and extend the scientist's ability to observe. We might call this *sophisticated* empiricism to distinguish it from the kind of *naive* empiricism that relies on the unaided use of one's senses.

Objectivity

An important feature of empirical evidence is that it is assumed to exist outside of scientists themselves. In this sense, it is sometimes held that scientists are, or should be, objective. However, in the usual sense of the term (to mean observation that is free from emotion, conjecture, or personal bias), objectivity is rarely, if ever, possible. Social psychologists have demonstrated that we do not see the world simply "as is." Rather, we interpret everything we see, and our interpretations depend on the sum total of our past learning and present experiences—including everything from our culture and language to our beliefs and expectations. It has been shown that if each eye is exposed to a different picture simultaneously, people will tend to "see" only the picture that is consistent with their past experiences. Mexicans, for instance, were more likely to see a bullfight scene when it was paired with a baseball game, while Americans were more likely to see the baseball game (Bagby, 1957). Emotional states also have been shown to affect what we see. In one study, people who were made to feel afraid were more likely to perceive another person as fearful and anxious than people who were unafraid (Feshbach and Feshbach, 1963). Clearly, then, our observation—or more properly, our "interpretation"—of the world is inevitably distorted to some extent by factors not under our conscious control. For this reason, scientists agree that objectivity, in the sense of observation free from bias, is a practical impossibility.

Fortunately, however, scientists assign a limited and far more useful meaning to the term objective. To the scientist, it merely means that a group of scientists can agree on the results of a given observation. In other words, it is possible for two or more independent observers working under the same conditions to agree that they are observing the same thing or event. The technical term for this is *intersubjective testability*. Psychologists Doherty and Shemberg (1978:5) provide the following example of its application in social research:

> If you were to send two observers into a classroom and instruct them to rate a child on "hostility," you may well expect to get two very different ratings. The term *hostility* is open to many different interpretations. So the observations would not be very objective. On the other hand, suppose you instructed the observers to count the number of times that a particular child punched or hit other children, defined what you meant by punched or hit, maybe showed the observers a training film to sharpen the definition, and *then* turned them loose to make the observation. You would very likely get very high agreement among the observers. That's objectivity.

Because of the requirement of objectivity, scientists are supposed to describe their research in detail, outlining their logic and methods of observation in such a way that other scientists may evaluate and repeat the investigation. In this way, others can decide for themselves whether a researcher's subjectivity has distorted the conclusions. In fact, ultimately "objectivity is the product of a community of thinkers, each offering unsparing criticisms of . . . claims that the others make. For no one scientist engaged in this process of criticism is infallible, and each has his [or her] own peculiar intellectual or emotional bias" (Nagel, 1967).

The importance of the public nature of science, and the sense in which this contributes to its objectivity, can be seen in the evaluation and reanalysis of some studies by the late British psychologist Cyril Burt. For several decades Burt was a very influential figure in scientific research on intelligence and its genetic basis. His research on identical twins reared apart, first reported in 1956, was a principal source of support for his own and others' theories that intelligence is determined primarily by heredity. However, beginning in the early 1970s Burt's articles underwent a close scrutiny that revealed several highly improbable and inconsistent results. No one can say for sure whether these flaws were the product of fraudulence or mere carelessness. Burt's preeminence has led many people to doubt that he fabricated his data just as it led scientists to accept his findings uncritically for many years. But the upshot of the reassessments of Burt's findings is that they are now considered unusable as scientific evidence (Wade, 1976; Dorfman, 1978). And so, the public nature of science permitted the discovery of some unwarranted conclusions about human intelligence.

Control

Even before scientists publish their findings, it is assumed that they have used procedures that eliminate, as far as possible, sources of bias and error that may distort their results. As we have said, the influence of certain biases is unavoidable, for language itself can structure our perceptions of the world. Biases even enter into the selection of problems for study and the preference for certain research strategies. However, there are many ways in which scientists, during the course of research, attempt to control for and minimize bias in order to maximize the trustworthiness of their observations. The use of such control procedures that rule out biases and confounding explanations of the events being studied is the principal way in which scientific inquiry differs from casual observation. In fact, the principle of control lies behind virtually every procedure and technique introduced in the remainder of this book. To get a glimpse of how scientists apply this principle, let us examine some applications from medical research.

Until this century nearly all medications had little, if any, beneficial pharmacological effect on the treated (Shapiro, 1960). In other words, the ingredients of most medications were worthless, and whatever beneficial effect they seemed to have was probably due to the power of suggestion or to the fact that people will improve naturally from many ailments irrespective of the medical treatment they receive. If most prescriptions were pharmacologically ineffective, however, why did so many people believe they were beneficial? The answer probably rests with the faulty evidence upon which beliefs in the effectiveness of treatments were based. For example, it was widely held at one time that cold salt water baths were beneficial to people suffering from high fevers. This belief appears to have been based upon repeated observations of improvement in the condition of people subjected to this treatment. But this evidence is insufficient to establish the validity of the cure, since the possibility exists that people not given such treatment might show a similar improvement. In short, those who accepted the belief failed to compare the course of the disease in patients receiving the treatment with its course in a control group who did not receive it, so that there was no rational basis for deciding whether the observed improvement could be attributed to the treatment (Nagel, 1967).

Yet even this kind of comparison may be inadequate for testing the efficacy of a new treatment or drug. When a treatment group is compared with a group that has received no treatment at all, there is still no control for the psychological effect of merely receiving some form of medication. A substantial part of medical practice appears to be based on the physician's and the patient's faith in the power of drugs to cure. It has been observed, for example, that persons given an inert substance such as a saline solution or sugar pill, called a "placebo," often react as favorably as persons given real medication. It is obviously important, therefore, to control for such placebo effects. One way that this is often done in medical research is through the use of "double-blind" investigations.

In a double-blind study, several doctors are asked to prescribe and administer the drug being tested to their patients. The doctors receive the drugs from the researcher in separate vials that are identified by number and contain only enough of the drug for one patient. Half of the vials contain the actual drug and half contain a placebo; and since neither doctors nor patients know which they are receiving, their beliefs about the drug cannot influence its effectiveness. Thus, in this type of study any difference observed between those receiving the drug and those receiving the placebo could not be attributed to either the doctors' or the patients' expectations about the drug.

Still, even if a double-blind procedure were used, there may be other problems of interpretation. One of the most important of these problems stems from the simple fact that people are different. As a consequence, they react differently to various treatments and drugs, so that most medications are not 100 percent effective. Therefore, if the patients used for testing tend to be people for whom a drug just happens not to work, the researcher may underestimate its effectiveness; and if the patients tend to be people for whom the drug does work, the researcher may overestimate its effectiveness. Fortunately, social researchers have devised methods—random selection procedures, discussed in chapters 6 and 7—that control for this problem by enabling one to estimate the likelihood of its occurring.

Other problems and mechanisms of control could be mentioned, but by now the point should be clear. While the researcher may devise studies and gather information to test a certain explanation or answer a certain question, findings are often open to a variety of interpretations. The idea of control is to employ procedures that effectively rule out all explanations except the one in which the researcher is interested. In medical research this takes the form of placebo groups and double-blind techniques designed to rule out the possibility of doctors' and patients' expectations contributing to the effectiveness of a treatment. In social research, as you will see, the application of the concept of control takes a wide range of forms, including (a) using several independent observers, not only to check for interobserver agreement (i.e., objectivity), but also to cancel out the personal biases of any particular observer, (b) withholding information from subjects, who may respond differently if they knew specifically what the researcher were investigating, and (c) employing instruments like tape recorders and counters or systematic observational methods that eliminate errors of omission and commission on the part of human observers. As we turn our attention exclusively to *social* research, we not only will introduce you to such techniques but also will help you to identify the sources of error and bias for which the techniques are intended to control.

Science: Ideal versus Reality

As we cautioned at the beginning of the chapter, we have presented a somewhat idealized view of science. It is a view often presented by philosophers who have analyzed the logic of the scientific process. Teachers of social research, however, sometimes ignore this "philosophical" model or even debunk it, reasoning that it gives students an unrealistic impression of what scientists actually do. But to disregard the picture of science outlined here is to fail to acknowledge a crucial fact: this model of knowledge and inquiry unifies and guides the activities of all scientists even if their work falls short of the ideal. Still, we would be remiss if we did not point out some of the more important realities of science, especially as practiced in the social sciences.

The first reality is that theoretical knowledge is not well developed in the social sciences. Indeed, there are those who claim that, at best, the social sciences have established only a few low-level principles, and certainly nothing comparable to the kinetic theory of gases examined earlier. Also, while we have defined "scientific theory" as a set of interrelated propositions from which testable hypotheses can be deduced, the term has a much looser meaning in the social sciences. In these fields, theory may refer to all sorts of speculative ideas offered as explanations for phenomena, and it is very common to see the terms "theory" and "hypothesis" used interchangeably.

With respect to scientific theory, it is also important to dispose of a popular misconception that the ideal view of science may serve to perpetuate. That is, theories do not have to be totally accurate to be judged as scientifically useful. Scientific predictions can never be exactly confirmed. There is always some degree of error. How much error depends on the level of development of both theory and research technology, which explains why theoretical predictions in the physical sciences, more advanced in both areas, are generally so much more accurate than in the social sciences. But this lesser degree of accuracy does not make social science theory any less scientific. In all sciences, theories are evaluated in a comparative framework in which one theory is judged superior to another according to criteria consistent with the aims of science. These criteria, as mentioned earlier, revolve primarily around the scope and accuracy of a theory's predictions.

The model of science outlined also may foster some distorted impressions about the practice of scientific inquiry. For one thing, scientific investigations seldom proceed along a smooth path from theory to hypothesis to observation to generalization, and so on. Reports of scientific research tend to follow this format, but that is mostly the product of hindsight and the condensation of a great many activities. Rather, the course of inquiry tends to be very irregular and circuitous, with no typical scenario. For example, the scientist may begin with a theoretical deduction, test the deduction, find that it is not confirmed, mull over the inconsistent results, revise the theory, test a new theoretical deduction, and so forth. Or, the scientist may begin with a problem from everyday life, make an educated guess about a suspected relationship, investigate the relationship, find that it does not hold, revise the idea, and formulate a new hypothesis for further study.

Sociologist Walter Wallace (1971:18–19) also points out that the process of scientific inquiry may occur

(1) sometimes quickly, sometimes slowly; (2) sometimes with a very high degree of formalization and rigor, sometimes quite informally, unself-consciously, and intuitively; (3) sometimes through the interaction of several scientists in distinct roles (of say, "theorist," "research director," "interviewer," "methodologist," "sampling expert," "statistician," etc.), sometimes through the efforts of a single scientist; and (4) sometimes only in the scientist's imagination, sometimes in actual fact.

As you can see, there is nothing mechanical or programmed about scientific work. The formulation of theory, the formulation of empirical tests of hypotheses, and the application of methods to carry out the tests all involve a great deal of imagination and insight and also can generate tremendous excitement and frustration.

This last observation brings us to a very important aspect of the reality of scientific practice. While the image of scientists projected by the ideal view is that of detached and dispassionate observers of the world, there is a pervasive subjective component in science. For example, scientists naturally develop an intense commitment to their work, and sometimes this commitment causes them to overlook or reject evidence that is contrary to their own ideas. In fact, such commitment may affect entire scientific disciplines. It has been shown that disciplines may adhere to theories for long periods in the face of much contradictory evidence, and that major theories are displaced only after prolonged "scientific revolutions" (Kuhn, 1962).

Also recall that as much as scientific norms and the scrutiny and skepticism of the scientific community foster objectivity, it is impossible to eliminate completely the influence of personal values and biases. Subjective judgments obviously affect problem selection, and they also enter into decisions about research procedures as well as the interpretation of results. Some social scientists even contend that the application of the model of science presented in this chapter can seriously bias interpretations of the social world. Indeed, we may regard this as the final reality of social science—that there are social researchers who reject what they call the "positivist" or "natural science" model.

According to these "phenomenologists," the positions of the natural scientist and social scientist differ because they deal with inherently different objects of study. The inanimate or nonhuman objects in the natural sciences "are not expected to interpret themselves or the environment or field in which they are located and move" (Gurwitsch, 1974:129). Therefore, the natural scientist can invoke his or her interpretations without regard to how facts and events may be interpreted by the objects themselves. Social scientists, on the other hand, deal with human beings who give meaning to their every action. Because of this—because the objects of study themselves interpret and act upon their own interpretations of the world— social scientists should aim to understand human behavior from the subject's frame of reference only. Otherwise, if one seeks to identify the external causes of phenomena, as natural scientists do, then one's interpretations of the social world are bound to be erroneous.

We certainly agree that it is important to understand the subject's point of view in addressing many sociological questions. Also consistent with the phenomenological position, we see certain methodological approaches as more amenable to this type of analysis than others (see chapter 11). However, many sociological issues need not take into account the subject's view of social reality. And regardless of whether one does incorporate the subject's interpretation into one's analysis, it is always best to use a variety of methodological approaches. Finally, no matter what methods they adopt, it is clear that most social scientists today are guided by the canons of scientific inquiry outlined here.

Summary

The aim of science in the broadest sense is to know and understand the world around us. In pursuing this aim, science addresses questions that can be answered by identifying the conditions under which observable events take place. Answering such questions requires concepts that describe the phenomena of interest and general laws and theories that show how events are instances of patterned relationships. Ideally, the events to be explained can be logically deduced from laws and theories, so that it is possible both to explain the past and present and to predict the future. Scientific theories also satisfy our curiosity and render a sense of understanding by positing the causal relationships and processes that connect events. This understanding is considered to be fragile and incomplete, however, since the observed patterns among events are always subject to change or reinterpretation. Thus, there are no ultimate explanations in science, and it follows that scientific theories should not be judged as true or false, only *useful*. In general, the greater the range of phenomena a theory is capable of explaining and predicting, and the more accurate and precise its predictions, the more useful it is considered to be.

The production of scientific knowledge requires the constant interplay of theory and research. The process of science therefore is cyclical, with theories leading to predictions, predictions to observations (or research), and observations to general-izations that have implications for theory. Throughout this process, scientists are guided by three canons of inquiry: empiricism, objectivity, and control.

Empiricism means that the only admissible evidence is that which we can know directly or indirectly through our senses. Objectivity, scientists agree, is not possi-ble in the sense of bias-free observation. On the other hand, it is possible if it means intersubjective testability—that independent observers are capable of agreeing about the results of observations. Ultimately, such objectivity is a product of sci-ence's public nature, for scientific knowledge rests with the consensus of scientists, and individual claims must be scrutinized by others. While certain biases are unavoidable, scientists do try to control for bias and error as far as possible. In fact, most of the procedures discussed in the remainder of this book could be regarded as mechanisms of scientific control.

Although the above model of science guides the activities of most social researchers, it is an ideal that in some ways does not match reality. Thus, theory in social science seldom takes the form of a deductive system of propositions and rarely, if ever, matches the accuracy of the natural sciences. Research can be very haphazard, sometimes exhilarating, and sometimes frustrating, so that to do scien-tific work requires a deep emotional commitment. This subjective element also affects science in other ways—to the extent that phenomenologists reject the very model of science that characteristically guides contemporary social research.

Key Terms

scientific versus nonscientific questions
concept
explanation
prediction
hypothesis
empirical generalization
law

cause/causal relationship
empiricism
objectivity
intersubjective testability
control
serendipity pattern

Review Questions and Problems

1. What is the ultimate goal of science?

2. Identify some of the untestable assumptions of science.

3. Give examples of scientific and nonscientific questions that could be asked about the following topics: (a) capital punishment; (b) abortion; (c) intelligence.

4. State the three rules about language usage in science.

5. How are scientific explanation and prediction alike?

6. Briefly differentiate the following terms: hypothesis, empirical generaliza-tion, law, and theory.

7. Short of direct empirical tests, what criteria are used for judging the relative superiority of competing scientific theories?

8. Explain how the structure of scientific theory ideally forms a *hierarchy* of explanations.

9. Why is the identification of causal processes thought to be crucial to the development of scientific knowledge?

10. Give an example of an empirical generalization that explains but cannot predict.

11. Why is all scientific knowledge considered tentative?

12. Describe the cyclical nature of the scientific process.

13. Why is the phrase "the scientific method" a misleading description of scientific research?

14. What are the three key principles underlying scientific inquiry?

15. What is meant by "indirect observation"?

16. Why is completely unbiased observation thought to be impossible to attain?

17. Briefly explain the scientific meaning of ":objectivity."

18. How does the public nature of science contribute to its objectivity?

19. What is the purpose of control procedures in scientific inquiry?

20. In what ways do the authors suggest that the depiction of science presented in this chapter is idealized?

21. Briefly explain the phenomenologists' position regarding the positivist model of science presented in this chapter.

NOTES

1. A distinction sometimes is made between basic or pure science, concerned exclusively with the production of knowledge, and applied science, involving the application of principles to specific, limited problems. The heart of science, however, is the search for understanding, not the solution of existing problems.

2. The division of philosophy that investigates the foundations of knowledge and understanding is called epistemology.

3. On the other hand, it would be possible to investigate scientifically the effects of prosecution on the incidence of pornography or the relationship between efficiency and morale.

3

The Logic of Scientific Reasoning

Like any serious intellectual endeavor, science involves thinking and reasoning. As an overall characterization, the reasoning process in science consists of attempts to draw conclusions about the order of the empirical world on the basis of observational evidence. As we study methods of social research, we will be concerned mostly with the nature of the evidence—with how to make scientifically valid observations and with how to judge the quality of scientific evidence. It is also important, however, to know something about evaluating the reasoning process itself. For such knowledge, we turn to logic, the study of the principles of reasoning.

Most people recognize that certain ways of reasoning are acceptable or valid while others are unacceptable or invalid. The aim of logic is to state the principles upon which we make this distinction. We will now introduce some of these principles for the purpose of applying them to scientific reasoning. Since reasoning is, of course, an activity occasionally practiced by everybody, learning a little logic also should help you to evaluate your own thinking as well as the persuasive messages that you encounter every day.

Logic and Reasoning

If we think of reasoning as an art or craft, then one of the true masters would have to be Sir Arthur Conan Doyle's famous detective Sherlock Holmes. The logician Wesley Salmon (1973:1–2) relates how in one of Holmes's adventures he comes across an old felt hat, whose owner is unknown to him. After carefully observing the hat, Holmes tells Dr. Watson several things about its owner, one of which is that he is highly "intellectual." Puzzled, Dr. Watson asks Holmes what the basis is for this assertion. In answer, Holmes puts the hat upon his head, where it comes down over his forehead and settles upon the bridge of his nose. "It is a question of cubic capacity," he says. "A man with so large a brain must have something in it."

This example contains the basic ingredients for logical analysis. Holmes has stated a conclusion along with supporting evidence. In his thinking he has proceeded from certain beliefs that he holds to be true (the evidence) to a claim (a conclusion) that he infers from them. Logic deals with the relation between evidence and conclusion (Salmon, 1973:3). Once an inference is made, logic can tell us whether or not the inference is correct, that is, whether the evidence properly justifies the conclusion.

Whenever we reason we proceed from certain information to conclusions based upon that information. The point at which logical analysis begins is *after* the act of reasoning has taken place. Once an inference has been made, it can be transformed into an explicit set of statements and subjected to logical analysis. In this way, logic can clarify our thinking. However, logic does not provide a description of actual thought processes, with acts of thinking, imagining, and creating. It cannot tell us what to infer or how to think and reason, but it can reveal whether our reasoning is sound. Although Dr. Watson and Sherlock Holmes were inevitably in possession of the same information, it was always the clever Holmes who drew the inferences. But after Holmes had expressed his reasoning, Watson could, through his understanding of the rules of logic, evaluate the correctness of the inference.

Elements of Logical Analysis

We will now introduce some of the technical concepts and rules that logic supplies for investigating reasoning. This excursion into logic will be highly selective, as we identify a few logical skills that are essential for studying the particular forms of reasoning found in science. Of necessity we will sidestep many issues that would be dealt with in more advanced logical studies. As in the previous chapter, we do not intend to dwell on knotty issues, but rather to fill in some of the background in the picture of social research, to provide a context for understanding the specific guidelines and procedures presented in the ensuing chapters.

The fundamental elements of logical analysis consist of terms, propositions, and arguments (Wheelwright, 1962). Let us examine the meaning of each of these elements as well as their relevance to science.

Terms

The simplest element of logical analysis is the term. A term is whatever is meant by a word or phrase. Some terms you will encounter in the following pages are antecedent, syllogism, valid argument, induction, and the fallacy of affirming the consequent. The distinctive feature of a term is its *meaning*. A term is neither true nor false. We can understand a term but cannot affirm or deny it. Terms are analogous to concepts in science.

Propositions

A proposition is an expression of a judgment about some term or terms. In the grammatical sense, it is a declarative sentence. Unlike terms, propositions are, by definition, either true or false. Logicians are interested in determining precisely what a given proposition says, that is, what is true or false according to the proposition, and in examining the logical role of propositions in reasoning.

There are several types of propositions in logical analysis. The traditional logic that stems from Aristotle deals primarily with what are called "categorical" propositions, for example, "All men are mortal," and "No events are uncaused." In this chapter we will concentrate on what are known as "conditional" or "hypothetical" propositions.[1]

A *conditional proposition* consists of two simple statements joined by the words "if" and "then." For example,

> a. If today is Friday, then tomorrow is Saturday.
> b. If the reader has taken a course in logic, then this chapter is largely a review.

In a conditional proposition the part that is introduced by the "if" is called the *antecedent* and the part that follows the "then" is called the *consequent.* "Today is Friday" is the antecedent of statement a; "the reader has taken a course in logic" is the antecedent of statement b. "Tomorrow is Saturday" is the consequent of statement a; "this chapter is largely a review" is the consequent of statement b.

A conditional proposition asserts that the antecedent implies the consequent, that the consequent is true if the antecedent is true. Beyond this common meaning, however, there are different kinds of relations between antecedent and consequent that can be asserted by conditional propositions. One kind of relation is definitional. In the conditional proposition "If the figure is a triangle, then it has three sides," the consequent follows from the antecedent by the very definition of the word "triangle" (Copi, 1973:15). Another sense of the "if-then" connection is causal. "If this metal is immersed in nitric acid, then it will dissolve" asserts that the antecedent (immersing the metal in nitric acid) causes the consequent (the metal's dissolution). Since scientists are concerned precisely with this kind of relation, the truth of which must be established empirically, our discussion of reasoning deals primarily with conditional propositions.

Arguments

In logic, an argument is a set of two or more propositions of which one is claimed to follow either necessarily or probably from the others. This technical definition of an argument should not be confused with its use in everyday discourse to mean some sort of disagreement, quarrel, or debate. Constructing arguments is the logician's way of making explicit a person's reasoning from evidence to conclusion. Once an act of reasoning has taken place, then the reasoning can be transformed into a group of verbal or written statements that constitute an argument. The statement that is claimed to follow from the others in an argument is, in fact, referred to as the *conclusion.* The other statements that supply evidence for accepting the conclusion are known as *premises.*

The principal kind of argument studied by logicians is the *syllogism.* Syllogisms are arguments composed of three propositions: two premises and the conclusion that the premises logically imply. A classic example of a syllogism, used by logicians for the past 2000 years, is

> 3.1 All men are mortal. (premise)
> Socrates is a man. (premise)
> Therefore, Socrates is mortal. (conclusion)

Although the arguments implicit in any act of reasoning will often contain more than three propositions, longer arguments can always be broken down into a series of syllogisms. Hence, the syllogism is the basic unit of logical analysis. To analyze the logic of scientific reasoning we must first identify the syllogistic structure of that reasoning and then examine the syllogisms with respect to their validity or invalidity.

Whereas terms are judged as to their meaning, and propositions primarily as to their truth, syllogisms are judged primarily as to their validity (Wheelwright, 1962:14). The *validity* of a syllogism depends solely on the relation between its premises and its conclusion. In a valid syllogism the premises have the following relation to the conclusion: if the premises are true, then the conclusion must also be true. Notice from this definition that to assess the validity of a syllogism we do not need to know whether the premises or conclusions are actually true. We only need to know whether the conclusion would be true *if* the premises *were* true. Thus, it is possible to have a valid syllogism that consists entirely of false propositions:

> 3.2 All students are seniors. (false)
> Some robots are students. (false)
> Therefore, some robots are seniors. (false)

It is also possible to have an invalid syllogism that contains exclusively true statements. One should be able to recognize, by common sense, the invalidity of the following syllogism:

> 3.3 All butterflies can fly. (true)
> All crows are birds. (true)
> Therefore, all crows can fly. (true)

These two examples do not exhaust the possible combinations, but they should clarify that the validity or invalidity of a syllogism is independent of the truth of its premises. That is, we can logically analyze arguments without knowing whether the premises are true. In fact, example 3.2 shows that we can analyze syllogisms that we know have false premises (although we, as social scientists, would ordinarily leave this task to logicians).

Validity and Truth: Logic and Science

With the aim of evaluating reasoning, logic can analyze relations among propositions irrespective of whether the propositions are factually true or false or whether they say anything at all about reality. Science, by contrast, has the broader goal of establishing knowledge about the empirical world. To justify their conclusions about reality, scientists must evaluate both the adequacy of their reasoning *and* the actuality of their statements, that is, both validity and truth. In other words, to justify conclusions, (1) the premises must be properly related to the conclusion so that the argument is logically correct or valid, and (2) the premises must be true (Salmon, 1973:3–4). Logic is concerned with the first question only. Logic can tell us if, given X and Y, we can reasonably infer Z, but it cannot tell us if X and Y are true. It is up to scientific observation to make that determination.

To clarify these two aspects of justifying conclusions, recall our Sherlock Holmes example. Holmes was interested in establishing as fact that the wearer of the hat was highly intellectual. To substantiate this assertion he presented an argument. Although we need not spell out his argument in complete detail here, let us examine one key syllogism that the argument contained (adapted from Salmon, 1973:3):

> 3.4 People with large brains are highly intellectual.
> The owner of this hat has a large brain.
> Therefore, the owner of this hat is highly intellectual.

The premises of this argument are alleged statements of fact that supply evidence for the conclusion. Therefore, if either of the premises is false, then the evidence does not justify the conclusion. But even if the premises are factually true, they still would not justify the conclusion unless the argument itself is correct. In point of fact, the argument is logically valid, and therefore Holmes's reasoning is sound. However, scientific research has shown the first premise to be false: the size of human brains is not directly related to intelligence. And the truth of the second premise rests upon the assumptions that hat size indicates skull size and that skull size indicates brain size. Hence, Holmes has not *justified* his conclusion. This does not mean that the conclusion is false. It may well be true, but Holmes has not provided adequate justification for accepting it as true.

Deduction and Induction

The two major types of reasoning are deduction and induction. The primary distinction between deduction and induction rests with the strength or certainty of the claim that is made about the conclusion on the basis of the premises. When a person uses deductive reasoning, or presents a deductive argument, he or she is claiming that the conclusion absolutely must be true if all the premises are true. (All the syllogisms that we have considered heretofore are deductive arguments.) When a person argues inductively, he or she is claiming that the conclusion is probably true but not necessarily true if all the premises are true.

Consider the following examples of each argument type:

> 3.5 *Deductive*: If Walter belongs to the union, then he votes Democratic.
> Walter belongs to the Union.
> Therefore, Walter votes Democratic.

3.6 *Inductive*: Hubert, Walter, and Joan, who are all union members, vote Democratic. Therefore, all union members vote Democratic.

In the first argument it would be inconsistent to deny the conclusion if the premises are true because the conclusion says nothing that was not already stated by the premises. The conclusion merely makes explicit the information contained in the premises (Salmon, 1973:14–15). In the second argument, on the other hand, it is possible for the conclusion to be false when the premise is true. The premise does not provide certain support for the conclusion because the conclusion goes beyond the information contained in the premise. Thus, a deductive argument, judged as to its validity, is either valid or invalid—there is no in-between. An inductive argument, by contrast, is judged as more or less sound depending on how probable it is that the conclusion is true, given the evidence provided in the premises.

It is sometimes said that deduction moves from general principles to particular instances, while induction moves from the particular to the general. For example, the above deductive argument might have begun with the general proposition that "all union members vote Democratic," from which we deduce that a particular union member votes Democratic. In our inductive argument, on the other hand, we observe that several union members vote Democratic and infer from this the general conclusion that they all do.[2]

This way of distinguishing between deduction and induction highlights the role of these logical processes in science. Recall from chapter 2 that science is a cyclical process. At one point in the cycle, the scientist reasons inductively, starting with particular observations and deriving general propositions and theories. Then the scientist reasons deductively, deducing certain observable consequences from his or her theory. Both of these applications are discussed as we consider different forms of deductive and inductive arguments in science.

Deductive Reasoning in Science

In chapter 2 we showed how the propositions of scientific explanations can be organized into deductive arguments. It is obviously important that such explanations represent valid deductive reasoning, for it is pointless to investigate a conclusion deduced from a theory if the deduction is invalid. To evaluate an act of deductive reasoning we must determine the validity or invalidity of the argument that represents the reasoning. So far we have done this informally, relying on the reader's common sense or intuition to recognize the validity or invalidity of an argument. However, such a procedure is notoriously fallible. In this section we first introduce a more rigorous technique for testing the validity of arguments containing conditional propositions. Then, we show how one can apply this technique to the reasoning inherent in scientific explanations.

Argument Forms

An argument is deductively valid if the truth of its premises necessarily implies the truth of its conclusion. We can recognize an invalid argument, then, as one in which the premises are true, but the conclusion is false. By this definition the following syllogism is clearly invalid:

> 3.7 If a person is President, then he or she is famous.   (true)
> Muhammad Ali is not President.   (true)
> Therefore, Muhammad Ali is not famous.   (false)

From the content of this syllogism we know that the premises are true and the conclusion is false; hence, it is invalid. However, since questions of truth and validity are independent of one another, we should be able to assess validity without reference to the content of the premises and conclusion. Recall that validity refers to the relation between premises and conclusion; this is something that we can check merely by examining the logical structure or *form* of the argument.

The form of an argument is identified by substituting letters for each of the sentences or phrases it contains. Thus, in argument 3.7 above, if we let the letter "p" stand for the proposition "a person is President" and "q" stand for the proposition "he or she is famous," then the form of this argument may be represented as follows:

> 3.8 If p, then q.
> Not p.
> Therefore, not q.

We can read 3.8 as "If p is true, then q is true; p is not true; therefore, q is not true." This particular argument form is invalid because we have shown that it is possible to have an argument of this form with true premises and a false conclusion. It follows, then, that any argument having this form is invalid.

In general, it is possible to determine the validity of a given argument by checking the validity of its form. Any argument with a valid form is a valid argument; any argument with an invalid argument form is an invalid argument. This method has its limitations, which we will not go into here (see Salmon, 1973:20–21; Copi, 1973:18–23). More sophisticated methods for testing validity such as Venn diagrams, syllogistic rules, and truth tables are introduced in textbooks on symbolic or formal logic. For our purposes, it will suffice to learn some common valid and invalid argument forms. Once you are able to recognize these forms, then you can understand and evaluate the soundness of much scientific reasoning.

Letting the letters "p," "q," and "r" stand for any statement whatever, the three simplest valid argument forms containing "if-then" statements (i.e., conditional propositions) are as follows:

1. *Affirming the antecedent*
   If p, then q.   e.g., If this metal is gold, then it will not dissolve in nitric acid.

   p.   This metal is gold.
   Therefore, q.   Therefore, it will not dissolve in nitric acid.

2. *Denying the consequent*

If *p*, then *q*.	e.g., If he can do long division, then he can add and subtract.
Not *q*.	He cannot add and subtract.
Therefore, not *p*.	Therefore, he cannot do long division.

3. *Chain argument* (or "hypothetical syllogism")

If *p*, then *q*.	e.g., If money gets tight, then interest rates will rise.
If *q*, then *r*.	If interest rates rise, then the volume of loans will be low.
Therefore, if *p*, then *r*.	If money gets tight, then the volume of loans will be low.

Note how the name of each of these forms is derived. In the form called "affirming the antecedent," the first premise is a conditional proposition, and the second premise affirms the antecedent of this conditional; in the form called "denying the consequent," the first premise is a conditional proposition, and the second premise denies or negates the consequent of this conditional (Salmon, 1973:25). Finally, in the chain argument form the two premises are linked, as in a chain, by a common statement (symbolized by "*q*" above) that is the consequent of the first premise and the antecedent of the second premise.

It is possible to construct longer chain arguments with any number of premises. The only requirements for a valid chain argument are (1) that the consequent of each premise be the antecedent of the next premise, and (2) that the conclusion have the antecedent of the first premise as its antecedent and the consequent of the last premise as its consequent.

Invalid argument forms are called *fallacies*. There are two common fallacies that are deceptively similar to the first two valid argument forms above:

1. *Fallacy of affirming the consequent*

If *p*, then *q*.	e.g., If he can do long division, then he can add and subtract.
q.	He can add and subtract.
Therefore, *p*.	Therefore, he can do long division.

2. *Fallacy of denying the antecedent*

If *p*, then *q*.	e.g., If you lock your car, then it will not be stolen.
Not *p*.	You did not lock your car.
Therefore, not *q*.	Therefore, it will be stolen.

Each of these arguments and argument forms is invalid because it is possible for the premises to be true and the conclusion false. One can see this in the first example if one realizes that long division can be performed (without calculators, of course) only if one can add and subtract, but that those who can add and subtract (e.g., third graders) cannot necessarily do long division. And one could imagine the same situation—that is, true premises and a false conclusion—in example 2, which, the reader should note, has exactly the same form as syllogism 3.7 above.

Fallacies are identified by one particular combination of truth and falsity among the premises and conclusion of an argument. That is, an argument is invalid or fallacious if it is possible for the premises to be true and the conclusion false. It is important to note, however, that a valid argument can contain any other combination of true and false premises and conclusion. For example, a valid argument with a true conclusion may have one or more false premises, as in the following:

3.9 If Harvard University is in California, then it is in New England.   (false)
Harvard University is in California.   (false)
Therefore, Harvard University is in New England.   (true)

3.10 If this animal is a whale, then it is a fish.   (false)
If it is a fish, then it lives in water.   (true)
Therefore, if this animal is a whale, then it lives in water.   (true)

The above arguments show that it would be a logical error either to infer true premises from a true conclusion or to infer a false conclusion from one or more false premises.

A useful summary of the various combinations of true and false premises, valid and invalid arguments, and true and false conclusions is contained in the following three statements (Manheim, 1977:35):

1. If all the premises are true and the argument is valid, the conclusion *must* be true.
2. If all the premises are true and the conclusion is false, the argument *must* be invalid.
3. If the argument is valid and the conclusion is false, at least one premise *must* be false.

These statements should help you to evaluate deductive reasoning. However, lest one be fooled by merely examining the truth or falsity of propositions, the best practice is to assess the validity of an argument strictly by its form. To identify the form of an argument, as we have shown, one must simply substitute letters for each of the simple statements in an argument. If an argument's apparent form is valid, the argument is valid; if the form is invalid, the argument is invalid.

The Deductive Pattern of Scientific Explanation

Now that we have the tools with which to evaluate deductive reasoning, let us apply them to scientific explanation. Recall from chapter 2 that a particular event or phenomenon is explained in science by showing how it can be subsumed under a general empirical proposition. Suppose, for example, that we want to explain why your friend John, who runs 2 miles daily, runs faster when people are watching him run than when he runs in isolation. We might say that because John runs daily, this is apparently not a terribly strenuous or difficult behavior for him, and people perform simple, well-learned tasks better in the presence of others than in isolation. Thus, we explain the phenomenon by showing that it is an instance of a general empirical (or causal) rule, which we call either a law or hypothesis according to how much empirical support it has.

Closer examination will show that the inference from law or hypothesis to a specific event can be put into the form of a deductive argument. The first premise of the argument consists of the law or hypothesis. This can be stated in the form of a conditional proposition that asserts a causal link between the antecedent and the consequent. The second premise specifies the antecedent conditions that are inherent both in the first premise and in the event to be explained. The conclusion logically deduced from these premises is then the event to be explained. For example, the above explanation can be represented as follows:

General law or hypothesis (premise 1): If a person performs a simple or well-learned task in the presence of others, then he or she will do better than when performing alone.

Antecedent conditions (premise 2): John ran 2 miles, a well-learned task, as others looked on.

Event explained (conclusion): John ran faster in the presence of others than he did alone.

The reader should recognize that this argument has a valid deductive argument form, namely, affirming the antecedent. Scientific explanations of this kind thus follow a deductive pattern. Just as the conclusion is an expected consequence of the premises in logical deduction, the given phenomenon or event to be explained is an expected occurrence in view of certain specified circumstances and general propositions (i.e., laws or hypotheses).

In chapter 2 we also pointed out that laws are explained deductively by theories. However, the logical form of a theoretical explanation is not quite the same as in the explanation of events. The simplest theory has the form of a chain argument, with premises consisting of lawlike propositions from which a given law can be deduced (or explained). For example, Cottrell's evaluation apprehension theory of the audience effect (1972) may be organized into the following set of propositions:

Theory

Proposition (premise 1): If a person performs a well-learned task in the presence of others, then the person will think that others are evaluating his or her performance.

Proposition (premise 2): If a person thinks that others are evaluating his or her performance, then the person's response drive will increase.

Proposition (premise 3): If response drive increases, then dominant or well-learned responses are strengthened.

Proposition (premise 4): If a person's dominant responses are strengthened, then the person's performance on well-learned tasks will be enhanced.

Law or hypothesis explained (conclusion): Therefore, if a person performs a well-learned task in the presence of others, then the persons' performance will be enhanced (i.e., will be better than the person's performance in isolation from others).

The above argument represents an interpretation of Cottrell's theory. As far as we know, the theory has not appeared before in this form. Indeed, most theories in the social sciences are presented informally in ordinary sentences and paragraphs, albeit couched in technical language. To analyze a theory logically, it is necessary first to break it down into a series of propositions and then to organize the propositions into an argument. The form of the argument then may be examined as to its deductive validity. (For some guidelines on how to transform arguments from everyday language into standard form, see Box 3.1.)

Expressing a theory in standard logical form facilitates logical analysis by enabling one to examine the form of the theory and the relations among theoretical propositions apart from their substantive meaning.[3] This makes it easier to detect implicit propositions and assumptions as well as possible contradictions that are often hidden in ordinary language. It also makes clearer the distinction between propositions that are directly testable and those that are not. For example, because the term "response drive" in the above theory refers to a hypothetical entity that has no immediate empirical referent, any proposition containing this term cannot be directly verified or tested. However, such propositions are logically connected within the theory to testable propositions, or hypotheses, containing terms with observable properties. It is this logical connection that makes propositions without immediate empirical referents, as well as the theory as a whole, testable.

Since scientific theories ideally explain events by showing how the phenomenon to be explained logically follows from a set of propositions, it is easy to see the relevance of deductive logic to scientific inquiry. The reasoning from theories to hypotheses should be deductively valid, for if the argument by which a testable conclusion is deduced from a theory is invalid, then it is pointless to investigate the truth of the conclusion.

Inductive Reasoning in Science

Deductive reasoning is either valid or invalid; either the truth of the conclusion necessarily follows when the premises are true, as in a valid argument, or it does not, as in an invalid argument. To meet the criterion of validity, the conclusion of a deductive argument cannot go beyond the content of the premises. Deduction therefore "only tells us things we knew already," but that we may not have realized that we knew prior to the deduction (Kemeny, 1959:113).

Induction, on the other hand, involves the drawing of conclusions that exceed the information contained in the premises. Because science seeks to establish *general* knowledge that goes beyond particular observations, it inevitably uses inductive reasoning. Indeed, the truth of a generalization, which is assumed in assessing the deductive validity of explanations, ultimately rests upon induction. That is, at some point we say that a generalization is justified because it is based upon one or more past observations. Our justification of the audience effect, for example, is our observation that in past situations people have performed better in the presence of others than alone. The fact that this effect has been observed frequently makes it

BOX 3.1

Recognizing and Reconstructing Arguments

In this chapter we examine arguments in which the premises are stated explicitly and the conclusion is always preceded by the key word "therefore." However, in everyday life as well as in science, arguments seldom appear in this neat form but come embedded in a variety of verbal and written expressions. Usually, premises and conclusion are not explicitly labeled. Often the conclusion is stated first or in the middle of an argument; and one or more of premises may be omitted because they seem obvious. The problem, then, is to be able to recognize arguments in ordinary discourse. The following guidelines should help you to recognize when an argument has been given and, if so, to identify its premises and conclusion. Keep in mind, however, that there is no precise set of instructions by which the arguments expressed in ordinary language can be mechanically and uniquely transformed into standard argument form.

1. A bit of discourse represents an argument if (a) it contains a sequence of at least two sentences (or the grammatical equivalent—a compound sentence), and (b) the claim is made that one sentence in the sequence follows in a certain way from the other (Blumberg, 1976:19).

2. Words such as "therefore," "hence," "consequently," and "so," and certain verb forms such as "must have been," announce that the claim, or conclusion, immediately follows. One logician (Barry, 1976:3) offers this useful rule for identifying the conclusion to an argument: "If we can insert the phrase *it follows that* before a statement in an argument so that the statement in context makes complete sense, then that statement is probably the conclusion of the argument." Note how this rule applies in the following arguments:

> "Rosie's pulse rate of 76 is much too high for a marathon runner; *therefore*, [it follows that] she could not have finished the marathon.
> "[It follows that] Rosie *must have been* a fraud, for she has refused to run in any race since the 1980 Marathon."

3. Words like "since," "for," and "because" indicate that the statement that follows is a premise. Just as the phrase "it follows that" indicates a conclusion, the phrase *for the reason that* signals a premise (Barry, 1976:3). Note how premises are indicated by key words in the following arguments:

> "*Since* [for the reason that] Rosie claims that her fastest time ever for a mile is 5:30, it is inconceivable that she could have averaged 5:46 for the 26 miles of the marathon."
> "Rosie has refused to run in subsequent races *because* [for the reason that] she did not complete the marathon in Boston."

4. In an argument with a missing or unstated premise, determining the unstated premise is a bit complicated. As a rough guide, first identify the conclusion and stated premise, and then determine the unstated premise by relating the appropriate term in the stated premise to the appropriate term in the conclusion (see Barry, 1976:214). For example, consider the following argument: "Rosie could not have run the marathon

BOX 3.1 (*continued*)

because she was not seen by anyone at checkpoints along the course." The premise, indicated by the key word "because," is "Rosie was not seen at course checkpoints." The conclusion is "Rosie did not run the marathon." The missing premise, relating terms of both stated premise and conclusion, is "If someone runs the marathon, then they will be seen at course checkpoints." Reorganizing these statements, we have the following argument:

> If someone runs the marathon, then he or she will be seen at course checkpoints.
> Rosie was not seen at course checkpoints.
> Therefore, Rosie did not run the marathon.

reasonable to assume that it will happen again under similar conditions; however, we can never be absolutely certain of its recurrence. That is the nature of induction.

As with deductive reasoning, in inductive reasoning we are interested in the relations between premises and conclusion. However, analyzing inductive arguments is more complicated than analyzing deductive arguments because we must take into account the *degree* to which the premises support the conclusion. When the premises of a valid deductive argument are true, then the conclusion is always true; however, when the premises of a correct inductive argument are true, the conclusion is only *probably* true.

Correct inductive arguments vary in the strength, or degree of probability, with which the premises provide evidence for accepting the conclusion. Further, the degree of support for an inductive conclusion can be increased or decreased by adding premises to the argument. For example, by inductive reasoning an actuary would claim that it is highly probable that a healthy, 20-year-old man will survive to age 65. This probability would increase somewhat if it is learned that the man exercises regularly and is not overweight. But if it is learned that the man smokes two packs of cigarettes per day or that he loves to practice hang-gliding, then the chances of survival to age 65 are reduced considerably.

We now examine two types of inductive reasoning common in the social sciences: inductive generalization and hypothesis testing. As each type of induction is considered, we look at the kinds of additional evidence that increase or decrease the strength of the argument.

Inductive Generalization

An inductive generalization says something about an entire class of objects or events on the basis of information on only part of the class. Suppose that each of the five union members that you know is a registered Democrat. You may argue inductively from this evidence that all union members are Democrats. This is the simplest type of inductive generalization. It has the following form:

> 3.11 All observed members of p are q.
> Therefore, all p are q.

A slightly more complicated variation of this argument asserts that if a certain percentage of observed *p* are *q*, then the same percentage of the entire class of *p* are *q*. For example, you might observe that four of five (80%) of the union members that you know are registered Democrats and from this evidence infer that 80 percent of all union members are Democrats. The only difference between this argument and the above is that "80 percent" has been substituted for "all" in both premise and conclusion. Since "all" means "100 percent," the general form of inductive generalization may be written as follows (Salmon, 1973:83).

> 3.12 *X* percent of the observed members of *p* are *q*.
> Therefore, *X* percent of *p* are *q*.

Like all inductive inferences, inductive generalizations go beyond the observed facts. Hence, the best that can be said for them is that they are probably true. But some inductive conclusions are more likely to be true than others; that is, some arguments are stronger than others. The strength of an inductive argument depends on how reasonable it is to suppose that the observed instances of a class (e.g., union members) are representative of the entire class. Several factors affect the reasonableness of this supposition (cf. Barker, 1974).

1. The more alike the observed instances of *p* in ways other than *q*, the weaker the argument. If, for example, all of the observed union members were over 40, lived in Detroit, and worked for an automobile manufacturer, then our conclusions about their Democratic political preference would be based on a relatively weak argument. The shared characteristics reduce our confidence that our observations are representative of the whole class of union members. It is possible that only those members over 40, or those who reside in Detroit, and so forth, are Democrats.

2. The more ways that the observed instances of *p* differ from one another, the stronger the argument. Thus, if we observe union members of all ages, from several cities, who are employed in a number of industries, then our argument is strengthened. We have increased the probability that our observations are representative of all union members, for we have excluded the possibilities that it is only members of a certain age, or residence, or occupation who are Democrats.

3. "The more sweeping the generalization that we seek to establish, the less is its probability relative to our evidence, and the weaker is our argument" (Barker, 1974:228). We can alter how much an inductive generalization says in two ways. First, we can alter the specificity of p, the class that is described. A conclusion about "all union members" is more sweeping than a conclusion about "all union members over 40 years of age." Because it is more limited and specific, we would be more confident in drawing conclusions about the latter generalization than the former one. Similarly, we could change the likelihood of a conclusion by changing the precision of *q*, our description. Thus the conclusions that "all are Democrats" or that "80 percent are Democrats" are not only more precise, but are also less probable, than the conclusion that "most are Democrats."

4. Ordinarily, the greater the number of observed instances, the stronger the argument. It is reasonable to assume that a conclusion based upon a thousand observations is more probable than one based on just five. Generally this will be the

case, since larger numbers of observations are likely to have fewer characteristics in common and therefore be more representative of an entire class. However, if the additional observed instances are all alike (as in 1 above), then the probability of the conclusion will not change.

5. The greater the relevance of the generalization to prior knowledge, the stronger the argument. The question that must be asked here is whether the connection between one property and another makes sense in light of other generalizations. For example, the expectation that members of labor unions are Democrats is consistent with the sociologist's knowledge that political ideology is often related to economic position in society. In light of such knowledge, the induction is more reasonable. If, however, the induction were incompatible with well-established knowledge, then it would be less reasonable.

In evaluating the strength of inductive generalizations, all five of these factors must be taken into account simultaneously. Thus, one must consider the number of observations (4) in conjunction with their degree of similarity (1) or dissimilarity (2) as well as the scope and precision (3) of the inductive generalization and its relation to prior knowledge (5). Larger numbers of observations produce stronger inductive arguments *if* the observations are dissimilar or *if* the generalization is limited in scope and precision. And generalizations consistent with established knowledge are more probable than those that are not consistent.

Reasoning by inductive generalization is common in science. The idea of strengthening conclusions with dissimilar observations directly parallels the idea of replicating studies with dissimilar procedures, which we discuss in chapter 13. Considerations about the representativeness of observations are central to the sampling procedures discussed in chapter 6. Moreover, this form of induction underlies the logic of many statistical techniques, such as those designed to estimate characteristics of whole populations from a sample of observations.

Perhaps even more commonly, scientists and nonscientists alike apply the logic of inductive generalization in their attempts to perceive order in the world around them. For example, a sociologist finds that 60 out of 100 students observed in a given school have smoked marijuana and concludes that the majority of students in the school have smoked marijuana. As a freshman you notice that all of your professors have doctorates and infer that all professors do. You find that your first course in sociology is interesting, have similar experiences in the second and third courses, and conclude that all sociology courses are interesting. Of course, none of these conclusions may actually be true. As with all inductive generalizations, they merely possess greater or lesser probability, depending on the strength of the evidence from which they are derived. Comparing the above conclusions about marijuana smokers, professors, and sociology courses, which inference do you think is strongest? Be sure to consider each of the five factors.

Testing Hypotheses: The Hypothetico-Deductive Method

The underlying logic of testing hypotheses in science is sometimes called the "hypothetico-deductive" method. The first part of this term signifies that the scientific explanations tested are *hypothetical* in the sense that they are assumed to be

true. Once this assumption is made about an explanation, then its observable consequences are *deduced* for testing—hence, the second part of the term. Forming a
hypothesis and deducing consequences from the hypothesis are actually the first two
of four steps in the hypothetico-deductive (h-d) method. Step 3 involves checking
by observation to see whether the deduced consequences are true, and step 4 entails
making inferences about the hypothesis on the basis of one's observations. We shall
forego a discussion of step 3 here because it is considered in the remaining chapters
in the book. For now we confine our attention to the logical characteristics of steps
1, 2, and 4.

In the section on deduction we saw how scientific explanations explain facts
deductively. However, while focusing on the logical form of explanations, we
ignored the inductive process by which the explanations are derived in the first
place. All scientific explanations—theories, generalizations, hypotheses—are
inductive conclusions. To impose an order on observations and make them meaningful, an explanation must go beyond the information contained in the observations
that it explains. Consider, for example, Emile Durkheim's generalization that high
social solidarity is related to low rates of suicide. This proposition was derived
inductively from several observations, such as that divorced and widowed persons
committed suicide more than married persons, childless persons more than people
who had children, and city dwellers more than rural people. To explain such facts,
Durkheim had to formulate an inductive conclusion—a hypothesis that went
beyond the facts available.[4] Once formulated, a hypothesis explains the facts from
which it is derived in that when it is assumed to be true, the facts logically follow.
More precisely, like all explanations, the hypothesis serves as a premise in deductive arguments in which the facts are conclusions. By deduction, Durkheim's
hypothesis explains the fact that the incidence of suicide is lower among married
people than among divorced or widowed persons:

3.13 If the social solidarity of one group is higher than another, then its suicide rate will be
     lower. (hypothesis)
     Social solidarity is higher among married people than among widowed or divorced
     persons.
     Therefore, the suicide rate is lower among married people than among widowed or
     divorced persons. (observed fact)

Explaining a set of facts in this fashion indicates that we have a legitimate
hypothesis, but it does not mean that the hypothesis is true, for some other hypothesis might explain the facts just as well. Considering Durkheim's data, for example,
perhaps widowed, divorced, and childless persons as well as city dwellers tend to
share the kind of social or religious philosophy that finds suicide morally acceptable. Or, it is possible that these same groups have higher rates of mental illness,
which may be the cause of suicide. Because such alternative explanations exist,
Durkheim's hypothesis should be thought of as more or less probable in light of the
facts that it explains. Like all inductive conclusions, it is drawn and accepted "in a
spirit of tentativeness" (Runkle, 1978:261).

Because any set of facts can have several explanations, we gain confidence in a particular explanation by testing its ability to explain additional observable facts. Basically, this means that we deduce other consequences from the hypothesis and then check to see if they are true. Thus, while formulated to explain existing events, hypotheses must be tested in terms of their capacity to predict future events. The second step in the h-d method therefore involves deducing consequences from the hypothesis. Let us now see what conclusions can be drawn when the hypothesis is confirmed and when it is disconfirmed.

The logic of confirming hypotheses. One of the consequences that Durkheim derived from his hypothesis was that Catholics in France will have lower suicide rates than Protestants in France. This follows from his hypothesis and from the assumption that Catholics have a higher degree of social solidarity than Protestants. Now suppose that the relevant observations are made and Durkheim's prediction is found to be true. In this case, the hypothesis is said to be "confirmed," and we conclude that it is more credible, or more probable. Notice that we are not saying that the supporting evidence *proves* the hypothesis, but merely that it increases the probability that the hypothesis is true. The added fact, or prediction, simply becomes an additional premise in the inductive argument upon which the hypothesis is based.

To conclude from a confirmation that the hypothesis is proven (or "true") would be to make the following argument:

> 3.14 If the hypothesis is true, then the predicted fact is true.
> The predicted fact is true.
> Therefore, the hypothesis is true.

However, this is a case of the "fallacy of affirming the consequent," an invalid deductive argument. The confirming fact is simply the consequent of the hypothesis. Just as existing facts may have more than one explanation, there is no guarantee that a "confirmed" hypothesis is the only hypothesis from which a predicted fact would follow. Sociologist Arthur Stinchcombe (1968:18) notes, for instance, that there are other explanations of Durkheim's prediction: "the higher suicide rate of French Protestants might be explained by their occupations, by the lesser emphasis on the sin of suicide in Protestant theology, by the fact that confessors are available to every Catholic in times of trouble and distress, and so forth." Deductively, therefore, we cannot say that a confirmation proves that a hypothesis is true. On the other hand, if the hypothesis implies a fact, and the fact is upheld by the evidence, then the fact does support the hypothesis inductively.

The proper inductive conclusion to the premises in argument 3.14 is that "the hypothesis is more probable." With this new conclusion we now have the kind of inductive argument that scientists use repeatedly in confirming hypotheses. There are two principal ways that additional evidence can strengthen such arguments: (1) by offering multiple confirmations of the hypothesis and (2) by eliminating alternative hypotheses.

1. The greater the number of tests and the greater the variety of tests that confirm a hypothesis, the more probable the truth of the hypothesis. The implication

from Durkheim's hypothesis that Catholics will commit suicide less often than Protestants suggests several independent predictions (Stinchcombe, 1968:19): that Catholic countries will have lower suicide rates than Protestant countries, that Catholic regions in Germany will have lower suicide rates than Protestant regions, and that Catholics in France will have lower suicide rates than Protestants. If all of these predictions are empirically supported, then the hypothesis is more convincing than if supported by a single test. Not only has the hypothesis stood up under more tests, but there are presumably fewer other explanations of all these facts taken together than there are of any one, isolated fact (Stinchcombe, 1968:19).

For the same reasons, one can intuitively see that an even stronger test is provided by testing different kinds of predictions than by merely repeating observations that are similar to those that have already been made. For example, suppose that suicide rates go down in France in times of parliamentary crisis, a prediction that also may be deduced from Durkheim's hypothesis.[5] When added to the facts above, this finding diversifies the confirming evidence. Consequently, it increases the credibility of the hypothesis far more than would, say, the additional but similar observation "that the various regions of Austria had higher suicide rates, the higher their proportion Protestant" (Stinchcombe, 1968:19).

2. The greater the number of plausible alternative hypotheses that have been disconfirmed, the more probable the truth of the hypothesis. Accepting a hypothesis as true on the basis of confirming evidence generally constitutes a weak inductive argument because alternative hypotheses may account for the same evidence. Therefore, if possible alternative explanations are eliminated, the inductive support for the hypothesis is strengthened. A significant part of scientific investigations is devoted to imagining alternative explanations of phenomena. Very often, then, separate tests are made of each of the alternatives. However, the best test is one that will confirm a hypothesis and disconfirm its principal alternative at the same time. This is sometimes called a "crucial" test.

Again, we use a substantive example that Stinchcombe (1968:25–26) has drawn from Durkheim's *Suicide*. A prominent alternative explanation in Durkheim's time was that suicide was the result of mental illness. Durkheim reasoned that if this were the case, then the same groups with high rates of mental illness ought to have high rates of suicide. On the other hand, Durkheim did not expect social solidarity to be related to mental illness; therefore, his own hypothesis did not imply an association between rates of mental illness and rates of suicide. Thus Durkheim could perform a crucial test: "he could describe a set of observations (the relations between rates of mental illness and rates of suicide, for various regions) which would show one result [an association] if mental illness caused suicides, and a different result [no association] if social causes were operating" (Stinchcombe, 1968:26). As it turned out, the association between mental illness rates and suicide rates was insignificant, thereby disconfirming a major rival hypothesis and making Durkheim's hypothesis more credible.

The logic of disconfirming hypotheses. In drawing conclusions about hypotheses, we apply a different argument with disconfirming evidence than we do with confirming evidence. Indeed, the reasoning from disconfirming evidence to the rejection of a hypothesis is deductively valid. The argument has the form of "denying the consequent":

> 3.15 If the hypothesis is true, then the predicted fact is true.
>   The predicted fact is false.
>   Therefore, the hypothesis is false.

Because such an argument is valid, some people argue that while hypotheses cannot be proven, they can be disproven. The major difficulty with this view, however, is that the conclusion that a hypothesis is false rests not only upon the validity of the argument but also on the assumed truth of the premise that the prediction is false. For example, before Durkheim could conclude that the mental illness hypothesis is false, he had to accept as true that no association exists between mental illness rates and suicide rates.

In other words, to reject a hypothesis we must assume that the prediction is clearly implied (i.e., a valid deduction) *and that the prediction is indeed false*. Likewise, to provide inductive support for a hypothesis, we must assume that the prediction is clearly implied *and that it is true*. However, the proposition linking a hypothesis with a prediction depends on assumptions whose truth can sometimes be questioned, and the evidence does not always indisputably establish that a prediction is true or false. Whether a lower suicide rate among Catholics than Protestants supports Durkheim's hypothesis depends on the truth of the assumption that Catholics as a group possess greater social solidarity than Protestants. The conclusion that the hypothesis is confirmed also makes assumptions about the accuracy of statistics on the number of persons who are Catholic or Protestant and the number of suicides committed in each of these groups. Similarly, the conclusion that mental illness does not explain suicide involves assumptions about the accurate identification and count of the incidence of mental illness. To reject the mental illness hypothesis, Durkheim assumed his data were accurate. But if this assumption were in error, then the decision to reject would be invalid. Because all tests of hypotheses implicitly or explicitly employ such assumptions, disconfirming evidence does not constitute grounds for categorically rejecting a hypothesis. Just as confirmed predictions increase the probability that a hypothesis is true, disconfirmed predictions decrease the probability.

Still, even though both confirmation and disconfirmation of hypotheses ultimately entail probabilistic conclusions, it would be a mistake to infer that these two types of evidence have equal bearing on hypotheses. Scientists generally regard disconfirming evidence as providing a much stronger basis for rejecting a hypothesis than confirming evidence provides for accepting a hypothesis. The reason for this may be found in the underlying logical arguments of confirmation and disconfirmation. The argument for rejecting a hypothesis, as we have seen, is based upon a valid deductive argument: If the hypothesis is true, then the prediction is true. The prediction is false; therefore, the hypothesis is false. Consequently, if we accept the prediction and disconfirming evidence as correct, we *must* conclude that the hypothesis is false. On the other hand, the argument for accepting a hypothesis is based upon an inductive argument, similar in form to the deductive fallacy of affirming the consequent. Therefore, if we accept the prediction and confirming evidence as correct, we can conclude only that the hypothesis is more probable. Thus, given equally compelling evidence, scientists tend to be more convinced by disconfirmation than by confirmation.

Confirmation or disconfirmation of a hypothesis completes the fourth step in the hypothetico-deductive method. Of course, given that the entire procedure of confirmation is inductive, no verification of a scientific hypothesis is ever really complete. In hypothesis testing, as in inductive arguments, no matter how strong the evidence, it is always possible for the evidence to be true and the hypothesis false. It is also possible for the evidence itself to be in error. To avoid these possibilities scientists must (1) make repeated applications of the h-d method to build up a large and diversified "body of confirming evidence, or to find disconfirming evidence if there is any"; and (2) take all steps necessary to ensure accurate, unbiased evidence (Salmon, 1973:116). In the ensuing chapters we intend to point out these steps, for as you can see, the edifice of scientific knowledge rests upon the quality of empirical evidence, hence, upon properly conducted research. (See Box 3.2 for an application of the hypothetico-deductive method from the history of medicine.)

BOX 3.2

The Hypothetico-Deductive Method:
An Example from the History of Medicine

Carl Hempel (1966), noted philosopher of science, provides an excellent example of the application of the hypothetico-deductive method in his story of Ignaz Semmelweis' work on a fatal illness known as puerperal fever or childbed fever. The physician Semmelweis did his work from 1844 to 1848 at the Vienna General Hospital. As a medical staff member of the First Maternity Division, he was distressed by the division's high incidence of childbed fever, especially as compared to the Second Maternity Division of the same hospital.

According to Hempel's account, Semmelweis entertained numerous explanations. "Some of these he rejected out of hand as incompatible with well-established facts; others he subjected to specific tests." For example, one view held that overcrowding was the cause; however, Semmelweis noted that overcrowding was in fact heavier in the Second Division than the first. Two other conjectures were similarly rejected "by noting that there were no differences between the two Divisions in regard to diet or general care of the patients." Among several other ideas suggested to Semmelweis was the position of the women during delivery: in the First Division, women delivered lying on their backs, while in the Second, they delivered on their sides. But when the lateral position was introduced in the First Division, mortality remained unchanged.

In a similar fashion, Semmelweis rejected idea after idea until finally, in 1847, an accident gave him the critical clue for solving the puzzle. While performing an autopsy, a colleague of his, Kolletschka, received a puncture wound from a scalpel and "died after an agonizing illness during which he displayed the same symptoms that Semmelweis had observed in the victims of childbed fever." Semmelweis reasoned

BOX 3.2 (*continued*)

that "cadaveric matter" introduced into Kolletschka's bloodstream from the scalpel "had caused his colleague's fatal illness."

> And the similarities between the course of Kolletschka's disease and that of the women in his clinic led Semmelweis to the conclusion that his patients had died of the same kind of blood poisoning; he, his colleagues, and the medical students had been the carriers of the infectious material, for he and his associates used to come to the wards directly from performing dissections in the autopsy room, and examine the women in labor after only superficially washing their hands, which often retained a characteristic foul odor (p. 5).

Semmelweis tested this idea by having all medical personnel who attended the women carefully disinfect their hands before making an examination. As a consequence, the mortality from childbed fever promptly decreased.

In seeking to explain childbed fever, Semmelweis repeatedly applied the hypothetico-deductive method. First, he formulated a hypothesis: that the illness was due to overcrowding, delivery position, or blood poisoning from cadaveric matter. Second, he deduced testable consequences from his hypothesis. That is, he reasoned that if his hypothesis were true, then certain facts or observations should follow: overcrowdedness will be greater in the First Division than the Second; adoption of the lateral position in the First Division will reduce the mortality; or having attendants disinfect their hands will reduce fatalities. Third, Semmelweis checked the observable consequences of the hypothesis against reality. In the case of the delivery position and blood poisoning hypotheses, this meant first establishing certain conditions for making his observations—changing the delivery procedure or requiring disinfection. Finally, having found the observable consequences to be true or false, Semmelweis drew conclusions about his hypotheses. When the consequences were disconfirmed (e.g., when it was shown that the lateral position did *not* decrease fatalities), then he rejected the hypothesis. When the consequences were confirmed (e.g., when disinfection lowered fatalities), he tentatively accepted the hypothesis as true.

Summary

Scientists apply the rules of logic to evaluate their reasoning. This does not mean that logicians can tell scientists how to think, but rather that logic provides the tools for analysis once an act of reasoning has taken place. The elements of logical analysis are terms (analogous to scientific concepts), propositions, and arguments. Arguments, which make explicit one's reasoning, consist of two or more propositions of which one (the conclusion) is claimed to follow from the others (the premises). In this chapter we focused on three-proposition arguments, called syllogisms, containing at least one conditional (or "if-then") proposition. Such propositions readily convey causal relations, in which science ultimately is interested.

One can logically analyze an argument without knowing the truth or falsity of its propositions; hence, logic is not concerned with actuality as such. Science, on the other hand, *is* concerned with reality. And to justify conclusions about the empirical world, scientists must establish both the validity of their arguments (or reasoning) and the truth of their propositions.

Scientists reason both deductively and inductively. In deduction, a valid argument is such that the conclusion necessarily follows if the premises are true; otherwise, it is invalid. In induction, arguments are judged by their strength, as the conclusion probably but does not necessarily follow if the premises are true.

One method of determining deductive validity is to examine the form of the argument, which is identified by substituting letters for each of the sentences or phrases it contains. Three valid argument forms are affirming the antecedent, denying the consequent, and the chain argument. Two invalid argument forms are the fallacy of affirming the consequent and the fallacy of denying the antecedent. The inference from a hypothesis to a specific event or observation is a deductive argument that can take the form of affirming the antecedent. Theories also have a deductive pattern that can be expressed in chain argument form. Placing scientific explanations in logical form makes it easier to detect implicit assumptions and contradictions that are hidden in ordinary language.

We examined two types of inductive reasoning found in scientific inquiry: inductive generalization and hypothesis testing. Inductive generalizations state something about an entire class of events on the basis of evidence on only part of the class. Such generalizations are strengthened by increasing the number and heterogeneity of one's observations and by limiting the scope and precision of the generalization.

Hypothesis testing involves four steps: (1) formulation of a hypothesis; (2) deduction of testable consequences from the hypothesis; (3) checking through observation (or research) to see if the consequences are true; and (4) drawing conclusions about the hypothesis on the basis of one's observations. Steps 1 and 4 involve inductive reasoning, whereas steps 2 and 3 involve deduction. The crucial point about steps 1 and 2 is that once a hypothesis is formulated, usually to account for existing evidence, it must be tested by examining new evidence. If the new evidence supports the hypothesis, then one may say that the hypothesis is more credible. However, it is logically inappropriate to conclude that the hypothesis is proven because the underlying argument is inductive and other hypotheses may account for the same evidence. One can increase the credibility of a hypothesis by repeated and varied testing, especially when such testing eliminates alternative hypotheses. If the evidence does not support a hypothesis, then one may logically conclude that the hypothesis is false. Such a conclusion, however, invariably rests upon the truth of certain test assumptions and the accuracy of one's data.

Key Terms

logic	*argument*
term	*premise*
proposition	*conclusion*
conditional proposition	*syllogism*
antecedent	*validity*
consequent	*deduction*

induction   *fallacy of affirming the consequent*
argument form   *fallacy of denying the antecedent*
affirming the antecedent   *inductive generalization*
denying the consequent   *hypothetico-deductive method*
chain argument (hypothetical syllogism)

Review Questions and Problems

1. Distinguish between logic and reasoning.
2. What are the three elements of logical analysis?
3. Why do the authors choose to focus on *conditional* propositions?
4. Explain the following statement: The validity of a syllogism is independent of the truth of its premises.
5. According to logicians, two questions arise when considering whether an argument or inference is justified: (1) Are the premises true? and (2) Are the premises properly related to the conclusion? Explain the relevance of each of these questions to (a) logical analysis and (b) scientific inquiry.
6. Briefly distinguish between deductive and inductive reasoning.
7. Indicate whether each of the following deductive arguments is valid or invalid by first identifying the argument form.

   a. If Ronnie Nosey reads the campus newspaper, then he will be up on the latest campus gossip.
      Ronnie Nosey does not read the campus newspaper.
      Therefore, Ronnie Nosey is not up on the latest campus gossip.
   b. If the sum of the digits of 261 is evenly divisible by 9, then 261 is evenly divisible by 9.
      The sum of the digits of 261 ($2 + 6 + 1 = 9$) is evenly divisible by 9.
      Therefore, 261 is evenly divisible by 9.
   c. If blood poisoning from bacteria causes childbed fever, then antiseptic washing to remove bacteria will reduce mortality (due to childhood fever).
      Antiseptic washing reduces mortality.
      Therefore, blood poisoning from bacteria causes childbed fever. (Adapted from Hempel, 1966:ch. 2)
   d. If someone gets all these questions right, then he or she will get an "A" on this exercise.
      No one got all the questions right.
      Therefore, no one will get an "A" on this exercise.
   e. If social reality is ambiguous, then people will rely upon others for information about reality.
      If people rely upon others for information about reality, then they will tend to conform to what others are doing.
      Therefore, if social reality is ambiguous, people will tend to conform to what others are doing. (Adapted from Festinger, 1954).

8. Given the following argument: If *X*, then *Y*; if *Y*, then *Z*; therefore, if *X*, then *Z*. (a) If the premises are true, what can we logically conclude about the

conclusion? (b) If the conclusion is true, what can we logically conclude about the premises? (c) If the conclusion is false, what can we logically conclude about the premises?

9. Find an example of an argument in a newspaper or on television. Reconstruct the argument in standard logical form and determine its validity or invalidity.

10. Describe the deductive pattern by which (a) a hypothesis explains a fact or event, and (b) a theory explains a hypothesis.

11. What does it mean logically to formalize a theory? What purposes does this serve?

12. What factors affect the strength of an inductive generalization?

13. Consider the following inductive generalizations. For each generalization, (1) add two premises that would increase or decrease the strength of the inference, and (2) alter the conclusion in such a way as to increase the strength of the inference.

    a. Steve has taken three sociology courses and has found them to be very stimulating. And so he concludes that all sociology courses are stimulating.

    b. You interview twenty-five students, asking them about the quality of the service in the campus cafeteria. Given that twenty of them rate the service as poor, you infer that the cafeteria provides poor service.

14. Identify the four steps of the hypothetico-deductive method. Which steps involve deductive reasoning? Which steps involve inductive reasoning?

15. Briefly explain why proof or certainty in science is a logical impossibility.

16. How can the inductive argument supporting a hypothesis be strengthened?

17. According to the authors, why is disconfirming evidence not always considered sufficient to reject a hypothesis, even though the underlying argument is deductively valid?

18. What are the deductive argument forms underlying the (a) confirmation and (b) rejection of hypotheses?

19. You have been very listless for the past 2 weeks. You don't have much of an appetite. Your friends bore you, and you can't seem to get very interested in anything. Your grades are beginning to go down. Formulate a hypothesis to account for this situation and then show how the facts of the situation can be deduced from your hypothesis. (Adapted from Runkle, 1978:281)

NOTES

1. Two other common types of propositions are "disjunctions (e.g., "That student is either very bright *or* she studies a lot") and "conjunctions" (e.g., "Ron read the chapter on logic *and* he found it interesting").

2. Though generally true, there are exceptions to this distinction. As Kemeny (1959:112) notes, an inductive conclusion need not be a generalized statement. From careful observations of electoral politics, a political scientist may reason that a Democrat will be elected President in 1992. This is a particular event, and yet it is also an inductive conclusion. "And deduction need not start with a generalization either. For example, from 'there are at least five students in the course' and from 'there are at most seven students in the course' we can deduce that 'there are either 5, or 6, or 7 students in the course.'"

3. The transformation of a theory into standard logical form to facilitate logical analysis is one type of *formalization*. A theory also may be represented with a graphic model, flow diagram, or system of mathematical equations. Formalizing a theory by any of these means enables one to see more clearly the logical structure or form of the theory.

4. As to how Durkheim conceived of this hypothesis, as well as how any other scientific explanation is thought up, philosophers (cf. Kemeny, 1959:115; Salmon, 1967:111) contend that this aspect of science requires insight and originality and may forever remain a matter of creative genius. The selection of hypotheses "may be aided by rules," such as the rules for inductive generalizations mentioned in the previous section, "but no such rules will ever replace original thinking" (Kemeny, 1959:115). Thus, while there exists a logic of confirming hypotheses, discussed in this section, the process of discovering hypotheses appears to be beyond the simple application of logic.

5. Durkheim (1951:208) argued that national crises "rouse collective sentiments, stimulate partisan spirit and patriotism, political and national faith, alike, and concentrating activity toward a single end, at least temporarily cause a stronger integration of society." This increased integration then causes a reduction in suicides.

II

RESEARCH DESIGN

Thus far we have placed social scientific inquiry in the contexts of science and logic. The goals and norms that regulate scientific inquiry have been outlined, as well as the logical framework within which that inquiry takes place. Having filled in the background, we are now ready to learn about the details of social research.

Science, as we have seen, is the process of producing generalized understanding through systematic observation. Research involves the planning, execution, and interpretation of scientific observation. The three chapters in this section deal with the planning phase. Focusing on the selection and formulation of the research problem, chapter 4 introduces the basic terminology of research. Chapters 5 and 6 then address two major problems in planning a study: devising operations to observe and measure the phenomena of research interest, and selecting cases for observation. Together these chapters specify the key elements and considerations in the overall plan, called the *research design*. The overview they provide will set the stage for the treatment, in the remainder of the book, of the execution and interpretation phases of research.

The language of social research introduced in chapter 4 represents a shift in terminology from our discussion of the nature and logical structure of scientific theory in chapters 2 and 3. As you will see, the tools of thinking on the abstract, theoretical level (concepts, assumptions, propositions) differ somewhat from the tools of research on the empirical level (variables, hypotheses). The process of moving from the abstract to the concrete is itself an essential part of social research that we consider in chapter 5.

4

Elements of Research Design

All research begins with the selection of a problem. In formulating the problem and putting it in researchable terms, the researcher makes several crucial decisions. Initially, the main concerns are (1) what entities (e.g., individual people, groups, formal organizations, nations) are to be studied; (2) what aspects or characteristics of these entities are of interest; and (3) what kinds of relationships among the characteristics are anticipated. Making decisions about these concerns is the object of research design, and clarifying the nature of these decisions is the object of the present chapter. But since research begins with a specific problem or topic, we first take a brief look at how problems are selected for study.

Selecting Topics for Research

The question of how research topics are chosen can be answered in several ways. In one sense we have answered it already. As stated in the first chapter, anything that is "social" and "empirical" is a relevant topic for social research. However, this suggests an incredibly broad range of potential topics and does not really indicate *how* specific topics are likely to emerge. A more informative answer would reveal that the following five factors affect topic selection in the social sciences.

1. *The structure and state of the scientific discipline.* Given the scientific goal of advancing knowledge, most researchers select topics suggested by the ongoing development of theory and research in their particular fields of study. The organization of fields of study casts the framework for topic selection. Social psychologists, for example, divide their discipline with respect to various forms of social behavior, such as aggression, altruism, interpersonal attraction, and conformity, which act as organizing themes or areas of research interest. Similarly, sociologists frequently study aspects of various institutions like religion, politics, education, and the family, around which the discipline is organized. As the knowledge in an area develops, inconsistencies and gaps in information are revealed that researchers attempt to resolve through research. Ordinarily only experienced researchers are able to tap this source of ideas, since it requires a thorough knowledge of the scientific literature.

2. *Social problems.* The focus and development of the social sciences are intimately related to interest in basic problems of the "human condition." Histor-

ically, this has been a major source of research topics, especially in sociology. The most eminent sociologists of the nineteenth and early twentieth centuries—people like Durkheim, Marx, Weber, and Park—concerned themselves with problems emanating from great social upheavals of their day, such as the French and Industrial revolutions, and massive foreign immigration to the United States. The problems wrought by these events—alienation, deviance, urban crowding, racism, and many others—have remained a major focus of the discipline ever since. Indeed, many people today are attracted to the social sciences because of their perceived relevance to social problems, and this is the most likely source of research ideas for the beginning researcher.

3. *Personal values of the researcher.* To carry out a research project, with its inevitable complications, obstacles, and demands for time and money, requires considerable interest and commitment on the part of the investigator. What sustains this interest more than anything else are highly personal motivations for doing research on a particular topic. Thus, an investigator may choose a topic not only because it is considered to be theoretically important, novel, or researchable, but also because it piques the researcher's interest. Social psychologist Zick Rubin (1976:508–509) mentions several such reasons for embarking on the study of romantic love. First, he needed a topic for his dissertation, and romantic love seemed particularly appropriate because it was distinctively social psychological and "yet almost completely untouched by nonpoetic human hands." Doing research on romantic love also was a way of extending the research on interpersonal attraction by his influential mentor Theodore Newcomb. And finally, since Rubin was "by temperament and avocation, a songwriter," studying romantic love was a way of measuring scientifically what he had often attempted to measure musically.

4. *Social premiums.* There are also powerful social determinants in topic selection. Through the availability of supporting funds, the prestige and popularity of the research area, and pressures within the discipline and within society, social premiums are placed on different topics at different times. Typically, these premiums will reinforce one another, with the social climate affecting funding, which in turn affects prestige. This was certainly true of the space program in the 1960s. Today, in the social sciences, the aging of the population as a whole appears to have raised interest and support for research on the elderly, just as it has caused a dramatic increase in federal expenditures on and services available to older people (Preston, 1984).

5. *Practical considerations.* An overriding concern in any research project is cost. Research requires time, money, and personnel. Limitations on these resources, as well as other practical considerations such as the skill of the researcher and the availability of relevant data (see chapter 12), will shape both the nature and scope of the problem that the researcher can pursue.

The choice of any given research topic may be affected by any or all of the factors mentioned. A topic defined as social and empirical may be chosen for its theoretical or practical relevance. Typically, it will be chosen by someone with an ongoing interest in a particular research area. For example, someone interested in aggression may investigate the effects of televised violence on subsequent aggression. Such research obviously would be relevant to the problem of violence in society, and it also may contribute to theoretical knowledge about aggression. The usual practice is to justify research on both practical and theoretical grounds. Of course, the selection of this topic will be influenced to some degree by the climate of concern in society about televised violence and by the funding of well-designed studies by granting agencies such as the Surgeon General's Scientific Advisory Committee on Television and Social Behavior.

Once a general topic has been chosen, it must be stated in researchable terms. This involves translating the topic into one or more clearly defined, specific questions or problems that are amenable to research. To get to this point the investigator usually conducts a literature search. In the process, he or she may discover several preliminary questions that must be answered before the main problem can be pursued; or the topic may be recast to fit a particular research strategy or to fit some other need. It is not uncommon, in fact, for the researcher's interest to become permanently shifted to one of these narrower or preliminary questions. Regardless of the direction it takes, however, formulating a researchable problem or question boils down to deciding what *relationships* among what *variables* of what *units* are to be studied. We will now turn our attention to these important terms.

Units of Analysis

The entities (objects or events) under study are referred to in social research as *units of analysis*. Social scientists study a variety of units, or cases as they are sometimes called. These include individual people, social roles, positions, and relationships, a wide range of social groupings such as families, organizations, and cities, as well as various social artifacts such as books, periodicals, documents, and even buildings. Ordinarily, the unit of analysis is easily identified. The unit is simply what or whom is to be described or analyzed. For example, a researcher wanting to determine if larger organizations (in terms of the number of employees) have more bureaucratic rules and regulations than smaller ones would treat the *organization* as the relevant unit and would gather information on the size and bureaucratic complexity of organizations. Alternatively, if one wanted to know what sort of people are attracted to the field of political science, then one would obviously need to gather information on characteristics of *individual people*, perhaps professional political scientists or graduate students in this field.

In these examples, the purpose of the study dictates what or whom is to be described, analyzed, and compared, hence what is the appropriate unit of analysis. Selecting and identifying the unit of analysis is not as simple as it may seem, however. Consider the problem of investigating a theory of cultural change. David Riesman (1950) proposed the theory that there has been a trend in this century toward "other-directedness," that people have become less motivated in their behavior by intrinsic values and more oriented toward the ways that other people behave. But how can one study such long-range trends in individual motivation when direct analysis of individuals from the past is impossible? One way that social scientists have resolved this issue is to rely on various social artifacts to study the past and to assume that such artifacts reflect the individual values and behavior of direct interest. To test Riesman's theory, for example, Dornbusch and Hickman (1959) chose as their units of analysis advertisements in a mass circulation women's magazine for the period 1890–1956, to see if the advertising had appealed increasingly over time to the standards of others (other-directedness), which indeed it had.

Another problem arises from the practice of combining information about individuals in order to describe the social unit to which they belong. Information about one set of units that is statistically combined and considered as a description of some larger social unit is called *aggregate data*. For example, by counting the number of members who are women or Caucasian or by adding up members' ages and performing the appropriate calculations, one could describe a local school board as being 70 percent women, all Caucasian, with an average age of 45 years. Where information about individuals (school board members) has been aggregated to describe a group (the school board), one might wonder whether the individual or the group is the unit of analysis. The answer depends on how the aggregate information is used and on the units about which one wishes to make descriptive or analytical statements.

If collective information about a particular group is used on a statistical summary basis simply to describe the makeup of individuals *within the group*, then the unit of analysis is the individual. Thus, in the above description of a local school board, the individual board members would be the units of analysis, provided that the research objective is simply to characterize the members of that particular board. However, if aggregate information is assumed to measure properties of the collectivity as a whole and is used in a comparison of *different groups* or collectivities, then the unit of analysis is the group. Suppose that the researcher wished to examine properties of school boards using aggregate data, say, on the proportion of members who are nonwhite and their average age, in order to determine how such properties affect school boards' support or opposition to a state busing plan. In this case, the school board itself is the unit because it is the actions and characteristic compositions of whole school boards that are being compared.

It is also possible to analyze individual persons while using aggregate data to characterize the groups or collectivities to which the individuals belong. Thus, an individual can be described as living in a county with a high or low average income, as attending a racially integrated or racially segregated school, or as being on a school board with relatively young or old members. In each instance, the individual is described in terms of characteristics of the group of which he or she is a part, while characteristics of the groups or collectivities are formed by aggregating information about individuals (e.g., average income of persons in a county or average age of school board members). Comparing individuals who are in different groups permits analysis of the effects of those groups on the individual. For instance, an investigator might examine whether members of "younger" school boards (as determined by the average age of the board members) are more likely to support a busing plan than members of "older" school boards, or whether members of boards in suburban or rural areas are more likely to support a busing plan than members of boards in urban areas. Since individual school board members are being compared in each case, the individual is the unit of analysis.

As this brief discussion reveals, identifying the unit of analysis can be less than straightforward when aggregate information is involved. Remember that in studying a particular unit a researcher ordinarily will compare a number of instances of that unit—for example, a number of individuals, or a number of cities, or a number of school boards. To identify the unit of analysis, therefore, ask yourself what is being described in each instance and what sort of units are being compared—individuals or groups.

One reason that it is important to identify accurately the unit of analysis is that confusion over units may result in false conclusions about research. Generally speaking, assertions from research can only be made about the particular unit under study. (Actually, assertions should be even more circumscribed than this, as we will see in chapter 6.) To draw conclusions about one unit on the basis of information about another is to risk committing a logical fallacy.

The most common fallacy involving the mixing of units is the *ecological fallacy* (W. S. Robinson, 1950). This occurs when relationships between properties of groups or geographic areas are used to make inferences about the individual behaviors of the people within those groups or areas. Political analysts who use aggregate data from elections to study individual voting behavior are particularly susceptible to the ecological fallacy. Suppose, for example, that a researcher wanted to know whether registered Democrats or Republicans were more likely to support an Independent party candidate in a city election, but that the only information available was the percentage of votes the candidate received and the percentages of Republican and Democratic voters *in each precinct*. In short, the researcher wants to draw conclusions about *individual voters* but only has collective information about *precincts*. Knowing that the candidate received a relatively larger number of votes in precincts with greater percentages of Republicans does not permit the conclusion that Republican voters were more likely to support the candidate than Democratic voters. We simply do not know how individual voters within each precinct voted. It is quite plausible that Democrats in predominantly Republican precincts were more likely to support the Independent party candidate than were Democrats in other precincts, but we do not really know this because the unit of analysis here is the precinct and not the individual voter.

Social scientists of a few decades ago frequently performed ecological analyses such as the one above. For example, numerous studies of crime and delinquency were conducted in which crime and delinquency rates and other characteristics of census tracts were analyzed to draw conclusions about characteristics of individual criminals and delinquents. A typical erroneous conclusion might be that foreign-born persons commit more crimes than native-born persons because the crime rate is higher in areas with greater proportions of foreigners. But such a conclusion is clearly unwarranted because we do not know who actually committed the crimes—foreign or native-born persons. Similarly, Durkheim's classic study of suicide was subject to the ecological fallacy by inferring that Protestants commit more suicides than Catholics from the observation that suicide rates were higher in predominantly Protestant nations than in predominantly Catholic ones. It is possible that Protestants were more often the victims of suicide, but it is also possible that they were not. The problem is that we do not know because conclusions about individuals cannot necessarily be drawn from data on groups.

The major implication for formulating a research problem is thus clear: carefully determine the units about which you wish to draw conclusions and then make sure that your data pertain only to those units. If you are interested in individuals but only aggregate data are available, then draw conclusions very tentatively, recognizing the possibility of an ecological fallacy.

Variables

While the researcher observes units of analysis in the process of research, it is relationships among characteristics of units in which scientists are primarily interested. Characteristics of units that vary, taking on different values, categories, or attributes for different observations, are called *variables*. Variables may vary over cases, over time, or over both cases and time. When observing individual people, for example, any set of characteristics that may differ for different people, such as age (range of years), gender (male and female), and marital status (single, married, divorced, widowed, etc.), is a variable. And when observing the same person, any characteristic that may vary from one time period to the next, such as age, level of education (first grade, second grade, etc.), and income (dollars earned per year), is a variable.

It is not unusual to see some confusion between variables and the attributes or categories of which they consist. Gender is a variable consisting of the categories male and female; "male" or "female" by themselves are not variables but simply categories into which a person's gender will fall. Likewise, "divorced" and "Republican" are not variables but categories of the variables "marital status" and "political party affiliation," respectively. To keep this distinction clear, note that any term you would use to describe yourself or someone else (e.g., sophomore, sociology major) is an attribute or category of a variable (academic class, major).

Types of Variables

Social scientists find it necessary to classify variables in several ways. One type of classification is necessitated by the complexity of social situations. While all social situations have a tremendous variety of aspects or properties, the researcher in any given instance will be directly interested in only a few of these and, moreover, will simply find it impossible to observe all of the potentially relevant properties. It is useful, therefore, to distinguish between those variables that are the focus of the research, called *explanatory variables*, and all other variables, which are *extraneous* (Kish, 1959).

There are two principal types of explanatory variables: dependent and independent. The *dependent variable* is the one the researcher is interested in explaining and predicting. Variation in the dependent variable is thought to depend on or to be influenced by certain other variables. The explanatory variables that do the influencing and explaining are called *independent*. If we think in terms of cause and effect, the independent variable is the presumed cause and the dependent variable the presumed effect. Independent variables are also called predictor variables because their values or categories may be used to predict the values or categories of dependent variables. For example, when the relationship between educational attainment (years of schooling) and income is studied, educational attainment is the independent variable and income the dependent variable. All other things being equal, knowing how many years of schooling a person has had should help us to predict roughly his or her level of income.

It should be noted that research studies in the social sciences often involve several independent variables and sometimes more than one dependent variable. Also, a variable is not intrinsically independent or dependent. An independent variable in one study may well be a dependent variable in another, depending on what the researcher is trying to explain. Finally, it is conventional in mathematics and science for the letter X to symbolize the independent variable and the letter Y the dependent variable. This is a practice we shall follow in the remainder of the book.

Extraneous variables also may be divided into two classes: controlled and uncontrolled. Controlled or, more commonly, *control variables* are held constant, or prevented from varying, during the course of observation or analysis. This may be done to limit the focus of the research or to test hypotheses pertaining to specific subgroups—for example, all males or all males under 18 years of age. Basically, the value or category of a control variable remains the same for a given set of observations. Several techniques for holding variables constant are discussed at length in the following chapters. Some examples would be selecting only individuals of the same age and gender, observing groups of the same size, creating uniform laboratory conditions or social settings in which to observe people or groups, and statistically controlling for specific attributes.

Whenever a variable is held constant in research, that variable cannot account for (or explain) any of the variation in the explanatory variables. Suppose, for example, that you wanted to explain differences (i.e., variation) between people in their level of aggression. If you controlled for gender by studying only males, then the variable "gender" could not account for any of the observed variation in aggression. Holding variables constant thus simplifies complex social situations. It is a means of ruling out variables that are not of immediate interest but that might otherwise explain part of the phenomenon that the investigator wishes to understand. Indeed, one aim of efficient research design is to identify potentially relevant extraneous variables in order to control as many as is feasible (Kish, 1959).

Another important distinction is made between quantitative and qualitative variables. Actually, this is a rather crude way of pointing to some significant differences in the numerical representation of variable categories. We make more precise distinctions along these lines in the next chapter, but for now appeal to the common understanding of quantitative and qualitative. A variable is *quantitative* if its values or categories consist of numbers and if differences between its categories can be expressed numerically. For example, the variable "income," measured in dollars, signifies a quantitative difference—a certain number of dollars—between people with different incomes. *Qualitative variables* have discrete categories, usually designated by words or labels, and nonnumerical differences between categories.

For example, with the variable "gender," consisting of the discrete categories male and female, we can make categorical, but not numerical, distinctions between people of different gender.

Relationships

Social scientists' ultimate objective is to make sense out of the social world by discovering enduring relationships among phenomena. Much research is therefore aimed directly at developing and testing relationships. However, there are other more immediate purposes for which research is conducted. When very little is known about something—for example, a new religious movement—the early stages of research are devoted necessarily to gaining insight into it and to isolating its central features. Later in this chapter we will also discuss a type of social research that has as its primary goal the precise, accurate description of groups and events. Yet, even when the researcher's goal is discovery or description, research findings will depend to a large extent on what particular *relationships* are anticipated. Research is not like the kind of fishing trip in which you drop your line anywhere hoping you will catch something. Investigators do not make random observations. Whatever their goals, they must decide what to observe or ignore, how to go about making their observations, and how to interpret them. Such decisions inevitably are based upon the researcher's expectations about how variables are related to one another.

To see how anticipated relationships guide research, consider the investigator who wants to study "everything" about families, but who wants to "let the facts speak for themselves" (Batten, 1971:9–11). Without any guiding expectations, how is the researcher to decide what constitutes a "family"? Should first cousins be included even if they lived far away or seldom kept in touch? Should a family include all persons living in the same household, no matter how remote the blood tie? (Batten, 1971) When collecting data, should the researcher include the hat size and shoe size of each family member? Obviously, it is extremely unlikely that these data would ever be gathered because they would be irrelevant to the social researcher's expectations about salient properties and relationships regarding families.

Whatever observations are made and whatever facts are established, they also must be interpreted, because facts never speak for themselves. Which facts are sought and how they are interpreted depends again on anticipated relationships—on what particular answers the researcher expects the "facts" to provide. A trenchant example is related by sociologist H. W. Smith (1975:22). According to Smith, it is a fact that American blacks save less money than whites. However, if the fact that blacks earn less than whites is taken into account, it turns out that blacks save proportionately more of their incomes than whites. Thus, blacks would appear to be *more* frugal than whites. But this conclusion would not have been reached if the researcher had not entertained the notion that the relationship between race and savings might be affected by a more complex set of relationships involving how much of his or her income a person saved.

It is clear, then, that all research carries expectations about the nature of what is being investigated. As a result, an important tenet of social research, which unfortunately is not always followed, is that one's expectations—that is, anticipated relationships and guiding theoretical explanations—should always be identified as far as possible.

Thus far we have relied on the reader's intuitive grasp of the term "relationship." Everybody has experienced relationships at some time in their lives. One might think of relationships among kin, "serious" relationships, as between lovers, and relationships among the members of teams and work groups. We also have a sense of a relationship when one event regularly precedes or follows the occurrence of another, as, for example, when the appearance of dark clouds is regularly followed by rain. All such relationships have two features. First, they always involve two or more entities: persons, objects, or events—such as parent and child, leader and follower, or clouds and rain. Second, the pairs or combinations of things usually occur together and change together; thus, the appearance of one thing signals the appearance of the other and the absence of one implies the absence of the other. For example, by definition every parent has a child and every child has a parent; we cannot have one without the other. Also, by observation we know that certain kinds of clouds produce rain and that without clouds it cannot rain.

The kind of relationships with which social scientists are concerned, relationships among variables, have these same two features. Two or more variables are related, or form a relationship, to the extent that changes in one variable are accompanied by predictable changes in the other(s). Since the manner in which the variables change or vary together will depend on whether the variables are qualitative or quantitative, we will consider the nature of relationships separately for each of these types of variables.

Relationships among Qualitative Variables

Consider the two qualitative variables, race and political party affiliation. If two individuals have the same party affiliation, say Democrat, then the category of this variable does not change as we look from one individual to the other. If they have different affiliations, say one is a Democrat and the other is a Republican, then the category of the variable does change. Assuming similar statements about race, we would say that a relationship exists between race and political party affiliation if a comparison of a pair of individuals reveals that a change in race is accompanied by a change in party affiliation. More generally, the basic idea of a relationship, or association, between qualitative variables can be incorporated into two assertions (Leik, 1972:26): (1) if one variable changes, the other variable changes; and (2) if one variable does not change, the other does not change. If these two assertions were true for all pairs of cases, the result would be a perfect one-to-one correspondence between the categories of one variable and the categories of the other. This can be seen in Table 4.1A, which depicts a perfect relationship between race and political party affiliation among twenty individuals.

In actual research, of course, we never see such perfect associations. To the researcher, therefore, the important question is not whether a given pair of variables

TABLE 4.1. Varying Degrees of Association between
Two Qualitative Variables: Race and Political Affiliation

Political affiliation	Race		Total
	White	Black	
A. *Perfect association*			
Democrat	0	10	10
Republican	10	0	10
Total	10	10	20
B. *Moderate association*			
Democrat	3	7	10
Republican	7	3	10
Total	10	10	20
C. *No association*			
Democrat	5	5	10
Republican	5	5	10
Total	10	10	20

are perfectly associated, but how strongly they are related. That is, how closely do the data approximate a perfect association between variables? Statistical techniques to assess this are called measures of association. These techniques, as well as the concept of "strength of relationship," are best understood if assertions about concomitant changes in variables are treated as predictions. Table 4.1A suggests two predictions: (1) if a person is black, then he or she will be a Democrat, and (2) if a person is white, then he or she will be a Republican. The proportion of times such predictions are correct for all pairs of cases is an index of the strength of the relationship. A high proportion indicates that the variables are strongly related; a low proportion of correct predictions indicates a weak relationship. Further, if the proportion is so low that knowledge of one variable is of no use in predicting the other, the variables are said to be unrelated. Table 4.1B gives one of the possible combinations showing a moderate relationship between race and political party affiliation. Table 4.1C gives the distribution indicating no relationship. Statistical indices of association may be computed for each of these distributions. Ordinarily, these indices will range from 0, indicating no relationship, to 1.00, indicating a perfect relationship.

Relationships among Quantitative Variables

As we move from qualitative to quantitative variables, it becomes possible to say whether a change in a variable represents an increase or decrease in value. With this additional property, we can measure not only the strength of the relationship but also two other aspects: direction and linearity.

A relationship may be either positive or negative in direction. A *positive* or *direct relationship* between variables exists if an increase in the value of one variable is accompanied by an increase in the value of the other, or if a decrease in the value of one variable is accompanied by a decrease in the value of the other. In other words, the two variables consistently change in the same direction. We would expect positive relationships between sons' heights and fathers' heights (e.g., the taller a father, the taller his son will tend to be), and between scores on the Scholastic Aptitude Test and college grade-point averages (e.g., among college students, as scores increase, grades tend to increase). A *negative* or *inverse relationship* between variables exists if a decrease in the value of one variable is accompanied by an increase in the value of the other. Thus, changes in one variable are opposite in direction to changes in the other. We would find negative relationships between a person's age and how long he or she is expected to live (as age increases, life expectancy decreases), and between the speed and accuracy with which people perform many tasks (the faster one does something, the less accurately one is likely to do it).

Relationships among quantitative variables are usually depicted with graphs, such as those in Figure 4.1. The lines in these two graphs illustrate the characteristic

FIGURE 4.1. Linear and curvilinear relationships between two quantitative variables.

A. Linear relationship

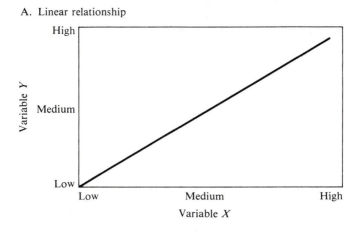

B. Curvilinear relationship

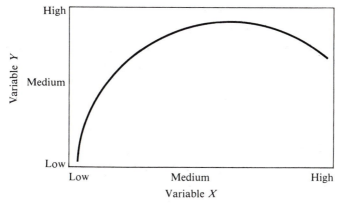

of "linearity." The straight line in Figure 4.1A depicts a linear relationship. (Actually, this line depicts a *positive linear* relationship. A straight line running from the upper left corner to the lower right corner would depict a *negative linear* relationship.) Notice that one variable changes at the same rate and in the same direction (positive) over the entire range of the other variable. The curved line in Figure 4.1B depicts a *curvilinear* relationship. In this case, the rate of change in one variable is *not* consistent over all values of the other: variable Y increases more rapidly for low values than for high values of variable X and then reverses direction. We would expect this pattern of relationship to occur between the age and annual earnings of adult workers. Earnings will generally increase with age up to retirement and then will decline.

Tabular and graphic representations of relationships between variables and other statistical analyses are discussed at length in chapter 14. There as well as elsewhere in the book we focus on linear relationships, since this is the most common pattern analyzed in the social sciences. A common statistical measure of the strength and direction of linear relationships between quantitative variables is called the Pearson product-moment coefficient of correlation, or *correlation coefficient* for short. Symbolized by the letter r, the correlation coefficient may vary between -1.00 and $+1.00$. The signs, $+$ and $-$, indicate the direction of the relationship, positive or negative; the magnitude of the coefficient, ignoring the sign, indicates the strength of association.

Relationships between a Qualitative and a Quantitative Variable

Another way of assessing relationships is used when both qualitative and quantitative variables are involved. Most often, in such cases, especially in experiments, the independent variable is qualitative and the dependent variable is quantitative. This is the type of relationship considered here.

It will be helpful, once again, to think in terms of predictions. A relationship is said to exist if the different categories of the independent variable predict different values for the dependent variable. Thus, if each category of the independent variable is treated as a distinct group, then a relationship can be described in terms of the *differences among groups* on the dependent variable. We might compute an average value on the dependent variable for each group. No differences in these averages across groups would then indicate no relationship. And, in general, the larger the differences, the stronger the relationship.

For example, suppose a researcher were interested in examining the relationship between race and annual income. Since annual income, as measured in dollars earned, is a quantitative variable, average incomes could be computed for each racial group (i.e., for each category of the qualitative variable race). If there is a difference in the averages across groups—say, whites earn $20,000 per year on the average and blacks earn $15,000—then it may be concluded that a relationship exists between race and income.[1]

So far we have examined some common ways of depicting relationships. Also, we have noted three properties of relationships: strength, directionality, and linearity. The strength of a relationship refers to the extent to which variables are associated or correlated. Directionality and linearity tell us *how* changes in one variable are related to changes in another. Do the variables change in the same or the opposite direction? Is the rate of change in one variable consistent over all values of the other? Together these two properties describe the *form* of the relationship. Knowing the strength and form of relationships will often satisfy the researcher's curiosity. However, if the interest is in explaining and predicting phenomena, then the researcher also will want to know about the causal link between variables. To establish a cause-and-effect relationship, the statistical properties mentioned above are never sufficient, as we will show.

The Nature of Causal Relationships

As we noted in chapter 2, for purposes of explanation and prediction, scientists find it helpful to think in terms of cause-and-effect relationships. But how does one identify such a relationship? What is meant by the term "causality"? At first glance, the task of defining "causality" seems simple. Since we are so accustomed to thinking causally, and causal terms are so frequently used in everyday life, the concept would appear to be widely understood. In lay terms, a cause is something that makes something happen or change. It seems obvious that a thrown rock will make, or cause, a pane of glass to shatter. And the fact that drinking too much soda causes the writer to get a stomachache is a causal relationship the reader can comprehend even if he or she fortunately has not had the same experience.

In contrast to the implicit understanding of causality that seems to exist in everyday life, the meaning of the concept of cause has been hotly debated by philosophers and scientists for centuries. Much of this debate stems from the philosopher David Hume's analysis (1748). Although we will not take up the debate here, one point of Hume's should be mentioned because it is central to current scientific thinking. Hume argued that all that one can observe is a constant or stable association between events. From such association we infer a causal connection; however, there is no way of logically or empirically showing that a causal connection actually exists. A causal relationship exists only in the observer's mind; it is something inferred from an observed association between events. Following Hume's line of reasoning, some philosophers and some scientists (e.g., Kerlinger, 1973) have maintained that the concept of cause ought to be discarded from scientific work. Yet many people regard causal relationships as the heart of scientific understanding. Further, even if such relationships cannot be "proven" empirically (just as no generalization can be proven by scientific evidence), scientists not only have found it helpful to *think* causally (Blalock, 1964:6) but also have found working with causal hypotheses to be a very productive way of doing science.

The important point of Hume's analysis, therefore, is that we should understand the bases for making causal inferences. In other words, what kind of evidence supports the belief that a causal relationship exists? Social scientists generally require at least three kinds of evidence to establish causality. These requisites are association, direction of influence, and nonspuriousness.

Association. For one variable to be a cause of another, the variables must be statistically associated. If the pattern of changes in one variable is not related to changes in another, then the one cannot be producing, or causing changes in the other. Thus, for instance, if intelligence is unrelated to delinquency—that is, if adolescents of high and low intelligence are equally likely to be delinquent—then intelligence cannot be a cause of delinquency.

Associations, of course, are almost never perfect; and so, a perfect association between variables is not a criterion of causality. According to logicians, in fact, the very idea of causation implies that imperfect associations between events will be observed. Causes can have invariable effects only in "closed systems" that exclude all other factors that might influence the relationship under investigation. Many of the laws of physics, for instance, are said to apply exactly only in a vacuum. However, vacuums are not found in nature; neither is it possible in real social situations to eliminate completely the influence of extraneous factors. Perfect associations may be expected, therefore, only under the theoretical condition that "all other things are equal," but not in the "real world" of observations.

Barring "perfect" associations, then, the application of this first criterion necessarily involves a judgment about whether an association is strong enough to imply a meaningful causal relationship. In the social sciences, causal relationships often are implied from comparatively "weak" associations. One reason for this is that many measurements in the social sciences are relatively imprecise. The primary reason, though, is that in explaining human action, it is assumed that there can be multiple causes operating independently or jointly to produce the same or similar effects. Consequently, a weak association may mean that only one of several causes has been identified, or it may mean that a causal relationship exists, but not under the conditions or for the particular segment of the population in which the weak association was observed.

Direction of influence. A second criterion needed to establish causality is that a cause must precede its effect, or at least the direction of influence should be from cause to effect. In other words, changes in the causal factor, or independent variable, must influence changes in the effect, or dependent variable, but not vice versa. For many relationships the direction of influence between variables can be conceptualized in only one way. Here are two examples: (1) ample rain and sunshine naturally occur prior to the growth of crops, and no amount of crop growth can produce changes in the weather; (2) characteristics fixed at birth, such as a person's race and gender, come before characteristics developed later in life, such as a person's education or political party affiliation, and it is hard to imagine how changes in the latter could influence changes in the former.

Direction of influence is not always so easy to determine. Suppose you found a correlation between racial prejudice and racial contact showing that the more contact a person has with members of other races, the less prejudiced he or she is apt to be. One possible interpretation is that racial contact increases familiarity and contradicts stereotypes, thereby reducing prejudice. An equally plausible interpretation is that prejudiced people will avoid contact while tolerant people will readily interact with other races, so that racial prejudice influences racial contact. Without any further information about the direction of influence between these variables, there is no basis for deciding which variable is causal and which is the effect. To take another example, a correlation between grades and class attendance may mean that greater attendance "increases the amount learned and thus causes higher grades" or it may mean that "good grades lead students who obtain them to attend class more frequently" (Neale and Liebert, 1973:84).

The requirement that causes influence effects has two major implications for research: (1) hypothesized relationships should always specify the direction of influence among variables, and (2) whenever the direction cannot be established theoretically, it should be tested empirically. As you will see, this task is relatively easy in experiments but often difficult in other kinds of research.

Nonspuriousness (elimination of rival hypotheses). If two variables happen to be related to a common extraneous variable, then a statistical association can exist even if there is no inherent link between the variables. Therefore, to infer a causal relationship from an observed correlation there should be good reason to believe that there are no "hidden" factors that could have created an accidental or "spuriousness relationship" between the variables. When an association or correlation between variables cannot be explained by an extraneous variable, the relationship is said to be *nonspurious*. When a correlation has been produced by an extraneous third factor, and neither of the variables involved in the correlation has influenced the other, then the relationship is called a *spurious relationship*.

The idea of spuriousness is obvious when we consider two popular examples in the social sciences. The first is a reported positive correlation in northwestern Europe between the number of storks in an area and the number of births in that area (Wallis and Roberts, 1956:79). Although this correlation might explain how the legend got started, one could hardly accept the conclusion that storks bring babies. The correct interpretation is that storks like to nest in the crannies and chimneys of buildings; and so, as the population and thus the number of buildings increases, the number of places for storks to nest increases. And as the population increases, so does the number of babies. We also would expect to find a positive correlation between the number of firefighters at a fire and the amount of damage done. But this does not imply that firefighters did the damage. The reason for the correlation is the size of the fire: bigger fires cause more firefighters to be summoned and also cause more damage.

In the above examples the original relationship is an incidental consequence of a common cause. In the first example, the size of the population accounts for both the number of storks and the number of births; in the second, the severity of the fire determines both the number of firefighters and the amount of damage. The examples are intuitively obvious and the third factor is fairly easy to identify. In actual research, however, spurious relationships are much less apparent, and since their detection depends on the investigator's knowledge and insight, the possibility always exists that an unknown variable may have produced an observed association.

To infer nonspuriousness the researcher ideally must show that the relationship is maintained when all extraneous variables are held constant. Circumstances seldom allow a researcher to control all variables, however. Therefore, one attempts to control or evaluate the effects of as many variables as possible. The greater the number of variables that are controlled without altering a relationship, the greater the likelihood that the relationship is not spurious. An example involving the relationship between smoking and cancer will show how this works (Labovitz and Hagedorn, 1976).

Smokers develop lung cancer at a rate eleven times greater than do nonsmokers (Brownlee, 1965). The belief that this indicates a causal link between smoking and cancer is strengthened by the fact that this rate remains the same when variables such as gender, urban-rural residence, and socioeconomic status are controlled. That is, when the incidence of lung cancer among smokers and nonsmokers is computed separately for males versus females, for urban versus rural residents, and for persons of high versus low socioeconomic status, smokers are, in every case, approximately eleven times more likely to develop lung cancer than nonsmokers. Each of these variables is a potential rival explanation to the interpretation that smoking *causes* lung cancer. An association but no causal connection between smoking and cancer could occur if males were both more likely to smoke and more likely (for some reason other than smoking) to get lung cancer. Similarly, urban-rural residence could produce a spurious association between smoking and lung cancer if urban areas have more smokers as well as sources of lung cancer (e.g., greater outdoor air pollution) than rural areas. Thus, if controlling for any one of these variables caused the differential rate of lung cancer between smokers and nonsmokers to disappear, then the relationship between smoking and cancer would be considered spurious. For example, the finding of no difference in the cancer rate between smoking and nonsmoking men and between smoking and nonsmoking women would suggest that the variable "gender" had produced a spurious association between smoking and cancer. (Box 4.1 provides another example of the importance of the nonspuriousness criterion. In this case, the causal interpretation that exercise reduces the risk of heart attacks was challenged by several rival explanations.)

BOX 4.1

Problems in Causal Interpretation:
The Case of Exercise and Heart Attacks

Of the three criteria needed to establish a causal relationship, the most difficult to assess is nonspuriousness. One can never be sure that a causal connection exists between correlated variables. Indeed, mistaken impressions of causality may remain undetected for years. An interesting example of this problem in social science research is related by psychologists Schuyler Huck and Howard Sandler (1979:151, 152, 227).

In recent years there has been much interest in the relative benefits of regular exercise. One claim, not well documented as yet, is that exercise can reduce the risk of heart attacks. An early study by Dr. J. N. Morris of London shows, however, how difficult this is to establish. Examining drivers and conductors of London's double-decker buses, Morris found that the drivers were far more likely to suffer from heart disease and to die from coronaries than the conductors. Since the drivers sat in their seats all day while the conductors ran up and down stairs to collect fares, he concluded that it was the differential amount of exercise inherent in the two jobs that brought about the observed differences in health. Before reading further, you might try to think of variables other than exercise that could have produced the difference in heart problems between the drivers and conductors. Morris uncovered one variable in a follow-up study, and Huck and Sandler mention two others.

Some time after the publication of the above results, Morris examined the records maintained on the uniforms issued to drivers and conductors and discovered that drivers tended to be given larger uniforms than conductors. Therefore, he concluded, differences in weight rather than exercise might be the causal factor. That is, heavier men, who were more coronary-prone to begin with, may have chosen the sedentary job of driver, whereas thinner men chose the more physically active job of conductor.

Another explanation is related to the amount of tension associated with the two jobs. As Huck and Sandler (1979:227) point out,

> The conductors probably experienced very little tension as they went up and down the bus collecting fares from the passengers; the worst thing that they probably had to deal with in their jobs was a passenger who attempted to ride free by sneaking around from one seat to another. Normally, however, we suspect that the conductors actually enjoyed their interaction with other people while on the job.
>
> But on the other hand, each driver had the safety of everyone on the bus as his responsibility. And as anyone who lives in or visits a city knows, driving in rush-hour traffic is anything but restful. Having to dodge pedestrians, being cut off by other vehicles, watching for signal changes—these activities can bring about temporary outbursts of anger and chronic nervousness. Imagine how it would affect your heart to be in the driver's seat of a bus for eight hours each working day!

Finally, a third variable that could account for the different rate of heart problems is age. If mobility or seniority or some other function of age were related to job assignment, then employees assigned to the driver jobs may have been older and those assigned to the conductor jobs younger. And since we would expect more heart attacks among older persons, age rather than the nature of the job could be the causal variable.

In this example it is difficult if not impossible to tell which cause—exercise, weight, job stress, or age—may have produced the observed differences in health between drivers and conductors. Since neither weight nor age provides a causal link *between* job type and heart disease, the association between the latter two variables would be defined as spurious if either weight or age were the true cause. However, if exercise or job stress were the correct interpretation, then the original relationship would not be spurious, since exercise and job stress specify intervening mechanisms through which the job itself can make a person more or less susceptible to heart problems. Of course, it is possible that two or more of these variables are operating jointly to produce the health differential between the two groups. The only safe conclusion is that we really do not know which interpretation is correct.

In general, correlation does not imply causation. All correlations must be interpreted; like any fact, they do not speak for themselves. To infer a causal relationship from a correlation, an investigator must detect and control for extraneous variables that are possible and plausible causes of the variable to be explained. The fatal flaw in Morris's study is that relevant extraneous variables were not controlled; without directly assessing the effects of such "hidden" causes, we cannot tell which interpretation is valid.

In one way or another, tests for spuriousness entail controlling for extraneous variables. The type of statistical control employed in our smoking-cancer example is very common in nonexperimental research. Its major drawback is that one can control statistically only for those variables that have been observed or measured as part of the research. Hence, the effects of any unknown or unmeasured variables cannot be assessed. A stronger test of nonspuriousness is provided in experiments through a process called randomization that makes it theoretically possible to control for all extraneous variables. Experimental controls are discussed in chapter 7, and causal analysis techniques involving statistical manipulation of nonexperimental data are discussed in chapter 15.

Causation, intervening mechanisms, and theory. In addition to association, direction of influence, and nonspuriousness, one other criterion is sometimes advocated to show that one variable causes another: one or more intervening mechanisms must link the independent and dependent variables (see Hyman, 1955). For example, one may argue that the belief that smoking causes lung cancer will be enhanced considerably if and when it is established that certain chemical agents from cigarettes produce cancerous cells. Knowing the causal process through which smoking produces cancer would provide one last shred of evidence against a spurious correlation. However, once the criterion of nonspuriousness is firmly established, a causal relationship is generally inferred even if the intervening mechanisms are not known. Few scientists today doubt that smoking causes cancer. Thus, while specifying the intervening mechanisms in a relationship may lead to a better theoretical understanding and more accurate prediction, it is "not part of the minimum requirements for demonstrating causality. Holding a match to a pile of leaves is a cause of their bursting into flame, even if one cannot describe the intervening chemical reactions" (Hirschi and Selvin, 1967:38).

Though not a necessary causal criterion, intervening mechanisms are nonetheless an essential part of scientific inquiry. Often, in fact, this is what the development of theory is all about. For example, Durkheim's theory of suicide stipulated the intervening causal mechanism—social integration—for a number of relationships. The reason that fewer suicides are found among Catholics than Protestants and among married than single people, according to the theory, is that being a Catholic and being married each engenders a greater sense of social integration that, in turn, reduces the likelihood that anyone within the group will commit suicide. For another illustration, recall from chapter 2 that the kinetic theory of gases explained the intervening processes in the relationship between the temperature and pressure of a gas; also, each of the various theories of the social facilitation effect postulates a different mechanism through which an audience will enhance the performance of a task.

Yet, theory plays a much larger role in causal analysis than specifying intervening variables. Theories not only render a more complete understanding of the causal processes that connect events, but also provide the general framework for investigating the nature of all relationships. Theories tell the researcher which relationships to observe, what extraneous variables are likely to affect what is being studied, and the conditions under which a causal relationship is likely to exist. It is only in terms of some theory, in short, that the researcher can determine how to assess

the meaningfulness of a "weak" association and how to test for direction of influence and nonspuriousness. Thus, we see again the importance of the interplay
between theory and research in science. Theory guides research, and research
provides the findings that validate and suggest modifications in theory.

Stating Problems and Hypotheses

Having introduced the language of units of analysis, variables, and relationships,
we are now ready to examine statements of the research problem. Scientific investigations always start with a problem or question that can be solved or answered
empirically. Arriving at this starting point for research can be a long and difficult
process. Experienced as well as novice researchers often begin with only a vague
notion of the problem, or they may be motivated by a question so broad in scope
that it provides little or no immediate direction for research. Many well known
social scientists seem to have been stimulated by just these kinds of "grand questions." For example, Stanley Schachter, well known in part for his work on affiliation, was interested initially in what motivates people to be around others (Evans,
1976:159), a question nearly as encompassing as the entire field of social psychology. In tracing the development of the ideas for his study *The Adolescent Society*,
sociologist James Coleman (1964:184) says that his major interest, from the time he
entered graduate school, was in "the relation of the individual to society," or, being
only slightly less general, "the dilemma that confronts each society, on the one
hand, to maintain social order and, on the other, not to restrict the freedom of the
individuals within it." These are certainly important questions, but they are too
broad to be scientifically answerable. Before Schachter and Coleman could begin to
do research, they had to reformulate their problems so that they pointed to identifiable variables and relationships. After reading and speculating about "affiliative
tendencies," Schachter eventually focused on the problem of how fear affects the
desire to be with others. Coleman, having been influenced by a casual discussion
among friends about high-school experiences, decided to study various determinants and consequents of high-school status systems.

To provide sufficient direction for research, the statement of a research problem
should always suggest observations that offer some solution to the problem. For
most research this means that a problem statement should, first of all, express or ask
a question about a relation between two or more variables (Kerlinger, 1973:17). This
rules out moral, philosophical, and religious issues as well as any questions of the
general form, "What causes *A*?" or "What are the effects of *B*?" Second, the variables in the problem statement should be observable or at least potentially observable. A major difficulty with the problems with which Schachter and Coleman
began is that their concepts—"being around others," "social order," "freedom"—
are too complex to be amenable to observation.

Consider the following sample research problems taken from a variety of social
science journals:

> 1. Do news stories on prominent suicides trigger a subsequent rise in national
> suicides? (Wasserman, 1984)

2. Does political repression increase as the investment of foreign capital in a country increases? (Timberlake and Williams, 1984)

3. What factors affect the formation and stability of ability groups in schools and how does ability grouping in turn affect growth in academic achievement? (Hallinan and Sorenson, 1983)

4. Will children having greater contact with elderly persons have more positive attitudes toward them than children having less contact? (Caspi, 1984)

5. What technical, economic, and political factors have affected the use of solar energy technology in the United States? (Etzkowitz, 1984)

The tentative answers to research questions are called hypotheses. Formally defined, a *hypothesis* is an expected but unconfirmed relationship between two or more variables. Hypotheses come from a variety of sources, including everything from theory to direct observation to guesses and intuition. Sometimes the formulation of hypotheses is the principal outcome of research. At other times, hypotheses are never made explicit, even though they implicitly guide research activities. However, whenever the research objective is clearly one of testing relationships among variables, it is essential that hypotheses be formally and precisely stated so that they carry clear implications for testing the stated relations (Kerlinger, 1973:18).

While stated in a variety of ways, all hypotheses should speculate about the nature and form of a relationship. An adequate hypothesis statement about two variables should indicate which variable predicts or causes the other and how changes in one variable are related to changes in the other. For example, if we thought that education generally increases tolerance, we might hypothesize that "an increase in education will result in a decrease in prejudice." This statement implies two features about the relationship: first, which variable causes, explains, or predicts the other (education predicts prejudice); and second, how changes in one variable are related to changes in the other (as education increases, prejudice decreases). Hypotheses that specify the form of the relationship are said to be testable because it is possible, assuming each variable has been measured adequately, to determine whether they are true or false, or at least whether they are probably true or probably false.

Of the several ways of stating testable hypotheses, such as the one relating education and prejudice, the most common forms of expression found in scientific work are the following:

1. *"If-then" statements.* These statements say that if one phenomenon or condition holds, then another will also hold. An example would be "if a person has a high level of education, then he or she will have a low level of prejudice." Alternately, one could say, "if a person has a low level of education, then he or she will have a high level of prejudice." In logic, such statements are called *implications*. An implication consists of a connection between two simple statements, each pointing to a condition or category of a variable. As used in science, the connection asserted by an implication is that the condition (or variable category) following the "if" *causes* the condition (or variable category) following the "then." Although in social research hypotheses seldom are specified in this form, it is always possible to restate testable hypotheses as implications (Hempel and Oppenheim, 1948). This is

important; by stating hypotheses in certain standard logical forms we can ascertain the kinds of inferences that legitimately can be made from research findings to the hypothesis (McGuigan, 1978:52).

2. *Mathematical statements.* Many hypotheses may be stated in the form of the standard mathematical formula, $Y = f(X)$, which reads "*Y* is a function of *X*." An example is Einstein's famous formula $E = mc^2$ (i.e., energy equals mass times the speed of light squared). Of course, though once a hypothesis, $E = mc^2$ is now called a scientific law because it has been confirmed repeatedly. Mathematical formulas represent precise formal statements of hypotheses. Because variables in social research generally are measured with less precision than in the physical sciences, many social scientists choose not to state hypotheses in this form. Nonetheless, mathematical formulas are the ideal in science, because they yield precise predictions and express complex relationships parsimoniously. The mathematical form is also equivalent to the implication. $Y = f(X)$ merely says "If (and only if) *X* is this value, then *Y* is that value" (McGuigan, 1978:53).

Considering our education-prejudice example and assuming each variable could be measured numerically, an equation for the relationship might be $P = 10 - \frac{1}{2}E$; that is, prejudice (*P*) equals 10 minus one-half times education (*E*). Prejudice might be scaled such that zero indicated an extremely low level of prejudice and 10 an extremely high level, with intermediate values indicating intermediate levels. Education might be quantified in terms of the number of years of schooling. Thus, a person with a college education, or 16 years of schooling, would be hypothesized to have a prejudice level of 2, since $10 - \frac{1}{2}(16) = 2$; and a person who had only finished the fourth grade would be hypothesized to have a prejudice level of 8 $[10 - \frac{1}{2}(4) = 8]$.

3. *Continuous statements.* Hypotheses of the form "the greater the *X*, the greater (or lesser) the *Y*" indicate that increases in one variable (*X*), are associated with increases (or decreases) in another variable (*Y*). For example, as education increases, prejudice decreases; or, expressed in slightly different form, the higher the level of education, the lower the prejudice.

4. *Difference statements.* Statements in this form assert that one variable differs in terms of the categories of another variable. For example, people with high education are less prejudiced than people with low education. Whether "continuous" or "difference" statements are used to express a hypothesis will depend on whether the variables in the hypothesis are quantitative or qualitative. If both variables could be "quantified," as we assumed in the case of the formula $P = 10 - \frac{1}{2}E$, then the relationship could be stated in the continuous form. But if either variable consisted of discrete categories, such as "high" and "low" prejudice, then the relationship would need to be stated in the difference form.

Both continuous and difference statements clearly specify the *form* of the relationship. However, both types of statements are ambiguous about the causal connection between variables. Ordinarily a statement of the form "the greater the *X*, the greater the *Y*" is meant to imply that *X* causes *Y*. But it also can mean that *Y* causes *X* or that *X* and *Y* cause one another. As you saw in our discussion of causation, it is important to know which variable is presumed to cause the other; in addition, since most hypotheses take the form of continuous or difference statements, the causal linkage can be problematic. Fortunately, in most research articles and reports, researchers make this connection clear in their discussions of the hypothesis.

Once the causal variable has been identified, then it is easy to transform the hypothesis statement into the form of an implication. Thus, for example, the statement "the higher the level of education, the lower the level of prejudice" becomes "if education is high, then prejudice will be low."

At this point we should reiterate an important tenet of scientific research. Even though all of the above forms of expression would appear to assert that the relationship is absolutely true or false, hypotheses in science can only have probabilistic, not exact, confirmation. Thus, while the statement "If X, then Y" logically can only be true or false, it is assumed that observations will show it to be "probably true" or "probably false."[2] One often sees this kind of assumption built into statements of hypotheses in the form of qualifiers such as "tends to" or "in general." For example, one might say that "increased education will *tend* to reduce prejudice." Such statements acknowledge that tests of hypotheses are always restricted by the limited accuracy of our measures and our inability to specify and control all the variables affecting events.

How a hypothesis is expressed in a given study will depend on several factors: the researcher's discretion, the present state of knowledge about the research problem, and whether qualitative or quantitative variables are involved. Regardless of how hypotheses are expressed, however, they should indicate at least the form of the relationship between variables and, ideally, should specify the causal linkage between variables; for ultimately it is causal relationships in which scientists are interested. (To check your understanding of hypotheses, variables, and units of analysis, see Box 4.2.)

BOX 4.2

Putting It All Together: Writing Hypotheses and Identifying Variables and Units of Analysis

A thorough grasp of the terms introduced in this chapter is essential for understanding every phase of social research. Therefore, to check your mastery of the language of social research, let us consider some crude statements of relations among variables, identify the relevant variables and units of analysis, and then transform these statements into testable hypotheses. Suppose that you wanted to rewrite the following statements as formal hypotheses:

1. Poverty breeds illiteracy.
2. Women are underpaid.

Neither statement as it stands is adequate. The terms "poverty" and "illiteracy" are too abstract and pertain to a limited range of the underlying variables. "Women are underpaid" is completely ambiguous because it fails to indicate the relevant comparison: underpaid with respect to whom or what?

To derive testable hypotheses from these statements, first you would need to identify the variables implied by key terms. Some terms pertain to the category of a variable; for example, "women" is a category of the variable "gender." Other terms in noun form convey abstract concepts; usually adding phrases such as "degree of . . . " or "level of . . . " will identify the relevant variable. For example, the concept "violence" implies the variable "frequency of violent bahavior." Similarly, to the extent that "illiteracy" pertains to a characteristic of an aggregate, such as an area of a city or a whole nation, then "the number of" or "percentage of the population who are illiterate" could be the relevant variable. Still other terms pertain to a limited set of values. For example, "poverty" and "underpaid" refer to particular ranges of values of the variable "income."

After identifying the variables, determine if each variable is qualitative or quantitative; then determine which variable is independent, which is dependent, and whether there are control variables. Gender is a qualitative variable; so is illiteracy if it is defined as whether or not an individual can read and write. Income is a quantitative variable. Because of the word "breeds," which implies causal direction, level of income ("poverty") should be considered the independent variable in the first statement. Given that gender is an immutable trait (sex changes notwithstanding), gender is the independent variable in the second statement.

If both variables are quantitative, state the hypothesis in the form of a continuous statement. If one or both variables is qualitative, then put the hypothesis in the form of a difference statement. Thus, we might rewrite statement 2 as "Women tend to receive lower pay than men for the same jobs"; gender is the independent variable, salary or wage the dependent variable, and job or occupation becomes a control variable. If you choose to write a hypothesis in the form of an implication, then be sure to write at least *two* statements, so that you identify all the relevant categories and appropriate comparisons. Thus, the implication "if a nation's average family income is low, then its literacy rate will tend to be low" should be complemented by the implication "if a nation's average family income is high, then its literacy rate will tend to be high."

To identify the unit of analysis, ask yourself what the variables describe—individuals, groups, areas, organizations, social artifacts, or what? Also, what units would the researcher need to observe to test the hypothesis? Gender describes a characteristic of individuals. "Average family income" describes a social grouping, such as a nation; so does the variable "literacy rate." Individuals do not have literacy rates; they are either illiterate or literate.

Research Purposes and Research Design

In the previous pages we have emphasized the role of relationships in social research. The sense that social scientists make out of the social world is expressed in terms of relationships among variables. Furthermore, although they are often only vaguely defined or implicit and unbeknownst to the researcher, anticipated relationships structure the researcher's every activity, from deciding which variables to measure to deciding how observations should be made and interpreted. As mentioned earlier, however, not all research is conducted for the immediate purpose of testing relationships. Research is undertaken for three broad purposes: (1) to *explore* a phenomenon such as a group or setting in order to become familiar with it and to gain insight and understanding about it, frequently in order to formulate a more precise research problem for further study; (2) to *describe* a particular community, group, or situation as completely, precisely, and accurately as possible; and (3) to examine and formally to *test relationships* among variables. Whether a study is conducted primarily for the purpose of exploration, description, or testing relationships is important to know, for these three functions have different implications for research design.

Exploratory studies are undertaken when relatively little is known about something, perhaps because of its "deviant" character or its newness. Falling into this category of research would be observational studies of street gangs and of various radical political and religious movements, clinical case histories of persons, groups, and events, and anthropological accounts of entire cultures. When attempting to explore a topic or phenomenon about which one knows very little, one necessarily begins with a general description of the phenomenon. This sounds easy but in fact this is probably the most difficult kind of study for the novice researcher to undertake. There are no clearly delineated independent and dependent variables and, therefore, no categories within which to classify what one sees. The researcher may have few, if any, guidelines to help determine what is important, whom to interview, or what leads to follow up on. For these reasons, the research plan in an exploratory study is more open than in other kinds of research. Decisions are made about the kinds of instruments needed (e.g., photographic equipment, tape recorders) and the key persons with whom one will need to speak at first, but the paths that these initial steps may lead to are almost impossible to foresee. In chapter 11, on field research, we discuss some data-gathering approaches that frequently are devoted to exploration.

The objective of a *descriptive* study, as the name implies, is to describe some phenomenon. The nature of the description, however, differs considerably from exploratory research. A descriptive study is much more structured. Basically a fact-finding enterprise, it focuses on relatively few dimensions of a well-defined entity and measures these dimensions systematically and precisely, usually with detailed numerical descriptions. The information is gathered from a set of cases that are carefully selected to enable the researcher to make estimates of the precision and generalizability of the findings. Examples of descriptive studies are the various censuses conducted periodically at the local and national levels. A census may provide information about everything from the age and racial composition of a community to its employment and housing costs. Also having a descriptive purpose are the ubiquitous opinion polls that attempt to estimate the proportion of people in a specified population who hold certain opinions or views, or who behave in certain ways: for example, How many favor capital punishment? How many say they will vote for candidate A in the next election?

The third purpose for which research is conducted is to test relationships. Studies with this purpose are sometimes called *explanatory* studies, because they formally seek the answers to problems and hypotheses. Since all research involves description at some level, the primary difference between descriptive versus explanatory studies lies in the scope of the description. Purely descriptive research operates at a lower level of description by merely seeking information about isolated variables, whereas explanatory research goes beyond this step to a description of relationships among variables.

Both descriptive and relationship-testing research are highly structured and must be carefully planned. With these kinds of research it is important, therefore, to have a complete, detailed strategy worked out before the data are collected. This preliminary strategy or outline is what we have called the research design. Basically, it consists of a clear statement of the research problem as well as plans for gathering, processing, and interpreting the observations intended to provide some resolution to the problem. To formulate a research design is to anticipate the entire research process, from beginning to end. To do this, one needs to have an adequate knowledge of every stage of social research. Examining these stages now will serve not only to clarify the key components of research design but also to introduce the reader to the remainder of the book.

Stages of Social Research

Stage 1: Selection and Formulation of the Research Problem

Research begins with a question or problem. Problems initially chosen almost always require more precise formulation to be amenable to research. From a general idea, one must decide more specifically what one wants to know and for what purpose one wants to know it. The best ideas on how to refine the problem are likely to be found in the scientific literature. Indeed, a thorough review of previous research on the topic of interest in journals and books is considered absolutely essential in science. Besides helping to narrow and refine the problem, a review of the literature may reveal the broader theoretical significance of the problem. It also will help define relevant extraneous variables and should suggest relevant methods and procedures by indicating how other researchers have addressed the problem.

Stage 2: Preparation of the Research Design

Once the problem has been clearly formulated, the researcher must develop an overall plan or framework for the investigation. To do this, one must, in effect, anticipate all of the subsequent stages of the research project. Preliminary decisions have to be made about what sort of observations are needed to solve the research problem or to provide an adequate test of the hypothesis. One must then select an appropriate strategy for making the observations—experiment, survey, field research, or use of available data. As you will see in chapters 7–12, each of these approaches has its unique strengths and weaknesses that determine its suitability for given problems. Often the best strategy, as we argue in chapter 13, is a combination of approaches. Within the context of selecting an overall strategy, decisions also must be made on the unit of analysis, on which variables to observe and control and how they should be measured, and on how best to analyze the data. Thinking through all of these problems in advance should prevent serious mistakes and omissions in a study. Of course, not all problems can be foreseen, especially in exploratory research, and many of the decisions at the design stage will be arbitrary and subject to change.

Two problems—measuring variables and selecting units of analysis—warrant special attention and are ordinarily worked out in detail after the basic research design is complete. These are therefore considered to be separate, concurrent stages.

Stage 3: Measurement

Part of the research plan involves devising operations that will link specific concepts to empirically observable events. This process of operationalization and the measurement in which it results will be taken up in chapter 5, a substantial part of which describes techniques for assessing the quality or goodness of measures.

Stage 4: Sampling

Besides deciding on the unit of analysis, the researcher must also determine how many units should be selected and how to go about choosing them. The problems and methods related to making such determinations are addressed in chapter 6 on sampling.

Stage 5: Data Collection

Once the research design is completed, the researcher is ready to make the observations—to collect the data. Since the general approach to data collection affects decisions about both measurement and sampling, the approach to be taken is determined early in the design phase. As we have pointed out, there are four basic choices: experiment, survey, field research, and use of available data. The underlying logic of each of these approaches, as well as their distinctive problems, advantages, and disadvantages are covered in chapters 7–12.

Stage 6: Data Processing

Having made the observations, the researcher is ready to analyze and interpret them. In most cases, however, the form of the data does not allow easy interpretation. The data must be transformed or processed for analysis. In this era, most data processing involves, at some point, the "hardware" and "software" of computers. Chapter 14 begins with a discussion of data processing, giving special attention to the preparation of data for "computer analysis."

Stage 7: Data Analysis and Interpretation

Once the data are ready for analysis, they must be manipulated further to extract their meaning and bearing upon the problems and hypotheses that initiated the inquiry. There are several types of analysis, many of which involve statistical tests, a topic that is beyond this textbook. Without any training in statistics, however, one can learn how to read and to present data properly in tables and graphs. One can also learn when it is appropriate to apply certain statistical procedures. Finally, it is possible to develop a solid understanding of the logic of analyzing causal relationships. These topics are also covered in chapters 14 and 15.

Summary

Science requires that research findings be communicated in a precise manner. In this way an investigation can be evaluated on the basis of clearly stated and understood concepts, rather than on some assumption or interpretation of what "must have been meant." This requirement for precision leads to a considerable body of technical language. Our purpose in this chapter has been to introduce the basic terms in the technical language of social research as these terms relate to problem formulation and research design.

Many of the sources of ideas and factors affecting problem selection were pointed out at the beginning of this chapter. A basic requirement, of course, is that a problem be amenable to scientific research—that it be resolvable with reference to observational evidence. Beyond this requirement, problem selection is affected by such factors as theoretical and practical relevance, social premiums, and the personal values and resources of the researcher.

Problems are refined in the course of working out the overall study plan, or research design, the key elements of which are units of analysis, variables, and relationships. Units of analysis are the entities about whom or which the researcher gathers information. These may be individual people, groups and organizations of all kinds, communities, nations, and social artifacts. Researchers often aggregate information about individuals in order to describe the social unit that the individuals comprise. When this is done, conclusions should be restricted to the social unit; otherwise one risks committing an ecological fallacy.

Variables are the characteristics of units that may vary in successive observations. Research focuses on explanatory variables while attempting to eliminate the influence of extraneous variables. The dependent variable is the explanatory variable that the researcher tries to explain or predict; an independent variable is a presumed cause of the dependent variable. Quantitative variables have categories that express numerical distinctions, while qualitative variables involve differences in kind rather than in number.

Relationships occur when the changes in two or more variables form a predictable pattern. This pattern has two properties—strength and form—which are depicted differently according to whether the variables are qualitative or quantitative. Scientists are particularly interested in causal relationships. To establish that variable X causes variable Y, one must show that X and Y are statistically associated, that the direction of influence is from X to Y, and that the association between X and Y is nonspurious.

Problem statements ideally express or ask a question about a relation between two or more variables. A hypothesis is a conjecture about a relationship between variables. In social research, a hypothesis may take the form of an implication, a mathematical equation, a continuous statement, or a difference statement. Although much social research is undertaken to test hypotheses, it also may be done for the purposes of exploration and description.

Key Terms

research design   correlation coefficient
unit of analysis   causal relationship
aggregate data   association
ecological fallacy   direction of influence
variable   spurious relationship
   explanatory variable   nonspuriousness
   extraneous variable   hypothesis
   independent variable   implication
   dependent variable   mathematical statement
   control variable   continuous statement
   qualitative variable   difference statement
   quantitative variable   exploratory research
relationship   descriptive research
   positive (direct) relationship   hypothesis testing research
   negative (inverse) relationship

Review Questions and Problems

1. What are some of the factors that influence topic selection in social research?

2. Indicate the unit of analysis (individual, social grouping or aggregate, social artifact) suggested by each of the following statements.

   a. Homicide rates are lower in European countries than in the United States.

   b. Ecks College has a lower proportion of minority students than any other college in the state.

   c. In a study of the influence of imitation and suggestion on suicide, D. P. Phillips (1974) charted the number of suicides committed in the United States before and after suicide stories that appeared on the front page of the *New York Times*.

   d. Grade-point average is directly related to class attendance.

   e. Over the last 20 years, the typical size of American families has declined from three to two children.

3. What is the "ecological fallacy"?

4. A researcher examining data on the characteristics of schools finds that the higher the average income level of the parents whose children attend a school, the higher is the average achievement test score for a school. What is the unit of analysis of these data? Can the researcher conclude from the data that the higher the income level of a student's parents, then the better his or her achievement test score will be? Why or why not?

5. Specify the type of variable (independent, dependent, extraneous, control) that applies to each underlined term in the following statements.

    a. We feel that the effect of <u>school quality</u> on <u>academic achievement</u> found in prior research is spurious, because researchers have not examined the <u>social class level</u> of the schools studied.

    b. When <u>pay rate</u> was held constant, we found no influence of <u>job satisfaction</u> on <u>productivity</u>.

    c. Sherif's camp studies demonstrated that <u>conflict between groups</u> increases <u>cohesion within groups</u>.

6. Explain how anticipated relationships guide the collection and interpretation of research evidence.

7. Give one example, other than those mentioned in the text, of (a) a positive and (b) a negative relationship between two quantitative variables.

8. Distinguish between the strength and form of relationships. Which of these aspects may be applied to relationships among qualitative variables? Which may be applied to relationships among quantitative variables?

9. What are the three criteria necessary to establish causality in the social sciences?

10. Explain the function of "intervening mechanisms" in delineating causal relationships.

11. Explain the meaning, and give an example (other than one mentioned in the text) of the statement "correlation does not imply causation."

12. In a sociological study, Galle, Gove, and McPherson (1972) found a positive statistical association between population density, or crowding, and several measures of social pathology (e.g., mortality rate, juvenile delinquency rate). Identify a variable that might have created a spurious relationship between crowding and social pathology. Then, briefly explain how the spurious relationship could occur.

13. Suppose that you want to test the hypothesis that students who have taken a course in methods of social research will receive higher grades in subsequent sociology courses than students who have not taken such a course.

    a. Identify the independent and dependent variables in this hypothesis.

    b. List three extraneous variables. One of them must be of the kind that reasonably could be expected to produce a spurious relationship between the independent and dependent variables.

    c. Briefly explain how one of your extraneous variables could make the hypothesized relationship spurious. (You may assume that methods of social research is not a required course.)

14. Evaluate the following statements as hypotheses. That is, discuss how clearly each spells out the nature of the relationship.

    a. Social class is related to party affiliation.

    b. As the frequency of interaction with a person increases, the degree of liking for the person increases.

    c. Among adults, intellectual ability declines with age.

    d. Broken homes cause delinquency.

15. Formulate three hypotheses, each relating two variables from the following list. For each hypothesis, specify the independent and dependent variables.

Gender (male/female)
Level of education (highest grade completed)
Marital status (married/widowed/divorced/separated/never married)
Party identification (Republican/Democrat/Independent/none)
Ideological orientation (radical/liberal/moderate/conservative/reactionary)
Belief in life after death (yes/no)
Attitude toward busing (favor/oppose)

16. Express one of the hypotheses formulated in question 15 in the form of an (a) implication, (b) continuous statement (if possible), and (c) difference statement.

17. What are the three broad purposes for which research is undertaken?

18. Explain the difference between exploratory research, on the one hand, and descriptive and hypothesis-testing research, on the other. Now differentiate between descriptive and hypothesis-testing research.

19. Outline the stages of social research.

NOTES

1. Determining the level of confidence in the conclusion that a relationship exists, as well as estimating the strength of the relationship, is the job of statistics and is therefore beyond the scope of this textbook. In general, confidence and strength will be greater to the extent that (1) the observed differences between groups are large, (2) the computation of averages is based upon a large number of people, and (3) people in the same group are quite similar to one another and different from those in other groups.

2. Determining whether a statement is probably true or probably false, like assessing the existence and strength of a relationship, is a matter of applying the laws of probability, which is the subject of statistics.

5

Measurement

Measurement is the process of assigning numbers or labels to units of analysis in order to represent conceptual properties. This process should be quite familiar to the reader even if the definition is not. For example, we measure every time we "rate" something, such as a movie, restaurant, or blind date: "the movie was 'pretty good'"; "the new restaurant definitely merits a four-star rating—the decor, service, and food are excellent, and the price is right"; "on a scale of 1 to 10, I would give him a 2—not the worst date I have ever had but close to it." In a somewhat more refined manner, you may have "measured" someone's "intelligence" by inferring this from his or her grade-point average; and you probably have measured your weight on a bathroom scale. Each of these examples contains the essentials of measurement: labels or numbers ("pretty good," "four-star," a "2," a particular GPA, a pointer reading on a scale) are assigned to objects (movies, restaurants, people) to represent properties (the overall quality of a movie, restaurant, or date, intelligence, weight).

There is a difference, of course, between these everyday examples of measurement and the process of measurement in social research. In the above examples, the rules for assigning labels or numbers to objects are more or less intuitive, whereas in social research these rules must be spelled out in detail. Scientific norms require that we specify the guidelines and procedures followed to obtain a measurement so that others can repeat our observations and judge the quality of information yielded by our measurement procedures. In this chapter we outline the measurement process, provide several examples of measurement in social research, and then discuss three criteria for evaluating the nature and quality of measurements.

The Measurement Process

The measurement process begins as the researcher formulates his or her research problem or hypothesis. Every problem or hypothesis contains terms—concepts or variables—that refer to aspects of reality in which the researcher is interested; problem formulation invariably involves thinking about what these terms mean in both an abstract and an empirical sense. The ultimate goal of measurement is to specify clearly observable referents of the terms contained in one's hypotheses, but to get to this point one must first consider the abstract meaning of the terms. Thus, the entire measurement process consists of moving from the abstract to the concrete. We can break this process down into three steps: conceptualization, specification of variables and indicators, and operationalization.

Conceptualization

The development and clarification of concepts is called conceptualization. Because we cannot identify observable representations of a concept unless its meaning is clear, the initial step is to clarify the mental imagery conveyed by one's concepts with words and examples, ultimately arriving at precise verbal definitions. For example, the researcher interested in testing the hypothesis that "education reduces prejudice" would begin by defining the meaning of "education" and "prejudice." Education might be defined as the "extent of one's intellectual and moral training and knowledge," and prejudice as "an emotional, rigidly held prejudgment about an individual based upon his or her group membership." The usual practice, recommended for the beginning researcher, is to rely on existing definitions in the social science literature. However, investigators sometimes formulate their own definitions, especially when disagreement exists in the literature over the exact meaning of a concept.

Because of their complexity, many sociological concepts, such as prejudice, alienation, group cohesiveness, and social status, have been analyzed into various components or dimensions. In our example, education could be broken down into formal and informal education, prejudice into negative feelings, stereotypes, and tendencies to discriminate. We also could distinguish among different targets of prejudice, such as antiblack prejudice, anti-Semitism, and prejudice toward other groups. Specifying dimensions of concepts, which contributes to the theoretical development of a discipline, facilitates measurement in two ways. First, it allows for more refined statements of problems and hypotheses, often suggesting a more limited and practical research focus. For instance, rather than examine the general relationship between education and prejudice, one might decide to restrict oneself to assessing the relationship between formal education and antiblack prejudice. Second, dimensional analyses often suggest empirical manifestations of concepts. For example, identifying "derogatory beliefs about blacks" and "unwillingness to associate with blacks" as components of antiblack prejudice readily indicates ways of observing the presence or absence of this concept.

Specification of Variables and Indicators

Two aspects of concepts lead us to the second step in the measurement process. First, a concept may signify a single category, such as male or prejudiced, or a concept may imply several categories or values, such as gender and degree of prejudice. Measurement assumes the possibility of assigning *different* values or categories to units of analysis; hence, we measure concepts that vary, which we refer to as *variables*. Second, many sociological concepts are not directly observable. For example, we cannot "see" education or prejudice in the same sense that we can see a table or a horse or the color red. On the other hand, while we cannot see education, we can observe how knowledgable people are and how much formal schooling they have; and while we cannot see prejudice, we can observe whether people avoid interacting with blacks, make derogatory statements about members of ethnic groups, and oppose integrationist policies. After conceptualization, the next step is to identify such manifestations of one's concepts, and it is at this point that we move from a language of concepts to a language of variables.

Where this shift in language occurs is difficult to pinpoint, and researchers often use the terms "concept" and "variable" interchangeably. The important point is that these terms connote different levels of abstraction and different stages in the measurement process. Once the researcher begins to speak in terms of a "variable," he or she generally has some observable events in mind that represent the underlying concept. At a still lower level of abstraction are the specific events, called *indicators*, that signify concrete instances of a variable. Thus, we go from the abstract to the concrete—from concepts to variables to indicators. To continue with our example, we have (1) the concept "education," its variable substitute, "level of education," and the indicator "years of schooling"; and (2) the concept "prejudice," the variable, "degree of prejudice toward blacks," and the indicators, "willingness or unwillingness to move into a racially integrated neighborhood."

Many different indicators can be chosen to measure a given concept. If each indicator classified units in exactly the same way, then the choice would be wholly arbitrary. However, no two indicators measure a given concept or variable in the same way, and no single indicator is likely to correspond perfectly to its underlying concept. Indicators provide imperfect representations of concepts for two reasons: (1) they often contain errors of classification, and (2) they rarely capture all the imagery of a concept. Consider willingness to move into a racially integrated neighborhood as a measure of antiblack prejudice. A white person may be unwilling to move into the neighborhood, not because of its racial composition, but because he or she prefers to live elsewhere—closer to work or to family. Furthermore, someone may be willing to move into a racially mixed neighborhood, even though he or she expresses prejudice in other ways.

Because of the imperfect correspondence between indicators and concepts, researchers often choose to rely on more than one indicator when measuring a concept. Sometimes several measures of a given concept are analyzed separately, yielding multiple tests or cross-checks of a hypothesis. At other times, indicators are combined to form a new variable, as when answers to several questions, each a distinct indicator, are combined to create the variable "IQ score." A derived variable such as this, formed from a combination of indicators, is referred to as an *index* or *scale*. With a complex concept like prejudice, researchers are very likely either to devise their own or to use an existing "prejudice" scale, consisting of answers to several questions that are summarized in a prejudice score. With simpler concepts like education, a single indicator will generally suffice. James Davis (1971:18) suggests this rule for deciding whether to use single or multiple indicators to represent a concept: "If you have to ponder about the best way to measure a key [concept], it is worth measuring in two or more different ways . . . ."

Operationalization

Variables and indicators designate the set of values or categories to which units of analysis are assigned, but they do not indicate precisely how such assignments are made. Thus, the final step in the measurement process is to delineate the procedures for sorting units into categories. This step is called *operationalization*. The detailed description of the research operations or procedures necessary to assign units of analysis to the categories of a variable is called an *operational definition*. In our example the variables, years of schooling and degree of prejudice toward blacks, might be operationalized by asking people questions. The complete operational definitions would consist of the specific questions asked, together with response categories and instructions for gathering the data and assigning cases to categories.

To understand better the notion of operational definitions, let us consider a simple illustration from everyday life. Suppose your friend bakes you a delicious carrot cake. You ask your friend how he made it, since you would like to make one. Your friend says, "Oh, you take some carrots, flour, sugar, eggs, and so forth, add some nuts, bake it, and voila!—you have a carrot cake." Would you be able to make an identical cake with these directions? Not likely. What you need is an operational definition of your friend's concept of carrot cake. You would need to have the complete directions—that is, details such as all of the ingredients, the amount of each ingredient to use, the steps necessary to combine the ingredients, the oven temperature, and baking time. In short, your friend's operational definition should look like an ordinary recipe card. Using the recipe (operational definition), you should be able to produce a very similar cake.

As with the selection of indicators, many operational definitions are possible; social scientists must choose or develop one that they believe corresponds reasonably well to the concept in question. To return to the carrot cake example, how could you be certain that your friend's recipe represented an "authentic" carrot cake? Are nuts really an essential ingredient? Suppose you substituted whole-wheat flour for white; would you still have a carrot cake? If you compared his recipe to others, you would no doubt find some differences. How are you to conclude which is the correct recipe? In the end you would find that there is no correct recipe, but you would still have to decide for yourself whether your friend's operational definition (recipe) "really" corresponded to your idea of what a carrot cake is. As you can see, operational definitions, so essential to social research, are somewhat arbitrary and restricted expressions of what a concept "really" means.

Operational Definitions in Social Research

There are two general kinds of operational definitions in social research: manipulated and measured. *Manipulation* operations are designed to change the value of a variable, whereas *measurement* operations estimate existing values of variables. Both types are nicely illustrated in a study of people's reactions in a common situation—a car failing to proceed immediately when a traffic signal turns green. Doob and Gross (1968) used this setting to investigate unobtrusively the relations among status, frustration, and aggression. They hypothesized that frustration in traffic caused by a higher status person would elicit fewer aggressive responses than would frustration caused by a lower status frustrator. The independent variable, status of the frustrator, was *manipulated* by blocking traffic with two different automobiles: a new luxury automobile for the high-status condition and an older vehicle for the low-status condition. To operationalize the dependent variable, aggression, they used a *measured* definition—number and frequency of horn-honking responses by drivers blocked by the experimental vehicle. The hypothesis was confirmed: for example, 84 percent of the blocked drivers in the low-status condition honked at least once in 12 seconds, compared to only 50 percent of those blocked in the high-status condition.

The operations involved in the manipulation of frustrator's status are spelled out in detail by Doob and Gross. These include such fine detail as the models and ages of the experimental cars, the clothes worn by drivers of these cars, and the amount of time the drivers remained stopped after the signal changed to green. Similarly, precise details are given on the measured operations (observers, stopwatches, and tape recorder) used to determine horn honking. Unless investigators explicitly spell out the details of their manipulations and measurements, other researchers will not be able to replicate or judge the quality of the research.

Manipulation of an independent variable is by definition experimental, and we will have a good deal more to say about this in chapter 7. For now, let us examine some of the various approaches to operationalization of measured variables.

Verbal Reports

By far the most common form of social measurement is the *verbal* or *self-report*. These consist of replies to direct questions, usually posed in interviews or on questionnaires. Self-reports provide simple and generally accurate measures of background variables such as age, gender, marital status, and education. They also are used extensively to measure subjective experiences, such as knowledge, beliefs, attitudes, feelings, and opinions.

The variables in a study of the education-prejudice relationship can be operationalized easily by means of self-reports. Here is a standard question for operationalizing years of schooling:

> What is the highest grade or year that you finished and got credit for in regular school or college?

The following question is one of several indicators that have been used repeatedly in national surveys to operationalize antiblack prejudice:

> How strongly would you object if a member of your family wanted to bring a black friend home to dinner?
> Would you object strongly, mildly, or not at all?

In self-report attitude measurement, responses to several questions frequently are combined to create a scale. For example, the Interpersonal Judgment Scale (IJS), a widely used measure of interpersonal attraction devised by social psychologist Donn Byrne (1971), derives a single score or rating from the following two questions:

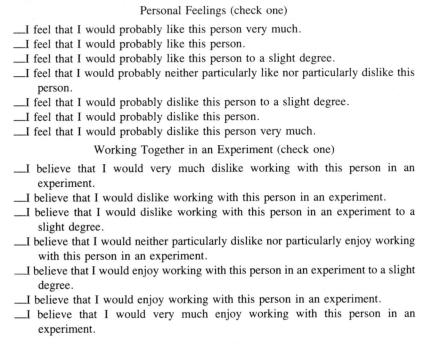

Personal Feelings (check one)

___I feel that I would probably like this person very much.

___I feel that I would probably like this person.

___I feel that I would probably like this person to a slight degree.

___I feel that I would probably neither particularly like nor particularly dislike this person.

___I feel that I would probably dislike this person to a slight degree.

___I feel that I would probably dislike this person.

___I feel that I would probably dislike this person very much.

Working Together in an Experiment (check one)

___I believe that I would very much dislike working with this person in an experiment.

___I believe that I would dislike working with this person in an experiment.

___I believe that I would dislike working with this person in an experiment to a slight degree.

___I believe that I would neither particularly dislike nor particularly enjoy working with this person in an experiment.

___I believe that I would enjoy working with this person in an experiment to a slight degree.

___I believe that I would enjoy working with this person in an experiment.

___I believe that I would very much enjoy working with this person in an experiment.

To obtain an IJS rating, Byrne assigns numbers to the response categories of each question, starting with 1 = "dislike this person very much" and "very much dislike working with this person" and ending with 7 = "like this person very much" and "very much enjoy working with this person." An individual's responses to the two questions are then added together to produce a single scale score that can range from 2 (strong disliking) to 14 (strong liking). (Scales are discussed further in chapter 13. Also see Box 5.1 for another example of a scale and a description of how it was constructed.)

Verbal reports vary widely with respect to question wording and response formats. The number of response categories ranges from two to ten for most attitude measures, but the researcher may provide many more categories or none at all. Instead of labeling all points on a response scale, as in the IJS above, only the endpoints may be labeled. Or, a graphic scale might be used, in which respondents are asked to place a check mark along a line whose endpoints represent opposite ends of a continuum. Verbal reports also are elicited with pictures and diagrams, which can simplify complex issues and are particularly useful with children. To measure attitudes toward residential integration, for example, Reynolds Farley and his colleagues (1978) presented respondents with diagrams of a number of neighborhoods with different interracial mixtures. Among the questions asked were how uncomfortable respondents would feel and whether they would be willing to purchase a home in each of the neighborhoods.

BOX 5.1

The Development of the FEM Scale

A great deal of social measurement, especially attitude measurement, involves the construction of scales. A scale is a composite measure that combines responses to two or more indicators into a single score. (See chapter 13 for a further discussion of scales.) While a variety of scaling techniques exists, all scales serve similar purposes. For abstract concepts that cannot be measured adequately with a single indicator, scales increase the precision and reliability of measurement by rank ordering cases along the underlying dimension of the concept. Let us see how this works by examining the construction of a scale intended to measure attitudes toward feminism.

Eliot Smith, Myra Marx Ferree, and Frederick Miller (1975) developed their FEM Scale at the height of the Women's Liberation Movement in the mid-1970s. To do so, they used the most popular scaling technique in social research: *summated ratings*. The following steps in the development of the FEM Scale illustrate how summated ratings scales are constructed.

Step 1. Smith, Ferree, and Miller initially developed fifty-seven items, each stating either the acceptance or rejection of a feminist belief. The sources of ideas for specific items are limited only by the researcher's imagination. In this case, the researchers drew many items from an earlier study by Kirkpatrick (1936); for other items they may have considered the published statements of avowed feminists and antifeminists. Below are five sample items that eventually were included in the scale.

    1. Women have the right to compete with men in every sphere of activity.
    2. As head of the household, the father should have final authority over his children.
    3. The unmarried mother is morally a greater failure than the unmarried father.
    4. A woman who refuses to give up her job to move with her husband would be to blame if the marriage broke up.
    5. A woman who refuses to bear children has failed in her duty to her husband.

Step 2. The researchers asked thirty-nine students to indicate whether they agreed or disagreed with each item as they role-played a "strong profeminist" or a "strong antifeminist." The purpose of this step, not always a part of scale construction, was to eliminate items that were ambiguous—that is, items that were not clearly perceived as representing either a profeminist or antifeminist position. When there was sizeable disagreement over the direction of an item, the item was discarded. This left forty-eight items.

Step 3. The next step is to select a subset of items that best discriminates among persons who hold different attitudes. To make this selection, researchers administer an initial item set to a group of respondents who are similar to those for whom the scale is intended. Smith, Ferree, and Miller shortened their scale in two stages. First, they asked the same students who role played to give their own opinions. From an analysis of these responses, they selected twenty-seven items. The basis of their selection was the items' variability. Greater variability generally indicates better discriminability

BOX 5.1 (*continued*)

(the ability to discriminate among individuals with different attitudes); for if an item shows low variability, meaning that it elicits similar responses from all individuals, then it does not reveal how individuals differ in their attitudes.

Next, the researchers administered the preliminary twenty-seven-item scale to 100 Harvard summer school students. Again, they assessed the items' ability to discriminate among respondents, this time using a technique called "factor analysis." Factor analysis is one of several ways to assess an item's discriminability. A simpler approach is to calculate each individual's scale score, determine the highest and lowest 25 percent of the scores, and then identify those items that best differentiate between the high and low scores. For example, if both high and low scorers are equally likely to endorse a profeminist statement, then that statement would have poor discriminability. For the final scale, Smith, Ferree, and Miller selected the twenty items with highest discriminability.

Step 4. In its final form, a summated ratings scale consists of a series of statements with which respondents are asked to indicate their agreement or disagreement. Agreement with FEM Scale items is expressed in terms of a Likert response format. Devised by psychologist Rensis Likert, such a format permits several categories of response. For the FEM Scale, there are five: "strongly agree," "agree," "undecided," "disagree," and "strongly disagree." To arrive at a scale score, these categories are assigned numbers from 1 to 5, the highest number representing strong agreement with a profeminist statement (or conversely, strong disagreement with an antifeminist statement). Adding item responses, we get a possible range of 20 to 100 for the twenty-item scale. This range corresponds to a dimension that at the low end indicates a very unfavorable attitude toward feminism and at the high end indicates a very favorable attitude toward feminism. The scale thus provides a more precise kind of measurement than would be obtained with a single indicator.

Step 5. At this point, the scale is ready to test for reliability and validity, a process that we describe in Box 5.2.

Since slight changes in phrasing can drastically alter the meaning of a question, wording is very important. We will discuss question formats and wording at length in chapter 10, which deals with interview and questionnaire construction.

Observation

Doob and Gross measured drivers' levels of aggression by direct observation of behavior: they observed how quickly and how often the drivers honked at a blocking vehicle. Observation provides direct and generally unequivocal measures of overt behavior, but it also is used to measure internal states such as feelings and attitudes. In contrast to the IJS, for example, we could measure interpersonal attraction by observing and recording the physical distance that two people maintain between themselves, with closer distances indicative of greater liking. Similarly, Zick Rubin (1970) operationally defined romantic love by observing the length of time couples spent gazing into one another's eyes.

Besides physical distance and eye contact, researchers have used exterior physical signs (e.g., clothing), gestures, and language to measure behavior. The categories of observational measures often involve the frequency and duration of acts, as in the horn-honking measure of aggression. Also, hardware such as videotapes, audiotapes, and counters are commonly used for recording purposes. To measure which television programs people watch, the Nielsen Organization attaches an electronic monitoring device to the television set of each person in their sample that automatically records, minute by minute, the channel to which the set is tuned.

Archival Records

Archival records, which refer to existing recorded information, provide another invaluable source of measurement. The various types of archival data, discussed in chapter 12, include statistical records, public and private documents, and mass communications.

An example of an operational definition derived from archival records comes from a study mentioned in the last chapter. Recall that Dornbusch and Hickman (1959) analyzed advertisements in a popular magazine, *Ladies Home Journal*, sampled over a 67-year period, to test Riesman's hypothesis that there has been a trend in this century from "inner-" to "other-directedness." An advertisement was operationally defined as other-directed if it used endorsements by persons or groups (e.g., "Billie Burke wears Minerva Sweaters," "Housewives like the Singer Sewing Machine"), or claimed that use of a product would benefit interpersonal relations ("He'll like you better if you use Revlon"). Beginning about 1920, the authors found a dramatic shift upward in the frequency of other-directed advertising themes, thus supporting Riesman's hypothesis.

Selection of Operational Definitions

Given that you have a concept in mind, how do you decide on an appropriate operational definition? First of all, your decision will be made in the context of an overall research strategy, the choice of which depends to a degree on the specific research problem or hypothesis. As we shall see, each of the four basic approaches has its distinctive strengths and limitations, which must be taken into account in deciding how to study a given problem. Some hypotheses, for example, contain variables that may be impractical or unethical to manipulate, hence, study experimentally. No one would propose inducing varying amounts of emotional suffering in people to study effects on physical health.

Each of the different approaches favors certain types of operational definitions. For the most part, survey research involves verbal reports; field research entails observational measurement; and the use of available data, by definition, includes archival records. Experiments, on the other hand, use a combination of measures—verbal reports and/or observation in addition to manipulation procedures. Field researchers often supplement their observations with verbal reports. And survey researchers sometimes use observational measures; for example, an interviewer may observe the type of household and neighborhood in which an interviewee resides as a measure of social class.

With an overall research strategy in mind, the most basic requirement is to select an operational definition that fits the concept well. The researcher conjuring up empirical indicators of a concept must repeatedly ask himself or herself if these measures encompass what he or she understands the given concept to mean. While we have said that no operational definition can capture a concept's meaning perfectly or completely, this does not license the researcher to select just any measure. It is still desirable to get the best possible fit between concept and measure, and the best way to do this is by carefully considering the meaning of the concept, especially as it relates to the theory in which it is embedded.

An example of a study in which theory guided the selection of an appropriate operational definition is Pierce's test (1967) of Durkheim's (1951) hypothesis that suicide rates increase in periods of rapid economic change independently of the direction of change (boom or bust). Durkheim theorized that marked economic changes can disturb the existing goals and norms toward which people orient their lives, can thrust individuals into new social settings in which they are ill-suited to manage, and hence increase the probability of suicide. Data for white males during the peacetime years 1919–1940 were examined. At first Pierce correlated the suicide rate with various *objective* measures of economic change, such as income, percentage of labor force unemployed, and housing construction, with indecisive results. Finally he struck upon the notion of using a measure of economic change—the "index of common stock prices"—that would reflect the *public definition* of the economic situation, which is more in tune with Durkheim's theory. That is, rapid fluctuations of stock market prices may be viewed as indicators of public economic uncertainty, resulting in disruption or discontinuities in perceived goals and norms. Pierce's analysis revealed that suicide rates correlated highly with the rate of change in the public definition of economic conditions as operationally defined by the index of stock market prices.

Beyond attending to the basic research strategy and the concept's meaning, the choice of operational definitions is largely a matter of creativity, judgment, and practicality. One's selection also should be aided by considering three characteristics that describe the quality of information provided by operational definitions: level of measurement, reliability, and validity.

Levels of Measurement

Speaking now in terms of variables, we can modify our definition of measurement as "the assignment of numbers or labels to units of analysis to represent variable categories." One characteristic of measurement emerges from the nature of the variable categories. It turns out that we tend to use four different empirical rules for sorting cases into categories, and each rule results in different interpretations of the numbers that may be assigned to the various categories. Unlike the numbers derived from the measurement of length, time, mass, and so forth, in the physical sciences, the numbers assigned to different categories in social research do not always have a simple and straightforward interpretation. The various meanings of these numbers, which reflect basic empirical rules for category assignment, are what is meant by *levels of measurement*. The four levels usually identified are nominal, ordinal, interval, and ratio.

Nominal Measurement

The lowest level, nominal measurement, is a system in which cases are classified into two or more categories on some variable, such as gender, race, religious preference, or political party preference. Numbers (or more accurately, numerals)[1] are assigned to the categories simply as labels or codes for the researcher's convenience in collecting and analyzing data. For example, political party preference might be classified as:

1. Democrat
2. Republican
3. Independent
4. Other
5. No preference

Since we are merely using numbers as labels, no mathematical relationships are possible at the nominal level. We cannot say that $1 + 2 = 3$ (Democrat plus Republican equals Independent) or that $1 < 2$ (Democrats are "lower" on political preference than Republicans). We can say, however, that all "1's" share the same political preference and that "1's" differ from "2's" in their political preference.

With nominal measurement, the empirical rule for assigning units to categories is that cases placed in the same category must be equivalent. Also, the categories of the variable should possess two characteristics; they must be both exhaustive and mutually exclusive. The requirement to be *exhaustive* means that there must be sufficient categories so that virtually all persons, events, or objects being classified will fit into one of the categories. The example below does not meet this criterion:

Race: 1. Black
2. White

You can probably think of categories to add to make the measure exhaustive, especially if you happen to be Japanese or an American Indian or of some other racial group.

The criterion of *mutual exclusivity* means that the persons or things being classified must not fit into more than one category. Suppose that a researcher hastily came up with the following categories for the variable place of residence:

1. Urban
2. Suburban
3. Rural
4. Farm

You can see that some persons would fit into both categories 3 and 4. The following set of categories would be an improvement:

1. Urban
2. Suburban
3. Rural—farm
4. Rural—nonfarm

Ordinal Measurement

In ordinal measurement, numbers indicate only the rank order of cases on some variable. Psychologist S. S. Stevens (1951), who developed the idea of measurement level, used hardness of minerals as one example of ordinal measurement. We can determine the hardness of any two minerals by scratching one against the other: harder stones scratch softer ones. By this means, we could number a set of stones, say five, from 1 to 5 according to their hardness. The numbers thus assigned, however, would represent nothing more than the order of the stones along a continuum of hardness: "1" is harder than "2," "2" is harder than "3," and so on. We could not infer from the numbering any absolute quantity, nor could we infer that the intervals between numbers are equal; in other words, we could not say how much harder one stone is than another.

Another example of ordinal measurement would be an individual's ranking of certain leisure activities in terms of the pleasure derived from them. Suppose you ranked three activities as follows:

1. Playing tennis
2. Watching television
3. Reading sociology

From this ordering we could not make any statements about the intervals between the numbers; it may be that you enjoy watching television almost as much as playing tennis but that reading sociology is not nearly as pleasurable as watching the tube. In this sense ordinal measurement is like a very elastic tape measure that can be stretched unevenly; the "numbers" on the tape measure are in proper order, but the distances between them are distorted.

One virtue of ordinal measurement, as Julian Simon (1978:231) notes, is "that people can often make an accurate judgment about one thing *compared to another*, even when they cannot make an accurate *absolute* judgment." Simon (1978:231) illustrates the accuracy of comparative judgments with a familiar example:

> [Y]ou can often tell whether or not a child has a fever—that is, when the child's temperature is two or three degrees above normal—by touching the child's face to yours and comparing whether her skin is warmer than yours. But you would be hard-put to say whether the temperature outside is 40° or 55°F, or whether a piece of metal is 130° or 150°F.

Similarly, in the realm of social measurement one can probably say with some certitude whether security or chance for advancement is the more important job characteristic without being able to say just how important either characteristic is.

The ability of human observers to make such comparative judgments permits a wide range of reasonably accurate social measurements at the ordinal level—for example, measures of socioeconomic status, intelligence, political liberalism, various preference ratings, and attitude and opinion scales. On the other hand, ordinal measurement is still rather crude. At this level we cannot perform most mathematical (statistical) operations in analyzing the data. We cannot add, subtract, multiply, or divide; we can only rank things: $1 < 2$, $2 < 3$, $1 < 3$.

Interval Measurement

Interval measurement has the qualities of the nominal and ordinal levels, plus the requirement that equal distances or intervals between "numbers" represent equal distances in the variable being measured. An example is the Fahrenheit temperature scale: the difference between 20° and 30°F is the same as the difference between 90° and 100°F—10 degrees. We can infer not only that 100°F is hotter than 90°F but also how much hotter it is. What enables us to make this inference is the establishment of a standard measurement unit, or *metric*. For Fahrenheit temperature, the metric is degrees; similarly, time is measured in seconds, length in feet or meters, and income in dollars.

When numbers represent a metric, the measurement is "quantitative" in the ordinary sense of the word. Thus, we can perform basic mathematical operations such as addition and subtraction. However, we cannot multiply or divide at the interval level. We cannot say, for example, that 100°F is twice as hot as 50°F, or that 20°F is one-half as hot as 40°F. The reason is that interval measures do not have a true or absolute zero but an arbitrary one. That is, the zero point on the scale does not signify the absence of the property being measured. Zero degrees Fahrenheit does not mean that there is no temperature; it is simply an arbitrary point on the scale. Its arbitrariness is illustrated by comparison with another interval scale designed to measure the property of temperature: 0°F equals about −18°C (Celsius or centigrade), and 0°C equals 32°F.

While social researchers often aim to create interval measures, most of what passes for this level of measurement is only a very rough approximation. IQ score, for example, is sometimes treated as an interval level measure, even though it makes no sense to add IQ scores or to infer that equal numerical intervals have the same meaning. (Is the difference between IQ scores of 180 and 190 equal to the difference between 90 and 100?) The empirical rule defining interval measurement is to create equal intervals between numbers. Some attitude scaling techniques attempt to do this, although most scales have ordinal level measurement.

Ratio Measurement

The fourth level, called ratio measurement, includes the features of the other levels plus an absolute (nonarbitrary) zero point. The presence of an absolute zero makes it possible to multiply and divide scale numbers meaningfully and thereby form ratios. The variable income, measured in dollars, has this property. Given incomes of \$20,000 and \$40,000, we can divide one into the other (that is, form a ratio) to signify that one is twice (or one-half) as much as the other.

Many measures in social research have a well-defined metric and a zero point that meaningfully signifies none of the property being measured. Besides income, other examples are age in years, number of siblings, and years of schooling. Ratio level measures often are obtained by simply counting—for example, number of horn honks, number of siblings, number of people in a group. Also, aggregate variables, which characterize collectivities of people, frequently are measured at this level by counting and then dividing by a population base—for example, crude birth rate (number of births per 1000 people in the total population), divorce rate (number of divorces per 1000 existing marriages), percentage of labor force unemployed, percentage Democrat.

In most social science research, the distinction between interval and ratio levels of measurement is not very important compared to the difference between interval and ordinal measurement. The latter distinction corresponds to that between quantitative and qualitative variables. Many statistical techniques assume interval measurement, and several other techniques are well suited to nominal measurement, so that researchers often divide variables into "quantitative" (interval, ratio) and "qualitative" (nominal). Special statistical techniques also exist for ordinal level measurement, but these are seldom used by social scientists. Instead, the usual practice is either to treat ordinal measures as nominal, ignoring the information provided by ranking, or to assume that ordinal categories approximate equal intervals, and treat them as quantitative.

A good rule to follow in operationalizing variables is to measure at the highest possible level. Do not settle for a lower level of measurement when you can be more precise by measuring a variable at a higher level.

It is interesting to note that the four levels of measurement themselves form an ordinal scale with regard to the amount of information they provide. Each level has the features of the level(s) below it plus something else. Table 5.1 illustrates this.

TABLE 5.1. Information Provided by the Four Levels of Measurement

Information provided	Nominal	Ordinal	Interval	Ratio
Classification	X	X	X	X
Rank order		X	X	X
Equal intervals			X	X
Nonarbitrary zero				X

Reliability and Validity

Level of measurement provides a framework for interpreting the categories of a variable. It tells us what sort of inferences we can make about cases assigned to different categories. (Are they merely different? Can we say that one is greater or lesser than the other? And so on.) But what about the adequacy of the set of categories as a whole and of the operationalization procedure for assigning cases to categories? In other words, how does one evaluate the goodness of specific operational definitions?

We have seen that for any concept a large number of operational definitions are possible, and that creative insight, good judgment, and relevant theory aid in the development of operational definitions. Admittedly these aids are rather subjective in nature; however, once an operational definition is selected, there are more objective ways to evaluate its quality. Social scientists use the terms "reliability" and "validity" to describe issues involved in evaluating the quality of operational definitions.

Reliability is concerned with questions of stability and consistency. Is the operational definition measuring "something" consistently and dependably, whatever that "something" may be? Do repeated applications of the operational definition under similar conditions yield consistent results? If the operational definition is formed from a set of responses or items (e.g., a test score), are the component responses or items consistent with each other? An example of a highly reliable measuring instrument is a steel tape measure. With such an instrument, a piece of wood 20 inches long will measure, with negligible variation, 20 inches every time a measurement is taken. A cloth tape measure would be somewhat less reliable in that it may vary with humidity and temperature, and in that we can expect some variation in measurements depending on how loosely or tightly the tape is stretched.

Measurement *validity* refers to the extent of matching, congruence, or "goodness of fit" between an operational definition and the concept it is purported to measure. Does this operational definition truly reflect what the concept means? Are you measuring what you intend to measure with this operational definition? If so, you have a valid measure. An example of a valid measure is amniocentesis, a technique for determining various genetic characteristics of an unborn child, including gender. It is a valid measure because it can determine with virtually perfect accuracy whether the unborn will be a boy or a girl. At one time, a number of invalid "measures" of the unborn's gender existed in the form of folk wisdoms. One belief, for example, involves tying a string to the pregnant woman's wedding band and holding it suspended over her abdomen. If the band swings in a circle, the baby will be a girl; if, however, the band swings back and forth, the child will be a boy.

A highly unreliable measure cannot be valid; how can you get at whatever you want to measure if your results fluctuate wildly? But a very reliable measure still may not be valid; that is, you could be measuring very reliably (consistently) something other than what you intended to measure. To take a facetious example, let us suppose we decide to measure the "intelligence" of students by standing them on a bathroom scale and reading the number off the dial (J. A. Davis, 1971:14). Such an operational definition would be highly reliable, as repeated measurements of an individual's "intelligence" would yield consistent results. However, this measure obviously would not be valid.

Sources of Error

Measurement results in the identification of differences in the cases observed—different labels, ranks, ratings, scores, or whatever. To understand the ideas behind reliability and validity assessment, one needs to be aware of three factors that contribute to the differences obtained from an operational definition. These three factors, or sources of variation, are (1) true differences in the concept the operation is intended to measure, (2) biases inherent in the method or operational definition, and (3) errors of measurement due to random or chance factors.

One would hope that the first of these sources of variation, true differences in the concept, would account for most of the variation in the measurements; after all, this is what validity is all about! In the ideal situation, with a perfectly valid operational definition, *all* of the measured variation would reflect differences in the concept under study. Differences in IQ scores obtained with an IQ test, for example, ought to reflect only differences in intelligence and nothing else. However, since perfect measurement is unobtainable, a realistic approach is to be aware of other possible sources of variation and to try to eliminate or reduce their effects as much as possible.

Social scientists refer to sources of variation other than true differences in the variable being studied as "error." The main problem in interpreting the results of a measure is to determine what part of the results can be explained by true differences and what part is due to one or more sources of error. There are two basic types of measurement errors: systematic and random.

Systematic measurement error results from factors that systematically influence either the process of measurement or the concept being measured. Assuming interval level measurement, systematic error would be reflected in ratings or scores that are consistently biased in one direction—either too high or too low. A cloth tape measure that has stretched with wear would create error in the form of constant underestimates of length. An example of systematic error in social measurement is the cultural bias of IQ tests. Most IQ tests contain problems and language that tend to favor particular groups in society. Given the same "true" intelligence level, the person familiar with the test problems and language will always score higher than the person who is unfamiliar with the test problems or who speaks a different language than the one in which the test is communicated. Thus, differences in IQ scores may reflect a systematic error introduced by the cultural bias of the test, as well as differences in intelligence.

Many of the systematic errors that contaminate social measurement arise from respondents' reactions to participating in research. When the respondent's sensitivity or responsiveness to a measure is affected by the process of observation or measurement, we refer to this as a *reactive measurement* effect (Webb et al., 1966:13). Just as we behave differently alone than in front of an audience, or with friends than with strangers, we tend to react differently when in a research setting. Awareness of the presence of a social scientist "observer," for example, can increase or decrease the incidence of some observed behaviors.

It has been shown that people are less willing to admit to holding undesirable positions and attitudes when they are aware of being "tested." Indeed, for this reason verbal report measures generally underestimate (a systematic error) the prevalence of socially unacceptable traits, behaviors, and attitudes such as psychiatric symptoms, deviant behaviors, and racial prejudice. To give a concrete example, some researchers have questioned the extent of the decline in racial prejudice in recent years, as revealed by measures that ask respondents directly to express their racial attitudes. It may be that the decline is more a function of social desirability effects than of real changes in attitudes (Crosby, Bromley, and Saxe, 1980). That is, respondents openly express less racial prejudice because it has become less socially acceptable to do so.

Besides this *social desirability effect*, there are other response tendencies that can introduce systematic measurement error. Respondents are more likely to agree than to disagree with statements irrespective of their content (called the "acquiescence response set"); also, when sequences of questions are asked in a similar format, respondents tend to give stereotyped responses, such as endorsing the right-hand or left-hand response (Webb et al., 1966). If such tendencies are systematically related to the measurement of a characteristic, then the responses of individuals may reflect the particular tendency as much as the characteristic being measured. For example, if a question measuring political liberalism is worded such that agreement indicates a liberal view, then the researcher could not be sure whether a person's agreement indicated a liberal view or simply a tendency to agree with statements regardless of their content.

Systematic errors are recurring. They are consistent across measurements taken at different times or are systematically related to characteristics of the cases being measured. Such errors bias measurements, affecting their validity. However, because of their constancy, such errors do not adversely affect reliability. Reliability is undermined by inconsistencies in measurement that arise from random errors.

Random measurement error is unrelated to the concept being measured. It is the result of temporary, chance factors, such as transitory upswings and downswings in the health and mood of subjects and respondents, temporary variations in the administration or coding of a research measure, momentary investigator fatigue, and other transient factors. A tired or bored respondent, for example, may give erroneous responses by not attending carefully to the questions asked. Similarly, an ambiguously worded question will produce random errors by eliciting responses that vary according to respondents' interpretations of the question's meaning.

Such error is random because its presence, extent, and direction are unpredictable from one question to the next or from one respondent to the next. Thus, random errors in a measure of the variable age would not be consistently high or low, but rather would fall on either side of respondents' real ages, so that the average error would be zero. Random error could be demonstrated by asking someone whose visual acuity is impaired (perhaps by drunkenness) to measure the length of an object several times. It is likely that this person's measurements will vary about the object's true length. Sometimes the errors will vary in one direction and sometimes in the other; sometimes they will be large and sometimes small. Random errors produce imprecise and inaccurate measurements, affecting reliability; however, because they are unsystematic, random errors tend to cancel each other out with repeated measurements. Thus, they do not bias the measure in a particular direction.

Reliability Assessment

So far we have said that reliability indicates consistency, or the extent to which a measure does not contain random error. Because we can never know for certain the precise true value of that which we measure, measurement errors can only be examined indirectly. In fact, we infer random error from the degree of consistency observed across measurements. If a measure yields the same result time after time, then it is free of random error; furthermore, the greater the variation in repeated measurements, the greater the random error. Reliability assessment is essentially a matter of checking for such consistency—either over time (as when the same measurements are repeated) or over slightly different but equivalent measures (as when more than one indicator or more than one observer/interviewer/recorder is used).

Test-Retest Reliability

The simplest method for assessing reliability, the test-retest procedure, involves testing (i.e., measuring) the same persons or units on two separate occasions.[2] One then calculates the statistical correlation between the sets of "scores" obtained from the two measurements, and the resulting value serves as an estimate of reliability. Such correlations range from 0 to 1.00. For the test-retest procedure, the correlation tends to be high, with anything less than .80 considered dangerously low for most measurement purposes.

While simple in principle, the test-retest method has several problems that limit its usefulness as an estimate of reliability. First, either the persons responding to questions or the persons recording observations may remember and simply repeat the responses they gave the first time, thereby inflating the reliability estimate. Second, real change in the concept being measured may occur in the interim between the two "tests." In attitude measurement, new experiences or new information may result in a shift in attitude. The loss of a job, for example, may change one's attitudes toward unemployment insurance or social welfare programs. Because such true changes are inseparable from random errors in test-retest correlations, they falsely lower the reliability estimate. Third, the first application of a measure may itself bring about conceptual changes in the persons under study. Suppose, for example, that a scale designed to measure antifeminine stereotypes is administered on two occasions to the same group of persons. If, after the first administration, the persons began to think through some of their assumptions about women and as a consequence changed some of their beliefs, a subsequent administration of the scale would yield different scores and a lowered estimate of reliability.

To a certain extent, these problems are manageable. For example, one can try to time the second measurement optimally so that responses to the first testing will have been forgotten but little real change in the concept will have had time to occur. Also, the above difficulties may be more or less problematic depending on the type of measure under study. Using a test-retest reliability estimate for an attitude measure would be fraught with problems, as such measures tend to be highly reactive and genuine changes in attitudes are likely to take place over time. On the other hand, the test-retest procedure provides a good evaluation of the reliability of many relatively stable concepts such as characteristics of organizations or political units and individual background variables.

Parallel Forms, Split-Half, and Internal Consistency Reliability

Rather than obtain a *stability* estimate based upon consistency over time, as in test-retest reliability, the remaining procedures for assessing reliability estimate the *equivalence* among measurements made on the same occasion. Equivalence may be assessed with respect to either different indicators of the same underlying concept or different interviewers, observers, or coders applying the same operational definition. Like the test-retest estimate, all of the statistical estimates of equivalence yield coefficients that run from 0 to 1.00.

One type of equivalence estimate is the *parallel* or *alternate-forms procedure*. Two alternate forms of a measure, designed to be as similar as possible, are administered successively to the same group of persons. The correlation between the "scores" on the two forms indicates the degree of reliability of either form taken separately.

Although this resembles the test-retest procedure in that two administrations are necessary, the parallel-forms approach has several advantages: (1) because the forms differ, respondents' recall of specific responses to the first form would be unlikely to affect responses to the second form; (2) with no danger of recall, the researcher does not have to wait the usual period before administering the second form; and (3) when both forms are administered very closely together, the chance of real change taking place in the concept being measured is very slight. A serious disadvantage is the difficulty of constructing two truly equivalent measures, as each item in one form must be carefully matched with an item in the second form.

A logical extension of the parallel-forms approach is the *split-half method*. In this procedure, a scale or index (i.e., a measure containing several items) is applied once to a sample of cases, after which the items of the scale are divided into halves, usually by random selection; each half is then treated as a subtest with the results of the two subtests correlated to obtain an estimate of reliability. The higher the correlation, the more equivalent the halves, and the greater the reliability of the measure.

Because the problem of directly creating two equivalent forms is avoided, this method is an improvement over the parallel forms procedure. On the other hand, the split-half technique still assumes the existence of equivalent subsets of items. From there it is a short step to the assumption that every item in a scale is equivalent to every other item. This gives rise to another technique for assessing reliability, called *internal consistency*. With this approach, the researcher examines the relationships among all the items simultaneously rather than arbitrarily splitting the items or comparing the results of parallel forms. The basic question is, to what extent are the items homogeneous—that is, to what extent do they measure the same concept? Homogeneity or internal consistency may be estimated via a number of statistical procedures that are beyond the scope of this text. One procedure involves computing the average of the correlations among the responses to all possible pairs of items; another involves computing the average of the correlations between responses to each item and the total scale score.

Intercoder Reliability

A second group of equivalence measures examines the extent to which different interviewers, observers, or coders using the same instrument or measure get equivalent results. Assuming that the different users have been properly trained, a reliable operational definition must yield comparable results from user to user. From the records of trained persons independently applying the same operational definition, various estimates of equivalence may be calculated. For example, in the aforementioned study of other-directedness (Dornbusch and Hickman, 1959), two coders were directed to judge whether magazine advertisements contained some form of other-directed appeal. A reliability check was made by comparing the number of such appeals independently analyzed by each coder in two issues of the magazine. The level of agreement, or intercoder reliability, was very high.

It is the norm in social research to check for intercoder reliability whenever measures are derived from systematic observation or from archival records. With regard to the other types of reliability, the split-half and internal consistency techniques are the most frequently used, even though they are limited to multi-item measures. The test-retest approach is less common, not only because of the problems mentioned above but also because of the impracticality of applying the same measure twice to the same sample of cases. The parallel-forms approach is rarely used outside of psychology. Yet, even here, alternate forms generally are not created expressly for the purpose of reliability assessment but rather because repeated testing with the same individuals makes it desirable to have more than one test form.

Improving Reliability

At some point in this discussion of reliability assessment you might have wondered, "What can be done if your measure turns out to have low reliability?" Should you discard it and start over with another measure? In some cases you may decide to do just that. However, there are ways to raise the reliability of an operational definition to an acceptable level.

1. Exploratory studies, preliminary interviews, or pretests of the measure with a small sample of persons similar in characteristics to the target group are ways to gain information that will lead to better measures. The need for preliminary work with actual respondents before the final form of an instrument is completed cannot be overstated. Indeed, it is a topic we will consider again in relation to experiments and survey research.

2. Simply adding items of the same type to a scale will usually increase reliability. Other things being equal, a measure containing more items will normally be more reliable than a measure having fewer. There are two reasons for this. First,

as we noted earlier, random errors deviate on either side of the "true" value. Thus, with repeated measurements or additional items, such errors will tend to cancel each other out, yielding a more stable and accurate measure of the true value. Second, since any given set of items represents a sample of the possible measures of a concept, adding items increases sample size. As you will see in the next chapter, a basic principle of sampling is that the larger the sample, the more precise and reliable the estimate.

3. An item-by-item analysis will reveal which items discriminate well between persons scoring or measured at various levels. Those items that do not discriminate appropriately should be omitted. For instance, if both persons scoring high and persons scoring low on a test measuring knowledge of research methods are equally likely to miss a certain item, the item may be ambiguous or misleading. By keeping only those items that correlate highly with the total score, reliability may be greatly improved.

4. Clues for improving reliability may be found in the instructions to respondents. Are they clear, or is there some room for misinterpretation? One should also examine the conditions under which the instrument is used or administered. Are they consistent? Finally, one might question whether the users of the instrument have been adequately and uniformly trained.

Of course, it is important to bear in mind that although a highly unreliable measure cannot be valid, it is possible to have highly reliable but invalid measures. Therefore, unless validity has been demonstrated, caution should be used in drawing conclusions about the "goodness" of even the most reliable measure.

Validity Assessment

Reliability assessment is relatively simple; the major forms outlined above use straightforward procedures that yield precise estimates of consistency and random error. These procedures are independent of the theories under investigation; that is, they can be applied and interpreted without regard to what is actually being measured. Validity assessment, by contrast, is more problematic. Systematic errors, which affect validity but not reliability, are more difficult to detect than random errors. And the issue of measurement validity generally cannot be divorced from larger theoretical concerns; sooner or later you must ask what the nature of your concept is, what it means, and whether your operational definition faithfully represents this meaning or something else.

Validity cannot be assessed directly. If it could—if we knew a case's true position on a variable independently of a given measure—then there would be no need for the measure. Therefore, to assess validity, one must either (1) subjectively evaluate whether an operational definition measures what it is intended to, or (2) compare the results of the operational definition with the results of other measures with which it should or should not be related. As you will see, the kinds of subjective judgments and objective evidence considered relevant depend on the purpose of measurement.

Subjective Validation

There are two methods of validity assessment based upon subjective evaluation of an operational definition: face validity and content validity. *Face validity* refers simply to the judgment that an operational definition appears, on the face of it, to measure the concept it is intended to measure. In some cases this claim alone would seem reasonable to establish a measure's validity. Few would dispute the face validity of common indicators of background variables such as age, gender, and education. Many observational measures of behavior have similar palpable validity, for example, "hitting another person" as an indicator of aggression and "offering assistance to a stranger" as an indicator of helping. However, as a method of validity assessment, face validity is generally not acceptable. Most operational definitions have it. After all, why would an instrument be offered as a measure of some concept if it did not appear to be valid? But face validity is based solely on personal judgment rather than objective evidence. Furthermore, it suggests that validity is an all-or-none matter when, in fact, measures have degrees of validity. For example, several operational definitions of age are possible. One could ask respondents directly what their age is, ask for their age at their last birthday, or ask them when they were born. These all have face validity but are not equally accurate.[3] One would not know which is most accurate without resorting to a validation method other than face validity.

Content validity concerns the extent to which a measure adequately represents all facets of a concept. A more acceptable form of subjective evaluation, this type of validation is used most often in psychology and education where it is applied to measures of skill, knowledge, and achievement. An instructor testing the reader's knowledge of this chapter, for example, ought to be concerned with whether the test has content validity—that is, with whether it includes questions on all sections of the chapter. Such a test would not have content validity if it omitted questions on reliability and validity and only contained questions on the measurement process and levels of measurement.

Psychologists and educators speak of the performance or content "domain" in relation to content validity. To demonstrate content validity, one must be able to define clearly and identify the components of the total domain and then show that the test items adequately represent these components. This is not too difficult for most tests of knowledge. With respect to knowledge of the present chapter, one could list all the major topics and subtopics, then develop test items for each of these, making sure that the number of items per topic was proportionate to the breadth of coverage. However, such a process is considerably more complex when measuring the abstract concepts typical of the social sciences. The domain of concepts like modernization, alienation, and social status is not easily specified; therefore, it is difficult to determine how adequately the domain has been tapped by specific indicators.

To some extent, the problems associated with face and content validity are not unique. All forms of validation are subjective in the sense that judgments on the validity of an operational definition ultimately rest with the verdict of the scientific community. However, social scientists generally do not find content validity evidence as persuasive as the kinds of "external" evidence provided by the validation procedures examined in the next two sections. Evidence that is external to the investigator is less subject to unintentional distortion and less difficult to replicate.

Criterion-Related Validation

Criterion-related validity applies to measuring instruments that have been developed for some practical purpose other than testing hypotheses or advancing scientific knowledge. One may wish to devise measures that will identify children with learning disabilities, determine a person's ability to fly an airplane or drive a car, or predict success in college. Under these circumstances, the investigator is not interested in the content or apparent meaning of the measure but in its usefulness as an indicator of a specific trait or behavior. The trait or behavior is called a criterion, and validation is a matter of how well scores on the measure correlate with the criterion of interest. The higher the correlation, the more valid the measure with respect to that criterion. As Nunnally (1970:34) notes, with this form of validation, the criterion variable is the only necessary standard of comparison. "If it were found that accuracy in horseshoe pitching correlated with success in college, horseshoe pitching would be a valid measure for predicting success in college."

There are two types of criterion-related validity. *Concurrent validity* refers to the ability of a measure to indicate an individual's *present* standing on the criterion variable. For example, a mental health inventory designed to identify those in need of psychiatric care could be given to a sample of "well" persons and a sample of persons currently under psychiatric care. Its concurrent validity would be indicated by the degree to which the inventory distinguishes between these two groups. With *predictive validity*, the measure is validated with reference to *future* standing on the criterion variable. A college entrance examination, for example, might be validated by comparing the exam scores of high-school students with a criterion measure of their success in college, such as grade-point averages or whether or not they graduate.

Since criterion-related validity rests on the correspondence between a measure and its criterion, it is only as good as the appropriateness and quality of the criterion measure. Unfortunately, this may present major difficulties. By what standards do you choose the criterion? What if no reasonable criterion exists? What if the criterion exists but practical problems prevent using it? For example, how would you demonstrate the predictive validity of a county civil service test developed to assist in the hiring of probation officers? Logically you could suggest that the county hire high-, average-, and low-scoring persons; then at a later time you could compare some measure of their job performance, such as supervisors' ratings, with their scores on the civil service test. Most likely, however, the county will hire only the top scorers; and regardless of their performance on the job, you would not know how it might have compared to the job performance of those who scored average or low. Thus you could not assess the predictive validity of the measure.

Despite such problems, evidence of criterion-related validity is crucially important when a test or measure serves a specific, practical end. Thus, if a test is designed to screen and select candidates for certain jobs or to place students in ability tracks or special programs, then it is important to know how well it works for the given purpose. Except for applied areas of psychology and education, however, social science measures are not developed to help solve practical problems of this sort. Operational definitions are created to reflect the meaning of certain concepts, and there is seldom a clear and adequate criterion variable for evaluating validity.

Construct Validation

When neither a pertinent criterion of prediction nor a well-defined domain of content exists for determining validity, investigators turn to construct validation. (The term "construct" is interchangeable with the term "concept"; a concept developed for scientific purposes is sometimes called a construct.) *Construct validation* emphasizes the meaning of the responses to one's measuring instrument. How are they to be interpreted? Is the instrument measuring the intended concept (or construct) or can it be interpreted as measuring something else? While this sounds like face validity, the orientation is quite different; construct validity is based upon an accumulation of research evidence and not mere appearances.

According to the logic of construct validation, the meaning of any scientific concept is implied by statements of its theoretical relations to other concepts. Thus, the validation process begins by examining the theory underlying the concept being measured. In light of this theory, one formulates hypotheses about variables that should be related to measures of the concept. At the same time, one considers other variables that should *not* be related to measures of the concept, but that might produce systematic error. Then, one gathers evidence to test these hypotheses. The more evidence that supports the hypothesized relationships, the greater one's confidence that a particular operational definition is a valid measure of the concept.[4]

An example of construct validation is Morris Rosenberg's validation (1965) of his self-esteem scale. Self-esteem refers to an individual's sense of self-respect or self-worth; those with high self-esteem have self-respect, those with low self-esteem lack it. To measure this concept, Rosenberg asked respondents whether they strongly agreed, agreed, disagreed, or strongly disagreed with ten items. Sample items were "On the whole, I am satisfied with myself" and "I feel I have a number of good qualities." Rosenberg reasoned that "if this scale actually did measure self-esteem," then scores on it should "be associated with other data in a theoretically meaningful way" (p. 18). Thus, because clinical observations indicated that depression and neurosis often accompany low self-esteem, people who score low on the scale should appear more depressed to outside observers and reveal more symptoms of neurosis. Also, given the sociological proposition that an individual's self-esteem is determined largely by what others think of him or her, students with high self-esteem scores should be chosen more often as leaders by classmates and described more often as commanding the respect of others. Evidence confirmed these and other theoretical expectations, thereby supporting the construct validity of the self-esteem scale.

Construct validation differs from criterion-related validation in several ways. With criterion-related validity, the test of validity is the ability of the measure to classify, group, or distinguish persons (or other units of analysis) in terms of a single criterion. What the measure means aside from its ability to make such distinctions is of little concern. What is important is the strength of the correlation between a measure and its criterion; the lack of a high correlation indicates that the measure lacks validity. In construct validation, on the other hand, one is less interested in the accuracy of a prediction per se than in what the prediction reveals about the meaning of the concepts being measured. One does not necessarily expect correlations between measures of two theoretically related concepts to be extremely high because the two concepts are not intended to mean exactly the same thing. Furthermore, all of the tested predictions contribute toward the evaluation of construct validity; it is their cumulative effect that supports or disputes the validity of the measure.

Evidence of construct validity consists of any empirical data that support the claim that a given operational definition measures a certain concept. Because such evidence may be derived from a wide variety of sources, construct validation is not associated with a particular approach or type of evidence. We will now consider four of the more common types of evidence used to establish construct validity. Remember, though, that no single study or piece of evidence is sufficient; the construct validity of a concept is only as compelling as the amount and diversity of evidence supporting it.

1. *Correlations with related variables.* If a measure is valid, then it should correlate with measures of other theoretically related variables. M. Rosenberg (1965) validated his self-esteem scale in this way by showing that scores on it were correlated with symptoms of depression and neurosis and with peer ratings.

2. *Consistency across indicators and different methods of measurement.* Different measures of the same concept should be correlated, and because each methodological approach is subject to different sources of systematic error, measures of concepts should not be tied to a particular method. Thus, one of the most convincing evidences of construct validity is the correspondence of results when a concept is measured in different ways. This is called *convergent validity* because the results converge on the same meaning, namely that conveyed by the underlying concept.

Glock and Stark (1966) provided such evidence for their Index of Anti-Semitic Beliefs. Scores on the index were determined by level of agreement with six statements about Jews; hence, respondents were forced to agree or disagree with characteristics imputed by the authors. To measure anti-Semitism in a different way, Glock and Stark had respondents furnish their own images of Jews by requiring them to complete the following sentences: "It's a shame that Jews . . ." and "I can't understand why Jews . . ." When their answers were divided into those indicating negative, neutral, or positive images of Jews, it was found that 73 percent of those scoring high on the beliefs index as opposed to 27 percent of the low scorers projected a negative image.

3. *Correlations with unrelated variables.* To be a valid measure of a particular concept, a measure should differentiate that concept from other concepts from which it is intended to differ. In other words, there are some variables (representing systematic errors) with which a measure should not be highly correlated. This is called *discriminant validity*.

A good example is Zick Rubin's validation (1970) of his thirteen-item Love

Scale. A valid measure of love should differentiate love from liking, as these two concepts are empirically related but conceptually distinct. Rubin therefore developed a parallel scale of liking. When both the love and liking scales were administered, he found that their scores were only moderately correlated. Also, whereas respondents liked their dating partners only slightly more than they liked their friends, they loved their dating partners much more than their friends. Additional evidence showed that the Love Scale tapped an attitude toward a specific other person rather than a general response tendency. For example, Love Scale scores were uncorrelated with scores on the Marlowe-Crowne Social Desirability Scale, designed to measure the tendency to give socially desirable responses.

4. *Differences among known groups.* When certain groups are expected to differ on the measure of a concept, one source of validating evidence would be a comparison of the groups' responses. Milton Rokeach (1960) used this approach to test the validity of his Dogmatism Scale. This scale consisted of items intended to tap the degree to which a person is closed-minded in his or her thinking and beliefs, irrespective of the content of the beliefs. Rokeach administered the scale to several groups, such as friends and acquaintances whom graduate students identified as open- or closed-minded, and Catholics, Protestants, and nonbelievers among American college students. Consistent with expectations, Catholics and persons perceived by peers as closed-minded had higher scores than their comparison groups. (See Box 5.2 for an example of construct validation that uses a variety of evidence.)

While construct validation is now considered the model validation procedure for most social measurement, it is not without its problems. Obviously it is cumbersome and requires abundant evidence; more importantly, however, it can lead to inconsistent and equivocal outcomes. If a prediction is not supported, this may mean that the measure lacks construct validity. On the other hand, such negative evidence may mean that the underlying theory is in error or that measures of other variables in the analysis lack validity. Only if one's theoretical predictions are sound and the measures of other variables are well validated can one confidently conclude that negative evidence is due to lack of construct validity (Zeller and Carmines, 1980).

BOX 5.2

The Validation of the FEM Scale

There is unusually good evidence validating the FEM Scale, previously described in Box 5.1. The creators of the scale, Smith, Ferree, and Miller (1975), tested its reliability as well as its construct validity based upon data from 100 Harvard summer school students. Royce Singleton and John Christiansen (1977) also assessed the scale's validity with data from a larger, more heterogeneous sample of respondents. Below is a summary of the evidence regarding the scale's reliability and validity.

Reliability

Both of the above studies obtained a reliability estimate, based upon internal consistency, of .91, which is quite acceptable for attitude measurement.

Intercorrelations and Convergent Validity

Smith, Ferree, and Miller tested the validity of the FEM Scale by correlating it with three other variables: measures of identification with the Women's Movement, activism in the movement, and the Rubin-Peplau Just World Scale. High scores on the latter scale reflect a belief that the world is a just place, that people generally get what they deserve. Smith, Ferree, and Miller reasoned that feminists are unlikely to view the world in general as a just place, since they tend to perceive that women have been treated unjustly. Consistent with expectations, the results showed that FEM Scale scores were positively correlated with the identification and activism measures (evidence of convergent validity) and negatively correlated with scores on the Just World Scale.

Singleton and Christiansen correlated scores on the FEM Scale with measures of dogmatism, antiblack prejudice, and identification with the Women's Movement. They reasoned that dogmatism, a tendency to adopt traditional views, would include an antifeminist orientation. Also, prejudice toward blacks would reflect a general tendency toward prejudice with which antifeminist attitudes would be consistent. The correlations of individuals' scores on the FEM Scale with their scores on these other measures were in fact uniformly high.

Discriminant Validity

In addition to the above measures, Smith, Ferree, and Miller administered the Rotter I-E Scale to their respondents. "I-E" stands for internal-external locus of control. High "internals" are persons who believe that they have a great deal of personal control over their lives; high "externals" are persons who tend to believe that their lives are controlled by forces outside themselves. Because there was reason to expect that feminism would be mildly correlated with both of these tendencies, Smith, Ferree, and Miller expected no correlation with the FEM Scale when internality and externality were treated as a single scale. Once again, the results supported their prediction.

Known-Groups Validity

Singleton and Christiansen also administered the FEM Scale to members of two groups with opposing views on women's issues: the National Organization for Women (NOW) and Fascinating Womanhood. NOW is the largest and most prominent organization in the women's movement; Fascinating Womanhood was an antifeminist organization of the early to mid–1970s that strongly advocated a traditional, dependent role for women. FEM Scale scores of the members of these two organizations were widely divergent as expected. Recall that the scale has a range of 20 to 100. NOW members had an average score of 91, whereas members of Fascinating Womanhood had an average score of 51.

A Final Note on Reliability and Validity

The procedures for assessing validity and reliability may seem so complex and cumbersome that one may wonder if investigators ever pass beyond this stage of research.[5] Fortunately, many investigators avoid the issue by borrowing, from prior studies, measures that have established records of validity and reliability. Also, few researchers apply more than one of the simpler procedures discussed above to ascertain the reliability or validity of their new measures. What usually happens is that once a new measure of some sort is introduced (perhaps with minimal evidence of reliability or validity), the measure is widely used for awhile until invalidating features are found (such as the middle-class bias of IQ tests) and the instrument is revised or replaced. Thus, validity and reliability assessment is not confined to intrastudy or intrainvestigator efforts, but is an ongoing process that extends across studies and investigators and over a considerable length of time.

It is also true that the most elaborate procedures were developed in response to the difficulties of operationalizing some concepts, such as attitudes, that are relatively unstable and pose reactivity and other measurement problems. More stable and less reactive measures are not as problematic.

In speaking about the issues validity raises, James Davis (1971:14–15) aptly observes that "[a]t the extreme [validation] constitutes a philosophical thicket which makes a dandy hiding place from which antiempirical social scientists can ambush the simple-minded folk who want to find out what the world is like rather than speculate about it." Although it is true that such difficulties can immobilize die-hard perfectionists, for most social scientists the validation problem presents challenging opportunities to exercise their creativity. No measure is perfect, but an imperfect measure is better than none at all. Or, as Davis further notes, "Weak measures are to be preferred to brilliant speculations as a source of empirical information" (p. 15).

Summary

Measurement is the process of assigning numerals to units of analysis in order to represent conceptual properties. This process involves three steps: (1) conceptualization—the development and clarification of concepts; (2) specification of variables and indicators to provide empirical manifestations of one's concepts; and (3) operationalization—the description of the research procedures necessary to assign units to variable categories. Because indicators do not correspond perfectly to concepts, researchers often use multiple indicators, which may be combined to create an index or scale. Operational definitions may be formed either by experimentally manipulating a variable or through nonmanipulative procedures such as verbal reports, observations of behavior, and archival records. One selects operational definitions in the context of an overall research strategy with an eye toward obtaining the best possible fit with the concept being measured.

Operational definitions are described in terms of their level of measurement and evaluated with respect to their reliability and validity. Measurement level alerts us to the various ways that we can interpret the numerals assigned to different variable categories. In nominal measurement, the numbers are simply labels that signify differences of kind. Variables measured at this level form a classification system that should be exhaustive and mutually exclusive. In ordinal measurement, different numbers indicate the rank order of cases on some variable. In interval measurement the numbers form a metric, so that different numbers imply not only rank order but also countable distances. Ratio measurement contains these features plus an absolute zero point, making it possible to form ratios of the numbers assigned to categories.

Reliability refers to the stability or consistency of an operational definition; validity to the goodness of fit between an operational definition and the concept it is purported to measure. A valid measure is necessarily reliable, but a reliable measure may or may not be valid. One can see this in relation to the three sources of variation in all measures: true differences and systematic and random measurement errors. A completely valid measure reflects only true differences, which means it is free of both systematic and random error. A completely reliable measure is free from random error but may reflect true differences and/or systematic error.

We assess reliability by calculating the correlation between (1) repeated applications of the measure (test-retest reliability), (2) responses to different but equivalent forms of the measure (parallel-forms reliability), and (3) responses to subsets of items from the same measure (split-half reliability); by (4) examining the consistency of responses across all items (internal consistency); or by (5) observing the correspondence among different interviewers, observers, or coders applying the same measure (intercoder reliability). Of these approaches, the last three are used most often. One can increase reliability by adding items to a scale, omitting items that do not discriminate well, and by clarifying questions and instructions contained in one's operational definition.

We assess validity by subjectively evaluating an operational definition, by checking the correspondence between the operational definition and a specific criterion, or by determining whether the operational definition as a measure of a given construct correlates in expected ways with measures of several other constructs. Subjective validation involves judgments either of whether an operational definition appears to be valid (face validity) or of whether it adequately represents the domain of a concept (content validity). Content validity is important in educational testing, but otherwise subjective judgment per se is unacceptable as a source of validation. Criterion-related validation applies to measures (or "tests") that are intended to indicate a person's present (concurrent validity) or future (predictive validity) standing on a specific behavioral criterion. It is especially important to assess when a measure is a practical, decision-making tool. Construct validation is based upon an accumulation of research evidence. This evidence may include differences among groups known to differ on the characteristic being measured, and correlations with related variables, with different measures of the same concept (convergent validity), and with measures from which the concept should be differentiated (discriminant validity).

Key Terms

conceptualization   *reactive measurement effect*
indicator   *social desirability effect*
index   *test-retest reliability*
scale   *parallel-forms reliability*
operationalization   *split-half reliability*
verbal report   *internal consistency reliability*
level of measurement   *intercoder reliability*
   nominal scale   *subjective validation*
   ordinal scale   *face validity*
   interval scale   *content validity*
   ratio scale   *criterion-related validation*
exhaustive   *concurrent validity*
mutually exclusive   *predictive validity*
reliability   *construct validation*
validity   *convergent validity*
systematic measurement error   *discriminant validity*
random measurement error

Review Questions and Problems

1. What are the three steps in the measurement process?
2. Why do researchers use multiple indicators to measure a concept?
3. Differentiate between an indicator and a scale (or index).
4. What is an operational definition?
5. Explain the difference between manipulated and nonmanipulated operational definitions, and give an example of each.
6. Give an operational definition of any two of the following concepts: leadership; campus involvement; quality of life; social class; interpersonal attraction.
7. Indicate whether the source of each of your operational definitions in question 6 is a verbal report, observation, or archival record.
8. What do the numbers assigned to variable categories signify with nominal measurement? With ordinal measurement?
9. Indicate the level of measurement of each of the following variables.
   a. *Seriousness of criminal offense*: measured by having judges rank offenses from the most to the least severe
   b. *Political activism*: measured by the total number of politically related activities in which an individual participates
   c. *Ethnic group membership*: measured by having respondents check one of these categories: black, Hispanic, Oriental, Caucasian, other
   d. *Educational attainment*: measured by asking respondents to check one of the following categories: eighth grade or less; 9 to 11 years; high-school graduate; some college; college graduate
   e. An item measuring an attitude or opinion that uses a Likert response format (usually, "strongly agree," "agree," "undecided," "disagree," "strongly disagree")
10. Although only one level of measurement typically is associated with a

given variable, it is frequently possible to measure a variable at more than one level. For example, while the variable "age" generally is measured at the ratio level, one could also measure age at the ordinal level by placing respondents in one of the following age categories: under 20 years, 20–39, 40–59, 60 and over. How might you measure the variable "income" (i.e., what categories would you establish) if you treated it as (a) a nominal variable, (b) an ordinal variable, and (c) a ratio variable?

11. Compile a list of categories for the variable "religious affiliation." Make sure that the list is *exhaustive* and *mutually exclusive*, but also keep the list fairly short (say, no more than six categories).

12. For each variable, indicate whether the list of categories is exhaustive and mutually exclusive. Then indicate, where necessary, the changes or additions to the categories that would have to be made to meet these two requirements.

    a. Income: $3000–7999; $8000–11,999; $12,000–14,999; $15,000–24,999; $25,000 and over

    b. Employment status: working full-time; working part-time; student; housewife; unemployed

    c. Age: under 18 years; 18–30 years; 30 years and over

13. Carefully state the relationship between the reliability and validity of measures. Is it possible to have a reliable but invalid measure? To have an unreliable but valid measure?

14. What are the three primary sources of variability in operational definitions?

15. Suppose members of a class in research methods were given an examination on this chapter. Assuming the examination is designed to measure students' knowledge of the material in the chapter, describe three possible sources of measurement error (either systematic error or random error) in the set of examination scores. For each source of error explain whether it is likely to affect measurement validity, reliability, or both.

16. Which type of measurement error—random and/or systematic—affects reliability? Which type of error affects validity?

17. What are some of the problems involved in using a test-retest procedure (or stability estimate) to estimate the reliability of a measure?

18. What is the difference between stability and equivalence estimates of reliability? Which of these estimates is preferable if a change in the variable is likely to occur over time? Explain.

19. What is the major disadvantage of the parallel-forms procedure for estimating reliability?

20. How is the logic behind split-half and internal consistency reliability similar?

21. What is intercoder reliability?

22. Identify two ways of increasing reliability.

23. Why is face validity generally an unsatisfactory method of validation?

24. When is content validity most appropriate as a method of validation?

25. In what sense are all forms of validation "subjective"?

26. Under what conditions is it important to use criterion-related validation? What are its drawbacks?

27. Explain the difference between predictive validity and construct validity.

28. Identify four types of evidence used to establish construct validity.

29. Indicate the type of reliability (test-retest, split-half, parallel forms, internal consistency, intercoder) or validity (face, content, concurrent, predictive, construct) to which each of the following assertions refers.

    a. The correlation between scores on the odd and even items of the multiple-choice exam was very high.

    b. The study indicated a moderately strong association between total score on the Graduate Record Examination and performance in graduate school, as measured by grade-point average.

    c. Zick Rubin (1970) found that scores on his Love Scale were correlated with marriage probability and the feeling of being "in love."

    d. The set of final examination questions was judged to be thoroughly representative of the material covered in the course.

    e. The scale is an improvement over previous measures of authoritarianism, in which right-wingers tended to score higher than left-wingers, because both left- and right-wing authoritarians tend to score high.

    f. The scale was administered twice to the same group. Scores obtained the second time were nearly identical to scores obtained the first time (coefficient of correlation = .98).

    g. Armer and Schnaiberg (1972) found that four measures of modernity (a set of attitudes and behavior that facilitates life in modern society) were no more highly correlated with one another than they were with measures of anomia and alienation.

30. Look through recent issues (1980-present: Vols. 59 and up) of *Social Forces* and find an article reporting an empirical study.

    a. Give a full bibliographical citation for the article (i.e., author, "article title," *Journal name*, year, volume number, pages).

    b. State the problem or hypothesis being tested (if more than one problem/hypothesis, state only one).

    c. Briefly describe how each concept or variable in the problem/hypothesis is measured.

    d. What is the level of measurement of each variable?

    e. Evaluate each measure from the standpoint of reliability. Do the author(s) cite or provide evidence of reliability?

    f. Evaluate each measure from the standpoint of face validity. Do the author(s) cite or provide evidence of construct validity?

NOTES

1. At times we will use the word "number" where technically the term "numeral" is more accurate. The difference, simply put, is that numbers are abstract concepts (such as the number two), whereas numerals are the squiggly lines used to represent the concepts. In the nominal level of measurement, numerals do *not* represent the number concept but rather are arbitrarily assigned to categories for coding purposes.

2. As the terminology suggests, most of the procedures for determining reliability were developed in connection with psychological testing.

3. Studies have shown that if a single question is used, it is best to ask respondents in what year they were born. However, the way to get the most accurate measure is to ask both date of birth and age at last birthday, check one against the other, and then inquire about any discrepancies (Sudman and Bradburn, 1982).

4. As you can see, this process is quite similar to general hypothesis testing. In fact, construct validation "is not simply a matter of validating a [measure]. One must try to validate the theory behind the [measure]" (Kerlinger, 1973:461).

5. The foregoing discussion of reliability and validity does not exhaust the use of these concepts in the social sciences; for in addition to judging the adequacy of operational definitions, the terms are also applied in the evaluation of other aspects of a research study. For example, the term validity is used in reference to logic (chapter 3) and to the adequacy of a research design (chapters 7 and 8). The concept of reliability is used frequently in judging the quality of a sample (chapter 6).

6

Sampling

Sampling, whether we are aware of it or not, is part of everyday life. For instance, after eating at one of a chain of restaurants, a person may decide that all the restaurants in the chain serve poor food and provide poor service. A student's decision to take a given course may be based upon the opinions of friends who have already taken it. Having met a few people from New York, or having seen one or two on television, someone may conclude that New Yorkers are pushy and aggressive. In each of these examples, inferences about a whole class of objects are made from observations of a subset of such objects. The examples implicitly contain the basic idea behind sampling: (a) we seek knowledge or information about a whole class of similar objects or events (usually called a *population*); (b) we observe some of these (called a *sample*); and (c) we extend our findings to the entire class (Stephan and McCarthy, 1958:22).

While simple in principle, sampling can be fraught with difficulties in practice. Consider some possibilities. The restaurant patron may have picked a day when the head cook had quit and been replaced by the busboy, or she may have patronized the worst franchise in the chain. The student talked to friends, who are likely to have highly similar opinions that may differ markedly from the opinions of other students who have taken the course. (Insofar as people tend to share the opinions of their friends, this sort of biased sample may be sufficient for this special purpose.) Finally, characterizations of groups of people, like the one of New Yorkers, seldom apply to even a majority of the group. Generalizations such as the above, drawn from casual observation, are likely to err because they are based upon inadequate samples of information. In this chapter we discuss some rigorous yet surprisingly simple techniques that are designed to reduce the hazards of generalizing from incomplete information.

The preceding chapter dealt with the measurement of variables. Before actual measurements are taken, researchers must select an appropriate set of units (or cases). How cases are selected depends on answers to several crucial questions. The first of these was addressed in chapter 4: What is the unit of analysis—individual people, married couples, newspaper editorials, cities? The answer to this question, recall, hinges largely on the research topic, which determines what the researcher seeks to describe and compare. Thus, research on the relationship between a nation's literacy rate and its economic development would use nations as units; a study of the effects of televised violence on aggression would concern individuals. The decision about *what type of unit* to examine will not be considered further in the present chapter; we will assume that the appropriate type of unit has been selected. The interests here will be with *how many* such units of *what particular description* should be *chosen by what method*. But before examining each of these issues, let us take a brief look at some of the reasons why sampling in social research, as in everyday life, is a practical necessity for informed decisions.

Why Sample?

Scientists seek to establish the broadest possible generalizations, applicable to infinitely large classes of events. Yet, it is obviously impossible to observe all relevant events. In the physical sciences, the nature of the elements studied simplifies this problem. Particular physical and chemical elements are assumed to be identical or nearly identical with respect to pertinent properties. Thus, any sample of one or more cases suffices; one test tube of hydrogen, or distilled water, or nitroglycerine will be like any other. As we move from the physical to the biological and social sciences, however, this assumption of homogeneity becomes increasingly risky. Because social objects such as people vary widely on nearly every imaginable property, studying any one case simply will not suffice as a basis for generalizing. The heterogeneity of cases requires careful procedures designed to ensure that the range of variation in the population will be represented adequately in one's sample of observations.

Beyond the need to represent population variability adequately, practical considerations usually necessitate sampling. Researchers often want to know something about a specific social group or population that, for reasons of size, time, cost, or inaccessibility, cannot be studied in its entirety. Indeed, unless the researcher is willing to restrict his or her inferences to a very small set of narrowly defined cases or unless one has unlimited time and funds, there is no getting around sampling.

To interview the entire 20,000-student population at a university, a population that is relatively small by survey research standards, would require a long period of time or a large number of interviewers. However, time is often of the essence. A lengthy period of data collection would render obsolete some data, such as attitudes about current issues or voter preferences, by the time the information was completely in hand. Moreover, the responses of persons interviewed late in the investigation could not be considered comparable to those of persons interviewed early. Responses could be affected by current events, or rumors and scuttlebutt about the ongoing survey may influence the responses of persons interviewed late. A large staff of interviewers also would present problems. Not only would this add to the total costs of the study but it would be more difficult to train and supervise interviewers adequately. To employ a large number of interviewers, one may also be forced to hire some who are not well qualified, thereby reducing the accuracy of the data.

This last point brings us to a third reason for sampling. Paradoxically, the attempt to observe all cases may actually describe a population less accurately than a carefully selected sample of observations, especially in survey studies of large populations. The reason is that the planning and logistics of observation are more manageable with a sample. Greater attention can be given to the design of interviews or questionnaires, to procedures for locating difficult-to-find respondents, and, once again, to the hiring, training, and supervision of a competent staff of interviewers, all of which will increase the quality of the data collected. In support of this point, Sudman (1976:3) notes that data from the Current Population Survey, a sample survey of over 60,000 households conducted monthly by the Bureau of the Census, are considered more accurate for many purposes than the decennial census, a complete enumeration of the U.S. population made every 10 years.

We hasten to add that only in the case of very large populations would we expect a sample to yield more accurate information about a population than a survey of the population itself. But the justification for sampling need not rest on a claim of greater accuracy. More to the point, carefully selected samples are an efficient way of producing accurate information. You can see this for yourself on the next election day. Note the accuracy with which the major news networks are able to predict certain election outcomes, long before all the votes have been tabulated. This accuracy is made possible by the careful sampling procedures of expert pollsters. (The polls have not always been so accurate, however, as revealed in Box 6.1.)

BOX 6.1

Sources of Errors in Survey Sampling:
Two Notorious Failures in Political Forecasting

In recent years political pollsters have been able to predict elections with amazing accuracy. Using sophisticated probability methods to select the sample, a Gallup poll of registered voters conducted just prior to the 1984 presidential election estimated that Ronald Reagan would receive 59 percent of the two-party vote and Walter Mondale would receive 41 percent. That is precisely what each candidate received. Although it is unusual to see this level of accuracy, most preelection polls fall within a few percentage points of the actual vote. Political polls, however, have not always been so accurate, as two infamous examples from the annals of sample surveys will reveal.

Perhaps the biggest polling debacle occurred in the presidential election of 1936, when *Literary Digest* magazine predicted that Alfred Landon would be a landslide winner, by 57 to 43 percent, over Franklin Roosevelt. At this time, the *Literary Digest* was well known for its polls on public issues and enjoyed considerable prestige, having predicted the winner in every presidential election since 1920. Its 1932 poll erred by less than two percentage points. However, in 1936 it missed calling the election by a wide margin. What went wrong? With over 2 million individuals polled, the *Digest's* sample was certainly large enough. Indeed, it was enormous by current standards. In 1984, a sample of only 2000–3000 people was required to predict accurately the voting behavior of over 90 million voters.

There were two major reasons for the failure of the *Literary Digest* poll. The first was the manner in which the sample was selected. The *Digest* conducted its polls by mailing ballots to millions of people. The names and addresses of these people came from a variety of sources, including phone books, automobile registration lists, and the *Digest's* own subscription list. Because such sources tended to exclude the poor, who could not afford telephones or automobiles, the sample did not provide a representative cross section of American voters. With rich and poor voting similarly prior to 1936, this bias against the poor apparently had little effect on the predictions. But in 1936, the rich tended to vote for Landon, the poor voted overwhelmingly for Roosevelt, and the bias inherent in the *Digest* poll produced a substantial error.

A second problem with the *Digest* poll has to do with what is called *nonresponse bias*. With any survey, there will be a certain percentage of the selected sample who do not respond or who cannot be contacted. Studies have shown that these nonrespondents tend to differ in important ways from respondents. For example, both lower-class and upper-class people are less likely to respond to questionnaires or personal interviews than the middle class. Respondents are also likely to have a stronger interest in the subject at hand than nonrespondents. Although 10 million sample ballots were mailed to prospective voters, the *Digest* based its predictions on 2.4 million responses. Statistician Maurice Bryson (1976) contends that this reliance on voluntary responses was the primary source of error in the 1936 poll. Feeling more strongly about the election than did the pro-Roosevelt majority, the anti-Roosevelt minority was more likely to respond, thereby creating another source of bias in the *Digest's* sample.

Another notorious polling failure occurred in 1948, known as "the year the polls elected Thomas E. Dewey President." All three major polls—Gallup, Crossley, and Roper—that covered the 1948 campaign projected that Dewey would be the winner with 50 percent or more of the popular vote, but he ended up with just over 45%. Several factors combined to produce this failure. For one thing, those who were undecided about their election choice when the polls were taken went predominantly for Truman. Critics of the 1948 polls, however, agree that the way the samples were selected also contributed to the prediction error.

By this time the pollsters were using a procedure called quota sampling (see text discussion). With quota sampling the population is divided into subgroups (e.g., men and women, blacks and whites), and interviewers are assigned a fixed quota of persons to interview in each of the subgroups. For example, an interviewer might be required to interview three men under 40 years of age and four over 40, four women under 40 and four over 40. Quotas are determined so as to guarantee that the sample will be representative of the voting population with respect to important characteristics thought to affect voting behavior. One shortcoming of this method is that the quotas are theoretical; they are an indirect means of creating a representative sample of the voting population *before the election*. However, demographic characteristics of the voting population cannot be known with certainty until after the election is held. Another problem is that the interviewers, who are free to choose anybody they like within the assigned quota, may be subject to selection bias. In fact, Gallup and Crossley poll results from 1936 to 1948, based on quota sampling, revealed that interviewers consistently preferred Republicans (Katz, 1949). With Democratic candidate Roosevelt possessing a large lead in 1936, 1940, and 1944, Gallup and Crossley were able to predict the winner in spite of the Republican bias of their polls. But this was too much to overcome in an election as close as that of 1948.

Population Definition

After determining the unit of analysis, the first task in sampling is to define the population of interest—to describe the particular collection of units that make up the population. Sociologist Kenneth Bailey (1982:86) notes that the experienced researcher always gets a clear picture of the population before selecting the sample, thus starting from the top (population) and working down (to the sample). "In contrast, novice researchers often work from the bottom up." Rather than making explicit the population they wish to study, they will select a predetermined number of conveniently available cases and assume that the sample corresponds to the population of interest. Consider a sample consisting of "randomly" chosen passersby at a shopping center on a Saturday afternoon. While one may assume that such a sample would be representative of the people in a given community, it is likely to differ from this population in several respects. For example, weekend shoppers would probably overrepresent people who work during the week and underrepresent the retired and unemployed. If the shopping area happens to be a luxurious shopping mall, the sample is likely to be heavily weighted in favor of the financially well-off. At best, this sample would represent Saturday afternoon shoppers at the shopping center in question on the day the data were collected, which is indeed a strange definition of the population and surely not the one in which the researcher would be interested.

Defining the population is a two-step process. First, one must clearly identify the *target population*, that is, the population to which the researcher would like to generalize his or her results. To define the target population, one must keep in mind (1) the scope of the planned generalizations and (2) the practical requirements of drawing a sample. This implies that the limits of inclusion and exclusion should be specified in terms of a few objective criteria rather than a flexible general description. For example, "in a study of the effects of noise on residents near an airport, it is better to define the population as all those living within one mile of the airport rather than defining the population as all those affected by airplane noises" (Sudman, 1976:14). While the distance criterion may exclude some who are affected by aircraft noises, only with this definition would it be possible to determine prior to data collection which cases are included in the population and which are not.

The relevant criteria for defining the target population depend on the type of unit and the research topic. With individual people, some combination of locale, age, and selected demographic variables such as gender, race, marital status, and education is ordinarily used (Sudman, 1976:12). For example, a national fertility study, in which it was important to identify married women of childbearing age, delineated the population this way: "ever married women under 45 years of age residing in the continental United States" (Westoff and Ryder, 1977). In his study of the Boston antibusing movement, Useem (1980) defined the target population as "white Boston residents between the ages of 25 and 53 who were United States citizens." Both of these examples provide good definitions of the target population because they clearly indicate who is to be included and who is to be excluded.

If the unit is groups or organizations, then organizational type and size as measured by number of members or employees are often specified. For instance, a recent study of organizations limited the population to social service agencies with staffs of ten or more in a large midwestern city (Lincoln and Zeitz, 1980). Studies of families also invoke unique definitional criteria: for example, presence or absence of children, number of generations, and intact or single-parent. Which set of criteria is used depends on the researcher's purposes.

Two defining characteristics that are always implicitly or explicitly part of the target population are its geographic and time referents. Notice that each of the above examples of target populations has a clear geographic boundary (e.g., continental United States; city of Boston); and although it was not made explicit, each has a distinctive time frame (e.g., mid-1970s).

With the target population clearly defined, the researcher next must find a way of making it operational. This involves the second phase of population definition: constructing the sampling frame. The *sampling frame* denotes the set of all cases from which the sample is actually selected. Since the term can be misleading, please note that the sampling frame is *not a sample*; rather, it is the *operational definition of the population* that provides the basis for sampling.

There are two ways of constructing a sampling frame, which correspond to the two ways to define a set (or subset) in logic: (1) listing all cases and (2) providing a rule defining membership. For example, in a city telephone survey, the sampling frame could consist of the city phone book (a listing) or the set of all telephone numbers with certain telephone exchanges (a rule). In survey research, establishing a sample frame often amounts to obtaining an adequate listing—either of the population as a whole or of subgroups of the population. But listing is not always possible or preferable. As long as cases can be identified, a rule procedure can usually be devised for finding and selecting cases. Suppose that you wanted to observe the behavior of inmates in a mental institution. Listing all acts before they occur is obviously impossible. However, if we consider that all acts within the institution occur at specified places, days, and times, then this would provide a three-dimensional rule (site, time, and day) for identifying and selecting cases. Similarly, if you wanted to interview people attending a rock concert, the fact that everyone must arrive at the concert at a particular time allows you to establish a rule based on time of arrival.

It is the researcher's hope that the sampling frame and the target population will be identical. Unfortunately, this usually occurs only for very small, geographically concentrated populations. Because it is often impossible or impractical for the researcher to create an accurate list of the target population, one must rely on existing lists; and such lists are inevitably incomplete. For Useem's antibusing study, the sampling frame consisted of the 1977 City of Boston "Annual Listing of Residents," which provided names, addresses, birthdates, and citizenship information. However, not only was it likely that many names were inadvertently omitted from this list, but through deaths and migration in and out of Boston, the target population was bound to have changed somewhat by the time the interviews were actually conducted. Thus, the sampling frame could not have matched precisely Useem's population of interest.

Strictly speaking, inferences should be made only about the population represented by the sampling frame. Yet, it is the target population to which we wish to generalize. Therefore, one should always evaluate cases in the target population that have been omitted from the sampling frame. How many omissions are there? How do they differ from cases included in the sampling frame? Because they frequently differ in a systematic way from those included in the frame, excluded cases can seriously bias findings. Telephone directories, for example, exclude the poor who cannot afford telephones and the more wealthy who tend to have unlisted numbers. Whenever such biases are known to exist, the researcher should decide whether to use the list or to find an alternative sampling frame. Regardless of the frame that is used, however, the nature of possible excluded cases should be discussed within the research report and carefully taken into account when making inferences about the target population.

Obviously, the problem of omitted cases is solved best by finding a good list to begin with. At the local level, many organizations (e.g., unions, schools, churches, professional associations) have membership directories, which constitute excellent sampling frames when appropriate. For most medium sized cities in the range of about 50,000 to 800,000, population and household directories are available (Sudman, 1976:58). Street address directories of households can provide particularly good sampling frames when the unit of analysis is the individual, such as head of household, or the family. At the national level few lists exist. A complete list of people or households in the United States is simply not available (Sudman, 1976:58). To sample national populations, researchers have developed a procedure in which sampling is carried out in stages. In this way, as we discuss below, one can select subpopulations for which lists either are available or can be created practically.

Finally, some populations defy identification and listing. If people can be trusted to classify themselves correctly, then they can be screened from a general population. For example, in a study of the elderly, the sampling frame might consist of people identifying themselves as over 65 years of age, even though the actual sample is selected from a sampling frame of the general population. But imagine trying to identify for sampling purposes members of a terrorist group or other radical political groups such as the Communist party of the United States of America, or deviant populations such as drug abusers and criminals. For obvious reasons, political radicals and deviants tend to resist identification by anyone outside their own group. In studying such populations, therefore, the process of population definition breaks down because an adequate sampling frame is unobtainable. More than likely, case selection will depend on a few crucial contacts, who provide the names of additional respondents.

Sampling Designs

Ideally in sampling we would like to obtain a sample that will be representative of the target population. To be "representative" means to provide a close approximation of certain characteristics of the target group. If the population consists of the students at Alpha College, then a perfectly representative sample would be like Alpha College students in all respects. The sample would contain the same proportion of freshmen, sophomores, juniors, and seniors, the same proportion of commuter students, the same proportion of sociology majors, and so forth, as are contained in the student body as a whole.

While intuitively appealing, however, the concept of representativeness has nearly disappeared from the technical vocabulary of sampling (Kish, 1965). Not only is it extremely unlikely that one will be able to draw a *perfectly* representative sample; it is rarely possible to evaluate a specific sample in terms of its representativeness. Because the populations we study are not known in all respects (which is, of course, the reason we study them), there is no way of knowing just how representative a given sample is. In the following pages, therefore, we use the term representative in reference to specific, known population characteristics but not in reference to the overall quality of the sample.

The quality of a sample must be judged in terms of the procedure that produced it, that is, in terms of its sampling design. *Sampling design* refers to that part of the research plan that indicates how cases are to be selected for observation. Sampling designs are generally divided into two broad classes: probability and nonprobability. *Probability sampling* is scientifically more acceptable, although it is not always feasible or economical. Its essential characteristic is that all cases in the population have a known probability of being included in the sample. This characteristic is made possible through a process of random selection. In nonprobability sampling, the chances of selecting any case are not known because cases are nonrandomly selected.

Probability sampling designs offer two major advantages over nonprobability sampling designs. The first advantage is that they remove the possibility that bias on the part of the investigator will enter into the selection of cases. Probability sampling is thus another important mechanism of scientific control. The second advantage is that by virtue of random selection, the laws of mathematical probability may be applied to estimate the accuracy of the sample. With probability sampling, one knows to which population the sample may be generalized as well as the limits of generalizability, but with nonprobability sampling, the population itself is undefined and the laws of probability do not apply.

Probability Sampling

Random Selection

Probability sampling always involves the process of random selection at some stage. In popular usage, "random" describes something that occurs or is done without plan or choice; random events or choices are haphazard or nondeliberate. As used in sampling, however, "random" has a more specific, technical meaning. It refers to a process that gives each case in the population an equal chance of being included in the sample. This means that characteristics of cases are irrelevant to their selection, and that the selection of one case has no bearing whatsoever on the selection of any other case. If for any reason the selection process favors certain cases, or if the selection of one case increases or decreases the likelihood that another case will be selected, then the selection is *biased*. By this definition, your circle of friends would clearly be biased as a sample of the student population at your college. So also would a variety of other, more or less haphazardly chosen samples, such as the students enrolled in introductory sociology classes, or students who happen to be in the library on a weekday night, or those students who pass in front of the campus center at a given time. In each of these samples, it is a good bet that certain types of students are more likely to appear than others, and therefore it would be unsafe to use any of these samples as a basis for generalizing about the whole student body.

To satisfy the condition of randomness, the investigator cannot simply pick cases haphazardly or in any hit-or-miss fashion; subtle and often unconscious biases will invariably enter into the selection process. Rather, sampling theory requires that mechanical or electronic aids be used to assure that chance alone dictates selection. "Mechanical" procedures used to convey randomness in sampling and statistics include tossing a perfect coin, drawing a card from a well-shuffled deck, or drawing perfectly round, numbered balls from a thoroughly mixed urn. However, processes of mixing and shuffling and the like not only are impractical as applied to populations of sociological interest but also have proven inadequate on occasion due to insufficient mixing.[1] In actual practice, social researchers achieve randomness by using either computer programs that provide random selection or specially prepared tables of mechanically generated random numbers. A table of random numbers (more precisely, the digits 0–9 randomly distributed) is shown in Table 6.1.

To illustrate the use of a table of random numbers, suppose that you want to select a sample of 100 students from a population totaling 2500 (say, all students enrolled at a certain school during the current semester). Before you can begin to use the table, you must first obtain a complete list of the population and number all individuals on the list from 1 to 2500. Because the population totals 2500, it will be necessary to select four-digit numbers from the table. (In general, the number of digits required depends on population size: a population of 50,000 requires five digits, a population of 100,000 requires six digits, etc.) The four-digit numbers in the table then are presumed to correspond to the numbered individuals in your population.

Now, notice that Table 6.1 is arranged in rows and columns of five-digit numbers. The numbers are arranged this way merely to make the table easier to use. One can read the digits in blocks of two, three, or more to produce two, three, or more digit numbers. Because the integers in the table are completely random, it makes no difference where you start in the table or whether you choose numbers by moving across rows or down columns. The important point is to decide where to start and how to proceed *before* you begin, so that the start can be truly random and columns or rows are not repeated. Suppose that you elect to move down the columns, using the first four of each set of five digits as your random number selection. A good (random) start can be made by simply closing your eyes, sticking your pencil into the table, and starting on the number where your pencil point lands. Let us say that the point lands on the tenth number down in the third column—03529. Using the first four digits, the first case selected will be number 0352. Proceeding down the

TABLE 6.1. Random Numbers

10097	32533	76520	13586	34673	54876	80959	09117	39292	74945
37542	04805	64894	74296	24805	24037	20636	10402	00822	91665
08422	68953	19645	09303	23209	02560	15953	34764	35080	33606
99019	02529	09376	70715	38311	31165	88676	74397	04436	27659
12807	99970	80157	36147	64032	36653	98951	16877	12171	76833
66065	74717	34072	76850	36697	36170	65813	39885	11199	29170
31060	10805	45571	82406	35303	42614	86799	07439	23403	09732
85269	77602	02051	65692	68665	74818	73053	85247	18623	88579
63573	32135	05325	47048	90553	57548	28468	28709	83491	25624
73796	45753	03529	64778	35808	34282	60935	20344	35273	88435
98520	17767	14905	68607	22109	40558	60970	93433	50500	73998
11805	05431	39808	27732	50725	68248	29405	24201	52775	67851
83452	99634	06288	98033	13746	70078	18475	40610	68711	77817
88685	40200	86507	58401	36766	67951	90364	76493	29609	11062
99594	67348	87517	64969	91826	08928	93785	61368	23478	34113
65481	17674	17468	50950	58047	76974	73039	57186	40218	16544
80124	35635	17727	08015	45318	22374	21115	78253	14385	53763
74350	99817	77402	77214	43236	00210	45521	64237	96286	02655
69916	26803	66252	29148	36936	87203	76621	13990	94400	56418
09893	20505	14225	68514	46427	56788	96297	78822	54382	14598
91499	14523	68479	27686	46162	83554	94750	89923	37089	20048
80336	94598	26940	36858	70297	34135	53140	33340	42050	82341
44104	81949	85157	47954	32979	26575	57600	40881	22222	06413
12550	73742	11100	02040	12860	74697	96644	89439	28707	25815
63606	49329	16505	34484	40219	52563	43651	77082	07207	31790
61196	90446	26457	47774	51924	33729	65394	59593	42582	60527
15474	45266	95270	79953	59367	83848	82396	10118	33211	59466
94557	28573	67897	54387	54622	44431	91190	42592	92927	45973
42481	16213	97344	08721	16868	48767	03071	12059	25701	46670
23523	78317	73208	89837	68935	91416	26252	29663	05522	82562
04493	52494	75246	33824	45862	51025	61962	79335	65337	12472
00549	97654	64051	88159	96119	63896	54692	82391	23287	29529
35963	15307	26898	09354	33351	35462	77974	50024	90103	39333
59808	08391	45427	26842	83609	49700	13021	24892	78565	20106
46058	85236	01390	92286	77281	44077	93910	83647	70617	42941
32179	00597	87379	25241	05567	07007	86743	17157	85394	11838
69234	61406	20117	45204	15956	60000	18743	92423	97118	96338
19565	41430	01758	75379	40419	21585	66674	36806	84962	85207
45155	14938	19476	07246	43667	94543	59047	90033	20826	69541
94864	31994	36168	10851	34888	81553	01540	35456	05014	51176
98086	24826	45240	28404	44999	08896	39094	73407	35441	31880
33185	16232	41941	50949	89435	48581	88695	41994	37548	73043
80951	00406	96382	70774	20151	23387	25016	25298	94624	61171
79752	49140	71961	28296	69861	02591	74852	20539	00387	59579
18633	32537	98145	06571	31010	24674	05455	61427	77938	91936
74029	43902	77557	32270	97790	17119	52527	58021	80814	51748
54178	45611	80993	37143	05335	12969	56127	19255	36040	90324
11664	49883	52079	84827	59381	71539	09973	33440	88461	23356
48324	77928	31249	64710	02295	36870	32307	57546	15020	09994
69074	94138	87637	91976	35584	04401	10518	21615	01848	76938

TABLE 6.1 (continued)

09188	20097	32825	39527	04220	86304	83389	87374	64278	58044
90045	85497	51981	50654	94938	81997	91870	76150	68476	64659
73189	50207	47677	26269	62290	64464	27124	67018	41361	82760
75768	76490	20971	87749	90429	12272	95375	05871	93823	43178
54016	44056	66281	31003	00682	27398	20714	53295	07706	17813

Source: RAND Corporation, 1955. *A Million Random Digits with 100,000 Normal Deviates.* New York: The Free Press, p. 1. Copyright 1955 and 1983 by the RAND Corporation. Used by permission.

table, the second case selected will be number 1490. You then come to the number 3980, which is beyond the sample size. Whenever you encounter such a number, simply ignore it and move on to the next number. Also, after a while, a number already selected is bound to appear a second time. When this occurs, omit the second appearance to avoid having a repetition of cases in your sample. When you get to the bottom of the page, turn to a new page of random numbers, and continue with the procedure until you have selected a sample of 100 cases.

Simple Random Sampling

If carried out, our illustration of the use of a random numbers table would yield what is called a simple random sample. This is the basic probability sampling design that is incorporated in all the more elaborate probability sampling designs discussed below. The defining property of a simple random sample is that every possible *combination* of cases has an equal chance of being included in the sample. For example, in a population of four cases, numbered 1, 2, 3, 4, there are six possible samples of size two: (1, 2), (1, 3), (1, 4), (2, 3), (2, 4), and (3, 4). In a simple random sample, each of these pairs of cases would have the same chance of selection. To guarantee this property, two requirements are necessary: a complete list of the population, and the random selection of cases to be included in the sample.

With the concepts of random selection and simple random sampling now in mind, we are in a position to examine the principles of probability sampling theory. Although a complete understanding of the theory would require advanced mathematical training, the reader can gain a good intuitive grasp of the essential concepts through the following small-scale hypothetical example.[2]

Suppose that you are interested in conducting a study of alcohol consumption in a campus pub. Your interest perhaps stems from recent reports that problem drinking is increasing among college-age youth. The design of the study calls for a measure of alcohol consumption among various categories of students patronizing the pub on a Tuesday night. The population consists of all patrons of the pub during the period of observation. Because all patrons must possess student identification cards, an accurate count and list of the population are possible. Ordinarily, however, it is not feasible to observe *all* patrons on the night in question. Obviously, then, you need a sample.

Ignoring certain practical problems such as how selection is carried out with a nonstationary population, let us look at some characteristics of samples drawn from an imaginary population of just eight students, say, all the students who happen to be in the pub on a very slow night. Since the pub serves only beer, your measure of consumption consists of the number of 10-ounce glasses of beer consumed. The following tabulation contains hypothetical data for the population of eight students:

Student	Ann A	Bea B	Cora C	Dee D	Ed E	Fred F	Greg G	Hal H
Gender	F	F	F	F	M	M	M	M
Class standing	U	L	U	L	U	L	U	L
Glasses of beer	3	1	0	2	3	4	6	5

Notice that, in addition to beer consumption, information on gender and class is given. There are four females (F) and four males (M); four upperclass (U) and four lowerclass (L) students. These two variables will be considered later.

The average (or mean) number of glasses of beer consumed by our population of eight students is 3.0, which is determined by adding up all of the glasses (24) and dividing by the number of cases (eight). Of course, if this were the actual population of interest, then the mean would not be known, and our task would be to obtain an estimate of the mean from a sample of observations. To get an idea of how sample estimates will vary, let us examine all possible simple random samples of two students and of four students that could be drawn from the population. By seeing how the samples vary in relation to the population, we also can see the kinds of generalizations about a population that are possible from a single sample.

There are twenty-eight possible combinations of two cases each that can be drawn randomly from eight cases; thus, there are twenty-eight simple random samples of size two. You can check this for yourself by systematically arranging the possibilities in the following manner: AB, AC, . . . , AH, BC, BD, . . . , GH. In

TABLE 6.2. List of All Possible Samples of Size Two

Combination of cases	Mean number of beers	Combination of cases	Mean number of beers
AB (Ann, Bea)	2.0	CE (Cora, Ed)	1.5
AC (Ann, Cora)	1.5	CF (Cora, Fred)	2.0
AD (Ann, Dee)	2.5	CG (Cora, Greg)	3.0
AE (Ann, Ed)	3.0	CH (Cora, Hal)	2.5
AF (Ann, Fred)	3.5	DE (Dee, Ed)	2.5
AG (Ann, Greg)	4.5	DF (Dee, Fred)	3.0
AH (Ann, Hal)	4.0	DG (Dee, Greg)	4.0
BC (Bea, Cora)	0.5	DH (Dee, Hal)	3.5
BD (Bea, Dee)	1.5	EF (Ed, Fred)	3.5
BE (Bea, Ed)	2.0	EG (Ed, Greg)	4.5
BF (Bea, Fred)	2.5	EH (Ed, Hal)	4.0
BG (Bea, Greg)	3.5	FG (Fred, Greg)	5.0
BH (Bea, Hal)	3.0	FH (Fred, Hal)	4.5
CD (Cora, Dee)	1.0	GH (Greg, Hal)	5.5

FIGURE 6.1. Frequency distributions of sample means for simple random samples of two cases and four cases drawn from a hypothetical population of eight cases with a mean of 3.0.

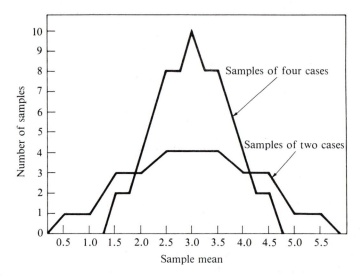

fact, we have done this for you in Table 6.2, which also gives the mean number of beers for each combination.

Similarly, there are seventy simple random samples of size four. To see how the estimates of beer consumption will vary from sample to sample, let us calculate the mean number of glasses consumed for each possible sample of size two and size four. Calculating a statistic, such as the mean, for all possible samples of a given size results in a *sampling distribution*. The sampling distributions of the mean for samples of size two and size four are presented in Figure 6.1 and in columns two and four of Table 6.3. Note first the sample of two cases: only one combination (BC) yields a sample mean of 0.5, only one combination (CD) has a sample mean of 1.0, three combinations (AC, BD, CE) have sample means of 1.5, and so on. Now examining samples of four cases: two combinations (ABCD and BCDE) yield sample means of 1.5, two combinations (ABCE and BCDF) yield sample means of 1.75, and so on.

From the sampling distributions one can calculate the probability that any given sample will be selected. Recall that with simple random sampling, each possible combination of cases is equally likely to be selected. This means that the likelihood, or probability, of selecting any particular combination of two cases (e.g., BC) from the above population will be equal to one divided by the total number of combinations (or $1/28 = .036$).[3] This is also the probability of drawing a sample with a mean of 0.5 and of drawing a sample with a mean of 1.0, since each of these means is the result of one and only one combination of two cases. To get the probability of selecting a sample with a mean of 1.5, we simply add the probabilities of each combination that yields a mean of 1.5 ($1/28 + 1/28 + 1/28 = .107$), which, as you can see, equals the number of such combinations (3) over the total (28). The remaining probabilities are given in columns three and five of Table 6.3. From the

TABLE 6.3. Means and Probabilities of Simple Random Samples of Two Cases and Four Cases Drawn from a Hypothetical Population of Eight Cases with a Mean of 3.0

	Samples of two cases		Samples of four cases	
Sample means	Number of samples	Probability	Number of samples	Probability
0.50	1	.04		
0.75				
1.00	1	.04		
1.25				
1.50	3	.11	2	.03
1.75			2	.03
2.00	3	.11	4	.06
2.25			6	.09
2.50	4	.14	8	.11
2.75			8	.11
3.00	4	.14 }.64	10	.14 } .89
3.25			8	.11
3.50	4	.14	8	.11
3.75			6	.09
4.00	3	.11	4	.06
4.25			2	.03
4.50	3	.11	2	.03
4.75				
5.00	1	.04		
5.25				
5.50	1	.04		
Total number of samples	28		70	
Mean of sample means	3.0		3.0	

table, notice that the probability of obtaining a particular sample mean increases as the estimate approaches the actual population mean of 3.0 glasses of beer. By the same token, the more a sample mean deviates from the population mean, the lower its probability of selection.

It is also possible to calculate the probability of obtaining sample estimates within a given range of the population mean. For example, there are eighteen samples (count them) of two cases with means between 2.0 and 4.0; thus, the probability of obtaining a sample mean within this range is $18/28 = .64$. Similarly, with samples of four cases, the probability of getting a sample mean within the range of 2.0 to 4.0 is $62/70 = .89$; and with samples of six cases (not shown), the "probability" is 1.0 (i.e., all samples have means between 2.0 and 4.0). This illustrates a very important principle in sampling theory: the larger the sample, the closer its mean is likely to be to the population mean. The amount that a given sample estimate deviates from the population value it estimates is known as *sampling error*. For example, in our hypothetical population, a sample mean of .5 has a sampling error of 2.5 because this is how much it differs from the known population mean of 3.0. The statistical measure of the "average" of such errors for an entire sampling distribution is called the *standard error*. Using this concept, then, another way of stating the principle about sample size is, the larger the sample, the smaller the standard error.

So far, we have demonstrated that a knowledge of the sampling distribution of the mean enables one to make the following kinds of statements regarding the accuracy of a sample mean: the probability is .89 that the mean of a randomly selected sample of four cases will deviate from the population mean by one or less (i.e., will fall within the range of 2.0–4.0). Of course, in the above example, the sampling distributions were constructed by calculating means for all possible random samples from a known population. In actual research, we select only one sample in order to estimate an unknown population characteristic. The key to being able to make the same kind of statement about sample accuracy in the actual research situation is provided by the mathematical theory behind probability sampling. According to this theory, the sampling distributions of various characteristics (such as the mean) form stable, predictable patterns. Consequently, even though the population value is not known, the theory indicates *how* sample estimates will be distributed (by specifying the sampling distribution) and provides a statistical formula for calculating the standard error, a measure of *how much* the sample estimates will tend to vary.

More rigorous accounts of sampling theory and sample estimation procedures can be found in the inferential statistics section of most statistics textbooks. In actual research, sample inferences about a population are arrived at in the following manner. From a single sample, drawn randomly:

1. The sample estimate (e.g., the sample mean) is considered the best single estimate of the population value.

2. The extent to which the sample estimate will tend to deviate from the population value (standard error) is calculated on the basis of variation within the sample.

3. Theoretical knowledge about the sampling distribution is utilized to attach a probability, or level of confidence, to a calculated range within which the population characteristic should fall.

This range, called a *confidence interval*, is established around the sample estimate. From this procedure we end up with statements such as the following: "We are 95 percent confident that the population mean is between 2.0 and 4.0."

A major advantage of probability sampling is that the size of the confidence interval (i.e., its precision), or the amount by which the sample estimate is likely to differ from the population value, can be determined *before* a study is carried out. Recall that the possible error in sample estimates is a function of sample size: the larger the sample, the smaller the standard error. Therefore, one can get a more precise sample estimate by selecting a larger sample. Sample precision also may be increased by using a more complex sampling design known as stratified random sampling.

Stratified Random Sampling

In stratified random sampling, the population is first subdivided into two or more mutually exclusive segments, called *strata*, based on categories of one or a combination of relevant variables. Simple random samples then are drawn from each stratum, and these subsamples are joined to form the complete, stratified sample.

To illustrate, let us return to our hypothetical data. Note that the population of eight cases can be broken down into two strata—male and female—according to categories of the variable gender, or into two strata—upperclass and lowerclass—according to categories of the variable class standing (frosh/sophomore versus junior/senior). A stratified random sample of four cases could be drawn by randomly selecting an equal proportion of males and females. In other words, one could draw independent random samples of two cases from each stratum, male and female, and then combine these into a single sample. This would not produce a simple random sample since there are several combinations of cases that are not possible, for example, the combinations of all females (ABCD) or all males (EFGH). There are thirty-six possible stratified random samples of four cases with equal proportions of males and females. By computing the mean beer consumption for each of these possible samples, we again obtain a sampling distribution of the mean. This distribution can be compared to the sampling distribution based upon simple random sampling to demonstrate the effect of stratifying on sample precision.

Table 6.4 presents the sampling distributions for samples of four cases based on simple random sampling, stratified random sampling with gender as the stratification variable, and stratified random sampling with class as the stratification variable. Notice that, compared to simple random sampling, sampling with gender stratification yields a distribution of sample means that cluster more tightly about the population mean. Thus, it is possible for a stratified sample to give a better estimate than a simple random sample. On the other hand, stratifying by class standing offers no such improvement; indeed, the percentage of sample means that deviate from the population mean by as little as .5 (next to last row) is lower than the comparable percentage in simple random sampling.

Clearly, as these comparisons reveal, stratifying can contribute to sampling efficiency. Whether it does or not depends partly on whether the stratifying variable is related to the dependent variable under study. In our hypothetical population, gender is related to beer consumption but class standing is not; that is, males tend to drink more beer than females, whereas lowerclass and upperclass students drink about the same amount. Consequently, stratifying by gender increases sample precision but stratifying by class standing does not.

Technically speaking, stratifying by variables correlated with the dependent variable in a study increases precision because it systematically introduces relevant sources of variability (or heterogeneity) in the population into the sample. The effect of this is to eliminate a source of sampling error—for example, the error that could occur if our sample of beer drinkers contained all men or all women. Thus, when there are differences across strata, stratified sampling ensures that these

TABLE 6.4. Means of Samples of Four Cases Drawn by Simple Random Sampling and Stratified Random Sampling with Gender and Class Standing as Stratifying Variables

Sample means	Simple random samples	Samples stratified by gender	Samples stratified by class standing
1.50	2		2
1.75	2		
2.00	4	1	2
2.25	6	2	6
2.50	8	5	2
2.75	8	6	2
3.00	10	8	8
3.25	8	6	2
3.50	8	5	2
3.75	6	2	6
4.00	4	1	2
4.25	2		
4.50	2		2
Total number of samples	70	36	36
Mean of sample means	3.0	3.0	3.0
Percentage of sample means between 2.5 and 3.5	60	83	44
Percentage of sample means between 2.0 and 4.0	89	100	89

differences are accounted for and are not free to vary within the sample. However, simple random sampling can reduce the variation across strata that contributes to sampling error only by increasing sample size. What this all boils down to is that a stratified random sample will be comparable in precision to a *larger* simple random sample, and hence more efficient, provided that the stratifying variable is related to the variable under study. Since we can also increase sample precision by increasing sample size, the greater efficiency of stratifying also depends on whether the cost of stratifying is low relative to the cost of sampling more cases. Obtaining a stratified sample necessitates classifying cases according to categories of the stratifying variable; however, this is not always possible or practical.

In addition to increasing efficiency, stratified random sampling may be used to guarantee that variable categories with small proportions of cases in the population are adequately represented in the sample. Suppose, for example, that we wanted to examine ethnic attitudes among various ethnic groups on a campus where 90 percent of the students are white, 5 percent are black, and 5 percent are Oriental. A simple random sample of 100 would yield, on the average, 90 whites, 5 blacks, and 5 Orientals. However, the number of cases in the latter two sampled groups is so small that statistical estimates derived from them would be very unreliable and imprecise. To get around this problem we could obtain a stratified random sample in which we select a greater proportion of blacks and Orientals for our sample than are found in the population. We might select 40 whites, 30 blacks, and 30 Orientals. This is called *disproportionate* stratified random sampling, because the proportion of cases in each stratum of the sample does not reflect the proportion in the population.

When strata are sampled proportionate to the population composition, then each case has an equal probability of being selected and one can generalize directly from sample to population. But with disproportionate sampling, the probability of selection varies from stratum to stratum and one must make a statistical adjustment before generalizations are possible. Basically, this is accomplished by a weighting procedure that compensates for oversampling in some strata. The necessary mathematical formulas, which are beyond the present discussion, can be found in Kish (1965). Although the probability of case selection varies from stratum to stratum, disproportionate stratified random sampling still constitutes a probability sample because the probability of case selection is *known*. Furthermore, probability sampling theory applies, since the subsamples drawn from each stratum are simple random samples.

Cluster Sampling

Returning to our beer drinking problem, suppose that instead of a central pub each of twelve dormitories on campus has social rooms in which beer is served. The population of beer drinkers now consists of all students who consume beer in the social rooms. To get an estimate of beer consumption on a given night with either a simple random or stratified random sample, our researcher would have to be in twelve places at the same time. A solution to this problem would be to hire a couple of assistants and to select randomly three dormitories for observation. Such a selection constitutes a cluster sample.

In *cluster sampling*, the population is broken down into groups of cases, called clusters, and a sample of clusters is selected at random. The clusters generally consist of natural groupings, such as college dormitories, or geographic units such as counties, census tracts, and blocks. Unlike stratified sampling, which draws cases from each stratum, cluster sampling draws cases only from those clusters selected for the sample. If all cases in each sampled cluster are included in the sample, the design is called a single-stage cluster sample in that sampling occurs once—at the cluster level. More frequently cluster sampling involves sampling at two or more steps or stages, hence the term *multistage cluster sampling*. An example of a two-stage cluster sample with our hypothetical population would be a random selection of dormitories (first stage), followed by a random selection of beer drinkers within each sampled dormitory (second stage). The sampling units in the first stage of a multistage sample are termed *primary sampling units* (or PSUs); units in the second stage are termed secondary sampling units, and so on.

While stratified random sampling is used to increase sample precision, the principal reason for cluster sampling is to reduce the costs of data collection. In interview studies of large, widely scattered populations, two major costs are interviewer travel and the listing of population elements. Simple random and stratified random methods produce isolated interviews at dispersed localities, which can create substantial costs for travel to and from interviews. However, clustering concentrates interviews within fewer and smaller geographic areas, thereby spreading the travel costs over several cases and saving on the costs of any one interview.

Since the listing of elements is a prerequisite for simple random or stratified random methods, clustering also can reduce the costs of listing by allowing lists to be compiled only for selected clusters rather than for the entire population. In fact, often it is either impossible or impractical to compile an exhaustive list of population elements, but it is possible to obtain lists of subpopulations (clusters) into which the population is naturally grouped or can be subdivided (Babbie, 1983:167). Examples would be the populations of a state or nation, all high-school students in the United States, and all cases of homicide in metropolitan areas. With such populations, a multistage cluster sample design is the only viable alternative. Thus, although a single list of U.S. high-school students does not exist and would be difficult and extremely costly to compile, lists of school districts within each state could be obtained fairly easily. To arrive at a nationwide sample of high school students, therefore, one could initially sample school districts, then obtain a list of high schools within selected districts and sample high schools, then list and sample students within each school. (Box 6.2 provides an example of a multistage sampling design for a national survey of the adult population.)

BOX 6.2

Sampling Design for a Nationwide Survey

Survey organizations such as the Survey Research Center (SRC) at the University of Michigan use multistage cluster sampling to conduct nationwide surveys. The steps involved in selecting the SRC's national sample are roughly diagrammed in the accompanying figure. The steps are numbered and labeled according to the type of unit selected.

Step 1. The United States is divided into *primary areas* consisting of counties, groups of counties, or metropolitan areas. These areas are stratified by region and a proportionate stratified sample of seventy-four areas is selected.

Step 2. The seventy-four areas are divided into *locations* such as towns, cities, and residual areas. After these have been identified and stratified by population size, a proportionate stratified sample of locations is drawn within each area.

Step 3. All sample locations are divided into *chunks*. A chunk is a geographic area with identifiable boundaries such as city streets, roads, streams, and county lines. After division into chunks, a random sample of chunks is drawn.

Step 4. Interviewers scout each sample chunk and record addresses and estimates of the number of housing units at each address. They then divide the chunks into smaller units called *segments*, and a random sample of segments is selected.

Step 5. Within each sample segment either all or a sample of the housing units, usually about four, are chosen for a given study. Finally, for every housing unit in the sample, interviewers randomly choose one respondent from among those eligible, which ordinarily consists of all U.S. citizens 18 years of age or older.

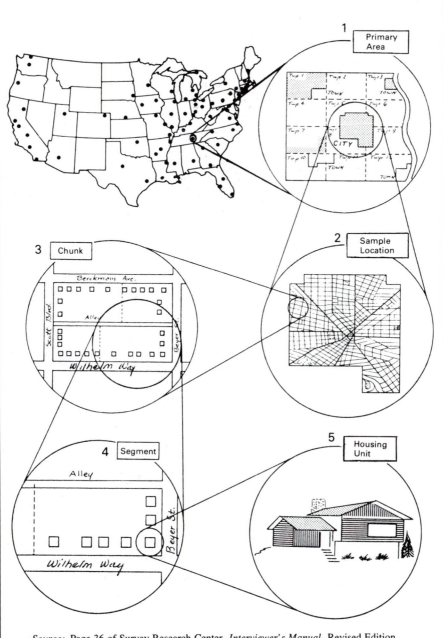

Source: Page 36 of Survey Research Center, *Interviewer's Manual*, Revised Edition (Institute for Social Research, The University of Michigan, 1976). Used by permission.

Multistage sample designs may involve either simple random sampling or stratified random sampling at each stage of the design. In other words, one can stratify clusters just as one stratifies individual cases. In fact, because natural clusters often vary considerably in the numbers of cases they contain, it is common practice to stratify clusters by population size. In this way, a relatively few clusters with extremely large populations can be sampled from a separate stratum to guarantee that they are represented in the sample. Otherwise, with simple random sampling one runs the risk of not selecting clusters that account for a major proportion of the population. Imagine, for example, drawing a cluster sample, with counties as the primary sampling units, of the population of Nevada, in which over 80 percent of the people reside in two of the state's sixteen counties. Any sample that excludes these two counties would be a biased sample of Nevada residents. Yet, the chances are fairly high that neither of the state's two largest counties would be included in a simple random sample (e.g., the probability that neither would be selected is 55 percent in a sample of four counties and 23 percent in a sample of eight counties). The best procedure, therefore, would be to stratify by county size, placing the two most populous counties in the topmost stratum, and then sample 100 percent from this stratum (i.e., select both counties).

One problem is that while cluster samples are more cost efficient, they are less precise, size for size, than either simple random or stratified random samples. Whereas the latter designs have a single source of sampling error, there are sampling errors associated with each stage of a cluster sample. For example, in the above two-stage example the sample of dormitories will represent the population of dormitories within a range of error, and the sample of beer drinkers within a selected dormitory will represent all beer drinkers in the dormitory within a range of error. The sampling error in the total sample is thus compounded and can be quite large relative to the error produced by one simple random selection.

In stratified sampling, efficiency increases to the extent that strata are internally homogeneous; for example, the beer drinking behavior of women is similar and the beer drinking behavior of men is similar. By contrast, the ideal in cluster sampling is for clusters to be internally heterogeneous compared to the differences between clusters. In general, however, there is much less variability (hence sampling error) within than across natural clusters. For example, residents in a single block are likely to be fairly homogeneous with respect to income, but quite different in terms of average income from the residents in another block. For this reason, one way of increasing efficiency is to select more clusters and fewer elements within the clusters. By increasing the number of clusters, sampling error is reduced at the stage that is subject to the greatest error.[4]

Although increasing the number of clusters generally increases precision, it also increases the cost of cluster sampling. A greater number of clusters means more widely scattered interviews, hence, more time and expense invested in travel, and more time and expense required for listing elements constituting the selected clusters. Reducing costs, of course, is the reason for cluster sampling. Consequently, researchers are likely to resolve this dilemma by simply selecting as many clusters as they can afford (Babbie, 1983:169).

Systematic Sampling

In conjunction with your study of campus beer consumption, you also might be interested in student perceptions of consumption. In other words, you might want to compare how much beer is consumed with how much beer students *think* is consumed. You therefore may want to conduct an interview or questionnaire survey of student perceptions. To select your sample of respondents, we recommend a very simple and direct probability sampling design called systematic sampling.

Systematic sampling consists of selecting every *K*th (e.g., fifteenth or twentieth) case from a complete list or file of the population, starting with a randomly chosen case from the first *K* cases on the list. Such a procedure has two requirements: a sampling interval (*K*) and a random start (Sudman, 1976). The *sampling interval* is merely the ratio of the number of cases in the population to the desired sample size. A *random start* refers to the process of using a table of random numbers or some other device to select at random the initial case between 1 and *K*. For example, suppose you wanted to draw a sample of 100 students from the 2500 students listed in the campus directory. Dividing 2500 by 100, you obtain a sampling interval of 25. You would then select at random a number between 1 and 25, and starting with that number, select every twenty-fifth student thereafter. Suppose the random number turns out to be 19. Your sample then would consist of cases numbered 19, 44, 69, 94, 119, . . . , 2494.

Whenever the population list is very long or the desired sample is large, it is usually much easier to draw a systematic sample than to draw manually a simple random sample. For this reason, systematic sampling is widely used in lieu of simple random sampling. In fact, if the list of cases is effectively random, then these two designs are equivalent. However, many available lists of populations are not random, but rather are ordered in some fashion, such as alphabetical, or by rank, age, or size of unit. Such ordering presents both advantages and disadvantages.

Because ordered lists often contain an implicit stratification of the population, a systematic sample may closely approximate a stratified sampling design. This, of course, could be advantageous because stratified samples generally are more efficient than simple random samples. A common example of implicit stratification is the stratification of ethnic groups inherent in alphabetical listings. Large proportions of certain ethnic groups have surnames beginning with the same letters (e.g., a disproportionate number of Irish surnames begin with M—McCarthy, McKenna; and O—O'Brien, O'Leary). Hence, taking every *K*th case is likely to yield the proper representation of each group (Blalock, 1979:559). In the student directory example, an important stratification effect might be provided if the listing is by gender (which is unlikely) or by some other characteristic related to perceptions of drinking (if alphabetical, then perhaps ethnicity).

The danger in systematic sampling is that the available population listing may have a periodic or cyclical pattern that corresponds to the sampling interval. This can create serious sample biases, as Blalock (1979:559) points out in the following example:

> [I]n a housing development or apartment house every eighth dwelling unit may be a corner unit. If it is somewhat larger than the others its occupants can be expected to

differ as well. If the sampling [interval] also happens to be [eight], one could obtain a sample with either all corner units or no corner units depending on the random start.

While systematic sampling thus offers the advantages of simplicity and implicit stratification, it also can create biased samples. Fortunately, the danger of periodicity in a systematic sample is actually quite small. Still, to counteract this possibility, the researcher should carefully examine the list from which a systematic sample will be drawn. If the list has a cyclical pattern, then steps should be taken (e.g., randomizing the start before selection on each page of the student directory) to eliminate the possibility of bias.

Nonprobability Sampling

Nonprobability sampling refers to processes of case selection other than random selection. Without random selection, nonprobability samples have two basic weaknesses: (1) they do not control for investigator bias in the selection of units, and (2) their pattern of variability cannot be predicted from probability sampling theory, thereby making it impossible to calculate sampling error or to estimate sample precision. However, while one should be ever mindful of these weaknesses, it would be a mistake to rule out nonprobability sampling. In many instances this form of sampling is either more appropriate and practical than probability sampling or the only viable means of case selection.

1. Consider the situation in which very few cases can be included in the sample. For an investigator doing an intensive study in which the unit of analysis is the city, corporation, or university, the expense of studying more than one or a few cases would be prohibitive. As we have seen, probability sampling is less reliable the smaller the sample. With extremely small samples of one or few cases, generalization from sample to population essentially becomes a matter of judgment. The selection of cases is therefore better left to expert judgment (in other words, nonrandom selection) than to the whims of chance (Wallis and Roberts, 1956:117–118).

2. When studying past events, the archeologist or historian often finds only a fraction of relevant materials available or accessible. Similarly in contemporary societies, certain individuals or institutions may refuse to cooperate in an inquiry. Under these circumstances, the researcher must either accept a nonprobability method of case selection or abandon the study altogether.

3. In the early stages of investigating a problem, when the objective is to become more informed about the problem itself, probability sampling simply may be unnecessary. It will suffice to select a range of cases nonrandomly without concern for precise statistical generalization.

4. If the population itself contains few cases or if an adequate sampling frame cannot be obtained or constructed, then there is no point in considering probability sampling. With small populations (say, less than 100), each case should be studied in its own right in comparison with all others. If the population is unknown or not

readily identifiable, as in many sociological studies of deviance, then sampling generally will consist of studying any and all identifiable and cooperative units.

Because nonprobability sampling is a residual category pertaining to any method of *non*random case selection, the various types of nonprobability samples are far ranging and less precisely defined than the probability sampling designs examined in the previous section. With this in mind, let us now examine three primary types of nonprobability samples: convenience, purposive, and quota.

Convenience Sampling

In this form of sampling (also called "haphazard," "fortuitous," and "accidental" sampling), the researcher simply selects a requisite number from cases that are conveniently available. In terms of the study of campus alcohol consumption, you might decide to (1) ask a professor for permission to administer a questionnaire to all the students in his or her classes, (2) interview whomever comes down the dormitory hall when you happen to be there, or (3) find a convenient spot in the campus pub from which to observe behavior. Television stations and newspapers wanting to tap public opinion on specific issues may interview conveniently available commuters, shoppers, store clerks, and others (Chein, 1981). Such methods of case selection are easy, quick, and inexpensive. If the research is at an early stage and generalizability is not an issue, then they may be perfectly appropriate. However, *convenience sampling* is a matter of catch-as-catch-can. There is no way of determining to whom, other than the sample itself, the results apply. Thus, in attempting to make inferences from such a sample, "one can only hope that one is not being too grossly misled" (Chein, 1981:424).

Purposive Sampling

In this form of sampling, the investigator relies on his or her expert judgment to select units that are "representative" or "typical" of the population. The general strategy is to identify important sources of variation in the population and then to select a sample that reflects this variation. One might select a single unit or subpopulation that is thought to be typical of the population in important respects or select a few units that correspond to key population differences. For example, in his study of "place ideology"—the values and beliefs associated with different kinds of communities—Hummon (1986) selected residents of four distinct communities in northern California: a central city, an upper-class suburb, a working-class suburb, and a rural small town. Because the type of community in which people lived was likely to affect their place ideology, this was a crucial variable in Hummon's study. He therefore wanted to be sure that it was represented adequately in his sample. Furthermore, in selecting the specific communities, Hummon carefully examined census data to identify typical areas or towns and to avoid populations that contained relatively large proportions of aged, minority, or institutionalized persons. Such *purposive sampling* fit the aims of the study extremely well, because Hummon's interest was not in estimating the distribution of various beliefs about communities within a particular population, but in identifying the key elements in various community ideologies.

Another purposive sampling technique, applied to election forecasting, is the selection of "barometer" states or precincts that have served as reliable predictors of overall election returns in previous years. Still another is the selection of deviant or extreme cases in order to discover why they deviate from the norm. Finally, one may select both typical and extreme instances within the same study. For example, if one were testing an innovation in the schools, then it would be wise to investigate at least one instance of the "typical school" in a particular city (or state or nation) and at least one instance of the best and worst problem schools (Cook and Campbell, 1979:76). If comparable results were found in all three instances, then one would have a reasonably firm basis for inferring that the effect applies to the full range of schools.

As with any nonprobability method of case selection, purposive sampling for heterogeneity and/or typicality is an unacceptable substitute for probability sampling when precise and accurate generalizations are required. However, with studies of more limited scope or in situations that preclude random selection, purposive sampling is an acceptable alternative. It generally offers much stronger, less tenuous inferences than convenience sampling, although such inferences are very much dependent on the researcher's expert judgment and intuition. The major weakness of purposive sampling is that it demands considerable knowledge of the population before the sample is drawn.

Quota Sampling

Quota sampling is a form of purposive sampling that bears a superficial resemblance to proportionate stratified random sampling. Like the latter, quota sampling begins by dividing the population into relevant strata such as age, gender, race, geographic region. The fraction of the population in each stratum is then estimated or determined via external data such as the census, and the total sample is allocated among the strata in direct proportion to their estimated or actual size in the population. Finally, to obtain the correct proportions in the sample, interviewers are asked to speak to a fixed quota of respondents in each stratum: so many men and so many women, so many of a given age or income, and so on. To fill the quotas interviewers are free to choose anyone who meets the quota requirements (see Stephan and McCarthy, 1958:37–38). For example, in the study of campus alcohol consumption, one might decide to obtain a quota sample, with a quota-control for gender, in light of the known effects of this variable on consumption. Suppose the campus population was 55 percent male and 45 percent female. Then a sample of 200 would require quotas of 110 males and 90 females. How these respondents were chosen would be up to the investigator.

The difference between quota sampling and stratified random sampling lies precisely in how cases are selected once quotas have been set. In stratified random sampling, the requisite number of cases within each stratum must be drawn by simple random sampling. But in quota sampling, the quota of cases within a stratum may be filled in whatever way the investigator chooses. Each stratum in a quota sample thus constitutes a convenience sample of the corresponding stratum of the population (Chein, 1981:426); moreover, the total sample is also a convenience sample, albeit one that resembles the population with respect to some key characteristics.

The quota method assumes that a sample that agrees with the population in important characteristics should be like the population in other ways as well. Experience has shown, however, that this is an unsafe assumption. Interviewers allowed to self-select respondents are subject to several kinds of bias. If left to their own devices, they will interview their friends in excessive proportions; they also have been known to fill quotas by concentrating on areas where there are large numbers of potential respondents, such as transportation or entertainment centers, college campuses, business districts (Chein, 1981:426). When quotas are filled by home visits, interviewers tend to select houses that are perceived as more attractive or as housing persons with relatively high income (Carter, Troldahl, and Schuneman, 1963). The potential biases in such procedures are obvious: friends are likely to resemble closely the interviewers themselves; people who gravitate to population centers may differ sharply from those who do not; and a preference for nicer neighborhoods and homes will almost certainly create a strong socioeconomic bias. Thus, representative quotas on some characteristics do not ensure representation on others.

For some years prior to the election forecast failure in 1948 (see Box 6.1), quota sampling was the predominant sampling design in opinion surveys. Also, in spite of its problems, it continues to be used by market research and opinion survey organizations, chiefly because it is cheaper and quicker than probability sampling.[5] To reduce the hazards of the quota technique, investigators have introduced tight geographic controls, specifying the section of the city, block, and even household where respondents may be selected. This will not eliminate sample biases entirely, but it does refine quota sampling to the point that it "is clearly superior to loose judgment or convenience samples" (Sudman, 1976:200).

Combined Probability and Nonprobability Sampling

In addition to the above "pure" forms, it is possible to combine probability and nonprobability sampling in one design whenever sampling is carried out in stages (Chein, 1981:438–439). Cases can be selected according to nonprobability procedures at one stage and by probability procedures at another. Two combinations are common in social research. The first involves multistage probability sampling of clusters, with a quota sampling of individual respondents at the final stage. Thus, one might "select a probability sample of counties in a state; within each of these counties, a probability sample of neighborhoods; and within each of the selected neighborhoods, a quota sample controlled for, say, age and sex" (Chein, 1981:438). While sometimes called "probability sampling with quotas," such a design produces, strictly speaking, a *non*probability (quota) sample—with geographic restrictions that sharply reduce interviewer selection bias.

The second type of mixed sampling design reverses the first strategy by drawing a probability sample of cases within a nonprobability (purposive) sample of areas. For example, in a study of crime and deterrence, Tittle (1980) surveyed the population aged 15 and older in New Jersey, Iowa, and Oregon. Within each state, he drew a probability sample of respondents. But the states themselves formed a purposive national sample, carefully selected to represent various degrees of urbanization and industrialization and to avoid unusual age, gender, and racial distributions. With this design, mathematical sampling theory applies to inferences from each probability sample to its respective state population, while more risky investigator judgment must be used in making generalizations to the total population.

Factors Affecting Choice of Sampling Design

Now that we have examined the basic sampling designs, let us look more closely at some of the factors that enter into the researcher's selection of an appropriate design. Which sampling design is adopted depends on several preliminary considerations:

1. What is the stage of research?
2. How will the data be used?
3. What are the available resources for drawing the sample?
4. How will the data be collected?

As you will see, these considerations are interrelated and vary in their relative importance in affecting the choice of a sampling design.

Stage of Research and Data Use

The first two considerations—stage of research and data use—dictate how accurate the sample must be as a description of the population (Sudman, 1976). Accuracy is least important in the exploratory phases of research, when the goal is to discover interesting patterns and generate hypotheses for later study. In fact, under these circumstances, generalizing to a specified population and estimating sample precision are usually unimportant or irrelevant. The researcher often must rely on his or her judgment in drawing a sample and may end up selecting cases for such reasons as availability or willingness to participate in one's research; therefore, convenience or purposive sampling is appropriate.

Accuracy would appear to be most important in large-scale fact-finding studies that provide input for major policy decisions. Perhaps the best example of this is the aforementioned Current Population Survey (CPS). The CPS is the only up-to-date source of information on a number of important characteristics of the total population—providing, for example, monthly estimates of unemployment and employment. As Sudman (1976:3) notes, "major government economic and welfare programs are influenced by changes of a few tenths of a percent in CPS data from month to month." Consequently, a very large (approximately 60,000) and carefully controlled probability sample is necessary to guarantee a high degree of precision.

Obviously, the desired level of precision in most studies lies somewhere in between exploratory data gathering and the CPS. The important point here is that the researcher must have some sense of how good the sample must be in order to meet the objectives of the research. For example, if you need to assess opinions about student government among students at your school for the purpose of documenting support for government reforms, then a haphazard, poor-quality sample would be inappropriate. You would need to make sure that the sample is adequate for the task of making reasonably accurate generalizations about the student population. On the other hand, if you merely wanted to get some sense of the variability in opinions about student government, for a class project, then a small-scale convenience sample would suffice.

Available Resources

If sample accuracy were the sole criterion, then selecting an appropriate sampling design would be a simple matter of using the procedure that yields the most precise results. However, precision ultimately must be balanced against cost. Available resources such as time, money, materials, and personnel place limitations on how cases can be selected. The primary reason for multistage cluster sampling, as we have seen, is that it reduces time and expense due to interviewer travel and the compilation of necessary case listings. Therefore, some form of this design is recommended for all large-scale surveys. Because it requires less time, systematic sampling often is used in lieu of simple random sampling. And the popularity of quota sampling similarly rests on a critical savings in time in comparison with probability sampling.

For the student doing unfunded research, such comparisons probably seem irrelevant. The underlying message, however, is that one should make efficient use of available resources in designing one's sample. The sampling design should be appropriate for available resources, but lack of funds should not be used as an excuse for drawing a haphazard, low-quality sample. As a general rule, one should define the target population to fit the scope of the study, for if the study is small enough, then a well-designed and executed sample is possible with very limited resources.

Method of Data Collection

A common impression of sampling is that it is only a tool of survey researchers. Social scientists who employ the other major forms of data collection (experimentation, field research, and documentary research) have been seen as having a peripheral interest in sampling. The truth is, however, that all researchers must deal with case selection. The four data collection strategies simply handle the issue of sampling in different ways. As you will see in subsequent chapters, convenience sampling is the rule in experiments, which tend to use small samples drawn from readily available populations. Some form of probability sampling is found in most surveys, purposive or judgmental sampling typifies field research, and—to the extent that the population is definable—probability sampling often is used in the analysis of available data.

Factors Determining Sample Size

Having carefully defined the target population, obtained a good sampling frame, and come up with an appropriate sampling design, the researcher finally must decide on an adequate sample size. As with the choice of a sampling design, several interrelated factors affect the decision about sample size: (1) heterogeneity of the population, (2) desired precision, (3) type of sampling design, (4) available resources, and (5) number of breakdowns planned in data analysis. The most sophisticated research applications enter these factors into mathematical equations for determining sample size. Such technical matters are, of course, largely beyond the scope of this book. Still, we think it is important to understand some of the statistical sampling theory underlying sample size considerations. The few mathematical principles that we introduce in the following discussion apply directly to simple random sampling. However, they also apply, in a more complex fashion than we discuss, to other forms of probability sampling, and, in both a logical and intuitive sense, to nonprobability sampling designs.[6]

Population Heterogeneity

Heterogeneity refers to the degree of dissimilarity (and conversely, homogeneity to the degree of similarity) among cases with respect to a particular characteristic. In general, the more heterogeneous the population with respect to the characteristic being studied, the more cases required to yield a reliable sample estimate. The logic of this principle can be seen by considering the extremes: if all cases were exactly alike, a sample of one case would suffice; and if no two cases were alike on a given characteristic, then only a complete census could satisfactorily represent the population.

The populations studied by social scientists are rarely uniform on any characteristic; indeed, it is their natural heterogeneity that compels us to sample in the first place. The degree of heterogeneity or variability depends on the specific population and variable in question. In a study of a college student population, political attitudes should be more heterogeneous, and therefore require a larger sample, than attitudes toward higher education. On the other hand, both of these sets of attitudes (or variables) should be more heterogeneous, and therefore require an even larger sample, in an urban population than in a college population.

The best statistical measure of population heterogeneity for a quantitative variable is the *standard deviation*, conventionally symbolized by the Greek letter sigma (σ). There is a direct link between this measure and the concept of standard error, introduced earlier in our discussion of probability sampling theory. The standard error, recall, indicates the degree of error or reliability of a sample estimate (the "average" amount by which a sample estimate deviates from the population value it estimates). The formula used to calculate the standard error is $\sigma/\sqrt{N}$, that is, the standard deviation divided by the square root of the sample size N. From this formula, one can see that the standard error is directly related to the heterogeneity of the population as measured by σ and inversely related to sample size. Also, the formula itself is a statement of the first principle regarding sample size: the greater the heterogeneity of the population, the larger the sample necessary to achieve a given level of reliability.

Desired Precision

Technically speaking, precision refers to the degree of variability or error in a sample estimate, hence, to the standard error. Intuitively, however, the concept of precision is perhaps best conveyed by relating it to the size of the confidence interval used to estimate a population value. Thus it is more precise to say that the average number of beers consumed is likely to fall between 2.0 and 4.0 than to say that the average is likely to fall between 1.0 and 5.0. For a given confidence level (say, 95 percent), the size of the confidence interval is directly related to the standard error; that is, the smaller the standard error, the smaller the confidence interval and the *more* precise the sample estimate. Of course, the larger the sample, the smaller the standard error. Therefore, it follows that the larger the sample, the greater the precision of the sample estimate.

Two facts about this relationship are especially noteworthy because they defy intuition to a certain extent. First, ordinarily it is the absolute size of the sample rather than the proportion of the population sampled that determines precision. As long as the population is relatively large, the proportion of the population sampled has a negligible effect on precision. For example, in 1980 the population of Vermont was a little over 500,000 and the population of Massachusetts was about 5.7 million. Now, if one were to take a simple random sample of 2000 in each of these states, the sample proportion of the total population would be 1 of every 250 persons in Vermont and 1 of every 2850 persons in Massachusetts. Yet, based on these samples, an estimate (say, of average income) would be just about as precise for Massachusetts as for Vermont.

We can get a mathematical understanding of this relationship by reexamining the formula for the standard error. Although the formula given above shows that the standard error is determined only by the standard deviation and sample size, this formula actually applies to populations of theoretically infinite size. For finite populations, the formula should be multiplied by a correction factor equal to $\sqrt{1-f}$, where f is the *sampling fraction*, or proportion of the population included in the sample (Kish, 1965:43–44). Notice, however, that if the sampling fraction is very near zero, then the correction factor becomes $\sqrt{1}$, or 1, which has no effect on the standard error. In most practical examples, the population is so much larger than the sample that f is extremely small—near zero—and the correction factor can be ignored. Only with small populations would we expect f to be much larger than zero; however, for a small population, a small f implies a small sample size, and it is the latter that has the greater impact on the standard error.

While precision is governed primarily by the absolute numerical size of the sample rather than the proportion of the population sampled, the sample need not be

TABLE 6.5. Standard Error of a
Percentage of 50 Percent,
Broken Down by Sample Size[a]

Sample size	Standard error (percent)
100	5.0
400	2.5
2,500	1.0
10,000	0.5

[a]Standard errors are smaller for percentages greater than or less than 50 percent.

enormous in size to yield very precise results. This is the second crucial fact about precision and sample size. The sampling error tends to be quite small for a sample of size 2000–3000, and increasing the sample size beyond this number decreases the error by so little that it usually is not worth the additional cost.

The mathematical explanation for this once again can be found in the standard error formula. Notice that the standard error goes down as the *square root* of the sample size goes up. Because of the square root function, each time we wish to decrease the standard error by one-half we must increase the sample size fourfold. At this rate, the precision gained with increased sample size reaches a point of minute, diminishing returns after a few thousand units. Consider, for example, how sample size affects the standard error of a percentage, such as the estimated percentage of the vote a candidate will receive in an election. With two candidates and an evenly split vote, the standard error will be 5.0 percent for a sample size of 100. This error decreases to 2.5 percent when the sample reaches 400, and 1.0 percent when the sample reaches 2500, as Table 6.5 shows. To get the error down to 0.5 of 1 percent would require a sample of size 10,000.

The reader should now begin to understand how election forecasters can make accurate predictions using samples of a few thousand out of millions of voters. The huge size of the population has no effect on the precision of sample estimates. And a sample size of 2000–3000 is large enough to predict accurately all but the closest elections.

We hasten to add that 2000–3000 should not be regarded as *the* standard size for reliable sample results. Not only does sample size depend on factors other than precision, but necessary levels of precision also vary widely from one study to the next. At one extreme, the CPS requires a sample of some 60,000 housing units, a sample "large enough so that the sampling errors of the total estimates of unemployment are only about 0.1%" (Sudman, 1976:3). At the other extreme, 30 cases generally is regarded as minimally adequate for statistical data analysis, although most social researchers would probably recommend at least 100.

Sampling Design

The type of sampling design also affects decisions about sample size. Recall that one way of increasing precision other than selecting a larger sample is to use stratified rather than simple random sampling. In other words, for the same level of precision a stratified random sample requires fewer cases than a simple random sample. A cluster sample, on the other hand, requires a somewhat larger number of cases for precision equal to that of a simple random sample. A nonmathematical explanation for these comparisons rests on the concept of heterogeneity.

Remember that stratified random sampling provides greater sampling efficiency (or precision) when the stratifying variable is related to the dependent variable of interest. Such correlation means that a good deal of the population heterogeneity resides in differences between the strata, and each stratum tends to be relatively homogeneous. With respect to beer consumption, for example, there is much less variability among males or among females than between males and females. By sampling every stratum, the effect of stratified random sampling is to eliminate this *between* source of heterogeneity, leaving only the variation within the strata. Because of their homogeneity, each stratum requires a relatively small sample.

Although cluster sampling has the advantage of low cost, it lacks efficiency in precision. In two-stage cluster sampling, for example, there is variability both between and within the clusters. By sampling among the clusters the "between source" of heterogeneity that was eliminated in stratified sampling is still present in cluster sampling. (For this reason, we want clusters to be heterogeneous compared to differences between the clusters—just the opposite of the strategy in stratified sampling.) If the variability between clusters tends to be large compared to the variability within the clusters, then the sampling error could be considerable, depending on how many clusters are selected. Furthermore, each stage in a multi-stage cluster design contributes a source of variability or error to the total sample; consequently, the more stages, the larger the total sampling error tends to be, and the larger the sample required for a given level of precision.

Available Resources

Each individual case requires an expenditure of available resources. Consequently, at some point cost must enter into the equation for determining sample size. When a fixed amount of money and/or time has been allocated for a project, Sudman (1976:88–89) offers the following rule of thumb for survey research: allocate one half of both money and time to data collection (and the other half to data analysis). Once the data collection procedure is specified, then the sample size can be determined on a time and cost per case basis. That is, the number of cases will be equal to the total time for data collection divided by the time per case or the total funds for data collection divided by the cost per case.

Number of Breakdowns Planned

The number of variables and variable categories into which the data are to be grouped and analyzed also must be taken into account in determining sample size. In general, the more breakdowns planned in the analysis—the more complex the relationships under investigation or the more distinct subcategories of separate interest—the larger the sample must be. Consider, for example, what happens when a sample of 1000 is divided into males/females, then into blacks/whites, then into people over/under 18 years of age, then into urban/rural residence. If we were interested in describing rural black young men, we might find that a breakdown of the 1000 cases looks something like this:

Sample	1000
Males	489
Black males	60
Young black males	20
Rural young black males	4

With just four cases available, the sample clearly would be too small for a reliable analysis of this particular subgroup. To avoid this kind of problem, it is important to estimate the number of breakdowns during the data analysis and to make sure that the total sample size will provide enough cases in each subcategory. If the requisite sample size turns out to be rather large, then it might be more efficient to sample the relevant subcategories separately, as in stratified and quota sampling.

Other Considerations

In sections on probability sampling and sample size considerations, we spoke repeatedly of sampling error—the deviation of a sample estimate from the true population value. The sampling error referred to in our discussions is random error, produced by the random selection of elements. Though unavoidable in sampling, this error can be estimated and reduced by increasing the size or efficiency of one's sample. There is, however, another type of sampling error, called sample bias,[7] which is nonrandom, difficult to detect, and often much more damaging to sample accuracy.

In probability sampling designs, the two most common sources of *sample bias* are incomplete sampling frames and incomplete data collection. As an example of the first problem, we mentioned earlier that telephone directories provide inadequate sampling frames to the extent that they exclude the poor who cannot afford telephones and the more wealthy who tend to have unlisted numbers. The second problem arises when through refusals to cooperate, unreturned questionnaires, missing records, or some other means, the sample turns out to be a fraction of the number of cases originally selected for observation. The crux of this problem is that nonobservations tend to differ in systematic ways from observations. Thus in surveys, mail surveys in particular, highly educated respondents are more likely to cooperate than poorly educated ones. Also, those who feel most strongly about the topics or issues of a study are more likely to respond than those in the middle.

Obviously, the researcher should do everything possible to avoid such biases. With respect to incomplete sampling, this may entail several call-backs to not-at-home respondents, three or four mailings of questionnaires, or interview follow-ups of respondents not returning questionnaires. Despite such efforts, however, in virtually all surveys some respondents designated for the sample ultimately will not be included. With probability sampling, the greater the proportion of this nonresponse, the greater the likelihood of bias. Therefore, it is very important to pay attention to response rates. For interview surveys, a response rate of 85 percent or more is quite good; 70 percent is minimally adequate; below 70 percent there is a serious chance of bias. In questionnaire surveys, response rates tend to be about 20 percent lower than in comparable interview surveys. (For a further discussion of response rates, see chapter 9.)

The manner of selecting cases in research determines to whom the results of the research may be applied. However, the issue of generalizability pertains not just to units of analysis but to all features of research, including the time of the study, the research setting, and the operational definitions. We might ask, for example, whether the same results would be obtained if a different set of questions were asked, if the study were conducted in a different place or at a different time of day or year. One reason that we have dealt here exclusively with generalizing over units of analysis is that this is the primary generalization issue addressed in social science research. This is particularly true of survey studies, in which the sampling of units is such an integral part of the research design that such studies are often called "sample surveys." Survey researchers are also largely responsible for the development of many of the sampling techniques discussed in this chapter. So, it is no wonder that many of our examples came from survey studies and typically involved people as units. Just keep in mind that the issue of generalization is not limited to units of analysis, nor is the sampling of units solely the province of survey research.

Summary

Sampling is the process of selecting a subset of cases in order to draw conclusions about the entire set. Sampling is unavoidable given the scientific goal of generalization; and it requires special attention in social research given the inherent variability of social units of analysis. Sometimes sampling can yield more accurate information than "complete" enumerations of the population. Still, even if this were never true, we would still sample because it is usually impossible for practical reasons to examine all cases, and observing a sample of cases is simply more efficient anyway: it saves time and money and can be as accurate as research purposes demand.

Prior to sampling one must select the unit of analysis. Sampling then begins with a description of the target population, the collection of units about which one wishes to generalize. For sampling to be feasible, the target population should be defined by objective criteria that clearly indicate its limits of inclusion. Even then, there is often an imperfect fit between the target population and the sampling frame, which consists either of a list of cases from which the sample is actually selected or of a rule defining membership that provides a basis for case selection.

The procedure for selecting a sample is called the sampling design. The major distinction among designs is between probability and nonprobability sampling. Probability sampling is based on a process of random selection, which gives each case in the population an equal chance of being included in the sample. This process, which is absent from nonprobability sampling, eliminates investigator bias in selecting cases and permits the application of mathematical probability theory for estimating sample accuracy.

Probability sampling designs include simple random sampling, stratified random sampling, cluster sampling, and systematic sampling. In simple random sampling, random selection from the entire population makes it equally possible to draw any combination of cases. The distribution of a statistical property for all possible combinations of random samples of a fixed size is called the sampling distribution. A given sample estimate differs from the population value estimated by an amount known as the sampling error; an index of the size of such errors in a given sampling distribution is called the standard error. In general, the larger the sample, the smaller the standard error. To take into account random sampling error, researchers use interval estimates, called confidence intervals, in making inferences from a sample to its population.

In stratified random sampling, the population is divided into strata and independent random samples are drawn from each stratum. The number of cases in each stratum of the sample may be either proportionate or disproportionate to the number of cases in the population. Stratifying improves sampling efficiency, provided that the stratifying variable is related to the variable under study and that the cost of stratifying is low compared to the cost of increasing sample size. It also may be used to increase the number of cases in certain variable categories that would prove too small if a simple random sample were drawn.

In cluster sampling, the population is divided into natural groupings or areas, called clusters, and a random sample of clusters is drawn. When this is done in stages, as it usually is, moving from larger to smaller clusters, it is referred to as multistage sampling. Clustering reduces the costs of interviewer travel and sampling frame construction, but it does so at a loss of sample precision. Systematic sampling, which often provides a reasonable approximation to simple random sampling, consists of selecting cases from an available list at a fixed interval after a random start.

Nonprobability sampling designs include convenience, purposive, and quota samples. Convenience sampling is a rubric for various nonrandom and unsystematic processes of case selection that offer no basis for generalizing. Purposive sampling involves the careful selection of typical cases or of cases that represent relevant dimensions of the population. Quota sampling allocates quotas of cases for various strata and then allows for the nonrandom selection of cases to fill the quotas. While this procedure has been abused in the past, it can be used effectively in combination with probability sampling and with tight controls on respondent selection.

Factors affecting the choice of a sampling design include (1) the stage of research and data use, with research in later stages intended to provide accurate population description requiring the most sophisticated probability sampling designs; (2) available resources such as time, money, and personnel; and (3) the method of data collection. In general, the more heterogeneous the population, the greater the desired precision and available resources, and the larger the number of breakdowns planned during the data analysis, the larger the sample should be. Holding sample size constant, one will generally get the greatest precision with a stratified sample, followed by a simple random sample, and then a cluster sample.

Key Terms

population
sample
nonresponse bias
target population
sampling frame
sampling design
probability sampling
   simple random sampling
   stratified random sampling
   cluster sampling
   systematic sampling
random selection
biased selection
table of random numbers
sampling distribution
sampling error

standard error
confidence interval
stratum
disproportionate stratified sampling
multistage sampling
primary sampling unit
sampling interval
nonprobability sampling
   convenience sampling
   purposive sampling
   quota sampling
heterogeneity
standard deviation
sampling fraction
sample bias

Review Questions and Problems

1. Give three reasons for sampling.

2. Why is a sample sometimes more accurate than a census of the population?

3. What were the principal reasons for the failures of the *Literary Digest* presidential poll of 1936 and the Gallup presidential poll of 1948?

4. Describe the two-step process involved in population definition.

5. How does one go about constructing a sampling frame?

6. In judging sample quality, why do social researchers prefer to assess the quality of the sampling design rather than sample representativeness?

7. Briefly distinguish between probability and nonprobability sampling.

8. When is case selection biased? How do researchers meet the requirement of random selection?

9. What is the defining property of a simple random sample?

10. How can one increase the probable accuracy of a simple random sample?

11. When is stratified random sampling more efficient than simple random sampling?

12. When is it advantageous, or even necessary, to employ *dis*proportionate stratified random sampling?

13. Explain the difference between a single-stage cluster sample and a stratified random sample.

14. What is the primary reason for using cluster sampling?

15. Assuming relatively homogeneous clusters, how can one reduce sampling error in a cluster sampling design?

16. What are the advantages and hazards of systematic sampling?

17. Explain how a systematic sample may approximate a stratified random sample.

18. When is nonprobability sampling justified?

19. What is the difference between convenience and purposive sampling?

20. What is the difference between quota sampling and stratified random sampling?

21. What are some of the potential biases in quota sampling?

22. How can one combine probability and nonprobability sampling within the same sampling design?

23. List four considerations affecting the selection of a sampling design and briefly indicate *how* each affects design selection.

24. Identify the five factors to consider in determining sample size. How does each factor affect the decision about sample size?

25. Because of your developing expertise about social research, someone approaches you and asks, "What proportion of the population should I sample to give me adequate precision?" How would you respond to this question?

26. What are the two most common sources of sample bias?

27. Indicate the type of sample that you think is most appropriate for each of the following research objectives, and state the rationale for your choice.

    a. A study of the career plans of sociology majors at your college or university

    b. An in-depth study of the gay community in Boston to determine their social and psychological characteristics

    c. A national survey of Democrats' favored candidates for the next presidential election

28. (Adapted from Kiecolt, 1978). This exercise will help familiarize you with some types of probability sampling. First, using the "A" section of the latest issue of your campus telephone directory as a starting point, draw up a sampling frame composed of the first fifty names listed.

    a. *Simple random sample*. Using your sampling frame and the list of random numbers in Table 6.1, select a random sample of ten names. List all the random numbers you use, even those that are not matched with names (i.e., random numbers beyond 50), and circle each number that is matched with a name. Now list the ten names in your sample. Repeat this procedure in drawing a random sample of five names.

    b. *Stratified systematic sample*. Divide the names in your sampling frame into strata on the basis of gender. Begin with a random start, and indicate the random number in each stratum with which you began. Then select a 1/5 systematic sample within each stratum. List the names that you obtain.

29. You would like to do a survey of students on your campus to find out how much time on the average they spend studying per week. You obtain from the registrar a list of all students currently enrolled and draw your sample from this list.

    a. What is your sampling frame?

    b. What is your target population?

    c. Explain how you would draw a simple random sample for this study.

    d. Assume that the registrar's list also contains information about each student's major. One then could select a stratified random sample, stratifying on major. What main benefit can result from using a stratified random sample instead of a simple random sample? Would you expect this benefit to be obtained by stratifying on major? Explain.

e. How might you obtain a cluster sample? When should you consider using this type of sampling design?

f. Which type of sampling design is most appropriate for this research problem? Explain.

30. Now you want to find out the same information (as in question 29) for all college students in the state of Massachusetts. To do so you obtain a list of all 4-year and community colleges in the state. As a first step you draw a random sample of colleges. Then you get a list of students enrolled in each of the colleges you selected in the first step. Finally, you draw a random sample of students from these lists.

a. What type of sample is this?

b. A significant proportion of students in 4-year colleges go to a few large schools in the state (e.g., University of Massachusetts, Boston University, Northeastern). If you were to give each school in your first stage of sampling an equal chance of being selected, you might not obtain any of the larger schools (because there are more smaller than larger schools). This could create problems in obtaining an accurate estimate of the time students spend studying since larger schools may require more (or less?) work. How would you resolve this problem while still drawing a probability sample?

31. Refer to the article from *Social Forces* that you used in question 30 of chapter 5.

a. Describe the sampling procedures employed in the study reported in this article. Did the authors use one of the sampling designs reported in this chapter? If so, which one?

b. What is the target population? What is the sampling frame? Does the sampling frame provide a good fit with the target population?

c. What particular sampling problems (e.g., incomplete lists, missing cases, nonresponses), if any, did the authors encounter? How were these problems dealt with?

NOTES

1. Two dramatic examples of this problem are the military draft lotteries of 1940 and 1970. Statistical analyses convincingly have shown that both lotteries were biased, apparently due to the failure of physical mixing to achieve randomness (Fienberg, 1971). The 1970 lottery, based on birthdays, was set up in the following way: 366 cylindrical capsules with rounded ends were used; slips of paper with the January dates were inserted in 31 capsules and placed in a large, square wooden box; the February dates were then placed in the box and mixed with the January dates, and this procedure was repeated for each of the remaining months, in turn; the box then was shut and shaken several times; finally, the 366 capsules were poured from the box into a large bowl, from whence they were drawn. When the lottery drawing sequence was analyzed, it was shown that the sequence was not random, but rather a reflection of "the order in which capsules were placed in the wooden box during the initial mixing procedure" (Fienberg, 1971:260). As a result, those with birthdays in the later

months of the year had lower lottery numbers, hence were more likely to be drafted, than those with birthdays in the early months of the year.

2. This example is modeled after presentations by Slonim (1957, 1960) and Chein (1981).

3. If each one of a set of events is equally likely to occur, then the probability of any one event occurring is defined as one divided by the number of events. Assuming a perfect coin, for example, we have two events—a head and a tail—with the probability of one event (say, a head) in a single flip equal to 1/2.

4. Another problem with cluster sampling is that, except for rare cases in which clusters are equal in size, the probabilities of case selection may vary widely from cluster to cluster. Consequently, estimates of population characteristics require some rather complex statistical solutions, which are beyond the scope of this book.

5. To obtain all the cases selected in a probability sample may require several call-backs to predesignated respondents who are not at home. However, call-backs are not necessary in a quota sample, as anyone meeting the relevant quota criteria may be selected. For this reason interviewing can be completed more quickly and at lower cost in quota studies.

6. Inferences from samples to populations are essentially inductive generalizations (see chapter 3). Consequently, the same factors that affect the strength of inductive generalizations affect the quality of a sample. Compare, for example, the discussions of sample size, heterogeneity, and desired precision (below) with the five factors affecting the strength of inductive generalizations discussed in chapter 3.

7. These two types of error—random sampling error and sample bias—are analogous to random and systematic measurement error.

III

METHODS OF DATA COLLECTION

The chapters in this section cover the four most distinctive and widely used approaches to social research: experiments, surveys, field research, and research using available data. Which of these basic approaches an investigator decides to take may be determined by many things: the nature of the research problem, research goals, available resources, disciplinary and personal preferences. All too often the choice is bound to a particular theoretical perspective, which makes the researcher unduly committed to one means of making observations. Indeed, each of these approaches has developed largely independently of the others, and as a consequence, tends to have its own distinctive terminology for describing various features of the method. This is reflected, for example, in the terms applied to units of analysis, which are labeled variously as "subjects" (experiments), "respondents" (surveys), "informants" (field research), and "items" (available data research).

Once a given approach is selected, it has an overriding effect on nearly every other facet of the research, from measurement and sampling to data analysis. Thus, even though we already have dealt broadly with elements of research design, in the following chapters we will return again and again to design issues. In fact, we devote whole chapters to technical design features of experiments (chapter 8) and surveys (chapter 10). Otherwise, our principal aim in the four main chapters (7, 9, 11, and 12) is to describe each approach's unique process of executing a study. Then, in chapter 13, concluding this section, we present some strategies for using a combination of methods and approaches.

7

Experimentation

People readily associate the term "experiment" with scientific research. Typically they have read about or conducted experiments in elementary and high-school science courses. Many have learned that experimentation is the hallmark of "the scientific method." In fact, we have found that some students refer to any scientific study as an experiment. This usage of the term, however, is technically incorrect and can be misleading. For as you will see, in social research "experiment" is reserved to denote studies with several distinctive features.

The key features of the experimental approach are manipulation and control. In order to test hypotheses, the experimenter deliberately manipulates or introduces changes into the environment of subjects and observes or measures the effects of the changes. Because greater control is exercised over the conditions of observation than in any other research strategy, experiments more effectively eliminate the possibility of extraneous variables offering alternative interpretations of research findings. For this reason, experimental studies long have been regarded as the optimal way to test causal hypotheses. Even when a "true" experiment is impractical or impossible and some other approach must be used, the logic of experimentation serves as a standard by which other research strategies are judged.

In this chapter we introduce the essential features and causal logic of experiments as found in social research. We outline the process of "staging" an experiment, and then discuss the social nature of experiments, including ways to prevent this from adversely affecting their scientific value. Finally, we discuss some variants of the experimental approach: experiments conducted in natural settings, the application of experimental design to social surveys, and the use of units of analysis other than individuals.

The Logic of Experimentation

The main reason for doing experiments is to test a hypothesis that one variable causes a change in another variable. Thus all experiments possess certain basic requirements that permit strong inferences about cause and effect. Research designs that fill these requirements are called "true experimental designs"; those that do not, which are discussed in chapter 8, are called "preexperimental" or "quasi-experimental designs." In this section we focus on the logic of experimentation by first identifying those essential features that make true experiments a model for testing causal relationships, and then relating these features to the criteria for inferring causality.

Testing Causal Relations

The basic features of an experimental design are nicely illustrated by a simplified version of Page's study (1958) of teacher comments and subsequent student performance. Page wanted to determine whether teacher comments written on test papers would motivate students to improve their scores on the next test. (This seems like a relevant question to study in view of the hours teachers spend writing comments on students' papers!) To conduct the experiment, teacher "Smith" gave one of her classes a scheduled objective test and scored the tests in her usual way, assigning grades A through F. Then she assigned the test papers, by tossing a coin, to one of two piles. One pile of papers received the experimental treatment, a specified comment that depended on the letter grade, as follows (Page, 1958:174):

A: Excellent! Keep it up.
B: Good work. Keep at it.
C: Perhaps try to do still better?
D: Let's bring this up.
F: Let's raise this grade!

Papers assigned to the second pile received no comment, providing a control group. The effect of the comments on student performance was judged by comparing the scores of students in the two groups on a subsequent test given and scored in the usual way. Results showed that the group that had received the written comments scored higher on the second test than the group that had received no comments.

What basic features of an experimental design are illustrated in the foregoing experiment? A *manipulated* independent variable, referred to as the *treatment* (teacher comments on the first test), is *followed by* a measured dependent variable (student performance on the second test). There are two groups: one receives the experimental treatment, and another, the control, does not receive the treatment. Except for this experimental manipulation, the treatment and control groups are treated *exactly alike* to avoid introducing extraneous variables and their effects. Finally, subjects (or in this case their first test papers) are assigned to one or the other group *randomly*.

How do these features meet the requirements of causal inference? While we can never prove beyond all doubt that two variables (say, X and Y) are causally related, recall that certain types of empirical evidence are regarded as essential for causal statements: (1) association (i.e., evidence that X and Y vary together in a way predicted by the hypothesis); (2) direction of influence (evidence that X affected Y rather than Y affected X); and (3) the elimination of plausible rival explanations (evidence that variables other than X did not cause the observed change in Y). The first two kinds of evidence show that X could have affected Y; the third kind shows that the relation between X and Y is nonspurious—that other variables are not responsible for the observed effects. Let us refer back to our simplification of Page's experiment to see how these types of evidence were provided.

1. *Association.* It was found that the independent variable, teacher comments, was associated with the dependent variable, scores on the subsequent test, in the manner hypothesized. That is, the treatment group, which received comments, scored higher on the test than the control group, which received no comments.

2. *Direction of influence.* Evidence that the independent variable (X) influenced the dependent variable (Y) and not the other way around is based on time order in experiments: Y cannot be the cause of X if it occurred after X. In the above experiment, we know that the subsequent test scores (Y) could not have caused or affected the teacher comments (X), because the experimenter made sure that the comments occurred first.

3. *Elimination of rival explanations.* What might be plausible reasons why one group of students would score higher than another group on a test? Personal qualities such as intelligence and motivation might have an effect; experiences such as having a cold on the test day, missing breakfast, or being in love also might affect individual scores. These extraneous variables are controlled by random assignment of persons to the treatment and control groups. *Random assignment* means that the procedure by which subjects are assigned (in this case, by tossing a coin) ensures that each subject has an equal chance of being in either group. By virtue of random assignment, individual characteristics or experiences that might confound the results will be about evenly distributed between the two groups. Thus, the number of students who are bright or dull, motivated or unmotivated, fully nourished or hungry, in love or not in love, and so forth, should be about the same in each group.

In addition to controlling preexperimental differences through random assignment, the researcher makes every attempt to ensure that both groups are treated exactly alike during the experiment except for the experimental treatment that one group receives. In the Page experiment the tests given, time of testing, and intervening classroom experiences were the same for both groups. Examples of violations of this principle would have been if the treatment and control groups had not had the same teacher or if students had been told that they were in an experimental or control group.

In an airtight experimental design, there is only one rival explanation: the results could have occurred by chance. This would mean that the process of randomly assigning persons to the experimental and control groups resulted, by chance, in an unequal distribution between the groups of variables related to test performance, such as intelligence, interest in school, and health. The lower test scores of the control group in the Page experiment, for example, could have resulted from the chance assignment of fewer of the brighter students to this group than to the treatment group.

To assess the likelihood that the results of an experiment could have occurred by chance, a statistical procedure called a *test of statistical significance* is used. Such tests express the likelihood or probability of a chance difference in decimal form. Thus, when we read that the results of an experiment were found to be significant at the .05 level, this means that only about 5 percent of the time, or 5 times in 100, would differences this large between the experimental and control groups occur by chance when the experimental variable actually has no effect. With such a low probability it would be reasonable to rule out prior differences uncontrolled by the randomization process as a plausible rival explanation of the experimental results. On the other hand, if the results were not found to be statistically significant, then it would not be reasonable to rule out differences due to chance assignment and we could not have much confidence that the experimental treatment caused the effects. In short, a statistical test of significance is used to assess the likelihood that the observed differences between the groups is real (significant) and not of a magnitude that would occur frequently by chance.[1]

Matching and Random Assignment

Some researchers attempt to eliminate prior differences between groups by *matching* subjects on characteristics that logically seem to be related to the experimental outcome. If, for example, an experimenter wanted to learn which of two methods of teaching Russian is most effective, potential students for the two language methods groups might be matched on variables such as grade-point average and verbal aptitude test scores. For each student with, say, above-average verbal aptitude and average grades, a second student who scored very nearly the same on the two variables would have to be found. Then, each matched pair would be split so that one of the pair would be in each group, thus assuring that the composition of the groups would be highly similar on the matching variables.

The reader should note carefully that matching should be used in conjunction with and *not* as a substitute for randomization. Matching is a powerful technique whose object is similar to that of stratification in random sampling: to increase the efficiency of the experimental design by creating treatment groups that are similar with respect to characteristics related to the dependent variable. However, matching on some characteristics does not guarantee an equal distribution on other possibly relevant extraneous variables. For example, in the study of language teaching methods, another variable that might affect the learning of a foreign language is auditory discrimination, the ability to discriminate similar sounds. Only with randomization can one be sure of the approximate equivalence on *all* extraneous variables, including those unknown to the researcher.

One problem with matching is that, unless the pool from which the subjects are drawn is extremely large, it may be difficult to find enough pairs of subjects who scored alike on the relevant variables to make up similar matched groups. In other words, it may be difficult to form treatment groups large enough to produce reliable results. This is especially the case when more than one or two matching variables are involved.

There are several ways to assign subjects randomly to experimental and control groups. The method previously mentioned was tossing a coin for each subject; "heads" meant one group and "tails" the other. For experiments with more than two groups we recommend using the table of random numbers, described in chapter 6. After numbering each group in the experiment, assign each subject to a group according to the number selected from the table. If matching procedures are used, then one should first match subjects on relevant variables and then randomly assign the members of each matched pair to different groups.

A final word of caution relates to the difference between the random assignment of subjects in experiments and the random selection of cases in probability sampling. While both processes invoke randomness, they occur at different points in the research process and serve different purposes. Sampling occurs first, for example, when a pool of subjects is selected for an experiment; although random sampling facilitates inferences from sample to population, it is seldom used in experiments. Random assignment occurs after the sample has been selected, when subjects are assigned to different experimental groups; its function is to make groups approximately equal on all uncontrolled extraneous variables, and it is an essential aspect of true experiments.

Internal and External Validity

The Page study possessed all the basic requirements of a true experiment. Besides random assignment, these included the manipulation of the independent variable, a measure of the dependent variable, at least one comparison or "control" group (i.e., at least two groups—experimental and comparison), and, excluding experimental manipulations, the constancy of conditions across groups. Experiments with these minimum characteristics, which provide relatively sound evidence of a causal relationship, will be generally high in *internal validity*. We will have more to say about this in chapter 8; suffice it to say here that an experiment is internally valid to the extent that it rules out the possibility that extraneous variables, rather than the manipulated independent variable, are responsible for the observed outcome of the study. As we saw in the Page study, experiments eliminate rival explanations associated with extraneous variables in two ways. First, effects of prior differences between subjects, such as personal qualities and experiences, are "neutralized" by randomly assigning subjects to treatment and control groups, thus initially assuring approximate equivalence of the groups. Second, aside from the introduction of the experimental variable, treatment and control groups are treated exactly alike, thus assuring equivalence of the groups during the experiment.

A related concern is that experiments have *external validity*. This is basically a question of generalizability, or what the experimental results mean outside of the particular context of the experiment. For example, regarding Page's study of teacher comments and student performance, we might question whether the same results would be obtained with different classes, teacher comments, subject matter, or age groups. At this point we will describe the Page study (1958) more completely, as it also provides an excellent example of an experiment high in external validity.

For his experiment, Page selected seventy-four teachers at random from twelve secondary schools (grades 7–12) in three school districts. These teachers were given detailed instructions in how to carry out the experiment, including the random selection of one of her or his classes for the experiment. This procedure ensured that the experiment would include a great variety of subject matter as well as students at every grade level. Over 1200 students participated, unaware that they were experimental subjects.

In addition to the "no comments" group (the control group) and the "specified comments" group that received the comments listed in our earlier discussion, a third group, called the "free comments" group, received whatever comments the teachers felt were appropriate in the circumstances. Random assignment of the initial set of test papers to one of the three groups was actually carried out by means of a specially marked die. The "specified comments" group scored significantly higher than the "no comments" group on the subsequent set of tests, with the "free comments" group scoring highest of all. Analysis of the data showed consistent results regardless of the particular class, school, or grade level (grades 7–12). Because of the consistency of the experimental results in different settings, with different teachers and students, we can say the experiment was high in external validity.

Sampling in Experiments

The relatively high external validity of the Page study is rare in experiments. External validity is usually very limited, especially with regard to generalizing from sample to population. Because experimental manipulation often involves a laboratory setting and/or elaborate staging, it is usually impractical either to sample subjects over wide areas or to utilize a large number of subjects. As a consequence, experimenters tend to use small samples drawn from readily available populations. In fact, because most experimentation is done in universities, very frequently the subjects are either college students (estimates run as high as 75 percent; Higbee and Wells, 1972), volunteers, or—worse yet—college students who have volunteered. Differences between college students and people in general would include average socioeconomic level, age, occupational goals, education, and interests. Differences between volunteers and nonvolunteers are also considerable (see Rosenthal and Rosnow, 1969).

With such circumscribed samples, generalizations from any one experiment are severely limited. Yet experimenters have not been too bothered by this lack of population generality. One apparent reason is that differences in subject characteristics are assumed to have no effect on subjects' reactions in the experimental situation. For example, men would be expected to react the same as women, old people the same as young people, and someone from New England the same as someone from the Southwest.

Some investigators (e.g., Festinger, 1959; Oakes, 1972) also take the position that sampling considerations are of minor importance as long as one is interested in examining the causal relationship between variables, which is the main task of experiments. In an experimental investigation of altruism, for example, the primary concern would be designing a valid test of the hypothesis under study, such as the effect of mood on helping behavior. The researcher would, of course, like to be able to generalize to a variety of persons, settings, and helping behaviors, but this is deemed less important than demonstrating the existence of a relationship between mood and helping. Once the relationship is established for a given sample of subjects, the researcher can then address, through subsequent research, the issue of whether the relationship extends to other, unsampled populations and to other settings and measures of helping.

Thus, experimenters often skirt the issue of population generality. They choose cases for convenience because this enables them to gain the necessary control over subjects required for experimentation, and they deemphasize the importance of generalizing to a population. Yet, despite the trade-off for experimental control and other justifications for convenience sampling, this is a major weakness of experimentation. If the experimenter has specified a target population of persons or settings, then a probability sampling design should be used if at all feasible. But even if the experimenter has no specific target group in mind, it is still desirable to utilize probability sampling or purposive sampling for heterogeneity to ensure that a wide range of cases is included in the study. As our discussion of inductive logic in chapter 3 revealed, the broader the range of cases included in the sample, the more generalizable the findings. Thus, the inferences that could be drawn from a study with a homogeneous sample of college sophomores enrolled in introductory psychology are far more restricted than the inferences possible from a probability sample of people from the town where the college is located. One might therefore draw the latter sample, not because it is meaningful to generalize to all residents of the town, but because the greater heterogeneity among town residents permits stronger inferences about generalizability.

The issue of external validity applies not only to samples of subjects but also to experimental settings, observers, or experimenters, and to the time of the study. Because all of these aspects limit the external validity of individual experiments, the usual strategy for increasing the generalizability of experimental findings is replication. That is, the experiment is repeated—by the same or another investigator who conducts the research at a different time, in a different setting or with slightly different procedures, or with a different sample of subjects. Indeed, the strongest argument for generality is that widely varying experimental tests have produced similar results.

Staging Experiments

Experiments are most frequently conducted in laboratory settings to which the experimenter brings subjects to have them participate in some individual or social activities. Planning and carrying out a laboratory experiment is much like producing a play. There are "scripts" to write and rewrite, a sequence of "scenes," each contributing something vital to the production, a "cast" of experimental assistants to recruit and train, "props" and "special effects," and "rehearsals." And once the stage is set, the experimenter must publicize the experiment and sell potential subjects on participation, for without an audience there can be no play.

In writing a play the playwright must consider how each scene will contribute to the success of the play; likewise a researcher designing an experiment must consider how each part of the experiment will contribute to the entire production. The basic parts of an experiment are (1) introduction to the experiment, (2) manipulation of the independent variable, (3) measurement of the dependent variable, and (4) concluding activities, which usually include a debriefing and sometimes a postexperimental interview. In order to illustrate these parts, we first summarize an experiment and then refer back to it as we describe each part.

An Example: Who Will Intervene?

Why do bystanders sometimes fail to aid people immediately in crisis situations? An experiment investigating bystander intervention in an emergency was designed by Darley and Latané (1968), who hypothesized that the more bystanders there are to an emergency, the less likely it is that any one bystander will come to the victim's assistance and the greater the amount of time that will elapse before intervention.[2] The setting was a simulated group discussion where the experimental subject witnessed (over an intercom system) and believed others to be witnessing an apparent epileptic seizure of one of the discussants.

College students served as subjects. On arrival they were met by an assistant to the experimenter who led them to a small room, seated them, and had them fill out a background information form. Each subject was then given headphones with a microphone attached and was instructed to listen for further directions. Over the intercom system the experimenter stated that the research involved the personal problems of college students and that, because of the personal nature of the discussion in which he or she would be participating, measures had been taken to minimize embarrassment for the students and to protect their privacy. First, anonymity would be preserved by their physical separation. (In reality, the separation permitted tape-recorded simulation of other subjects' participation and of the emergency.) Second, the experimenter would not be listening to the discussion but would obtain their reactions afterward. (This explanation permitted the experimenter's absence from the scene of the emergency.)

The experimenter went on to say that some organization of the discussion was necessary and that each person in turn would present his problems to the group. Next, each person in turn would respond to the others' remarks, with further discussion at the end. Each person's microphone would be on for 2 minutes and then would automatically shut off, allowing only one person to be heard at one time. (These instructions ensured that the subjects would realize two things at the time of the "emergency": that only the "victim's" microphone was on, and that they had no way to determine what the other discussants were doing.)

The simulated discussion then began. The "victim" spoke first and, among other problems, mentioned a proneness to seizures. Then the other "participants" and the subject spoke. In the second round of the discussion, the "victim" made several comments and then, after about 70 seconds, began in a distressed, and somewhat incoherent voice to ask for help, as he was having a seizure. After 125 seconds the "victim's" speech was cut off. The length of time it took the subject to report the emergency was measured from the start of the apparent epileptic fit.

The number of other people the subject believed to be in the group discussion was the major independent variable. The discussion groups (three treatment conditions) consisted of two persons (the subject and the "victim"), three persons, or 6 persons. The major dependent variable was the length of the time from the onset of the seizure until the subject left the room. If the subject did not leave the room in 6 minutes, the experiment was ended.

Subjects who left the room before 6 minutes found the experimental assistant seated in the hall. As soon as the emergency was reported, or at the end of 6 minutes, debriefing began. The real purpose of the experiment was then explained and the subject's emotional reactions discussed. Then, the subject was asked to complete a questionnaire and several personality trait scales.

Briefly, results showed that the number of discussants believed to be participating strongly affected the odds that the subject would report the incident. All subjects in the two-person groups reported the emergency, with approximately 80 percent of those in the three-person groups and 62 percent of those in the six-person groups reporting. In regard to speed of response, subjects in the three-person groups reported about as quickly as those in the two-person groups; the small difference obtained was not statistically significant. However, subjects in the six-person groups took significantly longer to report.

The experiment by Darley and Latané provides an excellent example of the work and planning involved in staging an experiment. The subject is brought into the setting where the production will take place. Appropriate "props" have been prepared and are in place: desk, chair, headphones, microphone, background information form, prerecorded tapes, chair in hallway, and additional scales and a questionnaire. There is a cast of characters. In addition to the experimenter and persons clearly perceived by subjects to be assistants to the experimenter, frequently there are also "confederates," or persons who appear to be subjects participating in the experiment but who are actually persons trained by the experimenter to play the subject role in order to affect the real subject in some way. The Darley and Latané experiment had a cast consisting of the experimenter's assistant, the experimenter, and confederates posing as subjects. (In this experiment the subject's only contact with the experimenter and confederates was through the tapes.) The cast carefully follows a script memorized in advance; only the subject is free to vary his or her behavior, some measure of which is the dependent variable. Every effort is made to ensure that the same "play" is presented to each subject in order to preserve internal validity. (For a further description of Darley and Latané's program of research on bystander intervention, see Box 7.1.)

Introduction to the Experiment

The first "scene" of an experiment consists of some sort of introduction to the experiment.[3] Basically this involves an explanation of the purpose or nature of the research, together with instructions to the subject. In the bystander intervention study, subjects were told that the research involved the personal problems of college students, and that in order to avoid embarrassment they would carry on a discussion with other students who were physically separated from them. Then they were told how the discussion would proceed.

It is essential that the first "scene" have enough impact on the subject to arouse interest. Obviously, if the subject is not paying attention to the directions or to the

BOX 7.1

External Validity and the Social Inhibition of Helping

The epileptic seizure experiment was part of a program of research carried out by social psychologists John Darley and Bibb Latané on bystander intervention in emergencies. The program consisted of a series of experiments, each designed to examine the kinds of factors that influence a person's decision to help or not to help another. A description of additional experiments by Latané and Darley will show how successive experimentation can increase external validity as it extends our knowledge of a social phenomenon.

Latané and Darley (1970) believed that a key factor in determining whether a bystander will intervene in an emergency is the presence of other bystanders. They hypothesized that as the number of bystanders increases, any one bystander will be less likely to *notice* an emergency incident, less likely to *interpret* it as an emergency, and less likely to *intervene* or take action. In ambiguous situations, which most emergencies are, people tend to look to others to gauge their reactions. Thus, others' apparent lack of concern and inaction will inhibit helping. When others are present, one also runs the risk of embarrassment by misinterpreting the situation. Moreover, the costs for not helping are reduced because one feels less personally responsible for taking action.

In their initial test of this explanation, Latané and Darley had subjects fill out questionnaires in a waiting room either alone or in the presence of two strangers. As the subjects worked, smoke was piped into the room through a wall vent. The experimenters, observing subjects' reactions through a one-way mirror, found that the majority of subjects who were alone noticed the smoke in less than 5 seconds and reported it to the experimenter in less than 2 minutes; subjects in the presence of others took an average of 20 seconds to notice, and most failed to report before the 6-minute experimental period had ended. In a postexperimental interview, the researchers also found that many of the latter subjects had interpreted the smoke as a nondangerous event—that is, as something other than fire. The "smoke" was explained variously as "steam or air-conditioning vapors," "smog, purposely introduced to simulate an urban environment," and "truth gas."

A second experiment, involving a woman in distress, was similar in design to the smoke-filled room study. After setting subjects to work on a questionnaire, a female researcher exited the waiting room through a curtained doorway to work next door in her office. Four minutes later she could be heard climbing up on a chair (to reach a book) and then crashing to the floor and screaming as the chair fell over. She then cried, "Oh, my God, my foot . . . I . . . I . . . can't move . . . it. Oh, my ankle, I . . . can't . . . can't . . . get . . . this thing off . . . me." This was followed by moaning and struggling for about 2 minutes until she limped out of her office door. The main dependent variable was whether subjects intervened to help the victim: 70 percent of the alone subjects did, but in only 40 percent of the pairs of strangers did either person offer help to the injured woman.

Besides these two studies and the epileptic seizure study, Latané and Darley conducted several other experiments on the social inhibition of helping, each producing similar findings. These experiments utilized a wide range of emergency situations. The situations varied in their seriousness. Some, such as the smoke-filled room, involved danger to the subject, while others, such as the fall and the seizure, involved danger to the victim. The experiments also utilized a range of subject populations. In addition to the male and female college students who participated in the above experiments, other studies included males and females from the general public. Finally, Latané and Darley performed field experiments as well as the laboratory experiments reported here. Thus, the external validity of the basic finding, which would be low in any one experiment, was made impressively high by a succession of studies that varied in their settings, procedures, measures, and samples.

In the decade following the publication of Latané and Darley's research, more than fifty studies were performed on bystander intervention in emergencies. About 90 percent of these studies showed that the presence of others inhibits helping (Latané and Nida, 1981). This research not only further documented an important social phenomenon; it also extended our knowledge by refining our theoretical understanding and by identifying some conditions under which the effect is reduced or eliminated. It is now clear, for example, that the presence of others is much less inhibiting when the emergency nature of the situation is made less ambiguous.

events being staged, experimental "findings" will be worthless. The explanation of the research purpose also must make sense to the subject; that is, it must be understandable and believable. This is especially important because the explanation often is intended to deceive the subject, through a *cover story*, as to the real nature of the research. While this practice raises ethical questions, many investigators believe it is necessary because subjects will often try to guess the hypothesis and sometimes even try to "help" the experimenter by behaving in ways consistent with the guessed hypothesis. A cover story may prevent this preoccupation with the true purpose of the study. Also, without deception some topics probably could not be explored at all. Think, for example, how the behavior of the subjects in the Darley and Latané study would have differed had they known that the experimenter was really interested in their willingness to intervene in an emergency.

The Experimental Manipulation

The manipulation of the independent variable may be thought of as the second "scene" of the experiment. This is the point at which some set of stimuli is introduced that serves as an operational definition of the researcher's independent variable and to which the subject is expected to respond. The major independent variable in the foregoing study was the size of the simulated discussion group. There were three levels of the independent variable or three conditions to which subjects were assigned randomly: the two-person condition, the three-person condition, and the six-person condition. The group size was manipulated by means of an assistant's comments pertaining to the size of the group and by the number of voices heard over the earphones.

A major concern in experiments is the possible meanings that subjects may attribute to the experimental manipulation. Essentially a matter of measurement validity, this has been referred to as the problem of "multiple meanings" (Aronson and Carlsmith, 1968). For example, a manipulation meant to arouse embarrassment in the subject is invalid if it produces disgust or anger instead. In general, the more complex the set of stimuli presented to the subject, the less sure the researcher may be that a manipulation appropriately measures the independent variable. When interpreting the results of any experiment, therefore, one must be sensitive to possible alternative explanations for any effects found. Evidence that the manipulation had the intended effect is gained by conducting a series of experiments in which the same theoretical concept is operationally defined differently, and by performing "manipulation checks."

Manipulation Checks

An immediate way to obtain evidence that the manipulation of the independent variable was experienced or interpreted by the subject in the way the experimenter intended is to incorporate some sort of *manipulation check* into the experiment. This might involve asking subjects, either directly or by means of a written instrument, what they felt or thought during or immediately after the experimental manipulation. A manipulation check may also be used to determine whether subjects understood or recalled essential directions or facts related to the manipulation.

In the Darley and Latané study, subjects were given a fifteen-item checklist of thoughts that might have occurred to them during the seizure. In addition, subjects were asked whether at the time of the seizure they had been aware of other persons who might be witnessing it—an awareness crucial to the meaning of the independent variable. (Data from two subjects who found the seizure unconvincing were not included in the statistical analysis.)

Different viewpoints exist regarding the best place in an experiment to administer a manipulation check. Frequently a manipulation check is taken after the independent variable is manipulated but before the dependent variable is measured. The advantage here is that the manipulation is still fresh and the subject's memory of it has not been distorted by later events. However, it may not be feasible at this point, as in the Darley and Latané study, where the check was made part of the postexperimental interview. (Certainly it was more appropriate for the subjects to respond at once to the "emergency" than to a checklist!) An additional problem with having a check administered between the experimental manipulation and the dependent variable is that of reactivity; that is, the manipulation check may alter subjects' subsequent behavior (the dependent variable) by calling attention to or emphasizing the manipulation.

One solution to this dilemma may be found through pretesting, in which the experiment is tried out on a number of subjects. The pretest subjects might be run in the usual manner through the manipulation of the independent variable and then interviewed as to how it affected them (Aronson and Carlsmith, 1968). In this way a manipulation check is carried out without affecting the data of the actual experiment. This procedure makes good sense also in view of the fact that there would still be time to make changes in the experiment before it is conducted with actual subjects whose data would be collected and analyzed.

Measurement of the Dependent Variable

The dependent variable, which always follows the introduction of the independent variable, is measured in experiments with either self-reports or observations of behavior. Darley and Latané used behavioral observation, with the dependent variable consisting of the length of time from the onset of the seizure until the subject left the room to report the emergency. A behavioral measure of the dependent variable—namely, grades on a second test—also was used in the Page study of the effect of teacher comments on student performance.

The use of verbal versus observational measures of the dependent variable is a controversial point among experimenters. Our examples notwithstanding, verbal reports are more common, even though they often contain serious weaknesses. Verbal measures have the advantage of being easy to devise, allowing for more numerous and varied assessments of the dependent variable. They also tend to be high in face validity. Using a verbal measure, for example, the experimenter interested in willingness to help could simply ask: "To what extent are you willing to help?" The principal problem with such self-reports is that subjects may censor their responses, especially when they construe the "truth" to reflect negatively upon themselves.

With observations of behavior, on the other hand, subjects tend to be less aware or even unaware of the measure. Behavioral measures also can be more precise; recall that Darley and Latané recorded the length of time to respond to the emergency in seconds. Finally, when a specific behavior (e.g., helping) is of interest, it is better to get a direct measure of that behavior than an indirect measure of how subjects *say* they will behave.

Debriefing

The closing "scene" of the experiment is a debriefing session in which the experimenter discusses with the subject what has taken place. When subjects have been deceived, it is ethically imperative that they be told at this point about the nature of and reasons for the deception and that their feelings about being deceived be explored fully (see chapter 16). The experimenter also may try to learn what the subject experienced throughout the experiment: Did the subject understand the directions? If a cover story was used, did the subject believe it? Why did the subject respond as he or she did to the experimental manipulation? Did the subject experience psychological stress or discomfort? How does the subject feel about the experiment as a whole?

The experimenter should be aware that the manner in which the debriefing session is conducted may make a great deal of difference in the feelings of the subject about being deceived (if the subject has been deceived), about this research and researcher, and about social science research in general. Thus the experimenter should explain the real purpose of the research and why it is of importance. If deception has been used, the subject must be gently informed of this and the reasons why it was necessary. If the manipulation aroused the subject's emotions, this, too, should be justified and every effort made to relieve any remaining discomfort. Any negative feelings of the subject toward the study should be brought into the open and discussed. The subject should be encouraged to ask questions about the study. Because many subjects in their experiment experienced stress and conflict, Darley and Latané took great care in explaining the necessity of the deception and seeing that subjects left the experiment feeling positive about their participation.

Finally, subjects must be convinced not to talk to others about the experiment. This is a serious problem in that frequently potential subjects are acquainted with one another. Certainly experiments requiring deception will not yield valid results if subjects coming to the experiment have been informed of its true purpose. Even experiments not requiring deception will usually suffer if subjects previously have been told the hypothesis or what the experimental manipulation is. If the debriefing process has been an open, satisfying experience for the subject up to this point, it would seem more likely that he or she would respect the researcher's wishes in regard to secrecy.

Pretesting

Pretesting an experiment may be compared to rehearsals of a play in that the pretests provide an opportunity for the director of the research (1) to train the "cast," (2) to test the "props," instructions, and cover story, (3) to check whether the manipulation has the intended effect, (4) to revise and practice the "script," and so forth. Pretests are carried out on a few preliminary subjects to see how the experimental procedures affect them. Feedback provided by pretest subjects may be used to modify the manipulation of the independent variable (e.g., by increasing the level of a stimulus such as praise, or by changing the behavior of confederates in some way), to change the dependent measure, or to improve some other part of the experiment such as the instructions, setting, or cover story. The time it takes for the actual performances of a play is usually a fraction of the time required to write the play and prepare for its performance. Similarly, the amount of time spent by a researcher in planning and pretesting an experiment will typically be many times greater than the time spent running subjects through the experiment.

Experimental and Mundane Realism

One thing the experimenter may learn from pretesting is the extent to which pretest subjects become involved in the experiment—that is, whether the experiment has impact upon them or, on the other hand, whether subjects remain detached. When an experiment is found to have impact upon subjects and to seem real to them, it is said to have *experimental realism* (Aronson and Carlsmith, 1968). The bystander intervention study achieved a very high degree of experimental realism for subjects. As Darley and Latané (1968:381) report,

> Subjects, whether or not they intervened, believed the fit to be genuine and serious. "My God, he's having a fit," many subjects said to themselves (and were overheard via their microphones) at the onset of the fit. Others gasped or simply said

"Oh." Several of the male subjects swore. One subject said to herself, "It's just my kind of luck, something has to happen to me!" Several subjects spoke aloud of the confusion about what course of action to take, "Oh God, what should I do?"

Frequently, as a researcher designs or pretests an experiment, tension develops between the goal of experimental realism and the goal of control over the events or stimuli presented. Situations that have high impact tend to be complex in terms of the stimuli presented, increasing the likelihood of "multiple meanings" from subject to subject. For example, sometimes experimenters provide instructions to subjects by means of audio or videotape recordings rather than by a "live" experimenter or assistant, in an attempt to provide exactly the same set of stimuli to each subject. This averts the possibility of an experimenter unknowingly introducing differences in the intended manipulation through slight variations in voice quality, inflections, and volume, by smiling more at some subjects than at others, and so forth. On the other hand, subjects are likely to be more attentive to a "live" experimenter. Besides having a "live" experimenter, other ways to increase experimental realism include making the cover story more interesting, selecting a confederate with substantial acting ability, and developing elaborate apparatus or other props.

A second type of "realism" that experiments may have to different degrees is called *mundane realism* (Aronson and Carlsmith, 1968). This type of realism refers to the similarity of experimental events to everyday experiences. The Page experiment on teacher comments, which took place in a natural setting, was clearly high in mundane realism. Receiving general comments on exams is something that every student has encountered. The Darley and Latané experiment, however, was low in mundane realism. Carrying on a highly regulated discussion with unseen peers over an intercom is not likely to be a common experience.

Experiments may be high in both experimental and mundane realism, high in one type of realism but low in the other, or low in both. Of the two types, mundane realism is considered less important in that an experiment is by nature a contrived situation (Aronson and Carlsmith, 1968). Therefore, mundane realism is of less concern in planning and pretesting. In order to control many variables and isolate others for study, some degree of mundane realism must be sacrificed. However, as long as an experiment is properly designed, so that the relationship between variables is interpretable, then its findings will be important even if it is artificial in a mundane sense.

The Experiment as a Social Occasion

Unlike an audience for a stage play who assume a passive role, subjects in a laboratory experiment are both "audience" and active participants. As participants, they bring to the experimental setting their own personal qualities, needs, and expectations. And as they interact with the experimenter (or the experimental assistants), the event takes on social as well as scientific aspects.

Scientifically, an experiment is an occasion to measure subjects' responses to certain intentionally and systematically varied stimuli. However, other stimuli related to the social aspects of the occasion may have unintended effects, which account for subjects' responses as much or more than the intended experimental manipulation. A good example of this was the famous Hawthorne experiments, mentioned in chapter 2 (see Box 2.1). Measuring the production rate of workers in response to a series of changes in working conditions (e.g., working hours, temperature, method of payment), the investigators found to their surprise that every change introduced resulted in an increase in productivity. This heightened productivity was not a response to the specific changes, however, but to the special attention given the group of workers as participants in an important experiment.

In chapter 5, we referred to the responses that are due to subjects' awareness of being studied as *reactive effects*. An example was the self-censoring that occurs with verbal report measures. While such effects are present in varying degrees in survey and field research, they are most problematic in laboratory experiments. Subjects in a laboratory experiment are acutely aware that they are participants in an experiment. Usually, their participation has brought them to a place they have never been before to interact with people whom they have never met before. They realize that they may be asked to do some strange things in the name of scientific inquiry, and they are likely to suspect that the true nature of the experiment is being concealed from them. They are aware that they are being observed and that certain behaviors are expected of them. Let us take a look now at how such thoughts and expectations might affect subjects' behavior.

Demand Characteristics

In any situation, from classroom to athletic field to experimental laboratory, there are norms and role expectations that govern behavior. Subjects entering an experiment, for example, implicitly agree to place themselves under the control of the experimenter and to perform a wide range of tasks without questioning their purpose or duration (Orne, 1962). These expectations were strikingly demonstrated by psychologist Martin Orne (1962) in the course of his research on hypnosis. In order to study the difference between the degree of control inherent in the hypnotic relationship and in a waking relationship, Orne tried to develop boring, meaningless, or unpleasant tasks that waking subjects would refuse to do or would stop doing after a short period of time. However, Orne found instead that subjects would persist hour after hour in apparently meaningless tasks. In one of these, subjects were instructed to perform additions of adjacent numbers on a sheet filled with hundreds of random numbers, to tear up the sheet in a prescribed manner, and then to go on to the next sheet and do the same thing, continuing in this manner until told to stop. Despite many efforts, Orne could find no task that would be refused or quickly discontinued by subjects once they agreed to participate in an experiment.

To Orne, these results revealed that a previously unimagined degree of control exists in the experimental setting. As a consequence of "being in an experiment," subjects feel justified in carrying out all sorts of tedious, noxious, even dangerous tasks. In one experiment, Orne and Evans (1965) found that subjects fearlessly complied to a request to reach into a cage containing a poisonous snake, only to be prevented from doing so by an invisible pane of glass. The reason that subjects will perform such tasks is that the "demands" placed upon them in an experiment go beyond the experimenter's verbal instructions. Because of the knowledge that one is in an experiment, endlessly boring tasks are viewed as endurance tests and seemingly dangerous acts are seen as really safe.

The particular cues in an experimental situation that communicate to subjects what is expected and what the experimenter hopes to find are called *demand characteristics* (Orne, 1962, 1969). These cues, which frequently are very subtle, range broadly. They can be communicated through campus scuttlebutt about the experiment, information provided during the recruiting of subjects, experimenter qualities such as appearance, the laboratory setting, experimental procedures, and communications during the experiment. According to Orne (1962), what makes subjects especially susceptible to such cues is their determination to play the role of "good subject." The "good subject" believes in the value of social science research and hopes by his or her participation to make a contribution toward the advancement of science. Whatever the purpose of the experiment, he or she assumes it to be worthwhile. Such subjects will gladly comply with virtually any request of the experimenter. And in order to "help" the experimenter, they are sensitive, consciously or unconsciously, to cues that indicate how to behave so as to validate the experimental hypothesis. Support for this viewpoint is provided by the fact that subjects often express concern about their behavior at the close of an experiment, saying something like, "I hope I didn't ruin the experiment."

The crux of the problem is that, in some experiments, demand characteristics, rather than the intended independent variable, may influence subjects' responses. Consider, for example, laboratory studies of the effect of persuasive messages on attitude change. When presented with a message or argument, followed by attitude or opinion measures, most subjects realize that their acquiescence to the message is being studied. If they are motivated to conform to the experimenter's expectations, then compliance to demand characteristics rather than the persuasiveness of the message accounts for their responses. One study in which this was demonstrated (Silverman, 1968) presented subjects with a 250-word report advocating the use of closed-circuit television tapes to present lectures in large classes. It was found that subjects showed more agreement with the message when they were told that they were in an experiment than when this was not explicitly conveyed to them.

Evaluation Apprehension

Besides their concern about being helpful and cooperative, subjects in experiments often experience anxiety about being evaluated. Viewing the experimenter, typically a psychologist, as having special skills to determine one's true character or personality, subjects come to experiments expecting the possibility that they will be evaluated. When this suspicion is confirmed, they are likely to experience *evaluation apprehension*. According to Milton J. Rosenberg (1965), who coined the term, subjects whose evaluation apprehension is aroused are concerned that they "win the positive evaluation of the experimenter, or at least that [they] provide no grounds for a negative one" (p. 29). This may cause the subject to be overly sensitive to cues regarding what constitutes a good, healthy, able, or "normal" performance on the task, and thus not to respond spontaneously to the independent variable.

Evidence that subjects may behave in a way that is thought to project a favorable image comes from an experiment by M. J. Rosenberg (1969). Subjects who believed they were participating in a social perception study were asked "to judge how much they liked or disliked various pictured persons." Before carrying out this task, however, one group of subjects was told that past research indicated that psychologically mature and healthy people show greater liking for strangers than do immature people, while a second group was told the opposite. For both groups, subjects' "liking" judgments reflected their beliefs about how psychologically mature individuals would respond.

For many subjects in the Rosenberg experiment, "looking good" may have seemed consistent with "being a good subject" and complying with demand characteristics. What happens, however, when there is a conflict between projecting a favorable image and confirming the experimenter's hypothesis? The evidence suggests that subjects will choose to look good. In one experiment (Sigall, Aronson, and Van Hoose, 1970), for example, subjects who knew the experimenter's hypothesis responded so as to disconfirm it when they thought that cooperating would reveal an unfavorable personality type.

Other Motives of Experimental Subjects

Motives of experimental subjects are not limited to those of the "good subject" who carefully attends to demand characteristics in order to "help" the experimenter or to the anxious subject intent on putting his or her best foot forward. When 110 experienced subjects were questioned regarding what they liked about the last experiment in which they participated (Straits and Wuebben, 1973), responses referred to the nature of the experimental task or the experimenter, the challenge of a new experience or of being successful in the experiment, the opportunity to learn something, and figuring out the experiment's purpose. Other common motivators are course credit or pay.

Another possible subject role is that of the negative or "bad" subject who tries to sabotage the research by deliberately providing useless or invalid responses. Argyris (1968:188) has written, for example, that

> [i]n one major university, a formal evaluation was made of the basic psychology course by nearly 600 undergraduates [and] the students were very critical, mistrustful, and hostile to the requirement [that they had to participate in experiments]. In many cases they identified how they expressed their pent-up feelings by "beating the researcher" in such a way that he never found out.

Why would subjects feel this way? Argyris, borrowing from organizational theory, has argued that experiments "tend to place subjects in situations that are similar to those organizations create for the lower level employees" (p. 193). Unaccustomed to being subordinates in a highly authoritarian system, research subjects may react by adopting employee ploys such as covert withdrawal or opposition.

Despite Argyris' claim, the negativistic subject seems to be less prevalent than the apprehensive or good subject (S. J. Weber and T. D. Cook, 1972). On the other hand, studies on the motivation of experimental subjects, taken together, seem to suggest that human subjects are too complex and diverse to describe by simple models presuming good, bad, or anxious subjects. For example, subjects may hold both hostile and favorable feelings toward experimentation and the social sciences. Certain features of experiments, such as required participation or unpleasant tasks, may evoke bad subject motives and behavior; other features such as an impressive or attractive experimenter may stimulate good subject motives. Certainly we can no longer assume the subject to be a passive responder to the experimental manipulation. Furthermore, there is always the strong possibility of subject bias whenever experimental procedures make the hypothesis transparent.

Experimenter Effects

Another source of bias due to the social nature of experiments is the experimenter. Experimenters can affect the results of their research in many ways that are not unique to experimentation, for example, by making recording errors, computational errors, and errors of interpretation, or by intentionally falsifying their data (recall from chapter 2 the case of the late Cyril Burt). However, the most problematic experimenter effects are influences on subjects' behavior. Robert Rosenthal (1966, 1967, 1969), who investigated such effects extensively, showed that numerous experimenter traits, including gender, race, status, anxiety, and warmth, affect the behavior of subjects. Just what effects these traits have depend on the particular experiment and on characteristics of the subject. Also, to a certain extent, such effects can be limited through training and appropriate controls.

More unsettling and operating at a more subtle level are effects due to the *experimenter's expectations* about how the experiment will turn out. Several studies by Rosenthal and others have shown that experimenters may unintentionally communicate to subjects their expectations about how the subjects "should" respond so as to confirm their hypotheses. One study involved a "person-perception" task (Rosenthal and Fode, 1963). Graduate student experimenters, who believed they were replicating a previous study, were told to present a set of photographs of individuals and ask subjects to rate each photograph as to how successful the individual appeared to be. The pictures had been selected on the basis of pretests to include only individuals who appeared neither especially successful nor unsuccessful. However, half the experimenters were informed that subjects would generally perceive the persons photographed as experiencing success (high ratings); the other half were led to expect that subjects would perceive the individuals as unsuccessful (low ratings). Even though the experimenters read identical instructions to their subjects, those experimenters expecting high ratings tended to get higher ratings from their subjects than those expecting low ratings.

The means by which experimenters communicate their expectancies to subjects is not yet well understood, although there have been a number of studies on this question. Some studies have demonstrated the importance of auditory cues—voice quality or tone of voice. For example, Zoble and Lehman (1969) showed that if subjects performing the person-perception task described above were denied visual contact with the experimenter, about one-half of the expectancy effect remained. This study, as well as others (Rosenthal, 1969:253–254), also provides indirect evidence that visual cues such as facial expressions and gestures may mediate expectancy effects.

Fortunately, although there is little question of the existence of experimenter expectancy effects, it is doubtful that such effects are either very strong or widespread. Those studies designed to demonstrate an expectancy effect, such as the study involving person perception, differ from most other experiments in two regards: (1) the stimulus was highly ambiguous, which may have caused the subject to pay unusual attention to any possible cues from the experimenter; and (2) the experimenters for the most part ran subjects in one experimental condition only. Aronson and Carlsmith (1968:67) have pointed out that an experimenter would be less likely to bias subject behavior when running subjects in more than one condition, because he or she would probably notice any systematic differences in his or her behavior toward subjects. Still, the general problem of experimenter bias is one that researchers can ill afford to ignore.

Minimizing Bias Due to the Social Nature of Experimentation

While experiments provide an ideal model for testing causal relations, the success of that model depends on the ability to eliminate or minimize potential biases emanating from an experiment's social nature. Several strategies have been developed for handling the problems raised by demand characteristics and experimenter bias.

The most straightforward way of detecting demand characteristics is simply to ask subjects about their perception of the experimental situation (Orne, 1969). Did the subjects entertain any hypotheses? Did it appear to them that the experimenter expected them to behave in a certain way? How do they think others might have reacted in the situation? This sort of probing could take place in a pretesting phase, in which subjects are asked for their impressions at different points in the experiment, or during the debriefing.

The most widely used means of controlling for demand characteristics is a cover story that provides the subject with a false hypothesis about the purpose of the study. If a cover story satisfies subjects' suspicions about the purpose of the experiment, they will not be busily trying to figure out the true hypothesis; therefore, they will be less likely to act deliberately in ways consistent or inconsistent with it. Similarly, experiments high in experimental realism (partly achieved with a good cover story) have such an impact on subjects that there is little chance for them to be distracted by "evaluation apprehension" or other suspicions.

A second approach to circumventing the problem of demand characteristics is to measure the dependent variable in a different setting than the one in which the independent variable is manipulated. By separating these processes physically, the experimenter hopes the subjects will dissociate the events psychologically. For example, M. J. Rosenberg (1965) arranged for subjects to participate in two apparently unrelated studies conducted by different experimenters. In the first study, conducted in the education department, subjects were paid to write essays counter to their own views on a particular issue, the size of the payment being the independent variable. Then, in a subsequent opinion survey, conducted in the psychology department, subjects' attitudes on the same issue were measured. A less elaborate separation of these parts of the experiment occurred in three studies testing the hypothesis that increased guilt will lead to increased compliance (Freedman, Wallington, and Bless, 1967). The investigators first manipulated subjects' feelings of guilt. Then, when the experiment appeared to be over and the subject was about to leave the laboratory, they measured compliance by asking subjects if they would be willing to take part in another study, without pay, being conducted by another person in the department.

A third technique for controlling demand characteristics is to keep subjects unaware that they are actually participating in an experiment. In this way, subjects should behave naturally without wondering about the "true" nature of the situation. The best place to conduct such "disguised experiments" is in a natural rather than a laboratory setting (Campbell, 1969). A good example is the Page experiment on teacher comments.

Finally, there is some evidence that the effects of demand characteristics can be minimized by asking subjects to adopt the role of the "faithful subject." Faithful subjects believe that they should follow instructions scrupulously, regardless of their suspicions about the true purpose of the experiment (S. J. Weber and T. D. Cook, 1972). Getting subjects to adopt this role, however, might be difficult if the experiment is likely to evoke a high level of evaluation apprehension.

A number of approaches also have been developed to eliminate or reduce bias introduced by the experimenter. One possibility, the *double-blind technique*, prevents the experimenter from knowing which condition a subject is in. This would be akin to studies of new drugs in which neither the subject nor the research assistant interviewing the subject knows whether the subject received the drug or a placebo (inert substance). With this method, a coding system enables the research supervisor to keep track of which subjects received which treatment.

In most studies it is not possible to keep the experimenter blind to the subjects' condition, because differences in the treatment conditions are obvious to the experimenter. In these cases, a partial solution may be to utilize two or more experimenters, with each "blind" to some part of the experiment. For example, when the manipulation of the independent variable is separated from the measurement of the dependent variable, as in the guilt-compliance study mentioned above, these two processes could be carried out easily by different experimenters.

Another effective means of controlling the effects of experimenter bias is to have a single experimental session that includes all subjects. The experimenter might read general instructions to all subjects, but manipulate the independent variable by varying additional written instructions. If the latter instructions were randomly assigned, then the experimenter could not systematically influence the subjects in any one group. Finally, one could reduce the amount of contact between the experimenter and subjects through the use of audio or videotapes. As indicated earlier, however, this approach also would reduce experimental realism.

Experimentation Outside the Laboratory

In the last two sections we have focused on experiments carried out in a laboratory. By far the most common setting for the experimental approach, the laboratory permits a great deal of control—control over subject assignment and of the events to which subjects are exposed. Control is obtained, however, at some cost: the sample of subjects is usually small and from a highly restricted population; the setting is often unrealistic in the mundane sense; and the subjects are aware that the experimenter has created the situation to test some hypothesis about their behavior.

Some experimental designs avoid these particular problems by moving outside the laboratory into a more natural social setting. When experiments take place "in the field," mundane realism tends to be high and demand characteristics are minimized because subjects often are unaware that they are participating in a study. Experimental designs also may be incorporated into nonexperimental research approaches, such as social surveys. Finally, as further evidence of the versatility of the experimental approach, the "subjects" randomly assigned to experimental conditions may consist of social units such as families, classrooms, clinics, and organizations, as well as individuals.

Field Experiments

Field experiments refer to studies that meet all the requirements of a "true" experiment but are conducted in a natural setting. As in a laboratory experiment, there is a staging of events in a field experiment. But this staging occurs in an environment that is familiar to the subject and is rendered in such a way that it appears to be a "natural" (albeit slightly out of the ordinary) part of that environment. Recall, for example, Isen and Levin's experiment on the effects of mood on helping, described in chapter 1. To manipulate mood, these investigators stocked a telephone booth with a dime; to measure helping, they staged an accident—someone dropping a folder of papers—and then recorded whether the subject stopped to help. The experiment took place as subjects were going about a common activity, and the manipulations and observations were so subtle and unobtrusive that subjects' normal behavior was not disrupted.

In recent years social researchers increasingly have gone outside the research laboratory to conduct experiments in a wide variety of settings. In the study of helping behavior alone, field experiments have been performed in department store and municipal parking lots (Bryan and Test, 1967; Shotland and Stebbins, 1983), in an enclosed shopping mall (Isen and Levin, 1972), in a college library (Isen and Levin, 1972), on a highway (Bryan and Test, 1967), and in the New York City subway (Piliavin and Piliavin, 1972). Conducting experiments in such settings offers several advantages. Without being aware that a study is in progress, subjects should not respond self-consciously to demand characteristics. External validity generally increases, not only because the setting and measures are more realistic but also because it is possible to observe the behavior of a more heterogeneous sample of subjects. Field experimentation also lends itself well to applied research, that is, research intended to provide input into problem solving. Some of the field experiments on helping behavior, for example, have been directed at factors affecting blood donating (Piliavin, Callero, and Evans, 1982) and contributions to charitable organizations (Cialdini and Schroeder, 1976). We will now examine one of these studies to illustrate the utility and nature of experiments carried out in a real-life setting.

Research has shown that heightening concern about one's self-image may predispose one to help others as a means of maintaining or restoring a favorable image. Robert Cialdini and David Schroeder (1976) demonstrated this in a field experiment performed in a door-to-door fund-raising context. With the permission of the American Cancer Society, they asked pairs of college students to solicit contributions for the society in a middle-class suburban area. Solicitors requested contributions in one of two ways. In the first method, they made a standard request: "I'm collecting money for the American Cancer Society. Would you be willing to help by giving a donation?" In the second strategy, solicitors added the sentence, "Even a penny will help." Cialdini and Schroeder predicted that helping would be greater when the latter statement was added, because it legitimizes trivial requests and makes the solicitation more difficult to turn down without damaging one's self-image. Supporting their hypothesis, 29 percent of the subjects in the standard request condition contributed, averaging $1.44 each, as opposed to 50 percent of the subjects in the even-a-penny condition, who averaged $1.54 each. (See Box 7.2 for the story behind the origins of this study.)

With the advantages cited above, one may wonder why the field has not supplanted the laboratory as the primary setting for experimental research. Alas, there are disadvantages, the major drawback being the lower degree of control present in field experiments. Often researchers can only approximate a true experimental design in the field. It may not be possible to assign subjects (or other units of analysis) randomly to the various treatment conditions. Sometimes it is not possible to have a true control group because of ethical considerations or subject preferences. Furthermore, field experimenters often relinquish some control over the experiment by their dependence on other persons such as administrators or teachers to carry out parts of the study (a potential problem in the Cialdini and Schroeder study). Consequently, it is much more difficult outside the laboratory to ensure that there are no systematic differences in the experiences of subjects other than those resulting from the manipulation of the independent variable.

A related problem with field experimentation is that the manipulation of the independent variable may be less controllable and more open to interpretation. This is apparent in studies that attempted to evaluate the educational impact upon American preschoolers of the television series, "Sesame Street" (Ball and Bogatz, 1970; Cook and Conner, 1976; Liebert, 1976). Ideally, to investigate the effects of viewing it would be desirable to have a treatment group that viewed the series and a control group that did not. However, because there was no practical way to prevent the control group children from viewing the series in their homes, it was decided that the experimental treatment would be "encouragement to view." This treatment included weekly visits by trained staff who encouraged parents and children to watch the programs and who brought along literature, toys, and games designed to stimulate viewing. The control group children received no "encouragement" and

BOX 7.2

On the Origins of Research Ideas

In chapter 4 we outlined some of the sources of ideas for social research. As we noted, many studies derive from existing theory. This is especially true of the hypothesis-testing research that characterizes experiments. Occasionally, however, investigators get their research ideas from everyday observations and experiences. This was, in fact, the origin of two of the experiments described in this chapter.

According to John Darley, his and Bibb Latané's research on bystander intervention stemmed from a widely publicized incident in New York City. A young woman named Kitty Genovese was brutally murdered while thirty-eight of her neighbors watched from their windows without so much as calling the police until her assailant had departed. Shocked by this incident, Darley and Latané met over dinner and began to analyze the bystanders' reactions.

> Because we were social psychologists, we thought not about how people are different nor about the personality flaws of the "apathetic" individuals who failed to act that night, but rather about how people are the same and how anyone in that situation might react as did these people. By the time we finished our dinner, we formulated several factors that together could lead to the surprising result: no one helping. Then we set about conducting experiments that isolated each factor and demonstrated its importance in an emergency situation (reported in Myers, 1983:394).

Robert Cialdini (1980:27–28), whose research involves social influence processes, tells how a personal experience led him to investigate a highly effective fund-raising tactic.

> I answered the door early one evening to find a young woman who was canvassing my neighborhood for the United Way. She identified herself and asked if I would give a monetary donation. It so happened that my home university has an active United Way organization and I had given in-house a few days earlier. It was also the end of the month and my finances were low. Besides, if I gave to all the solicitors for charity who came to my door, I would quickly require such service for myself. As she spoke, I had already decided against a donation and was preparing my reply to incorporate the above reasons. Then it happened. After asking for a contribution, she added five magic words. I know they were *the* magic words because my negative reply to the donation request itself literally caught in my throat when I heard them. "Even a penny will help," she said. And with that, she demolished my anticipated response. All the excuses I had prepared for failing to comply were based on financial considerations. They stated that I could not afford to give to her now or to her, too. But she said, "Even a penny will help" and rendered each of them impotent. How could I claim an inability to help when she claimed that "even a penny" was a legitimate form of aid? I had been neatly finessed into compliance. And there was another interesting feature of our exchange as well. When I stopped coughing (I really had choked on my attempted rejection), I gave her *not* the penny she mentioned but the amount I usually allot to charity solicitors. At that, she thanked me, smiled innocently, and moved on.

Together with his then-graduate student Dave Schroeder, Cialdini analyzed the situation and concluded that two sources of social influence had been activated by the addendum "Even a penny will help." First, it removed any excuses for not offering at least some aid. Second, it made it more difficult to maintain one's altruistic self-image without contributing. Cialdini and Schroeder then set out to find a naturalistic fund-raising context for testing their ideas.

could view or not. Both groups of children were given a battery of tests prior to the first viewing season and at its end, and the results showed that the group encouraged to view made greater gains on the posttests. Unfortunately, this did not establish that viewing the programs caused the gains, as there were systematic differences in the experiences of the two groups aside from the viewing experience; that is, the effects of viewing were confounded with the effects of "encouragement." It may have been that the social and intellectual stimulation provided by the "encouragement" alone was sufficient to cause the gains.

Finally, field experiments often raise ethical and legal issues. Is it ethical or legal, for example, to expose passersby to someone who collapses or feigns a heart attack, as has been done in bystander intervention research? In laboratory experiments, subjects' rights are protected by obtaining their prior consent to participate and by debriefing. But these safeguards may be impossible to incorporate in a field experiment. Obtaining "informed consent," for instance, in many cases would destroy the cover for the experiment. Thus, there is a greater demand on field experimenters to demonstrate that their research presents no more than minimal risk of harm to subjects. (Ethical issues are discussed further in chapter 16.)

Experimental Designs in Survey Research

The versatility of the experimental approach is evidenced not only by extensions into the field but also by the use of experimental design in survey research. For example, several surveys have investigated the effects of slight changes in the wording of a question during an interview. Generally, as part of a larger survey, a miniexperiment is conducted by directing a question with one wording to a randomly selected subsample of respondents and directing a differently worded question to the remaining respondents. (See Box 10.1 for a specific example.)

Another common way of incorporating an experimental design into surveys is through the use of vignettes. Vignettes are short, detailed, and concrete descriptions of situations that contain references to factors that are thought to be important in decision making. Some survey researchers believe that vignettes produce more valid responses than the briefer but more general or abstract questions normally used in opinion surveys (see Alexander and Becker, 1978). In order to test experimentally which factors in a given situation significantly affect respondents' decision making, a number of versions of the vignettes are developed by systematically varying the details of the situation. The different versions are then randomly assigned to respondents. For example, to study college women's fertility plans, Straits (1985) used six vignettes, each of which described a married woman facing a decision directly or indirectly bearing upon her childbearing plans. The information that was varied in each vignette concerned the direct costs of children due to changes in earning power and living standards, the indirect costs of children due to the loss of other opportunities for self-fulfillment (foregoing further schooling or occupational advancement, for example), and the perceived cultural support for parenthood. Contrary to some journalistic accounts, Straits found that the college women in his sample had a strong commitment to motherhood that took precedence over a career and other direct and indirect costs of childbearing.

It is also possible to perform an experiment via a sample survey by constructing different sets of questionnaires. Consider, for example, a study by Navazio (1977) on the so-called bandwagon effect. This is the idea that voters are influenced by public opinion poll results to the extent that they tend to "get on the bandwagon" and support what they believe to be the majority opinion on an issue. To study this phenomenon, Navazio (1977) mailed experimental and control questionnaires to two samples of respondents. The questionnaires contained four opinion questions evaluating then-President Nixon's performance. On the experimental questionnaire, each question followed a statement of recent national poll results that showed that a majority of people had responded negatively to the question. On the basis of "bandwagon psychology," one would predict that the experimental group, having access to the critical responses of others, would respond more negatively than the control group. However, the results did not support this hypothesis.

Units of Analysis Other Than Individuals

Experimental designs do not always use individuals as the unit of analysis. Numerous laboratory experiments have been performed over the years treating pairs of subjects or small groups as units. Though less common, experimental units of analysis also have consisted of larger groupings such as organizations or neighborhoods.

One illustrative field experiment on patrol staffing in San Diego, California used police "beats" as the units, assigning them to either a one-officer or two-officer condition. The object of this study was to evaluate whether staffing police patrol cars with two officers as opposed to one officer resulted in increased quality of service, efficiency, and safety, making the practice cost effective (Boydstun et al., 1978). It had been determined that the difference in cost between fielding a two-officer patrol unit and a one-officer patrol unit was over $100 per unit for an 8-hour period. Pairs of beats were matched on various characteristics and then randomly assigned to the one-officer and two-officer staffing conditions, with forty-four patrol units involved. The findings revealed that quality of performance and efficiency were as high with the one-officer units as with the two-officer units and that the two-officer units were more often associated with suspects resisting arrest or assaulting officers. The study concluded, therefore, that the staffing ought to be primarily one-officer units.

Another study, a massive field experiment carried out on the island of Taiwan in the city of Taichung, used neighborhoods as units of analysis (Berelson and Freedman, 1964). This study sought to determine the extent to which "family planning" would be implemented with information and service programs that required different levels of effort and cost. Each of Taichung's 2389 *lin's* (neighborhoods of twenty to thirty families) was randomly assigned to one of four experimental treatments. The treatments varied in terms of the cost of providing family planning information; in the lowest-cost treatment, educational posters were distributed and neighborhood meetings were held, and in the highest-cost treatment a nurse-midwife visited the home of every married couple. The researchers found that the proportion who accepted contraceptives was highest in the highest-cost condition as expected. But there was also a marked indirect effect by word-of-mouth communication from the high-cost home visit *lin's* to *lin's* receiving lower cost treatments. The researchers therefore concluded that contraception use can be spread economically by a mixture of low- and high-cost programs.

Summary

Experimental research is intended for the purpose of testing hypothesized causal relationships. Controlling extraneous variables is the key to doing this effectively. First, random assignment of subjects to treatment and control groups assures that preexperimental differences will be "neutralized" or distributed approximately evenly among the groups. Then, treatment and control group subjects must experience the same events during the experiment except for the manipulation of the independent variable. Only in this way can we be confident in inferring that the experimental manipulation produced differences in measures of the dependent variable.

Because experiments permit relatively strong inferences about cause and effect, providing clear evidence of direction of influence and controlling effectively for extraneous variables, they are high in internal validity. On the other hand, experiments, especially those performed in research laboratories, tend to be limited in generalizability—that is, low in external validity. This is most apparent with respect to the sample of subjects, who typically are college student volunteers. While external validity is sometimes increased by using more heterogeneous samples, more often it is achieved through replications that test the same hypothesis, but in a different setting, with different variable manipulations and measures, and with subjects drawn from different populations.

The staging of an experiment has four parts: (1) an introduction, which provides subjects with instructions and a rationale for the experimental procedures; (2) manipulation of the independent variable, ideally accompanied by a manipulation check that examines subjects' interpretations of the manipulation; (3) measurement of the dependent variable, either by verbal reports or, preferably, by behavioral observation; and (4) a debriefing session, which is intended to explain the purpose of the experiment, to explore subjects' reactions, and to assuage subjects' anxieties about their "performance" or participation.

Before experiments are carried out, they should be pretested on a few preliminary subjects to check the efficacy of the procedures. At this time, one can determine the study's experimental realism, or the extent to which the experiment engages and has an impact on subjects. Also important, though generally of lesser concern, is the study's mundane realism, which refers to the similarity of experimental procedures to "real-world" events.

Perhaps the most problematic aspects of the laboratory experiment stem from its social nature. Subjects react not only to experimental manipulations but to the social meaning of the situation. Thus their responses may be determined by their sensitivity to cues, called demand characteristics, which communicate the hypothesis being tested, by their apprehensiveness about the evaluation of their performance, or by their resentment about being "coerced" into taking part in an experiment. Experimenters, on the other hand, may nonverbally communicate their own expectations to subjects.

To a large extent, these potentially biasing factors can be controlled. Subject biases might be detected by pre- and postexperimental interviews. Methods of controlling such biases include using a good cover story that inhibits subjects' suspicions, placing the manipulation of the independent variable and the measurement of the dependent variable in different contexts, conducting a disguised experiment, or asking subjects to adopt the role of the "faithful subject." Experimenter biases are controlled most effectively by keeping experimenters blind to the subjects' conditions. One also may use two experimenters, each blind to a part of the experiment, or carry out the experiment in a single session. Also effective, though less desirable, is the automation of the experiment through the use of audio or videotapes.

One other means of controlling for biases is to perform an experiment in a natural setting where subjects are unaware that a scientific investigation is taking place. Such field experiments also increase external validity and are an effective tool for applied research. However, in moving from the laboratory to the field, one generally sacrifices control over extraneous variables and over the manipulation of the independent variable, and one may find it more difficult to protect subjects' rights and safety.

Evidence of the versatility of experimentation comes from the incorporation of experimental design methodology into sample surveys and from the use of units of analysis other than individuals. Because of this versatility as well as its greater degree of control, experimentation is the preferred approach for testing causal hypotheses. However, there are frequently problems in applying true experimental designs to social research that may result in a less-than-ideal execution of the experiment or in a compromise in the design itself. In the next chapter, we will consider a variety of research designs, some of which are extensions and some of which are approximations to the model of the true experiment presented in this chapter.

Key Terms

treatment	*matching*
random assignment	*internal validity*
test of statistical significance	*external validity*

cover story   reactive effects
manipulation check   demand characteristics
debriefing   evaluation apprehension
pretesting   experimenter expectancy effect
experimental realism   double-blind technique
mundane realism   field experiment

Review Questions and Problems

1. Briefly explain *how* experiments provide the types of evidence required to establish causality: association, direction of influence, and elimination of rival hypotheses.

2. What purpose does a test of statistical significance serve in an experiment?

3. Should matching be substituted for random assignment in an experiment? Explain.

4. Differentiate random assignment from random sampling.

5. Briefly distinguish between internal and external validity.

6. Describe the typical sample of subjects in an experiment.

7. How do experimenters rationalize the lack of population generality typical of experiments?

8. How can one increase external validity?

9. What are the four parts or stages of an experiment?

10. What is the purpose of a cover story?

11. Explain the problem of multiple meanings in experimental manipulation.

12. What is the purpose of manipulation checks?

13. Why are behavioral measures generally preferred over self-report measures of the dependent variable in experiments?

14. What purposes does debriefing serve?

15. When is an experiment high in experimental realism? When is it high in mundane realism?

16. What are the advantages and disadvantages of using a "live" experimenter rather than a tape recording to provide instructions to subjects?

17. Why is it important to consider the social nature of an experiment?

18. Describe the role expectations of the typical experimental subject.

19. Briefly describe Orne's model of the "good subject." How is this model related to the problem of demand characteristics?

20. Explain the motives of the "anxious subject" and the "bad subject" in experiments.

21. Describe various ways in which the experimenter can affect the outcome of an experiment.

22. How are experimenter expectancies communicated to subjects?

23. How do experiments demonstrating experimenter expectancy effects differ from most other experiments?

24. Identify two methods for minimizing demand characteristics and two methods for reducing experimenter effects.

25. Compare the advantages and disadvantages of field experiments versus laboratory experiments.

26. How can the experimental approach be incorporated into survey research?

27. Do the units of analysis in experiments always consist of individuals? Explain.

28. Refer to the article "Misogyny and the Single Girl," by Philip A. Goldberg (pp. 147–153 in Golden, 1976).

    a. State the hypothesis under investigation.

    b. What is the principal independent variable? How was it manipulated?

    c. What is the dependent variable? How was it measured?

    d. Identify any control variables present in the study.

    e. Do the results of the study support the hypothesis? Explain.

    f. Evaluate this experiment in terms of its experimental and mundane realism.

29. Refer to the article "Status of Frustrator as an Inhibitor of Horn-Honking Responses," by Anthony N. Doob and Alan E. Gross (pp. 481–486 in Golden, 1976).

    a. What is the hypothesis being tested in this study?

    b. What is the independent variable? How is it manipulated?

    c. What is the dependent variable? How is it measured?

    d. What type of experiment—laboratory or field—is this? Which of the four parts of an experiment is missing?

    e. Comparing the experiments by Goldberg (question 28) and Doob and Gross, which is higher in mundane realism? Which is higher in experimental realism? Explain.

NOTES

1. Note that in this sense the word "significance" does not refer to the importance or triviality of the research findings.

2. This hypothesis is explained by the theory that the presence of others at an emergency is likely to create a "diffusion of responsibility" for helping. That is, with others present, we feel less personally responsible for taking action and we are more likely to rationalize that "someone else is doing something."

3. Prior to the start of the "production," other procedures must be carried out. These include the recruitment of subjects, random assignment of subjects to treatment conditions, and, most importantly, the acquisition of the subjects' "informed consent." Informed consent, which we discuss in chapter 16, is an ethical guideline requiring that subjects learn about foreseeable risks and discomforts before agreeing to participate in an experiment.

8

Experimental Designs

By now you should have some pretty clear ideas about the experimental approach—its key features, strengths and weaknesses, and the steps involved in carrying out an experiment. This chapter will provide you with additional knowledge necessary to become an informed consumer of research. Your increased sophistication regarding experimentation should be especially valuable to you as a citizen, since experimental designs increasingly are applied to the study of important social policy issues.

Although the topic of experimental design may sound formidable, and some experiments with their statistical baggage do appear rather complex, the basic principle of good design is simply the idea of "doing only one thing at a time." For the results of an experiment to be as unequivocal as possible, the only plausible explanation of changes in the dependent variable must be the manipulated independent variable. Therefore, a good design is one that rules out explanations of the results other than the independent variable. We learned in the last chapter that this is best accomplished by random assignment of subjects to experimental conditions (thereby controlling for preexisting subject differences) and by making sure that the events occurring within each experimental condition are exactly the same except for the manipulated independent variable (thus controlling for extraneous factors and experiences during the experiment). The principle, then, is to allow only one factor, the independent variable, to vary while controlling the rest.

In this chapter, the first three designs we consider are inadequate; they do not follow the above principle of good design. Before we examine the flaws in these "preexperimental" designs, we identify the kinds of uncontrolled variables, or threats to internal validity, which provide plausible rival explanations of study results. Next we consider three basic, true experimental designs, which stand up better against threats to validity and thereby yield less ambiguous results. Then we examine designs for testing the joint effects of two or more independent variables. The need for these more complex "factorial" designs exists because in the "real world," unlike in the typical laboratory experiment, many variables may be at work simultaneously. Finally, we examine some "quasi-experimental" designs, used when it is not practical or possible to meet all of the conditions of true experiments.

Threats to Internal Validity[1]

Suppose a psychologist conducts an experiment to determine whether a program of assertiveness training is effective in helping shy, introverted persons become more

socially outgoing. She recruits subjects from undergraduate psychology and sociology classes and tests them with a previously validated scale of extroversion. The
most introverted subjects—those who scored in the bottom quartile—are assigned
to the experimental condition, where they undergo an 8-week assertiveness training
program. The remaining subjects serve as a control group, receiving no such training. At the end of 8 weeks, both groups are retested. The psychologist finds that, on
the average, the control group subjects score about the same as they did at the
beginning of the experiment; but the experimental group shows a significant gain in
extroversion. Can she conclude that the assertiveness training program has produced this gain?

The answer is that she cannot safely draw such a conclusion because the
research design is inadequate; that is, the experiment lacks internal validity. Recall
that an experiment has internal validity when it is possible to make strong inferences
about cause and effect, enabling one to say with confidence that the independent
variable has produced the observed changes in the dependent variable. We now
introduce some common *threats to internal validity*—"threats" because they represent extraneous variables that, if uncontrolled, pose explanations of the results that
rival the hypothesized effects of the independent variable. Each threat, then, signifies a class of extraneous variables.

One threat to internal validity is *history*. This consists of events in the subjects'
environment, other than the manipulated independent variable, that occur during the
course of the experiment and that may affect the outcome. In this sense a "historical
event" may be a major event of social or political importance, such as an assassination of a public figure or a prolonged strike, or it may be a minor event that occurs
within the experimental setting and has no significance outside of it, such as a
hostile remark by a subject. For example, suppose that you are studying the impact
of a series of written persuasive communications upon attitudes toward U.S. immigration policies. During the course of your experiment, many of your subjects
happen to view at home a feature television program on the plight of illegal immigrant workers. Should the results of your study show that subjects' attitudes toward
U.S. immigration policies have changed, it would be impossible for you to tell
whether this change was caused by your independent variable (written communications) or by the television program. When we cannot separate the effects of the
independent variable from possible effects of extraneous variables, we say the
effects are *confounded*. In this case, the confounded effects of the experimental
manipulation and history preclude a clear causal interpretation of the results.

Another frequent rival explanation for research findings is *maturation*. By this
we mean any psychological or physical changes taking place within subjects that
occur with the passing of time regardless of the experimental manipulation. Even
during a 1- or 2-hour experiment, subjects may become hungry or tired. Over a
long-term experiment, subjects may grow physically or intellectually, become more
rigid or more tolerant, and develop health problems or improved health. The effects
of such maturational factors may be confounded with treatment effects. For example, in a study of the effectiveness of a new physical therapy program for stroke
victims, any progress that the stroke victims would make naturally over time with-

out therapeutic intervention (a phenomenon known as spontaneous remission) might incorrectly be attributed to the therapy.

Testing represents a third possible source of internal invalidity. Similar to reactive effects discussed in chapters 5 and 7, testing effects refer to changes in what is being measured that are brought about by reactions to the process of measurement. Typically, people will score better or give more socially desirable or psychologically healthier responses the second time a test or scale is administered to them. This is true even when a different but similar measure is used. There are a number of reasons why this occurs. On some measures, such as intelligence tests, the tasks simply become easier after practice. Attitude scales, on the other hand, may alert subjects to the purpose of the scale, causing them to give socially desirable responses or perhaps to reexamine their own attitudes. Such effects are potentially confounded with the effects of the independent variable whenever subjects are measured twice in the same study and the measuring device arouses their awareness of being studied.

A fourth threat to internal validity, *instrumentation*, refers to unwanted changes in characteristics of the measuring instrument or in the measurement procedure. This threat is most likely to occur in experiments when the "instrument" is a human observer, who may become more skilled, more bored, or more or less observant during the course of the study. Instrumentation effects also may occur when different observers are used to obtain measurements in different conditions or parts of an experiment. Such an effect would be analogous to a shift in an instructor's grading standards while grading a set of essays, or to inconsistent standards on the part of two instructors grading subsets of the same essays.

The fifth threat to internal validity is *statistical regression*, the tendency for extreme scorers on a test to move (regress) closer to the mean or average score on a second administration of the test. Also known as *regression toward the mean*, this phenomenon is likely to affect experimental results when subjects are selected for an experimental condition because of their extreme scores. Our opening example of an inadequate research design illustrates this problem. The students chosen for assertiveness training were those scoring in the bottom 25 percent on a measure of extroversion. Because of this, the observed increase in extroversion scores may have been due to statistical regression rather than the training program.

Statistical regression can explain many events in everyday life. An example should clarify how its effects occur. Suppose that Instructor Young gives his class two exams. In each case the average grade is "B." Table 8.1 compares the performance of individuals on the two tests. Young is disappointed to see, from the first row of Table 8.1, that of the fifteen persons who received A's on Exam I, only ten received A's on Exam II, with four receiving B's and one receiving a C. He concludes that five of the students became overconfident after the first exam and slacked off. Then he looks at the C scorers and is delighted to see that of the fifteen who scored C initially, two raised their scores to A and four to B. He feels some satisfaction that at least these students hit the books to bring their grades up. Such conclusions could be correct, but it is more likely that the results are due to regression toward the mean.

TABLE 8.1. Grade on Exam II by Grade on Exam I (Hypothetical Data)

Exam I grade	Exam II grade			
	A	B	C	Total
A	10	4	1	15
B	3	22	5	30
C	2	4	9	15
Total	15	30	15	60

Because measurement error is always present, there is never a perfect correlation between scores from separate administrations of the same test or measure. A relatively large amount of measurement error will be reflected in a low correlation of scores and will result in more regression toward the mean. Another way to think of it is that the extreme scorers, as a subgroup, are affected more by chance factors we might call luck. On the first exam, some of the high scorers are particularly lucky and some of the low scorers particularly unlucky; but their luck tends to change on the second exam, which results in subgroup scores closer to the mean. Initially average scorers, on the other hand, are likely to include about as many lucky as unlucky individuals, so that changes in luck will tend to cancel out and not influence results on the second test.

A sixth threat to internal validity, *selection*, is present whenever there are systematic differences in the composition of the control and experimental groups. Such selection bias is especially likely when naturally existing groups are studied. Suppose, for example, a study compared 1-year recidivism rates of apparently recovered alcoholics who received help through Alcoholics Anonymous with the recidivism rates of those who received in-hospital treatment. One possible systematic difference in the two groups that might affect abstinence is economic standing. If economic well-being aids recovery, and if those choosing in-hospital treatment were in fact more affluent, then the hospital treatment group might have a better record of recovery because of their economic status, apart from any benefits of the treatment.

An additional example where selection would be a confounding factor is a study comparing the academic progress of pupils in an alternative school with that of pupils in a conventional school. Even if attempts were made to match the alternative school to a conventional school on such relevant characteristics as class size and socioeconomic status of pupils, there still might be confounding differences between the two groups. For example, the parents of the alternative-school children might be more permissive or differ in other unknown ways from the parents of the conventional-school pupils. Whenever the groups are not equivalent at the beginning of the experiment, it is difficult to interpret differences on the dependent variable.

Another rival explanation for experimental results involves the loss of subjects from the experimental groups. The reasons for subjects dropping out range from illness or moving out of the area to disenchantment with the experience of being a subject. The loss of subjects in an experiment is called *mortality*. This poses the greatest threat to internal validity when there is *differential mortality*, that is, when the conditions of an experiment have different dropout rates. Invariably, those subjects who drop out differ in important ways from the ones who remain, so that the experimental conditions are no longer equivalent in composition. In an experiment to test the effectiveness of certain behavior modification techniques on fingernail biting, for example, nail biters might be randomly assigned either to the experimental treatment or to the control group. But what if nail biters who are making the least progress dropped out of the experimental group? The measure of nail biting at the end of the treatment would tend to reflect greater success than if all subjects remained in the experimental group. Thus the effect of differential mortality would be confounded with the treatment.

Finally, experimental findings may be confounded by an *interaction* between two or more of the threats to internal validity we have discussed. This simply means that two of these threats, say selection and maturation, act together to affect the outcome on the dependent measure. You will recall the example we used to illustrate the possible confounding effects of maturational processes, a hypothetical study of the effectiveness of a new physical therapy program for stroke victims. It was pointed out that some degree of spontaneous remission might be confounded with the therapy effects. Now suppose that patients were allowed to select either the new therapy program, where treatment took place at a hospital, or the usual program, which involved visits by a physical therapist to the patient's home. We can conjecture how this process of selection might interact with effects of the normal recovery process (maturation). Those patients who volunteered for the new treatment program would differ from those who did not in one obvious way: they would have to have transportation to the hospital. For most patients this would mean a family member or some other person available and willing to take and wait for them while they had the therapy. Perhaps stroke victims who have someone around who is willing to make such an effort are also receiving more social and emotional support (and perhaps other benefits) than are those patients who do not have such a person available. Such benefits could possibly facilitate spontaneous remission for patients in this therapy group. Thus the interaction effects of selection and maturation would be confounded in this study with the effects of the therapy program.

We now examine three research designs in which threats to internal validity pose rival explanations for the results, thus preventing meaningful interpretation. Because these designs lack one or more features of true experimental designs, they are termed "preexperimental."

Preexperimental Designs

Design 1: The One-Shot Case Study

$$X \qquad O$$

In the simplest possible design, dubbed the one-shot case study, some treatment is administered to a group, after which the group is observed or tested to determine the treatment effects. The above diagram illustrates this design; X stands for the treatment condition of the independent variable and O for the observation or measurement of the dependent variable. Time moves from left to right.

To illustrate this design, imagine a teacher who is having a problem with her fourth-grade pupils frequently talking out of turn. She decides to conduct the following "experiment" one day. Every time a child speaks out of turn, the teacher says, "You are talking out of turn," and then immediately turns her attention to the pupil who was interrupted or to another who is modeling desirable behavior. Toward the end of the day a teacher's aide carefully records the number of incidents for each child and finds that few children are talking out of turn and that the number of incidents is low. The teacher concludes that her treatment is effective and recommends it to other teachers.

Unfortunately for the teacher's efforts, such a conclusion is clearly unwarranted; several other explanations may account for the apparent change in behavior. Maybe one of the more recalcitrant talkers left after lunch for a date with the dentist; this would result in a mortality effect. Maturational variables also might threaten the study's internal validity if, for example, some of the children were particularly tired that day. Finally, history could offer an alternative explanation for the results; perhaps early in the day the class had a music lesson in which they let off steam by doing a lot of energetic singing and so felt less inclined to interrupt during class discussions. Mortality, maturation, and history represent threats to the internal validity of any study based on the one-shot case study design.

The critical flaw in this design is that it provides no adequate basis for comparing the findings to other observations; and some process of comparison is essential to scientific inference. We cannot tell in our example what the incidence of talking out of turn would have been with a different intervention, with no intervention, with a different group of students, or on a different day. All we know is that the teacher intuitively sensed that talking out of turn decreased.

Many of our day-to-day assumptions about causality are based on "experiments" similar to one-shot case studies. Suppose a jogger buys a new brand of running shoes and afterwards finds that she is running faster than before. Concluding that the shoes have "helped" her, she recommends them to you. Can you think of other explanations for her increase in speed?

Design 2: The One-Group Pretest-Posttest Design

$$O_1 \qquad X \qquad O_2$$

A second preexperimental design, the one-group pretest-posttest design, involves observing or measuring a group of subjects (the pretest), introducing a treatment (the independent variable), and observing the subjects again (the posttest). The pretreatment observations are represented by O_1, the independent variable by X, and the posttreatment observations by O_2. For example, the performance of a group of joggers might be timed before (O_1) and after (O_2) they received a new brand of running shoes (X). Design 2 is commonly found in educational, organizational, and clinical research. It is an improvement over design 1 because it provides a basis of comparison, but it is still subject to major sources of invalidity.

We may illustrate this design by changing our design 1 example slightly. Suppose the teacher's aide counted talking-out-of-turn incidents on the day prior to as well as the day of the experiment. How would this change in design affect the study's internal validity? First, the mortality threat is controlled effectively in design 2 studies, because only the data from those subjects observed both before and after the treatment would be used in analyzing the effects of the independent variable. In addition, the pretreatment observation makes it possible to determine whether those who dropped out before the second observation differed initially from those who remained.

Two other threats found in the one-shot design, maturation and history, also are found in one-group pretest-posttest designs. In fact, the longer the period between pretest and posttest, the greater the likelihood that either of these threats will confound the results. If in our example a weekend or holiday intervened between pretest and posttest, the children might be "talked out" or worn out on the posttest day.

Additional threats to internal validity—testing, instrumentation, and sometimes statistical regression—may present rival explanations to the hypothesis in design 2 studies. To continue with our example, it is possible that recording talking-out-of-turn incidents could inhibit children who notice their behavior is being observed and recorded; this would be a testing effect. Instrumentation would threaten internal validity if the teacher's aide was not consistent in measuring the problem behavior. For instance, he might record every incident zealously during the pretest but become bored during the posttest and fail to count some incidents. On the other hand, he might be more accurate on the second day of observation due to practice. Finally, statistical regression can be a problem in design 2 studies if a group representing an extreme position on the dependent variable is used. This was not the case in our classroom example as the whole class served as subjects.[2]

Design 3: The Static-Group Comparison

$$X \qquad O_1$$

$$O_2$$

A third preexperimental design, the static-group comparison, like design 2 is an improvement over the one-shot case study in that it provides a set of data with which to compare the posttreatment scores. While design 2 provided pretreatment scores on the same group, design 3 provides the scores of a control group. As symbolized above, the rows represent separate groups. X stands for the experimental treatment, the blank space under X for the no-treatment control, and O represents the dependent-variable measure. Notice that each group is measured just once.

Our classroom example again may be altered slightly to fit this design. Let us suppose that, because of rapid growth in the area, the school is on double sessions, so that the teacher has one class in the morning and a different one in the afternoon.

On the treatment day she tries out her new approach on the morning class only, but records talking-out-of-turn incidents for the pupils in both groups.

Although the static-group comparison does a better job of controlling threats to internal validity than do the other two preexperimental designs, some threats remain. The threat of history confounding the findings is controlled, for the most part, as the two groups should experience the same major environmental events. Since there is no pretest, the threats of testing and statistical regression are absent. And as long as measurements are equally reliable and valid for the two groups, instrumentation is not a problem. On the other hand, mortality is uncontrolled and there are no pretest data by which one may learn whether subjects who drop out of a group are similar or dissimilar to those who remain. Groups that were similar in all important aspects at the beginning of a study may become dissimilar through differential mortality. Maturation also may be a threat if maturational factors are operating differently in the two groups. Indeed, it seems plausible that the afternoon class will be less lively and less likely to talk out-of-turn than the morning class, simply because it is later in the day. Finally, selection is perhaps the most serious threat to internal validity. For without the random assignment of subjects to the experimental and control groups, there is no control of possible pretreatment differences.

We turn now to a discussion of true experimental designs, in which threats to internal validity are better controlled.

True Experimental Designs

The designs described in this section differ from the preexperimental designs in that there are always two or more groups, and subjects are assigned to them randomly to ensure approximate equivalence of the groups.

Design 4: The Pretest-Posttest Control Group Design

$$R \quad \begin{matrix} O_1 & X & O_2 \\ O_3 & & O_4 \end{matrix}$$

The pretest-posttest control group design involves measuring the experimental group before and after the experimental treatment. A control group is also measured at the same time but does not receive the experimental treatment. As symbolized before, the rows represent separate groups, and time moves from left to right. The R to the left indicates that subjects are randomly assigned to the groups; each O stands for an observation; the X symbolizes the treatment condition of the independent variable; and the blank space under the X indicates the no-treatment control condition.

Our earlier example of the study of assertiveness training effectiveness may be altered to illustrate this design. In the original example, which was not a true experiment, subjects who scored in the bottom 25 percent on an extroversion scale were assigned to the experimental treatment with the remaining 75 percent serving as controls. To fit design 4, the entire pool of available subjects would be randomly assigned to the treatment and control groups. Both groups then would be given the extroversion scale (O_1 and O_3 pretest measurements). Only the experimental treatment group would receive the assertiveness training; then, at the conclusion of the training, both groups would again be given the extroversion scale (O_2 and O_4 posttests).

How does this design deal effectively with the common threats to internal validity? To consider history first, any event in the general environment that would produce a difference between the pretest and posttest in the experimental group ($O_1 - O_2$) would produce about the same difference in the control group ($O_3 - O_4$).[3] Similarly, changes due to maturation, testing, or instrumentation would be felt equally in both groups. Therefore, these factors cannot account for differences between the posttests, O_2 and O_4. Random selection also eliminates the factors of selection and regression, within the limits of chance error. Comparison of O_1 and O_3 provides a check on the randomization procedure with regard to initial differences on the dependent variable. And even if the subject pool consisted only of extreme scorers—for example, all introverts—random assignment of these subjects to experimental and control groups should ensure initially equivalent groups that regress about the same amount on the posttest. Finally, this design permits the assessment of possible mortality effects; one can compare both the number of subjects and the pretest scores of those who drop out of each group.

Since true experimental designs adequately control threats to internal validity (without which we cannot tell whether the independent variable was responsible for the results), it is appropriate to examine these designs for possible threats to external validity. You will recall that external validity refers to the extent to which a study's findings have meaning outside the particular circumstances of the experiment, that is, the extent to which the results may be generalized.

The pretest-posttest control group design suffers from the external-validity threat of testing interacting with the independent variable, called *testing-X* or *testing-treatment interaction*. This simply means that the effect of the independent variable may be different when a pretest is present than when it is not. Sometimes an independent-variable effect can be produced only with subjects who have been sensitized to the experimental treatment by pretesting. To continue with our example, it may be that the assertiveness training is effective in helping people become more socially outgoing only when they have been made particularly conscious of their introversion (or extroversion) by responding to the pretest extroversion scale. If that were true, results of the study could be generalized only to other similarly pretested groups.

The extent to which one need be concerned about an interaction between testing and treatment depends on the experimental situation. In educational settings, where test-taking is the norm, the effects of a testing-treatment interaction would probably be negligible; and the learning situations to which one would be generalizing are likely to involve testing. The classroom experiment described in the last chapter on the effects of teacher comments on student achievement (Page, 1958) is an example of the usefulness of the pretest-posttest control group design. Since regular classroom tests and procedures were used in this study, there is no reason to believe the pretests interacted with the treatment to any significant extent. On the other hand, in studies of attitude change or persuasion, a pretest may very well alert subjects to the treatment to follow in such a way as to make them more receptive (or resistant) to it. In such cases, the findings would have little external validity, and it would be better to use the following design.

Design 5: The Posttest-Only Control Group Design

$$
\begin{array}{ccc}
 & X & O_1 \\
R & & \\
 & & O_2
\end{array}
$$

The simplest of the true experimental designs, the posttest-only control group design incorporates just the basic elements of experimental design: random assignment of subjects to treatment and control groups, introduction of the independent variable to the treatment group, and a posttreatment measure of the dependent variable for both groups. Notice that, except for one crucial difference—subject randomization—design 5 resembles the preexperimental static-group comparison design. Unlike this design, however, design 5 controls for the common threats to internal validity adequately.

Some researchers seem to feel more confident that groups are equivalent prior to the experimental manipulation when they can check pretest scores. Yet, in reality the random assignment of subjects is sufficient to ensure approximate equivalence. Therefore, under most circumstances, design 5 is preferable to design 4, the pretest-posttest control group design. By eliminating the pretesting step, design 5 has two major advantages. First, it is more economical. Second, and more importantly, it eliminates the possibility of an interaction between the pretest and the experimental manipulation. Still, there are special situations requiring a pretest and other situations in which a pretest would be useful. Imagine, for example, a long-term experiment in which you expect a higher than usual number of subjects to drop out. In such a situation, pretest scores on each group would help in determining if there was an interaction between mortality and the experimental manipulation.

Design 6: The Solomon Four-Group Design

$$
\begin{array}{cccc}
 & O_1 & X & O_2 \\
 & O_3 & & O_4 \\
R & & & \\
 & & X & O_5 \\
 & & & O_6
\end{array}
$$

A third true experimental design, the Solomon four-group design, is really a combination of designs 4 and 5, as may be seen in the above symbolic representation. Here we have an experimental group and a control group that are pretested, as well as experimental and control groups that are not pretested.

The Solomon four-group design has the advantages of both of the two pre-viously discussed experimental designs; information is available regarding the effect of the independent variable (O_2 and O_5 compared with O_4 and O_6), the effect of pretesting alone (O_4 versus O_6), the possible interaction of pretesting and treat-ment (O_2 versus O_5), and the effectiveness of the randomization procedure (O_1 versus O_3). While this design provides more information than either of the other two experimental designs, the requirement of two extra groups makes it much more expensive to use.

Overview of True Experimental Designs

Many simple variations of experimental designs are possible. Although designs 4 and 5 were presented as having just two groups (an experimental group and a control group), the logic of either design may be extended easily to three or more groups: one might, for example, want to compare several clinical approaches to treating depression or a number of methods of teaching reading. Similarly, groups may be added to vary the intensity of the independent variable; for example, we might induce a high level of frustration in one group, a moderate level in another, and a low level in a third group.

Sometimes ethical considerations preclude withholding treatment from a control group. This is frequently the case in the fields of correction, clinical psychology, medicine, and education. Also, a true no-treatment control group, one that is exactly identical to the treatment group except for the treatment manipulation, is impossible to implement in many situations. The hypothetical study discussed ear-lier, in which a new approach to physical therapy for stroke victims was compared to a standard approach, illustrates the common variation of experimental design in which there is no true control group; rather, two or more treatments are compared for their relative effectiveness.

We have pointed out the importance of random assignment of subjects as a means of controlling for preexisting differences (known and unknown) in subjects. However, randomization introduces one other threat to internal validity: the observed results might have occurred by chance rather than being caused by the experimental variable. Recall that tests of statistical significance are used to deter-mine the likelihood of this occurring, thereby screening out trivial results that could have occurred easily by chance. Having noted this, we stress again that the random assignment of subjects is an integral part of any true experimental design.

The matter of external validity warrants further comment. According to the terminology introduced here, external invalidity results from an interaction of the treatment, or independent-variable manipulation, with some other variable. The presence of such interaction means that treatment effects only apply under certain conditions inherent in the experiment. Earlier, for example, we discussed the threat of a testing-treatment interaction as a particular concern in the pretest-posttest control group design. This interaction limits the generalizability of results to situa-tions in which subjects have been pretested. External validity similarly may be threatened by interactions of the treatment with characteristics of the subject population, time, or some other feature of the experimental setting. We now elaborate on a few of these sources of external invalidity.

Sample selection often restricts external validity. Because the sample of subjects participating in an experiment typically consists of homogeneous groups such as college students, the possibility of selection interacting with the independent variable may be present in any of the experimental designs. Thus, extreme caution must be used in generalizing any effect of the independent variable to dissimilar groups. A cigarette smoking cessation treatment, for example, might succeed with volunteer subjects (who are highly motivated) but be ineffective with the general population of smokers who wish to quit.

Maturation also may interact with the independent variable; that is, the effect of the treatment may occur only with subjects in a certain physical or mental state. For example, the findings of an experiment conducted at four o'clock on a hot summer day may be generalizable only to hot, tired subjects. Solutions to this problem include (1) deliberately varying the conditions that would seem to affect maturational states as part of the experimental design, or (2) replicating the basic experiment under varying conditions.

Finally, the effect of the treatment might be peculiar to the historical circumstances surrounding the experiment. For example, a study of the effects of certain experiences on Christians' attitudes toward Jews might produce significant results only because the experiment took place at the time of a highly rated television series on the Holocaust. In viewing it, subjects became more receptive to the treatment. Replicating experiments under different historical circumstances is an effective way of ruling out the threat of such treatment-history interactions.

Factorial Experimental Designs

Social events often are caused or influenced by a number of variables. Therefore, it frequently makes sense to study several possible causes, or independent variables, at the same time. When two or more independent variables are studied in a single experiment, they are referred to as *factors*, and the designs that enable us to explore their effects jointly are called *factorial designs*. Although more than one variable is manipulated, it is possible to assess the effect of any manipulated variable while controlling for the impact of other variables. Hence, the basic principle of good design, "doing only one thing at a time," still applies.

Factorial designs are not especially difficult to understand or use, as they are simple extensions of the basic experimental designs. In fact, we already have introduced one design, the Solomon four-group design, which may be viewed as a factorial design. We depicted this design as follows, with each row representing a separate group.

		O_1	X	O_2	First group
R		O_3		O_4	Second group
			X	O_5	Third group
				O_6	Fourth group

TABLE 8.2. Solomon Four-Group Design
Represented as a 2 × 2 Factorial Design

Treatment condition (factor A)	Pretest condition (factor B)	
	Pretest	*No pretest*
Treatment	First group O_2	Third Group O_5
No treatment	Second group O_4	Fourth group O_6

Table 8.2 presents this design in factorial form. Note that both levels (categories) of one factor are combined with both levels of the second, forming the four experimental groups in the cells of the table. When a design has two independent variables, each having two levels, we call it a 2 × 2 ("two by two") factorial design. A design that had three levels of one factor and four levels of another would be a 3 × 4 factorial design having twelve cells. In every case the number of cells of a factorial design may be determined by multiplying the number of levels of the first factor by the number of levels of the second factor, and, if there are additional factors, by the number of levels of each in turn. Theoretically, a factorial design may utilize any number of factors, although there are practical limits.

Ideally, each cell will have the same number of subjects. When this is not possible (because of subject mortality or other reasons), the dependent variable data in the various cells can be analyzed after statistical adjustment has been made to compensate for the uneven number of subjects. As always with true experimental designs, subjects are assigned to the various conditions (cells) by a random device to control for preexperimental differences.

You may be wondering how the effects of the various factors are determined in a factorial design. To answer this question, let us consider a hypothetical study of the effect of a sympathetic movie portrayal of the gay community (the treatment) on attitudes toward gay rights (the dependent variable). The results from the Solomon four-group experiment are shown in Table 8.3. Each cell contains the average (mean) posttest attitude score for that experimental group. A higher score indicates a more positive attitude toward gay rights.

The first information that one looks for in a factorial design is the *main effect* of each factor, that is, the overall effect of the factor by itself. We have labeled the treatment variable "factor A" and the pretest variable "factor B." The main effect

TABLE 8.3. Hypothetical Results of a Study Using a 2 × 2 Factorial Design

Treatment condition (factor A)	Pretest condition (factor B)		Overall means of A
	Pretest	*No pretest*	
Treatment	40	10	25
No treatment	20	10	15
Overall means of B	30	10	

of factor A is determined by comparing the overall mean score of subjects who received the experimental treatment (which in this case is 25) with the overall mean score of subjects who did not receive the experimental treatment (in this case 15).[4] Clearly, subjects who saw the movie were then more supportive of gay rights than those not exposed to the movie. Whether or not this treatment effect is "significant" would have to be determined by an appropriate statistical test. Let us assume that all effects are statistically significant.

Likewise, the main effect of factor B is determined by comparing the overall mean score of pretested subjects (30) with the overall mean of subjects not pretested (10). Thus, exposure to the pretest also enhanced posttest attitudes toward gay rights. While this result is not unexpected, it is nonetheless discouraging, since ideally treatment effects (the movie) should be much more powerful than measurement artifacts (pretesting effects).

Interaction Effects

A major advantage of factorial designs is that they also provide information about the joint effects of the factors. If there is an interaction between two factors, the effect of one factor on the dependent variable varies according to the value or level of the other. In other words, the effects of the factors together differ from the effects of either alone. The presence of the pretesting effect in our example should lead us to question the generalizability of the movie effect. Specifically, there may be an interaction between the pretest and the movie, with the pretest sensitizing subjects to the topic and thereby enhancing the movie's impact. Inspection of the cell means in Table 8.3, graphed in Figure 8.1, does indeed reveal a testing-treatment interaction: The movie has an impact only on pretested subjects. Consequently, its value outside the laboratory as an attitudinal change agent appears to be very limited.

Interaction effects do not always look like the idealized results in Figure 8.1. Some other possible outcomes are graphed in Figure 8.2. The movie treatment may

FIGURE 8.1. Graph of cell means from Table 8.3.

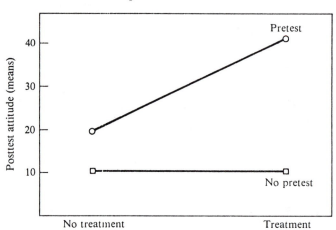

FIGURE 8.2. Illustrative outcomes for 2 × 2 factorial designs. Symbols are same as in Figure 8.1.

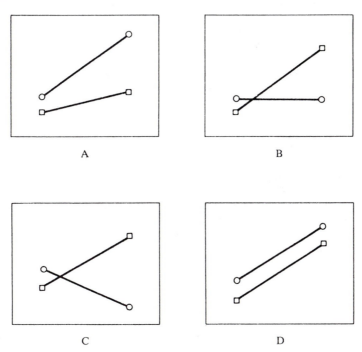

A   B

C   D

affect all subjects but more so for those pretested (Figure 8.2A), may have no effect on pretested subjects (Figure 8.2B), or even may have a reverse effect on pretested subjects (Figure 8.2C). Finally, when there is no interaction, the lines connecting the mean scores for pretested and not-pretested subjects will be parallel as shown in Figure 8.2D. (Box 8.1 describes a factorial experiment that produced an interaction effect.)

Besides providing information on interaction effects, factorial designs are cost efficient. A factorial design can increase the amount of information provided by a study with little increase in cost over a nonfactorial experimental design. Suppose, for example, an investigator wished to study the usefulness of an aversive conditioning program for people who wish to stop cigarette smoking. One design possibility would be simply to compare thirty subjects receiving aversive conditioning with thirty control subjects receiving pseudoconditioning. However, with little effort and no additional subjects, this design could be expanded by including another relevant independent variable. For instance, evidence suggests that the expectation of success conveyed to subjects in some smoking cessation programs may be an important placebo factor in effecting success. Such a possibility could be explored easily in a factorial design by adding a manipulation of expectancy as the second independent variable. The first design would examine only one research question: What is the effect of aversive conditioning on smoking cessation? The factorial design, however, would address two additional questions: (1) What is the

BOX 8.1

An Example of a Factorial Design: Beautiful But Dangerous

In an interesting study employing a 2 × 3 factorial design, Sigall and Ostrove (1975) investigated the effects of type of criminal offense (swindle or burglary) and physical attractiveness of the offender (attractive, unattractive, or no information) on the severity of the sentence received. Subjects in each of the six conditions were presented with a case account describing the offender and the crime. Then they were asked to circle a number between 1 and 15 to complete the statement, "I sentence the defendant, Barbara Helm, to _____ years of imprisonment" (p. 412).

For the factor "type of criminal offense," the researchers chose a swindle and a burglary. Swindles appeared to be attractiveness-related, in that the offender could use his or her attractiveness to commit the crime. The crime of burglary, however, appeared to be unrelated to attractiveness. In the swindle account, the defendant Barbara Helm had become friendly with a middle-aged bachelor and persuaded him to invest $2200 in a nonexistent corporation. In the burglary account, the defendant had illegally entered a neighbor's apartment and had stolen $2200 in cash and goods. To manipulate the attractiveness factor, the researchers attached a photograph of a physically attractive woman to one-third of the case accounts, a photograph of a physically unattractive woman to one-third of the accounts, and no photograph to the remainder.

Sigall and Ostrove predicted an interaction: when the crime was unrelated to attractiveness (the burglary), subjects would sentence the attractive defendant to a shorter prison term than the unattractive defendant. But when the offense was attractiveness-related (the swindle), the attractive defendant would receive a more severe sentence. The first prediction follows from evidence that attractive people are better liked and that liking for a defendant increases leniency. In the case of the second prediction, the authors reasoned that a beautiful criminal would be regarded as more dangerous and as having taken advantage of a "God-given gift" if her attractiveness helped her to commit the crime. As shown below, the data supported the hypothesis, with a statistically significant interaction of attractiveness and offense.

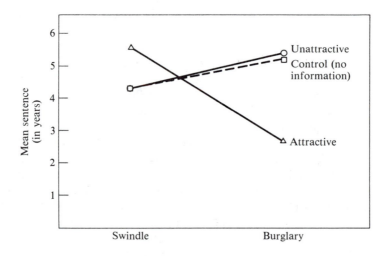

effect of expectancy of success on cessation? (2) Is the effect of aversive conditioning different when expectancy of success is low than when it is high?

A factorial design also may enhance external validity by permitting one to determine the effects of a key variable under several conditions. When the effects are consistent under diverse conditions, we are more confident that the findings generalize to additional situations. For example, we may want to study the effects of counseling on troubled marriages, our dependent measure being the percentage of participant couples still together 1 year after completion of counseling. A $2 \times 3 \times 2$ factorial design might utilize two counseling approaches, let us say "behavior modification" and "eclectic"; three counselor conditions, such as "male-female counselor team," "male counselor only," and "female counselor only"; and two cost-of-counseling conditions, perhaps "fixed fee" and "free." Since this design explores the effects of marriage counseling under twelve conditions, the study should be high in external validity.

Quasi-Experimental Designs

Legal, ethical, or practical considerations make it impossible to employ a true experimental design in some research situations. Frequently random assignment of persons (or other units) is not possible. At other times control or comparison groups cannot be incorporated into the design. Sometimes random assignment to treatment and control groups can be carried out but the researcher cannot exercise the tight control over subjects' experiences required for a true experiment. To deal with these problems, researchers have developed a number of *quasi-experimental designs*, so named because they take an experimental approach without having full experimental control.

In terms of complexity and effectiveness in controlling extraneous threats to validity, these designs generally lie between preexperimental and true experimental designs. Some of them resemble preexperimental designs but with added features. Others are similar to true experimental designs but with something lacking, such as a control group or the process of randomization.

An example of the first type is the *separate-sample pretest-posttest design* (Campbell and Stanley, 1963), diagrammed below.

$$R \quad \begin{matrix} O_1 & X & \\ & X & O_2 \end{matrix}$$

The top line represents the group randomly selected for pretreatment measurement. This group receives the treatment but is not measured afterward. The second group is randomly selected for posttreatment measurement. Since the treatment effect is estimated by comparing pretest (first-group) scores with posttest (second-group) scores, this design resembles the preexperimental one-group pretest-posttest design $(O_1 \ X \ O_2)$. However, some of the threats to validity found in the latter (e.g., testing and testing-X interaction) are eliminated by using separate samples. The most serious challenge to the internal validity of the design is history.

The separate-sample pretest-posttest design may be useful in those circumstances in which the entire population of interest, such as residents of a city, employees of a large firm, students in a university, or soldiers in a military unit, receives the same treatment. Although one cannot randomly assign subjects to different treatments, the design may be applied if one can determine the timing of the measurement of the dependent variable and randomly select those who are measured. For example, measurement might take the form of an attitude survey conducted prior to and following alcohol education week (the treatment) at a certain college.

Nonequivalent control group designs exemplify those quasi-experimental designs that are similar to but lack a crucial feature of true experiments. These designs often are used when the experimental treatment is administered to intact groups, such as school classes, making random assignment of individual subjects impossible. In one such design, symbolized below, pretests and posttests are administered both to the experimental group and to a nonequivalent but similar control group.

$$O_1 \qquad X \qquad O_2$$
$$O_3 \qquad\qquad O_4$$

Except for the missing "R" representing randomization, this design looks exactly like the pretest-posttest control group design. Randomization, of course, should be used if at all possible. But if it is not possible, then this quasi-experimental design is often worth using. The inclusion of a control group, especially one highly similar to the experimental group in known respects, makes it superior to the one-group pretest-posttest design. For if the groups are similar in recruitment and history, then the design controls for history, maturation, testing, and regression.

Since the design possibilities are so numerous, we limit further discussion of quasi-experimental designs to some general ideas and a detailed description of a quasi-experimental study.[5] The objective of such studies, as with true experiments, is to determine treatment effects by eliminating plausible rival explanations of experimental results. Lacking subject randomization or other features of true experiments, however, quasi-experimental studies use a variety of approaches to establish internal validity. Threats to internal validity are ruled out individually in several ways (Cook, Cook, and Mark, 1977): (1) including special design features; (2) examining additional data that bear on each threat; and/or (3) reasoning, based on theory or on common sense, that a particular threat is an unlikely alternative explanation.

An example of a design feature that strengthens causal inferences in a quasi-experiment is the use of a pretest. This is a nonessential feature in most true experiments because randomization creates initially equivalent groups. But in a quasi-experimental study, a pretest permits a vital check on the initial difference between nonequivalent groups (Cook, Cook, and Mark, 1977). An example of the second approach—examining additional data—comes from a study of a smoking cessation treatment (Berglund et al., 1974). The researchers obtained a measure of motivation from pre-treatment interviews with participants. By showing that motivation scores were unrelated to subjects' success in withdrawing from smoking, they eliminated one selection threat as a possible rival explanation. Finally, an example of the third approach would be ruling out testing as a serious threat in an educational setting where the measures are similar to typical classroom testing procedures.

Let us further examine how these approaches are applied in a carefully conducted quasi-experimental study.

An Example: Interracial Attitudes and Behavior at a Summer Camp

Can contact between "opposite-race" children under favorable circumstances improve interracial attitudes and behavior? To test this idea, social psychologist Gerald Clore and his colleagues (1978) set up a summer camp for underprivileged black and white children that was designed to provide a positive interracial experience. Previous research suggested that prolonged, intimate contact between racial groups of equal size and similar socioeconomic background could significantly reduce prejudice. Therefore, the camp was structured so that blacks and whites of similar status were equally represented among the campers, counselors, and staff. For example, children were assigned to tents that accommodated three black and three white campers of the same sex and age group (8–10 or 11–12), as well as one black and one white counselor. In all, 196 children were randomly assigned to attend one of five 1-week camp sessions.

The experimenters used three dependent measures to assess whether the camping experience affected racial attitudes and behavior. First, they administered an attitude measure, based on four questions regarding feelings toward children of the "opposite" race. The procedure approximated the separate-sample pretest-posttest design, with half the children administered the measure on the first day of camp and the other half near the end (fifth or sixth day). Results showed the camp to be effective for girls but not for boys. While the girls had somewhat more negative cross-race attitudes at the beginning and shifted toward neutrality, the boys were relatively neutral at the beginning and showed no change.

A second measure, obtained for three of the five weeklong sessions, involved making inexpensive loaded cameras available to the children and allowing them to photograph whatever and whomever they wished. Within age, sex, and race categories, children were randomly assigned to either a pretest group that took pictures on the second day or a posttest group that took pictures on the fifth or sixth day. The dependent variable was the proportion of persons in the resultant photographs who were not of the photographer's race. Thus, this measure, like the first, was based on the separate-sample pretest-posttest design. But unlike the first measure, the photo taking was unobtrusive and behavioral. Analysis of the photos revealed a slight but nonsignificant overall treatment effect: for only one of the 3 weeks measured did photos taken at the end of the week reveal a significantly higher proportion of cross-race persons than photos taken at the beginning.

A third set of measures, also behavioral, consisted of interpersonal choices the children made in three games played on the first day of camp and again on the fifth or sixth day. Counselors recorded the choices, the dependent variable being the proportion of choices that were interracial. The design for this measure, referred to by the researchers as a "multiple-group pretest-posttest design," resembled the preexperimental one-group pretest-posttest design but was an improvement over it in that it was replicated over five camp sessions ("multiple groups"). Results showed a slight shift toward more cross-race choices from the beginning to the end of the sessions. As with the attitude measure, the change was evident for girls only. While showing no significant change from pretest to posttest, the boys made a higher proportion of cross-race choices overall than did the girls.

Thus, the dependent measures, taken together, indicated that the camp experience was effective in changing the interracial attitudes and behavior of the girls but not of the boys, who evidenced more positive attitudes and behavior from the beginning. The authors of the study described how they were able to rule out rival explanations to the hypothesis that the camp experience itself caused the observed changes. To do so, they invoked special design features, additional data, and reasoning based on common sense.

Some crucial design features incorporated in the study enabled Clore and co-workers (1978) to eliminate several validity threats. These included the use of two different quasi-experimental designs, three very different dependent measures (attitude questions, photographs, and interpersonal choices), and replications. Using more than one quasi-experimental design strengthens a study, because different designs ordinarily will not share the same weaknesses. For example, testing effects cannot be ruled out in the multiple-group pretest-posttest design (which produced the shift in cross-race choices), since pretests and posttests are administered to the same persons. However, testing is not a threat in the separate-sample pretest-posttest design (which produced the change in attitudes), since individuals receive either the pretest or the posttest but not both.

The use of dissimilar measures also strengthens inferences by controlling for systematic error in any one measure. Moreover, the measurement processes were replicated three to five times (weekly camp sessions), controlling for the most part the threats of instrumentation and history. Instrumentation could be ruled out because with pretests and posttests repeated over several weeks, it was unlikely that scorers' expertness, effort, or enthusiasm would differ systematically from pretest to posttest across all sessions. And since the measurements were replicated at different times and produced consistent results for both the attitude and choices measures, the rival explanation of history was ruled out for these two measures. On the other hand, one could not rule out entirely the possibility that historical conditions were responsible for the change in the photo measure, implausible as this explanation seems, since this measure showed significant effects for only 1 week.

Two possible rival explanations for certain of the findings were ruled out through the examination of additional data. First, it was conjectured that the changes in the interpersonal-choices data might be attributable to children making their choices from among their acquaintances. That is, if children were acquainted with more same-race children than cross-race children at the beginning of camp, they might choose more same-race children on the pretests and move toward a higher proportion of cross-race posttest choices as they became acquainted with the cross-race children. Since the names of initial acquaintances of each child were available (the children had been asked in one game to circle the names of all the other children whom they knew), it was possible to test this argument. Data for two camp sessions were reanalyzed, discarding choices of children known to the subject before camp. The results of the reanalysis were consistent with the original findings, ruling out this rival explanation.

A second possible explanation for the choices data, that choices in the posttest games might reflect allegiance to the child's living unit, was also evaluated. The choices data were reanalyzed using the proportion of cross-unit choices as the dependent variable. No significant effects were found, thereby ruling out this second possibility.

Finally, Clore and colleagues were able to rule out some other threats through reasoning based on common sense. For example, maturation was an unlikely explanation for the changes as the camp sessions lasted only 1 week each. The threat of regression was implausible, because subjects were not selected on the basis of extreme attitudes or behavior. (See Box 8.2 for another example of quasi-experimental research.)

BOX 8.2

The Connecticut Crackdown on Speeding: An Example of Quasi-Experimental Time-Series Analysis

In late December 1955, Governor Abraham Ribicoff of Connecticut instituted a crackdown on speeding in the hope of reducing the number of deaths from automobile accidents, which had risen to a high point of 324 in 1955. New, stiffer penalties for speeding involved automatic suspension of the offender's driver's license: 30 days for the first offense; 60 days for the second offense; and indefinitely for the third offense, with a hearing after 90 days. Though opposed by many, the crackdown was carried out and suspensions for speeding increased dramatically. When the number of traffic fatalities declined to 284 in 1956, Governor Ribicoff was quoted as saying, "With the saving of 40 lives . . . we can say the program is definitely worthwhile" (Campbell and Ross, 1968).

But did the program actually cause the reduction in traffic deaths? Campbell and Ross (1968) addressed this question while demonstrating the utility of various quasi-experimental designs. First, they presented the data that Ribicoff cited—"before crackdown" and "after crackdown" statistics—shown in Figure A. Note how impressive the decrease appears in the figure. If these data alone were used in determining whether the crackdown (the treatment) caused the decrease in deaths (the dependent variable), the design would be the one-group pretest-posttest design, which fails to control for most of the common threats to validity.

BOX 8.2 (*continued*)

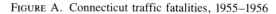

Figure A. Connecticut traffic fatalities, 1955–1956

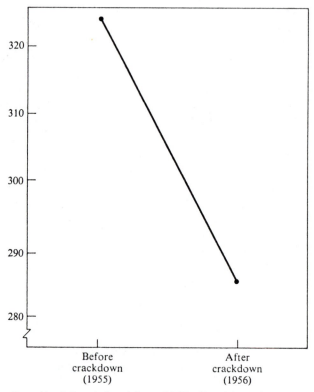

Source: Page 38 of Campbell and Ross (1968). Copyright 1968 by the Law and Society Association. Used by permission.

Because of the weakness of the one-group pretest-posttest design, Campbell and Ross next did an analysis based on an *interrupted time-series design*. This design resembles the one-group pretest-posttest design but with a series of observations before and after the treatment manipulation.* One way to symbolize it would be this:

$$O_1 \quad O_2 \quad O_3 \quad O_4 \quad X \quad O_5 \quad O_6 \quad O_7 \quad O_8$$

Data for this design are graphed in Figure B, which shows the number of traffic fatalities from 1951 through 1959. The decrease in traffic fatalities in 1956 now appears much less impressive in view of the comparable decreases shown in 1952 and 1954 and the unusually high number of fatalities in 1955.

Campbell and Ross then extended their evaluation by using a *multiple time-series design*, in which a series of observations are made on nonequivalent control groups as well as on the treatment group. The researchers obtained traffic fatality statistics for the years 1951–1959 for four states adjacent to Connecticut, which were assumed to be

---

*There are no limitations, other than practical ones, on the number of observations in the series.

FIGURE B. Connecticut traffic fatalities, 1951–1959.

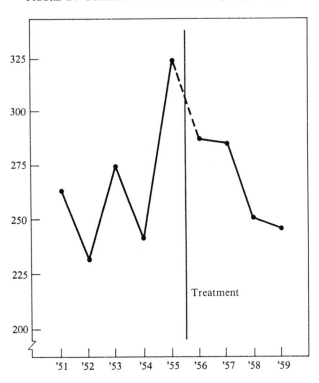

Source: Page 42 of Campbell and Ross (1968). Used by permission.

similar in weather and driving patterns. Figure C shows the time-series data for the five states. Note that for the year 1955 four of the five states showed an increase in fatalities over the previous year, with Connecticut showing the greatest increase. All five states showed a decrease for 1956. These facts, as well as the fact that the 1956 decrease in Rhode Island closely resembled that in Connecticut, might argue against the hypothesis that the decrease in Connecticut was caused by the crackdown. However, Connecticut was the only one of the five states to show consistent year-to-year decreases following the crackdown; Rhode Island, by contrast, showed consistent increases after 1956.

Let us now examine how the major threats to validity were dealt with in this study.

History is a possible threat in that some event of 1956 other than the crackdown may have caused the reduction in fatalities. Possible rival explanations included better weather conditions in 1956 than in 1955 and improved safety features on 1956-model automobiles (Campbell and Ross, 1968). While the researchers reasoned on the basis of available data that neither of these explanations appeared plausible, the threat of history cannot be ruled out altogether, especially in view of the fatality rate decreases for 1956 in all of the four control states. Some event common to all five states still may have caused the decrease in fatalities. However, history is not a plausible rival explanation for the post–1956 decreases in Connecticut, since the adjacent states failed to show the same pattern.

BOX 8.2 (*continued*)

FIGURE C. Traffic fatalities (per 100,000 persons) for Connecticut, New York, New Jersey, Rhode Island, and Massachusetts.

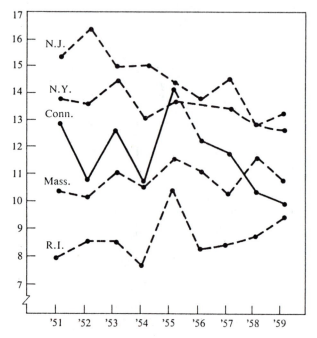

Source: Page 45 of Campbell and Ross (1968). Used by permission.

Maturation is normally associated with human physical and psychological processes. In the Connecticut study, maturation would be a threat if, for example, the driving population as a whole were becoming more skilled drivers. Although this is rather implausible, Campbell and Ross extend the idea of maturation to processes external to subjects. Thus, they defined as a maturation threat the possibility of a long-term trend toward a reduction in death rates due to such factors as improved medical services or improved highways. But since no such trend appears in the time-series or multiple time-series data, this threat may be ruled out.

The threat of *testing* must also be evaluated: could the pretest by itself have caused the change? In this case, the pretest consists of the 1955 traffic fatalities statistic. It seems unlikely that mere keeping of records would have much impact on the next year's statistic, but the widespread publicizing of the high 1955 figure conceivably could have increased driver caution, thus lowering the subsequent year's statistic. This threat cannot be ruled out with certainty for 1956; however, it seems implausible that publication of the 1955 figure would result in the continued year-to-year decreases that were observed in Connecticut.

Instrumentation would be a threat if there had been a postcrackdown change in record keeping. Campbell and Ross reported that they found no evidence of this.

Regression is a threat whenever a treatment is administered on the basis of a high pretest score. It may be argued that this was the case with the Connecticut crackdown on speeding, which was instituted following an extreme year. Based upon the data from 1951 through 1956, regression or simple instability of the data would indeed offer plausible rival explanations. However, since the rate of traffic deaths continued to decrease in the years following the crackdown, these factors do not explain the findings adequately.

The Campbell and Ross study is an example of rigorous quasi-experimental research. While the absence of a true experimental design made it impossible to exert optimal control over the threats to validity, the researchers gained valuable knowledge by making use of better quasi-experimental designs, relevant available data, and common sense. By these means they were able to conclude with a large degree of confidence that the Connecticut crackdown on speeding had some effect.

Evaluation Research

Intended to show how quasi-experimental analysis could be used to assess the effects of social policy, the Campbell and Ross study (Box 8.2) was reported at a time when there was a flowering of interest in applied social research. This interest was produced largely by legislation in the 1960s that called for mandatory evaluations of federal social action programs (Rossi, 1972). Now, over 20 years after the first enabling legislation, *evaluation research* is firmly established as a distinct area of study in the social sciences. The goal of evaluation research is to analyze the extent to which social policies and social programs achieve particular effects. Thus, it focuses on cause and effect and takes as its primary methodological model the true experiment.

In the last chapter we mentioned some evaluation studies that were true experiments: the "Sesame Street" study (Ball and Bogatz, 1970) and the San Diego study of patrol staffing (Boydstun et al., 1978). In many evaluation research situations, however, a true experimental design is not possible. For various reasons, random assignment may not be used or breaks down. Frequently the treatment program is already in existence before the evaluation researcher is consulted; and it may not be possible, legal, or ethical to create a control group by withholding treatment from qualified persons. Under these circumstances, a quasi-experimental design must suffice.

Besides the greater difficulty of drawing causal inferences in quasi-experimentation, evaluation research poses special problems of its own. We now consider these in relation to internal and external validity.

Internal Validity

Internal validity is limited in many evaluation studies by the infeasibility of random assignment. Yet, even when subject randomization is feasible, resistance to the idea may come from project sponsors, administrators, and staff, who may feel that assignment to the treatment should be based upon the individual's need or some similar criterion. At this point researchers must be persuasive and diplomatic. They may explain the logic and mechanics of randomization, and point out that the effectiveness of the treatment is unknown and will remain so until a scientific test of it is carried out. They may also argue that, since the effects of the treatment are unproven and since there might even be undesirable effects in some cases, the only fair way to assign persons to the groups is by a random method (Cook, Cook, and Mark, 1977).

Many times random assignment is incorporated into an evaluation research design but it breaks down somewhere along the line. For example, at the very beginning of implementation, the person responsible for processing applicants may fail to randomize appropriately because of personal biases, such as the belief that persons should be assigned to the program on the basis of merit, or because of carelessness (Cook, Cook, and Mark, 1977). This problem may be circumvented by more extensive training of the staff person or by using research personnel rather than regular program staff to implement the randomization procedure.

A greater problem is treatment-related loss of participants, which would lead to dissimilarity of the treatment and control groups. This may occur either when individuals who have been assigned to a treatment or control group refuse to participate in the assigned group (selection) or when individuals drop out of the experimental groups at different rates (differential mortality). Treatment-related refusals to participate may be minimized by restricting the subject population to persons who agree at the outset to participate in any condition to which they are assigned. Solutions proposed by Cook and Campbell (1976) for minimizing treatment-related attrition include (1) paying subjects to remain in the experiment, (2) omitting the control group and making the treatment groups approximately equal in attractiveness to subjects, (3) and requesting those who drop out of treatment groups to continue with the measurement aspects of the experiment so that data on these persons may be compared with data on those who fully participated.

Another internal-validity issue involves the tests of statistical significance used to determine the probability that research findings may be due to chance factors. We pointed out in chapter 7 that these statistical tests assume subjects have been randomly assigned to treatments, which is often not the case in evaluation research. Although social statisticians are in sharp disagreement over the use and meaning of significance tests in nonexperimental designs (see Morrison and Henkel, 1970), we share D. Gold's position (1969) that results that easily could have occurred by a chance process (i.e., a "nonsignificant" result) should not be taken seriously. Consequently, as a minimal but not sufficient condition for attributing importance to a treatment program, the results should be statistically significant.

On the other hand, discovery that a treatment has had a statistically significant effect does not have the same meaning or importance to the evaluation researcher that it would have for a researcher testing hypotheses. While in pure science the researcher is most interested in whether or not a predicted effect is present, the evaluation researcher is more interested in the magnitude of the effect and its practical significance. Consider, for example, a new, expensive program for the vocational rehabilitation of disabled persons. If this program were found to have statistically significant effects, but resulted in only a few more persons being placed in permanent jobs than the standard program, then it would most likely be abandoned.

External Validity

The issue of external validity is particularly important in evaluation research. Such research frequently is undertaken so that an informed decision may be made regarding the extension of a program or policy to other participants or beneficiaries. Yet generalizing results is difficult for several reasons.

With regard to the sampling of units, the target population often is too difficult or too expensive to enumerate, thereby precluding probability sampling. In fact, a survey of evaluation researchers in 1970 indicated that only 59 percent used random sampling, and only 50 percent observed a sample representative of the target population (Bernstein and Freeman, 1975). When nonprobability samples are used in evaluation research, several selection procedures may further threaten external validity. Sometimes subjects self-select themselves into a treatment; sometimes program participants are selected because they are most likely to generate positive results; and sometimes units are chosen because of their availability (Bernstein, Bohrnstedt, and Borgatta, 1975). As long as a program is designed only for volunteers who seek treatment, self-selection should permit reasonable generalization to the target population. Otherwise, self-selection, as well as selection for availability and presumed excellence, is likely to produce samples that differ systematically from the target population.

Other features of evaluation research may also threaten external validity (Bernstein, Bohrnstedt, and Borgatta, 1975).

1. The effectiveness of a social program may be dependent on the personal qualities of the staff who administer it. Thus, results would not be generalizable to later, widespread implementation of the program by staff who are less able, committed, or enthusiastic about its success.

2. Knowledge that one is a participant in the evaluation of a social program can produce biased results. This raises the question of whether findings are generalizable to settings where the program is no longer experimental or being evaluated.

3. The program may be effective only at the historical time in which and/or in the particular geographic setting where it takes place.

4. Measurement may be inadequate for assessing a program's effectiveness. Unreliable measuring instruments, for example, will produce underestimates of treatment effects, affecting both internal and external validity. And while external validity is limited to the particular effects that are in fact measured, it is often difficult to specify program goals clearly. Frequently in evaluation research, treatment (independent variables) and desired goals (dependent variables) are conceptually and operationally defined by policy makers or program administrators before the evaluator is called in, which results in vague or ambiguous definitions. Commonly, the treatment program is relatively clear but the goals are stated very broadly for political reasons (e.g., to attract or keep support of a government agency or other sponsor). In such a case, the adequacy of evaluation research depends on the evaluator's ability to perform the delicate task of translating politically acceptable goals into measurable outcomes without losing the support of the program administrator and other interested parties. (For a more complete discussion, see Rossi and Wright, 1977.)

There are no easy solutions to these external validity problems. To begin, one should draw a probability sample of the target population if possible. Whether or not this is done, one should also attempt to vary those factors—time, setting, staff, etc.—that are likely to limit the generality of study results. Another approach is to attempt to make the conditions of the experimental program (e.g., sample, setting, staff) representative of the conditions under which the program ultimately would be implemented. Cook, Cook, and Mark (1977) refer to this approach as "generalization to modal instances." It requires first that one describe the manner in which the program would be carried out if it became formal policy (the modal setting). Then one selects or creates a research setting in which the program is implemented in a manner very similar to that of the modal setting. If, for example, the modal program involved health education services directed to the urban poor, then the pilot program should involve urban poor. One would not choose to evaluate a program located in a small town or one directed to a wider range of socioeconomic groups.

Summary

The basic principle of good experimental design is "doing only one thing at a time," that is, allowing only one independent variable to vary while controlling all other variables. In this chapter we examined preexperimental designs, true experimental designs, and quasi-experimental designs in the light of this basic principle. We found that the preexperimental designs violate this principle by permitting a number of variables to go uncontrolled, presenting serious threats to the internal validity of the study. Features of the true experimental designs, on the other hand, permit researchers to rule out these threats as rival explanations to the hypothesis. Although quasi-experimental designs control extraneous variables imperfectly, rival explanations frequently may be ruled out through the intelligent use of design features, additional data, and common sense.

Experimental designs are evaluated in terms of how well they control for extraneous variables that threaten a study's internal and external validity. Thus, we began by identifying several common threats to internal validity: history (specific events other than intended experimental manipulations that occur during the course of an experiment), maturation (psychological and physiological changes in subjects), testing (the effects of being measured once on being measured a second time), instrumentation (unwanted changes in the measuring instrument or procedure), statistical regression (the tendency for extreme scorers on one measurement to move closer to the mean score on a later measurement), selection (differences in the composition of experimental and control groups), mortality (the loss of subjects during the course of an experiment), and interactions with selection (differences between treatment groups due to the combined effect of initial differences and history, maturation, or testing). These threats, or classes of extraneous variables, are sources of invalidity insofar as they can account for study results.

Preexperimental designs lack one or more features of true experiments, such as a comparison group or random assignment. Therefore, they are subject to several validity threats and their findings cannot be interpreted meaningfully. Three preexperimental designs are the one-shot case study, the one-group pretest-posttest design, and the static group comparison.

All of the basic true experimental designs control adequately for the major sources of internal invalidity. However, the external validity of the pretest-posttest control group design suffers from the possibility of a testing-treatment interaction, in which experimental effects occur only for pretested subjects. This threat is eliminated in the more economical posttest-only control group design, albeit at the loss of pretest information. The Solomon four-group design offers the advantages of both of the latter designs by combining them in a single experiment. While strong in internal validity, studies incorporating these three designs may still be weak in external validity. Besides testing-treatment interaction, external validity may be threatened by the interactions of the treatment with sample characteristics, history, and maturation.

External validity is generally better in factorial designs. These are simple extensions of basic experimental designs in which two or more independent variables are manipulated. Other advantages of factorial designs include their ability to demonstrate both main effects and joint effects and cost efficiency. Each manipulated variable in a factorial design is called a factor. Main effects refer to the effects of a single factor by itself. Joint or interaction effects refer to outcomes in which the effect of one independent variable depends on the level or value of another.

Quasi-experimental designs, like preexperimental designs, lack some feature (usually randomization) of true experiments. However, by virtue of special design features and supplementary data that test specific validity threats, and by rendering threats implausible through reasoning, quasi-experiments often permit relatively strong inferences about cause and effect.

Quasi-experimentation frequently is used in evaluation research, which investigates the effect of social policies and social programs. As an increasingly important area of investigation, evaluation research presents unique problems and is fast evolving a methodology of its own. Evaluation researchers, for example, often must contend with resistance to randomization and extensive treatment-related loss of participants. They must attend to the magnitude as well as the statistical significance of effects; in addition, they must be keenly concerned about external-validity issues, since the ultimate objective in evaluating trial programs is to decide whether they should be extended in time and geography and to larger numbers of people.

Key Terms

threats to internal validity
history
maturation
testing
instrumentation
statistical regression
selection
mortality
differential mortality
preexperimental designs
one-shot case study
one-group pretest-posttest design
static-group comparison

true experimental designs
pretest-posttest control group design
posttest-only control group design
Solomon four-group design
factorial experimental designs
main effect
interaction effect
quasi-experimental designs
separate-sample pretest-posttest design
nonequivalent control group design
interrupted time-series design
multiple time-series design
evaluation research

Review Questions and Problems

1. What is the basic principle of good design?

2. What is meant by "threats to validity" in a research design?

3. Complete this statement: If "history" or some other threat to internal validity is present in an experimental design, then the possible effects of an extraneous variable are *confounded* with the _____.

4. Explain the difference between history and maturation effects. Between testing and instrumentation effects.

5. Under what circumstance is regression toward the mean likely to be a threat to internal validity?

6. The authors give an example of an experiment in which the *interaction* effect of selection and maturation is a threat to internal validity. Imagine the following hypothetical experiment. To study the effects of new writing-intensive courses at a college, a researcher examines two groups of students during a single semester. One group, mostly freshmen, consists of students enrolled in writing-intensive courses, and the other group, mostly upperclass, consists of students who are not enrolled in such courses. Tests given at the beginning and end of the semester reveal a much greater improvement in writing skills for the group enrolled in writing-intensive courses than for the group not enrolled. How could a selection-maturation effect account for this outcome?

7. Which threats to internal validity are likely to be present in the (a) one-shot case study, (b) one-group pretest-posttest design, and (c) static-group comparison?

8. Explain how the pretest-posttest control group design adequately controls for each of the major threats to internal validity.

9. (Adapted from Dane, 1981:13). Explain why random assignment to experimental conditions can or cannot be used to rule out the following threats to internal validity: (a) maturation, (b) history, (c) instrumentation, (d) selection, (e) statistical regression.

10. What is the principal threat to *external* validity in a pretest-posttest control group design?

11. Why is the posttest-only control group design generally preferred over the pretest-posttest control group design?

12. The interaction of the independent variable with some other variable (e.g., a variable represented by history or maturation) poses a threat to external validity in experiments. What are some solutions to problems of (a) selection-X interaction, (b) maturation-X interaction, and (c) history-X interaction? (Recall that X is an independent variable.)

13. The Solomon four-group design may be viewed as a 2×2 factorial design. What are the factors and the levels of each factor in this design?

14. What kind of effect—main or interaction—was found in the Sigall and Ostrove experiment (Box 8.1)? Suppose they had found that the defendant's attractiveness had no effect on sentencing, irrespective of type of crime, but that sentences were significantly longer for the burglary than the swindle. What kind of effect is this?

15. What are the principal advantages of factorial over nonfactorial (i.e., single-factor) experimental designs?

16. How do quasi-experiments differ from true experiments?

17. What are the three ways that rival explanations are ruled out in quasi-experimental designs? Describe one application of each of these techniques in (a) the Clore and co-workers camp study, and (b) the Campbell and Ross study of the Connecticut speeding crackdown (Box 8.2).

18. What are some of the special problems in evaluation research with regard to establishing internal validity and external validity?

19. Why is the magnitude of an effect of greater importance to the evaluation researcher than statistical significance alone?

20. Aside from nonrandom selection of subjects, what other common features of evaluation research limit external validity?

21. Over 30 years ago social psychologists Morton Deutsch and Mary Evans Collins (1951) conducted a study on the impact of an interracial residency pattern on racial attitudes. To assess this impact they interviewed tenants of two *integrated* interracial housing projects in New York (families were assigned to apartments without consideration of race) and tenants of two *segregated* biracial housing projects in Newark (black and white families were assigned to different buildings or different parts of the project). In general, they found less prejudice among tenants in the integrated housing projects. Identify three threats to internal validity in this study. Briefly explain how each threat (or extraneous variable) could account for the observed difference in prejudice between the two projects.

22. (Adapted from McGuigan, 1978:171–172). "The problem of whether children should be taught to read by the word method or by the phonics method has been a point of controversy for many years. Briefly, the word method teaches the child to perceive the word as a whole unit, whereas the phonics method requires that he break the word into parts. To attempt to decide this issue an experimenter plans to teach reading to two groups, one by each method. The local school system teaches only the word method. 'This is fine for one group,' the experimenter says. 'Now I must find a school system that uses the phonics method.' Accordingly, a visit is made to another town that uses the phonics method.

"A sample of third-grade children in town is tested to see how well they can read. After administering a long battery of reading tests it is found that the children who used the phonics method are reliably superior to the children who used the word method. It is then concluded that the phonics method is superior to the word method."

    a. What is wrong with this study design?

    b. Briefly explain how you would redesign this study to provide an adequate test of the researcher's hypothesis.

NOTES

1. This section and the next two sections draw heavily upon Campbell and Stanley's classic treatment of these subjects (1963).

2. However, if the teacher initiated the experiment one day because of a sharp increase in talking out of turn, the incidence of this behavior may regress toward a more typical classroom level on the posttest.

3. However, this design does not by itself control for effects of unintended events that might occur *within* a treatment group. For a discussion of this problem and suggestions for dealing with it, see Campbell and Stanley (1963:13–14).

4. Notice how the principle of "doing only one thing at a time" applies in interpreting factorial results. The only difference between the first-row and the second-row groups is the factor A manipulation. The two groups are equivalent on factor B (each row has an equal number of pretested and nonpretested subjects) and should be approximately equivalent on extraneous variables as a result of subject randomization.

5. For a more complete discussion, see Campbell (1969) and Cook and Campbell (1976, 1979).

9

Survey Research

Survey research in its many forms has become a very common activity in our society, and most of us have had some experience with it in one form or another. Perhaps you have been stopped on the street by a radio news reporter and asked your opinion on some issue of local or national importance. You may have responded to a reader survey found in a popular magazine. Or perhaps you have filled out and returned a brief questionnaire that came with a small appliance or other product you purchased. You or someone else in your household very likely responded to the last U.S. Census, which attempted to enumerate and gather confidential information about every person living in the United States. You have been a consumer of survey research if you have read in the newspaper the results of Gallup or Roper public opinion surveys. You have done a little "survey research" of your own if you moved to a new community and asked a number of residents about local restaurants or where to obtain various services.

General Features of Survey Research

The survey examples above differ in their degree of formality and in the extent to which they conform to these typical features of professional survey research:

1. A large number of respondents are chosen through probability sampling procedures to represent the population of interest.
2. Systematic questionnaire or interview procedures are used to elicit information from people in a reliable and unbiased manner.
3. Sophisticated statistical techniques are applied to analyze the data.

As we now elaborate on these three features through reference to actual studies, we will also describe exceptions to the general rule for each feature.

Large-Scale Probability Sampling

Professional surveys normally make use of large samples chosen through scientific sampling procedures to ensure precise estimates of population characteristics. In the 1970 National Fertility Study, for example, the national probability sample interviewed consisted of 6752 ever-married women (i.e., women who were married, separated, divorced, or widowed) (Westoff and Ryder, 1977). Among the many important findings, it was determined that in 1970 one factor alone, the elimination of unwanted births, would bring fertility down almost to replacement level—that is, the level that would keep the population stationary, an average of 2.1 births per couple. And by 1975 it had become apparent that the elimination of unwanted births would bring U.S. fertility to below replacement level.

Budget and other practical considerations frequently limit national samples to 1500–3000 respondents. At times, however, they are much larger, such as the sample of 28,043 persons included in the first Health and Nutrition Examination Survey (HANES I). Respondents to the HANES I survey submitted to measures of nutrition status as well as to various medical examinations, which resulted in a wealth of information about the nutrition and general health status of the U.S. population (USDHEW, 1973).

Sometimes when large samples are desired it is possible to obtain them economically by combining samples from previous studies. For example, in their study of the long-term effects of education, Hyman, Wright, and Reed (1975) drew together fifty-four surveys conducted between 1949 and 1971, involving 76,671 respondents, from three sources: the Gallup Poll, the National Opinion Research Center (NORC) of the University of Chicago, and the Survey Research Center, University of Michigan. Not surprisingly, a very strong positive relationship was found between amount of education and correct answers to knowledge questions. However, this was true not only for "academic"-type questions taken from the arts and sciences, but for questions relating to current affairs and popular culture as well. Furthermore, the relationship persisted over time, suggesting that one of the lasting effects of education is a lifelong openness to learning or tendency to seek information.

The sample of respondents for a study is not necessarily confined to one country. In *comparative* or *cross-cultural studies*, equivalent sample surveys are conducted in different countries. In a study of the process by which individuals in developing countries become modern in personality, a sample of 6000 men were interviewed, 1000 from each of six countries (Inkeles and Smith, 1974). Modern attitudes and outlook were found to be determined largely by just three of the many factors examined: total years of education, exposure to the mass media, and years of factory experience.

Units of analysis. While in most surveys the units of analysis are individuals, this is not always the case. An example of a survey treating cities as units involved community decisions about whether or not to fluoridate water supplies in order to reduce tooth decay. A controversial issue in many communities in the 1950s, the proposal to fluoridate provided social scientists with an excellent opportunity to study the political decision-making process in cities. To learn how cities had dealt with the issue of fluoridation, Crain, Katz, and Rosenthal (1969) sent questionnaires to three informants in each of 1181 cities: the public health officer, the publisher of the largest city newspaper, and the city clerk. The units of analysis were, again, the cities. One finding was that when the issue was decided by referendum, the odds against fluoridation were five to one.

Systematic Procedures: Interviews and Questionnaires

Although the popular impression of surveys may be that they obtain information through interviews, some survey studies use a combination of interviews and self-administered questionnaires, and many others use questionnaires only. Regardless of whether the survey researcher makes use of interviews only, questionnaires only, or some combination of the two, professional survey research typically requires that procedures be standardized for all respondents so that the data obtained will be high in reliability.

The National Fertility Study illustrates the use of interviews; the U.S. Census uses a combination of interviews and self-administered questionnaires; and the 1969 study by Crain et al. of political decision making in cities made use of questionnaires only.

An additional example of the use of questionnaires is a study in which the researchers sought to discover the factors responsible for the career choices of college men (J. A. Davis, 1964a, 1966). Questionnaires covering such topics as academic performance, occupational interests, intended career, expectations for graduate study, personal characteristics and values, and background factors were completed by 33,982 university and college seniors representative of American students graduating in the spring of 1961. In addition, the researchers rated the 135 institutions from which the students were drawn in terms of their selectivity, as measured by the intellectual caliber of their students. Results showed that while grade-point average (GPA) was strongly associated with the choice of a demanding profession, the caliber of the institution was not. The study's authors concluded that students compare their grades with those of others at their institution, and that this information plays a stronger part in determining career choice than does "pure" intellectual ability. Thus, a student of moderately high ability who attends an excellent university and who achieves a mediocre GPA is less likely to choose a demanding profession requiring graduate school than a student of comparable ability who attends a less selective institution and achieves a high GPA. It may indeed be more advantageous to be a "big frog in a little pond" than a "little frog in a big pond."

Unstructured versus Structured Interviewing. Although the term "survey" generally implies highly standardized procedures, informative and scientifically useful interviewing is sometimes carried out in a less formal or structured manner. In an *unstructured interview*, the objectives may be very general, the discussion may be wide ranging, and individual questions will be developed spontaneously in the course of the interview. The interviewer is free to adapt the interview to capitalize on the special knowledge, experience, or insights of respondents. An everyday example of an unstructured interview might be a journalist's interviewing a celebrity to learn more about his or her personal background, interests, and lifestyle.

At the other extreme is the highly *structured, standardized interview* in which objectives are very specific, all questions are written beforehand and asked in the same order for all respondents, and the interviewer is highly restricted in such matters as the use of introductory and closing remarks, transitions or "bridges" from topic to topic, and supplementary questions to gain a more complete response (probes). In between the two extremes, the *partially structured interview* would have specific objectives, but the interviewer would be permitted some freedom in meeting them. The scope of the interview would be limited to certain subtopics, and key questions probably would be developed in advance.

The choice of a highly structured, partially structured, or unstructured approach depends on the researcher's objectives. For example, in her study of the relationship between contraception and abortion in an environment where both are readily accessible, Kristin Luker (1975) wanted an interviewing approach that would allow maximum flexibility in the development of hypotheses and theory. By using a relatively unstructured approach in interviewing a sample of fifty abortion-seeking women who had prior experience with effective methods of contraception but who had taken risks during their last menstrual cycle, Luker was able to develop a theory of contraceptive risk-taking. She found that a woman's decision not to contracept was not a symptom of psychological problems, as often has been assumed by health care professionals, but rather a rational decision in terms of the perceived costs and benefits to the woman of contracepting and the perceived risks, costs, and benefits of pregnancy. That is, each woman did her own cost accounting, although it may not have been explicit. Costs associated with contraception included medical side effects, inconvenience, lack of spontaneity, male resistance, and so forth. To most of the women interviewed, the risk of pregnancy seemed slight, and all were aware of the possibility of obtaining an abortion. Benefits to getting pregnant included testing fertility (many were of the impression that they had some physical problem that decreased their chances of getting pregnant) and testing the partner's commitment.

Komarovsky (1976) combined the use of unstructured, in-depth interviews with standardized personality tests and questionnaires in her study of the masculine role strains of seniors at a male Ivy League college. In the process of generating hypotheses, she was able to compare the information gained from the interviews to the data from the tests and questionnaires. The areas of role strain most troublesome to the seniors were sexuality (72 percent), followed by anxiety over future work roles (53 percent) and family relationships (33 percent).

For some research purposes a social scientist might utilize two or three sets of interviews, beginning with very loosely structured interviews and progressing to a final set of highly structured interviews. A freer interviewing style in the preliminary stages would yield rich and varied information. This would assist the researcher in formulating or refining hypotheses, clarifying objectives, and specifying subtopics for subsequent partially structured interviews. Findings from a second set of interviews might be applied to the development of a highly structured questionnaire.

Sophisticated Data Analysis

Data analysis techniques depend on whether the survey's purpose is descriptive, explanatory, or a combination of the two. Surveys that are primarily descriptive seek to describe the distribution within a population of certain characteristics, attitudes, or experiences and make use of simpler forms of analysis. Explanatory surveys, on the other hand, investigate relationships between two or more variables and attempt to explain these in cause-and-effect terms. Sorting out the relationships between the variables in an explanatory survey requires the use of more sophisticated data analysis techniques. (Data analysis will be dealt with further in chapters 14 and 15.)

The Health and Nutrition Examination Survey (HANES I), mentioned earlier, which gathered data on the eating habits and health status of Americans, illustrates surveys whose purpose is mainly descriptive (USDHEW, 1973).

Descriptive surveys also may be illustrated by *social indicators* research. Although existing definitions of social indicators vary in emphasis, basically the term refers to a broad measure of some important social condition that has relevance to government policy decisions. Social indicators would include measures of crime, family life, health, job satisfaction, satisfaction with government services, schools and public transportation, and so forth; these may be contrasted to familiar economic indicators such as the consumer price index, the gross national product, and the unemployment rate. Like economic indicators, social indicators may be measured at repeated intervals to study changes. Andrews and Withey (1976) developed a comprehensive set of social indicators that were used in several surveys, with a total of 5422 respondents. The purpose of their research was to measure individual perceptions of well-being. One of the findings was that the life concerns related most strongly to a measure of overall well-being involved personal relationships. Economic factors played a very small role in respondents' perceptions of well-being.

The *explanatory* potential of survey research may be illustrated by a study of elderly persons' self-images in regard to aging (Blau, 1955). Citing a survey that found that elderly individuals' self-images regarding age (whether they see themselves as "old" or "middle-aged") are highly correlated with their idea of how others perceive them, Blau asked this question: Does the changing of an elderly person's self-image from middle-aged to old bring about a change in the way the person perceives that others view him or her; or, does the changing view of others in regard to "elderliness," and the perception of this changing view, precipitate a change in the person's self-image? The former was found to be the case; that is, the changing self-images of the elderly lead to a change in their perceptions of the way others view them.

Survey Research Designs

The character of survey data analysis depends not only on the purpose of the study—descriptive or explanatory—but also on the type of design used. The basic types of designs are cross-sectional designs, trend studies, panel studies, and sociometric and contextual designs.

The most commonly used survey design by far is the *cross-sectional design*, in which data on a cross section of respondents chosen to represent the larger population of interest are gathered at essentially one point in time. By "one point in time"

we do not mean that respondents are interviewed or that self-administered questionnaires are collected simultaneously (although questionnaires might be in some studies). Rather, the data are collected in as short a time as is feasible. Most of the
studies just cited are cross-sectional designs.

Trend studies and panel studies are two types of *longitudinal designs*, that is,
designs in which the data are gathered over an extended period of time. In *trend
studies* a research question is investigated by repeated surveys of independently
selected samples of the same general population. That is, for each survey a different
sample of respondents is obtained. This allows for the study of trends or changes in
the population as a whole. In *panel studies*, on the other hand, the same individuals
are surveyed more than once, permitting the study of individual as well as group
changes.

Trend studies may be illustrated by social indicators research, by repeated
public opinion polls of candidate preferences as an election approaches, and by the
monthly government surveys used to estimate unemployment. Ideally, all trend
information would be obtained through measures repeated frequently at regular
intervals. However, much of our trend survey data come from infrequent replications of classic studies. For example, a classic study by Stouffer (1966) surveyed
opinions regarding the threat of communism and attitudes toward civil liberties
among a cross section of the American population and a separate sample of community leaders. One finding was that, while a solid majority of community leaders
expressed support for the rights of dissidents to freedom of expression, a minority of
the sample from the general population did so. Stouffer predicted a future trend
toward increased tolerance. A careful replication of this study did indeed find an
increase in the proportions of civic leaders and of the general public expressing
tolerance, but as a group the civic leaders remained somewhat more tolerant than
the population in general (Nunn, Crockett, and Williams, 1978). The replication
also revealed that the relationships found in the Stouffer study between support of
civil liberties and such variables as gender, section of country, and education still
held.

Whereas trend studies identify which *variables* are changing over time, panel
studies can reveal which *individuals* are changing over time because the same
respondents are surveyed again and again. Lazarsfeld, Berelson, and Gaudet's
classic 1948 study of voter behavior, *The People's Choice*, exemplifies the panel
method. Prior to the 1940 presidential election, 600 persons were interviewed
repeatedly between May and November. The analysis revealed that persons who
expressed a clear preference for Roosevelt or Wilkie at the first interview were
unlikely at the second interview 1 month later to remember having seen or heard any
campaign propaganda from the party of the opposing candidate. Because of this
phenomenon of selective attention, few voters changed their preferences over the
course of the study.

Another panel study, Project TALENT, involved a huge random sample of
American students who were in grades 9–12 in the spring of 1960. The approximately 375,000 students in the sample were given numerous intelligence, personality, and interest tests and were asked detailed questions about home and family,

study habits, and future plans for education and work. Follow-up questionnaires regarding educational achievement and plans, work history and plans, and personal history were administered to the same individuals 1, 5, and 11 years after their expected high-school graduation dates. Among the many analyses that have come out of this massive research effort is one that examined the long-term effects of teenage parenting on the parents' personal and professional lives (Card and Wise, 1978). A comparison of those who became parents before age 20 with a matched group of classmates who did not revealed a number of differences between the groups that persisted up to age 29. The adolescent parents, for example, averaged much less schooling, with a minority completing high school; held lower-status jobs; had more children than their comparison group and had a larger number than they considered to be ideal; and were more likely to have experienced separation or divorce.

Cross-sectional and longitudinal survey designs typically gather information about individuals. The last group of designs we will introduce, sociometric and contextual designs, look more closely at the group of which the individual is a part.

Sociometric designs require the interviewing of every person in the group under study. This makes possible the delineation of networks of personal relationships by asking respondents to provide such information as who their best friends are, whom they most like to work with on a certain project, or to whom they would go for advice. Sociometric procedures were among the methods used in a well-known study by James S. Coleman on the social status systems of high schools (1961). Among other questions, students were asked to identify their friends, student leaders, best students, students most popular with the opposite sex, and so forth.

Contextual designs study the relationship between certain characteristics of the social environment or *context*, and the characteristics or behavior of individuals in that environment. For example, a contextual design was employed to study the political activism of union members in relation to the type of shop in which they worked (Lipset, Trow, and Coleman, 1956). On the basis of voting records from union elections, shops were classified as radical or conservative and as high or low in political consensus. The analysis revealed that an individual in a shop having a high degree of political consensus was about four times as likely to be a union activist as a worker in a shop of low consensus.

Advantages and Disadvantages of Surveys

Now that we have examined a wide range of surveys, we are in a position to consider some of the advantages and disadvantages of this method compared to the experimental approach.

Whereas experiments are used almost exclusively for explanatory, hypothesis-testing research, surveys are used extensively for both descriptive and explanatory purposes. A principal advantage of surveys, therefore, is that they can provide detailed descriptions of populations. Indeed, surveys permit one to describe large and heterogeneous populations accurately and economically. By using probability sampling, one can be certain (within known limits of error) that the attributes, opinions, or behavior of a sample accurately describe the larger population from which it was drawn.

The major disadvantage of surveys relates to their use in explanatory research. Beyond association between variables, the criteria for inferring cause-and-effect relationships cannot be established as easily in surveys as in experiments. For example, the criterion of directionality—that a cause must influence its effect—is predetermined in experiments by first manipulating the independent (or causal) variable and then observing variation in the dependent (or effect) variable. But in cross-sectional surveys this is often a matter of interpretation, since variables are measured at a single point in time. Consider also the criterion of eliminating plausible rival explanations. Experiments do this effectively through randomization and other direct control procedures that hold extraneous variables constant. In contrast, surveys must first anticipate and measure relevant extraneous variables in the interviews or questionnaires, and then exercise statistical control over these variables in the data analysis. Thus, the causal inferences from survey research generally are made with less confidence than inferences from experimental research.

On the other hand, surveys can address a wider range of research topics compared to experiments. Ethical considerations preclude studying some topics experimentally—for example, the effect of emotional traumas on mental health—while practical considerations rule out many others; for instance, one normally cannot experimentally manipulate organizations or nations. Besides this flexibility, surveys can be a very efficient data-gathering technique. While an experiment usually will address only one research hypothesis, numerous research questions can be jammed into a single large-scale survey. The wealth of data typically contained in a completed survey may yield unanticipated findings or lead to new hypotheses. In fact, secondary analysis of surveys originally conducted for other purposes is a strong tradition in the social sciences that we discuss further in chapter 12. Still, surveys are less flexible than experiments in the sense that it is difficult to change the course of research after the study has begun. That is, once the survey instrument is in the field it is too late to make changes. The experimenter, in contrast, can modify the research design after running a few subjects with the loss of only those subjects.

Finally, an inherent weakness of surveys is that they deal almost exclusively with reports of behavior rather than observations of behavior. A brief encounter for the purpose of administering a survey also does not provide a very good understanding of the context within which behavior may be interpreted over an extended period of time. For this kind of understanding, the best approach is field research, discussed in chapter 11.

Steps in Survey Research: Planning

The activities in doing surveys fall into three broad categories: (1) planning, (2) field administration, and (3) data processing and analysis. The remainder of this chapter is devoted to planning and field administration. Chapters 14 and 15 deal with data processing and analysis.

FIGURE 9.1. Key decision points in planning a survey.

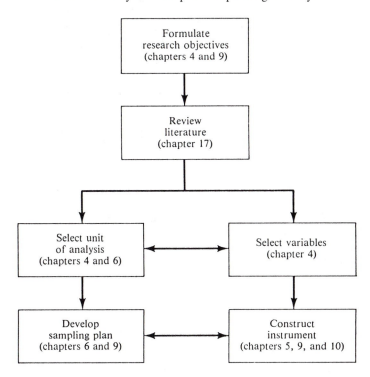

In planning a survey, a few activities may be thought of as key decision points. These are represented in the above flowchart. Under each major activity we have indicated the chapters that deal with it.[1]

The initial stages in planning a survey are essentially the same as in other forms of research. The first step is to select a topic and formulate a problem in researchable terms. One then reviews relevant journal articles, books, and other published materials to determine what is known about the topic and what work remains to be done. During the course of this review the researcher inevitably will refine and further specify his or her objectives; also he or she may become aware of existing definitions, approaches, or survey instruments that may be incorporated into the prospective study. The selection of units of analysis and variables occurs in light of research objectives. In survey research, the units of analysis are either individuals or groups of individuals (including families, organizations, cities); the particular variables selected depend on which characteristics should be studied in order to meet research objectives.

Constructing the Instrument

Constructing the survey instrument requires a great deal of time and thought and the making of many decisions. The most important decisions to be made are whether to use a structured or unstructured instrument (or something in between) and whether to use questionnaires, personal interviews, or telephone interviews.

Structured versus Unstructured approaches. As pointed out before, the research purpose largely determines whether structured or unstructured survey procedures are chosen. When the research objective is to test hypotheses, a structured approach is usually chosen. However, when the purpose is to acquire preliminary data in an area in which little research has been done in order to generate hypotheses, unstructured interviewing is generally preferred.

One reason to use highly structured procedures is to improve the quality of the data by minimizing measurement error. If slight changes in the wording of questions or in the behavior of interviewers (tone of voice, friendliness, appearance) can greatly influence responses, as studies have shown, then controlling these factors by presenting questions with exactly the same wording, in the same order, and in the same manner should reduce error and increase reliability. The typical procedures in large-scale, highly structured studies are intended to accomplish this, although complete standardization can only be approximated with human interviewers.

On the other hand, such standardization may not always improve data quality from the standpoint of validity. Standardization may reduce validity if the structured interview or questionnaire has different effects on respondents, for example, if respondents with varying personal, socioeconomic, or cultural backgrounds interpret the same questions differently. In this case, standardized questions are less useful than questions that can be adapted to the respondent. A related validity problem is the effect of standardization on respondent motivation. Some respondents feel irritated by the unilateral nature of a structured survey; they cannot converse with the researcher or interviewer, they cannot qualify or expand answers, and they may be forced to choose among alternative answers that they find unsatisfactory. Argyris (1968) reported that a questionnaire irritated a significantly higher proportion of top-level managers than did an interview with similar content.

Still, even when unstructured interviews are clearly preferable from the standpoint of validity, they may not be adopted. Unstructured interviews require much more highly trained personnel and more complex data analysis, so that they are much more expensive per interview. This is why in-depth interviews generally are done with very small samples.

Choice of data collection mode. Survey research may be conducted through personal face-to-face interviews, telephone interviews, or self-administered questionnaires (usually delivered and returned by mail). The choice of one or a combination of these modes is a critical decision step in the planning of the survey, with the decision depending partly on other planning decisions such as the research objectives, units of analysis, and sampling plan. For example, in the J. A. Davis (1964a, 1967) study of factors influencing students' career choices, the sampling plan required contact with a very large number of respondents at 135 geographically dispersed colleges and universities. These requirements ruled out both face-to-face and telephone interviews as too expensive, time-consuming, and impractical, and questionnaires were used. In the study of contraceptive risk-taking by Luker (1975), personal interviews were necessitated by the sensitivity and complexity of the topic and by the researcher's need for an approach flexible enough to permit the development of hypotheses.

Developing the Sampling Plan

The choice of survey mode, in addition to the overriding factor of cost, will determine the optimum sampling design. The most expensive and time-consuming mode of survey research is face-to-face interviewing, the major costs of which are incurred from direct interviewing time and travel to reach respondents. If respondents are widely dispersed geographically, this method also will require an efficient sampling procedure for locating respondents. Under these circumstances, the most cost-efficient procedure is multistage cluster sampling. Almost all large-scale surveys are multistage, with stratification at one or more stages. Many of these same surveys also use geographically controlled quota sampling at the final stage.

If respondents are reached by mail or phone, there is no reason for using clustering. Simple random or systematic sampling may be implemented easily, with or without stratification, provided that an adequate sampling frame can be obtained. Unfortunately, for phone surveys telephone directory listings often provide inadequate sampling frames because they exclude new and unlisted numbers, which constitute as many as 40 percent of the phones in the largest cities. This problem has been circumvented in recent years by a procedure called random-digit dialing, which is described later.

Decisions about the survey mode and basic sampling plan are made concurrently, since each affects the other and both depend on the objectives and resources of the researcher. In relation to the latter, each survey mode has its distinctive advantages and disadvantages, which we will now consider.

Face-to-Face and Telephone Interviewing

Both the face-to-face interview and the telephone interview require trained interviewers proficient in the use of the survey's *interview schedule*. The interview schedule consists of instructions to the interviewer, together with the questions to be asked, and, if they are used, response options. Interviewers and an interview schedule permit a great deal more flexibility than is possible with a self-administered questionnaire. For example, when research objectives necessitate the use of *open-ended questions*, which require respondents to answer in their own words, in contrast to *closed-ended questions*, for which specific response options are provided, an interviewer usually will be able to elicit a fuller, more complete response than will a questionnaire requiring respondents to write out answers. This is particularly true with respondents whose writing skills are weak or who are less motivated to make the effort to respond fully. In addition, interviewers can easily utilize question formats in which certain questions are skipped when they do not apply to a particular respondent, while such a format may be confusing for respondents completing a questionnaire. Further, in cases where it is important that questions be considered in a certain order, the self-administered questionnaire presents problems because the respondent may look over the entire form before beginning to answer.

Other advantages of interviewing include the ability of an interviewer to clarify or restate questions that the respondent does not at first understand. An interviewer may also help respondents clarify their answers by using *probes*, such as "I'm not sure exactly what you mean," or, "Can you tell me more about that?" Interviewers help to ensure that every relevant item is answered; tedious or sensitive items cannot be passed over easily as in self-administered questionnaires. Even when a respondent initially balks at answering an item, a tactful explanation by the interviewer of the item's meaning or purpose frequently results in an adequate response.

In addition to these characteristics that both modes of interviewing share, each has its own set of advantages and disadvantages.

Face-to-Face Interviewing

The oldest and most highly regarded method of survey research, face-to-face interviewing has a number of advantages in addition to the ones already mentioned. The *response rate*, the proportion of people in the sample from whom completed interviews (or questionnaires) are obtained, is typically high—approximately 80 percent except in large cities where the rate declines for surveys of the general public (Dillman, 1978). A high response rate means less bias is introduced into the data as a result of nonparticipation of sampled persons (since nonparticipants may differ in some important ways from participants). Reasons for the high response rate probably include the intrinsic attractiveness of being interviewed (having someone's attention, being asked to talk about oneself, the novelty of the experience); the difficulty of saying "no" to someone asking for something in person; and possibly the fact that the importance and credibility of the research is conveyed best by a face-to-face interviewer who can show identification and credentials.

This survey mode is appropriate when long interviews are necessary. Face-to-face interviews of 1 hour's length are common, but they sometimes go much longer. It also enables one to use visual aids such as photographs and drawings in presenting the questions, as well as cards that show response options. The cards may be useful when response options are difficult to remember or when it is face-saving for respondents to select the option or category on the card rather than to say the answer aloud. Finally, face-to-face interviewing permits unobtrusive observations that may be of interest to the researcher. For example, the interviewer may note the ethnic composition of the neighborhood and the quality of housing.

There are some disadvantages to this method, the greatest of which is cost. The budget for a face-to-face survey must provide for recruiting, training, and supervising personnel, interviewer wages and travel expenses, plus lodging and meals in some cases. In one experiment by Shosteck and Fairweather (1979) in which comparable surveys of physicians were conducted by mailed questionnaires and by personal interviews, the field cost per initial respondent—that is, the data-gathering expenses divided by the number in the sample—amounted to approximately $63 for personal interviews and $24 for the mailed questionnaire. These figures excluded the costs of initial planning and data coding, processing, and analysis. In 1986, the full cost of the National Opinion Research Center's General Social Survey, which involves a national probability sample with 90 minute interviews, was $325 per respondent (T. W. Smith, personal communication, 1986).

The difficulty of locating respondents not at home when the interviewer first calls is another disadvantage of this survey mode. In more and more households, no adult is at home during the day, necessitating call-backs in the evening. Unfortunately for the survey researcher, many persons in large cities will not open their doors to strangers in the evening, and many interviewers refuse to go into certain areas of cities at night. Fear of strangers and the desire for privacy may be the causes of another disadvantage: the response rate for heterogeneous samples in metropolitan areas has been declining for several years. However, this is not true for rural areas or among specialized target groups.

Staff supervision presents special difficulties. Frequently, interviewers, data coders, and the researcher are geographically dispersed. If an interviewer has not recorded responses adequately, effective coding is impossible. Furthermore, several more interviews may be completed by an interviewer before feedback gets to the individual. This is less of a problem when interviewer supervisors go over each interview schedule soon after it is completed.

Finally, with the personal interview method, interviewers may introduce bias into the data in a number of ways. For example, they may fail to follow the interview schedule in the prescribed manner or may suggest answers to respondents. Bias also may be introduced through a respondent's reaction to the interviewer's sex, race, manner of dress, or personality. In chapter 7 we spoke of the experiment as a "social occasion" and the related possibilities of bias. A face-to-face interview is no less a "social occasion" than an experiment; consequently, interviewers must be carefully trained to be sensitive to the ways in which they may wittingly or unwittingly affect their interviewees' responses.

Telephone Interviewing

Like face-to-face interviewing, telephone interviewing has its advantages and disadvantages. Substantial savings in time and money are two of the reasons survey researchers choose to use this method. Large survey research organizations that have a permanent staff can complete a telephone survey very rapidly, and even those researchers who must hire and train interviewers can complete a telephone survey faster than one requiring face-to-face interviews or mailed questionnaires. The costs for sampling and data collection in telephone surveys have been estimated to be 45–64 percent of those for face-to-face interview surveys (Groves and Kahn, 1979). However, telephone survey costs will exceed those for mailed questionnaires, even with several follow-up mailings included. The cost of long-distance telephone interviews has been greatly reduced by the use of Wide Area Telephone Service (WATS) lines, for which the researcher pays a flat monthly rate for a line permitting unlimited long-distance calls.

Administration and staff supervision for a telephone survey is much simpler than for a personal interview survey. No field staff is necessary; in fact, it is possible to have the researcher, interviewers, and coders working in the same office. This cozy arrangement has several advantages:

1. It permits supervisors to listen in on interviewers, allowing immediate feedback on performance and helping to minimize interviewer error or bias.
2. Coders may be eliminated and the interviewers can enter numbers corresponding to respondent answers directly into a computer terminal. If they are used, coders may provide immediate feedback to interviewers and their supervisors.
3. The researcher can be in touch with each aspect of the survey.

Response rates for this survey mode approach those for face-to-face interview studies, and may exceed them. Groves and Kahn (1979) report response rates about 5 percent below what may be attained with face-to-face surveys. Dillman (1978), on the other hand, has reported a response rate average of 91 percent for thirty-one telephone surveys using a precise step-by-step approach he calls the Total Design Method. For metropolitan areas, telephone surveys usually will attain higher response rates than will face-to-face interview studies. In addition, required callbacks may be made more easily and economically with telephone surveys than with face-to-face surveys.

In terms of sampling quality, the telephone survey mode falls between the face-to-face interview and the mailed questionnaire. In the past, lists of telephone subscribers were used in the sampling process, creating a problem of sampling representativeness. Two groups went unsampled: (1) that part of the population who did not have telephones and (2) those who had unlisted telephone numbers. The problem of bias resulting from the omission of nonsubscribers has diminished as an increasingly larger percentage of U.S. households, about 90 to 92 percent, have telephones (Groves and Kahn, 1979). However, certain groups are still underrepresented, such as rural people and the poor. The second problem, missing those with unlisted numbers, may be resolved through *random-digit dialing* or *modified random-digit dialing*. In the first procedure, telephone numbers are chosen independently by means of a table of random numbers. In modified random-digit dialing, known residential prefixes are sampled and the last four digits of the telephone number are chosen randomly. Using either of these procedures should result in a sample adequately representative for many purposes.

The complexity of the questions asked is an issue with telephone surveys. While the interviewer may repeat a question, it is desirable to develop questions simple enough to be understood and retained by respondents while they formulate an answer. A related issue is the adequacy of data attained by open questions. Groves and Kahn (1979), as well as others, have found that open-ended questions yield shorter, less complete answers in telephone interviews than in face-to-face interviews. Further, closed questions may present difficulties in that the interviewer cannot present the options on cards but must read, and, if necessary, repeat them to respondents at the risk of boring them. For these reasons, the telephone survey mode lacks the advantages of the face-to-face mode in regard to the types of questions that are used.

Another disadvantage of the telephone interview is that it is more difficult for interviewers to establish trust and rapport with respondents than it is in face-to-face interviews; this may lead to higher rates of nonresponse for some questions. Groves (1979) compared the results of two identical telephone surveys based on separate samples with the results of a face-to-face survey asking the same questions. At the end of the questionnaire were items about respondents' reactions to the interview. Among other questions, respondents were asked if they felt uncomfortable talking about certain topics, such as income, their income tax refund, political opinions, or racial attitudes. For each of the sensitive topics, more telephone respondents felt uncomfortable, with the largest differences for the income and income tax questions. Not surprisingly, the telephone surveys showed lower response rates to the income questions.

Despite these disadvantages, telephone surveys have become the most popular survey method in the United States in recent years. Reduced time and cost are a major advantage; and developments in random-digit dialing and the fact that over 90 percent of American households have telephones make the quality of telephone surveys only slightly inferior to face-to-face interviewing (Schuman and Kalton, 1985).

Self-Administered Questionnaires

Occasionally, the site of a self-administered questionnaire is a school or organization, where the questionnaire may be hand-delivered and filled out in a group or individually. Most often, however, the setting of either an interview or questionnaire survey is the home (Schuman and Kalton, 1985). To get to this setting, almost all self-administered questionnaires are mailed to respondents. Therefore, we will discuss the pros and cons of this method as a *mail survey*.

This is the least expensive of the three survey modes, even though the budget for printing and postage must be sufficiently high to permit follow-up mailings. No interviewers or interviewer supervisors are needed, there are no travel or telephone expenses, and very little office space is required. In some surveys, the staff may consist of just one or two persons in addition to the researcher.

The time required to complete the data collection phase of the survey is greater than that for telephone surveys but usually less than that for face-to-face surveys. The sample size may be very large, and geographic dispersion is not a problem. Further, there is greater accessibility to respondents with this method, since those who cannot be reached by telephone or who are infrequently at home usually receive mail.

On the other hand, sample quality can be a problem with this survey mode. The researcher must sample from a mailing list, which may have some incorrect or out-of-date addresses and which may omit some eligible respondents. Also, the response rate with mailed questionnaires tends to be much lower than with other survey modes. However, even though rates of 50 percent or lower are fairly common, it is possible to obtain high response rates. Dillman (1978) reports response rates from 60 to 75 percent in surveys of the general public that used his Total

Design Method. Furthermore, over one-fourth of the ninety-eight experiments on mailed questionnaire response rates reviewed by Heberlein and Baumgartner (1978) showed a final return of more than 80 percent. According to Heberlein and Baumgartner, the most important factors in generating high return rates are reducing the costs for the respondent and increasing the perceived importance of the survey. Costs are reduced by including postpaid return envelopes, offering monetary incentives, and making the questionnaire shorter and easier to complete. The importance of the survey is impressed upon respondents by using special forms of mailings and by repeated follow-ups.

Bias due to response selectivity is another concern with self-administered questionnaires. Certain groups of persons, such as those with little writing ability and those not interested in the topic, would be less likely to respond to a mailed questionnaire than to a personal interview request. Also, more questions are left unanswered with self-administered questionnaires than with interview methods. The problem of item nonresponse may be alleviated to some extent by instructions explaining the need for every item to be answered, by assurances of confidentiality, and by making items easy to understand.

While interviewer bias is eliminated, so are the advantages of an interviewer. There is no opportunity to clarify questions, probe for more adequate answers, or control the conditions under which the questionnaire is completed or even who completes it. A mailed questionnaire usually yields the most reliable information when closed questions are used, when the order in which questions are answered is unimportant, and when the questions and format are simple and straightforward.

The questionnaire may serve the research purposes well under the following conditions: with specialized target groups who are likely to have high response rates,[2] when very large samples are desired, when costs must be kept low, when ease of administration is necessary, and when moderate response rates are considered satisfactory.

A Final Note on Planning

By now you may sense that our flowchart oversimplifies the planning process. Rather than a linear series of decisions, survey planning actually requires the simultaneous consideration of a number of factors or choices. Also, as planning progresses, revisions in previous decisions and plans frequently are needed. One very effective planning device is to work backward mentally from the final steps in the study to the earlier steps in the planning phase. Serious mistakes can be avoided by anticipating the data analysis. To do this, one works out the actual data analysis along with the steps likely to be taken in the event of various outcomes. One might ask questions such as these: If the data support my hypothesis, what will I do next? If the data are the opposite of my hypothesis, what will I do next? (I might decide that I need to control additional variables to test the hypothesis properly.) Have I included all the variables I might want to use? By anticipating the data analysis in this way, the survey content can be planned better. (But, then again, this is not as easy

---

BOX 9.1

An Informal Account of a Large-scale Survey

Researchers do not, as a rule, report the false starts, unsolvable roadblocks, embarrassing problems, and mistakes that are a normal part of the process of doing surveys. James Davis (1964b), however, has provided a humor-filled account of a national survey, the Great Books study, from its inception to the publication of a book. Davis describes the events as an illustration of how survey research is carried out in a large research organization.

The parties involved in the Great Books study included the National Opinion Research Center (NORC), with James Davis as study director, the Fund for Adult Education as client, and the object of the study, the Great Books Foundation. The Fund for Adult Education, a subsidiary of the Ford Foundation, had been supporting, through grants, various educational activities and programs, including Great Books. The Fund hoped by commissioning an evaluation study to gain concrete evidence of the value of the Great Books program and to determine whether the continuation or expansion of support was merited. The Great Books Foundation, a nonprofit corporation, believed in its program, according to Davis, but seriously doubted the usefulness of a survey in evaluating it. The parties in the study agreed at the outset that the study would be concerned with the effects on participants of participation in Great Books.

The Great Books program in 1957–1958 involved approximately 1960 discussion groups throughout the United States, with additional groups in Canada and elsewhere, which met every 2 weeks, September to June. At each meeting the members discussed an assigned selection. Selections were organized into blocks of 1 year. Size of the groups varied, with the sample average eleven. The groups were sponsored chiefly by public libraries, but also by churches, businesses, and individuals. One or two persons served as leaders of each group. No tuition was charged and no certificates of completion were given. Readings could be bought from the Foundation inexpensively if desired.

The design of the study fell naturally into two parts: sampling and questionnaire construction. In regard to sampling, the "ideal" design would have been a field experiment in which a large probability sample of persons were randomly assigned to a control group or to a Great Books discussion group. After a specified period, both groups would be measured on the dependent variables. However, such a design clearly was not feasible. Among other problems the effects were expected to take a long time to appear, and a report had to be delivered in about a year. The compromise design would use beginning participants as a control group and compare them to advanced-year members on a number of variables. The sample was stratified to overrepresent the advanced-year groups where the effects might be expected to show. Groups were asked to distribute and complete self-administered questionnaires at a regular meeting. Thus, although it would have been ideal to have had a sample of randomly assigned *individuals* in and out of the Great Books program, practical considerations resulted in a stratified sample of Great Books discussion *groups*.

Constructing the questionnaire presented more difficulties than devising the sampling plan. The Fund for Adult Education, the Great Books Foundation, and the study director Davis had different ideas about the program's effects. The Fund, interested in community participation, argued that participants would become more involved in

BOX 9.1 (*continued*)

community affairs as a result of their exposure to great literature. Davis and the Great Books Foundation doubted this was the case. The Great Books Foundation insisted that their program did not have any specific purposes that could be evaluated by a survey. Under pressure from Davis, the Foundation was able to make some very general statements regarding the program's objectives: participants should become more open-minded, develop more critical thinking skills, become more intellectually sophisticated, and so forth, effects that would be difficult to measure. Davis was interested in members' philosophies, ideologies, and tastes. He also wanted to include some sociometric items to see how a person's acceptance or nonacceptance by the group affected his or her reactions to the program. However, the Great Books Foundation ruled out the sociometric items as possibly offensive to participants. Instead, questions were asked about roles played by the respondent and others in the group. The final questionnaire contained items reflecting the Fund's interest in community participation; a few items related to aesthetics, open-mindedness, and critical thinking; materials on tastes, ideologies, and philosophies; and the role questions.

Over 90 percent of the sampled groups returned the questionnaires. Analysis of the survey results showed marked differences in knowledge between beginners and advanced-year members, slight differences in tolerance and open-mindedness, and few behavioral differences.

A report for the sponsor was completed on time in August 1958. The project, however, was not finished. Davis immediately conceived the idea of doing a follow-up study to find out which respondents had dropped out of the groups during the year, so that data from these individuals could be subtracted. The remaining data would be reanalyzed to see whether omission of the dropouts affected the findings. The Fund agreed to sponsor the follow-up study. It turned out that controlling for dropouts had little effect.

A new study then was conceived to analyze, with the budget money remaining, the factors associated with dropping out. The idea was not only to learn why Great Books members drop out, but to view the data more broadly as "why some small-scale social systems lose the commitment of their members" (p. 228). Davis admitted he hoped by this study to impress his colleagues that he was capable of theory-building research, as opposed to purely empirical work. The study was to lead to the publication of *Great Books and Small Groups*.

The study showed that retention of participants was greatest where a large percentage of members played active roles. Theories that the content of the roles is important were not supported, nor was Davis's hunch that retention was related to a balance of power in the group.

At the end of Davis's account (1964b:233–234) of the Great Books study, he gives a beautiful description of the satisfactions of doing research:

> There is a lot of misery in surveys, most of the time and money going into monotonous clerical and statistical routines, with interruptions only for squabbles with the client, budget crises, petty machinations for a place in the academic sun, and social case work with neurotic graduate students. And nobody ever reads the final report. Those few moments, however, when a new set of tables comes up from the machine room and questions begin to be answered; when relationships actually hold under controls; when the pile of tables on the desk suddenly meshes to yield a coherent chapter; when in a flash you see a neat test for an interpretation; when you realize you have found out something important that nobody ever knew before—these are the moments that justify research.

as it sounds, as James Davis reveals in his report of a social survey that we recount in Box 9.1.)

Field Administration

Once the planning is completed, fieldwork can begin. This phase of the research begins with the recruitment and training of interviewers, continues with the field interviews, and concludes when follow-up efforts have been completed on initially unresponsive persons in the sample. Figure 9.2 is a flowchart that summarizes the various aspects of a survey's fieldwork phase.[3]

Interviewer Selection

Although there are no universally agreed-upon criteria for the selection of inter- viewers, experience and common sense suggest that certain qualities are desirable. These would include articulateness, a pleasant personality that inspires cooperation and trust, a neat, businesslike appearance, freedom from prejudices or stereotypes toward the population being interviewed, interest in the survey topic, a legible handwriting, and the ability to listen, use neutral probes when needed, and record responses accurately. The presence of these qualities may be evaluated to some

FIGURE 9.2. Flowchart illustrating a survey's fieldwork phase.

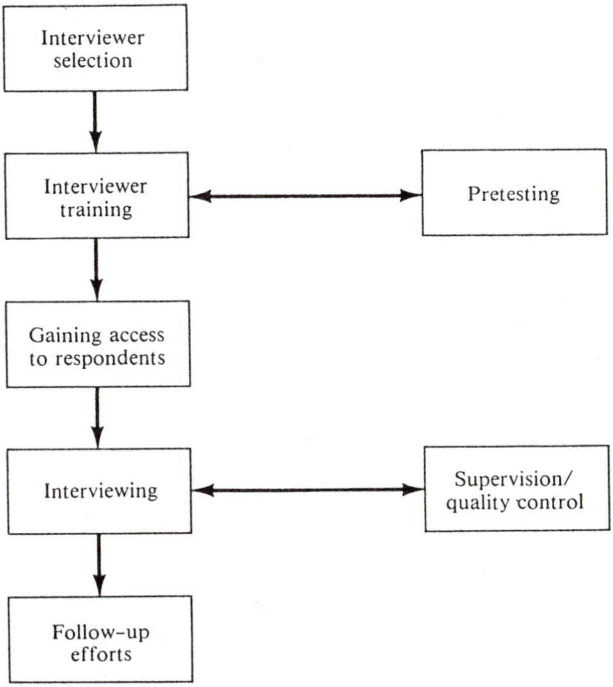

degree during the selection process, but further evaluation and screening must take place during training.

Unless the survey is being done by a large research organization that has a permanent staff, the researcher must recruit and select all interviewers within a short time. Usually a researcher will advertise for interviewers. Persons responding to the advertisements will be given a more detailed description of the position and its requirements as well as an application form to be handwritten. The completed application forms will be screened, and those who seem qualified will be invited for a job interview. During the interview, the applicant may be required to conduct a mock survey interview of the researcher or another person with an interview schedule provided. Those who perform best will be invited to begin training.

Interviewer Training

Interviewing requires of the interviewer a successful blending of three roles: the friendly, understanding, trustworthy listener; the teacher; and the data collector/recorder. The interviewer must be warm and nonthreatening in the listener role and yet be able to "teach" the respondent the appropriate role to facilitate meeting the interview objectives within a limited time frame. A major part of the interviewer's task in teaching the respondent role is to indicate in some way when responses are adequate and when they are incomplete, digress, or are otherwise inappropriate (*ISR Newsletter*, 1977). Restraining the verbose respondent is a related part of the teacher role. At the same time, the interviewer must accurately "collect" or record the responses of the interviewee.

The training process must accomplish several goals:

1. Provide interviewers with information regarding the study's general purpose, sponsor, sampling plan, and uses or publication plans.

2. Teach basic interviewing techniques and rules, such as how to gain respondents' cooperation, establish rapport without becoming overly friendly, ask questions and probe in a manner that will not bias the response, deal with interruptions and digressions, and so forth.

3. Acquaint interviewers with the interview schedule and special instructions for its use, such as how to introduce a topic or record responses.

4. Provide demonstrations and supervised practice with the interview schedule.

5. Weed out those trainees who do not possess the motivation and ability to do an acceptable job.

Training usually consists of a series of informal group sessions. The researcher might begin the first session with a general introduction to the study, followed by a discussion of basic interviewing techniques and rules. The second session would consist of familiarizing interviewers with the survey questionnaire or interview schedule and the user instructions. The researcher would go over the entire instrument item by item, explaining the importance of each item, giving instructions for recording responses and examples of problematic responses and ways to deal with them. Next, the researcher would conduct a demonstration interview with another staff member or volunteer. Finally, the interviewers would be divided into pairs to practice interviewing and recording responses while the researcher observes and gives assistance. The third and subsequent training sessions would involve more practice, including experience in the field, and further evaluation by the researcher.

Pretesting

A pretest consists of trying out the survey instrument on a small number of persons having characteristics similar to those of the target group of respondents. The basic reason for conducting a pretest is to determine whether the instrument serves the purposes for which it was designed or whether further revision is needed. Pretesting may be carried out prior to, at the same time as, or after the interviewers are trained. An advantage to completing the pretest prior to interviewer training is that the final instrument may be used during training. An advantage to delaying pretesting is that the interviewers can assist with this step, either during the field practice part of interviewer training, or after the formal training is completed. A disadvantage to delaying pretesting is that there may be a time gap between the completion of training and the start of the "real" interviews while the instrument is being revised. The subject of pretesting is discussed in more depth in chapter 10.

Gaining Access

The next step is gaining access to respondents. This involves two steps: gaining "official" permission or endorsement when needed or useful; and mailing a cover letter introducing the study to persons or households in the sample.

When doing a community interview survey, it is usually a good idea to write a letter to the local sheriff or chief of police describing the general purpose of the study, its importance, the organization sponsoring it, the uses to which the data will be put, the time frame, and so forth. A follow-up visit to the sheriff or chief of police may be made. In addition, endorsements from relevant local organizations may be sought, such as the county medical society if doctors will be interviewed, or the chamber of commerce if businesses are being sampled. Press releases to local newspapers and television stations also may help to open doors.

Respondent cooperation also will be enhanced by a good *cover letter*. In interview surveys, the cover letter is usually mailed a few days before the interviewer is to call on the respondent. In surveys using mailed questionnaires, the cover letter is sent with the questionnaire either as a separate sheet or attached to the questionnaire. The objective of the cover letter, to persuade the respondent to cooperate with the survey, may be met by (1) identifying the researcher and survey sponsor, (2) communicating the general purpose and importance of the study, (3) showing how the findings may benefit the individual or others (e.g., the results will be used to improve health care or to increase understanding of marriage relationships), (4) explaining how the sample was drawn and the importance of each respondent's cooperation to the study, (5) assuring individuals that they will not be identified, that their responses will be kept confidential and will be combined with those of others for data analysis purposes, (6) explaining that the questionnaire will take only a few minutes to fill out or that the interview will be enjoyable and will be held at the respondent's convenience, and (7) promising to send respondents a summary of the study's findings. (See Box 9.2 for an example of a cover letter.)

Interviewing

In interviewing, as in every research activity, one must be aware of the possible effects of random and systematic error. Random errors, you will recall, tend to cancel each other out and are due to temporary and changing factors. In contrast, systematic errors affect the data in one direction and are due to more stable factors, for instance, biased questions or the tendency of respondents to answer in such a way as to appear socially acceptable. The general term for such errors in survey research is response effects. More precisely, a *response effect* is "the amount of the error in response to a question that is associated with a particular factor" (Sudman and Bradburn, 1974). For example, a response effect may be associated with the respondent's misunderstanding of the question or an intentionally falsified answer. The following chapter, on survey instrument design, suggests ways in which to minimize response effects in the interview schedule (or questionnaire). Here we focus on effects due to the interaction of interviewer and respondent.

Perhaps the most serious weakness of surveys is one they share with laboratory experiments: they are susceptible to reactivity. This is especially true of interviews, where biases may be produced not only by the wording, order, and format of the questions, but also by the interaction between interviewer and respondent. Like the subject in an experiment, the respondent's chief concern often is with gaining the interviewer's social approval, or at least with avoiding his or her disapproval (D. L. Phillips, 1971). And even though the interviewer's main goal is to obtain valid responses, interviewers may unknowingly introduce response effects in myriad ways. Let us briefly examine some of the ways that response effects may occur in interview situations. (For a somewhat fuller discussion, see Warwick and Lininger, 1975:199–202, and for an extensive treatment of this subject, see Sudman and Bradburn, 1974.)

One source of response effects is the interviewer's physical characteristics. For example, the race of the interviewer has been shown to have a considerable impact on certain types of responses. In recent studies, the effect of race is for blacks to express fewer antiwhite sentiments to white than to black interviewers, and for whites to give fewer antiblack answers to black than to white interviewers (Schuman and Kalton, 1985). With regard to other characteristics, Schuman and Kalton (1985:686) observe: "There is little information on whether sex, age, or other visible interviewer characteristics have the same effects as race. It seems likely that they may whenever respondents classify the interviewer into a larger category and believe they know what would offend or please persons in that category."

In a fashion similar to experimenter effects, interviewers also may inadvertently communicate their expectations to respondents about how they should respond. To illustrate, if an interviewer believes a respondent to be of limited intelligence and inarticulate, he or she may expect shorter, less articulate responses and may communicate this indirectly by short pauses. Since the respondent is looking to the

BOX 9.2

Sample Cover Letter for Household Survey,
with Key Features Identified in Left-hand Margin

Official letterhead	**WASHINGTON STATE UNIVERSITY** PULLMAN, WASHINGTON 99163 DEPARTMENT OF RURAL SOCIOLOGY Room 23, Wilson Hall
Date mailed	April 19, 1971
Inside address in matching type	Oliver Jones 2190 Fontana Road Spokane, Washington 99467
What study is about; its social usefulness	Bills have been introduced in Congress and our State Legislature to encourage the growth of rural and small town areas and slow down that of large cities. These bills could greatly affect the quality of life provided in both rural and urban places. However, no one really knows in what kinds of communities people like yourself want to live or what is thought about these proposed programs.
Why recipient is important (and, if needed, who should complete the questionnaire)	Your household is one of a small number in which people are being asked to give their opinion on these matters. It was drawn in a random sample of the entire state. In order that the results will truly represent the thinking of the people of Washington, it is important that each questionnaire be completed and returned. It is also important that we have about the same number of men and women participating in this study. Thus, we would like the questionnaire for your household to be completed by an <u>adult female</u>. If none is present, then it should be completed by an <u>adult male</u>.
Promise of confidentiality; explanation of identification number	You may be assured of complete confidentiality. The questionnaire has an identification number for mailing purposes only. This is so that we may check your name off of the mailing list when your questionnaire is returned. Your name will never be placed on the questionnaire.
Usefulness of study "Token" reward for participation	The results of this research will be made available to officials and representatives in our state's government, members of Congress, and all interested citizens. You may receive a summary of results by writing "copy of results requested" on the back of the return envelope, and printing your name and address below it. Please <u>do not</u> put this information on the questionnaire itself.
What to do if questions arise	I would be most happy to answer any questions you might have. Please write or call. The telephone number is (509) 335-8623.
Appreciation	Thank you for your assistance.
Pressed blue ball point signature	Sincerely, Don A. Dillman Project Director
Title	

Source: Page 169 of Dillman (1978). Copyright © 1978 by John Wiley and Sons, Inc. Used by permission.

interviewer for clues to the appropriateness of his or her behavior, he or she will likely provide short responses, thus fulfilling the interviewer's expectations.

On the other side, the respondent's reports to an interviewer may easily be distorted by such things as poor memory, desire to impress the interviewer, dislike for the interviewer, or embarrassment. Similarly, a respondent's feelings about the topic of the study or toward the organization sponsoring it may also affect the quality of data obtained. Finally, settings for interviews may present problems. A housewife who is being interviewed while supervising children may not be able to focus on the tasks of the interview sufficiently to provide as full and accurate responses as she might in another situation. A study by Zanes and Matsoukas (1979) showed that eleventh graders were more likely to report incidents of drug use when questioned at school than when questioned at home.

Organizations sponsoring surveys usually produce an interviewers' manual that explains rules and procedures to follow in order to minimize the effects of error. (See, for example, Survey Research Center, 1976.) The guidelines that follow have been adapted from an interviewers' manual used in a community survey conducted by a research team in a middle-sized southern California city. The project involved some 2000 subjects whose families had been interviewed 9 years earlier. The rules and guidelines, however, are generalizable beyond this particular type of survey project.

When reading the following section, bear in mind that in each interview the potential exists for influencing the respondent. Interviewers, if not careful, can introduce bias into the situation, thereby altering the responses obtained.

Rules. Three basic rules are suggested.

1. *Courtesy, tact, and acceptance.* It is of utmost importance that your manner be at all times courteous, tactful, and nonjudgmental. Under no circumstances are you to argue or debate anything that is said. The primary function of the interviewer is to learn what the respondent believes about the items on the schedule without judging or influencing that response in any way. No matter what the respondent says, the interviewer should accept it without showing surprise, approval, or disapproval. Respondents will be less likely to share confidential data about their personal lives, for example, with an interviewer who appears to disapprove of them.

2. *Dress.* Three things should be kept in mind in selecting clothing for interviewing: the expectations that surround the role of the interviewer, the persons being interviewed and their probable response to one's dress, and comfort. Within the limits of good taste, the individual interviewer should make adjustments for the neighborhood in which he or she is working.

3. *Confidentiality.* Under no circumstances is the interviewer to give out to anyone except the supervisor any information gathered in the course of interviews. Incidents that occur or any information gained while interviewing are strictly confidential and should not be discussed with anyone who is not part of the project. Project workers should never discuss interview data, even among themselves, in a public place where the conversation could be overheard.

Procedures in conducting an interview. The following procedures have been found to be helpful in conducting interviews and obtaining accurate, honest responses. In many cases, deviating from these procedures will influence the respondent and introduce bias.

1. *Initiating the interview.* When the respondent comes to the door, introduce yourself by name. Show identification. Explain briefly what the study is about and whom it is you wish to interview. Be prepared to answer briefly questions regarding who is sponsoring the study and how or why the respondent was chosen. Letters of endorsement and newspaper clippings may be presented.

Proper groundwork by the researcher and a positive approach on the part of the interviewer will help to minimize the problem of refusals. In addition, the interviewer can frequently overcome an initial refusal by listening to the respondent's concerns and then addressing those concerns. For example, is the respondent "too busy"? Stress the brief and enjoyable nature of the interview, or, when necessary, make an appointment to call back. Does the respondent appear suspicious about the uses to which the data will be put? If so, explain again the study's purpose, provide an assurance of confidentiality, and explain that the data will be combined so that no individual's responses can be identified or linked to that person. Of course, firm refusals must be respected.

2. *Put the respondent at ease.* This is a major part of successful interviewing. A conversational, convivial attitude may help put the respondent at ease. Try to be relaxed and "natural."

3. *Be businesslike.* While it should be relaxed, an interview should not be long-winded. Remember that you and the respondent are busy people. If the respondent strays far afield from the point of a question, politely pull him or her back on the track.

4. *Keep the interview situation as private as possible.* If you are in a room with other people, do not let your attention wander to other parts of the room. Direct your questions to the respondent and maintain eye contact. This will help both you and the respondent focus on the task.

5. *Avoid stereotyping.* Do not try to "peg" the respondent, as your preconceptions may interfere with your objectivity and may influence the respondent. You can also help to prevent the respondent from stereotyping you by not identifying yourself with any particular group or ideology.

6. *Be thoroughly familiar with the survey instrument.* Know the instrument so well that you can look at the respondent while asking questions.

7. *Ask every question in its proper sequence and exactly as written.* The interview schedule should have been carefully constructed. Questions are in the order presented because it is easier for interviewers to ask them in this order, because there is a logical flow of the topics, in order to help respondents think through or recall material, or for similar reasons. Remember that very slight changes in the wording of items have been shown to affect the results.

8. *Do not assume the answer to any question.* A respondent may imply the answer to a question in answering a previous question but may respond differently when asked the question formally.

9. *Speak slowly in a clearly understood, well-modulated voice.* If respondents are to give reliable answers, they must understand the questions.

10. *Do not put answers in the respondent's mouth.* This is one of the most common mistakes of interviewers. If a respondent seems unsure of an answer, pause, then repeat the question exactly as worded. Do not suggest an answer or series of answers. Not all interviewers would suggest the same responses, and therefore, respondents would not be choosing from the same suggestions. This would result in biased data.

11. *Use an appropriate, neutral probe when needed.* Probing is used when the initial response is incomplete, ambiguous, or irrelevant. A variety of probes are possible, but they must be neutral; that is, they must stimulate a more valid response without suggesting an answer. Sometimes, as suggested above, pausing or repeating the question may be sufficient to motivate the respondent to add to or clarify the response. At other times a neutral question such as one of the following may be needed: Is there anything else? Can you tell me more? In what ways? The survey instrument designer may include on the interview schedule certain probes to use with particular items when needed.

12. *Record responses on the interview schedule as you go along.* Do not try to recreate the interview later. Before leaving the residence, skim the instrument to be sure all questions have been answered. Later, check to be sure responses will be understandable to the coders. Add notes in parentheses if necessary.

Supervision and Quality Control

The researcher or an interviewer supervisor must carefully oversee all aspects of the interviewing phase of the research, including (1) ensuring that sampled respondents are interviewed according to schedule, (2) keeping records on each interviewer, providing materials, and paying for work done, (3) collecting and checking returned interview schedules, (4) holding regular meetings with interviewers, (5) remaining available to interviewers to answer questions or provide help, and, if possible, (6) sitting in on a few interviews to provide continued feedback and reinforcement throughout the interviewing period.

To assure that the sampled respondents are being interviewed, they should be checked off a master sampling list as interview schedules are returned. A subset of respondents should be contacted by phone to determine whether the interview actually took place and to check accuracy by asking a few predetermined questions. In order to complete the interviewing phase in a timely manner, it may be necessary to assign additional interviews to more efficient interviewers or to those willing to work longer hours.

Records kept on each interviewer would include number of schedules taken and interviews completed, adequacy of work done, amount of supervision required, refusal rate, and amount paid. Ideally, all interview schedules should be gone over by a supervisor shortly after completion. Uncodable responses can be clarified and interviewers can receive prompt feedback on the quality of their completed schedules. The checking of schedules is particularly important early in the fieldwork, but it is desirable to continue to check at least a few randomly selected schedules of each interviewer.

The supervisor should meet with interviewers on a regular basis to discuss progress and problems and to reinforce skills and motivation. In addition, the supervisor should be available to interviewers by phone. The development of interviewer feelings of isolation should be prevented. The need for continued reinforcement of interviewing skills and for attention to the issue of morale and motivation has not received a great deal of attention by survey researchers, who have assumed that interviewers will do better work as they gain experience. Studies have shown that the opposite may be the case. For example, several validity studies of reports of hospitalizations and physician visits have shown that the more interviews an interviewer has done, the greater the problem of underreporting (Cannell, Marquis, and Laurent, 1973). If possible, the supervisor should sit in on randomly selected interviews throughout the interviewing period not only to provide continuing feedback and reinforcement of skills but also to communicate the importance of good interviewing. Staff meetings, a team spirit, and individual attention by the supervisor may all help maintain quality of interviewing.

Follow-up Efforts

The final phase of fieldwork consists of following up on nonrespondents in an attempt to gain their cooperation. Follow-up efforts help to ensure that an adequate response rate is obtained. When the response rate is low, the adequacy of the sample will be in question because nonrespondents may differ in important ways from respondents. Follow-ups therefore are an important component of all kinds of surveys.

Regardless of the response rate, the researcher should inspect the data for systematic bias in response patterns. If it is discovered, for example, that younger people were less likely to cooperate in the survey, additional efforts must be made to obtain data from this group, or adjustments in the data analysis will be required.

The question of what constitutes an adequate response rate has no definitive answer, but in surveys of the general public, response rates of approximately 80 percent for face-to-face interviews, 75 percent for telephone interviews, and 60 percent for mailed questionnaires are frequently considered acceptable. With concerted effort from the planning stage through follow-up, and with specialized groups, higher rates can be obtained (Dillman, 1978). Besides follow-up efforts, response rates may be improved (1) by appropriate efforts to gain access, discussed earlier; (2) in interview surveys, by proper interviewer training and supervision; and (3) for mailed questionnaires, by inclusion of a stamped return envelope and by attention to the length, difficulty, and appearance of the questionnaire (see chapter 10).

The particular follow-up activities depend on the survey mode. For telephone and face-to-face surveys, the problem is that of dealing with refusals. The same or a different interviewer may be able to gain the respondent's cooperation on the second try. However, in response to a refusal, one follow-up call should be the limit to avoid respondent feelings of harrassment.

Since response rates are typically lower for mailed questionnaires, follow-up efforts are especially important with this mode. Typically, the first follow-up mailing is sent out about 2 weeks after the original mailing, to allow time for completion and for transit in both directions. If questionnaires have been coded so that the researcher knows who has responded, there can be a savings in postage and paper, as only nonrespondents need receive the follow-up mailings. If the questionnaire is truly anonymous, all persons in the sample must be sent the subsequent mailings. In the latter case, a letter must be enclosed thanking those who have completed the questionnaire and urging those who have not to do so. We recommend enclosing a new questionnaire with each follow-up mailing, although some researchers merely send out a reminder letter for the first follow-up. Approximately 2 weeks after the first follow-up mailing, a second is sent with a questionnaire enclosed. The enclosed letter should contain a thank you to those who have responded, a more thorough explanation of why each respondent's cooperation is important to the study, and all the basic information in the original cover letter. A deadline for completion may be added to spur well-meaning procrastinators. In the aforementioned study by Heberlein and Baumgartner (1978), third contacts via a special class of mail or by telephone were one of the most significant factors affecting response rates to mailed questionnaires. However, additional follow-up mailings are generally fruitless and seldom used.

Summary

Social surveys have three common features: a relatively large number of respondents generally chosen by some form of probability sampling, formal observation procedures involving interviews and/or questionnaires, and computerized statistical analysis of data. The units of analysis in sample surveys are typically individuals selected from a single community or nation; however, surveys with social units are not uncommon, and samples from different countries are sometimes combined, as in comparative studies. While usually fairly standardized, data collection procedures vary along a continuum from highly formal and structured to less formal and structured, the choice of which depends on the researcher's objectives. Social indicators research represents one type of formal, descriptive survey.

The basic survey research designs include (1) cross-sectional studies, in which data are gathered from a community or larger grouping at essentially one point in time; (2) longitudinal studies, in which data are gathered at two or more points in time from either the same sample of respondents (panel study) or independently selected samples of the same population (trend studies); (3) sociometric studies, in which every individual in a group is studied in order to delineate networks of personal relationships; and (4) contextual studies, in which different social environments are sampled in order to examine the effects of the environment or context on individuals.

Relative to experiments, surveys are more flexible in that they can be used with equal facility for both descriptive and explanatory research, can address a wider range of research topics, and can gather more information from much larger samples of cases. On the other hand, surveys present greater problems for inferring causal relationships, are less easily altered once the study has begun, are limited to reports of behavior rather than observations of behavior, and, like laboratory experiments, are subject to reactive effects.

Of the three steps in conducting a survey, planning and field administration were considered in this chapter, with data processing and analysis covered in chapters 14 and 15. The initial stages in planning a survey depart from other research strategies primarily in the construction of the survey instrument (interview schedule or questionnaire), which we discuss at length in the next chapter, and the development of the sampling plan.

Interviews, in comparison to questionnaires, offer greater flexibility in the type and format of questions, provide the opportunity to clarify questions and elicit fuller responses, and tend to have higher response rates. Face-to-face interviews also permit lengthy interviews with complex questions, although they may introduce greater bias through interviewer-respondent interaction, and they tend to be very expensive. By comparison, telephone interviews offer a substantial savings in time and money and are easier to administer, although they require simpler questions and may elicit less complete responses. Mailed self-administered questionnaires are the least expensive survey mode, but they tend to have lower response rates, result in more nonresponse to items, and must contain simpler questions for reliable responses.

Field administration in survey research begins with interviewer selection and training and instrument pretesting, continues with interviews and staff supervision, and ends with follow-up efforts to reach initial nonrespondents. Interviewers must be able simultaneously to put the interviewee at ease, to ask questions and guide the interview to its completion, and to record responses. To accomplish this requires careful interviewer selection and training. Prior to gathering data from respondents, the survey instrument should be pretested and access to respondents should be gained by contacting appropriate community officials and mailing a cover letter. During the course of interviewing, interviewers must (1) be wary of introducing bias; (2) be courteous, tactful, dress appropriately, and guard the confidentiality of respondents' replies; (3) be relaxed but businesslike; and (4) be thoroughly familiar with the instrument so as to maintain rapport, use probes when necessary, and record answers as they go along. Supervision of interviewees—keeping a record of each interviewer, checking their completed interview schedules, and so forth—is essential for quality control, while follow-up efforts to contact initial nonrespondents are essential to obtain an adequate response rate, especially in mail surveys.

Key Terms

cross-cultural surveys	*contextual design*
unstructured interview	*interview schedule*
structured interview	*response rate*
partially structured interview	*face-to-face interview*
social indicators	*telephone interview*
descriptive and explanatory surveys	*random-digit dialing*
survey research designs	*modified random-digit dialing*
cross-sectional design	*self-administered questionnaire*
longitudinal design	*pretesting*
trend study	*cover letter*
panel study	*response effect*
sociometric design	

Review Questions and Problems

1. What are the three principal features of professional survey research?

2. Give an example of a survey study in which the unit of analysis is not the individual.

3. Contrast the objectives of unstructured, structured, and partially structured interviews.

4. What is the difference between a trend study and a panel study? Which of these study designs permits the assessment of individual change?

5. Discuss the advantages and disadvantages of surveys in relation to experiments.

6. Outline the major decision points in planning a survey.

7. What are the relative advantages and disadvantages of structured versus unstructured survey procedures?

8. Which sampling design is likely to be used with face-to-face interviews? Why?

9. Explain how interviews provide greater flexibility than self-administered questionnaires.

10. What particular problems are associated with face-to-face interviewing?

11. Relative to face-to-face interviewing, what advantages does telephone interviewing offer?

12. Compare face-to-face interviews, telephone interviews, and self-administered questionnaires with respect to (a) response rates and sampling quality; (b) time and cost; and (c) type—complexity and sensitivity—of questions asked.

13. Under what conditions is a questionnaire survey recommended?

14. Outline the key steps in the field administration phase of survey research.

15. What qualities are desirable in an interviewer?

16. Describe the steps involved in interviewer training.

17. Explain the purpose of pretesting.

18. What should a cover letter communicate to the respondent?

19. Describe some sources of measurement error in surveys attributable to the (a) interviewer and (b) respondent.

20. What three basic rules are described in the text for minimizing error in survey interviews?

21. (true or false) According to the interview procedures outlined in the text (which are designed for structured interviews), one should

   a. Pull the respondent back on track if he or she strays far afield from the point of a question.

   b. Change the wording of a question if it seems appropriate for a particular respondent.

   c. Change the order of questions if a respondent's response suggests a question that appears later in the interview schedule.

   d. Ask every question in its proper sequence and exactly as written.

   e. Record responses immediately after the interview is completed rather than during the interview.

     f. Pause, repeat the question, or use probes such as "Is there anything else?" when an initial response is incomplete, ambiguous, or irrelevant.

22. What activities does the supervision of interviewers involve?

23. Why is it suggested that supervision and contact with interviewers be maintained throughout the interviewing period?

24. Why are follow-up efforts necessary? At what point do they become fruitless?

NOTES

1. Whereas the flowchart shows the top-to-bottom and sideways influences, in reality later decisions may result in modifications of earlier decisions. For example, sampling plan cost considerations may bring about a change in the research objectives.

2. See Shosteck and Fairweather (1979) for a study comparing physician response rates to mailed and personal interview surveys.

3. Fieldwork is not always carried out exactly in this order. Pretesting, for example, may occur prior to, during, or after the training of interviewers. Efforts to gain access to respondents may well begin earlier than depicted.

10

Survey Instrumentation

The two most critical features for successful survey research are the sample and the survey instrument. Accurate generalizations about populations of interest depend on the quality of the sample. But no matter how carefully the sample is selected, a sample survey is only as good as the design of the questionnaire or interview schedule.

Survey instrument design is a creative process, partly art and partly science. Like an artist, the survey designer selects "raw materials" and combines them creatively within certain principles of design. For the artist, raw materials may consist of paper or canvas; pencil, charcoal, chalks, watercolors, acrylics, or oils; brushes; and so forth. The survey designer's "raw materials" are such things as free response and fixed-choice questions; direct and indirect questions; question-and-response formats; overall physical layout; and instructions.

However, the survey designer is unlike the artist in at least one important way. An artist is mainly concerned with expressing his or her own personal ideas, emotions, or other subjective experience, whereas the designer of a survey instrument must be concerned ultimately with getting reliable and valid reports of other people's experiences. This concern is what makes the survey designer a scientist rather than an artist. The reports may be of subjective experiences such as values, opinions, fears, and beliefs, or they may be of overt experiences such as job history, salary, political behavior, place of residence, consumer behavior, or leisure activities.

The verbal reports obtained in surveys are, of course, answers to questions; survey instrumentation is thus the science of asking questions. In this chapter we focus on standardized instruments, in which the wording and order of questions is the same for all respondents. Yet many of the principles discussed here apply to less structured interview approaches. Also, we do not treat separately the three modes of asking questions (self-administered mail questionnaire, face-to-face interview, and telephone interview), although these sometimes require different questions and formats. The survey designer generally has fewer options with self-administered than with interviewer-administered questionnaires. Questions, response formats, and instructions must be simpler in mail surveys, and certain questions—for example, questions of knowledge in which consulting other sources would be undesirable—are inappropriate.

We begin by considering available "materials"—types of questions and response formats. Next we examine the overall design or "sketch" of the instrument. Then we look at practical guides for "filling in the sketch"—writing items to arrive at a finished product.

Materials Available to the Survey Designer

Like the artist, the survey designer has a number of choices about "raw materials." We now offer some guides regarding choices among certain types of questions and response formats and regarding the use of visual aids and questions from previous research.

Open and Closed Questions

A major choice among "materials" concerns open-ended and closed-ended questions. The *open-ended* (also called the free-response) *question* requires respondents to answer in their own words (in written form on a questionnaire or aloud to an interviewer). The *closed-ended* (or fixed-choice) *question* requires the respondent to choose a response from those provided. Here are examples of two questions written in both open and closed forms.

1. How would you rate the President's performance in office so far? (OPEN)
1. How would you rate the President's performance in office so far? (CLOSED)
 ( ) Poor
 ( ) Below average
 ( ) Average
 ( ) Above average
 ( ) Excellent

2. What do you think is the number one domestic issue the President should be concerned with? (OPEN)
2. Which one of the domestic issues listed below should the President be most concerned with? (CLOSED)
 ( ) Unemployment
 ( ) Inflation
 ( ) Reform of the welfare system
 ( ) Balancing the budget
 ( ) The energy crisis
 ( ) Other

The choice between open- and closed-ended questions is a complex one, as each has a number of advantages and disadvantages. The greatest advantage of the open question is the freedom the respondent has in answering. The resulting material may be a veritable goldmine of information, revealing respondents' logic or thought processes, the amount of information they possess, and the strength of their opinions or feelings. Frequently the researcher's understanding of the topic is clarified and even completely changed by unexpected responses to open questions. But alas, this very quality of open questions, the wealth of information, has a drawback: the

"coding" problem of summarizing and analyzing rich and varied (and often irrelevant and vague) responses. Coding such material is a time-consuming and costly
process that invariably results in some degree of error (Sudman and Bradburn,
1982). (See chapter 14 for a further discussion of coding.)

Other problems with the open question include (1) the varying length of
responses (some people are unbelievably verbose, others exceedingly reticent); (2)
the difficulty with inarticulate or semiliterate respondents; (3) the difficulty interviewers have in getting it all down accurately; and (4) the reluctance of many
persons to reveal detailed information or socially unacceptable opinions or behavior. Open-ended questions also entail more work, not only for the researcher but
also for the respondent. Indeed, open questions should be used sparingly if at all in
self-administered questionnaires, where respondents must write rather than speak.

Closed-ended questions are easier on the respondent as they require less effort
and less facility with words. They may also make self-disclosure less painful by
presenting to the respondent a range of (presumably) "typical" responses. When
used in an interview, less work and training are required to administer closed
questions, and the interview may be shortened considerably.

On the other hand, good closed questions are difficult to develop. It is easy to
omit important responses, thereby forcing respondents to choose among alternatives
that do not correspond to their true feelings or attitudes. Some survey designers add
a response such as "Other _____ (please explain)," but this is not as satisfactory as
knowing the range of possible responses and including suitable response options.
The recommended procedure for designing closed-question alternatives is to use
open questions in preliminary interviews or pretests to determine what members of
the study population say spontaneously; this information then may be used to
construct meaningful closed alternatives for the final instrument. Unfortunately,
this procedure is not always followed; time and financial limitations may prevent
pretesting of sufficient scope to yield adequate information on the population's
responses.

Another serious drawback of closed questions is the lack of spontaneity permitted the respondent (the boon and bane of open questions). If the survey instrument
employs mainly closed questions, the respondent may not feel as involved or highly
motivated and may not complete the interview or questionnaire. If the options
presented are not exhaustive of all possible responses, respondents may feel frus-
trated and conclude that the study is "dumb" and not worth the effort.

Are there other important considerations in choosing open or closed questions?
Kahn and Cannell (1957) have suggested these five: (1) the objectives of the survey,
(2) the level of information possessed by respondents in regard to the topic, (3) how
well respondents' opinions are thought out or structured, (4) motivation of respondents to communicate, and (5) the extent of the researcher's knowledge of respondents' characteristics.

1. Consider first the study's objectives. If you simply want to classify respondents with respect to some well-understood attitude or behavior, the closed question
would probably be appropriate and most efficient. However, the open question is
usually preferable when the survey objectives are broader and you are seeking such

information as the basis upon which opinions are founded, the depth of respondent knowledge, or the intensity with which respondents hold opinions.

2. A second consideration is the amount of information respondents already have on the topics of interest. If you believe the vast majority will have sufficient information regarding the survey's topics, the closed question may be acceptable. On the other hand, if you are uncertain as to the level of information of the respondents or if you anticipate a wide range in the amount of knowledge, the open question is more appropriate. With closed questions, uninformed respondents may conceal their ignorance by making arbitrary choices, yielding invalid reports. And even adding the response option "don't know" may not resolve the problem, since this option is unlikely to be popular with respondents who are sensitive about appearing ill-informed.[1] It is easier, for example, to respond "approve" or "disapprove" of the Equal Rights Amendment than to admit not knowing what it is.

3. A related consideration is the structuring of respondent thought or opinion. Are respondents likely to have thought about the issue before? Can they take a position or express a definite attitude? If respondents are likely to have given previous thought to the matter *and* the range of typical responses is known to the researcher, the closed question may be satisfactory. This might be the case, for example, with a survey designed to measure the attitudes of suburban parents toward the busing of schoolchildren to achieve racial balance. However, if respondents' ideas are less likely to be structured, open questions may be preferable. Suppose you wanted to ascertain why college freshmen chose XYZ University or why couples desired a certain number of children; for such questions the reasons may be numerous and not always immediately accessible to respondents. A series of open questions would allow respondents time to recall, think through, and talk about various aspects of their decisions, rather than hastily selecting a possibly incomplete or inappropriate response provided by a closed question.

4. Motivation of respondents to communicate their experiences and thoughts is a further consideration. In general, the open question will be successful only when the respondent is highly motivated, because this question type is more demanding in terms of effort, time, and self-disclosure. Therefore, closed questions may lead to better-quality data with less-motivated respondents. On the other hand, closed questions sometimes dampen respondent motivation, in that some people prefer to express their views in their own words and find being forced to choose among limited fixed-choice responses very irritating.

5. A fifth important consideration in choosing between open and closed questions is the extent of the researcher's prior knowledge of respondent characteristics. That is, how well does the researcher understand the vocabulary and amount of information possessed by the respondents, the degree of structure of respondents' views, and their level of motivation? Unless the researcher has done similar studies previously or has done extensive preliminary interviewing, the most likely answer is "not very well." If this is the case, open questions should yield more valid (albeit more difficult to summarize and analyze) data.[2]

One approach is to use the different types of questions at different stages of research, first utilizing open questions in preliminary interviewing and using the information provided by these early interviews to develop closed questions or a combination of open and closed questions on the final instrument. Or, you may decide from the start upon some combination of open and closed questions appropriate to your purposes. (For a further comparison of open and closed questions, see Box 10.1.)

BOX 10.1

An Experimental Comparison of Open and Closed Questions

Discussions of the advantages and disadvantages of open and closed questions are based largely upon common sense and the unsystematic experiences of survey researchers. One of the few exceptions is Schuman and Presser's use (1979) of an experimental design within large-scale sample surveys to compare systematically responses elicited by parallel open and closed questions. Shown below is the outcome of one of their 1976 experiments, in which half of the respondents were randomly assigned to an open version and half to a closed version of the same question.

Closed question		*Open question*	
This next question is on the subject of work. Would you please look at this card and tell me which thing on this list you would *most* prefer in a job?		This next question is on the subject of work. People look for different things in a job. What would you *most* prefer in a job?	
1. *High income*	12.4%	1. *Pay* Remuneration (e.g., "the money is what counts")	11.5%
2. *No danger of being fired*	7.2	2. *Security* Steady employment and source of income (e.g., "no danger of being fired," "a good retirement plan," "insurance plan")	6.7
3. *Working hours are short; lots of free time*	3.0	3. *Short hours/lots of free time* Jobs that give time for other things (e.g., "the chance to be with the family")	0.9
4. *Chances for advancement*	17.2	4. *Opportunity for promotion* Chance for advancement (e.g., "the chance to get ahead")	1.8
5. *The work is important and gives a feeling of accomplishment*	59.1	5. *Stimulating work* Work that makes some demand on the worker (e.g., "work that is challenging," "varied," "creative," "work that gives a sense of accomplishment or leads to fulfillment," "helping people," "interesting work")	21.3

Closed question		Open question	
		6. *Pleasant or enjoyable work* Usually concerns pleasant social relations (e.g., "congenial people," mention of happiness or social situation of work)	15.4
		7. *Work conditions* Factors affecting how job is done (e.g., "being able to set one's own pace," "safety," "being free from interference," "an understanding boss")	14.9
		8. *Satisfaction/liking the job* Unspecific answers not codable in 5 or 6 (e.g., "doing what I like," "being satisfied with the job is most important")	17.0
		95. *Specific job* "I would want to be an accountant."	3.0
		96. *More than one codable response*	1.4
		97. *Other*	2.1
8. *"Don't know"*	0.2	98. *"Don't know"*	1.4
9. *No answer*	0.9	99. *No answer*	2.7
	100.0%		100.0%
(Numbers of respondents)	(460)		(436)

Source: Adapted from page 696 of Schuman and Presser (1979). Used by permission of the authors and the American Sociological Association.

The two versions differ in the manner by which response information is coded or summarized for analysis. In the closed or self-coded version, the respondents select the most appropriate of the provided response categories to represent their work values. In the open version, research personnel code the spontaneous responses recorded by the interviewer into general categories. For example, the general category "work conditions" included such responses as "being able to set one's own pace," "safety," and "an understanding boss."

The two versions produced quite different results. Nearly one in five closed-version respondents cited advancement as the most important work value, whereas less than 2 percent preferred promotion opportunities in the open version. Almost 60 percent of the open-version responses fell outside of the five given categories of the closed version. In a subsequent experiment, Schuman and Presser (1979:698–704) demonstrate that discrepancies between the two versions are due partly to inadequate development of the closed categories; that is, the five alternatives of the closed version (first used in the 1950s) match poorly the major responses people gave spontaneously in the 1976 survey. Yet, even with adequate closed categories, the two versions yielded somewhat different results. Although Schuman and Presser provide some

BOX 10.1 (*continued*)

suggestive (but not conclusive) evidence that properly constructed closed questions may provide more valid information than open questions, they acknowledge that open questions are necessary in many survey circumstances (e.g., pretesting; "why" follow-ups to closed questions; when alternatives are too complex or too many to present easily in a closed version; and when rapidly changing events undermine the adequacy of closed alternatives).

Direct and Indirect Questions

Another choice of "materials" concerns the use of direct and indirect questions. A direct question is one in which there is a direct, clear relationship between the question that is asked and what the researcher wants to know. The bulk of questions used in survey research are direct. "What is your total family income?" and "What do you think is the ideal number of children for your family?" are examples of direct questions.

With indirect questions, the link between the researcher's objectives and the question asked is less obvious. An investigator interested in studying the sex role attitudes of male factory workers, for example, might ask the indirect question, "Do you believe your co-workers would mind having a woman as supervisor?" instead of the direct question, "Would you mind having a woman as supervisor?" Although the investigator really wants to determine the respondents' own sex role attitudes, he or she may suspect that they will be unwilling to admit personal sexist sentiments to an interviewer. Knowing, however, that individuals' attitudes and beliefs shape the way they perceive the world about them, the researcher assumes that respondents will impute their own attitudes to their co-workers.

Indirect questions may be appropriate when the researcher is interested in characteristics or experiences that the respondent is unwilling or unable to reveal in direct terms. Respondents may be unwilling because the behavior in question is considered socially undesirable or unacceptable; they may be unable because the characteristics—motives, needs, fears—are below their level of conscious awareness.

Most indirect measurement is based on the notion of projection: that individuals tend to attribute their own inner needs, feelings, opinions, and values to the outer world. Thus, an individual presented with ambiguous stimuli will tend to interpret the material in ways that reflect his or her own needs and values. Some of the more common projective techniques are word association, sentence completion, and storytelling. In word association, respondents say the first thing that comes to mind in response to each of a list of words read by an interviewer. Sentence completion requires respondents to finish incomplete sentences, such as "When I think of cities, I think of . . ." Storytelling involves asking respondents to interpret such ambiguous stimuli as inkblots and pictures.

Most indirect measures were developed for clinical use and designed to aid in the diagnosis of emotional disorders by revealing an individual's personality and needs. This remains their principal use, although they also have been used in attitude and motivation research, especially in marketing. To illustrate the indirect approach, let us examine a classic study from marketing research, conducted in 1950. (For a more complete discussion of the use of indirect questions and approaches, see Kidder and Campbell, 1970.)

Mason Haire (1950) was interested in attitudes toward instant coffee, one of the early instant food preparations. Using direct questioning, Haire found that when women who reported not using instant coffee were asked, "What do you dislike about it?" most of them said that they did not like the flavor. Suspecting, however, that this was a stereotypic response that concealed other motives, Haire developed an indirect approach to measure consumer's attitudes. He prepared two grocery shopping lists that were identical, except that one contained "Nescafé instant coffee" and the other "1 lb Maxwell House coffee (drip grind)." He then asked subjects to read one or the other shopping list and to describe the personality and character of the woman who made it out. As it turned out, Nescafé and Maxwell House coffee users were perceived quite differently. For example, nearly half of the subjects described the Nescafé user as lazy and failing to plan household purchases, whereas the Maxwell House purchaser was rarely described in these terms. The evidence from the indirect approach thus suggested that the decision to buy instant coffee was influenced as much by prevailing attitudes about what constitutes good housekeeping as by the flavor of instant coffee. Although a 1968 replication of this study produced essentially the same results (Webster and von Pechmann, 1970), it would be interesting to see if the findings would be repeated today, given the apparent changes in attitudes toward women and housework in the last two decades.

While one should be aware of the possibility of indirect questioning, it is used relatively infrequently in survey research today. One likely reason is that its use often requires intensive training in the administration, scoring, and interpretation of responses. Some researchers also question the validity of such measures. On the infrequent occasions that tests of validity and reliability have been done, the results have not been encouraging (Kidder and Campbell, 1970). Further, there are some serious ethical concerns with the use of indirect questions. To what extent are respondents giving their "informed consent"? To what extent is deception being used, and is its use justifiable?

Response Formats

In addition to making decisions about the broad categories of open and closed questions and direct and indirect questions, the creative survey designer will also consider the possibilities offered by various response formats for closed-ended questions. The simplest response option is a simple "yes" or "no." This would be appropriate for such questions as "Do you belong to a labor union?" or "Have you ever been threatened with a gun, or shot at?" However, even though many types of information form natural dichotomies, this kind of question appears less frequently than you might think. With many apparently dichotomous items, respondents may prefer to answer "don't know," "uncertain," or "both." About 10 percent of national samples, for instance, respond "don't know" to the question, "Do you believe in life after death?" (J. A. Davis and T. W. Smith, 1985).

For questions having more than two response options, the researcher usually is interested in measuring the strength or intensity of respondents' feelings. Several ordinal scales exist for doing this. One of the most popular formats, used in Likert scaling, consists of a series of responses ranging from "strongly agree" to "strongly disagree." This is a common way of measuring attitudes. The respondent is presented with a statement and asked to indicate the extent of his or her agreement. For example,

> Rent control is necessary in order for many of the people of River City to obtain adequate housing.
>
> ( ) Strongly agree
> ( ) Agree
> ( ) Uncertain
> ( ) Disagree
> ( ) Strongly disagree

Besides degrees of agreement, a variety of other rating scales exist for assessing attitudes and opinions. To evaluate objects ranging from consumer products to personal attributes to government policies, respondents could be given the categories "excellent," "good," "fair," and "poor," as in the following question.

> Compared with the jobs that your friends have, would you say that your job is excellent, good, fair, or poor?
>
> ( ) Excellent
> ( ) Good
> ( ) Fair
> ( ) Poor

One can also create scales by asking respondents "how" they feel and then using a series of adverbs to modify the intensity of opinion. For example,

> On the whole, how satisfied are you with the work you do—would you say you are very satisfied, moderately satisfied, a little dissatisfied, or very dissatisfied?
>
> ( ) Very satisfied
> ( ) Moderately satisfied
> ( ) A little dissatisfied
> ( ) Very dissatisfied

It is also common to use numerical rating scales, with verbal ratings provided for the numerical endpoints, as below (J. A. Davis and T. W. Smith, 1985).

> I am going to name some institutions in this country. Some people have complete confidence in the *people running* these institutions. Suppose these people are at one end of the scale at point number 1. Other people have no confidence at all in the *people running* these institutions. Suppose these people are at the other end, at point 7. And, of course, other people have opinions somewhere in between at point

2, 3, 4, 5, or 6. Where would you place yourself on this scale for banks and financial institutions?

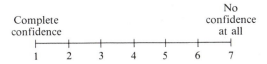

Another popular rating approach measures people's reactions to stimulus words or statements on a seven-point scale with endpoints anchored by opposing adjectives (such as "good" and "bad," or "fast" and "slow").[3] Respondents are asked to rate the stimulus word or statement as it relates to each pair of adjectives. For example:

President Reagan

Fun:	:		:	x	:	:	:	:	:Boring
Real:	:		:		:	:	x	:	:	:Fake
Strong:	x	:		:		:	:	:	:	:Weak
Cold:	:		:		:	x	:	:	:	:Warm

Here a hypothetical respondent evaluated President Reagan to be slightly fun and fake, extremely strong, and was neutral or undecided on the cold-warm dimension.

A particular advantage with this format is that it is easily adapted for people from different backgrounds by using words appropriate to their vocabulary. Robert Gordon and colleagues (1963) adopted this format to test predictions from several delinquency theories regarding the values of gang, nongang lower-class, and nongang middle-class boys. Using such adjective pairs as "clean-dirty," "good-bad," "brave-cowardly," and "smart-sucker," the boys studied were asked to rate various stimulus descriptions (e.g., "someone who works for good grades at school," "someone who shares his money with his friends," "someone who knows where to sell what he steals," "someone who stays cool and keeps to himself"). The gang boys were found to endorse middle-class norms to a much greater extent than predicted.

Ranking questions present another possibility to the survey designer, as in this example:

A number of factors influence a supermarket shopper's choice of food items. Rank the factors listed below from 1 to 5, according to their importance to you in buying groceries:

_____Convenience
_____Taste appeal
_____Cost
_____Nutritional value
_____Advertising, displays

Although ranking questions frequently are handy and appropriate to use, we have chosen this example to illustrate several potential problems. First, unless pretesting with an open question has been done, who can say these five factors are the most salient to the respondents? (This, of course, is a general problem with closed questions.) Even if these factors have been shown to be the most important ones, further questions of validity may be raised. Do people really *know* why they choose certain food products? If so, will they tell you? How many respondents would freely admit that, to them, "convenience" or "advertising" is the most important factor? Would "nutritional value" tend to get a spuriously high ranking? (See Sudman and Bradburn [1982:158–165] for several additional examples of ranking questions.)

Visual Aids

An effective survey instrument also may include miscellaneous aids such as illustrations, photographs, films, and cards that contain written material. The use of illustrations in a self-administered questionnaire may improve clarity and appeal, increasing respondent motivation and perhaps improving the completion rate. In interviewing, photographs and films sometimes are used to acquire data not obtainable through questioning alone. In a study of early socialization practices, for example, photographs of mothers with their young babies might be taken to stimulate the mothers to discuss their childrearing attitudes and behavior, especially if the mothers have difficulty answering highly abstract questions.

Other aids used with an interview may speed up the interview or make it easier for the respondent to answer accurately. The latter purpose may be served by presenting respondents a card containing the responses to a fixed-choice question, so that the respondent can view the choices while answering the question. As a rule, cards are used whenever the response categories are lengthy or more than five or six in number. For example, interviewers from the National Opinion Research Center hand respondents a card similar to the one shown below when they ask, "Which of the categories on this card come closest to the type of place you were living in when you were 16 years old?" (J. A. Davis and T. W. Smith, 1985).

> In open country but not on a farm 1
> On a farm 2
> In a small city or town (under 50,000) 3
> In a medium-size city (50,000–250,000) 4
> In a suburb near a large city 5
> In a large city (over 250,000) 6

Existing Questions

Of all the raw materials available to the survey researcher, perhaps the most important are questions that have been used in previous research. Most survey instruments contain existing questions, at least in adapted form, and it is easy to understand why. The use of existing questions shortcuts the measurement and testing processes. It also enables researchers to compare results across studies, to estimate trends, and, under certain conditions, to estimate response reliability (Sudman and Bradburn, 1982:14). Lest one be concerned about the ethics of using another person's questions, Sudman and Bradburn (1982:14) note that "the mores of social science in general and survey research in particular not only permit but encourage the repetition of questions." Unless questionnaire items have been copyrighted, no permission is required.

Many sources of questions are available on most topics. Literature reviews on the research topic should uncover references with pertinent questions. One may also consult more general sources of questions, such as the CBS-*New York Times* poll, as indexed in the *The New York Times Index*, and the Polls Section of *Public Opinion Quarterly*, or data archives, such as the Roper Center and National Opinion Research Center. (See Sudman and Bradburn [1982:15–16] for a useful suggestive listing of general sources and data archives.) Finally, since every survey contains some demographic questions on age, gender, marital status, and so forth, an indispensable resource is the Social Science Research Council's *Basic Background Items* (Van Dusen and Zill, 1975). Created in an effort to standardize basic descriptive information on respondents, this document contains recommended question wordings and coding procedures.

"Sketches" or Preliminaries

Having considered likely "raw materials," the survey designer, like the artist, will go on to make a "sketch." The sketch for the survey designer essentially is an outline of the topics to be covered in the interview or questionnaire.

The Opening

At this point one should decide what the opening topic will be and draft the opening questions. It is best to have an interesting and nonthreatening topic at the beginning that will get respondents involved and motivate them to cooperate in completing the interview or questionnaire. The first question should be congruent with respondents' expectations: it should be a question they might reasonably expect to be asked, on the basis of what they have been told by the interviewer about the study. This sometimes involves using a question that has no research purpose other than motivating respondents by conforming to their preconceptions about what should occur in a competent survey. The first question also should be relatively easy to answer, thus preventing respondents from becoming discouraged or feeling inadequate to fulfill their role as respondents.

If both open and closed questions are used, the beginning is a good place to have an open question.[4] Most people like to express their views and have someone listen and take them seriously. An interesting opening question is a good way to meet this need of respondents and also get them to open up and warm to the respondent role. Here are two examples:

As far as you're concerned, what are the advantages of living in this neighborhood?
What do you like about living here?

Let's talk first about medical care. What would you say are the main differences
between the services provided by doctors and hospitals nowadays compared to
what they were like when you were a child?

The Placement of Sensitive and Routine Questions

It would be prudent to avoid both boring, routine questions and sensitive, personal
questions in the beginning; build up interest, trust, and rapport before risking these.
Uninteresting routine questions such as background information (age, gender, marital status, etc.) are often placed toward the end of the survey instrument. Asking
personal questions (e.g., racial prejudices, income, sexual activity, alcohol or drug
use, religious beliefs) prematurely may embarrass or otherwise upset respondents
and possibly cause them to terminate the interview or question the researcher's
motives.

Some researchers place sensitive or personal topics at the end of an interview,
arguing that, if the respondent fails to cooperate at this point, not much information
will be lost. However, this may leave respondents with a bad taste in their mouths
and may promote negative feelings toward survey research. Probably it is best to
introduce such questions after the interview is well under way, as the respondent
will have invested time and effort by then and possibly will have developed trust
toward the research and/or interviewer. In addition, sensitive questions should fit
into the question sequence logically; they should be preceded when possible by
related but less sensitive questions or topics, so that the relationship of the personal
questions to the topic and to the research is clear to the respondent. It also may be
helpful to precede the most sensitive questions with a direct explanation of their
importance to the research and to repeat an assurance of confidentiality.

Order, Flow, and Transition

After decisions have been made regarding the first topic and questions and you have
a general idea of how you plan to introduce both sensitive and routine questions, the
next task would be to put the remaining topics in some reasonable order. What
additional considerations go into the organization of topics?

The respondent's point of view must be considered as the researcher attempts to
order the topics. The order must seem logical to respondents if their thinking about
the questions is to be facilitated and motivation enhanced. Early topics should be
easy to answer and of interest to the respondent; subsequent topics should seem to
flow naturally from them. It may even be that the survey instrument will begin with
topics of little or no interest to the researcher but that will facilitate the introduction
at a later point of topics more pertinent to the research objectives. An excellent
example of topic flow is provided by the University of Michigan Surveys of Consumer Finances. According to Kahn and Cannell (1957:161–162),

[T]he objectives of these annual surveys [was] to ascertain the respondent's
income, his savings patterns and the amount he has in various forms of savings, his

buying intentions and major items purchased over the past year, his indebtedness, and his feeling about his own financial situation, both present and anticipated. The questionnaire starts with broad attitudinal questions on how the respondent feels about economic conditions generally, and moves to questions on his feelings about his own financial position and his expectations for the next few years. The interview then considers the respondent's assets, beginning with home ownership. How much is the house worth? When did he buy it? Does he have a mortgage? How much does he still owe on the mortgage? Similarly, ownership of automobiles is discussed. Then other major purchases are discussed. Next comes the topic of plans to purchase goods in the near future, which leads logically to the problem of sources of funds for such purchases. Will the money come from savings, from current income, or where? This introduces the topics of how much income is available and how much savings the person has. Last, to round out the picture, the amount of money already committed (debts) is discussed.

If there are to be questions that demand hard work on the part of the respondent, these should not be at the beginning but included sometime later when commitment and momentum have been developed but before the respondent could become tired.

The researcher also must be sensitive to the problem of reactivity or "mental set." A topic or question appearing early in the instrument may start the respondent thinking in a way that will affect later responses; changing the order of questions can influence responses to related questions. For example, questioning cigarette smokers early in an interview about their beliefs in a link between cancer and smoking could influence their responses to later questions about perceived benefits and drawbacks of continued smoking. One way to deal with this problem (really a validity check) is to have two forms of the instrument in which the order of related questions differs and to compare responses on the two forms.

After the researcher has made an outline of the topics, considered the location of routine and sensitive questions and the problem of reactivity, and has written the opening questions (and perhaps a few others), transitions between major topics should be considered. Transitions indicate that one topic is completed and another topic is to be discussed; the main objective is to focus the respondent's attention on the new topic. Transitions also may be used to explain briefly why the new topic will be discussed or how it relates to the research purposes. Although they are not needed between every change in topic, transitions can improve the flow of an interview or questionnaire as well as respondent understanding and motivation. The following are examples of topic transitions:

"Now I would like to ask some questions about your family. As you were growing up, let's say when you were around 16, how much influence do you remember having . . . ?"

"Okay, now I'd like to change the subject slightly to one part of campus life that we're particularly interested in. As you may know . . ."

"I would like to shift the subject slightly and get some of your opinions about . . ."

"Fine. Now we have just a few background questions."

The "sketch" of the instrument will be completed by the drafting of an introduction to the questionnaire or interview. The introduction should explain briefly the general purpose of the study, assure the respondent of confidentiality, and provide basic instructions for responding to the interview or questionnaire. Of course, the researcher never divulges specific hypotheses or relationships of interest during the introduction, for to do so would be an invitation to respondents to give the desired or expected responses.

Filling in the Sketch: Writing the Items

Drawing upon the "raw materials" outlined earlier, the survey designer is now ready to "fill in the sketch" by writing the individual items. An artist has elements such as line, perspective, light effects, and color to aid in filling in a sketch. Are there principles or "elements of design" by which the survey designer likewise may be guided?

The most general principle to follow is to formulate your research objectives clearly before you begin to write questions. We could not agree more with Sudman and Bradburn's recommendation (1982:41), especially for beginning researchers, "that—before you write any questions—you put down on paper the aims of the study, hypotheses, table formats, and proposed analyses." This material then "should not become a straightjacket for you," but should guide you in writing items, clarifying their meaning to respondents, and organizing them into a meaningful sequence.

Beyond a formal statement of objectives, certain practices in survey design have been shown to enhance the effectiveness of the research instrument. For instance, when a topic is somewhat abstract, using a number of items or questions results in better-quality data. In general, the more abstract the topic, the more items are required; however, this principle must be balanced by the need to keep the instrument reasonably short. The principle may be illustrated by a hypothetical interview schedule investigating job satisfaction. Topics to be included might be wages, hours or shift worked, opportunities for learning and advancement, whether the work is interesting, supervisor-worker relations, and other working conditions. The topic concerning hours or shift worked might well be covered by a couple of questions, whereas "supervisor-worker relations" is a bit more abstract, and several distinct questions probably would be needed in order to get an accurate picture of the worker's satisfaction or dissatisfaction in this area.

We now consider useful principles for wording questions, for grouping questions to achieve greater effectiveness, and for avoiding common problems.

Using Language Effectively

In writing question items, using language effectively presents a real challenge. Even slight altering of the wording of a question can greatly affect responses to the item, whether open or closed.[5] And with closed items, slight changes in the wording of a response option can greatly affect the frequency with which the option is chosen.

Guidelines for using language to obtain better data have been developed on the basis of survey researchers' experiences and of validity and reliability testing. While some of these guidelines seem to be self-evident or commonsense suggestions, the plethora of poorly worded items continually being produced would seem to indicate a need for more attention to the language of items. The following questions provide a framework for examining the language of the items.

1. Are the items unambiguous, easily read, and sufficiently brief? Clarity and precision are essential qualities of well-worded items. At times an item that appears perfectly clear to the designer may be very confusing or carry a different meaning to someone with a different background and point of view. The point is easily illustrated by the question, "How many years have you been living here?" To one respondent "here" may mean the present house or apartment, to another the city, and to another the United States. If you have tried to order a "medium-rare" steak in New York City and in Dallas, you can appreciate that using the same words in different social settings does not necessarily convey the same meaning.

Especially troublesome are indefinite words such as "usually," "seldom," "many," "few," "here," "there"; these will have different meanings to different respondents. Following are two alternative items illustrating the problem; the second is an improvement over the first because the responses are specific and thereby have the same precise meaning for both researcher and respondent.

> A. How frequently do you eat meals in restaurants?
> ( ) Seldom or never
> ( ) Often
> ( ) Very often
> ( ) Every day
>
> B. How frequently do you eat a meal in a restaurant?
> ( ) 0 to 1 time(s) per month
> ( ) 2 to 4 times per month
> ( ) More than once per week but not every day
> ( ) Every day

Items also should be easy to read or hear accurately. Succinct wording of items will enhance the accuracy of responses, as will avoiding the use of negative words such as "not." Some respondents will skip over or tune out the negative word in an item and respond the opposite of the way the question is actually intended. If negative words must be used, it is wise to print them in all capitals, underline, or verbally emphasize them.

2. Is the instrument's vocabulary appropriate for the respondents you intend to interview? If the intended study population is highly heterogeneous, the vocabulary must be kept extremely simple and the survey designer should be aware of regional and other group differences in the meanings of words. To exemplify the problem of translating social science concepts into language understandable by nearly everyone, let us assume for a moment you are studying "socialization" among a random sample of American parents. You decide to start the interview with a broad, open question. While any of the three examples that follow could be used, the third would doubtless be most effective.

What do you consider to be the most important factors in the socialization of
children?

What childrearing practices do you think are most important?

What things do you think are most important for parents to do if they want to bring
up their children right?

On the other hand, with some surveys "talking down" may be a potential
problem. When sampling a more homogeneous or specialized group (say, city
managers, doctors, or nuclear engineers), use vocabulary that is appropriately
sophisticated and technical for that group.

3. Do the questions contain a single idea, or are any of them "double-barreled"? A *double-barreled question* is one in which two separate ideas are presented
together as a unit. An example (perhaps from the "socialization" study) might be:
"What factors contributed to your decision to marry and have children?" The
researcher seems to assume that marrying and having children is a single act or
decision, whereas in fact there are two questions being asked here. It is a good idea
for the survey designer to examine all questions with the word "and" in them to be
sure they are not double-barreled.

4. Are the items free of emotionally loaded words and other sources of bias?
Emotionally loaded words and phrases, such as "communists," "capitalist,"
"cops," or even "the President's statement," may result in some "gut-level" or
reflexive responses that have little to do with the real attitudes or opinion of the
respondent regarding the issue the researcher is attempting to study. In general, try
to word questions in a neutral way, and avoid identifying a statement or position
with any controversial or prestigious person or group. Notice the loaded words
("union czars," "forcing," "knuckle under") in the following question (Sudman
and Bradburn, 1982:2):

Are you in favor of allowing construction union czars the power to shut down an
entire construction site because of a dispute with a single contractor, thus forcing
even more workers to knuckle under to union agencies?

This question was part of a questionnaire distributed by a political lobbying group
for fund-raising purposes, a practice that social scientists consider deceptive and
unethical.

Another source of bias is *leading questions*. Leading questions suggest a possible answer or make some responses seem more acceptable than others. A question
that begins, "Do you agree . . . ?" may suggest to some persons that they ought to
agree. The question, "How often do you smoke marijuana?" may seem to imply
that everyone indulges at least occasionally.[6]

An unbalanced or incomplete listing of alternatives either in the question or in
the response options given is another common error. An example of the former
would be the question, "When you discipline your children, do you spank them,
take away privileges, or what?" It would be better to give a complete listing of
alternatives or none. The problem of making sure the responses to a closed question

are exhaustive was discussed earlier in the chapter; it is also important that the responses be balanced. For example, if the responses represent attitudes toward the United Nations, it would be judicious to have an equal number of positive and negative statements, as well as a neutral statement. Furthermore, you would want to represent both extreme and moderate attitudes in each direction.

5. On personal and sensitive questions, is the wording as tactful, diplomatic, and face-saving as possible? The topic of sensitive questions was discussed earlier in reference to their placement in the instrument. It was pointed out that motivation could be enhanced not only by logical placement of the item but also by showing the relevance of the question to the research purpose, reassuring the respondent of confidentiality, and including a wide range of response options. In addition to these efforts, careful diplomatic wording of the items may boost motivation and facilitate more candid responses. A housewife may feel irritated or defensive if asked, "Do you work?" but perhaps not if asked, "Do you work outside the home?"

A sensitive question might also be preceded by a statement that in effect sanctions the less socially desirable response, such as, "Some people feel that smoking marijuana is pleasant and harmless, while others feel that it is harmful. What do you think?" or "Many people have taken an item from a store without paying for some reason. Have you ever done this?"

Finally, in order to make the best use of language, the survey designer will usually need to make several successive drafts of the questions. Early drafts should be subjected to careful scrutiny by both the researcher and his or her associates with the aforementioned questions in mind. Then, to facilitate further improvements in the language of the items, a semifinal draft should be pretested with a population similar to the one for which the survey instrument is designed.

The "Frame of Reference" Problem

Often the questions we ask people seem clear in meaning to us but can be answered from several perspectives or frames of reference. For example, suppose a survey of second-semester college freshmen asked: "Generally speaking, how satisfied are you with your decision to attend State University?" Students giving the same response, such as "relatively satisfied," could have very different reasons for doing so. One may feel "relatively satisfied" because she has a generous scholarship and feels the school is as good as most others from an academic standpoint. Another student may be thinking of the social life, and a third of intramural sports activities. Yet, from their answers, the researcher would not know what the respondents' reasons were for their satisfaction or dissatisfaction.

There are a number of ways to determine or to control the respondent's frame of reference. A straightforward way to determine the frame of reference is to follow the question with a probe such as "Can you tell me why you feel that way?" "What things specifically do you feel are satisfactory (or unsatisfactory) about State University?" Another simple means of controlling the frame of reference for individual questions is to specify the frame of reference within the question, such as, "Compared to other universities in the state system, how do you feel about the intellectual life at Caufield State?"

By particular arrangements of questions, the researcher also can direct the respondent to the investigator's frame of reference. A *funnel sequence* (Kahn and Cannell, 1957:158–160) moves from a very general question to progressively more specific questions. Suppose one wanted to study the impact of inflation on people's attitudes about the performance of the President. Asking questions about inflation first might impose this frame of reference on respondents, so that later questions about the President's performance are judged with reference to the President's inflation efforts. Instead, a funnel sequence could start out with general questions about achievements ("What do you think about the President's performance in office?" "Why do you feel this way?"), which will likely disclose the respondents' frame of reference. These questions then could be followed by questions on inflation ("Do you think we have a serious inflation problem?" "Has it had much effect on you?"), and, finally, specific questions about the President's activity in this area ("Do you believe the President is doing a good job of fighting inflation?").

The previous example illustrates the effectiveness of a funnel sequence when the researcher wants to avoid the possibility that asking more specific questions first would bias responses to more general questions. This sequence also offers the advantage of beginning with the respondent's ideas and perspectives, which may increase interest and motivation. Funnel sequences may consist entirely of open questions or of an open question (or questions) followed by closed questions.

A common frame of reference also may be established through an *inverted-funnel sequence* of related questions (Kahn and Cannell, 1957:160). Here one begins with the most specific questions and ends with the most general. While this approach lacks the advantages of the funnel sequence, it is useful in some situations. First, it may be used to assure that all respondents are considering the same points or circumstances before expressing their general opinions. For example, if we wanted to make sure that respondents were judging the President's performance in office upon similar bases, an inverted-funnel sequence would enable us to bring up and question performance in specific areas (inflation, unemployment, foreign policy) before asking for a general evaluation. A second advantage of the inverted-funnel sequence is that, whether or not respondents have previously formed an opinion regarding the final question in the sequence, all will have time to think through certain aspects of a complex issue before giving their opinion. Instead of asking respondents to express immediately their attitude toward liberalizing laws on abortions, for example, one might ask about approval of abortion in various specific circumstances (if there is a strong chance of a birth deformity, if the woman became pregnant as a result of rape, if the woman's own health is seriously endangered, if the woman is married and does not want the child, if the family cannot afford any more children), at the end of which the respondents' general opinion would be sought. (See Box 10.2 for additional examples of a funnel sequence and inverted-funnel sequence.)

Reason Analysis

The funnel sequence illustrates the benefits of using a sequence of questions to explore complex issues. Similarly, a well-devised series of questions is invariably

BOX 10.2

Examples of Funnel and Inverted Funnel Sequences of Questions

Here is a sample funnel sequence from a study of union printers (Lipset, Trow, and Coleman, 1956:493–494).

7. (a) All things considered, how do you like printing as an occupation?
     Do you dislike it?
     Are you indifferent?
     Do you like it fairly well?
     Do you like it very much?
   (b) Why do you feel this way?
8. (a) Is there any occupation you would like to have other than the one you now have—either in or outside the printing trade?
     (If so) Which one?
9. Let's look at it another way: If you were starting all over again, what occupation would you want to get into?
10. (a) How would you rate printing as an occupation? For example:
     (1) Would you rate the *pay* as excellent, good, fair, or poor?
     (2) How about *job security* in the printing trade? Would you rate it as excellent, good, fair, or poor?
     (3) How about the *prestige* printing receives from people outside the trade?

A brief inverted-funnel sequence used to measure perceptions of well-being (Andrews and Withey, 1976:376) is reproduced here.

13. Here are some faces expressing various feelings. Below each is a letter.

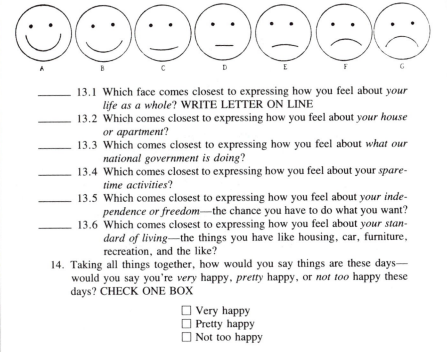

A   B   C   D   E   F   G

_____ 13.1 Which face comes closest to expressing how you feel about *your life as a whole*? WRITE LETTER ON LINE
_____ 13.2 Which comes closest to expressing how you feel about *your house or apartment*?
_____ 13.3 Which comes closest to expressing how you feel about *what our national government is doing*?
_____ 13.4 Which comes closest to expressing how you feel about your *spare-time activities*?
_____ 13.5 Which comes closest to expressing how you feel about *your independence or freedom*—the chance you have to do what you want?
_____ 13.6 Which comes closest to expressing how you feel about *your standard of living*—the things you have like housing, car, furniture, recreation, and the like?
14. Taking all things together, how would you say things are these days—would you say you're *very* happy, *pretty* happy, or *not too* happy these days? CHECK ONE BOX

        ☐ Very happy
        ☐ Pretty happy
        ☐ Not too happy

more effective than the simple question "Why?" in finding out the reasons for people's behavior.[7] Suppose we ask undergraduates why they decided to attend UCLA, and receive the following responses: Mary—"My parents convinced me"; Sam—"because I live in LA"; Pascual—"for a scholarship"; Irma—"to be with my boyfriend"; Reuben—"It's a fun school and I wasn't accepted at the other schools I applied to." Not only are these reasons brief and quite diverse, they seem incomplete; surely these students selected UCLA for more than one reason (only Reuben mentioned two reasons). Perhaps Mary and Sam also were influenced by scholarships; maybe Irma was not alone in having a close friend at UCLA or Reuben was not the only one turned down by other schools. Also, other determinants of the respondents' choice of UCLA may have been overlooked, such as the recommendations of high-school teachers, the academic reputation of UCLA, and the climate of southern California.

How, then, can we go about discovering the main factors that influenced our respondents to attend UCLA? Fortunately, Hans Zeisel (1968) has systematized the process of asking "Why?" The key idea in Zeisel's *reason analysis* is the development of an "accounting scheme" outlining the general categories of reasons, or dimensions of the decision, which, in turn, provides a model or structure for formulating a comprehensive series of questions.

The accounting scheme is based upon the research objectives (not all reasons may be of interest), upon the researcher's creativity, and usually upon informal exploratory interviewing with members of the group under study. Unless one is reasonably well informed about the various categories of reasons for an action (perhaps from previous research or experience), these are sought through exploratory interviewing. The information from these preliminary interviews is culled for reasons not pertinent to the research objectives,[8] and the remaining responses are creatively grouped into an integrated model of relevant categories to form the accounting scheme.

Often an accounting scheme is structured in terms of the typical stages in a decision process. To return to our example, for many students the decision to attend UCLA involved (1) a decision to attend college, (2) the selection of schools to apply to for admission, and (3) the final choice of UCLA. At each of these stages the respondent's behavior may be influenced by sources of information (knowledge, gossip, rumors learned from the media, friends, and strangers), advice from significant others (recommendations of friends, parents, teachers), constraints or limitations (financial needs, health requirements, need to live with or near a friend or relative), the respondent's particular needs (academic interests, vocational objectives, social and recreational interests), perceived characteristics of the schools considered (reputation or image, strengths and weaknesses, location and climate, housing availability, costs), and responses by the schools (offers of aid or scholarships, athletic awards, special recruitment efforts, or rejection of admission application).

After systematically outlining the accounting scheme just sketched out, the final step in our reason analysis would be to write a series of questions to assist the respondents in reviewing the stages of their decisions to attend UCLA: "When did you first seriously consider going to college?" "How did you reach this decision?"

. . . "Did you apply to any other colleges or universities? Which ones?" . . . "What were the characteristics of UCLA that you particularly liked?" . . . "Did your parents, friends, teachers or any other persons help you come to your decision? Who?" "How much influence did this have on you?" Although the process of reason analysis in this situation obviously calls for intense mental labor, we would end up knowing immensely more about the college decisions of Mary, Sam, Pascual, Irma, and Reuben than had we simply asked, "Why UCLA?"

The sequence of stages of a decision process is not the only basis for accounting schemes. Zeisel (1968) discusses in detail several common schemes. In studies of why people move from place A to place B (or shift jobs, or, in general, change preferences from A to B), the reason analysis focuses particularly on the negative aspects of A and the positive aspects of B. This is called the "push-pull" scheme in migration studies since the decision to move may be precipitated either by factors that push one out of the old location (e.g., an increase in rent, a change in neighborhood character, the loss of a job) and/or factors that pull or attract one to a new habitat (e.g., the anticipation of employment, or a better wage, or a better environment). Another common accounting scheme used in studies of consumer behavior has three major dimensions: the perceived attributes of the consumer product (e.g., its effects, price), the motives or needs of the respondent to be satisfied by the product, and the influences that affect the purchase decision (e.g., advertising, recommendations of friends).[9]

Reason analysis thus is a very useful and general technique for guiding questionnaire construction and for avoiding superficial and incomplete answers to important questions. The researcher basically is asking many specific "why's?" rather than a general "why?" question.

Memory Problems

There are two kinds of memory problems. First, respondents may be unable to recall information the researcher is seeking about life events. According to Cannell and Kahn (1968), the ease with which material may be recalled depends on three factors: how long ago the event occurred, how significant the event was when it occurred, and how relevant the event is to the respondent's life currently. Generally, respondents will have a longer memory for significant rare and costly events in their lives, such as getting married or having major surgery, than for more trivial habitual occurrences, such as small gambling losses or the content of the previous evening's television programs. Furthermore, they will remember more effectively events of continuing importance in their lives. The presence of an unsightly scar, for example, is a reminder of the accident that produced it.

A second difficulty arises from memory distortion. People do not uniformly recall events objectively; rather, memories seem to be distorted either in the process of organizing one's past and making it consistent or in an unconscious effort to maintain a positive self-image. One common type of memory distortion in responses to survey questions is called *telescoping* (Sudman and Bradburn, 1974). This occurs when a respondent erroneously recalls the timing of an event, for example, remembering an event as having occurred more recently than it did.

What can be done to stimulate accurate recall? Here are some suggestions (see Cannell and Kahn, 1968; Sudman and Bradburn, 1982):

1. Provide a helpful context and question sequence as in "reason analysis." Rather than asking a respondent, for example, "At what addresses have you resided in the last 10 years?" begin with the present, asking, "How long have you lived in Atlanta?" A second question might ask if the respondent had lived at other addresses in Atlanta, and a later question might ask about residences prior to moving to Atlanta. Or one might ask the respondent to recall an important past event, such as completing school or leaving the parental home, and then guide the respondent to recall subsequent events (marriage, first job, etc.) in a forward time sequence.

2. Some questions demanding accurate memory may be best asked by means of closed questions utilizing lists. Doctors sometimes present new patients with a list of illnesses and ask them which they have had. Social researchers likewise may present lists for aiding recall of such things as magazines read, television programs watched, and organizational memberships.

3. Conduct a household inventory with the respondent. Studies of consumer behavior have revealed that even the current day's grocery purchases (type, brand, size) are best documented by examining with respondents their refrigerator and pantry provisions.

4. Where appropriate, ask respondents to check their records (birth and marriage certificates, school records, financial information, scrapbooks, photographs, etc.).

5. In some circumstances indirect questions may be used to gain information about experiences that are likely to be repressed or distorted.

The first three suggestions, involving the use of "aided-recall" procedures, deal directly with the problem of forgetting but may contribute to some memory distortion. The use of records deals most effectively with both kinds of memory problems, although this information is often difficult to acquire.

Response Bias Problems

Another instrumentation problem arises from the social situation surrounding the administration of interviews and questionnaires. Just as experimenters must be concerned about how the laboratory setting may produce disingenuous subject behavior, the survey researcher must be alert to how the social situation in surveys may produce responses irrelevant to the object of measurement. We discussed this problem briefly in the previous chapter in relation to response effects introduced by the interaction between interviewers and respondents. Here we focus on biases produced by respondent tendencies to answer in certain ways as a function of the content or form of survey questions.

One frequent response tendency is to answer in the direction of *social desirability* (see DeMaio, 1984). We all have our private self-image to maintain; in addition, many respondents will want to make a good impression on the researcher by appearing sensible, healthy, happy, mentally sound, free of racial prejudice, and the like. Some individuals and groups demonstrate this tendency more than others. Indeed, D. L. Phillips (1971:87–88) suggests that the consistent finding of greater happiness, better mental health, and lower racial prejudice among middle-class compared to lower-class respondents may not reflect true class differences in these variables but instead a greater concern among the middle class to give socially desirable responses. Some common techniques for minimizing social desirability bias have been mentioned previously: use of indirect questions, careful placement and wording of sensitive questions, assurances of anonymity and scientific importance, statements sanctioning less socially desirable responses, and building rapport between interviewer and respondent.

A second response bias is the *acquiescence response set*. This is the tendency for respondents to be very agreeable: presented with a question having such options as "yes/no" or "agree/disagree," they are more apt to "agree" or say "yes" than to "disagree" or say "no." This tendency also extends to such formats as the Likert, where there are gradations of agreeing or disagreeing. One way of circumventing the problem is to give specific content to the response options. For example, one may construct the second item below to avoid a possible acquiescence effect in response to the first item.

A. Rent control is necessary in order for many of the people of River City to obtain adequate housing.
( ) Strongly agree
( ) Agree
( ) Uncertain
( ) Disagree
( ) Strongly disagree

B. From the following statements, select the one that most closely represents your opinion about the need for rent control in River City.
1. Rent control is necessary in order for many of the people of River City to obtain adequate housing.
2. Rent control is necessary in order for some of the people of River City to obtain adequate housing.
3. I am uncertain whether rent control is necessary or not.
4. Very few people are really helped by rent control.
5. Rent control is unnecessary.

One problem with this approach, however, is that it requires much greater effort on the part of the survey designer.

Another way to control as well as check for an acquiescence response set when the researcher wishes to retain a yes/no or agree/disagree format is to include within the instrument two items measuring the same concept that are roughly opposite in meaning. Obviously, the items should be located at different points in the instrument. The following item pair from the F scale, a measure of authoritarianism, illustrates this approach (Bass, 1955:619):

A. Human nature being what it is there will always be war and conflict.
B. Human nature being what it is, universal peace will come about eventually.

Responses to the two conflicting statements may be compared to see whether a significant number of persons answered both statements affirmatively. The major problem with this approach is the difficulty of constructing truly contradictory items. It would not necessarily be inconsistent, for example, to reject both of the above statements.

Ordinal or position biases represent a third response tendency. Some respondents mark options located in a certain position, such as the first choice in a multiple-choice format or a particular position in a horizontal rating scale. This is a potential problem whenever questions are asked in a very similar format. Hence, one way of addressing this type of response set, as well as the tendency to acquiesce, is to vary the arrangement of questions and the manner in which they are asked. A second approach is to give response options more specific content, as in the rent control question above.

Format Considerations

Finally, the format or physical organization of the survey instrument must be planned. Obviously there are many possibilities, but a few main points should be considered.

Probably most important, the physical form of the instrument should be appealing to respondents. In addition, the design should facilitate the tasks of reading, completing, and coding. Numbering items consecutively throughout, using clear type, and allowing sufficient space between items and between response options can help greatly. With interview schedules, different type styles (or capitalization and underlining) should be used to differentiate instructions to the interviewer from material to be read aloud to interviewees.

While planning the physical organization, it would be appropriate to consider whether using "filter" and "contingency questions" would improve the instrument. *Contingency questions* are intended for only a part of the sample of respondents. By addressing only those persons for whom the questions are clearly relevant, contingency questions avoid the waste of time and possible decline in respondent motivation that may occur when the same questions are asked of all respondents. Responses to a *filter question* determine who is to answer which of subsequent contingency question(s). One format is illustrated below from a hypothetical survey of adolescent sexual attitudes and practices.

19. Have you ever had sexual intercourse?   (FILTER QUESTION)
    ( ) Yes (Please answer questions 20–29.)   (CONTINGENCY QUESTIONS)
    ( ) No (Go to question 30. Please skip questions 20–29.)

BOX 10.3

Examples of Filter and Contingency Questions

The following is one page from an interview schedule for a longitudinal study of the educational and labor market experience of young women (U.S. Department of Labor, 1978). The physical layout is designed to facilitate interviewing and computer processing.

26. What were you doing most of **LAST WEEK** – working, going to school, or something else?

(087)
1 ☐ WK – Working – SKIP to 27b
2 ☐ J – With a job but not at work
3 ☐ LK – Looking for work
4 ☐ S – Going to school
5 ☐ KH – Keeping house
6 ☐ U – Unable to work – SKIP to 30
7 ☐ OT – Other – Specify ⌐

_____

27c. Do you **USUALLY** work 35 hours or more a week at this job?

(088)
1 ☐ Yes – What is the reason you worked less than 35 hours **LAST WEEK?**
2 ☐ No – What is the reason you **USUALLY** work less than 35 hours a week?

(Mark the appropriate reason)

(089)
1 ☐ Slack work
2 ☐ Material shortage
3 ☐ Plant or machine repair
4 ☐ New job started during week
5 ☐ Job terminated during week
6 ☐ Could find only part-time work
7 ☐ Labor dispute
8 ☐ Did not want full-time work
9 ☐ Full-time work week under 35 hours
10 ☐ Attends school
11 ☐ Holiday (legal or religious)
12 ☐ Bad weather
13 ☐ Own illness
14 ☐ On vacation
15 ☐ Too busy with housework, personal business, etc.
16 ☐ Other – Specify ⌐

_____

(SKIP to 31a and enter job worked at last week)

27a. Did you do any work at all **LAST WEEK**, not counting work around the house?

(090)
1 ☐ Yes   2 ☐ No – SKIP to 28a

b. How many hours did you work **LAST WEEK** at all jobs?

(091) _____ Hours

CHECK ITEM I

Respondent worked –

(092)
1 ☐ 49 hours or more – SKIP to 31a and enter job worked at last week
2 ☐ 1–34 hours – ASK c
3 ☐ 35–48 hours – ASK d

27d. Did you lose any time or take any time off **LAST WEEK** for any reason such as illness, holiday, or slack work?

☐ Yes – How many hours did you take off?

(093) _____ Hours

0 ☐ No – GO to 27e

NOTE: Correct item 27b if lost time not already deducted; if item 27b is reduced below 35 hours, ask item c, otherwise SKIP to 31a.

e. Did you work any overtime or at more than one job **LAST WEEK?**

☐ Yes – How many extra hours did you work?

(094) _____ Hours

0 ☐ No

NOTE: Correct item 27b if extra hours not already included and SKIP to 31a.

(If "J" in 26, SKIP to b)

28a. Did you have a job (or business) from which you were temporarily absent or on layoff **LAST WEEK?**

(095)
1 ☐ Yes
2 ☐ No – ASK 29a

b. Why were you absent from work **LAST WEEK?**

(096)
1 ☐ Own illness
2 ☐ On vacation
3 ☐ Bad weather
4 ☐ Labor dispute
5 ☐ New job to begin within 30 days } ASK 29c and 29d(2)
6 ☐ Temporary layoff (less than 30 days)
7 ☐ Indefinite layoff (30 days or more or no definite recall date) } ASK 29d(3)
8 ☐ School interfered
9 ☐ Other – Specify ⌐

_____

_____

c. Are you getting wages or salary for any of the time off **LAST WEEK?**

(097)
1 ☐ Yes
2 ☐ No
3 ☐ Self-employed

d. Do you usually work 35 hours or more a week at this job?

(098)
1 ☐ Yes
2 ☐ No

(GO to 31a and enter job held last week)

Notes

Another common format uses arrows to point from the filter response options to the appropriate contingency questions (see Box 10.3).

The Final Product

Once the survey instrument has been drafted and the draft has been revised in light of reviewer comments, there is one more critical step to take. This step, one of the field activities of survey research outlined in the last chapter and also a crucial aspect of experimentation, is called *pretesting*. It is the final technique for troubleshooting and improving the survey instrument, and without it, you could not know for sure that respondents would understand the questions the way you intended.

Pretesting

Pretesting a survey instrument consists of trying it out on a small number of persons having characteristics similar to those of the target group of respondents. The pretest group is normally not a probability sample, since you are not planning to generalize your findings. However, it should be as heterogeneous as the target population. For example, if your target group is a national sample of college and university students, the pretest group should include college students at all levels (freshmen through graduate students) and from different types of institutions (large, small, religious, secular, liberal arts, technical, etc.).

The responses of the pretest group are examined for such problems as a low response rate to sensitive questions, items where everyone makes the same response, confusion as to the meaning of questions, or complaints about the length of the interview. Pretesting also should provide answers to questions such as these:

> Does the level of language match the sophistication of respondents? Are instructions to respondents and to interviewers clear? Are transitions smooth and informative?
>
> Are response sets a problem?
>
> Are responses to open questions so diverse as to be impossible to analyze?
>
> Are the choice options to closed questions clear and exhaustive?
>
> Are interviewing aids such as cards or photographs effective and practical?
>
> Are there questions that respondents resist answering?
>
> How long, generally, does the interview take to complete?
>
> What is the completion rate?

The information gained by pretesting will give direction to further revision efforts. Often, several pretests and revisions may be necessary to arrive at a good instrument.

Sometimes aspects of the instrument are deliberately changed or varied during pretesting to check out suspected problems or weaknesses. For example, a new attitude scale may be suspected of evoking socially desirable responses. This suspicion might be examined by deliberately varying the content of the scale's introduction (perhaps omitting the usual reassuring preamble, "There are no right or wrong answers") or by rewording the questions.

Failure to conduct pretests can result in a meaningless study. Once the study has been conducted, it is too late to benefit from the information, for example, that in one item, 99 percent of the respondents chose the same option, or that a large number of respondents misunderstood the meaning of a question. Experience has shown that the amount of effort expended on study planning and pretesting is related directly to the ease with which data may be analyzed and to the quality of results.

Summary

Survey design is indeed an art as well as a science. The design of the instrument must (1) assure effective two-way communication between the respondents and the researcher, (2) assist the respondents in recalling and clarifying their experiences, attitudes, and thoughts, and (3) keep the respondents interested and motivated. The principles and procedures discussed in this chapter are intended to facilitate these tasks.

In gathering "raw materials," the survey designer chooses among open and closed questions, direct and indirect questions, and a wide variety of response formats. The researcher may also select visual aids and will almost certainly draw upon questions developed in previous research. Open questions are most appropriate in face-to-face interviews when the researcher is unsure of response categories or is dealing with complex issues that require an in-depth understanding. They often are used effectively in preliminary interviewing in order to determine appropriate closed questions and response alternatives. However, the use of open questions in the final survey instrument is somewhat limited because responses are difficult for researchers to code and require more time and effort on the part of respondents. Closed questions are best used when both researcher and respondent have ample information on the topic. While easier for researchers to analyze and for respondents to complete, closed questions are more difficult to develop, may bias results by structuring responses, and may dampen respondents' interest in the survey. Most questions in surveys are linked apparently or directly to what the researcher wants to know. However, when examining characteristics that respondents are unable or unwilling to report directly, researchers may use indirect questions that disguise the researcher's intent.

After considering raw materials, the survey designer makes a "sketch" of the instrument—an outline of topics to be included. The researcher decides at this point on opening questions, on the placement of sensitive and routine questions, and on the order of topics. Opening questions are critical for motivating respondents to complete the survey; therefore, they should be interesting, relatively easy to answer, and consistent with respondents' expectations. Sensitive questions are best placed somewhere between the middle and end of the instrument; routine background items are usually placed at the end. But all questions should be ordered in a way that seems natural and logical to the respondent. Transitions also may improve the flow from topic to topic.

As one begins to fill in the sketch—to write the items—one should keep the objectives of the study in mind. Properly worded items are clear and precise, are written in a vocabulary appropriate for the respondents, contain a single idea, are free of emotionally loaded words and phrases, and are tactfully worded. To control the respondent's frame of reference in investigating complex topics, one can arrange questions in a funnel sequence, moving from general to progressively more specific questions, or an inverted-funnel sequence, moving from the most specific to the most general questions. Complex issues also can be examined through reason analysis. This involves the development of an accounting scheme, based on preliminary interviewing, that identifies the key dimensions of reasons for an action and integrates them into a model of the action.

Besides the error and bias introduced by improper question wording, the survey designer must be alert to problems of forgetting and memory distortion and to various response bias tendencies. Response accuracy may be improved by aided-recall procedures, such as providing a helpful context or list, or by encouraging the use of records. Among the ways to minimize the social desirability bias are careful placement and wording of questions as well as assurances of anonymity. Response set problems are best handled by varying the type of questions and response format. It is also important for the format of the instrument to be neat and appealing. To save time and prevent adverse reactions, the format might include filter questions that direct respondents to appropriate contingency questions.

Once a draft of the instrument has been prepared, it should be reviewed by one's colleagues and then pretested on a group of respondents similar to those in the target population.

Key Terms

open versus closed questions	inverted-funnel sequence
direct versus indirect questions	reason analysis
response format	response bias tendency
Likert response format	social desirability bias
sensitive question	acquiescence response set
routine question	position response set
double-barreled question	contingency question
leading question	filter question
funnel sequence	pretesting

Review Questions and Problems

1. Compare the advantages and disadvantages of open versus closed questions. When is it advisable to use open rather than closed questions? Why should open questions be used sparingly in self-administered questionnaires?

2. For each of the following research conditions, indicate whether an open or closed question is most appropriate.

    a. The survey seeks broad, in-depth information.

    b. Respondents have a high level of information about the topic of interest.

    c. Respondents are not likely to have given much thought to relevant issues.

    d. Respondents are not highly motivated.

    e. The researcher has little prior knowledge of respondents.

3. Schuman and Presser's (1979) experiment (Box 10.1) showed that people responded differently to open and closed versions of a question regarding preferred job characteristics. What were the major differences in responses to the open and closed versions?

4. Why do researchers resort to indirect questions? What special problems do they present to the researcher?

5. Is it considered unethical to borrow questions from previous research? Explain.

6. Describe some characteristics of a good opening question in an interview or questionnaire.

7. Suppose you are constructing a questionnaire for the purpose of conducting a survey of sex role attitudes. What would be the best placement (beginning, middle, end) of the following questions?

    a. How many sisters do you have?

    b. Does your mother work outside the home?

    c. Mothers should put their children before themselves.

        ( ) Strongly agree

        ( ) Agree

        ( ) Disagree

        ( ) Strongly disagree

    d. Would you say that women nowadays are more likely to work outside the home than they were when you were growing up?

8. Give an example, other than one cited in the text, of a "transition." What purpose do transitions serve?

9. As a general guide to writing items and organizing the entire survey instrument, what should you do before you begin to write individual questions?

10. The text identifies five common wording problems in constructing survey questions: (1) lack of clarity or precision, (2) inappropriate vocabulary, (3) double-barreled question, (4) loaded word or leading question, and (5) insensitive wording. Identify the wording problem(s) in each of the following questions and then rewrite the questions to make them more satisfactory.

    a. How many siblings do you have? ( ) 0–2 ( ) 3–7 ( ) 8 or more

    b. Do you think the man should initiate and pay for the first date?

    c. In divorce or separation cases, the man has just as much right as the woman to have custody of the children.

        ( ) Strongly agree

        ( ) Agree

     ( ) Disagree

     ( ) Strongly disagree

  d. Because women are less aggressive than men, a woman's place is in the home.

     ( ) Strongly agree

     ( ) Agree

     ( ) Disagree

     ( ) Strongly disagree

  e. Do you hold traditional sex role attitudes?

  f. Does your mother work?

  g. Is the leadership in your family matriarchal, patriarchal, or egalitarian?

11. How can a funnel sequence or inverted-funnel sequence solve the survey researcher's frame-of-reference problem?

12. Suppose you wanted to know why students choose a specific major (e.g., sociology). Applying reason analysis, construct a series of questions to find out the reasons for students' choice of major.

13. What are the two types of memory problems with which survey researchers must deal? Identify three ways of increasing the accuracy of respondents' recall.

14. How can one minimize the tendency to give socially desirable responses?

15. Identify two methods of avoiding acquiescence and positional response sets.

16. What is the relation between a filter question and a contingency question?

17. What does it mean to pretest a survey instrument? What purposes does pretesting serve?

NOTES

1. For experimental investigations of the effects of including "don't know" options in opinion questions, see Schuman and Presser (1978).

2. Even when the researcher has had relevant personal experiences, this should not take the place of pretesting.

3. This response format is used in, but not limited to, the semantic-differential scaling technique. For details, see Osgood, Suci, and Tannenbaum (1957).

4. This rule applies to interviews only. As indicated earlier, open-ended questions are usually inappropriate in mail surveys, and if placed at the beginning of a self-administered questionnaire, may discourage respondents from completing the survey.

5. For example, an item might be written, "What is your annual income?" or "What is your total annual income from all sources?" A person answering the first item might neglect to consider income from such sources as interest on stocks or savings, sale of stocks, and rental income. In a test of question wording, Schuman and Presser (1977) compared the responses to two freedom-of-speech questions: "Do you think the United States should allow public speeches against democracy?" and "Do you think the United States should forbid public speeches against democracy?" When these questions were asked in separate but comparable 1974 national sample surveys, approximately 16 percent fewer people wanted to "forbid" than "not allow" such speeches.

6. On the other hand, for certain underreported behavior, this type of question may be necessary (Sudman and Bradburn, 1982). While the marijuana question appears to assume that the respondent smokes, it is still possible to answer "never."

7. This section is adapted, in part, from the discussion in Zeisel (1968).

8. If the UCLA Administration had hired us to study the impact of financial aid programs on the quality of undergraduate admissions, for example, our accounting scheme would definitely incorporate financial considerations; and the sample under study also should include UCLA applicants who are accepted but choose to go elsewhere to school. If, instead, our client were the UCLA student government, which wanted to improve programs serving the needs of incoming freshmen, our accounting scheme would focus on these needs and would likely omit information about other schools considered.

9. Sometimes an accounting scheme guides the entire research design, not just the wording of a few questions. Nine years after the first major announcement in 1953 of a possible link between cigarette smoking and lung cancer, Straits (1967) conducted a survey to study why the health reports were apparently having only slight effects on cigarette smokers. His study was designed around the accounting scheme that this anxiety-arousing information was having negligible impact on smokers because they (1) were unaware of the reports, (2) disbelieved them, (3) were not motivated to give up smoking, or (4) were unable to translate their motivation into action.

11

Field Research

Virtually all experiments and many surveys are conducted for the purpose of explanation; they seek to answer "why" questions by testing hypotheses about causal relationships. We emphasized this side of science in the previous chapters; and at times the studies we examined may have seemed far removed from common experience. However, social science involves more than explanation and prediction and most certainly is not the product of unusual experience. It also involves exploration and description. This chapter examines methods for the exploration, description, and understanding of naturally occurring events. As you will see, social scientific inquiry is as much about "how" people do things as about "why" they do them (J. Lofland, 1976).

We have chosen to call the methodological approach examined in this chapter *field research*. Some call it "qualitative" (as opposed to "quantitative") research (see Filstead, 1970; Schwartz and Jacobs, 1979; Taylor and Bogdan, 1984). But this is somewhat misleading, as it implies that there is no place for counting or enumerating. Field research may, in fact, give central place to data on the frequency of certain behaviors and events. Therefore, to refer to it as "qualitative" distorts the possibilities of this approach.

Others have referred to this approach as "observational" research or, more commonly, *participant observation* (see Bruyn, 1966; McCall and Simmons, 1969). But these labels also are misleading. Not only is observation basic to all scientific inquiry, but the picture of detached observation that science sometimes conjures up is contrary to the kind of understanding that field researchers seek. Field researchers often aim to see the world from the subject's own frame of reference. To do this requires more than a backstage view of reality; indeed, field researchers may actively participate in the lives of the people and situations that they are studying. Yet, to call this approach simply "participant observation" is too limiting. Anything that allows the researcher to obtain firsthand information and to get close to the subjects being studied—for example, direct observation and open-ended interviewing—is likely to find its way into field research. What brings these activities together, aside from the desire to describe the social world as subjects see it, is that they always take place *in the field*—in a natural social setting familiar to the subject (see Emerson, 1983; Shaffir, Stebbins, and Turowetz, 1980).

Substantively, field research has tended to focus on community or ethnic groups, deviance and powerlessness, occupations and professions, and, more recently, aspects of everyday life. Some field studies of corporate power have been done (e.g., Domhoff, 1974), but field research generally has entailed "studying down," focusing on the poor, the powerless, and the marginal members of society.[1] Perhaps it is more difficult to gain access to persons in the seats of power than it is to gain access to the "common person." Similarly, everyday aspects of social life are easier to locate than sporadic and uncommon events.

As you might imagine, there are an extraordinarily large number of "fields" in which to do field research. Consider, for example, some of the topics of studies that have been conducted in this tradition: becoming a doctor (Becker et al., 1961), being a milkman (Bigus, 1978), frequenting singles bars (Allon, 1979), selling used cars (Browne, 1976b), shopping in secondhand clothing stores (Wiseman, 1979), dealing with chronic back pain (Kotarba, 1977), playing Little League baseball (Fine, 1979), driving a cab (F. Davis, 1959), visiting a pornographic bookstore (Karp, 1973), acquiring privacy in public places (Henderson, 1975), having a baby (Danziger, 1979), managing a corporation (Kanter, 1977), living in a new community (Gans, 1967), and experiencing a religious conversion (Bromley and Shupe, 1979).

Although we take the position that most research topics in social science can and should be studied via a variety of methods, we recognize that some topics are more amenable to certain approaches. It is possible to identify specific conditions that best lend themselves to the field approach. We begin our examination of field research by considering some of these conditions, as well as some of the limitations of this approach compared to experiments and surveys. Thereafter, we describe some key aspects of field observation, research design, and sampling. Then we turn our attention to the various stages of field research, culminating with a synopsis of a field study of the cocktail waitress.

When to Adopt Field Methods

A major reason for doing field research is to get an insider's view of reality. For example, one of the fundamental goals of Meredith McGuire's study (1982:19) of a religious movement was to obtain "an understanding of believers' actions from their point of view." This, she tells us, "means trying to take the role of the other, seeing things as believers see them and using their categories of thought in the organization of experience." She refers to this position as *methodological empathy*, which "differs from sympathy in that it is not necessary to agree with a perspective in order to understand it." The religious beliefs and practices that McGuire observed were understood by her as they were understood by those in the movement. But to say this is not to say that she believed in them as they did, only that she empathized. (McGuire's research is discussed further later in the chapter.) Methodological empathy is a hallmark of field research. It enables researchers to understand the substance, coherence, and maintenance of views that may seem implausible in relation to the dominant culture. Indeed, insofar as field research is descriptive, it may have little more than this as its goal.

Because of its flexibility, the field approach lends itself well to studies of dynamic or rapidly changing situations. Suppose you are interested in how people cope with the aftermath of a natural disaster. (Recall from chapter 1 Louis Zurcher's 1968 study of a volunteer work crew formed after a tornado struck Topeka, Kansas.) People's responses are likely to depend on the severity of the disaster and the length of time since the disaster occurred. To determine the immediate impact of a calamitous event you would have to act quickly to get to the site and observe; otherwise, the opportunity to understand certain reactions may be lost. Drafting a questionnaire or designing a probability sample of households would result in the loss of valuable time and information.

Besides fleeting situations, certain kinds of substantive problems may require a field approach. This approach is recommended (1) when it is essential to preserve "whole" events in all their detail and immediacy (Weick, 1968); (2) when a situation is complex, involving interrelated phenomena that must be studied simultaneously and as a whole—for example, the study of a prison as an institution (Weiss, 1966); and (3) when the focus is on the relationship between the person *and* the setting, so that it is important not to separate one from the other (Weick, 1968). Similarly, field research may be used when methodological problems preclude other research strategies—for example, when subjects are unable (young children) or unwilling (deviants) to participate in a formal survey.

One also may be inclined to adopt a field approach when certain kinds of resources are limited. Research can be costly. All research strategies require time, space, money, and personnel. Conducting interviews with a large sample of individuals can be expensive in terms of sampling, interviewer training, data collection, and so forth. Similarly, experiments, while generally on a smaller scale than surveys, can be complex and expensive to conduct. Field research, on the other hand, if it is to be conducted at some nearby location, can be the least expensive approach. It does not require elaborate tools or equipment and, since it is typically conducted entirely by a single investigator, requires no additional personnel or training period beyond the preparation of the investigator. The major resource consumed in field research is time. Investigators have been known to spend years in the field. Bettylou Valentine (1978), for example, in her study of ghetto life-styles, spent 5 years in the Blackston community. Thus, the most important resource to field researchers are field researchers themselves.

In addition to cost, ethical constraints may preclude the use of other research approaches. The control and manipulation necessary for experiments are not always possible for ethical reasons. For example, it would be too dangerous to stage many kinds of events (e.g., a riot) in order to study their consequences experimentally. Nor could one ethically use potentially harmful manipulations (e.g., randomly label some children as "dumb") or, needless to say, create certain medical conditions (e.g., physical disabilities such as blindness or paraplegia) in order to study them sociologically. In such cases, field research is often a viable option. This is not a unique feature of field research, of course, as other strategies also may be ethically sound in certain circumstances. The point is simply that a field approach can avoid some ethical problems presented by experiments and surveys. (This approach also raises other ethical issues that we address in chapter 16.)

Finally, one may turn fruitfully to field research when one knows relatively little about the subject under investigation. The less you know about the subject, the less you can afford to limit data collection. The less you know, the more you must be open to all possibilities. Experiments and surveys generally require a great deal of prior knowledge about the topic being investigated. Such knowledge is essential for deciding what to manipulate and control, or what to ask about and what to ignore. In field research, however, you must resist carrying preconceived notions into the field, since these notions may bear little resemblance to the experience of the people being studied.

Field research thus lends itself best to investigating dynamic situations, settings where it is important to preserve the natural order of things, and where the researcher's minimal understanding makes it crucial to understand the subjects' interpretation of reality. This approach takes time, however, and may not be a very efficient way of gathering certain kinds of information. For enumerating the distribution of certain demographic characteristics (e.g., age, gender, occupation) or beliefs and attitudes within a certain population, surveys are much quicker and more reliable. For testing causal hypothesis, experiments are far superior because of their greater control. In addition, because it typically is carried out by a single observer who interacts with a limited number of people in a limited number of settings, field research is highly dependent on the observational and interpretive skills of the researcher, is difficult to replicate and compare, and may lack generalizability.

Field Observation

The foremost characteristic of field research is observation. Field researchers nearly always begin with field observations; even when they turn to other data sources by interviewing "informants" or analyzing personal documents, these data generally serve as supplemental evidence or cross-checks on their observations.

The kind of observation conducted by field researchers differs from both casual, everyday observation and generic "scientific observation." In contrast to the casual observation in which each of us engages every day, field observation is planned, methodically carried out, and intended to extract meaningful interpretations of the social world. McCall (1984) notes that "while nearly everyone who goes to a zoo *sees* the animals there, and many even *watch* some of those animals, very few can be said to *observe* their behavior." In this sense, a good field researcher is like a good detective (Sanders, 1976). Sherlock Holmes, for example, was a master observer of social life, able to see and interpret the hidden meanings of things that other people simply would overlook. Holmes's colleague Dr. Watson would see an average tradesman; Holmes would observe a snuff-taking Freemason who had done manual labor and been to China (see the story of the "The Red-Headed League"). Watson would see footprints; Holmes would interpret the prints to have been made by a tall, left-handed man who walked with a limp, wearing a gray cloak, and smoking Indian cigars ("The Boscombe Valley Mystery").

Field observation differs from other forms of scientific observation in two important ways. First, while the latter can be both direct and indirect, field observation involves direct observation with the naked eye, unaided by instruments such as questionnaires or mediated by respondents' reports. Second, field observation takes place in a natural setting, not a laboratory or other contrived situation. Observations made in the field also tend to be less structured and systematic than those made in the laboratory, although this is not an essential difference. Field research varies in structure, but it differs primarily in terms of the extent to which the researcher actively participates in the social setting being observed. At one extreme is the passive and intentionally unobtrusive, nonparticipant observer; at the other is the active and intentionally involved, participant observer.

Nonparticipant Observation

The nonparticipant observer is, in effect, an eavesdropper, someone who attempts to observe people without interacting with them and, typically, without their knowing that they are being observed. This form of observation often is used in conjunction with participant observation, especially in the early stages of research when one is reconnoitering a social setting as preparation for more intensive study (R. L. Gold, 1958). As a separate, inclusive method, however, nonparticipant observation is comparatively little used, in spite of its amenability to studies of social phenomena. It has been applied most routinely in the field by psychologists studying children and animals.

Direct scientific observation involves the selection, recording, and encoding of behavior and events. Selection refers to the fact that scientific observers make intentional and unintentional choices about what to observe and record (Weick, 1968). Recording consists of making records of events (e.g., by taking field notes), while encoding involves the simplification of records (e.g., by categorizing or counting the frequency of different behaviors) (Weick, 1968). All of these processes may be more or less structured. Observation is structured or systematic when it uses explicit and preset plans for selection, recording, and encoding of data; it is unstructured to the extent that these processes are implicit and emergent (McCall, 1984).

The early phase of most field research involves relatively unstructured observation. As the researcher gains a greater understanding of the setting, his or her observations may become more structured. For example, the investigator may become increasingly specific about when and where to observe; what specific aspects of the setting or behavior to observe; and how to make and record the observations. As the research is delimited in this way, even more structure may be introduced in the form of area and time sampling of observation sites and checklists or other more elaborate schemes for categorizing behavior.

A good example of unstructured, nonparticipant observation is Lyn Lofland's study (1971, 1973) of how people in cities—strangers in public places—relate to one another in terms of appearance and spatial location. Although Lofland drew upon other materials, her study was based largely on hundreds of hours of observations. She made the observations in and around Ann Arbor and Detroit, Michigan, in bus depots, airports, libraries, stores, restaurants, bars, theaters, and parks, aboard buses, and on the streets. In most of these settings, she was able to "blend into the scenery," even for periods of several hours. Imagining herself viewing others through a one-way mirror, Lofland attempted to record everything within her line of vision. She did not systematically sample observation sites or resort to checklists for recording behavior. As the study progressed, she concentrated at times on certain kinds of behavior—for example, seating patterns and entrance behavior—but in general she simply recorded as much as she could.

One of Lofland's observation sites was a glass-walled hallway, called the "Fishbowl," between two buildings on the University of Michigan campus. Here she became sensitized to the "grooming" actions which people go through as they are about to enter a public setting. Lofland (1971:303) describes how she made this discovery.

> One wall of the Fishbowl, the one which contains the doors, is solid glass, so that whenever I happened to be observing from a bench close to the doors, I could not fail to be struck by the preparation behavior that occurred over and over again as student after student neared the door, stopped, groomed himself, and then entered. There were many instances of this behavior recorded in my notes before I ever "recognized" it as a pattern, but once I did, I was led to look for similar activities in other settings and eventually to "see" the full entrance sequence.

Lofland maintains that some of her discoveries were made possible by her prolonged periods of observation in only a few sites. This provided sufficient familiarity with the settings to enable her to recognize faces and to make important distinctions among the different inhabitants, such as residents, patrons, customers, and newcomers. If her observations had been more systematic, it seems unlikely that she would have discovered many of the patterns she reports. On the other hand, more systematic observation could have provided other important kinds of sociological information, such as the duration and frequency of occurrence of the behavior patterns Lofland observed.

The advantage of systematic observation lies in its greater control of sampling and measurement error, which permits stronger generalizations and checks on reliability and validity. We can see how this is possible in one of the relatively few sociological studies of this type, an investigation of crime and law enforcement by Albert J. Reiss (1967).

Among other things, Reiss observed police-citizen transactions in eight high-crime areas of three large cities. To do so, he assigned twelve observers and a supervisor to each city. Because he wished to generalize about transactions with citizens, Reiss (1968:358) sampled a number of units: "days of the week, watches of the day, and the officer based unit of the beat within precincts." He also used standardized procedures for recording observations. Following each 8-hour period of observation, observers completed booklets for each encounter of 2 or more minutes duration. Each booklet contained a sequence of questions about the transaction. By systematically recording observations and using multiple observers, Reiss was able to show that the race of the observer was related to differences in reporting of officer deviance: white observers were less likely than black observers to report the undue use of force among black officers. Thus, he was able to uncover a source of error that in all likelihood would have gone undetected in a solo unstructured observation study.

Unlike Lofland, Reiss's observers were unable to blend into the scenery, since the role of observer was unnatural in the context of police-citizen transactions. The observers therefore were cast by officers in the role of a plainclothes detective. In this way they entered the realm of participant observation, to which we now turn.

Participant Observation

Historically field research has been associated most strongly with participant observation. In ideal descriptions of this method, the observer is said to participate actively, for an extended period of time, in the daily lives of the people and situations under study (see Becker and Geer, 1957; McCall and Simmons, 1969). This may require that the observer live or work in an area; it clearly assumes that the observer will become an accepted member of the group or community, able to speak informally with the people—to "joke with them, empathize with them, and share their concerns and experiences" (Bogdan and Taylor, 1975:5).

Despite the tidiness of this description, however, there is a rather fine line between nonparticipant and participant observation. As with the dimension of structure in observational studies, participation is a matter of degree. Some would argue that even a relatively unobtrusive observer sitting at a table in a restaurant taking notes influences the situation by virtue of his or her mere presence; thus, however unwittingly, such an observer is also a participant. It is more accurate, therefore, to think of the two types of field observation as poles of a continuum. At one extreme is the participant observer who becomes completely absorbed in the group under observation; at the other is the nonparticipant observer who tries to remain aloof from it. "Usually," as Wiseman and Aron (1970:49) note, "a researcher participates to a degree somewhere between these two extremes by either *posing* as a member or announcing himself as a scientific investigator and hoping to be accepted by the group in that role."

Because field research is rarely either detached observation on the one hand, or embroiled participation on the other, participation oftens becomes a question of "how much"? To fully immerse oneself in the situation is to risk altering the events one observes and perhaps even losing sight of one's role as researcher. But field researchers argue that these risks are small compared to the benefits to be gained from being a participant. A stranger to a situation may easily take a word, a sigh or other gesture, or a relationship for something wholly different from what it means to a participant.

Consider, for example, the use of the Spanish phrase *de colores* in the contemporary religious movement known as Cursillo. Although the literal translation of this phrase from Spanish to English is "of colors," it means much more to those who have experienced the spiritual renewal of the Cursillo. Marcene Marcoux (1982:222), who studied the movement by participant observation, says this about the term:

> As a motto, de colores reminds members of the rainbow; the various colors merge
> into one phenomenon, representing the very brotherhood and sisterhood of the

movement. Moreover, it conjures up the excitement and elan of initiation where this phrase was first heard . . . the spirit of the movement in terms of caring, action, piety, and community . . . that is made evident in the concrete exchange of these particular words.

It is difficult to imagine how one could see this simple phrase in all its symbolic power without actually exchanging greetings with other participants in the Cursillo.

In addition to this "language barrier," there are many other potential problems of interpretation for the outsider, or nonparticipant. Just imagine that you are one of the subjects of someone else's field research. Assume for a moment that your place of work, a club you belong to, the church you attend, a class you are taking, or a favorite tavern you visit is the setting for the researcher's observations. Now think of all the things that the researcher would have to learn in order to make appropriate judgments about the activities of the group. What do you know so well that you take for granted about the job (e.g., how the places where people take their coffee breaks serve to reinforce territorial influence and status in the workplace), the conduct of the club's business (e.g., how the president influences the opinions of certain members), the symbols of your church (e.g., how the theology of your religion makes these symbols meaningful), the daily affairs of the class (e.g., what seating patterns mean in terms of social cliques), or about the differences among customers at the tavern (e.g., differences among regulars and casual visitors in terms of where they sit and how they are served)?

Even if this same researcher used you as an informant to help him or her to understand the situation, there will be features that you are likely to forget, not convey accurately and completely, or omit because their understanding is assumed. In short, it is difficult to imagine full comprehension without a heavy dose of participation. Everything that you know about these various settings you learned because of your activity as a participant.

On the other hand, field research carries with it some risks. It can be an emotionally stressful experience for the researcher (see J. Lofland and L. H. Lofland, 1984). Shaffir, Stebbins, and Turowetz (1980) describe fieldwork as "usually inconvenient, to say the least, sometimes physically uncomfortable, frequently embarrassing, and, to a degree, always tense." In the early days in the field, before learning the ropes, researchers are likely to experience awkward and embarrassing encounters; after awhile they may become sensitive to hostile and suspicious challenges to their intentions and "observer" role. Eventually, researchers may come to loathe the people under observation and wish to withdraw, or may identify so strongly with the group that they cease their research. Finally, after being in the field for so long and developing deep attachments, the researcher often finds it difficult to leave.

The problem that perhaps receives the most attention among field researchers is balancing the requirements of both participating and observing. Participant observation creates a difficult marginal existence; one usually participates in an alien setting, with a desire to be accepted, but a constant sense of separation from those observed that is part and parcel of the observer role. As researchers become more familiar with the setting, however, and are drawn into it more as participants, they may lose sight of their reason for being in the field. In fact, field researchers even have a label for this phenomenon: the researcher who ceases to be conscious of the observer role is said to be *going native*.

As an illustration of going native, Albert Reiss (1968: 362–363) describes an observer who had the role of plainclothes detective thrust upon him by the police officer he was observing:

> The officer arrested two citizens, and one began to flee. The officer in this case turned to the observer, handed him his nightstick, and said: "Hold him." He then chased the fleeing man. The observer obeyed and, what is more, as he held the man against the patrol car, the man resisted and attempted to flee. And then . . . the observer threatened the citizen with the nightstick.

The problem a field researcher constantly faces in such situations is judging where to draw the line between participation and observation. Reiss contends that his assistant in this case clearly went too far, that he should have responded as Reiss himself had in a similar situation—by refusing the nightstick and reminding the officer that he was an observer. On the other hand, subjects usually come to treat participant observers as at least "quasi"-members of the team or group and expect them to participate, such as by assisting a police officer in holding a suspect. Refusal to participate may jeopardize the observer's relations with subjects and his or her continued presence in the field.

To make the issue even more complicated, there may be sins of omission involved in maintaining observer distance. Sociologist Don Zimmerman (personal communication, 1986) once found himself in a situation where a social worker he was observing discovered a very young child abandoned by her caretaker. Leaving the child alone, the worker returned to the office to report the situation. Her supervisor responded by immediately calling the police and reprimanding the worker. For not assuming custody of the child, she and Zimmerman could have been held criminally culpable. Zimmerman was uncomfortable about leaving the child, but his research plan called for strict nonintervention in the work activities of the social workers. Thus, he faced a difficult dilemma in which his research plan conflicted with his personal values and civic duty. It also could be said, by the way, that Reiss's assistant performed a civic duty by assisting the officer in holding the suspect. As these examples show, the issues in balancing participant and observer roles are seldom as easy or clear-cut as they seem.

Research Design and Sampling

Unlike experiments and surveys, in which the elements of research design— hypothesis formation, measurement, sampling—are specified prior to data collection, design elements in field research usually are worked out during the course of the study. The one exception to this is systematic observation, which relies on a well-developed scheme for coding behavior. The researcher observing children at play, for example, may record specific features of the play that are designed to test clearly stated hypotheses. Perhaps the hypothesis is that boys' games are more complex than girls' games. This may lead the researcher to record characteristics such as the size of the play group, the rules of the games, the nature of the different task roles performed by players, and so forth (see Lever, 1978).

More typically, however, field researchers begin with (1) broad substantive and theoretical questions, and (2) a methodological approach based on observation in natural settings—that is, settings of activity that occur without the contrivance of the investigator. Neither of these desiderata permit a rigid research design. Because preconceived images may be very misleading, the researcher avoids preset hypotheses and instead lets his or her observations in the field guide the formulation of hypotheses, the asking of questions, and sampling. And because the observed setting is not under the researcher's control and its resident activities typically are not known to the researcher before entering the field, research design is necessarily emergent rather than predetermined. Let us examine sampling in field research to see the special design problems that this approach presents.

Sampling in Field Research

Initially, field research almost always involves the nonrandom selection of a small number of settings and subjects. The nature of field research generally focuses attention on interactive social units such as encounters, social relationships, organizations, and communities. These units are much less amenable to probability sampling techniques than the discrete individuals typically sampled in experiments and surveys. Smaller interactive units seldom can be enumerated before their occurrence; and studies of larger units—for example, a community, an area of the city, an organization—usually are restricted to the one case under investigation. The delicate operation of entering the field—of locating suitable observation sites and making fruitful contacts—also necessitates nonrandom selection. Convenience, accessibility, and happenstance by and large determine where researchers can begin to make observations, whom they will meet there, and whom they will find most informative. Finally, the time required to conduct field observations tends to restrict the possible sample size to a very small number of cases.

Though seldom possible before entering the field, rigorous sampling can occur in the field. The general strategy, sometimes called *dimensional sampling* (Arnold, 1970), is to sample relevant *dimensions* of units rather than units themselves. The determination of a sampling frame presupposes knowledge of the field setting, and knowing which dimensions capture the activities of interest may not be known in any detail in advance. Therefore, as with other aspects of field research, dimensional sampling plans may emerge during the course of the research. Typical dimensions include time and space; variations in either can serve to protect against bias and to increase the scope of the observations. For example, in a study of altruism in which you observe altruistic acts at the scenes of accidents, you may note that the nature of the acts differs according to the time of the day, the day of the week, or the particular place where the accident occurs. Sampling times and places, therefore, will make some degree of generalization possible if that is a goal of the research. Another dimension is role. In settings with formally defined positions (e.g., precinct captains, detectives, street officers), the field researcher could sample incumbents of these positions and observe them in the course of their daily activities. Observed uniformities across roles might reflect organizational constraints, while variation within roles might reflect individual factors or more local social influences.

Murray Melbin's research (1969) on behavioral disturbances in mental hospitals provides an example of the use of probability sampling techniques in a field study. Melbin found that among patients in a small private mental hospital, far more unusual disturbances (e.g., walking around naked, making animal-like noises, lying stiffly in front of a doorway) occurred on weekdays than on evenings and weekends, but that this pattern did not appear in a large state institution nearby. In making his observations, Melbin chose times and places according to a probability sampling design. First, he listed all sites in each hospital where patients could be found and apportioned the waking hours of the day into 2-hour units. Then, he randomly selected combinations of site, time, and day of the week for observation. Melbin concluded that patients tended to behave crazily when they could get the attention of professional treatment personnel—psychiatrists, social workers, and psychologists. The private hospital had an ample professional staff, which was present on weekdays and Saturday mornings, while the state hospital had far fewer professionals available at any time.

Another recommended technique in field research is to sample broad analytical categories in order to facilitate the development of theoretical insights. In other words, purposive nonprobability sampling could be carried out to extend and pursue ideas that emerge in the course of research (Glaser and Strauss, 1967). For example, you may decide that the time required to perform an altruistic act and the amount of physical risk or suffering incurred are important factors in developing a theory of altruism. In order to incorporate such variability in your study you might investigate acts that involve different time commitments (e.g., cash contributions versus volunteer work) and acts that cause different levels of hardship (e.g., donating blood versus donating a kidney).

Stages of Field Research

As we have noted before, scientific investigations rarely proceed smoothly in a neat sequence of steps; this is especially true of field research. Nevertheless, we can identify a series of essential problems faced by all field researchers, even if these do not always occur in a prescribed sequence. These problems, considered below, are (1) selecting a research setting, (2) gaining access to the setting, (3) presenting oneself, (4) gathering information in the field, and (5) analyzing the information and developing a theoretical scheme for interpretation.

Selecting a Research Setting

Obviously you must begin somewhere, and for the field researcher, the first problem is deciding *where* to begin. How do you select an appropriate site in which to conduct your study? Speaking of participant observation, Taylor and Bogdan (1984) describe the ideal setting as one that is directly related to the researcher's interests, easily accessible, and allows for the development of immediate rapport with informants. This ideal is seldom realized, however. One reason is that the broad research questions that guide field research rarely point to a particular setting. It also is not uncommon for investigators to end up in settings that are ill-suited to their interests (Geer, 1964). Consequently, the setting itself may dictate research interests; for it is only after entering the field and beginning to make observations that the researcher comes to know exactly what theoretical questions may be asked.

Regardless of the extent of one's participation, the setting should permit clear observation. To the nonparticipant, it is also important not to alter the naturalness of the setting by making participants aware that they are being observed. The counterpart of this rule for the participant observer is to select a setting where one can participate naturally and easily become an accepted and familiar part of the surroundings. Finally, given the time required for this type of research, the setting should be as accessible as possible.

Together, these criteria suggest that novice field researchers might do well to select a setting close at hand where they can readily fit in. This does not necessarily mean a setting with which you are intimately familiar. In familiar settings, especially where one has a direct personal or professional stake, researchers often experience problems in overcoming their own particular views of reality and of holding their feelings in abeyance (Taylor and Bogdan, 1984). It is extremely difficult to be able to treat the familiar as new and to observe more as a researcher in a familiar setting than you observed as a natural participant. On the other hand, J. Lofland and L. H. Lofland (1984) suggest that the best starting place for field research may be "where you are." Noting that a good deal of field research is born out of accidents of the "current biography" and "personal history" of the researcher, they say: "A job; a physical mishap; the development, loss or maintenance of an intimate relationship; an illness; an enjoyed activity; a living arrangement—all these and many other possible circumstances may provide you with a topic you can care about enough to study (p. 7)." Thus, for them, "starting where you are" is a matter of interest as well as access to a social setting.

This approach has a long history dating to the University of Chicago in the 1920s and 1930s where students were encouraged to build on their experience and to use the city as their "lab" (see Box 11.1). More specific examples of "starting where you are" cited by J. Lofland and L. H. Lofland (1984) include Julius Roth's study (1963) of the passage of time in a hospital, based on his experience as a tuberculosis patient; Fred Davis's study (1959) of the cab driver, developed from his work as a cab driver while in graduate school; and a study called *Synagogue Life* by Samuel Heilman (1976), who as an Orthodox Jew had joined the synagogue before the conception of his study. In each of these cases, the researcher "natu-

BOX 11.1

Origins of Field Research

Modern field research traces its origins to two related traditions, one in anthropology and one in sociology.* Ethnographic fieldwork, the study of native cultures by learning the native language and observing and taking part in native life, originated with the founders of modern anthropology: the German-trained Franz Boas (1858–1942) and the Polish-born British social anthropologist Bronislaw Malinowski (1884–1942). Before these two men, anthropology was largely an armchair discipline relying on the testimonies of explorers, missionaries, and colonial officials for its data.

Boas, who did research on American Indians, was particularly concerned about how the biases of Western culture affected one's understanding of native life. He believed that only by living among native peoples and learning the language of native thought could one come to see the world as natives saw it. Malinowski, whose major field studies took him to the Pacific islands, was the first anthropologist to provide a detailed account of how he carried out his fieldwork. These two field researchers reoriented the whole field of cultural anthropology. They and their students (e.g., Margaret Mead, Ruth Benedict, Alfred Kroeber, and others) made it possible by their methodology to get an insider's view of the culture. This goal of understanding the subject's point of view remains a central feature of field research.

Another major source of modern field research is the social reform tradition of sociology. This tradition is as old as sociology itself. However, it became more empirically oriented toward the end of the nineteenth century, as social reformers and sociologists turned first to social surveys and then to a more varied methodology based primarily on field observation. In the United States, the latter approach became identified with the so-called Chicago School of sociology. One of the key figures was W. I. Thomas (1863–1947), who, with his collaborator Florian Znaniecki, published a monumental study of *The Polish Peasant in Europe and America*. This work contributed to the field approach by its use of a variety of techniques, including the examination of letters and life histories. Thomas also advocated the importance of understanding the individual's own "definition of the situation" as part of a more self-conscious theoretical analysis.

More than Thomas, however, it was Robert Park (1864–1944) who established the place of field research in modern sociology. Educated in Germany and trained as a journalist, Park was for many years the chairman of the sociology department at the University of Chicago. Park and his associates at Chicago inspired a generation of researchers who used the city as their social laboratory. There they investigated pickpockets, police, juvenile gangs, the Jewish ghetto, hobos, taxi-hall dancers, and other assorted groups and areas of the city. They were guided by the desire to ameliorate the problems of city living, which they saw as the natural outcome of urban crowding. One might say that Park's participant observers contributed to our understanding of different urban subcultures in much the same way that Boas- and Malinowski-inspired ethnographers promoted our understanding of different cultures.

*Although it was not until the late nineteenth and early twentieth century that this became a self-conscious method of social research, some aspects of field research are as old as recorded history. (See Wax, 1971, and Hughes, 1960, for historical sketches of "fieldwork.")

rally" belonged in the setting, but was new to it, so his degree of familiarity did not encumber his observations.

"Starting where you are" also is likely to facilitate the researcher's efforts in other ways. Field research is not easy work. The good field researcher must be able to feel comfortable in the presence of informants who are almost always, at least at the outset, strangers—and be able to make these informants feel comfortable as well. The ability to develop rapport is not a skill that each of us possesses to the same degree. An optimal site, therefore, may be one that encourages ease in the researcher.

Gaining Access

Just how do you go about getting into a group that you wish to study? The answer to this question depends first of all on the nature of the group or setting. If the setting is a formal organization, then one should seek permission from those in charge, referred to as *gatekeepers* by field researchers (Taylor and Bogdan, 1984). Obtaining permission may be facilitated by having a friend vouch for the researcher or by getting one's foot in the door, as by first visiting or volunteering to serve the organization in some way.

If the setting is public (e.g., park, street corner, public restroom), then you may not need to negotiate access as an observer, although we recommend informing the police or other proper authority about what you are doing. If the setting is semi-public (e.g., bar, theater, store), then it is generally a good idea to speak to the manager or owner before you begin your research. It is almost impossible to spend long periods of time in public places without having to give a proper account of oneself. Observers can be arrested for loitering and may be suspected of shoplifting when hanging around a store. Therefore, the best practice is to seek the cooperation of those who are likely to question what you are doing.

As a participant, you also will have to figure out ways of interacting with people and, if necessary, of becoming an accepted member of the group (Taylor and Bogdan, 1984). The usual recommendation here is simply to station oneself at an active spot and try to engage people in casual conversation. Yet, there can be problems with this seemingly innocuous approach. Since people are wary of strangers, researchers must be careful that their intentions are not misconstrued. Consider the case of a highly regarded early field study conducted by William Foote Whyte (1981) in an Italian neighborhood in Boston. Having been advised that he could learn a great deal by visiting a tavern, striking up a conversation with a woman, and buying her a drink, Whyte decided to try this approach. As he recounts (p. 289),

> With some trepidation I climbed the stairs to the bar and entertainment area and looked around . . . . There were women present all right, but none of them was alone. Some were there in couples, and there were two or three pairs of women together. I pondered this situation briefly. I had little confidence in my skill at picking up one female, and it seemed inadvisable to tackle two at the same time. Still, I was determined not to admit defeat without a struggle. I looked around me

again and now noticed a threesome: one man and two women. It occurred to me that here was a maldistribution of females which I might be able to rectify. I approached the group and opened with something like this: Pardon me. Would you mind if I joined you? There was a moment of silence while the man stared at me. He then offered to throw me downstairs.

Later on Whyte had the good fortune to be introduced by a social worker to someone, referred to as "Doc," who would be instrumental in his gaining entry into "Cornerville." Doc became Whyte's closest friend, sponsor, and major source of information. The key to opening doors in the community, such persons are called *key informants* by field researchers. Not only was Doc able to introduce Whyte to a number of people from the neighborhood, but Doc himself was well regarded in the community. Being introduced as Doc's friend thus gained Whyte immediate acceptance by people who were willing to accept any friend of Doc. Still, just as Whyte was able to bask in Doc's light, so too would he have been cast into Doc's shadow if Doc had been held in low regard by the community.

One of the problems with relying on contacts in a strange group is that one cannot always be certain how well regarded the contact may be. Weinberg and Williams (1972) note that frequently it is easier to meet those more peripheral to the group than it is to meet those more central. At the outset of field research, most investigators will feel ill at ease and quite alone in a new setting. Marginal members of the group may have similar feelings and thus be easier to contact. They tell the story of the first day in the field doing a study of nudists (p. 172): "The first day . . . the researcher ended up spending too much time with an unmarried male who, it was later learned, was held in disrepute. The motive imputed to this nudist as well as to other single nudists was of being there to look at other members' wives." Such situations present a dilemma for field researchers. One must be careful about whom to accept as a friend. At the same time, as an outsider one cannot afford to offend others by rejecting their friendship.

Finding out how informants stand vis-à-vis the setting or community they "inform" is also critical because of its impact on research findings. William Labov (1973) discusses this issue in terms of what he calls the "linguistic consequences of being a lame." In his study of the linguistic habits of a group of young black men, Labov found that the men most accessible and willing to serve as informants were those men who were marginal to their groups, in a word, "lames." Thus, inferences concerning linguistic patterns among blacks might reflect the habits of informants on the periphery, and thereby be limited in generalizability.

Many of the settings and situations where Whyte ventured in the community were private: homes, social clubs, political campaign meetings, and places of illegal business operations. His means of gaining entry to these settings can be traced to his contact with the social worker, who introduced him to Doc, who in turn introduced him to other "street corner boys," politicians, and racketeers, who introduced him to still others. This *snowballing technique* is the basic approach to obtaining access to private settings. The key to its implementation is knowing where to start. Some successful strategies include checking with friends to see if they can arrange personal introductions; involving oneself in the community by using local stores and facilities and attending public meetings; going to agencies that serve the community such as churches, day-care centers, and neighborhood centers (where Whyte began); and advertising one's research interests in the local newspaper (Taylor and Bogdan, 1984:24–25).

Presenting Oneself

Related to the problem of gaining entry is deciding how to present oneself to those in the field. Certain aspects of this problem must be resolved before the researcher attempts to gain access to a setting, while other aspects cannot be anticipated fully and must be worked out during the course of the study.

As you consider how to gain access to a research setting, you must determine how to present yourself in the context of the research. This issue basically boils down to deciding what roles to play. Roles are strategic because they greatly affect what the researcher is able to learn. The role you assume will determine where you can go, what you can do, whom you can interact with, and what you can inquire about and be told (McCall and Simmons, 1969).

The four "master roles" from which other role relationships develop stem from the positions of scientific observer and participant (Junker, 1960; R. L. Gold, 1958). At one extreme is the *complete observer*, represented by our earlier description of nonparticipant observation. At the other is the *complete participant*, who conceals the observer role while becoming a fully accepted member of the in-group. In both of these cases, the researcher hides his or her true identity from those observed. This avoids the problem of reactivity and also has other advantages: for the complete observer, it is easier to play one role than try to balance two; and for the complete participant, one may gain access to information that would escape or be withheld from an observer. But such concealment has major disadvantages: the complete observer may wish to clarify points by questioning those observed; and, most importantly, such covert research invariably raises ethical questions.

Covert research generally does not present serious ethical problems when the setting is public and open, where anyone has a right to be (J. Lofland and L. H. Lofland, 1984). In this situation, no harm can come to the people observed, the researcher is likely to be a passive observer, and concealing one's status as a researcher is considered a mild form of deception. Many social scientists believe, however, that concealment can become a serious problem when the researcher enters a private or closed setting, especially when his or her identity is purposely misrepresented in order to gain entry (see Erikson, 1967). We consider some of the ethical questions raised by covert research in chapter 16. For now, we note that other social scientists defend covert research by maintaining that the scientific knowledge and social benefits of research may justify deceptive practices. Some research questions probably could not be investigated without complete cover for one's actions. In fact, some important, albeit controversial, studies have been conducted using a covert approach.

A well-known example is Laud Humphreys' study (1975) of impersonal sex in public places entitled *Tearoom Trade*. In this study the author posed as a voyeur and lookout who loitered around public restrooms waiting for opportunities to study brief sexual encounters among anonymous men. While engaging in this action Humphreys made note of participants' license plate numbers and had them traced. Then, a year later he conducted interviews at these men's homes in order to find out more about them than he could have learned during the covert observation of their homosexual behaviors. Humphreys' research created a heated controversy. Some applauded him for his courage in undertaking such pioneering research, for his scrupulous care in protecting the identity of the people he observed, and for contributing to the understanding of a sensitive and private aspect of social life. Others denigrated him for his vivid descriptions of homosexual activities, and, more importantly, for the blatant deception involved and the dangers posed, especially during the follow-up phase of his research (Glazer, 1972).

The other two master roles that the field researcher can play combine observation and participation. The *participant as observer* role emphasizes participation. The researcher's "observer activities are *not* wholly concealed, but are 'kept under wraps' as it were, or subordinated to activities as a participant" (Junker, 1960:36). Thus, others in the field generally relate to the researcher in his or her informal participant role, and the researcher is likely to spend more time participating than observing. This master role probably occurs most frequently in community studies, where relationships with informants develop over an extended period of time (R. L. Gold, 1958).

Finally, the field researcher can assume the role of *observer as participant*. In this role, observer activities are overriding, as the researcher intentionally draws attention to his or her status as an observer and may even be publicly sponsored by people in the situation studied (Junker, 1960:37). Relationships with informants are thus more formal. This master role is likely to be invoked in brief encounters that do not allow relationships to develop with informants to the point of personal friendship.

Being able to relate to the people studied as a participant is likely to help one gain a better understanding of the "native" point of view and perhaps even gain access to information hidden from an observer. But the reverse also may be true: people may be more willing to share confidential information with an observer than with a fellow participant. Also, at times field researchers will find it useful to call upon their status as an observer in order to gather information—for example, to schedule formal interviews. Most participant observation, therefore, involves both of these two master roles, albeit at different times and in relation to different informants.

Assuming, then, that the field researcher embraces the observer role to some degree, how much should be revealed about one's research? It is generally not a good idea—in fact, rarely necessary—to reveal the details of a study. One reason is that this may make people more self-conscious of the researcher's presence (Taylor and Bogdan, 1984). It is also unnecessary to volunteer information. Perhaps the best rule to follow is that suggested by the author of *Hard Living on Clay Street*. Joseph Howell (1973:381) advises the field researcher to "be honest about who you are and what you are doing. You need not tell more than is asked," he suggests, "but if you are caught lying, you are finished."

Besides these four dominant roles, there are other lesser, but no less important, roles that researchers may assume in the field. These roles are determined largely by the situation. In Humphreys' study of homosexual encounters in public bathrooms, mentioned above, he performed the role of "lookout" who watches for police or other unfriendly strangers. While conducting a study of Little League baseball, Fine and Glassner (1979) played the roles of supervisor, leader, observer, and friend in relation to the children they observed. One might also imagine researchers in this situation playing the roles of manager or coach.

Once researchers assume a particular role, then they are faced with decisions about how to present themselves in that role. Suppose, for example, that you are considering doing a study of medical technicians. You apply for a position as a laboratory assistant so that you will be able to observe the interactions of people in a medical research setting. How, then, will you present yourself? Will you allow people to teach you to do tasks that you might already know how to do? Will you pretend to be more naive than you are so that you can see how people will explain things to a know-nothing? Or will you flaunt your expertise so that you might become a valued member of the staff? Perhaps you think that people will tell you more if they have confidence in your abilities.

These are difficult choices, each with its particular consequences. Some field researchers recommend presenting oneself as naive or as an "acceptable incompetent" (J. Lofland and L. H. Lofland, 1984; Taylor and Bogdan, 1984). This can be an effective way of gaining information, as it gives the impression of someone who is ignorant, needs to be taught, and therefore is expected to ask questions. On the other hand, there are some settings—for example, in studies of higher-status people and "deviants"—where it is clearly better to show competence (see Gorden, 1975:227–228). Informants are likely to judge researchers on their knowledge as well as interest in areas in which the informant is expert. Asking people about their occupation from a starting point of total ignorance usually just irritates them. Moreover, criminals may con you unless you make it clear that you are in the know.

Ultimately, the best guideline for deciding what to do is to consider how one's behavior will affect the naturalness of the setting and how it will affect the development of trust and rapport with people in the setting. This appears to be the strategy which Joseph Kotarba (1980) followed in his study of acupuncture. His goal was to cultivate the trust of the physicians and staff people with whom he was in regular contact. Using what he calls the "good boy" approach, Kotarba was able to charm his way into everyone's good graces. And by being helpful and friendly to everyone, even people he personally disliked, Kotarba learned a great deal about the practice of acupuncture.

Establishing rapport requires interpersonal skills at which all field researchers are not equally adept. Some of these skills can be learned, but the best advice is recommended by Joseph Howell (1973:381): "*Be yourself.* Don't try to overidentify or be 'one of the boys.' Chances are you will be less threatening to the people you are studying if you are a little different from them anyway. This way you are not competing with them." The job of being yourself is really not hard work and has the added advantage of allowing each researcher to be a natural participant.

Gathering Information

Gathering information in the field presents several complex problems. To get some insight into the nature of these problems let us imagine a hypothetical field study.

Suppose that you are going to do some field research. You have solved the problem of site selection by deciding to study the class you are currently taking in research methods; therefore, the classroom in which it meets and the surrounding campus constitute the site. Choosing this site also simplifies the problem of self-presentation; after all, you are a *student* in the class. Given what you already know about the class and its participants, you also know that you want to do a participant observation study. You are ready, as Robert Park is reported to have encouraged his students at the University of Chicago, to "go get the seat of your pants dirty in *real* research" (McKinney, 1966). Or are you ready?

Before you begin your study, you should consider the nature of your participant-observer role in the class and the limitations that this places on what you can find out. As a student, it is extremely likely that your behavior and your perceptions of the instructor's behavior will be affected by your ego involvement in the class. You will, after all, be graded; you might even be graded on your class participation. Professional ethics will prevent the instructor from giving an honest account of his or her opinions about class members and the quality and significance of their participation. Thus you are probably in the best position to study the way a student culture develops in a class, as long as you do not play too central a role in it.[2]

With this objective in mind, how do you proceed? Immediately you are faced with the problem of how to take down class notes at the same time that you observe all the other activities in the classroom. In fact, you will probably find so much going on that you will have to forego note taking and borrow someone else's notes! How will you observe and remember: where people sit, who asks questions, how people address one another and interact with one another, who speaks to whom before, after, and during class, who attends regularly, who is absent or late, what people say about assignments, exams, the instructor, and so forth? If you just think about everything that goes on in a class, you will see the enormity of the problem. The vast amount of information afloat in any social setting seems especially overwhelming at the beginning of a study when you are uncertain about what is relevant or important and what is not.

The best approach to take in the early phases of field research is to provide as detailed and complete a *description* of events as you possibly can. Be concrete; take note of specific behavioral details; and avoid attaching your own abstract labels to things. As Joy Browne (1976a:77) advises, "it is crucial . . . to collect only data, not analysis. Don't interpolate or integrate—just remember. What is important or trivial is usually not evident until much later. So don't sift, just collect." In other words, force yourself to see first and conceptualize later. Earlier we alluded to Lyn Lofland's study, in which she observed the "grooming behavior" of people about to enter public places. "Grooming" was the conceptual category Lofland arrived at on the basis of more specific, concrete observations. Here are two examples of her observations of people preparing to enter a building.

> A young man approaches the door. He carries a briefcase in one hand; the other hangs free. As he nears the door he uses his free hand to brush the hair back from his forehead, then opens the door with that hand and enters.
>
> Two girls come toward the entrance. About three yards from the door, each begins to pass her hand over her hair, as though brushing it. They continue this until they reach the door. Apparently finished, they stop for a few seconds in front of the door while continuing the process (Lofland, 1973:141).

As the research progresses, you might want to intersperse your record of what actually happens with your own feelings and ideas. Both kinds of observations are important, but should be kept separate (Browne, 1976a). For example, you might observe in the classroom that two students are looking intently and steadily out the window during the instructor's lecture; at the same time you feel bored and sense that others are also. You should not, however, confuse or confound your impression of "boredom" with your factual observation of students "gazing" out the window.

How will you record your observations? For purposes of simplification, let us assume that you have three choices for managing and recording data: a tape recorder, a notebook and pencil, and your memory. Consider some of the implications of each of these choices. A tape recorder has the advantage of allowing you to record everything that is said. But there may be nonverbal behavior to observe; so you cannot rely solely on taping. Tape recorders also have the distinct disadvantage of being highly obtrusive. Taping a conversation with someone is the surest way to get that person to be very careful about his or her choice of words, at least at the outset.

Finally, the advantage of *getting* everything on tape also carries with it the problem of getting *everything* on tape. Tape recording individual interviews is common and may prove useful as a backup to the written record. Furthermore, in cases where talk in the setting is a major activity of observation, a verbatim record furnishes a primary source of data to which the researcher (and others) might return again and again. But for many purposes taped recordings of group interactions produce useless overload. Since it will take at least 3 hours to transcribe 1 hour of taped events, you can quickly find yourself overwhelmed with transcriptions. The tendency to be swamped with data in field research is great anyway; so most people shun the use of tape recorders except for dictating notes in the field.

What about the second strategy of note taking at the scene? This is generally less obtrusive than mechanical devices but can be a distraction to subjects and researchers alike. This technique probably would prove very easy for recording classroom observations. However, most situations circumscribe note taking. In interviews outside the class, for example, many people would find it annoying to be talking to someone who constantly looks away to take notes. Therefore, the field researcher needs to be alert to the opportunities naturally afforded for note taking. In her study of behavior in bars, Sherri Cavan (1966) went to the bathroom, an easily accountable act, to jot down her notes. If such opportunities do not present themselves, then the research must rely on quick jottings to serve as reminders of key words or observations and use these as aids to the basic short-term data collection system—human memory.

The most popular approach to gathering information at the scene is a well-developed memory. To guard against forgetting, most field researchers record field notes as soon as possible after their observations. They may unobtrusively make quick notes on the scene by using available materials (class notebook, paper napkin, shirt cuff, palm of the hand, whatever), but the essence of their data consists of thorough reconstructions of their observations recorded at a later time. The detail and completeness that these accounts require can be developed from the storehouse of a good memory. At first this may be difficult; some researchers have known a sense of panic in the early stages, fearing that they will not remember anything that happened. But with effort and practice, memory can provide surprising detail.

Once developed, the ability to recollect events becomes a permanent part of one's life. Joy Browne (1976a:77) offers the following personal insight into her own highly developed memory: "It becomes a bit of an occupational hazard in that I find it difficult to relate any event simply or briefly. If someone inquires three hours later about a party I have attended, they learn what everyone wore, drank, said, meant, and implied. Bored friends notwithstanding, it is pleasant to develop the skills of effortless observation."

Besides firsthand observation, which is the field researcher's primary source of data, you will probably also want to obtain information by questioning the professor and other students in the class. In field research, questioning takes a different form and serves different purposes than it does in survey research. Questioning in the field occurs either in casual conversations or in lengthy, *in-depth interviews*, sometimes called *intensive interviews*. Such interviews are much less structured than in surveys and also take much longer, often requiring several sessions. Indeed, in-depth interviews with one or two subjects can become the major method of collecting data in the field. Sociologist Robert Bogdan (1980) describes how the life stories of two people emerged as the principal focus of a participant observation study of the mentally retarded. Bogdan and a colleague met with one of the persons in 3-hour blocks of time once or twice a week for 2 years.

More commonly, field interviewing will occur as part of the process or as a natural extension of participant observation. It is impossible to observe everything at the scene; many relevant events will occur in the researcher's absence, and there may be other revealing information to which the researcher is not privy. For example, you may be absent from the class you are observing, or important conversations about the class may take place outside of class. In such cases, field researchers typically rely on the careful questioning of other participants, called *informants*, to gain information. Another important purpose of field interviewing is to question members or participants about their feelings, motives, and interpretations of events. These reactions are not only likely to be of direct interest to the researcher, but often serve as a critical validity check on the researcher's inferences.

Other sources of information frequently tapped by field researchers to supplement their observations are various official records (e.g., agency records, census data, court transcriptions) and personal documents (e.g., diaries, letters, scrapbooks). Documentary data may prove especially useful in the early stages of field research, as a means of learning about the history and the physical and social characteristics of a setting. Such data also can serve the same purposes as interviewing—that is, to gather and cross-check factual information. Kai Erikson (1976) drew widely upon this type of evidence in his study of the aftermath of a devastating flood in Buffalo Creek, West Virginia. This disaster resulted in a legal suit filed by the 650 survivors against the coal mining company whose land excavations and dam construction precipitated the flood. Taking a field research approach, Erikson consulted thousands of pages of legal depositions, psychiatric evaluations, and statements and letters written by the survivors to their attorneys.

One of the features of field research that makes describing it difficult is that it "is not a single method gathering a single kind of information" (Zelditch, 1962:567), but a blend of methods and techniques. The ways of collecting data outlined above constitute a very short list of the means for understanding the social world used by field researchers. For example, in Lyn Lofland's study of behavior in public places, she drew upon a broad range of materials, including not only field observations, but personal experiences, anecdotes, interviews, and historical and anthropological studies. Anything that promotes understanding is grist for the field researcher's mill.

Analyzing the Data and Formulating Theory

This brings us to the final phase of field research: data analysis and, as part of this process, the formulation of theory. This is almost a subset of gathering information because in this type of research, unlike some others, data analysis occurs throughout the period of data collection. The act of recording field notes itself is the beginning of analyzing and making sense of field data.

The data collected by the field researcher should render, first of all, a rich description of social life. And since such description should convey a "true-to-life" picture of reality, data analysis begins with an attempt to see things and to present them from the subjects' point of view. What to present from the mass of data and how to present it—for example, what "story line" to develop—are up to the researcher. But whatever one chooses to present should, as far as possible, describe the people on their own terms, graphically capturing their language and letting them speak for themselves. Pure description of this sort was the principal goal of the earliest field studies in anthropology and sociology (see Box 11.1), but most field research today integrates description with the development of theory.

Some field researchers contend that field studies can be used both to develop and verify theory (see Emerson, 1983). The more popular position, however, is that field research should be directed toward the development or "discovery" of theory. The most influential proponents of this view, Glaser and Strauss (1967), refer to theory that is generated from the data as *grounded theory*, as distinguished from theory logically derived from a priori assumptions and based on "a touch of common sense, peppered with a few old theoretical speculations" (p. 29). We believe that Glaser and Strauss's position distorts the nature of theory development outside of field research and unnecessarily places this mode of research in opposition to other approaches. But regardless of which position researchers take, the field approach to data analysis generally entails some attempt to lend coherence to the data by identifying themes, concepts, propositions, and theories. How, then, does one go about doing this?

A key process in theorizing from field data is the categorizing and sorting of information, called *coding* (Charmaz, 1983). Coding is a common aspect of all social research (see chapter 14). Typically, codes for variable categories are established prior to data collection, and the data are interpreted within this theoretical frame of reference. In grounded theory development, on the other hand, since one is working toward theory rather than from theory, the codes are developed from field observations. Thus, it is inappropriate to approach the field with preconceived notions or *pre*coded protocols detailing how the world is to be understood. Instead, codes (*post*codes if you will) are developed as part of making sense of the world. Let us reconsider your participant observation study of a research methods class. How might the emerging data be coded?

Perhaps you notice that a common activity in class is the asking and answering of questions. You might begin to organize your observations around an initial coding scheme so as to convey who asks and who answers questions. Some questions come from the professor and are answered by certain students. Others are asked by students and are answered by the professor. The more you observe the asking and answering of questions (including people's facial expressions, gestures, and body language), the more you realize that these question-answer dialogues do not all serve the same purpose; nor are their purposes always manifest. Sometimes the professor's questions are targeted to specific persons and sometimes they are thrown out to the entire class. Sometimes students' questions are substantive, sometimes they are procedural. Thus your initial coding scheme for "questions" might include these four types: professor (general, targeted) and student (substantive, procedural).

Additional observations, field interviews, and personal experiences in the classroom as a participant eventually may lead you to new insights and a more focused coding scheme. You might come to realize that students sometimes perceive the professor as asking questions (or answering them) in order to reward or to penalize certain students; you might interpret this as a sanctioning type of question. Other times you might infer that the effect of the professor's questions is to maintain a degree of social control over the class; for example, sometimes he or she asks questions that effectively end discussion on one topic and shift it to another. Questioning (and answering) thus becomes a demonstration of power. For their part, students may ask questions out of intellectual curiosity or out of a desire to ingratiate themselves with the professor. These interpretations may lead you to develop a more refined coding scheme than you had first imagined. Ultimately, you may come to see the asking and answering of questions as a dramatization of the power relations within the classroom, which may contribute to your formulation of a theory of interpersonal power.

As this example reveals, there is a constant interplay in field research between data collection and data analysis. Observations guide the creation of analytical categories and coding schemes. And whatever codes, tentative hypotheses, and theories you develop constantly are checked against and modified according to your observations.

To get an overview of the entire process of fieldwork, we now turn our attention to a participant observation study of a bar. The researchers spent 1 year in the field, from July 1971 to July 1972.

The Anthropological Study of Brady's Bar

Modern anthropology began with field studies of foreign, usually preliterate people, and the idea of studying one's own society was unheard of until recently. Studies of foreign cultures, however, are fast becoming a thing of the past for a number of political, ethical, economic, and social reasons. Anthropologists have turned more and more to the study of what is near at hand if not familiar. This is precisely what James Spradley and Brenda Mann (1975) did in their study of a bar that they called "Brady's." They were interested principally in the rules that govern the interactions of men and women in this particular work setting. Brenda Mann took a job as a cocktail waitress earning money to help pay her way through graduate school in anthropology. James Spradley, a professor of anthropology, studied Brady's as an observer who interviewed his colleague as though she were his informant. Thus, between the two of them, they had the opportunity to do team research involving very different levels of participation.

The *site* for the study presented no problem; it was a local bar frequented by college students and other neighbors. The decision as to *presentation of self* also was not a serious problem as they were, in fact, a cocktail waitress and a customer. *Access* was untroublesome as well, since there were many legitimate contacts that Brenda Mann developed as an employee. Most of the other waitresses, in a sense, became her informants.

Data collection involved many activities. It consisted largely of observing and recording observations on the scene. Spradley and Mann took note of such things as male and female roles, formal and informal social structure, including the relations among bartenders, waitresses, and customers, and the language peculiar to Brady's. They noted, for example, that the formal social structure of the bar included three major categories of people: customers, employees (bartenders, bouncers, and waitresses), and managers. Waitresses used various terms to describe different kinds of customers, such as "real regular," "loner," "drunk," "female," and "couple." They were quick to identify someone entering the bar in terms of one of these categories, which led them to anticipate certain kinds of behavior and to plan strategies for performing their role.

To supplement their firsthand observations, Spradley and Mann conducted intensive interviews with over half of the bar's waitresses several months after they began their research. In addition, after every one or two nights of work, they would have lengthy debriefing sessions that allowed them to compare their insights and discuss what they were observing. Spradley and Mann (1975:13–14) make the following observation about their experiences as field researchers doing an ethnography of Brady's.

> Before many weeks have passed the ethnographer *knows more than she can tell.* Much of the culture she is studying eventually becomes part of her own system of tacit knowledge. Although she will strive to record everything fully in field notes, it will be impossible to recall and record everything. Sometimes the most important information drifts outside our awareness. But as Brenda Mann acted as both participant observer *and* informant, our discussions of life at Brady's brought to light much of this tacit knowledge. Our debriefing sessions became opportunities to discover things about Brady's Bar that would have been difficult to know if either of us had done this research alone.

The final major issue—*analysis and theory development*—is one that develops gradually over the course of any field study. The book that came out of the study is in a general sense about contemporary American womanhood and the forces affecting women's perceptions of their place in the culture. It is about the sexual division of labor and how men and women differ in their claimed rights, perceptions, and power.

More specifically, *The Cocktail Waitress* reveals a number of insights about territoriality in the workplace; joking as a means of social control; speech patterns and the functions they serve; drinking behaviors of male versus female drinkers and of novices versus experienced drinkers; and how waitresses cope with sexual harassment, underage drinkers, regulars, and rowdies. The authors concluded, among other things, that the bar serves very different purposes for men and for women. For women, Brady's, and perhaps many other college bars, is an establishment for the purchase of goods, a sociable place to meet other people. For men, on the other hand, it is a ceremonial center for affirming male values, a place where male solidarity allows behavior that would be unacceptable in many other settings.

What Spradley and Mann have given us in their field study is the description of a bar from the cultural perspective of a cocktail waitress; they have revealed what it is like for a female at work in this male world. In short, they have given us *description*. They also have given us an *exploratory study* of the sexual division of labor in America. And, most impressively, they have provided well-grounded *theoretical formulations* about power in society and how culture operates to define women's accepted roles within the structure of that power.

The Products of Field Research

Some practitioners of field research explicitly reject the "positivist" view of science that we introduced earlier in the book (see Schwartz and Jacobs, 1979; Taylor and Bogdan, 1984). They believe that no real understanding of social phenomena can emerge without accounting for the actor's own point of view, and that a field approach offers the only means of learning about this view. We prefer, however, to see the strengths and the weaknesses of this approach in relation to the larger goal of theoretical understanding, for the products of field research are entirely consistent with a *science* of social life.

Rarely does a scientific study lead immediately to a great discovery; rarely are new laws formulated; rarely are theories supported without reservation. More typically, scientific studies lead to the gradual uncovering of empirical regularities, to the eventual realization of general principles. Yet, the end-product of science *is* theoretical understanding—however rarely this may occur. And because science is cumulative, the early steps and exploratory studies in the process are as important to the final product as are the key hypothesis-testing investigations.

Field studies are more likely to be important earlier in the scientific process than later. As we have seen, the field researcher typically enters the field without a well-developed picture of the research problem. An existing literature may help guide and inform the research, but the researcher can never be certain of just how a study of natural events in a natural setting will fit into that literature. Let us consider an example.

Suppose that you were interested in the process of religious conversion. A thorough reading of the literature would suggest that people make changes in their religious picture of the world based on social pressures, psychological predispositions, and the content of the belief system to which they are in the process of converting. Thus, an adequate theory of conversion would have to include social, psychological, and ideational variables. How, then, might you study the process of religious conversion with this information as backdrop?

To begin, you would not want to be closed to the possibility that other factors—say, the personal charisma of a religious leader or perhaps the lack of commitment to one's former religion—might affect religious conversion. Beyond this is the problem of exactly what or whom to study. Does a person who goes from being a traditional Catholic to being a pentecostal Catholic experience conversion in the same way as does someone who converts from Conservative Judaism to the Unification Church of Reverend Moon? Does someone who modifies or consolidates his or her beliefs experience something similar to the person who undergoes a more radical transformation? More to the point of the methodological issue, does studying a specific group, say a group of Catholic pentecostals in New Jersey, enable you to say anything about religious conversion in general or even Catholic pentecostals in general? When you observe a prayer group and afterward interact with and interview people present in the group, are you learning anything that describes the entirety of this group? What sort of generalizable information have you learned in doing a field study of some people in some group(s) within some movement that may be part of a larger cultural phenomenon that crosses denominational lines?

Meredith McGuire (1982), who conducted a field study of nine groups of pentecostal Catholics, generalized beyond her sample of subjects and groups to suggest answers to questions relevant not only to the Catholic pentecostal movement, but also to other religious movements and to the broad issue of religion and social change. She noted, for example, the consistent claim of members of the movement that they were countering the secularity of modern society. Catholic pentecostals typically bemoaned the lack of religion in the work world, education, and the family; they saw a lack of Christian norms in guiding behavior, as evidenced by parental permissiveness, "gay" liberation, widespread pornography, drugs and rock music, and restriction of prayer in the public schools. She further pointed out that in spite of the uniqueness of the Catholic pentecostal form of religion, and the specific historical processes that have given rise to the movement, her analysis of the movement corresponded to broader sociological theories of religion and social change. Thus, Catholic pentecostals' concern over "secularization" is one expression of the lack of integration in modern society. The Catholic pentecostal movement is an attempt to restore religion's role in premodern times, when religion provided a system of beliefs that unified all aspects of people's lives.

McGuire's conclusions are reasonable insofar as we recognize that all social science knowledge is tentative knowledge. She is fully conscious of the limitations of her fieldwork. She provides us not with axioms of fundamental truth but with a descriptive interpretation of one religious movement, not with social laws of religious ways of being but with an exploration of one of the ways in which people can be religious, not with predictions of how people will behave but with the beginnings of a theory of conversion.

These, then, are the products of field research: descriptions, explorations, and theoretical formulations. These products will be useful to other researchers seeking to understand pentecostal Catholics, to those working on other questions in the sociology of religion, and even to other social scientists who might gain insights for their own work on broader questions (e.g., interpersonal communication). What Meredith McGuire has done in her own limited study of nine groups is to help accumulate information that she and other social scientists can use in their struggles to understand social life. What she has written may not describe any other new religion, may not describe even any other pentecostal Catholic group, but it does suggest what might be. In this way it contributes to the cumulative work of science.

Summary

Field research implies an attempt to develop an understanding of human behavior as it is defined by the subjects themselves and/or as it is related to the situation in which the behavior occurs. To gain such understanding requires, first of all, the observation of persons in natural settings. It also may involve interviewing and the analysis of documents and virtually anything else that enables the researcher to get an insider's view of reality.

Traditionally field research has tended to focus on the downtrodden and, more recently, on aspects of everyday life. It is most advisable to adopt this approach under the following conditions: (1) when one wishes to study a fleeting or dynamic situation, (2) when it is essential to preserve the interrelatedness of the person and situation or other situational elements, (3) when methodological problems, resources, or ethics preclude the adoption of other research strategies, and (4) when very little is known about the topic under investigation. However, field research is an inferior way of testing specific causal hypotheses, a very time-consuming and sometimes inefficient method of gathering data, necessarily limited to a few settings, and highly dependent on the observational skills of the researcher.

The foundational method of field research is firsthand observation. Field observation varies in terms of structure, with less structured observation characterizing the early phases of research. Highly structured or systematic observation entails formalized rules for extracting information specifying when and where observations will take place, who will make the observations, and what will be observed. Field observation also varies according to the researcher's degree of participation in the setting being investigated. At one extreme is the intentionally unobtrusive, nonparticipant observer; at the other is the engaged participant observer. Participant observation is far more common than nonparticipant observation as an inclusive method, perhaps because being a participant is seen as crucial to gaining an insider's view of the world. However, the marginal position of the participant observer makes it a difficult and often stressful role to play.

Field researchers are flexible about research design, working out the specifics of their approach during the course of the study. In sampling, for example, a flexible approach is necessitated by the nature of the social units studied and by the delicate problems of entering the field and establishing field relations. Small nonrandom samples typify the selection of subjects and settings; however, once in the field, the researcher may use probability sampling techniques to sample times, observational sites, and other analytical dimensions relevant to the study.

Selecting an appropriate setting constitutes the first stage of fieldwork. For reasons of accessibility and interest, some researchers recommend "starting where you are," which has a strong tradition in field research. Gaining access to a setting is the second stage. In a formal organization this is usually a matter of getting the permission of those in charge. Public settings are more readily accessible, but require ingenuity in interacting with people and finding informants. In private settings, the principal means of gaining entry is the snowballing technique, whereby each contact is used to arrange additional introductions to others.

The third stage of field research, which begins with the task of gaining entry, is presenting oneself to those in the setting. Researchers must decide, first, on the extent to which they will reveal themselves as scientific observers and the extent to which they will participate in the setting. Although not uncommon, covert field research presents ethical problems and is frowned on by some investigators. More commonly, field researchers combine undisguised observation and participation, while varying the enactment of these two roles during the course of a single study. Other roles played by the researcher depend on the situation. In presenting oneself, one generally should try to develop trust and rapport with those in the setting. This is best accomplished by participating naturally.

The final two stages of field research, gathering and analyzing information, are concurrent. To collect data, field researchers rely primarily on well-developed memories to record detailed field notes as soon after their observations as possible. Besides firsthand observation, they also may question participants and consult records and personal documents. From this information, the researcher develops a rich description of events that conveys the experience of someone who "was there." Furthermore, throughout the process of gathering information, the researcher develops concepts and tentative hypotheses in order to make sense out of the data. Coding schemes are an aid to gaining such insights, and as the research progresses and theoretical insights emerge, the gathering of information becomes more focused and structured.

The products of field research thus consist of descriptions of settings and events from the unique perspective of the participants, exploratory studies of the social phenomena of which the settings and events are examples, and theoretical formulations grounded in firsthand observations.

Key Terms

field research	*key informants*
methodological empathy	*snowballing technique*
nonparticipant observation	*covert research*
participant observation	*in-depth interview*
going native	*informants*
dimensional sampling	*grounded theory*
gatekeepers	*coding*

Review Questions and Problems

1. Why is it misleading to use the labels "qualitative" and "observational" to characterize field research?

2. When is it advisable to adopt field research?

3. What is "methodological empathy"? How does it differ from sympathy?

4. How does field observation differ from casual, everyday observation? How does it differ from general scientific observation?

5. Distinguish between nonparticipant and participant observation. Which is more common in field research?

6. Describe how field observations can vary in structure. What are the advantages of structured, or systematic, field observation?

7. Why is it advantageous for a researcher to become a participant in the setting under observation?

8. How can participant observation be an emotionally stressful experience?

9. What is meant by "going native"?

10. How does the field researcher's approach to research design differ from that of the experimenter and survey researcher?

11. Why do field researchers generally use nonrandom selection of settings and subjects?

12. How are probability sampling techniques incorporated or approximated in field studies?

13. What are the principal stages of field research?

14. Why do J. Lofland and L. H. Lofland recommend "starting where you are" as a way of selecting a research setting?

15. Describe the basic approaches to gaining access to (a) formal organizations; (b) public settings; and (c) private settings.

16. Explain the functions of "gatekeepers" and "key informants" in relation to gaining access.

17. What are the four master roles for presenting oneself in the field? Which roles are most common in participant observation? Why is this the case?

18. When is covert research likely to pose ethical problems for the field researcher?

19. What guidelines should field researchers follow in deciding what to reveal about their research to those observed?

20. Why does Howell recommend "being yourself" as a guide to self-presentation in the field?

21. Discuss the disadvantages of a tape recorder and on-the-spot note taking as means of gathering information in the field.

22. Why is it important for the field researcher to have a well-developed memory?

23. How can interviewing and document analysis complement field observations as sources of information? That is, what kind of information do these methods provide?

24. Describe how coding contributes to data analysis in field research.

25. What is meant by "grounded theory"? How does this term apply to field research?

26. What are the typical products of field research?

27. How does field research contribute to the cumulation of scientific knowledge?

NOTES

1. Robert Park (see Box 11.1) was instrumental in establishing this focus. Trained as a journalist, Park was the press agent for the famous black educator Booker T. Washington when they coauthored a book entitled *The Man Farthest Down*. This book attracted the attention of sociologist W. I. Thomas, who invited Park to leave the Tuskegee Institute, where he had worked with Washington, to come to the University of Chicago. Park did so in 1913, ultimately becoming chair of the sociology department and establishing the intellectual tradition of studying "those farthest down."

2. By contrast, a student making the same kind of observations in a course in a different college, after getting the instructor's permission to observe, would face a different set of constraints. This setting probably would provide more access to the instructor's opinions, but less access to the student network outside of class. It also presents the problem of whether the student researcher should conceal his or her status in the class from other students.

12

Research Using Available Data

As different as experiments, surveys, and field studies may seem, they do have one common feature that distinguishes them from the methodological approach described in this chapter: each involves the firsthand collection of data. Doing any of these three kinds of research entails gathering information, either by questioning or direct observation, from the people and groups who are the objects of study. Thus the data originate with the research; they are not there before the research is undertaken.

By contrast, the fourth general strategy for doing social research is to make use of available data. Sometimes the researcher uses data that were produced by another investigator for a completely different research purpose. At other times, one may use available data that were not produced for any research purpose at all. The variety of such data is tremendous; it is limited only by the researcher's imagination. As you will see in this chapter, that imagination has found sources of data in letters and diaries, government and court records, newspapers and magazines. Even tombstones and graffiti have been used as the raw material for social research.

In spite of the extraordinary diversity of available data, a major problem with this approach is finding and procuring relevant information. We begin, therefore, by considering several studies that suggest the sources of and possibilities for using available data. With reference to these studies, we discuss the distinctive advantages and limitations of this approach. Then we consider issues related to sampling, measurement, and data analysis.

Sources of Available Data

The sources of available data may be placed in five broad categories: (1) public documents and official records, including the extensive archives of the Census Bureau, (2) private documents, (3) mass media, (4) physical, nonverbal materials, and (5) social science data archives. These categories provide a useful summary of data sources, although they do not constitute a mutually exclusive typology. Any data source may be placed in one or more of these categories.

Public Documents and Official Records

Exemplifying the available data approach is the historian who searches for traces of events and processes from the past. More than any other source of evidence, the historian relies on the written record. Writing is regarded as a mark of civilization. The ubiquity of the written record is easily demonstrated. Just attempt to compile a list of all the different written materials that you encounter on a given day. This book is one example; so is the bookstore receipt that you received with its purchase, or the checkout slip filed in order to remove a copy from the library. The advertising brochure that first brought this book to the attention of your instructor is part of the written record; so is your grade for the course in which the book is being used. Each of these could find its way into the hands of a researcher using available data. The researcher could be studying anything from the reading level of textbooks to the costs of higher education; from the marketing strategies of textbook publishers to the achievement of students in different types of schools.

A great deal of the written record is public. Documents created to assure the normal functioning of offices and departments are maintained at every level of government (not to mention by virtually every private business and organization) in every society throughout the world. These include the proceedings of government bodies, court records, state laws, and city ordinances. Many government agencies, most notably the Bureau of the Census, also maintain numerous volumes of official statistics. Add to this birth and death certificates, directories, almanacs, and publication indexes such as the *New York Times Index* and *The Reader's Guide to Periodic Literature*, and one can imagine the massive information available from public records.

An especially rich data source is *vital statistics*: data on births, deaths, marriages, divorces, and the like. By state law, all births must be recorded, and death records must be filed before burial permits can be obtained. Birth records provide information not only on the child born but also on the parents, including father's full name, address, age, and usual occupation. These data make possible research ranging from a study of social class and fertility to a study of maternal age and the incidence of twin births. Similarly, death records contain, in addition to the usual biographical information, data on cause of death, length of illness (where applicable), whether injuries were accidental, homicidal, or self-inflicted, and the time and place of death. With such data all sorts of demographic and epidemiological studies (studies dealing with the incidence or prevalence of disease in an area) are possible. Indeed, much of what we know about death has come from the analysis of death records. Ordinarily, the researcher obtains these records from an agency such as the National Center for Health Statistics in Washington, D.C., which compiles data for the nation as a whole, or from international organizations such as the United Nations, which compile such statistics for the world.[1]

One of the earliest sociological studies to make use of official records—in this case, death records—was Emile Durkheim's classic *Suicide* (1951), first published in 1897. Using statistics on suicides from official publications in several European countries, Durkheim related suicide rates to such variables as religion, season of the year, gender, and marital status. With these data, he rejected several hypotheses popular at the time, such as that suicide was the result of mental illness and that suicide increased with the temperature. Ultimately, he arrived at his influential theory that a lack of social integration contributes to suicides. Supporting his theory were data showing that suicide rates were lowest when social ties were strong (as among persons who are married and members of religions that emphasize social cohesion) and highest when social ties were weak (as among the divorced and members of religions that emphasize individualism).

Another early example of the use of public data sources is Sanford Winston's study (1932) of the sex ratio at birth (the ratio of males born alive to females born alive) among upper-class families in the 1920s. Winston hypothesized that upper-class families, because of social factors and their knowledge of methods of birth control, would show a strong preference for male children that would be evident in the sex ratio. He obtained data on 5466 families from genealogical records published in the *Abridged Compendium of American Genealogy*. First he identified the sex of each child in each birth order (first child, second child, etc.). Then he computed sex ratios (the number of males divided by the number of females multiplied by 100) for three groups: (1) for lastborn children in families estimated to be complete (e.g., where the mother was 45 years old or had been childless for at least 9 years), (2) "for all children of incomplete families," and (3) "for all children of completed families, omitting the last child" (p. 228). In comparison to the latter two groups, the sex ratio of lastborn children in completed families was higher (117.6 versus 108.8 and 109.3), indicating a preference for males and a concomitant decision to practice birth control when that preference was realized. Interestingly, when family size was controlled, the ratio of males to females among lastborn children was highest in completed two-child families (sex ratio = 133.1).

Kai Erikson (1966) used several public documents to study deviance in puritan New England. As a way of examining how the community defined deviance and, in so doing, defined its moral boundaries, Erikson examined three "crime waves" among the Puritans over a 60-year period. The first wave, called the antinomian controversy of 1636–1638, developed over a conflict concerning who was qualified to preach the Gospel in Boston and culminated in a civil trial for sedition and the banishing of two prominent citizens from the colony. The second wave involved violent, court-ordered persecutions of the Quakers from the 1650s to the 1660s, and the third wave consisted of the famous witchcraft hysteria centered in Salem in 1692. To analyze these events, Erikson relied on the extensive records of the Essex County Court and on the writings of some principals in these conflicts, such as Anne Hutchinson and the Puritan ministers John Winthrop and Cotton Mather. He concluded, in support of his hypothesis, that these historical events were in effect created by the community in order to establish its moral boundaries.

Stephen Sales (1973) made use of multiple sources of available data, including official statistics, in his study of threat and authoritarianism. Authoritarianism is a personality pattern characterized by a tendency to be unduly respectful of those in positions of authority. Authoritarians tend to admire power and toughness, to be superstitious, cynical, and opposed to introspection, and to believe in harsh treatment of those who violate group norms. Sales tested the hypothesis that these tendencies would be especially likely to occur in response to a threatening environment, such as exists in a period of economic depression. He compared existing data from the 1920s, a period of low economic threat in the United States, with data from the 1930s, the time of the Great Depression. For example, given that authoritarians wish to condemn and punish violators of in-group values, Sales expected an increase in support for police forces during the 1930s. He therefore examined the city budgets of two cities, New York and Pittsburgh, which were readily available to him. When he calculated the proportions of the budget devoted to the police force and the fire department (which he used as a control), he found that appropriations were higher for the police and lower for the fire department in the 1930s than in the 1920s. Moreover, this increase in budgeting for the police did not result from an increase in crime. For when Sales consulted the *Uniform Crime Reports for the United States*, he found a decline in crime from the 1920s to the 1930s.

Sales also found a variety of other data from public records consistent with the hypothesis that authoritarianism increased in the 1930s. For example, as indicated by the *The United States Catalog, Cumulative Book Index,* and *Reader's Guide to Periodical Literature*, there were more books and articles published on astrology (authoritarians are superstitious) and fewer books and articles on psychoanalysis and psychotherapy (authoritarians are opposed to introspection).

Perhaps the most widely used public storehouse of data is that collected and maintained by the U.S. Bureau of the Census. The bureau gathers an enormous amount of information. According to the Constitution, every person in the nation must be counted at least once every 10 years. Data from these decennial censuses, which began in 1790, are made available in two different forms: aggregate and individual. Aggregate data are released within months of their collection and describe various characteristics of the population of the states, counties, metropolitan areas, cities and towns, neighborhood tracts and blocks. The censuses of population and housing gather detailed information on the composition of every household in the country, including data on the age, gender, race, and marital status of each person, and numerous household characteristics, such as value of home or monthly rent, number of rooms, and presence of telephone.[2] Social scientists have used these data to study everything from the ecology of cities to residential mobility to racial inequality and segregation.

Using census reports from the 1950s, 1960s, and 1970s, for example, Reynolds Farley (1984) addressed the question of what blacks in the United States had gained from the civil rights struggle. Farley found undeniable progress on some measures, with the gap between blacks and whites narrowing on educational attainment, and occupation and earnings of the employed. But a few indicators (e.g., unemployment) showed no improvement, and some others (e.g., school and residential integration, family income) were mixed. Overall, Farley concluded, blacks have made significant gains, but the gap between blacks and whites is still great and will require many more decades of change similar to the 1960s and 1970s to disappear.

By aggregating data of this sort before release, the Census Bureau protects the privacy of individual persons, which the bureau is sworn to do. However, after a period of 72 years, individual census records—known as the *manuscript census*—also are released to the general public (Kaplan and Van Valey, 1980:78–79). (See Box 12.1 for an example of research using the manuscript census.) Beginning with the 1960 Census, the bureau also has made available individual-level data (actual census responses) on a sample of the population. To ensure confidentiality, these sample files (called the *Public Use Microdata Sample*) have had removed from them names, addresses, and all other personal identifying information. In addition,

BOX 12.1

Using the Manuscript Census in Social Research:
Nineteenth Century Shaker Demographics

Social scientists have been interested for many years in a religious group that has almost disappeared. The Shakers developed in England as a branch of the Quakers around the middle of the eighteenth century. In 1774 the group's prophetess Ann Lee came to America with eight others to start one of the most interesting chapters in the history of American religion. The Shakers lived a rigidly communitarian life, requiring that new members give up all personal property. They also did not believe in marriage, cohabitation, sex, or procreation. Men and women lived in different houses, and members of the opposite sex were prohibited from talking to one another in the halls or crossing one another's paths.

As celibates, the Shakers' principal means of gathering new members was voluntary joining. Yet, in spite of their austere living conditions, the sect survived for over 200 years and even thrived for a time, growing from the nine members who immigrated to America to a population that standard reference works estimate at 17,000 at the height of the movement. Some believe that this is an underestimate; indeed, the director of the Shaker Museum and Library at Sabbathday Lake, Maine, estimates that "total membership ran to about sixty-four thousand" (Kephart, 1982:208). Other estimates are more modest; Holloway (1966:70) claims that in 1830, 5000 members were scattered among eighteen different Shaker communities. What was the actual popular success of the Shaker experiment? How many Shakers were there? The fragmentary and scattered nature of the data make all of the foregoing estimates very rough guesses. However, William Sims Bainbridge (1982) recently put the original enumeration schedules of the U.S. census to good use in estimating the Shaker population in the latter half of the nineteenth century. In so doing, he also provides insights into the nature of recruitment, defection, and the gradual decline of this sect.

Seventy-two years after each census, the original schedules on which census enumerators recorded their data are released to the general public. These data are available on microfilm in twelve regional archives around the country. The organization of the data files facilitates the location of individuals by persons interested in learning more about their ancestors. In fact, the 1900 census files have a "soundex" system that allows the genealogist to trace the location of heads of households by identifying their names phonetically. The social scientist faces several problems in using these data. For the first six censuses, 1790–1840, relatively little information was collected on individuals, as only heads of households were identified by name. For later censuses the sheer volume of data presents a barrier to many researchers. Recently, methods have been developed for sampling census records (see Johnson, 1978). But the small population of Shakers made sampling inappropriate.

From historical accounts, Bainbridge first identified twenty-two colonies of Shakers in the period from 1840 to 1900. These colonies were located in eight states (five in Massachusetts, four each in New York and Ohio, three in Maine, two each in New Hampshire and Kentucky, and one each in Connecticut and Florida). Since Bainbridge could not know in advance the last names of Shakers, he was forced to search through some 150 rolls of microfilm reporting data for these eight states. And because the manuscript schedules for 1890 do not exist, having been destroyed in a fire, he decided to examine the data for every other census in the period 1840–1900. Describing the difficulties in researching the census of 1840, Bainbridge (1982:354) says that

> when one is scanning through a town which is supposed to contain a Shaker colony, and finds a household with 215 members, one may guess the Shakers have been located. But this presumption is not good enough. For one thing, Shaker colonies were divided into "families," sometimes as many as six of these subunits composing a colony, and some of the smaller families could be mistaken for other kinds of groups, and vice versa. Some families in 1840 were labeled "Shakers," but most were not. Many could be identified because the "head of household" whose name was recorded was a prominent Shaker mentioned in published histories.

Through painstaking cross-checking (e.g., using the 1850 census to identify some names listed in 1840), Bainbridge estimated the Shaker population at 3489 in 1840 and 855 in 1900. By analyzing the age and sex distributions of Shakers, he also showed that the proportion of females always was greater than in the general population and increased substantially over time, from 58 percent in 1840 to 72 percent at the turn of the century. Contributing to this transformation to a female society was "the defection of males, recruitment of destitute young mothers with children, and intentional differential acceptance of female children" (p. 363).

the bureau conducts a monthly survey of over 63,000 households sampled in 461 places throughout the fifty states. Known as the Current Population Survey (CPS), this provides, among other information, the monthly unemployment figures published by the government. Finally, there are regular censuses of business, manufacturers, agriculture, and other institutions.

An interesting application of census data is suggested by Marcus Felson (1983), who recommends using diverse available data sets, including the Census of Manufacturers, to measure social and cultural change. The *1977 Census of Manufacturers*, for example, shows that during the 1970s increases in sales of electronic musical instruments did not result in reduced sales of traditional acoustical instruments; the shipment of neckties sharply declined while shipments of baseballs, softballs, and baseball mitts increased; and shipments of girdles declined while shipments of women's and girl's athletic shoes increased.

Private Documents

A less accessible but no less important data source are private documents: information produced by individuals or organizations about their own activities that is not intended for public consumption. Diaries and letters long have been a favorite data source for the historian; other examples would be businesses' personnel and sales records, inventories, and tax reports, hospital patient records, and college transcripts.

Perhaps the best-known research using letters is W. I. Thomas and Florian Znaniecki's classic 1918 study, *The Polish Peasant in Europe and America*. The study dealt broadly with problems of immigration and assimilation into American society. The authors drew upon several sources of information, including newspaper accounts, autobiographies, and the records of social agencies such as the Legal Aid Society. But by far their largest single data source was a collection of over 750 personal letters exchanged between Polish immigrants in America and their relatives and friends in Poland. Thomas and Znaniecki's analysis of these materials was mainly descriptive. It consisted largely of introductions to sets of letters, commentaries on individual letters, and the letters themselves, nearly all of which were published as part of their study.

A second example of research using personal documents is Jerry Jacobs's analysis of suicide notes (1967). In order to understand how individuals justify their actions to themselves and others, Jacobs analyzed 112 notes left by persons committing suicide in the Los Angeles area. He was able to place nearly all of the notes in six general categories: "first form notes," "sorry illness notes," "not sorry illness notes," "direct accusation notes," "will and testament notes," and "notes of instruction." The largest category, "first form notes," pertains to accounts in which the person faced an intolerable problem for which death was seen as the only possible resolution.

Victoria Swigert and Ronald Farrell's study (1977) of the effects of a criminal stereotype on the adjudication of homicide defendants combined the use of both public and private documents. Swigert and Farrell's data came from two sources in the jurisdiction of a large northeastern city: publicly accessible indictment files of the office of the clerk of courts and confidential diagnostic records from a clinic attached to the court. All persons arrested for murder were seen in the clinic; and so Swigert and Farrell were able to relate the clinical diagnoses and background characteristics of defendants to legal data on prior convictions, access to legal resources such as a private counsel, and conviction severity. They found that the use of a diagnostic category of the violent offender had important consequences for the course and the outcome of the judicial process. Defendants labeled as "normal primitives" by the clinic were more likely than other defendants to be denied bail and access to trial by jury and, as a result, were likely to receive more severe sentences.

Mass Media

Also constituting part of the written record (as well as an oral and nonverbal record) are the mass media—newspapers, magazines, television, radio, films. By analyzing the content of these sources, social researchers have addressed a variety of issues.

In the aforementioned study of threat and authoritarianism, Sales (1973) also did a very simple analysis of comic strips. Because authoritarians tend to admire power and strength, Sales expected that popular fictional protagonists would become stronger and more powerful in the threatening 1930s than they had been in the relatively nonthreatening 1920s. Searching through Stephen Becker's *Comic Art in America*, Sales identified twenty comic strips that first appeared in the 1920s and twenty-one comic strips introduced in the 1930s. He and two other coders then judged whether the main character in each strip was either (1) "physically powerful or controlled great power, or (2) not particularly powerful." Supporting his hypothesis, Sales found that only two of the strips started in the 1920s emphasized the power of the main character ("Buck Rogers" and "Tarzan"), whereas twelve of the strips started in the 1930s were about powerful men (e.g., "Joe Palooka," "Dick Tracy," and "Superman").

While most research on the media has analyzed verbal content, one can also analyze visual content. Erving Goffman (1979) looked at hundreds of pictures from advertisements in newspapers and magazines to see what these pictures revealed about the meaning of gender in American society. One image that he identified was that of women as subordinate and dependent. This was evidenced by pictures consistently showing women bowing or otherwise on a lower plane than men, in a recumbent or reclining position, displaying a "bashful knee bend," canting (lowering) the head or upper part of the body, being victimized by men in playful games of "mocked assault," and in childlike, playful, or unserious poses.

Goffman provided a provocative description of "gender displays," but he neither chose nor analyzed his photographs in a systematic fashion. By contrast, Dane Archer et al. (1983) used more rigorous techniques to study one aspect of the stylistic representations of men and women in the media. They hypothesized that men and women differ in "facial prominence": the face and head—symbolizing intellect, character, wit, and other dimensions of mental life—are more prominent in depictions of men, and the body—symbolizing nonintellectual qualities like weight, physique, attractiveness, and emotion—are more prominent in depictions of women. Thus facial prominence may both reflect and influence societal images of men and women with regard to intellectual qualities. To measure facial prominence, Archer and his associates created an index consisting of the ratio of two linear measurements: the distance from the top of the head to the lowest point of the chin divided by the distance from the top of the head to the lowest visible part of the subject's body. They then calculated this index for men and women depicted in 1750 photographs from five American periodicals (e.g., *Time* and *Newsweek*), 3500 pictures from thirteen periodicals in eleven other nations, and in 920 portrait and self-portrait paintings spread across six centuries. Except for the fifteenth and sixteenth centuries, every comparison showed a significantly higher facial prominence score for men than for women.

Physical, Nonverbal Evidence

Although seldom used in the social sciences, nonverbal materials such as works of art, clothing, household items, and various artifacts constitute a rich source of evidence. Cave paintings, tools, and other artifacts are important data to archeologists studying past civilizations, and historians find invaluable evidence in sculpture and other works of art. Furthermore, as seen in the work of Archer et al. (1983), social scientists also make use of paintings. A study of tombstones provides a further example.

Between 1690 and 1765 the Puritans, in the words of historian Richard Bushman (1967), became Yankees. This historic transformation is evident in changes in attitudes toward death, available for all to see in the tombstones of New England's colonial cemeteries. Observing engravings on gravestones, David Stannard (1977) found that throughout the late seventeenth and early eighteenth centuries, stones invariably bore some version of the "death's-head" carving of a winged skull, representing the Puritans' rather grim vision of death. This visage dominated until the 1730s, when the death's-head motif and accompanying epitaphs steadily gave way to more romantic and optimistic designs of cherubs and angels. As this shift occurred, Stannard notes (1977:157), "the cemeteries in which those gravestones were placed began to become overcrowded while simultaneously falling into neglect and disarray. The Puritan community was becoming a relic of history. . . ."

Social Science Data Archives

Over the last 15–20 years, the social sciences have seen a tremendous proliferation of *data archives*, repositories of data collected by various agencies and researchers that are accessible to the public. Most of these archives contain survey data, but archives also exist for collections of ethnographies, in which the whole society is the unit of analysis. Thus the use of data archives is an extension of both survey research and field research. Some major advantages to using precollected data of this sort, which we discuss below, have made this the currently most popular method of social research.[3]

Social scientists refer to the analysis of available survey data as *secondary analysis*. Its earliest application was to census data, and then, beginning in the 1950s, to opinion poll data. However, these data were collected primarily for administrative and journalistic purposes; it was not until the 1970s that social scientists began conducting social surveys expressly for secondary analysis (Glenn, 1978). The first large-scale sociological survey conducted for this purpose was the General Social Survey (GSS), which began in 1972 and has been conducted annually, except for 1979 and 1981, ever since. Each GSS samples and interviews face-to-face about 1500 respondents, with questions pertaining to a wide range of attitudes and behavior. Many of the questions were asked one or more times in opinion polls conducted prior to the first GSS in 1972, and these and other questions have been repeated on subsequent GSSs. This became an important source of data in the following study. (We also make extensive use of GSS data in chapters 14 and 15.)

Noting that over 80 years lapsed between the Civil Rights Act of 1875 and the passage of further federal legislation protecting the rights of minorities, Paul Burstein (1979) investigated the circumstances under which Congress would act against discrimination. Burstein hypothesized that such action would occur only when a substantial and increasing majority of the public favors it. He then asked if this was indeed the case in 1964 when Congress passed its landmark Civil Rights Act prohibiting discrimination against minorities in employment, public accommodations, public schools and colleges, and federally assisted programs. To find out, Burstein traced changes in public attitudes toward discrimination, as measured by questions in several different surveys in the 1950s, 1960s, and 1970s. Among the sources of these data were the Gallup and Roper opinion polls and the GSSs of 1973, 1975, and 1976. The data were consistent with his hypothesis, but additional analyses also revealed that civil rights activity and demonstrations may have been instrumental in changing public sentiment and in directly influencing the passage of specific legislation.

Social scientists also do "secondary analyses" of data based on characteristics of whole societies. One valuable archive of such data, called the Human Relations Area Files (HRAF), contains information recorded on microfiche on over 300 societies. These files are in "raw data" form, with pages from ethnographic reports organized by topic. Another type of cross-cultural data are available in "coded" form, with numeric codes on several variables for each society. Examples of these sources are the *Ethnographic Atlas* (Murdock, 1967), containing codes on approximately forty variables for over 1100 societies, and the Standard Cross-Cultural Sample (SCCS) (Murdock and White, 1969), containing more extensive data on a smaller sample of 186 societies. The following study used all three of these sources.

Obtaining data from a sample of forty-eight tribal societies, Willie Pearson and Lewellyn Hendrix (1979) tested the hypothesis that divorce increases as the status of women increases. This follows from the reasoning that as women gain economic resources they become more autonomous and less dependent on their husbands. Pearson and Hendrix's findings showed that divorce rates were moderately correlated with female status even when theoretically relevant variables such as community size, marital residence, and descent rules were controlled.

Advantages of Research Using Available Data

The foregoing studies suggest several advantages as well as some problems with research using available data. Here we discuss the principal advantages, and then in the remaining sections we address specific problems. The first five of the six benefits listed below originally were outlined by Hyman (1972) with reference to the secondary analysis of survey data. All five apply to most other available data, whereas the final advantage pertains to sources other than survey data archives.

Understanding the Past

Available data provide the social researcher with the best and often the only opportunity to study the past. To study some aspect of American society 50 or more years ago, it might be possible to conduct a survey of people who were alive at the time. But to do so presents several methodological problems, from the inaccuracy of repondents' memories to survivor bias in the sample. To study periods prior to this century necessitates the search for available data. Documentary records and other archival evidence have therefore been a favorite source of data for historians, as we saw in Erikson's and Stannard's studies of the Puritans. Burstein's study of public attitudes and antidiscrimination legislation also shows how more recent events can be investigated with the aid of survey data archives. In fact, many social scientists see surveys from the past as a primary data source for historians of the future (see

Hyman, 1972). But studies of the past are not limited merely to understanding the past. They also can be done to test general propositions about social life, as we saw in Erikson's and Burstein's studies as well as several others—for example, Sales's research on threat and authoritarianism.

Understanding Social Change

Because of the commitment and cost involved, social scientists rarely conduct longitudinal surveys or do field research over long spans of time. The analysis of available data, however, is well suited to studies of social and cultural change. Trend studies, such as Farley's analysis of black and white inequalities, have a long tradition among social demographers who rely on the census and other demographic data. Stannard's analysis of the carvings on gravestones provides an example of another source of evidence on social change. Moreover, the establishment of data archives has resulted in a marked increase in the number of studies that trace relatively recent changes in various attitudes, opinions, and behaviors (see Glenn and Frisbie, 1977). The GSS was designed partly as a social indicators project to measure trends in social conditions. And as we noted, Felson has suggested a similar use for other available data sources such as the Census of Manufacturers.

Studying Problems Cross-Culturally

As with surveys of long-term change, there are few cross-cultural surveys. In fact, Hyman (1972:17) estimated "about ten documented examples of comparable large-scale multination surveys of the general population [existed] as of 1970." This is especially lamentable because many sociological generalizations pertain to societies as the unit of analysis. Once again, however, available data—in the form of existing survey data and ethnographies—provide the opportunity to study problems cross-nationally. Pearson and Hendrix's investigation of the relationship between divorce and the status of women is one example.

Improving Knowledge through Replication and Increased Sample Size

In contrast to experiments and field studies, which use samples of very limited size, and to most surveys, the use of available data often affords the opportunity to generate very large samples. Winston (1932) obtained data on 5466 families; Archer et al. (1983) measured facial prominence in over 5000 photographs in eighteen diverse periodicals from twelve nations. Sample size is important for two reasons. First, large samples generally enhance our confidence in study results; with random sampling, increases in sample size increase the reliability of findings, as we saw in chapter 6. Second, by increasing sample size, we may gain access to specialized problems and smaller populations that otherwise could not be studied. A national sample of 1500 adults, for example, may be inadequate for a study of persons 80 years of age or older, because they would only constitute about 50 cases. But this problem may be solved by combining data from several existing surveys, such as several years of the GSS.

By combining sample surveys and thereby increasing sample size, we are in effect replicating our research—repeating our analyses across the different surveys. Replications, which are relatively rare in the social sciences, often may be carried out easily with available data. A good example is Sales's research on threat and authoritarianism. Sales used diverse sources. We mentioned his use of municipal budgets, listings of books on astrology and psychotherapy, and comic strips. But he used several other sources that we did not mention and also analyzed changes in similiar indicators for two later periods in the United States: 1959–1964 and 1967–1970. And that is not all. Two other researchers (Padgett and Jorgenson, 1982) replicated part of Sales's analyses for Germany in the 1920s and 1930s, using, for example, the German equivalent of the *Reader's Guide* to chart the number of articles that appeared on astrology, mysticism, and cults. The data consistently supported the thesis that threat increases authoritarianism.

Savings on Research Costs

Insofar as research using available data bypasses the stage of data collection, it can economize greatly on cost, time, and personnel. This is especially true of the secondary analysis of surveys. The cost of obtaining available data sets is a small fraction of the cost of producing the data. Hyman (1972:6) estimates that the money required to conduct a survey up to the point of data analysis consumes about 40 percent of the total budget, and we would expect the savings in time and personnel to be even greater. When one adds to this the better quality of the data found in most survey data archives, which typically are produced by professional polling and research centers who obtain large, national samples, then secondary analysis becomes a particularly efficient way to do research.[4]

Research with sources of available data other than surveys also tends to be less costly than experiments, surveys, and field studies. These costs vary depending on the nature of the data source, and the time, money, and personnel required to obtain and to analyze the data. The tasks of the researcher using available data, such as searching for and coding relevant information, often are tedious and time-consuming. Imagine, for example, the efforts of Archer et al. in obtaining periodicals, identifying eligible pictures, and measuring the facial dominance and gender for some 5000 pictures, or the job faced by Swigert and Farrell in sampling and coding the information contained in court and clinic records for 444 cases of persons charged with murder. Yet, the cost per case in such studies is generally quite small compared to the cost of interviewing a respondent or running a single subject through an experiment.

Nonreactive Measurement

As we saw in our discussion of previous research strategies, a major problem in much social research is reactive measurement: changes in behavior that occur because of subjects' awareness that they are being studied or observed. Research with available data also encounters this problem to the extent that the data sources are surveys or documents like autobiographies in which the author is clearly aware that what is said will be in the public domain. Still, much available data are nonreactive. With physical evidence and many other available data sources, there is simply no reasonable connection between a researcher's use of the material and the producer's knowledge of such use. By analyzing genealogical records, Winston's study (1932) of the preference for male children is completely nonreactive. Imagine, however, the kind of self-censorship that might have occurred if he had interviewed prospective mothers in their homes or expectant fathers in waiting rooms (Webb et al., 1981). Needless to say, we would be much less confident in this kind of evidence.

The risk of reactivity is so high in some areas of study that available data may provide the only credible evidence. Consider, for example, studies of illegal activities such as consumption of illegal drugs. Survey evidence is likely to be contaminated by concealment and underreporting; police records such as number of arrests for controlled substances may be distorted by differential efforts at law enforcement. An ingenious use of available data, however, can provide nonreactive evidence on drug use. Noting that the federal government imposes a tax and keeps a record of taxes collected on cigarette papers and tubes, Marcus Felson (1983) observed that federal taxes collected on these items changed little during the 1950s and 1960s but jumped about 70 percent over 1960s levels in 1972. Meanwhile, loose tobacco sales declined during this same period. The conclusion Felson reached is that a new market had been created for cigarette papers in the production of marijuana "joints." That market, it would appear, opened up in 1972.

Obtaining and Sampling Available Data

From all that we have said so far, one may find it hard to conceive of a social science topic that cannot be studied using available data. Certainly this is a flexible and powerful approach to social research. Nevertheless, it is not without its problems. A major problem centers around the accessibility of existing data. While the material to study a given topic may exist, how do you know what to look for? And how do you find it, acquire it, and/or gain permission to use it?

Perhaps the best advice is to let the research problem or hypothesis serve as a guide to suggesting appropriate sources. In one sense, this is obvious. For example, researchers like Swigert and Farrell who are interested in the adjudication of criminals will readily entertain the possibility of using judicial records. But this advice holds true in another way. Aimlessly searching through records or dredging up data from survey archives is unlikely to yield anything of value. Even though the data preexist, that does not mean that the researcher should reverse the research process by analyzing the data and then developing some post hoc rationale for the analysis. More than likely, the outcome of such an approach will be a trivial and flawed study. It is far better to let your research problem dictate your methodology than to let your method override the substantive and theoretical focus of your research.

A second guide to locating pertinent data is to search the literature for studies by previous investigators. No doubt Erikson's study of deviance in Puritan New England was aided by the mounds of data already uncovered by earlier historians who investigated this era. It also helps to know where to go for tips on locating available data. You can learn about the location of many data sources by consulting a librarian. For a listing of social science data archives, together with addresses and telephone numbers, we recommend Kiecolt and Nathan (1985:76–80). Descriptions of other publicly available data sets may be found in Taeuber and Rockwell (1982). In addition, each February issue of *American Demographics* contains a "Directory of Commercial Data Suppliers."

Access to public sources varies among the archives and agencies holding the data. Much of these data, such as that compiled by the Census Bureau and other government agencies, is mandated for public use without restrictions. The greatest access problems pertain to private documents and confidential records. Obtaining such data may require a little ingenuity, such as Thomas and Znaniecki used in their study of letters written to and from Polish immigrants. They acquired the letters through advertisements in a Polish language newspaper which offered to pay 10–20 cents per letter. Gaining access also may depend on the permission and cooperation of others. Jacobs, for example, collected his suicide notes with the aid of an acquaintance who was a deputy coroner in the Los Angeles County Coroner's Office.

Once the researcher has located pertinent data, issues of sampling arise. Often the issue is not whether or how one should sample, but how adequate is the existing sample of information. Survey archives, as we have mentioned, often provide unusually good, broad-based samples. Sampling errors in U.S. censuses are among the lowest of all sources of survey data (Kasarda, 1976). Cross-cultural data banks, on the other hand, constitute nothing more than availability samples; they do not contain data on modern industrialized societies or even a representative sample of nonindustrial societies. This limits generalizations as well as the types of research that can be undertaken. Cross-cultural researchers cannot make predictions or esti- mate worldwide societal characteristics. But they can provide limited tests of hypotheses (Lee, 1984). In their study of divorce and the status of women, Pearson and Hendrix were forced to use only those societies—forty-eight in all—for which they could obtain adequate measures on key variables. Their rationale for this data set was that it included societies from all continents except Australia and contained sufficient variation in the key variables.

Sampling is even more problematic for researchers studying the more remote past who must rely on whatever traces of information they can find. These data are certain to be incomplete and are probably biased. This is especially true of physical evidence, which invariably is subject to selective survival and selective deposit. *Selective survival* refers to the fact that some objects survive longer than others. The fact that pottery and bone survive the elements better than wood and paper has long been a problem for the archeologist. A graver problem for users of the written record is *selective deposit*—systematic biases in the content of the evidence that is available. Records may be selectively destroyed; other information may be edited.

Webb et al. (1981) note that members of Congress are allowed to edit proofs of the *Congressional Record*, a transcript of the speeches and activities of the U.S. Congress, which means that this document hardly serves as a spontaneous account of events. As another example, Webb et al. (1981) cite a study of the longevity of the ancient Romans based on evidence from tombstones. Wives who died after their husbands may have been underrepresented insofar as they were less likely to get a tombstone than wives who died before their husbands. Also, middle- and upper-class Romans were probably more likely to have tombstones than the lower classes of Roman society. And because mortality rates are likely to have varied across class, this could bias estimates of longevity.

Similar sampling problems may exist in studies of the written record. Only about 10 to 20 percent of those who commit suicide leave notes. The question that must be asked of the Jacobs study, therefore, is whether the rational and coherent character of the notes he observed describes the mental condition of suicide victims *not* leaving notes. In other words, are persons who leave notes representative of the entire population of persons who commit suicide? More generally, Bailey (1982:305–306) observes that documents may be biased by educational level. Not only are poorly educated people much less likely to write documents, but the mass media are likely to be aimed at and to be more representative of well-educated people.

Under those circumstances where there is no choice in the selection of information, sampling design obviously is irrelevant. However, in studies of the more recent past, probability sampling of time and space are feasible and often necessary because of the massiveness of the information. Thus actuarial, political, and judicial records usually may be sampled over time; voting records may be sampled across precincts (Webb et al., 1981). Much of the research on the mass media also uses probability sampling, which we discuss below in relation to content analysis.

Measurement Issues in Available Data Research

The four basic approaches to social research differ according to the stages that require the greatest labor and creativity on the part of the researcher. In experimentation, experimental design (e.g., number of conditions, measurement of key variables, instructions to subjects) is crucial; therefore, much of the effort goes into perfecting the design and preparing for its implementation (pretesting), and the data analysis is simple and straightforward. When the design is not experimental, the data analysis requires great effort and skill. And when the data were collected for another purpose, evaluation and refinement of the data is an extremely important research phase as well as data analysis.

Using available data is a bit like wearing someone else's shoes. They may fit perfectly well. But more likely they will either be too small, pinching your toes, or too large, causing you to stumble. Seldom will available data be ideally suited to the purposes the researcher has in mind. At worst, the data may be inadequate to address the research question. At best, the data may require the creative construction of measures that provide indirect evidence of a given variable.

Inadequate and Insufficient Measurement

A major limitation of secondary analysis is that the surveys may not contain appropriate questions for measuring key variables. Suppose, for example, that you were interested in characteristics of the victims of child abuse. If you searched through the GSS data, you would find in the 1984 survey that respondents were asked three relevant questions. First, every respondent was asked:

"Have you ever been punched or beaten by another person?" (Nearly 40 percent of the 1473 persons in the sample answered "yes.")

Those answering affirmatively were asked two subsequent questions about their experiences as the victims of violence. First,

"Did this happen to you as a child or as an adult?" (Two-thirds—390—of those who were asked responded that they had been punched or beaten as children or both as children and as adults.)

These 390 respondents then were asked about the frequency of this experience:

"How many times would you guess this has happened to you?" (Some 55 respondents answered that it had happened only once; 146 persons said that it had happened two or three times; and 172 persons indicated that they had been the victims of this kind of violence four or more times.)

If we define respondents in this last category as victims of child abuse, then this group constitutes only about 12 percent of the sample. Aside from the relatively small sample, however, our measurement of child abuse presents problems. Surely among these 172 people were some who were beaten up as members of youth gangs, others who were the victims of violent crimes perpetrated on them by strangers. Should these respondents be considered "abused children"? On the other hand, some respondents who were physically neglected or emotionally abused by their parents may have been excluded from the 172 because they were not punched or beaten.

In a related way, existing survey data may be found wanting for what they do not contain at all. Suppose you used the GSS data to study some of the life experiences of persons whom you defined (for better or worse) as adult survivors of child abuse. You might want to know, for example, how likely these persons are to marry and to have children. The GSS data could answer these questions. However, if you are interested in whether child abuse victims are likely to abuse their own children, you will find no data available on this point. No such question was asked. (On the other hand, you could relate child abuse to tolerance of violence. See discussion of Sedgely and Lund's study [1979] in chapter 15.)

Similar problems are found in other sources of available data. Official records, including population statistics, may contain defective data, or the number and spacing of the data may be inadequate for research purposes. Demographers have developed mathematical and graphic procedures to adjust for defective data and to estimate intermediate values in a set of observations (Shryock et al., 1976:407–559). Users of historical documents often must make subjective inferences to fill in gaps in information.

Indirect Measurement

In much available data research, the investigator must develop creative measures that approximate variables of interest. Taxes collected on cigarette paper and tubes cannot be considered a direct measure of marijuana consumption. But taken in the context of loose-tobacco sales, they do provide a useful surrogate indicator, especially given the reactivity of other measures. Many of the measures in Sales's research on authoritarianism are similarly indirect. Unable to question individuals directly about their attraction to powerful people, Sales relied on the popularity of comic strip characters as an indicator of such attraction. And when no reference work covering new comic strips was available for the later periods he investigated, he speculated that individuals "attracted to strength and power in times of stress . . . might be more inclined to purchase strong and powerful dogs" (1973:52). Sure enough, an examination of American Kennel Club (AKC) registrations of some 116 breeds showed that 9.8 percent of all dogs registered by the AKC in the low-threat period (1959–1964) were in the attack-dog classes (German shepherds, Doberman pinschers, Great Danes), whereas these dogs accounted for 13.5 percent of the registrations in the relatively threatening period (1967–1970).

Sales's measurement of threat also is somewhat indirect, since it depends on the tenor of the times rather than on the measurable feelings of individuals. More direct measures of threat can be found in experiments where individuals have been "threatened" by telling them that they have failed tests of intelligence (see Sales and Friend, 1973) or by leading them to anticipate receiving electrical shocks. Sales, on the other hand, identified contiguous historical periods that appeared to pose contrasting environmental threats for the population as a whole. He ended up comparing periods marked primarily by differences in economic prosperity: the 1920s versus the 1930s, and 1959–1964 versus 1967–1970. These contrasts do not unambiguously represent low- versus high-threat conditions. For example, as Sales (1973:51) himself noted, the presumed "low-threat" period of 1959–1964 "included the abortive Bay of Pigs invasion, the Cuban missile crisis, and the assassination of J.F. Kennedy." But the facts that he used two sets of contrasting historical periods and that the relationship between threat and authoritarianism was so consistently demonstrated lend considerable credibility to his measurement of "threat." Indeed, Sales's historical measure would appear to provide a much more powerful test of his hypothesis than weak and short-lived, albeit direct, experimental manipulations of threat.

As we argue in the next chapter, the use of several different measures of a given variable is always a good practice in social research. This is even more imperative, however, in available data research that uses indirect and approximate indicators.

Reliability and Validity: Authenticity and Accuracy

Perhaps the most important general rule that applies to the use of available data, irrespective of the source, is that the researcher must reconstruct the process by which the data were originally assembled (Riley, 1963:252). If you gather the data yourself, you generally are aware of their limitations, possible errors and biases, and you can adapt your analyses accordingly. But such adaptations also may be required of available data. Therefore, it is crucial to try to determine, so far as possible, how, when, where, and by whom the data were collected. Only then can you begin to assess the validity of the data.

Researchers using historical documents must be especially concerned about their authenticity. Authentication is a highly technical matter that requires a thorough knowledge of the historical period from which the documents are purported to originate. Besides checking the logical consistency of the content, one must examine handwriting, writing style, and even the chemical composition of ink and paper. Historian Louis Gottschalk (1969) notes that doubts about authenticity arise frequently, and if they seem not to, it is only because a skilled historian has already authenticated the sources. For this reason, social researchers like Kai Erikson usually are spared the task of authentication. Assuming authenticity, however, one must still ask how the data were collected. Is the available evidence accurate, complete, and reliable? A recent series of studies of colonial Boston illustrate how easy it is to be misled if you do not have a thorough knowledge of the conditions of data collection.

According to historian G. B. Warden (1976), the traditionally accepted view of colonial Boston was that of a basically egalitarian community with a town meeting democracy and a relatively equitable distribution of wealth. These egalitarian conditions, moreover, are believed to have made the city a center of radical political agitation before the Revolution. In the 1960s this position was challenged by a group of scholars (see, for example, Henretta, 1965) who advanced the view that Boston experienced dramatic increases in social and economic inequality in the eighteenth century. Indeed, these scholars claim that it was the resulting socioeconomic tensions that contributed to radical political agitation. The arguments supporting the latter view are rather extensive, but are based largely on evidence from tax assessments in 1687 and 1771 (unfortunately, tax records for the intervening years are not available).

For example, one of the propositions put forth was that Boston experienced extraordinarily rapid economic growth in the eighteenth century, which increased stratification and the maldistribution of wealth. Evidence of this came from an observed increase in the total assessed wealth of Boston from 16,591 pounds in 1687 to 460,493 pounds in 1771, which translates into an annual growth rate of 33 percent per year. As Warden points out, however, these figures do not take into account how property was estimated for tax purposes. In 1687 all property was estimated for tax purposes at about 5 percent of its true market value, whereas in 1771 real property (land and house) was estimated at about one-twelfth of its market value, and personal property (e.g., stock in trade) was estimated at close to its actual value. If appropriate adjustments are made, then the estimated "simple annual growth rate is only about 2.3 percent which is relatively low compared with other colonial communities" (Warden, 1976:589).

Warden shows how similar problems exist with other interpretations of these data. Another proposition was that the richest Bostonians possessed an increasingly disproportionate share of the wealth. But once again, the data purported to support this proposition are flawed by inconsistencies. The different assessments of real and personal property in 1771, for example, magnifies the difference between the actual taxable wealth of propertyholders in the bottom and top halves of the distribution. As a consequence,

> there appears to be a heavy concentration of wealth in the upper half of the group; the apparent concentration occurred, however, not because the retailers and merchants were all that much richer than those in the bottom half but because the wealth of those in the top was estimated at a much higher rate than the wealth of those in the bottom half (1976:604).

Even for more recent data sources, the same general rule of carefully assessing the accuracy and consistency of the data applies. Consider, for example, the unwary user of crime statistics. There are two major sources of crime data: (1) self-report data from the National Crime Survey, in which people are asked to indicate crimes in which they have been personally victimized, and (2) data from official reports of crimes known to the police, which are compiled in the *Uniform Crime Reports* by the Federal Bureau of Investigation. These two sources clearly offer very different operational definitions of crime; one focuses on the victim and the other on the offense. And as it turns out, there is no simple relationship between the two measures. A single offense (e.g., a robbery of several persons in an establishment) may have more than one victim. Some offenses (murder) have no victims who can be interviewed, and other offenses (e.g., prostitution and gambling) have no victims in that the "victims" are also the offenders. Each of these measures also suffers from other methodological problems. Victimizations are limited to persons over the age of 12. Not all crimes are brought to the attention of the police (e.g., burglaries of uninsured items); also, the police themselves may fail to record incidents.

Such problems do not render crime statistics useless or totally invalid. But they do force the researcher to focus on a particular definition of crime—either offenses or victimizations—and to consider the implications of using data with a relatively large measurement error (Jacob, 1984). More generally, the flawed nature of these data point to the need for every researcher using available data to become acquainted with the process by which the information was gathered. How did the data collectors define categories (e.g., "crime" and "tax assessments")? If the data were collected repeatedly over time, have there been changes in record-keeping or data collection procedures? In the case of the media and first-person documents, how might the writer's ideological position have affected his or her interpretation of events? Without recourse to the usual checks on validity, knowing how the data were collected is often the only way to determine the authenticity and accuracy of available data.

Another procedure that is especially useful for evaluating reliability is the use of several different sources of evidence. As a rule, historians do not accept an account of an event as reliable unless it is confirmed by two or more independent primary sources.[5] Demographers, who analyze population statistics, often use several data sources and different estimation procedures. To estimate the annual net number of undocumented ("illegal") Mexican immigrants to the United States, David Heer (1979) used several reports of the CPS and came up with seven different estimates, each based on different assumptions about the data. Heer's estimates for the period from 1970 to 1975 ranged from 82,300 to 232,400, figures that are well below estimates of the gross flow of illegal aliens.[6]

Once the data have been evaluated, it may become necessary to refine measures. If measurement errors or changes in definitions are detected, then the researcher must make the necessary adjustments to allow for proper interpretation. The historian Warden's reanalysis of tax assessments in Boston offers one example of this.

Data Analysis and Interpretation

The analysis and interpretation of available data takes as many forms as the data themselves. In part, the type of analysis is a function of research purposes and research design. Descriptive accounts of a single event or historical period differ from tests of general hypotheses, which differ from trend studies. The analysis also depends on data sources. Researchers use very different techniques for analyzing population statistics, mass media communications, historical documents, and survey archives. Here we briefly discuss aspects of three sharply different types of analysis typical of research using available data: historical interpretation, content analysis, and cohort analysis.

Historical Interpretation

The historical analyst is interested in understanding the past. Partly this involves establishing what happened in a factual way. During the Salem witchcraft hysteria, for example, who was accused by whom? Who was executed? But analysis never stops here. To arrive at some *understanding* of what happened, the researcher must order the facts according to some interpretation of the materials. This is precisely what Kai Erikson did in his aforementioned study of deviance in Puritan New England.

One of the three crises that Erikson analyzed was the Salem witchcraft hysteria. The events of this well-known episode have been fairly well established through court depositions and writings of that period, and the reader may be familiar with them through popular accounts such as Arthur Miller's play *The Crucible*. In 1692 two daughters of the local minister Samuel Parris became ill, or at least they began to exhibit rather bizarre behavior. They would scream unaccountably, go into convulsions, their bodies would become contorted, and they would crawl around on all fours and bark like dogs. Possibly the girls suffered from hysteria, although nobody knew then or knows now precisely what afflicted them. Whatever it was spread quickly to other girls in the community, who began to manifest similar symptoms. In the wake of this panic, unable to bring this strange behavior under control, someone offered a diagnosis of witchcraft. And when the girls were pressed into identifying who was tormenting them, they implicated three women. One of the women was Parris's slave Tituba, who was from the West Indies and known for her practice of voodoo magic. She confessed and conveniently identified, among others, the two other women named by the girls as agents of the devil. Other confessions and accusations followed, supposed witches were arrested and put on trial, and before it was over, nineteen people were hanged and one was pressed to death.

Why did this unfortunate episode occur? Erikson, you will recall, saw this as one of three "crime" waves in the seventeenth century that served to reinforce the moral boundaries of the community. The need to reaffirm moral boundaries and community solidarity arises, according to Erikson, when the sense of community control and consensus is threatened. The threat to Salem Village, however, was not posed by the alleged witches; they were conveniently chosen deviants. Rather, it was the uncertain political status of the community. In the 1670s, Erikson points out, the colony was beset by strife between clergy and magistrates, whose alliance "had been the very cornerstone of the New England Way," and by a costly war with a confederacy of Indian tribes. Then, in the 1680s King Charles II of England imposed the establishment of an Anglican church in Boston and revoked the charter that had legally protected the colony for over half a century. At the onset of the witchcraft hysteria, colonial agents were visiting England in an attempt to restore the charter. Finally, there were many land disputes and feuds at the time, which undermined the harmony on which the community had depended. All of this, according to Erikson's interpretation, evoked a need to reaffirm the Puritan way of life.

Although Erikson's analysis of these events is thorough and persuasive, it has been challenged by other sociologists and by subsequent historical research. William Chambliss (1976) contrasts Erikson's "functionalist" explanation with "conflict" theory, siding firmly with the latter. He sees the witchcraft hysteria, in addition to the other two crime waves, as "indeed created for the consequences it had. But the consequences were not 'to establish moral boundaries'; rather, they aided those in power to maintain their position" (p. 15). Chambliss points out in support of this interpretation that the actions of court assistants were followed and criminal sanctions imposed so long as members of the ruling elite were not accused. However, when the witch finders began to overstep this bound, the witchcraft trials came to an end.

Historians Paul Boyer and Stephen Nissenbaum (1974) offer still another interpretation of these events. Using many of the same references as Erikson as well as some previously neglected sources of data, they noticed a split between accusers and accused that coincided with whether people supported or opposed Samuel Parris, the minister in whose home the girls first experienced their afflictions. As it turned out, this split between pro-Parris and anti-Parris factions existed prior to the witchcraft outbreak and went well beyond support for the local minister. Compared to supporters, for example, opponents of Parris tended to be more wealthy and to live and own land close to the adjacent commercial town of Salem, and were less likely to be members of the Salem Village church. Thus, in part, Boyer and Nissenbaum contend "that the accusations of 1692 represented a direct and conscious continuation of factional conflict" (p. 186).

All of this points to a major difficulty and an important caveat regarding historical analysis. Historical events invariably are subject to a variety of interpretations. It is possible for more than one interpretation to be valid, especially if the interpretations represent different levels (e.g., psychological versus sociological) or focus on different aspects of an event. For example, in explaining the witchcraft mania, one may not only account for why it took place at this point in time in the Massachusetts colony (which is what Erikson was attempting to explain), but also why it was focused in the community of Salem Village (which Boyer and Nissenbaum explained), why it began among these particular girls, why the citizens of the community actually could believe that there were witches in their midst [which historian Chadwick Hansen (1969) has attempted to explain], and so forth.

On the other hand, if the researcher assumes that some explanations may be valid while others are not, then it becomes important to entertain various plausible interpretations and to evaluate these critically in light of the evidence. How well does a given interpretation account for the evidence? What does the interpretation assume and what consequences follow from it? Chambliss assumes a singularly valid explanation in raising such questions about Erikson's hypothesis: If Erikson is right, then it follows that the witchcraft mania (as well as the other crime waves) should have increased community solidarity. Did this occur? If each crime wave increased solidarity, then why did the community experience three major crime waves in a period of 60 years? These are precisely the kinds of critical issues that must be raised about *any* historical interpretation. Better yet, the historical analyst should entertain and critically evaluate multiple interpretations and hypotheses and compare the relative plausibility of each. Only then can we reach an understanding of events in the scientific sense.

Content Analysis

William Chambliss and Kai Erikson have rather divergent perspectives on the functions of crime in society. So it is not surprising that they would arrive at different interpretations of the events in Salem Village. This difference points to one of the problems with the mere *reading* of written documents—the lack of agreement or reliability. One way to overcome this problem is to be explicit about how one should read the text. In fact, it is possible to develop systematic and objective criteria for transforming written text into highly reliable quantitative data. That is the goal of content analysis.

More than just a single technique, content analysis is really a set of methods for analyzing the symbolic content of any communication. The basic idea is to reduce the total content of a communication (e.g., all of the words or all of the visual imagery) to a set of categories that represent some characteristic of research interest. Thus, content analysis may involve the systematic description of either verbal or nonverbal materials.

Sales's analysis (1973) of comic strips and Archer and associates' measurement of facial prominence (1983) are examples of content analysis. However, Goffman's study (1979) of the meaning of gender roles as represented in magazine advertisements is not; he neither specified his content categories prior to the analysis nor systematically selected and described advertisements in terms of these categories. On the other hand, Goffman's study does suggest a set of gestures and body position cues that might be used to do a content analysis. Rather than casually look for evidence of such gestures, we would need to (1) identify the categories into which the ads are to be coded (e.g., male versus female; body position—standing, sitting, recumbent); (2) define the categories according to objective criteria that can be applied by anyone; (3) systematically select and then code the advertisements in terms of these objective criteria; and (4) report the frequency of the categories into which the ads have been coded.

The process just described is exactly the same as that found in systematic observation studies. It is also the same process that one would use in analyzing open-ended questions (see Box 14.1). Sociologists have used content analysis to analyze unstructured interviews, and psychologists have applied it to verbal responses that are designed to assess the psychological states of persons. So as you can see, its application is not limited to the analysis of existing data. Still, its most common application is to the available printed or spoken word. Content analysis has been applied to written documents with varied and complex content, including newspaper editorials (Namenwirth, 1969), political party platforms (Weber, 1985), novels (Griswold, 1981), and recorded speeches (Seider, 1974). Let us take a closer look at the steps in carrying out such an analysis: selecting and defining content categories, defining the unit of analysis, deciding on a system of enumeration, and carrying out the analysis (Holsti, 1969).

Selecting and defining content categories. To the extent that human coders are used, selecting and defining the categories for content analysis is analogous to deciding on a set of closed-ended questions in survey research. Instead of giving the questions to respondents who provide the answers, the content analyst applies them to a document and codes the appropriate category. The "questions" applied to the document should be adequate for the research purpose, and the categories should be clearly defined, exhaustive, and mutually exclusive.

Recall that Sales asked one question of the comic strips he analyzed: Is the central character strong and powerful? Wendy Griswold (1981), who analyzed a random sample of 130 novels published in the late nineteenth and early twentieth centuries, was interested in how the American novel might reflect unique properties of American character and experience. Accordingly, she asked several questions pertaining to characteristics of the protagonist (e.g., gender, age, social class at the beginning of novel, social class at the end) and to the plot (e.g., What is the setting of the main action? What is the time period? Is adult heterosexual love important to the plot? Is money important in the novel?).

Both Sales and Griswold used human coders to record category "answers." In fact, Griswold's study is unusual because of her large sample of novels, which required 10 readers/coders. Namenwirth (1969), on the other hand, used a computer in order to describe the editorial orientation of British elite and mass newspapers. First, he typed the text of 144 newspaper editorials into the computer. Then he provided the computer with a "dictionary" similar in structure to a thesaurus. The dictionary contained several hundred frequently used words from the editorials to be analyzed, which were entered into one or more of ninety-nine categories. For example, words referring to buildings and building parts were placed in the category "social place"; words such as job, ability, engineer, hunter, and print were included in the category "technological."

Regardless of whether one uses a human coder or a computer, the reliability and overall value of the content analysis depends on the clear formulation of content categories and of definitions or rules for assigning units to categories.

Defining the unit of analysis. Content analysts refer to their units of analysis as *recording units*. The recording unit is that element of the text that is described by the content categories. It could be the single word or symbol, the sentence, paragraph, or other grammatical unit, the whole text, or some other aspect of the text such as the character or plot. Namenwirth's recording unit was the word, whereas Griswold used three different units—character, plot, and whole novel. Sales's unit, on the other hand, was the character.

In general, smaller units may be coded more reliably than larger units because they contain less information (R. P. Weber, 1985). On the other hand, smaller units such as words may not be sufficient to extract the meaning of the message, and there may be too many such units for the researcher to manage. Imagine, for example, using the word as the recording unit in Griswold's analysis of 130 novels! These limitations apply to the use of computers in content analysis because, at this time, the only units programmable for computer analysis are words, word senses, and phrases such as idioms and proper nouns.

Because it may not be possible to place the recording unit in a particular category without considering the context in which it appears, content analysts also distinguish *context units* (Holsti, 1969). One of Namenwirth's findings was that British elite newspapers were more concerned about relations with Europe and less concerned about the Cold War than mass newspapers. Concern with Cold War issues was indicated by a large number of references to the word categories "Soviet," "American," and "Atlantic." From a simple analysis of words, however, one cannot infer the extent to which editorial positions on the Cold War generally were pro- or anti-American. To make this inference, the coder would need to consider the larger context unit—the sentence, paragraph, or whole editorial—in which the words are embedded. Similarly, Sales's coders would need to be familiar with the comic strip in order to make judgments about the power of the main character; thus his recording unit is the character and his context unit is the comic strip.

Deciding on a system of enumeration. There are many ways of quantifying the data in content analysis. The most basic systems of quantification are listed here.

1. *Time/space measures.* Early content analysis of newspapers often measured the space (e.g., in column inches) devoted to certain topics. Analogously, television content has been measured in time (e.g., the number of hours of televised violence). Another example is Archer and associates' measurement of facial prominence (distance from top of head to chin divided by length of whole body).

2. *Appearance.* Sometimes it is sufficient simply to record whether or not a given category appears in a recording unit. Sales's measurement consisted of classifying the central character in a given comic strip as powerful or not. Many of Griswold's categories were measured in this way: Is the main character a male? Is religion important to the plot?

3. *Frequency.* The most common method of measuring content is in terms of the frequency with which a given category appears in the contextual unit. Namenwirth counted the number of times categories appeared in each newspaper editorial. In an

analysis of the Democratic and Republican party platforms, R. P. Weber (1985) calculated the proportion of words in the category "wealth" (e.g., capital, inflation, unemployment).[7]

4. *Intensity*. When attitudes and values are the objects of the research, the content analyst may resort to measures of intensity. For example, rather than ask whether money is important to the novel's plot, one might ask *how* important it is. Devising mechanisms for making judgments of intensity is essentially the same as the construction of indexes and scales, which we discuss in chapter 13.

How the researcher decides to enumerate the data depends on the requirements of the problem under investigation. However, the choice of a system of enumeration carries with it certain assumptions regarding the nature of the data and the inferences that one can draw from the data (Holsti, 1969). Space-time measures may appropriately describe certain gross characteristics of the mass media, but they are too imprecise to serve as indicators of most verbal content. Appearance measures also tend to be rather imprecise, although they are more flexible and can be applied to a larger range of content than time-space measures. Frequency measures are better still, but involve two crucial assumptions that should be examined: first, they assume that the frequency of a word or category is a valid indicator of its importance, value, or intensity; second, they assume that each individual count is of *equal* importance, value, or intensity. It may be that some categories or some recording units should be weighted more heavily than others. It has been suggested, for example, that front-page articles might be more important and therefore weighted more than articles appearing elsewhere in a newspaper (Holsti, 1969). (Box 12.2 also discusses the problem of making inferences from frequencies of the "manifest" content of materials.)

Carrying out the analysis. To carry out the analysis, one first obtains a sample of material. As in survey sampling, the researcher should always be mindful of the population to which inferences are to be made. Three populations are relevant to content analysis: communication sources (e.g., types of newspapers, novels, speeches), documents (e.g., specific newspaper issues), and text within documents (e.g., pages). Often a sample of documents is drawn from a single source; for example, Griswold took a random sample of all novels published in the United States between 1876 and 1910. Namenwirth first sampled communication sources, purposefully choosing three British prestige newspapers and three mass papers. Then he randomly selected twenty-four documents—newspaper editorials—from each of the papers. Although researchers also have sampled text, R. P. Weber (1985:43) recommends that the entire text be analyzed when possible because this preserves its semantic coherence. If it is necessary to sample text, then meanings are best preserved by sampling paragraphs rather than sentences.

Having selected the sample, one proceeds to code the material according to the coding categories and system of enumeration. This gives the analyst a description of the communication content. Finally, the content analyst truly engages in *analysis* by relating content categories to one another or by relating the characteristics of the content to some other variable. Griswold compared the content of novels written by American and foreign authors, finding many similarities but also some interesting differences. For instance, American authors were likely to place protagonists in the

BOX 12.2

Perspectives on Gender Differences in Graffiti

The grist for the content analyst—recorded language and visual representations—are essentially messages in a communication process. The object of content analysis is to uncover the *meanings* of the message. Among the many possible meanings, at least one will be manifestly understood by the source as well as the receiver of the message, but a great many more meanings may be latent to one or both parties. Thus the message may reveal something about the characteristics or unconscious intent of the source or about the beliefs and values of a group or culture. But how one comes to understand these meanings depends on the theoretical orientation that informs the analysis. Nowhere else is this better illustrated than in research on restroom graffiti.

Thirty years of research on restroom graffiti shows that the inscriptions written by men differ from those written by women. Edward Bruner and Jane Paige Kelso (1980) divide this research into two types. One type establishes categories of manifest observations (e.g., sexual humor, racial insults, romantic, political), and then assigns each graffito to one of these categories. These studies show where gender differences lie (e.g., men use more insults, women are more romantic) but leave unclear the meanings of these differences. In this research, according to Bruner and Kelso, "there is an implicit theory of text which assumes that the meaning is the message, and that significance will be revealed by counting the frequency with which items of manifest content appear. The graffiti mean what the graffiti say, without any attempt to interpret the text" (p. 240).

The second type of research goes beyond the manifest meaning to a deeper level of interpretation. These studies interpret graffiti in terms of such Freudian imagery as unconscious impulses, infantile sexuality, and primitive thoughts. As Bruner and Kelso point out, however, the "connection between the data and the Freudian meaning is not readily apparent," and this approach suffers from "an over-attribution of meaning compared to the under-attribution" characteristic of the first approach.

By contrast, Bruner and Kelso offer a "semiotic perspective." Noting that graffiti are never found where others will not be able to see them, they argue that restroom graffiti constitute communication among anonymous partners. "The writing of graffiti," they say, "is an essentially social act that cannot be understood in terms of the expressive functions performed for an isolated individual. To write graffiti is to communicate; one never finds graffiti where they cannot be seen by others" (p. 241). Moreover, given the segregation of restrooms in American culture, restroom graffiti must be understood as same-sex communication—men writing for other men, and women writing for other women.

Approaching the data from this perspective, Bruner and Kelso find that on the surface, women's graffiti are more interpersonal and interactive than those written by men. Men tend to write egocentric and competitive inscriptions about sexual conquests and sexual prowess and derogatory inscriptions that attack, insult, or put down; women tend to raise serious questions about love, sexual relations, and commitment, often soliciting or giving advice regarding women's relationships with men. Going beyond this surface text, Bruner and Kelso conclude that "the underlying message in both male and female graffiti is fundamentally political." "Graffiti reflect the power positions of men and women in the social structure" (p. 250). Accordingly, "men

BOX 12.2 (*continued*)

write graffiti to tell themselves and other men that they have maintained their superior position and are still in control," while women write graffiti that "express the cooperation of the dominated and reflect the strategy of mutual help employed by those in a subordinate status" (pp. 249–250).

middle class; foreign authors favored the upper class. American authors also were more likely to set their novels in small towns and less likely to set the action in the home.

R. P. Weber's content analysis of party platforms (1985) showed how Democrats and Republicans have varied over time in their concerns. Figure 12.1 shows the pattern of change with respect to the percentage of each platform devoted to economic matters. The vertical axis is based on the percentage of words in the platform that fall into the category "wealth."[8] Weber points out several features of the figure: (1) the general rise between 1844 and about 1952 in the level of concern about economic matters, perhaps reflecting the increasing importance of the federal government in the management of economic affairs; (2) the relatively constant level of concern from 1952 to the present; (3) and the change over time in the relationship between the parties' concern with economic matters, with the parties manifesting

FIGURE 12.1. Democratic and Republican concern with wealth, 1844–1980. Diamonds, Republican platforms; stars, Democratic platforms.

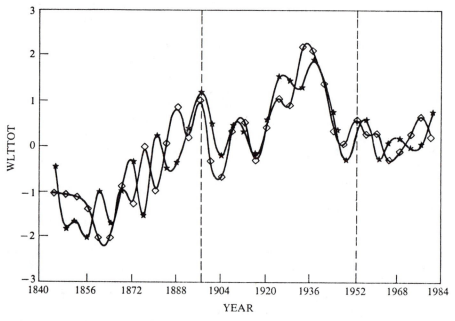

Source: Page 139 of R. P. Weber, "Computer-Aided Content Analysis: A Short Primer," *Qualitative Sociology*, vol. 7, 1984.

similar levels of concern between 1896 and 1952 and moving opposite to one another before and after this period.

Cohort Analysis

It is unfortunate that most social research is static and ahistorical, but it is easy to understand why. Experiments are by nature brief events, and for economic reasons, most surveys are cross-sectional and field research cannot be carried out over lengthy periods of time. Available survey data, however, are making it increasingly possible to analyze social change. Paul Burstein's study (1979) relating trends in attitudes toward discrimination to antidiscrimination legislation represents one form of such research: the analysis of trends in an entire population. The cohort study is another representative form of longitudinal research.

A *cohort* consists of persons (or other units such as organizations and neighborhoods) who experience the same significant life event within a specified period of time (Glenn, 1977). Most often the life event that defines a cohort is birth, but it also might be marriage, completion of high school, entry into medical school, and so forth. Demographers long have analyzed birth cohorts from census data to predict population trends. In the last 25 years social researchers also have begun to do cohort analyses using survey data archives. Such analyses identify cohorts by their age, and they trace changes through sample surveys taken at regular intervals. A sample of 18-year-olds in a 1980 survey, for example, would be represented by a sample of 28-year-olds in a 1990 survey and 38-year-olds in a 2000 survey.

Cohort analyses enable one to study three different influences associated with the passage of time. To get a sense of these influences and of the difficulty of studying them at a single point in time, consider a cross-sectional survey containing measures of age and alcohol consumption. If we found that alcohol consumption is negatively correlated with age, this could be due to one of two kinds of influences: *life course* (as people grow older, they drink less) or *cohort* (older generations drink less than younger generations). By the same token, if we found no association between age and alcohol consumption, this does not necessarily mean that alcohol consumption would not change in subsequent years. The absence of association may be due to a third influence of aging—the effects of specific *historical periods*. As times change, so might the consumption of alcohol (and so might other aging effects on the consumption of alcohol). The problem with cross-sectional data is that one cannot begin to disentangle these various effects. Let us see how we can begin to separate them in a standard cohort table.

Table 12.1 presents hypothetical data for the percentage of respondents who said they drank alcoholic beverages. The first column identifies the respondent's age at the time of the survey; the second column indicates the cohorts (diagonals A, B, etc.); subsequent columns present percentages for each of four cross-sectional surveys conducted in 1950, 1960, 1970, and 1980. Notice that the 10-year cohorts (e.g., B, C) correspond to the 10-year intervals between the survey dates. We can make three comparisons within the body of such a table: (1) by reading down the columns, we can compare different cohorts during the same time period; (2) by reading diagonally down and to the right, we can trace changes in a given cohort

TABLE 12.1. Percentage of Respondents Who Said They Drank Alcoholic Beverages, by
Age, for Four Time Periods (Hypothetical Age Effects)

Age interval	Cohort	Period			
		1950	1960	1970	1980
	A				
20–29	B	70	70	70	70
30–39	C	65	65	65	65
40–49	D	60	60	60	60
50–59	E	55	55	55	55
60–69	F	50	50	50	50
70–79		45	45	45	45

over time; and (3) by reading across the rows, we can compare trends at each age
level as different cohorts replace one another (Glenn, 1977:10).

In Table 12.1, we find systematic changes when reading down and diagonally,
but no change when reading across; that is, for any given period and for any given
cohort, we find a decrease in five percentage points for each 10-year increment in
age. This pattern suggests a life course or *age effect*: changes associated with
growing older cause a decrease in the consumption of alcoholic beverages.

Variation among the percentages in a cohort table also may be due to the effects
of membership in particular cohorts (called *cohort effects*) or to the influence of
time periods (called *period effects*). Table 12.2 shows the pattern of percentages
that represents a pure cohort effect. Notice that there is no variation within each
cohort (reading diagonally), but there are systematic changes across cohorts (reading either across or down). A pure period effect (not shown) would be represented
by no variation within periods (reading down) but changes across periods both
within (reading diagonally) and across cohorts (reading across).

With actual data most cohort tables show evidence of at least two of the three
effects. However, Glenn (1977) notes that the pattern predicted by pure age effects
(Table 12.1) is surprisingly frequent. He also points out that there may be other

TABLE 12.2. Percentage of Respondents Who Said They Drank Alcohol Beverages, by
Age, for Four Time Periods (Hypothetical Cohort Effects)

Age interval	Period			
	1950	1960	1970	1980
20–29	70	75	80	85
30–39	65	70	75	80
40–49	60	65	70	75
50–59	55	60	65	70
60–69	50	55	60	65
70–79	45	50	55	60

TABLE 12.3. Percentage of Respondents Who Said
They Drank Alcoholic Beverages, by Age, for Three Time Periods
(Actual Data)

Age interval	1956–1957 (N)	1966 (N)	1977 (N)
20–29	64.4 (839)	75.8 (557)	81.7 (644)
30–39	66.1 (1188)	74.0 (585)	76.9 (450)
40–49	62.5 (1120)	67.1 (735)	75.2 (439)
50–59	54.5 (785)	67.1 (656)	69.3 (362)
60–69	45.9 (569)	50.6 (518)	58.2 (335)
70–79	39.1 (307)	49.7 (310)	53.2 (190)

Source: Page 366 of Glenn (1981). Copyright 1981 by The Gerontological Society of America. Used by permission.

plausible explanations for the patterns predicted by pure age, cohort, or period effects. Moreover, the variations in the cells of the table may reflect still other sources of variability, such as those due to sampling or the death of some cohort members (Hyman, 1972:276–290). Consequently, one must be careful in interpreting cohort tables. With this in mind, try your hand at analyzing Table 12.3, which contains actual data from a series of Gallup polls.

Reading across the rows and down the columns reveals fairly systematic changes across cohorts: as age increases, the percentage who drink alcoholic beverages decreases. Reading diagonally within each cohort, we find no systematic change and, in fact, very little variation, most of which could be the result of sampling error. Thus the pattern appears to reflect a pure cohort effect: each cohort entering adulthood in recent years has contained a larger percentage of drinkers than the one before it. And it is apparently this trend that accounts for the overall increase in the percentage of drinkers in the adult population (Glenn, 1981:366). Another interpretation, however, is more consistent with other data on age and drinking. The data in Table 12.3 also may reflect a combination of positive period effects and negative age effects. That is, drinking does indeed decline with age, but this age effect is offset in the table percentages by an overall increase in drinking between the late 1950s and the late 1970s.

This table points to a fundamental problem with cohort analysis. The standard approach in data analysis is to allow one (independent) variable to vary while the others are held constant. However, no matter how we read the table (diagonally, across, or down), two variables vary at the same time. For example, when we read a cohort table diagonally, both period and age vary; when we read the table across, both period and cohort vary; when we read the table down, both age and cohort vary. Usually researchers get around this problem by ignoring or assuming the absence of one of the effects or by some rather complex statistical analyses (see Fienberg and Mason, 1979). A further discussion of these issues is beyond this text. Our purpose here is to introduce you to cohort analysis and to alert you to certain problems of interpretation that it presents.

Summary

In contrast to research strategies that rely on data collected firsthand, the available data researcher mines secondhand information. The sources of such information include the written public record, ranging from court proceedings, vital statistics, and publication indexes to the voluminous data files of the Census Bureau; private documents such as diaries, letters, business records, and tax reports; the mass media; nonverbal physical evidence such as works of art, clothing, and other artifacts; and social science data archives generated from surveys and ethnographies.

Available data research, especially the secondary analysis of existing survey data, is currently the most popular method of social research. Compared to other research strategies, it is better suited to cross-cultural research and to studies of the past and of social change. In addition, it often can provide the means to increase sample size and to replicate research, it generally costs less to the individual researcher, and it often provides nonreactive measures of concepts.

It is far more preferable to let the research problem guide the search for sources of available data than simply to dredge existing data sets for interesting findings. The research literature may provide useful leads to locating sources, which may be augmented by consulting a librarian or various listings of publicly accessible data sets. After gaining access to the data, one should consider their adequacy as a sample of information. Fortunately, much of the data from the census and various survey archives are based on unusually good, though not error-free, samples. Written records from the more remote past, however, invariably suffer from selective deposit, and physical materials are subject to selective survival. For voluminous data sets, probability sampling based on time and/or space is often possible.

When one uses data collected for another purpose, the evaluation and refinement of the data become extremely important research phases. Available survey questions, for example, may provide less than satisfactory measures, requiring the abandonment or modification of the researcher's hypothesis. Other sources of information may require the creative construction of substitute or indirect measures of key variables, or the use of multiple indicators. Whatever the data source, it is essential to assess the validity of the data—to determine their authenticity, whether definitions used in compiling records have changed over time, whether the meaning of words and phrases in written documents have changed, and so forth. Following such evaluation it is often necessary to refine or make adjustments to allow for proper interpretation.

Data analysis is equally important in available data research, although the kind of analysis depends largely on the source of information. In historical document analysis, a major problem is the variety of interpretations to which such data invariably are open. Ideally, the researcher should not focus on a single explanation, but instead critically evaluate and compare the relative plausibility of several explanations. To analyze the symbolic content of communication, especially verbal materials from the media, researchers use content analysis. This involves selecting and defining a set of content categories, defining and then sampling the elements of the text that are described by the categories, quantifying the categories such as by counting their frequency of occurrence, and then relating category frequencies to one another or to other variables. Among the analytical techniques for longitudinal research is cohort analysis, which attempts to assess the relative effects of age (life course), period (current history), and cohort (generation or past history).

Key Terms

public documents	*selective survival*
vital statistics	*selective deposit*
manuscript census	*content analysis*
Public Use Microdata Sample	*recording units*
private documents	*context units*
mass media	*cohort analysis*
physical, nonverbal evidence	*age effect*
data archives	*cohort effect*
secondary analysis	*period effect*
nonreactive measurement	

Review Questions and Problems

1. How does research using available data differ from the other three basic approaches to social research?

2. What are the five categories of available data described in this chapter?

3. Give three examples of public records other than those mentioned in the text that might serve as sources of data. In each case, identify a hypothesis that might be tested with the data.

4. What information is contained in birth certificates? In death certificates?

5. In what forms does the Census Bureau release information from the decennial census?

6. What is the manuscript census? When is it released to the general public? How else are individual-level data made available to the public?

7. What are private documents? Give an example of a private document available to you that might serve as a source of data. What research question might be addressed with these data?

8. How could you use the mass media to study changes in racial stereotypes? What period would you study? Which medium would you select?

9. What do the authors mean when they say that the "use of data archives is an extension of both survey research and field research"?

10. What is the General Social Survey? When did it begin?

11. What are the principal advantages of research using available data?

12. Compare research using available data with the other three methodological approaches in terms of the problem of reactive measurement.

13. Identify two guidelines for locating appropriate sources of available data.

14. Aside from research using survey data archives, what are the special sampling problems presented by research using available data?

15. What particular measurement problems are presented by research using available data?

16. What is meant by "indirect measurement"? How is Sales's study of authoritarianism an example of indirect measurement?

17. How do users of historical documents go about determining the validity and reliability of their data?

18. What are the three interpretations of the Salem witchcraft hysteria described in the text? Is it possible for all three of these interpretations to be valid? Why or why not?

19. What is content analysis? Why is Sales's study of comic strips an example and Goffman's study of gender displays *not* an example of this method?

20. What steps are involved in doing a content analysis?

21. Identify common units of analysis in content analysis. What is the difference between a recording unit and a context unit?

22. What are the basic systems for quantifying data in content analysis?

23. Using Box 12.2 as an example, discuss the problem of using frequency counts for content analysis.

24. Describe how you would carry out a content analysis to examine some of the issues raised by Goffman's study of gender displays. (a) What materials will you select for analysis? (b) How will you sample them? (c) How will you select and define content categories? (d) What is the recording unit? (e) What is the context unit? (f) What system of enumeration will you use?

25. What are the three kinds of influences examined in cohort analysis?

26. How do cohort tables violate the principle of allowing only one thing to vary at a time?

NOTES

1. For a comphrehensive listing of sources of demographic information, see Shryock et al. (1976).

2. For a complete list of population and housing items included in the 1980 census, see Kaplan and Van Valey (1980:170).

3. Hakim's analysis (1982:23) of articles in the two leading sociology journals, *American Sociological Review* and *American Journal of Sociology*, in 1979 showed that two-thirds of the articles were based on the analysis of existing survey data.

4. This refers, of course, to the cost to the individual secondary analyst. The cost of producing the data is considerable. In 1986, for example, the field and data collection costs for the GSS were $506,000.

5. *Primary* sources are eyewitness accounts of the events described, whereas *secondary* sources consist of indirect evidence obtained from primary sources. Kai Erikson used both types of evidence in his study of deviance in puritan New England: court records and the journals of those witnessing the events of the time (primary), and the writings of numerous historians (secondary).

6. The net flow of migration to a country is equal to the number of immigrants entering minus the number of emigrants returning. The gross flow is simply the number entering.

7. Word counts have proven especially useful in content analyses designed to determine who wrote a certain document. A study of the disputed authorship of several of *The Federal-*

ist papers showed, for example, that the disputed authors James Madison and Alexander Hamilton differed in known writings in their rate of use of noncontextual words like "by" and "to." When the papers were analyzed, the rate of use of these words corresponded closely in all but one paper to Madison's rather than Hamilton's writing (Mosteller and Wallace, 1964).

8. In order to eliminate differences of scale in the figure, the data were standardized for each party to a mean of zero and a standard deviation of 1.0 (R. P. Weber, 1985:84).

13

Multiple Methods

The preceding chapters described four principal research strategies for understanding the social world: experiments, surveys, field research, and research using available data. By studying these approaches separately, you may have gotten the idea that these are entirely separate ways to proceed, that decisions about methods are necessarily of the either-or variety. However, given the limitations and biases inherent in each of the main approaches—indeed, inherent in all research procedures—the best way to study most research topics is to combine methodological approaches. This chapter examines some of these "multiple methods" combinations, ranging from multiple measures of concepts within the same study to multiple tests of hypotheses across different studies.

Triangulation

In their everyday lives, people frequently use more than one means to solve a problem. Consider, for example, the simple problem of arising earlier than usual in order to catch a flight. Let us say a woman presented with this problem normally awakens by means of an electric clock radio set for 7:00 A.M. In order to make sure that she awakened by 6:00, she might employ several methods. She might set the clock radio for 5:55, set a windup alarm clock for 6:00, and ask an early-rising friend to phone her at 6:05. She would then have three independent and somewhat dissimilar methods for solving the problem. If the electricity should go off, the windup alarm would work. If the windup alarm were defective, then the friend should come through. If the friend proved unreliable, one of the other methods should work. By using multiple methods that do not share the same inherent weaknesses, we enhance our chances of solving the problem.

Social scientists have borrowed the term *triangulation* from the field of navigation to help describe how the use of multiple approaches to a research question can enable an investigator to "zero in" on the answers or information sought. To understand the conventional meaning of triangulation, imagine that you are an employee of the Federal Communications Commission (FCC) assigned the task of determining the location of a pirate (unlicensed) radio station (P). First, using a FCC mobile receiver with directional-finder antenna, you measure the direction to the pirate radio station from a certain point, point A, and again from a second point,

FIGURE 13.1. Triangulating a pirate radio station (P) from two points (A and B).

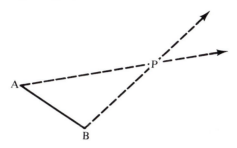

point B. Knowing the distance between points A and B, you can now determine the distance AP or BP, using trigonometry, and thus the position of P (Figure 13.1).

The process of triangulation in navigation requires accurate measuring instruments. Suppose, for example, that your directional-finder antenna was off calibration (biased), so that it always gave a figure that was 15 degrees below the true figure. In that case you would fail to locate the pirate station (Figure 13.2). After failing to find the station, you might suspect that the measuring instrument (the directional antenna) was inaccurate, or you might entertain the possibility that the "concept" being measured changed between the first and second measurements (i.e., the pirate is a mobile radio station).

In social research, the logic of triangulation applies to situations in which two or more dissimilar measuring instruments or approaches are used. These approaches are analogous to the different vantage points, A and B, in the figure. The key to triangulation is the use of *dissimilar* methods or measures, which do not share the same methodological weaknesses—that is, errors and biases. The observations or "scores" produced by each method will ordinarily contain some error. But if the pattern of error varies, as it should with different methods, and if these methods independently produce or "zero-in" on the same findings, then our confidence in the result increases. Previously, we encountered the triangulation principle in discussions of convergent validity assessment (chapter 5) and repeated and varied testing to increase the credibility of hypotheses (chapter 3).

Unfortunately, social researchers rely altogether too frequently on a single method or measure when a number of approaches could be brought to bear on the research question (Webb et al., 1981). Suppose, for example, you are investigating the hypothesis that airline disasters increase the anxiety of air travelers. Rather than rely on a single measure of anxiety, it would be better to use several. Webb et al.

FIGURE 13.2. Triangulating a pirate radio station (P) from two points (A and B), with directional-finder antenna off calibration by 15 degrees.

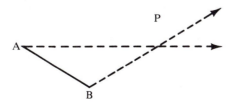

(1981) suggested the following indicators of anxiety: increased sales of alcoholic beverages at airport bars, increased sales of flight insurance policies, and decreased sales of air travel tickets following a disaster. Any one of these indicators, by itself, represents a relatively weak measure of anxiety. But note that the three measures do not share the same weaknesses: a downturn in the economy might decrease sales of tickets but would probably not affect the sales of inexpensive trip insurance policies to a great extent; publicity on insurance policy rip-offs could decrease policy sales but would not be expected to affect bar sales or ticket sales; an increase in the price of drinks might affect bar sales but would not be expected to affect the other measures, and so forth. Thus, if all three indicators of anxiety point to a relationship between airline disasters and travelers' anxiety, we can be relatively confident that such a relationship exists. For as the number of dissimilar indicators increases, the likelihood that the relationship is an artifact of measurement error or spuriously created by an uncontrolled extraneous variable (such as a downturn in the economy) decreases.

The use of *multiple methods* refers here to "methods" in the broadest sense. In addition to the use of multiple indicators of a single concept, as in the above example, triangulation can also involve multiple tests of a hypothesis. Each test ordinarily uses a separate sample of subjects and different measures of key variables. Multiple tests also may entail either the same research strategy or a combination of strategies, such as when a researcher uses both experimentation and the analysis of available data to test the same hypothesis. We now examine each of these multiple "methods," starting with the use of multiple indicators in the same study.

Multiple Measures of Concepts within the Same Study

Suppose we want to test the hypothesis that a mother's expression of love toward her infant is directly related to the mother having a positive self-concept. In Figure 13.3, an arrow pointing from the independent variable ("positive self-concept") to the dependent variable ("mother love") represents the hypothesis. "Mother love" is

FIGURE 13.3. Diagram of the relationship between positive self-concept and mother love, with three indicators per concept.

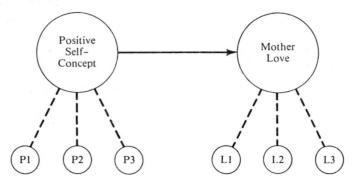

measured by the indicators L1 (amount of *time* a mother spends with the child), L2 (frequency of *physical contacts* such as lifting, holding, kissing, and stroking the child), and L3 (duration of *verbalizations* such as talking, singing, and cooing to the child); "positive self-concept" is also measured by three distinct indicators P1, P2, and P3. There are two general ways to analyze the results of a study such as this that uses multiple measures: (1) reduce the complexity of the data by combining all measures of each concept into a composite measure (an index or scale), and then determine whether the composite measures are related in the way hypothesized; or (2) formulate a model to represent the relationships among concepts as well as the measures of those concepts, and then test the model to see how well it fits the data. Let us examine each of these approaches in some detail.

Composite Measures: Indexes and Scales

Multiple measures are often combined into an index or scale. As we pointed out in chapter 5, it is difficult to measure a concept well with a single indicator or question. Not only do single indicators rarely capture all the meaning of a concept, but each indicator is likely to have distinctive sources of error or bias. By combining several indicators into a composite measure, we generally get a better overall representation of the concept, and the errors tend to cancel each other out, yielding a more reliable measure.

An example is provided by the questions on abortion included in the General Social Surveys (GSS) (Davis and Smith, 1985):

Please tell me whether or not you think it should be possible for a pregnant woman to obtain a legal abortion if . . . . [The interviewer then reads each of the following statements.]
  A. If there is a strong chance of serious defect in the baby?
  B. If she is married and does not want any more children?
  C. If the woman's own health is seriously endangered by the pregnancy?
  D. If the family has a very low income and cannot afford any more children?
  E. If she became pregnant as a result of rape?
  F. If she is not married and does not want to marry the man?

Responses to these questions may reflect attitudes unrelated to abortion per se, such as attitudes toward handicaps (A), large families (B), growing up in poverty (D), rape (E), or premarital sex (F). However, by combining these items into an index, we avoid the biases inherent in any single item. For example, if only question C were used as our measure, then the overwhelming majority of the U.S. population would be proabortion. If only question B were used, then the majority would be antiabortion (Davis, 1980). In either case we would have a biased estimate of the general attitude toward abortion in the United States. On the other hand, if all six items were used, then we would get a better overall estimate, one that is less likely than any single item to under- or overestimate the strength of individuals' attitudes.

How are separate measures combined or "aggregated"? The simplest and most common procedure is just to add or to take an average of the scores of the separate items; this is what we generally mean by an *index*. For example, public attitudes toward racial integration have been surveyed repeatedly with the use of a five-item index developed by Donald J. Treiman (Taylor, Sheatsley, and Greeley, 1978). Below are the items.

1. Do you think white students and black students should go to the same schools or to separate schools?
2. How strongly would you object if a member of your family wanted to bring a black friend home to dinner?
3. White people have a right to keep blacks out of their neighborhoods if they want to, and blacks should respect that right. (Do you strongly agree, agree, . . . , or strongly disagree?)
4. Do you think there should be laws against marriages between blacks and whites?
5. Blacks shouldn't push themselves where they're not wanted. (Do you strongly agree, agree, . . . , or strongly disagree?)

The index consists of the number of prointegration responses to these five items; thus, scores may range from zero (strongly antiintegrationist) to five (strongly prointegrationist). Interestingly, since 1963 the average score for the U.S. adult population has consistently increased.

Keyfitz (1976) provides another example of an index, one that is constructed from population estimates rather than questionnaire items. To study the relationship between use of natural resources and the growth of the world middle class, he needed some way to estimate the size of the world middle class in different years. He obtained this estimate by developing an index based on four separate indicators. Each indicator required mathematical operations that we will not describe, but briefly, the four indicators were based on the number of passenger cars in use, the number of telephones, electric energy produced, and the consumption of crude oil. The values yielded by the four separate estimates of the world middle class were then averaged. One of the conclusions of the study was that, if more of the poor are to enter the high-consumption middle class, ways must be found to support the middle class standard of living with less energy and natural resources.

In both examples above, each of the multiple measures (questionnaire items or separate population estimates) was assumed to be of equal value in determining the index score. In other words, each indicator was given the same "weight" in computing the index. One could, however, assign different weights by multiplying the separate indicators by different values (weights). Measures of socioeconomic status, for example, typically combine indicators of occupational prestige, education, and income. But because occupational prestige is thought to contribute more to socioeconomic status, it is generally weighted more heavily. Thus, in Hollingshead's (1971) two-factor Index of Social Position, an occupation score is given a weight of 7 and an education score is given a weight of 4. To compute the index, one would first determine an individual's occupation and education scores on separate seven-point measures; multiply each score times its respective weight; and then add the score-weight products.

The advantage of indexing may be illustrated as follows. Suppose the value of each observed measure (*X*) is equal to a true score corresponding to the concept being measured (*C*) and an error score (*e*); thus, $X = C + e$. Now suppose that we have four different measures, and pretend we know the true and error scores for a particular respondent (see tabulation).

Measure	Observed score (X)	True score (C)	Error score (e)
Item 1	2	4	−2
Item 2	3	2	+1
Item 3	7	5	+2
Item 4	5	8	−3
Total	17	19	−2

For each separate item, about one-third or more of the observed score represents error. If the error tends to be random (or if systematic but in different directions for the separate items), the error scores tend to cancel out when we sum over the items. Consequently, if we form an index by summing the four items, we obtain a greatly improved measure. For the particular respondent shown above, the index score would be 17 units, only a small fraction of which represents error (2 units).

While most composite measures constitute indexes, multiple indicators may also be combined to form *scales*. The distinction between an index and a scale is rather fuzzy, and some social scientists use the terms interchangeably. But we think it is a distinction worth making. An index usually refers to the arbitrary combination of indicators, such as when we simply add together the responses to separate items without regard to what each actually contributes to the measurement of the underlying concept. The chief problem with an index is ensuring *unidimensionality*, as it may be measuring more than the intended concept (e.g., "political liberalism" as well as "attitude toward racial integration"). A scale, on the other hand, combines indicators according to nonarbitrary rules that are ordinarily designed to reflect only a single dimension of a concept.

Some scales differ from indexes by assigning scores to patterns of responses to a set of items. To illustrate the idea of patterns of responses, let us return to the Treiman index of attitudes toward racial integration referred to earlier (Taylor et al., 1978:43). Suppose that two respondents, Earl and Rudolph, gave the responses shown here to the five questions (see tabulation). If the items were scored as an index, counting prointegration responses, Earl and Rudolph would receive the same score, even though they have very different response patterns. Can one say which of the two is more racially liberal?

Question number	Earl	Rudolph
1	Prointegration	Antiintegration
2	Prointegration	Antiintegration
3	Antiintegration	Antiintegration
4	Antiintegration	Prointegration
5	Antiintegration	Prointegration

This contrived example points out a problem with index construction, namely an issue of validity. If the same score may be achieved with very different responses, the possibility exists that the items are measuring more than one dimension or concept. Besides attitudes toward racial integration, Earl's and Rudolph's responses may reflect other concepts, such as a concern to give socially desirable responses.

The construction of scales assumes that a concept can be understood in terms of an underlying continuum; in the case of an attitude, the continuum may range from favorable to unfavorable or positive to negative. It is further assumed that scores on individual items and composite measures represent specific points along the relevant continuum (or "scale"). Each score, in other words, should uniquely reflect the strength or degree of something—for example, an individual's degree of prejudice or a nation's level of modernization. But whereas these assumptions are implicit in an index, scaling procedures make them explicit and are designed to test their validity.

To illustrate a scaling technique, we will describe the approach developed by Guttman (1950). Suppose we measure people's reading ability by testing their reading comprehension of items *ordered* in terms of difficulty, such as portions of a third-grade reader, a ninth-grade textbook, and a college textbook. Subjects would be tested on each item starting with the easiest, and the item at which someone changed from "passing" to "failing" the reading tests would indicate the subject's position on a scale of reading ability. Four response patterns are expected if the items form a perfect Guttman scale: (1) flunk each item, (2) pass only at the third-grade level, (3) pass all but the college text, and (4) pass all reading tests. Other response patterns, such as passing the ninth-grade test and flunking the other two, are called "nonscale" or "mixed types." By selecting a set of items that minimize the proportion of "nonscale" response patterns, the Guttman approach attempts to ensure a unidimensional scale.

The actual process of *Guttman scaling* is sometimes quite elaborate. A researcher may start with a large battery of items thought to measure a concept. Then subsets of these items are tested, often with a computer program, to determine if they satisfy the expectations of a Guttman scale. Let us illustrate part of this process using the six GSS abortion items referred to earlier. Based on the proportion of 1975 GSS respondents answering "yes" to each question, Clogg and Sawyer (1981) ordered the items from the "easiest" condition under which to approve of abortion (woman's health is seriously endangered by the pregnancy) to the "most difficult" condition (woman does not want more children). Table 13.1 shows this question ordering and the seven response patterns possible if the items form a perfect Guttman scale. Each column in Table 13.1 displays a different response pattern ("Y" and "N" denote "yes" and "no" answers, respectively), and the "yes" responses are totaled to obtain a scale score for each response pattern.

In contrast to an index, a respondent's score on a *perfect* Guttman scale uniquely identifies the person's response pattern. In Table 13.1, for example, a score of "2" is always the pattern "Y Y N N N N." Note also that a score on a perfect Guttman scale indicates the point at which the respondent shifts from one reponse to another (e.g., those who score "3" approve of an abortion in the three "easiest" conditions and then shift to disapproval). Whether or not a set of items are reasonably close to

TABLE 13.1. Response Pattern of a Perfect Guttman Scale

Approve of an abortion if:	*Response pattern*						
The woman's own health is seriously endangered by the pregnancy?	Y	Y	Y	Y	Y	Y	N
There is a strong chance of serious defect in the baby?	Y	Y	Y	Y	Y	N	N
She became pregnant as a result of rape?	Y	Y	Y	Y	N	N	N
The family has a very low income and can't afford any more children?	Y	Y	Y	N	N	N	N
She is not married and does not want to marry the man?	Y	Y	N	N	N	N	N
She is married and does not want any more children?	Y	N	N	N	N	N	N
SCALE SCORE	6	5	4	3	2	1	0

the ideal of a perfect Guttman scale is an empirical question. Clogg and Sawyer (1981:247) report that 16.8 percent of the 1975 GSS respondents had "nonscale" response patterns (e.g., "Y N Y N N N"). Using conventional measures of scalability, they conclude that the six questions form an acceptable Guttman scale for the 1975 GSS sample. The employment of Guttman scaling to ensure unidimensionality, however, is sample dependent. A set of items may be unidimensional among one sample of respondents, but not for another. Differences in scalability across samples reflect sampling and measurement error as well as population differences (see Clogg and Sawyer, 1981, for details and alternatives to the Guttman approach).

Various scaling procedures have been developed: some capitalize on the inherent pattern among a set of items, others on each item's placement with regard to an underlying continuum. The construction of scales is a topic beyond the scope of the present text. For a good overview of the subject of index and scale construction, see Dawes and Smith (1985).

Although we have presented composite measures from the standpoint of "triangulation," there are other good reasons for building indexes and scales. One is ease of analysis: the number of variables that must be considered is reduced. Another has to do with the variability in respondents' scores provided by the measure. Sometimes items provide very little information due to low variability (e.g., 90 percent of the respondents make the same response). By combining several items with low variability, it is possible to obtain an index with much greater variability, hence, a more informative measure.

Structural Equation Modeling

Until recently indexes and scales were almost always constructed when one had multiple measures of concepts. In part this was because most social scientists were unfamiliar with procedures for analyzing multiple measures simultaneously. However, over the past two decades, simultaneous testing has become increasingly popular as sociologists have become more knowledgable about a technique called *structural equation modeling*. The term "structural modeling" refers to the systematic identification of the possible relationships among a set of concepts and their indicators. Each distinctive model describes a different "structure" of relationships that can be represented with a unique system of mathematical "equations." When applying this technique, one essentially checks to see how well the data fit various models. The mathematics required to do this are rather advanced. Still, one can get a sense of the value of structural equation modeling by considering the following example.

Recall the hypothetical study described earlier in this section involving the relationship between mother love and self-concept. All the mothers in the study would have to be measured on each of the six indicators. Since measurement may be reactive, there is the possibility that measuring L1 may influence L2, L3, or even P1 or positive self-concept. For example, the presence of an observer might affect the extent to which the mother touches the infant or perhaps even the mother's self-concept. Consequently, an adequate representation of the relationships among the variables might be considerably more complicated than indicated in Figure 13.3.

Consider Figure 13.4. Notice the arrows leading from "mother love" and "positive self-concept" to each of their respective indicators; these represent the assumption that the unobserved concepts "mother love" and "positive self-concept" cause their measured indicators. This model also shows that P1 and P2 partly share the same methodological weaknesses (diagrammed by the curved arrow between them denoting this common bias), and that the measurement of P3 influences "mother love." Obviously, there are a large number of possible models depicting the variables in Figure 13.4. For example, deleting the arrow from P3 to "mother love" or adding a curved arrow beten L1 and L3 produces a different model. It is the job of the researcher to consider the more plausible models and to test each in order to determine which "fit" the data.[1]

Structural equation modeling differs from composite measurement in that it maintains the separate identity of each indicator throughout the analysis. This requires that the researcher specify how each indicator is related to the underlying concept it measures. An advantage of this approach is that it makes it possible to test for certain kinds of measurement error. One disadvantage is that it becomes

FIGURE 13.4. Diagram of a structural equation model of the relationship between positive self-concept and mother love.

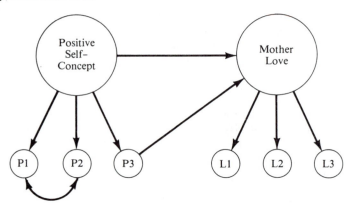

extremely difficult to consider all possible combinations of relationships as the number of indicators and concepts increases (Jacobson and Lalu, 1974). Modeling is discussed further in chapter 15.

Multiple Tests of Hypotheses across Different Studies

One of the best ways to increase our confidence in a particular finding is to repeat a study to see if we can obtain the same result. Although such replications frequently aim to duplicate the original study in as much detail as possible, they can never be exactly the same. At the very least, each *replication* is conducted at a different time, and generally will involve a different sample of cases. Thus, replications are inherently dissimilar. Further, the more dissimilar they are in terms of methods, time, place, and so forth, the greater the confidence that the findings support the research hypothesis rather than being an artifact of particular research conditions and procedures.

In spite of their value, replications are relatively infrequent in social research. Apparently, the cost of most studies cannot be justified solely for the purpose of replicating a finding. The one exception to this pattern is experimental research. Not only are small-scale experiments less costly to replicate than other kinds of research, but replication is the principal method of increasing the external validity of experimental results. In the following example, a team of investigators carried out an initial experiment and two replications to test versions of the same basic hypothesis. The experiments used different groups of subjects as well as different manipulations and measures of the hypothesis-linked concepts.

Replications Using the Same Research Strategy: Compliance without Pressure

How are people swayed to comply with a request they would prefer to refuse? Freedman, Wallington, and Bless (1967) hypothesized that one factor that leads to increased compliance is guilt: People who feel guilty are likely to try to relieve their guilt by either doing a good deed or willingly submitting to an unpleasant experience. To test this hypothesis, they designed three experiments.

In the first experiment, the investigators manipulated guilt by inducing some subjects to tell a lie while others did not. The subjects, sixty-two high school males, were randomly assigned to the experimental (lie) and control (nonlie) groups. A confederate of the experimenter, posing as the previous subject, introduced the manipulation while the experimenter was in another room "preparing the test." As the subject waited for the "test" to begin, the confederate struck up a conversation. In the lie condition, he described in detail the test the subject was about to be given; in the nonlie condition, he divulged no such information about the test. Before administering the test, the experimenter then asked each subject whether he had taken the test before or heard about it. Only one subject in the lie condition admitted that he had heard about the test; hence, all but one subject in this condition were induced to tell a direct lie, and it was assumed that they would experience guilt as a result. Each subject was then given the 40-minute test, after which he was thanked and paid for his participation. As he was leaving the room, the experimenter casually asked him if he would participate without pay as a subject in an experiment being done by someone else in the department. The study's hypothesis, that subjects who lied would be more likely to comply with the request than subjects who had not lied, was confirmed. Of the subjects in the lie condition, twenty volunteered for the additional experiment and eleven did not; the figures were exactly the opposite for the control subjects.

In the second experiment, guilt was manipulated by causing some subjects to upset "accidentally" a very large pile of carefully arranged index cards apparently containing notes for a dissertation. Sixty-seven college freshmen women served as paid subjects. The subject was greeted and led by the experimenter to a room which, she explained, had been lent to her by a graduate student. In the room was a confederate (purportedly another subject), seated at a small table on which were a pile of approximately 1000 note cards separated by topic. The manipulation occurred when the experimenter left the subject and confederate alone for 5 minutes while she went to get the tests. One leg of the small table, hidden by the confederate's chair, was 2 inches shorter than the other three legs and was supported by a small block. In two conditions, the block was removed before the subject entered the room; in the third, the block was left in place. In the "guilt" condition, the subject inevitably touched or brushed against the table, thus tipping it and scattering the cards. In the first control condition, the confederate upset the table; in the second control condition, with the block in place, no "accident" occurred. When the table had been tipped, the confederate and subject worked together to return the index cards to the table in neat stacks (but out of order). The experimenter returned, administered the test to the subject in the same room, and led the confederate out, ostensibly to take the test in another room. Later the experimenter returned, thanked and paid the subject, and, as the subject was leaving, either asked her if she would participate as an unpaid subject in an experiment to be conducted by the graduate student in whose room the experiment had taken place (relevant request) or asked her if she would participate in an experiment to be conducted by "a graduate student in the department" (irrelevant request). Compliance was measured by the number who agreed.

The study addressed two questions: (1) Did guilt affect compliance? and (2) Was the level of compliance among the guilty affected by whether the victim or some other person would be the beneficiary of compliance? The results showed that in general, scattering the note cards did affect compliance: 75 percent of those who knocked over the cards volunteered for the future experiment while less than 39 percent of those in the control conditions did so. This finding supported that of the first experiment described earlier. The results regarding the second question were more surprising. While it might seem that an opportunity to help the victim of one's guilty action might bring about compliance to a greater extent than an opportunity to help someone not associated with the guilty act, the reverse was found. The difference in compliance between guilty and nonguilty subjects showed up only when the request did not involve the injured party; no difference was found between these groups in volunteering to help the graduate student in whose office the accident took place. This perplexing finding led to the formulation of a new question: Is the guilty person under two pressures, one, to make up for the misdeed, and second, to avoid contact with the injured party? A third experiment was conceived with the dual purposes of testing this new question as well as providing additional confirmation of the hypothesis that guilt increases compliance.

The third experiment was much like the second, with the physical setting exactly the same. Subjects were seventy-four freshmen and sophomore women. Since there had been essentially no difference in scores of subjects in the two control conditions of the second experiment, one condition was eliminated, that in which the confederate spilled the cards. A confederate was present as before, but merely served as an assistant to answer questions the subject might have. The main difference between the second and third experiments lay in the nature of the request made at the conclusion of the experiment. While all subjects were asked to help the graduate student in whose room the experiment took place (the injured party), half were told they would be working closely with the graduate student in distributing a public opinion questionnaire (association condition), and half were told they would be working with another volunteer (nonassociation condition). As before, the number who agreed to help served as the measure of compliance.

As in the first two experiments, the hypothesis that guilt leads to compliance was confirmed, with over 55 percent of the guilty subjects acceding to the request compared to 28 percent of the controls. Results also supported the new hypothesis: guilty subjects complied more than the nonguilty when the request did not require subjects to associate with the injured party (nonassociation condition), but there was no difference in compliance between guilty and nonguilty subjects when the request required contact with the victim (association condition).

The fact that the main hypothesis was consistently supported across three different experiments greatly strengthens our confidence in the findings. Note that across the three experiments, operational definitions of guilt and compliance varied: guilt was manipulated in two ways (either by inducing subjects to lie or by causing subjects to scatter someone's research notes); and although the measure of compliance was always the number who agreed, the requests for the subjects' help differed somewhat (irrelevant or relevant to the victim, association or nonassociation with the victim). In addition, the populations from which subjects were drawn differed slightly in the three experiments. These differences in methods helped to eliminate rival explanations for the findings. For example, in the first experiment, a rival explanation might be that the lying subjects complied not out of guilt, but because they felt sorry for the person whom they had lied to and therefore would be more likely to comply with the request that was made (Freedman, Wallington, and Bless, 1967). However, because in experiments 2 and 3 the person making the request was not the person wronged, this explanation may be ruled out.

Replications Using Different Research Strategies: Interpersonal Influence

A group of studies of interpersonal influence in decision making may be used to illustrate further the application of multiple methods to test hypotheses across different studies. Unlike the group of studies just described, in which the same team of investigators and the same principal research strategy (experiments) were employed, this series of studies was performed by different research teams, in different geographic locations, utilizing not only different measures but different research strategies—interviews and analysis of available data. Each of the studies examined the role played by the mass media and by face-to-face contacts in decision making.

The stimulus for this research initially came out of a classic study of voting decisions made during the 1940 presidential election campaign, *The People's Choice* (Lazarsfeld, Berelson, and Gaudet, 1948). Prior to this study it was generally believed that the mass media exerted direct and powerful influences on individuals' behavior. However, in the course of the study it became apparent that the media had little effect on voting decisions (Katz and Lazarsfeld, 1955). This unexpected finding led the authors to look for other sources of influence. People who changed their minds during the campaign were asked what had led to the change, and replies consistently revealed that discussions with other people had influenced them. Additional investigation seemed to suggest that certain people—opinion leaders—frequently affected the decisions of others. The question then arose: Who or what affects the decisions of the opinion leaders? In questioning the leaders, Lazarsfeld and colleagues (1948) found that these individuals did attribute influence to the mass media. As a result of these findings, a two-step flow of communication was hypothesized. That is, information seemed to flow from the media to certain persons who then exerted disproportionate influence on the decisions of others.

To test the two-step flow of communication hypothesis, Katz and Lazarsfeld (1955) designed a study of decision making by women in Decatur, Illinois. Four areas of decision making were studied: daily household marketing, fashion, movie selection, and opinions on local public affairs. First, a cross section of women were interviewed, each being asked whether she had recently reached a decision or experienced a change in any of these areas. If so, the interviewer tried to determine which individuals and media had influenced her. In addition, opinion leaders were identified and interviewed. Leaders and nonleaders were compared on a number of variables, including social status, gregariousness, age, marital status, number of children, and most importantly, exposure to the mass media. Results of the study showed that the influential women had greater exposure to the mass media in general as well as more exposure to specific content related to their sphere of leadership. Thus the two-step flow hypothesis was supported.

While the two studies described above investigated the same hypothesis, they differed in locale selected, population surveyed, topics of decision making, and research personnel. On the other hand, both studies employed the survey interview and therefore share methodological weaknesses such as the biases inherent in self-reports and the various "demand characteristics" of the interview. For example, the respondents may have consciously or subconsciously cited sources of influence on decision making that were in accord with their perception of the study's purpose. It is also possible that the interviewers expected the opinion leaders to report greater exposure to the media and somehow subtly reinforced such responses.

We now turn to two studies of the effects of interpersonal influence among medical doctors on the decision to prescribe a new drug. In these studies (a pilot and a larger study), the investigators added sociometric measures to the survey interview and also made use of available data, thus avoiding reliance on a single research strategy.

The pilot study was conducted in a small New England city with forty practicing physicians, of whom thirty-three agreed to be interviewed (Menzel and Katz, 1955). In the interview, each doctor was asked a number of questions, including how they had learned about two of the drugs they had recently begun prescribing. Replies included mailings from drug companies, professional journals, drug salespeople, colleagues, and out-of-town medical meetings. In addition, three sociometric questions were asked to ascertain each physician's position in the local network of social and professional relationships: (1) "Can you name the three or four physicians you meet most frequently on social occasions?" (2) "Who are the three or four physicians in your conversations with whom the subject of drug therapy most often comes up?" and (3) "When you need added information or advice about questions of drug therapy, where do you usually turn?" (Menzel and Katz, 1955).

The hypothesis of a two-step flow of communication was supported somewhat in that the designated opinion leaders—physicians who were more frequently chosen for discussions about drug therapy—were more likely to learn about new drugs from professional journal articles and out-of-town meetings. In contrast, doctors who received no sociometric choices tended to rely more heavily on commercial sources—drug company mailings and salespeople. The finding that opinion leaders and nonleaders are differentially exposed to professional and commercial informational channels suggests that modifications are necessary in the two-step flow model to allow for multistep communication flow (Menzel and Katz, 1955).

The key dependent variable in the study was the date on which each physician first prescribed a new antibiotic drug, which was obtained from prescription records provided by local pharmacists. Adoption of the new drug was closely linked to sociometric relationships: doctors who first prescribed the drug tended to have direct sociometric contact with others who had already adopted the drug; members of social cliques who prescribed the new drug tended to do so within a few days of each other. While the opinion leaders were not among the first to adopt the drug, their adoption coincided within a few days with the dates of first prescription of the drug by most of the physicians in their clique.

The larger study was carried out later the same year, 1954, in four Illinois cities (Coleman, Katz, and Menzel, 1966), again studying the process by which a new drug was adopted by physicians. The same research methods—personal interviews that included sociometric questions and examination of the prescription records in local pharmacies—were used. The respondents included 125 pediatricians, internists, and general practitioners (85 percent of the physicians practicing those specialties in the four cities), as well as 103 doctors practicing other specialties who were mentioned by the original 125 respondents in response to the sociometric questions.

The hypothesis of a two-step flow in communication was supported, although the findings differed in detail from some of those of the pilot study. For example, in the larger study the innovators, or pioneers in the use of the drug, were also the opinion leaders within their profession. Thus, the specific role of the opinion leaders in the adoption of the drug differed in the two studies. However, in both the pilot and larger studies the opinion leaders were those who read professional journals and frequently attended out-of-town meetings in their specialty.

The studies of interpersonal influence described above illustrate the merits of a multiple-methods approach. Rival explanations of the earlier studies pertaining to the limitations and biases inherent in self-reports were eliminated in the later studies by augmenting the self-report measures of decision making and sources of influence with the analysis of available data (prescription records) and sociometric information. Not only does the application of different research strategies help rule out rival explanations, but repeated testing under dissimilar conditions may also suggest enhancements and modifications of the original hypothesis. For example, results of the drug studies suggested revision of the two-step model to permit multistep communication flow, and subsequent research has led to further theoretical refinements (J. P. Robinson, 1976; Weimann, 1982).

Summary

The logic of a multiple-methods approach is best conveyed by the process of triangulation in navigation. To locate a point in space, navigators calibrate the distance to that point from two different positions. Similarly, the key to triangulation in social research is the selection of research strategies and measures that do not share the same methodological weaknesses. If different methods produce similar findings, our confidence in the results increases.

Traditionally, triangulation through the use of multiple indicators has involved the construction of indexes and scales. Indexes combine indicators more or less arbitrarily in the absence of checks to see how well the indicators correspond to the underlying concept; scales combine indicators according to procedures designed to determine the degree of correspondence between indicators and a single underlying dimension. The primary benefit of indexes and scales is the reduction of measurement error. A more recent approach called structural equation modeling retains the identity of each indicator by incorporating all variables—observed indicators and their underlying unobserved concepts—into causal models. Unlike index measurement, this approach allows one to test for certain kinds of measurement error.

Triangulation also occurs through replications of studies. The most frequent replications in social research are of small-scale, low-cost experiments. Rather than duplicating an experiment exactly, investigators usually vary certain features, such as the subject population, the manipulation of the independent variable, and the measurement of the dependent variable. Less frequent, yet rendering even more confidence in research findings, are replications involving different research strategies.

Key Terms

triangulation
index
scale
unidimensionality
Guttman scaling
structural equation modeling
replication

Review Questions and Problems

1. What is the principle of triangulation? Explain how this principle applies to convergent validity assessment, discussed in chapter 5.

2. What is a composite measure? From the standpoint of triangulation, why are such measures better than single-item indicators? What are some other reasons for creating composite measures?

3. How does an index differ from a scale?

4. Although we describe the use of Guttman scaling to measure individual attitudes, social scientists also have used Guttman scaling techniques to measure characteristics of whole societies. For example, R. D. Schwartz and J. C. Miller (1964) proposed that the changes in societies' legal systems parallel changes in societal complexity (or, in Durkheim's terms, the societal "division of labor"). Fully developed legal systems were seen to have the following three characteristics:

  a. *Mediation*—regular use of third parties to settle disputes.

  b. *Police*—use of specialized, armed force to enforce laws.

  c. *Counsel*—regular use of specialized, nonkin advocates (e.g., lawyers). Assuming that these three characteristics, in order, respresent a progression of complexity, present a table that shows the response pattern of a perfect Guttman scale. Then give an example of a "nonscale" response pattern. How would you test these three items for Guttman scalability?

5. How does structural equation modeling differ from composite measurement?

6. How do replications constitute triangulation?

7. Each of the four basic approaches to social research examined in this book applies the principle of triangulation in various ways. Explain how triangulation typically is applied in: experiments, surveys, field studies, and research using available data.

8. Why is it preferable to use more than one of the four basic research strategies whenever possible?

NOTE

1. For an introduction to social science applications as well as some of the technical details involved in structural equation modeling, see Bielby and Hauser (1977), Goldberger and Duncan (1973), O. D. Duncan (1975), and Jöreskog and Sorbom (1979).

IV

DATA PROCESSING, ANALYSIS, AND INTERPRETATION

As with other facets of research, data analysis is very much tied to the researcher's basic methodological approach. In the chapters on field and available data research, we discussed certain data-analytical techniques at length, but in the case of experiments and surveys we only alluded briefly to this stage of research. The first two chapters in this section take up where our discussions in chapters 7 and 9 left off. Having collected data in an experiment or survey, the researcher must quantify it, put it in computer-readable form, and analyze the data statistically. Chapter 14 charts this process for survey research, outlining the key steps in processing data prior to analysis and describing elementary statistical analyses. Chapter 15 then considers some more advanced statistical techniques for assessing the causal relations among sets of variables.

Even though our attention in these two chapters is focused mostly on the analysis of survey data, the underlying logic and flow of the analysis described is basically the same as it is in other approaches. There is, for example, always a constant interplay between theory and data. The stage for data analysis is set by the researcher's theoretical model of anticipated relationships, as this limits and guides the kinds of analyses that can be carried out. The analysis, in turn, assays and elaborates this model and invariably suggests new models for further analysis. The first rule in all this is that "facts (data) never speak for themselves." Rather, they must be interpreted. Ultimately, that interpretation takes the form of a research report, book, or article that will be read and interpreted by others. Thus, in chapter 17, we examine the writing of research. All research also must be interpreted in terms of standards of research ethics, examined in chapter 16.

14

Data Processing and Elementary Data Analysis

As we consider the later stages of research, it is valuable to recall the broader process of scientific inquiry. Science is a means to understanding that involves a repetitive interplay between theoretical ideas and empirical evidence. Thus, data and facts lead to tentative theory, deductions from this tentative theory are compared with new facts, the theory is modified or discarded in light of discrepancies, new deductions are made, and so on. Data analysis takes place whenever theory and data are compared. This comparison begins in field research when an investigator struggles to bring order to, or to make sense out of, his or her observations. In surveys and experiments, the researcher typically begins to bring theory and data together when testing predictions from a hypothesis. In either case, however, initial data analyses set the stage for a continued interaction between theory and data.

This chapter and the next chapter focus on quantitative data analysis. We are concerned with how data are prepared for analysis (data processing) and then manipulated numerically (data analysis). Together the two chapters follow the typical development of a survey study following data collection: from handling the data and putting them in computer-readable form to preliminary analyses involving one and two variables (chapter 14) to more advanced statistical analyses (chapter 15). Both chapters are oriented toward the reader more as consumer than producer of research and in no way can substitute for a course in statistics. In fact, we eschew computational formulas in favor of verbal presentations. What we want to do is give the reader a sense of the *process* of data analysis—a learning process achieved through comparing empirical evidence with theoretical expectations.

Many of our examples are drawn from the General Social Surveys (GSS) conducted by the National Opinion Research Center (NORC) between 1972 and 1985 (Davis and Smith, 1985). These surveys consisted of interviews administered to national samples using a standard interview schedule.[1] Among the questions asked were (1) requests for standard background information on gender, race, occupation, religion, and so on, (2) questions about the quality of one's life in various areas (e.g., health, family, social relations), (3) items asking for evaluations of government programs, and (4) items tapping opinions and attitudes about a wide range of issues, such as drug usage, abortion, religious freedom, and racial equality. The GSSs were part of a national data program designed to provide high-quality data to social scientists. Literally hundreds of studies have been published analyzing data from these surveys.

Beginning the Analysis

Data analysis begins with the statement of hypotheses, the construction of a theoretical model, or, at the very least, implicitly anticipated relationships among a set of variables. These "models," to use the most general term, guide the collection of data and therefore determine not only the kind of statistical analyses that are possible but also what alternative relationships or models may be analyzed. To see how this works, let us examine a study of the effects of television viewing on perceptions of reality.

In several studies reported in the 1970s, George Gerbner, Larry Gross, and their associates (Gerbner and Gross, 1976a,b; Gerbner et al., 1977, 1978) hypothesized that heavy viewers of television see the world as a more dangerous and frightening place than lighter viewers. This hypothesis followed from the assumption that television programs shape conceptions of social reality and from an extensive analysis of program content that showed that "more than half of all characters are involved in some violence, at least one-tenth in some killing, and . . . over three-fourths of prime-time hours contain some violence" (1976a:192–193).

Gerbner and Gross realized that heavy television viewing tends to be associated with lower education and other socioeconomic variables that might also distort one's view of the world. Therefore, they were careful to measure and include such variables in their analysis. This enabled them to determine, for example, whether education affects both television viewing and fear of violence, creating a spurious causal relationship between the latter variables. It is crucial for the researcher to consider such alternative explanations or "models" before and during the data analysis. Only if the relationships are anticipated *before* data collection, however, can the researcher introduce appropriate procedures and measures, and be able to carry out the relevant statistical analyses. For example, if Gerbner and Gross had not gathered information on respondents' education, then they would not have been able to examine its effects on their hypothesized relationship.

Many other variables may influence the relationship between television viewing and fear of violence—for example, age, gender, race, number of hours worked per week, and the incidence of crime in the neighborhood. Indeed, all of these variables ultimately were included in the analyses by Gerbner and his associates or by others. In the next chapter we consider statistical techniques for controlling the effects of such variables. Before we get to that point, however, we need to know how to analyze the relationship between television viewing and fear of violence by itself. Before we can analyze the data, we also need to know how to prepare the data for computer analysis, as statistical analyses are seldom done without the aid of a computer. We now turn to these issues.

Data Processing

In investigating the relationship between television viewing and fear of violence, Gerbner and Gross and their associates (1978) have relied, in part, on questions from the 1977 GSS. The question measuring television viewing was, "On the average day, about how many hours do you personally watch television?" Since respondents' answers were recorded in number of hours (the range was 0–20), this variable may be considered a ratio scale measure. The question they used as a measure of fear of violence was, "Is there any area right around here—that is, within a mile—where you would be afraid to walk alone at night?" The alternatives to this question, "yes" and "no," insofar as they indicate degrees of fear, amount to ordinal measurement. Both of these questions were also included in the 1985 GSS, which we will use to replicate part of Gerbner and Gross's analysis. Interviewers collected the data by recording respondents' answers on an interview schedule. The schedule lists all acceptable answers to every question included in the particular GSS survey. But it also contains something else, a feature that marks the beginning of data processing—numerical codes for each answer.

The processing of data may be likened to the processing of most manufactured goods in which raw materials are changed step by step into some finished product. Steps in manufacturing are referred to as "value-adding," in that each contributes a certain increased value as the product takes form. In data processing, five essential steps constitute the process of making data serviceable for analysis: coding, editing, data entry, cleaning, and data modification.

Coding

Coding for computer analysis consists of assigning numbers or symbols to variable categories. In surveys such as the GSS, the categories are answers to questions; and the common practice, which simplifies data entry and analysis, is to use numerical codes only. If the answers to questions are expressed in numbers, as in the question on television viewing, then there is no need to code the data further. But if the answers are not expressed numerically, then numbers must be assigned to each answer. For the fear-of-violence question, a code of 1 was used for the answer "yes," 2 for "no," 8 for "don't know," and 9 for "no answer." The first three of these codes were listed on the GSS interview schedule, and interviewers were instructed to record answers by circling the appropriate code. The particular numbers used are arbitrary; a code of 2 might just as well have been used for the "yes" response and a code of 1 for "no."

For closed-ended questions such as the above, coding is straightforward: there are relatively few categories, and you simply need to assign a different code to each category. For open-ended questions, however, the number of unique responses may number in the hundreds. Coding for this type of question is very much like coding in content analysis (see chapter 12). The researcher tries to develop a coding scheme that does not require a separate code for every respondent or case, but which adequately reflects the full range of responses. The idea is to put the data in manageable form while retaining as much information as practical. (See Box 14.1 for an example of coding open-ended questions.)

If anything, the tendency for novice researchers is to use too few categories, which gloss over potentially meaningful differences. Once the data are coded and data analysis is under way, it is easy to combine code categories for purposes of

BOX 14.1

Reasons for Giving up Cigarette Smoking: An Example of Coding Responses to Open-Ended Questions

Developing coding categories for open-ended questions, like many other research activities, involves an interplay between theory and data. Let us follow the procedure used by Bruce Straits (1967) in a study based on personal interviews of ex-smokers ("quitters"), current smokers who tried but were unable to quit smoking ("unables"), and current smokers who have never made a serious attempt to stop smoking ("smokers"). Hypothesizing that specific factors precipitate and support smoking cessation, Straits asked "quitters" and "unables" the open-ended question: "Why did you want to stop smoking?" (Smokers were asked, "What reasons might you have for giving up smoking?") Individual responses to the question were too diverse and numerous to manage and analyze without grouping them into a smaller number of categories.

Both theory and data guided Straits' development of coding categories. Theoretical considerations included the hypothesis that current physical ailments (especially those easily connected with smoking) play a more important role in the discontinuation of smoking than health fears for the future (e.g., incurring lung cancer). The coding procedure involved first listing each reason given by the 200 respondents. (Typically studies use a sample of about 50 to 100 respondents to build codes.) Tally marks were used to note identical reasons. Here is part of the listing:

"I couldn't get over a bad cough"   卌 卌 ||||

"Job requirements"   卌 |

"Not good for health"   卌 卌 卌 |||

"It is too expensive"   卌 卌 |||

"Live longer"   卌 |

"Sore throat"   卌 卌 |

"To see if I could"   卌 ||||

"Heart attack" |

"Quit for Lent and didn't return" |

"Doctor's advice"   卌 卌 |||

"Sinus condition"   卌 卌 卌 |||

"Causes lung cancer"   卌 卌 |

"My wife hates it" |||

Next, coding categories were formed by grouping together reasons that seemed similar from the research perspective. For example, people with bad coughs were placed in the same category as those reporting sore throats. Although the distinction between a cough and a sore throat is important from a medical standpoint, it was not pertinent to Straits' hypotheses.

Empirical considerations also influenced construction of the coding categories. Some reasons had to be lumped together in "other" categories, because they occurred too infrequently. An unanticipated category had to be established for quitters who had not made a conscious decision to quit, but instead found themselves in situations where they were unable to smoke for a temporary period, such as while recovering from an operation.

The final coding scheme, which was used to code *each* reason given, is shown below.

Current health reasons

1. Didn't feel well (unspecified illness)
2. Nasal congestion (bad cold, sinus, etc.)
3. Cough, sore throat (smoker's cough, dry throat, etc.)
4. Shortness of breath (cutting down on wind, etc.)
5. Poor appetite, loss of weight
6. Other ailments (headaches, nervous condition, nausea, dizziness, etc.)

Advised by doctor

7. Unspecified (ordered by doctor, etc.)
8. Because of specific ailment (heart trouble, palsy, etc.)
9. Doctor said smoking harmful

Future health reasons

10. Smoking is harmful (unspecified)
11. Live longer
12. Fear of cancer (lung cancer, etc.)

Other

13. Sensory dislike (bad taste in mouth, smell, dirty house, etc.)
14. Pressure from close associates (wife, co-worker, etc.)
15. Financial reasons (waste of money, etc.)
16. Test of willpower (to see if could, control life, etc.)
17. Work requirement (smoking not allowed)
18. Quit temporarily (because of operation, illness, Lent, etc., and didn't return to smoking)
19. Other reasons
20. Don't know
21. No answer

The coding scheme represents a balance between too much and too little detail. The classification preserves possibly relevant distinctions such as identifying those who specifically mentioned cancer. The detailed categories are easily collapsed (recoded) when the analysis requires broader groupings. For example, Straits (1967:75) reports that a higher proportion (82 percent) of quitters mentioned current health ailments and/or advice from a doctor than did the unables (60 percent) or smokers (37 percent), who mentioned less immediate health threats or weaker reasons such as "waste of money" or "test of willpower" more frequently.

analysis, but impossible to recover lost detail. Consider a questionnaire study that needed a count of respondents' siblings: instead of asking for that number, respondents were asked to list the ages of any brothers and sisters. Now, one could code only the number of siblings. But consider what happens when all the available information is retained—when the age and gender of each sibling are coded and entered separately into the data base. Doing this makes it possible, by computer manipulation, not only to count the number of siblings but also to generate measures of number of brothers, sisters, older brothers, younger sisters, respondent's spacing from next sibling, and so on.

Before data are entered into a computer, coding schemes must be developed for every variable or question. In the early days of computers, it was common for survey researchers to do the coding for all questions after they collected the data, and then to record the coded data on *code sheets* before entry into the computer. Today researchers almost always develop coding schemes for closed-ended questions *before* the data are collected. GSS interviewers, as noted, record answers on the interview schedule, which has codes for each answer. This makes it easy to enter the information directly into the computer and minimizes the number of mistakes that are likely to be made in the process.

Questionnaires and interview schedules like that used for the GSS that contain answer codes as well as other data-processing instructions on the form itself are said to be *precoded*. Figure 14.1 gives an example of a precoded form with sample questions from the GSS. Codes either are written in by the interviewer (respondent ID number) or circled (respondent's gender). Notice the numbers in the right-hand margin: these indicate where the information is to be entered in the computer data file (more about this below). If an open-ended question were used, then space would be provided for the interviewer to write down exactly what the respondent says. After all the data have been collected and codes developed for open-ended questions, then each answer could be coded by writing the appropriate number in the margin of the schedule. This procedure is called *edge coding*; like precodes for closed-ended questions, it enables the researcher to transfer the data directly from the questionnaire to the computer without the aid of code sheets.

FIGURE 14.1. Sample precoded form with questions from the GSS.

1. Respondent ID number ☐☐☐☐   01–04/

2. Circle respondent's gender: 05/
   Male. 1   Female. 2

3. Is there any area right around here—that is,   06/
   within a mile—where you would be afraid to
   walk alone at night? (Circle one.)
   Yes 1
   No. 2
   Don't know. 8
   No answer. 9

Once codes are established for all data items and the data are ready to enter into the computer, then the researcher should prepare a *codebook*. A codebook is like a dictionary in that it defines the meaning of the numerical codes for each variable. Codebooks also indicate the location of each variable in the data file, and may contain coding and editing decision rules, such as how to handle two answers circled to a single-response question. If the questionnaire is precoded, and no open-ended questions are used, then a blank copy of the questionnaire may serve as the codebook. In fact, a codebook for the items in Figure 14.1 would look very much like the questionnaire itself. More often than not, however, the researcher will want to prepare a separate codebook for data processing purposes.

Editing

Editing is a quality control process applied mostly to surveys. Its purpose is to ensure that the information on a questionnaire or interview schedule is ready to be transferred to the computer for analysis (Sonquist and Dunkelberg, 1977). "Ready" means that the data are as complete, error-free, and readable as possible.

Editing is carried out both during and after the process of data collection, and much of it occurs simultaneously with coding. In interview studies, the editing process begins in the field. Interviewers should check over their completed forms for errors and omissions soon after each interview is conducted. Respondents should be recontacted if necessary or corrections should be made from memory. Field supervisors may also do some editing at this point, such as determining whether the interviews have been properly conducted from the standpoint of using the correct forms, legibly recording answers, and interviewing the correct respondents.

Most of the editing in large-scale surveys such as the GSS is done in a central office. Here an editor, who serves much the same function as a copy editor for a writer, goes over each completed form (1) to evaluate interviewers and detect interviewing problems (e.g., inadequate use of probes to obtain answers to open-ended questions), (2) to check for multiple answers to single items, vague answers, response inconsistencies (e.g., reporting zero hours of television watched in one section and the viewing of a specific TV program in another section), and the like, and (3) to make sure that the interview schedule or questionnaire is complete—that all items, especially those with "missing" responses, have answer codes. The editor may bring glaring errors to the attention of the principal investigator or the field supervisor, who provides feedback to interviewers, but mostly he or she simply will make corrections directly on the form.

Entering the Data

We assume at this point that the researcher has access to a computer and is ready to enter his or her data through a computer terminal.[2] A computer terminal is a device for communicating information to a computer. It generally consists of a typewriter keyboard connected to either a printer or a video monitor that looks like a television screen (called a cathode ray tube or CRT). When the researcher types information on a line and then depresses the "carriage return," the information is sent to the computer.

The data that are entered into the computer are stored on a disk or tape in a *computer file*, sometimes called a *data file*, because all the information in the file consists of data. One can think of a computer file as a sheet of graph paper. Each character or number you type occupies a particular row and column in the file. Each row of information in a file is called a *record*. Records are usually restricted to eighty columns in length (CRTs usually display eighty columns), although they can be much longer.

Before entering the data into the file, the researcher must decide on the arrangement or *format* of the data: how many records are needed for each case or respondent and in what columns to locate each variable. As noted above, precoded forms and questionnaires contain this information on the form itself. The numbers in the right-hand margin of Figure 14.1, for example, show that the respondent's identification number is located in columns 1–4, respondent's gender is coded in column 5, and responses to the fear-of-violence question are coded in column 6. The number of columns is a function of the maximum number of digits required to code the variable. If you are coding income in dollars and you want to record exact amounts up to $900,000, then you would need six columns. (You would record only the number, ignoring the dollar sign and comma.) The number of records depends on the volume of information collected. For a small-scale survey of twenty to thirty questions, all of the information for a given case can usually be recorded on a single line. By contrast, as of 1985 the GSS data file for all years, which contained over 1000 questions and other information, consisted of eighteen records per case.

Ordinarily, the data are arranged in the file so that the information for each variable is stored in the same column(s) for each case.[3] This is called a *fixed-column format*.[4] One of its advantages has to do with the next stage in data processing— data cleaning.

Cleaning

After the data have been entered into a computer file, the researcher should check them over thoroughly for errors. Eliminating errors in coding and transmitting the data to the computer is referred to as *cleaning* the data. This is an essential process. Researchers who have invested a great deal of time and energy in collecting their data do not want their work undermined by avoidable mistakes made at the stage of data processing. For unlike sampling error and certain kinds of measurement error, data-processing errors *are* avoidable. The way to avoid them is to be exceedingly careful about entering the data and to use every possible method of checking for mistakes. Here are a few ways to clean your data.

First, if the data are stored in a fixed-column format, then you can spot-check the data for errors by running your eye down the various columns. This will enable you to pick up glaring errors such as columns that have been shifted right or left, or characters where blanks should appear.

Second, if possible—for example, if there are relatively few cases and items of information—you should carefully proofread every column of every case. A better procedure would be to enter the data twice and then compare the two entries for errors. When punched cards were the means of recording and storing data, this was done on a machine called a verifier. Currently, the data are entered twice into computer files and a program instructs the computer to search the files for noncomparable entries. Although such verifying usually removes most data-entry errors, data cleaning seldom stops here, especially when it is important that the data be as absolutely clean as possible.

A third cleaning technique is sometimes called *wild-code checking* (Sonquist and Dunkelberg, 1977:211). Every variable has a specified set of legitimate codes. The fear-of-violence question, for example, has possible codes of 1 for "yes," 2 for "no," 8 for "don't know," and 9 for "no answer." Wild codes are any codes that are not legitimate. Wild-code checking consists of examining the values recorded for each item to see whether there are any wild codes, such as a "4" for the fear question. Some computer programs do this kind of cleaning to the point of identifying which particular cases contain wild codes. Alternatively, one can obtain a frequency distribution for the variable (see below), check to see if there are any erroneous codes, and then proofread or computer search the data file to find the errors. Of course, one should keep in mind that wild-code checking does not detect typographical or other errors involving legitimate codes.

Fourth, most large-scale surveys use a process called *consistency checking* (Sonquist and Dunkelberg, 1977:215). The idea here is to see whether responses to certain questions are related in reasonable ways to responses to particular other questions. For example, it would be unreasonable, and therefore an indication of coding error, to find a respondent who is married and age 5, or a medical doctor with 3 years of formal schooling.

One common type of consistency checking involves contingency questions. As you may recall from chapter 10, these are questions designed for a subset of the respondents. The GSS, for example, first asks people about their employment status last week. If the respondent is working full or part time, then he or she is asked the following contingency question: "How many hours did you work last week, at all jobs?" Consistency checking determines if a question such as this was answered only by those for whom the question was intended. We would not expect an answer to this question if the respondent was unemployed, retired, or in school. To identify such erroneous responses, one must break down the frequency distribution for the contingency question by pertinent subsamples of the population. One might check to see, for example, if any of the subsample of nonworking respondents answered the question on number of hours worked last week.

One can get an idea of the importance of editing and data cleaning by considering the measures taken to edit and clean the GSS data (T. W. Smith, personal communication, 1986). Before the data are entered, interviewers in the field go over their interview schedules after each interview to check for errors; the first two forms submitted by each interviewer are checked by editors at the National Opinion Research Center for systematic interviewer errors, and one out of every four forms submitted thereafter is also checked; responses to open-ended questions and other responses that are not precoded (e.g., "not applicable" or "no answer") are coded on the form; attempts are made to obtain missing data on crucial questions; and validation checks are carried out on all interviewers. The data are entered into the computer with the aid of a data-entry program, which automatically alerts the investigator to wild-code errors at the time of entry. Once data from all of the forms have been entered, data from 20 percent of the forms are entered a second time for verification. Then, another program is used that essentially does consistency checking for certain questions. Finally, frequency distributions for variables are generated for another round of consistency cleaning.

Data Modification

At this stage, having entered all the data into the computer and checked for errors, the researcher is ready to give the computer instructions for analyzing the data.[5] Although the instructions vary according to the particular computer and computer program the researcher chooses to use, they will always describe the content and format of the data file and will invariably contain commands for modifying the data.

Data modification frequently occurs prior to data analysis; and so we prefer to think of it as part of data processing. The reasons for modifying the data are many: for example, you may want to add together the responses to several items in order to create an index, rearrange the numerical order of categories, change one or more of the values for a variable, or collapse categories for purposes of analysis. In one phase of their analysis of the GSS data, Gerbner and associates (1978) chose to collapse the codes for the variable television viewing. Instead of using the entire range of responses from 0 to 20 hours watched per day, they divided respondents into three groups: those who watched 2 hours or less ("light" viewers), those who watched 3 hours ("medium" viewers), and those who watched 4 or more hours ("heavy" viewers).

Another example of data modification concerns the variable age. Investigators have found less measurement error when respondents are asked for their date of birth rather than directly for their age. Asking date of birth, however, necessitates a transformation of the data in order to obtain a respondent's age. Thus, for the GSS, age is computed by subtracting date of birth from the year of the survey: for the 1985 GSS, age = 1985 − birthdate. Of course, this transformation ignores the actual month and day of birth, but this is precise enough for most research purposes.

The Functions of Statistics in Social Research

The next steps would be to decide on the appropriate statistical analysis and then instruct the computer to carry it out. But how do you decide what kind of analysis to do? Naturally, that decision depends on what you want to know. Gerbner and Gross wanted to know whether watching a lot of television (the independent variable) tends to make people fearful of violence (the dependent variable). Of course, to establish a causal relation such as this, they would need to show that the two variables are associated (that changes in one variable accompany changes in the other), that the direction of influence is from the independent variable to the dependent variable, and that the association between the variables is nonspurious. To begin their analysis, they could examine the raw data respondent by respondent to see if changes in television viewing across repondents are associated with changes in fear of violence. But with some 1500 respondents, this task would be incredibly tedious and probably not very reliable. Therefore, what they need is a fast and efficient means of summarizing the association between these variables for the entire sample of respondents. This is precisely where statistics (and computers) enters in. A *statistic* is a summary statement about a set of data; statistics as a discipline provides techniques for organizing and analyzing data.

Traditionally, statistics has been divided according to two functions—descriptive and inferential. *Descriptive statistics* is concerned with organizing and summarizing the data at hand to make them more intelligible. The high and low scores and average score on an exam are descriptive statistics that readily summarize a class's performance. Gerbner and Gross needed a descriptive statistic that would summarize the degree of association between television viewing and fear of violence in their sample.

Inferential statistics deals with the kinds of inferences that can be made when generalizing from data, as from sample data to the entire population. Gerbner and Gross needed this form of analysis as a means of determining what their sample observations indicated about the effects of television on fear of violence in the population of adult viewers.

Based on probability theory, inferential statistics may be used for two distinct purposes: to estimate population characteristics from sample data (discussed in chapter 6), and to test hypotheses.[6] Traditionally, hypothesis testing is employed to rule out the rival explanation that observed data patterns, relationships, or differences are due to chance processes arising from random assignment (in the case of experiments), sampling error (in the case of probability sampling), random measurement error, or other sources.[7] In experiments (discussed in chapter 7), such testing determines if the differences between experimental conditions are "statistically significant"—that is, not attributable to random assignment. The appropriate role of significance tests in the analysis of nonexperimental data is a long-standing controversy (see Morrison and Henkel, 1970). Following D. Gold's argument (1969) that results which easily could have occurred by a chance process should not be taken seriously, we view tests of significance as an effective means of screening out trivialities and chance mishaps.

We have chosen in this chapter to focus on the analysis of data from cross-sectional surveys. The quantitative analysis of survey data has been greatly influenced by the advent of computers. Indeed, with the rapid development of high-speed computers, social researchers have begun to change their thinking about the role of statistics, seeing it more in relation to the analysis of models (Kenny, 1985). The key issues in analyzing models are (1) translating the theory into a statistical model, (2) deciding whether the data are adequate to estimate (test) the model, (3) obtaining estimates of the various effects hypothesized by the model, and (4) evaluating how well the data support or "fit" the model (Kenny, 1985). Technical aspects beyond the scope of this book prevent us from taking up the second issue. In the next chapter, we will consider briefly the issue of statistical modeling. Our ultimate concern, however, is with the third and fourth issues—for example, with analyzing the effect of television viewing on fear of violence, and determining whether certain models containing these and other variables provide a good fit with the data. To perform these tasks, we must examine statistical techniques for analyzing two or more variables simultaneously (*multivariate* analysis). But we focus our attention first on techniques for examining one variable at a time (*univariate* analysis).

Univariate Analysis

Univariate analysis may be conducted as part of the data-cleaning process, as a prelude to more complex analyses, or as part of a basic descriptive study. In any case, the goal is to get a clear picture of the data by examining one variable at a time. The data "pictures" generated by univariate analysis come in various forms—tables, graphs, charts, and statistical indexes. The nature of the techniques depends on whether one is analyzing variables measured at the nominal/ordinal level or variables measured at the interval/ratio level (discussed in chapter 5).

Gerbner and Gross might have done a univariate analysis simply to get a sense of the nature of the variation in the variables to be analyzed. It is generally a good idea, for example, to see if there is sufficient variation in responses to warrant including the variable in the analysis. As a rule, the less variation, the more difficult it is to detect how differences in one variable are related to differences in another variable. To take the extreme case, if no respondent expresses a fear of violence (which conceivably could occur in samples from certain communities), then it would be impossible to determine how *differences* in this variable were related to differences in any other variable.

Similarly, a univariate analysis can inform decisions about how to collapse the categories of a variable for further analysis. Collapsing decisions may be based on theoretical criteria and/or may hinge on the empirical variation in responses. Thus, years of education might be collapsed into "theoretically" meaningful categories (grade 8 or lower, some high school, high school graduate, some college, college graduate) based on the years of schooling deemed appropriate over time in the United States for leaving school and qualifying for certain occupations. Alternatively, one might collapse categories according to how many respondents fall into each category. If the sample contains only a handful of respondents with less than a college education, then these respondents may be placed in one category for purposes of analysis.

Suppose that we wanted to examine responses to the fear-of-violence question. One means is to organize responses into a table called a *frequency distribution*. A frequency distribution is created by first listing all of the response categories and then adding up the number of cases that fall into each category. If we instruct the computer to do this, then our output might look like Table 14.1, which gives the distribution of responses in the 1985 GSS to the fear-of-violence question. This certainly presents a clearer picture than a case-by-case listing of responses. However, this sort of table generally would serve as a preliminary organization of the data, because more readable formats can be derived from it. In particular,

TABLE 14.1. Frequency Distribution of Fear
of Violence,[a] 1985 GSS

CODE	LABEL	FREQUENCY
1	YES	617
2	NO	901
8	DON'T KNOW	13
9	NO RESPONSE	3
TOTAL		1534

[a]Question: "Is there any area right around here—that is, within a mile—where you would be afraid to walk alone at night?"

researchers often compute the percentage of respondents in each category. To see how this might create a still clearer picture, examine the raw figures in Table 14.1.

Notice that the number of "yes" responses in the sample is 617. This number by itself is meaningless unless we provide a standard or reference point with which to interpret it. More than likely as you peruse the table you will see the figures in relation to one another, invoking implicit points of comparison. You may note, for example, that there are more "no" than "yes" answers (about one and a half times as many) or that "yes" responses constitute about six-fifteenths of the sample. *Percentage distributions* provide an explicit comparative framework for interpreting distributions. They tell you the size of a category relative to the size of the sample. To create a percentage distribution, you divide the number of cases in each category by the total number of cases and multiply by 100. This is what we have done in Table 14.2. Now you can see more clearly the relative difference in responses.

It should be noted that the percentages in Table 14.2 are based on the total number of responses, excluding "missing data"—those in the "don't know" and "no response" categories. Since these are not meaningful variable categories (i.e., they say nothing about fear of violence), it would be misleading to include them in the percentage distribution.[8] However, the total number of nonresponses is certainly important information. If this information is not placed in the main body of a table, then it at least should be reported in a footnote to the relevant table or in the text of the research report. Also notice that the base upon which percentages are computed

TABLE 14.2. Percentage Distribution of Fear
of Violence for the Distribution in
Table 14.1

Response	%
Yes	40.6
No	59.4
Total	100.0
(Number of responses)	(1518)
(Missing data)	(16)

(1518) is given in parentheses below the percentage total of 100 percent. It is customary to indicate in tables the total number of observations from which the statistics are computed. This information may be found elsewhere—at the end of the table title or in a headnote or footnote to the table; often it is signified with the letter *N*.

The fear-of-violence question is, as noted, an ordinal-scale variable. Creating frequency or percentage distributions is about as far as the univariate analysis of nominal- and ordinal-scale variables goes. On the other hand, data on interval and ratio variables may be summarized not only in tables (or graphs) but also in terms of various statistics.

Consider the variable television viewing, which, you will recall, was measured by asking respondents how many hours of television they watched on an average day. We could get a picture of the number of hours watched, as we did with fear of violence, by generating a distribution of the responses. Table 14.3 presents a computerlike output for this variable. Though not a problem here, the relatively large number of values for most interval and ratio variables makes it necessary to collapse categories in order to get a compact, readable table. Had we generated the distribution for the variable of age, for example, we would have had so many values—over seventy—that they might not have fit on a single page of computer output. In this case, we might lump together respondents according to the first age digit—those under 20, between 20 and 29, 30 and 39, and so on.

Notice that Table 14.3 presents two kinds of distributions: frequency and percentage. Can you tell from the table what percentage of respondents report that they do not watch any television at all on the average day?

We also could get a picture of a distribution by looking at its various statistical properties. Three properties may be examined. The first consists of measures of *central tendency*—the mean, median, and mode. These indicate various points of concentration in a set of values. The *mean* is the arithmetical average, calculated by adding up all of the responses and dividing by the total number of respondents. It is the "balancing" point in a distribution, because the sum of the differences of all values from the mean is exactly equal to zero. The *median* is the midpoint in a distribution—the value of the middle response; half of the responses are above it and half are below. You find the median by ordering the values from low to high and then counting up until you find the middle value. The *mode* is the value or category with the highest frequency. The modal value in Table 14.3 is 2 hours. With the aid of a computer we calculated a mean of 2.98 hours and a median of 2.56 hours.

A second property that we can summarize statistically is the degree of variability or *dispersion* among a set of values. The simplest dispersion measure is the *range*. Statistically, this is the difference between the lowest and highest values, but it is usually reported by identifying these endpoints, such as "the number of hours of television watched ranged from 0 to 20 hours." Of several other measures of dispersion, the most commonly reported is the *standard deviation*. As we saw in chapter 6, this is a measure of the "average" spread of observations around the mean. One of its important uses in statistics involves the calculation of "standard scores." A standard score is calculated by dividing the standard deviation into the

TABLE 14.3. Number of Hours of Television Watched on Average Day, 1985 GSS

CODE	LABEL	FREQUENCY	PERCENTAGE
00	0 HOURS	78	5.1
01	1 HOUR	269	17.7
02	2 HOURS	396	26.0
03	3 HOURS	311	20.4
04	4 HOURS	209	13.7
05	5 HOURS	121	7.9
06	6 HOURS	65	4.2
07	7 HOURS	11	0.7
08	8 HOURS	33	2.2
09	9 HOURS	1	0.1
10	10 HOURS	13	0.9
12	12 HOURS	5	0.3
13	13 HOURS	2	0.1
14	14 HOURS	3	0.2
15	15 HOURS	2	0.1
20	20 HOURS	4	0.3
98	DON'T KNOW	1	MISSING
99	NO ANSWER	10	MISSING
TOTAL		1534	100.0
(VALID CASES)	(1523)	(MISSING CASES)	(11)

difference between a given value and the mean of the distribution. This converts the value from a "nonstandard" measurement (e.g., hours, years) specific to the variable and sample to a "standardized" measure expressed in terms of standard deviations from the mean. Similar in some ways to "percentaging" a table (see discussion of Table 14.2 above), standardizing provides a reference point for comparing individual responses in the same or different distributions.

With respect to the variable of television viewing, the standard deviation is perhaps best interpreted as an index of heterogeneity, which could be used to compare the degree of variability in hours watched among different subsamples or in samples from different populations. The standard deviation of the above distribution of all GSS respondents was 2.22. Among respondents with an eighth-grade education or less, the standard deviation in hours watched was 2.72, revealing more variability in this group than among those respondents with at least some college, for whom the standard deviation was 2.08. As a further example, the ages of GSS respondents in 1985 ranged from 18 to 89, with a standard deviation of 17.9 years. By comparison, the standard deviation for age in a sample of college undergraduates would be around 1.5 years; and the standard deviation for the inauguration ages of U.S. presidents, of whom the youngest was 42 (Teddy Roosevelt) and the oldest 69 (Ronald Reagan), is 6.1 years.

FIGURE 14.2. Percentage polygon for the distribution in Table 14.3.

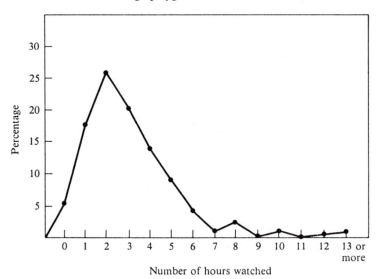

Number of hours watched

A third statistical property of univariate distributions is their *shape*. This property is most readily apparent from a graphic presentation called a *frequency* or *percentage polygon*. Figure 14.2 presents the percentage polygon for the data in Table 14.3. The figure reveals that the distribution has a single high point (or mode), with the data lopsided or "skewed" mostly to the right (or positive side) of this point. This shape also is typical of income distributions. Many variables in social research have "bell-shaped" distributions, so called because they form the general shape of a bell. In a bell-shaped distribution, the three measures of central tendency are identical, whereas in a positively skewed distribution like Figure 14.2 the mode has the lowest value, followed by the median and then the mean.

Collectively, these three statistical properties—central tendency, dispersion, and shape—provide such a good picture of quantitative data that they often obviate the need for tabular or graphic presentations. Most investigators, in fact, describe their data simply in terms of a mean or median, an index of dispersion, and overall form (for which there are also statistical indexes). As long as the reader understands these properties, then he or she should be able to visualize readily the distribution. (See Box 14.2 for another means of visualizing the data.)

Univariate analysis is seldom conducted as an end in itself, especially in explanatory research. One important function mentioned earlier is to determine how to collapse categories. As we will see in the next section, tabular analyses are not workable if the variables contain a large number of categories.

In the absence of theoretical criteria for collapsing, the best strategy is to try to obtain an approximately equal proportion of cases in each category. If the distribution is to be dichotomized, then this would mean a 50 : 50 split. Achieving such a split for a nominal variable is a matter of combining conceptually similar categories. For example, if we wanted to compare students with different majors on some

BOX 14.2

Television Viewing and Labor Force Status:
An Example of Graphing Data

Recent developments in graphic procedures for data analysis (Cleveland, 1985:1), when implemented in computer software, offer an attractive new alternative to strictly numerical analysis of data. One useful tool is the *box-and-whisker* or *box plot* (Tukey, 1977:39–41). Figure A presents box plots that summarize television viewing reported by the 1985 GSS female respondents grouped according to their current labor force status.*

Figure A. Average daily television viewing by labor force status, female, 1985 GSS.

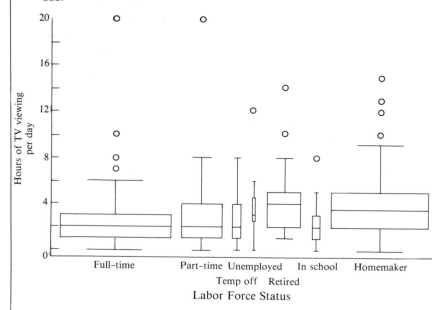

The box plots aptly display key aspects of each frequency distribution. The top and bottom of each box indicates respectively the 75th and 25th percentiles of television viewing, and the crossbar within each box shows the median (50th percentile). The height of a box is one measure of dispersion, showing the spread of television viewing among the middle 50 percent of the respondents (e.g., 1–3 hours for full-time female workers). An off-center position of the crossbar (median) within the box reflects skewness in the central 50 percent of the distribution (e.g., positive skewness for part-time workers). The width of each box is proportional to the number of respondents; this serves to flag patterns in the data that must be ignored or cautiously interpreted because of small sample sizes (e.g., the unemployed).

The vertical lines (or "whiskers") extending above and below each box include all

*The personal computer program STATA/GRAPHICS produced these examples.

BOX 14.2 (*continued*)

but the most extreme data values, which are plotted separately as circles.† The whiskers serve to fence out stray values, which are possibly *outliers* requiring special attention. Sometimes outliers result from measurement error, which seems likely here for the full-time worker who watches television 20 hours a day. Conversely, the reports of watching television 8 hours daily by a few full-time workers are not overly suspicious. Extreme outliers are usually excluded from the data analysis (especially if measurement error is suspected) or analyzed separately from the main data, since some statistical procedures may be adversely affected by a few unusual values.

Now you should be able to intepret the box plots in the figure. Which groups report the lowest median television viewing? Which has the lowest variation (dispersion) in viewing habits? How do the retired differ from those keeping house?

Box plots are one of a set of tools designed for exploratory data analysis, which has applications ranging from preparing data for testing prior hypotheses to dredging data for theoretically unexpected patterns. Because of their exploratory purpose, these techniques are relatively resistant to outliers and other data anomalies. And with an appropriate computer program it is quite easy to explore a data domain. When you studied the box plots in the figure, for example, you may have wondered about the large variation in television viewing among women working at home. Perhaps the viewing differences among the homemakers reflect, in part, educational differences. This hunch is easily checked by requesting the computer program to draw box plots for various educational groups (8 or fewer years of completed schooling, 9–11, 12, and 13 or more years), which is shown in Figure B. What do these box plots show?

Figure B. Average daily television viewing by education, female homemakers, 1985 GSS.

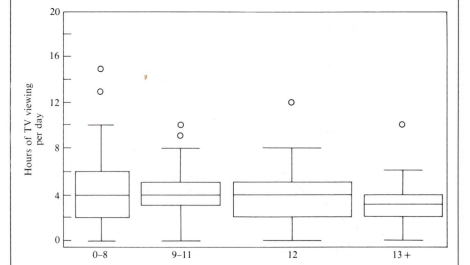

†Each whisker extends 1.5 times the height of the box or to the most extreme value if that distance is shorter.

relevant variable, and we found that 50 percent majored in mathematics or natural science, 30 percent in sociology, and 20 percent in psychology, then we might combine the latter two categories. At the ordinal, interval, and ratio levels, obtaining a 50:50 split means finding the appropriate cutting point between two contiguous categories. Problems arise, however, when the shape of the distribution does not enable one to create equal proportions. In fact, the more skewed the distribution, the more difficult it usually is to achieve a 50:50 dichotomy.

Gerbner and associates (1978) chose to trichotomize the distribution on television viewing. The nature of the distribution, however, prevented them from creating proportionate categories. Those in their "light" viewer category, who watched 2 hours or less, constituted nearly 50 percent of the respondents, while "medium" viewers, who watched 3 hours, made up 20 percent, and the remaining "heavy" viewers about 30 percent. This disproportionality, with no apparent theoretical rationale for the division, left these researchers open to criticism, because there is always the possibility of masking important information or distorting results when one collapses categories. In fact, sociologist Paul Hirsch (1980) has argued that nonviewers (0 hours of television per day) and "extreme" viewers (8 or more hours per day) tend to differ in nonpredictable ways from other respondents. Gerbner et al. (1981) effectively defend themselves against Hirsch's criticism. They point out, for example, that these two extreme groups represent less than 10 percent of the sample, and to separate them out "is a little like trying to study religion by comparing atheists and fanatic fundamentalists" (p. 46). But as you can see, deciding how to collapse categories can be a tricky business.

Bivariate Analysis

The object of bivariate analysis is to assess the relationship between two variables, such as that between television viewing and fear of violence. In general, this amounts to determining, first, whether or not the relationship is likely to exist (or whether it might be a product of random error), and second, how much effect or influence one variable has on the other. As with univariate analysis, the way in which this is done depends on the level of measurement.

Relationships Involving Nominal-Scale Variables

When the variables analyzed have only a few categories, as in most nominal- and ordinal-scale measurement, bivariate data are presented in tables. The tables constructed are known as cross-tabulations, cross-classifications, or contingency tables. A cross-tabulation requires a table with rows representing the categories of one variable and columns representing the categories of another. When a dependent variable can be identified, it is customary to make this the row variable and to treat the independent variable as the column variable, although this arbitrary convention is sometimes broken.

Before we get back to reported television viewing, which is a ratio-scale variable, let us consider the cross-tabulation of the two nominal-scale variables from the

TABLE 14.4. Attitude toward Capital Punishment by Gender,
1985 GSS

Attitude toward capital punishment	Gender		Total
	Male	Female	
Favor	547	607	1154
Oppose	115	182	297
Total	662	789	1451

1985 GSS shown in Table 14.4. The row variable consists of "attitude toward capital punishment," or, more precisely, whether the respondent favors or opposes the death penalty for persons convicted of murder. The column variable is "gender." Gender is the independent variable simply because, in one's lifetime, one's gender is determined earlier than one's attitude toward capital punishment. What sort of information does this table convey?

First, notice that the last column and bottom row, each labeled "Total," show the total number of respondents with each single characteristic, for example, 662 men. Because these four numbers (1154, 297, 662, 789) are along the right and bottom margin of the table, they are called *marginal frequencies*, or *marginals*. The row marginals (1154, 297) are the univariate frequency distribution for attitude toward capital punishment; the column marginals (662, 789) are the univariate frequency distribution for the variable gender. Also, the number at the lower right-hand corner is N, the total sample size excluding missing cases. N equals the sum of either the row or column marginals, or the sum of the four numbers (547 + 607 + 115 + 182) in the body of the table.

The body of the table where the categories of the two variables intersect contains the bivariate frequency distribution. Each intersection is called a *cell* and the number in each cell is called a *cell frequency*. Cell frequencies in a *bi*variate table indicate the numbers of cases with each possible combination of *two* characteristics; for example, there were 547 *men* who *favored capital punishment*. Because Table 14.4 has two rows and two columns, it is referred to as *2 × 2 table*.

Now that we know the meaning of the numbers in a cross-tabulation, how do we analyze these numbers to assess the relationship between the variables? What comparisons should we make? With gender the independent variable in Table 14.4, the relevant substantive questions are: Does gender influence attitude toward capital punishment? If so, how much influence does it have? If a relationship exists, then a change in gender should produce a change of favor/oppose responses in the distribution on the dependent variable. Either men will be more likely to favor and less likely to oppose than women, or women will be more likely to favor and less likely to oppose than men. Notice, however, that when we compare cell frequencies there are more women than men who both favor and oppose (607 versus 547 and 182 versus 115).

Obviously, there is a problem here. Although we are comparing the proper cells, the comparison is invalid because the cell frequencies for men and women are based on different total frequencies. To be valid, the cell numbers compared must

TABLE 14.5. Attitude toward Capital
Punishment by Gender (%), 1985 GSS

	Gender	
Attitude	Male	Female
Favor	82.6%	76.9%
Oppose	17.4	23.1
Total	100.0%	100.0%
	(662)	(789)

be expressed as parts of the same total. This is accomplished by creating separate percentage distributions for men and women, thereby converting each total to 100 percent. The result is a bivariate percentage distribution, presented as Table 14.5. Now when we compare responses across gender, we see clearly that men are more likely to favor capital punishment by a percentage of 82.6 to 76.9, and conversely, less likely to oppose (17.4 percent to 23.1 percent).

A bivariate percentage distribution enables one to compare the distribution of one variable across the categories of the other. In Table 14.5, we created such a distribution by percentaging *down* so that the column totals, corresponding to the categories of the independent variable, equaled 100 percent. The rule that we followed in deriving this table is to *compute percentages in the direction of the independent variable*. If gender had been the row variable and attitude toward capital punishment the column variable, then we would have run the percentages in the other direction—across rather than down. To interpret the relationship in Table 14.5, we compared percentages by reading *across* the table. In so doing, we followed a second rule: *make comparisons in the opposite direction from the way percentages are run*. Having percentaged down, we compared across; had we percentaged across, we would have compared down.

These are extremely important rules to follow, for cross-tabulations may be percentaged in either direction and are easily misinterpreted.[9] If we percentage Table 14.4 in the direction of the attitude variable, then the results would indicate whether those who favor capital punishment are more likely to be men than those who oppose, which is indeed an odd and unlikely research question.

One of the variables that Gerbner and Gross included in their analysis was gender. Table 14.6 presents the bivariate percentage distribution for gender and fear of violence. What does this table reveal about the relationship between these variables? It clearly shows that in this sample of respondents, women are more likely to fear violence than men. But does this necessarily mean that the relationship holds for the population from which the sample was drawn? And what does the bivariate table reveal about how much effect gender has on fear of violence?

As you read across Table 14.6, you saw that there was a difference of 24.9 (56.4 − 21.5) in the percentage of women as opposed to men who are afraid to walk alone at night. This "percentage difference" indicates that a relationship exists for these data; if there were no difference between the percentages, then we would conclude that no relationship exists. Remember, however, that these are *sample*

TABLE 14.6. Fear of Walking Alone at
Night by Gender (%), 1985 GSS

	Gender	
Afraid	Male	Female
Yes	21.5%	56.4%
No	78.5	43.6
Total	100.0%	100.0%
	(685)	(833)

data. The important question is not whether a relationship exists in these data; rather, do the observed cell frequencies reveal a true relationship between the variables in the *population*, or are they simply the result of sampling and other random error?

The latter judgment is made by means of *tests of statistical significance*. For cross-tabulations, the most commonly used statistic is the *chi-square (or χ^2) test for independence*. This chi-square test is based on a comparison of observed cell frequencies with the cell frequencies one would expect if there were no relationship between the variables. Table 14.7A shows the expected cell frequencies, assuming no relationship, and B the derived bivariate percentage distribution. Notice that the cell percentages in Table 14.7B (reading across) are the same as the marginals; this indicates that knowing whether a respondent is male or female is of no help in predicting his or her fear of violence, precisely the meaning of "no relationship" between variables. The larger the differences between the actual cell frequencies and those expected assuming no relationship, the larger the value of chi-square and the more likely that the relationship exists in the population. Chi-square values for the data in Tables 14.5 and 14.6 are both statistically significant.[10] This suggests that in the American population, women are less likely than men to favor capital punishment (Table 14.5), and women are more likely than men to fear violence (Table 14.6).

Knowing that these relationships exist in the population, however, does not tell us how much effect the independent variable has on the dependent variable. It is possible for a relationship to exist when changes in one variable correspond only

TABLE 14.7. Fear of Walking Alone at Night by Gender, 1985 GSS,
Assuming No Relationship

	A. Frequencies			B. Percentages		
	Gender			Gender		
Afraid	Male	Female	Total	Male	Female	Total
Yes	278	339	617	41%	41%	41%
No	407	494	901	59	59	59%
Total	685	833	1518	100%	100%	100%
				(685)	(833)	(1518)

slightly to changes in the other. The degree of this correspondence is a second measurable property of bivariate distributions. In a 2×2 table, the percentage difference provides one indicator, albeit a poor one, of the strength of the relationship: the larger the difference, the stronger the relationship. However, researchers prefer to use one of several other statistics to measure the size of this effect. These *measures of association* are standardized to vary between 0 (no association) and plus or minus 1.0 (perfect association). One such measure, commonly used for 2×2 tables, is Yule's Q, which equals .18 for the data in Table 14.5 and $-.65$ for the data in Table 14.6.[11] Although the choice of labels is somewhat arbitrary, the magnitudes of these values suggest a "low" association in the first table and a "substantial" association in the second (see J. A. Davis, 1971:49). In other words, gender is more strongly related to fear of encountering violence than to attitude toward capital punishment. (For variables with nominal categories, the sign, $+$ or $-$, does not reveal anything meaningful about the nature of the relationship.)

Relationships between Two Ordinal-Scale Variables

A third property—the *direction* of the relationship—may be measured when the categories of both variables can be ordered, that is, when one has at least ordinal-level measurement. Direction refers to the tendency for increases in the values of one variable to be associated with systematic increases or decreases in the values of another variable. Direction may be either positive or negative. In a positive relationship, lower values of one variable tend to be associated with lower values of the other variable, and higher values of one variable tend to go along with higher values of the other. The categories of the variables of education and income, for example, can be ordered from low to high. When we examine the association between these variables we expect it to be positive, with lower educated persons tending to have lower incomes and persons of higher education tending to have higher incomes. Table 14.8 illustrates this relationship with GSS data from 1985. Carefully examine this table before reading further.

Notice that, as in previous examples, Table 14.8 is percentaged down for each category of the independent variable, education; so comparisons should be made across. The percentage with low income (first row) drops sharply as educational attainment increases: 58.5 to 32.2 to 24.7 percent. Similarly, the percentage with

TABLE 14.8. Income by Level of Education, 1985 GSS

Income[b]	Level of education[a]		
	Low	Medium	High
Low	58.5%	32.2%	24.7%
Medium	34.3	44.9	38.4
High	7.2	22.9	36.9
Total	100.0%	100.0%	100.0%
	(147)	(692)	(580)

[a]Low, less than 12 years; medium, 12 years; high, more than 12 years.
[b]Low, $0–14,999; medium, $15,000–34,999; high, $35,000 or over.

TABLE 14.9. Number of Hours per Day Watching TV by Years
of Education, 1985 GSS

Number of TV hours	Years of education		
	Less than 12	12	More than 12
0–2	37.6%	43.2%	61.3%
3	18.7	22.7	19.7
4 or more	43.6	34.1	19.0
Total	100.0%	100.0%	100.0%
	(168)	(756)	(599)

high income (third row) rises with increasing education: 7.2 to 22.9 to 36.9 percent. It is this sort of pattern (higher income associated with higher education) that suggests a clearly positive (direct) relationship.

In a negative (inverse) relationship, there is a tendency for *lower* values of one variable to be associated with *higher* values of the other variable. Table 14.9 reveals such a relationship between education and the number of hours of television watched on an average day: as education increases, television viewing time decreases. (There are many possible explanations here: perhaps higher income persons are more apt to be exposed to and can better afford other, more expensive forms of entertainment, or perhaps higher educated people have less leisure time, or maybe they read more.)

The existence of a relationship between two ordinal-scale variables also may be tested with the chi-square statistic. Ordinal measures of the strength of association, while differing in name from nominal measures of association, are similar in concept. The magnitude of such statistics, ignoring the sign, indicates the strength of the relationship; and the sign (+ or −) indicates the direction of the association (positive or negative). One such statistic, gamma, equals .43 for the data in Table 14.8 and −.31 for the data in Table 14.9.[12] Thus, there is a moderate positive association between income and years of schooling and a moderate negative association between television hours and years of schooling, and the former association is stronger than the latter.

So far we have restricted ourselves to variables having only two or three categories and, consequently, to tables with four to nine cells. This is not unusual, as most cross-tabulation analyses in social research are limited to variables with relatively few categories. There are three important reasons for this. First, the size of the table increases geometrically as the number of categories for each variable increases. And the larger the table, the more difficult it is to discern the pattern of the relationship, which can be much more complex than the positive or negative relationships we have described. Second, as we pointed out in our discussion of sampling, the finer the breakdown of one's sample into various categories, the fewer cases there will be for any given breakdown (or cell of the table). Hence, larger tables may require impractically large samples for reliable assessments. Finally, variables with a relatively large number of categories either constitute or tend to approximate interval-scale measurement. With interval-scale variables, we can use a more precise and more powerful form of statistical analysis known as correlation and regression.

Relationships between a Nominal/Ordinal and an Interval/Ratio Variable

To create the cross-tabulation between the two ordinal-scale variables in Table 14.9, we collapsed the categories of variables that were measured at the ratio level. Thus, respondents were grouped into one of three categories based on the number of hours of television they watched and into three categories according to the number of years of education they had completed. We did this for heuristic purposes and for purposes of replicating the analysis of Gerbner and colleagues. When analyzing ratio-scale variables, it is generally better not to use such grouping procedures, because the grouping eliminates potentially important variation. For example, there may be important differences between people who watch 0 as opposed to 1 and 2 hours of television per day, but these respondents are treated as the same in Table 14.9.

When one of two variables of interest is measured at the interval or ratio level, the researcher has three basic options. The first option is to collapse the categories of the interval/ratio variable, as in Table 14.9. This is what Gerbner and associates chose to do in examining the relationship between television viewing and fear of violence. Table 14.10A replicates their bivariate analysis for the 1985 GSS data. Notice that the biggest difference is between "heavy" viewers and the other two categories: "heavy" viewers are most fearful, as predicted. This is what Gerbner and associates found in the 1977 data that they analyzed. In 1985, however, "medium" viewers are less fearful than "light" viewers, although this difference is not statistically significant.

The second option, and the one that we think is most appropriate, uses the actual number of hours of television that each person watched. In this case, one calculates the average—that is, mean—number of hours of television watched by respondents in each of the fear categories, as we have done in Table 14.10B. This table shows that the mean hours of television watched by respondents who were afraid to go out alone at night was 3.09, as compared to an average of 2.90 for those who were not afraid. Once again, the difference is in the predicted direction.

A third option when analyzing a variable with only two categories, such as fear of violence, is to create what is called a *dummy variable*. This is a variable that has been recoded so that one of its categories has a value of 1 and the other category has a value of 0. Dummy coding enables the researcher to manipulate the variable numerically and to use certain kinds of statistical analysis that would not be possible otherwise.

In a reanalysis of the Gerbner et al. analysis of 1977 GSS data, Michael Hughes (1980) dummy-coded the fear-of-violence variable while retaining the three-category coding of television viewing. We have replicated part of Hughes's analysis in Table 14.10C. Following Hughes, we assigned a value of 1 to "yes" responses and a value of 0 to "no" responses. The mean values for dummy variables indicate the proportion of responses coded as 1. In Table 14.10C this is the proportion of

TABLE 14.10. Alternatives for Analyzing
the Relationship between Television
Viewing and Fear of Violence

A. Cross-tabulation after Collapsing Categories

	Television viewing		
Afraid	Light	Medium	Heavy
Yes	39.3%	37.4%	45.5%
No	60.7	62.6	54.5
Total	100.0%	100.0%	100.0%
	(737)	(310)	(462)

B. Mean Hours of Television Viewing

Afraid	Mean	N
Yes	3.09	(616)
No	2.90	(893)
Total	2.98	(1509)

C. Mean Fear of Walking Alone at Night,
with 1 = Yes and 0 = No

	Television viewing			
	Light	Medium	Heavy	Total
Mean	.393	.374	.455	.408
N	(737)	(310)	(462)	(1509)

respondents who said they were afraid to walk alone at night. Notice that the proportions in this table are equivalent to the percentages in the cross-tabulation in Table 14.10A. The reason is that these two tables make use of the same information on each variable. However, by dummy-coding the fear-of-violence question, we have made possible the application of more powerful techniques for analyzing bivariate relationships, which we cover in the next section.

Deciding which of these options to take is not a matter of style, but of technical considerations such as sampling variation and the level and quality of measurement. For the novice researcher unfamiliar with these issues, we recommend the second strategy because it retains all of the available information. One happy note is that for most data, it will not matter much which strategy you adopt. All three subtables in Table 14.10, for example, reveal basically the same relationship: a small effect (gamma = .08 in Table 14.10A) that reaches the same level of statistical significance.[13] In other words, the association between television viewing and fear of violence is very weak for the 1985 GSS, as it was for the 1977 GSS.

Relationships between Two Interval/Ratio Scale Variables

In chapter 4, we showed how relationships between two quantitative variables are depicted by plotting the values of each variable in a graphic coordinate system. In conjunction with this form of presentation, social researchers use a statistical method called *regression analysis* to analyze the effect of one interval/ratio variable on another. This is done by finding the mathematical equation that most closely describes the data.

Let us begin our examination of regression analysis by looking at a *scatterplot* of television viewing and education for a random sample of 100 respondents in the 1985 GSS (Figure 14.3). We have chosen a sample of the over 1500 respondents simply to make the plot easier to read. Each plot or point in the graph represents the values of one of the 100 respondents on two variables. With the vertical axis as our reference, we can read the value of the dependent variable (number of television hours); and with the horizontal axis as our reference, we can read the value of the independent variable (years of education). Thus, the circled symbol in the figure represents a respondent with 14 years of education who reported watching an average of 6 hours of television per day.

The scatterplot gives the researcher a rough sense of the form of the relationship: whether it is positive or negative, and whether it is best characterized with a straight or curved line. This is crucial information because regression analysis assumes that the data have a particular form. If a straight line provides the best fit with the data,

FIGURE 14.3. Scatterplot of television viewing by education, 1985 GSS.

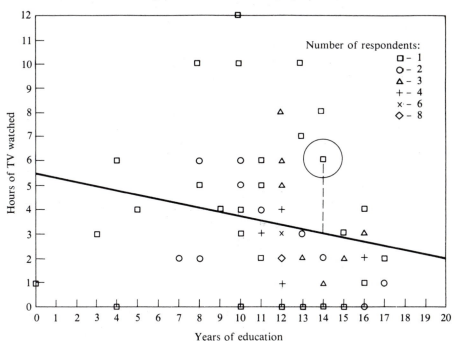

Years of education

then one should do linear regression; if a curve provides the best fit, then one should use special techniques for fitting curvilinear relationships (which are beyond the scope of this book). As a first step in our analysis, we will examine the scatterplot to make a judgment about form. The overall form of the data in Figure 14.3 is somewhat difficult to discern; however, since the relationship does not appear to be sharply curvilinear, we can assume that a straight line offers as good a fit as a curved line. The trend of the data also suggests that the number of hours watched per day declines as education increases, a pattern that we observed earlier in Table 14.9.

Having decided to fit a straight line to the data, and therefore to do *linear* regression analysis, we need to know two things: (1) the mathematical equation for a straight line, and (2) the criterion for selecting a line to represent the data.

The general form of the equation for a straight line is $Y = a + bX$, where Y is the predicted value of the dependent variable and X is the independent variable. Thus, an equation for a straight line relating hours of TV watched to years of education is

$$\text{Number of TV hours} = a + b \text{ (years of education)}$$

The value a, called the *Y-intercept*, is the point where the line crosses the vertical axis (where education $= 0$). The value b, called the *slope* or *regression coefficient*, indicates how much Y increases (or decreases) for every change of 1 unit in X; in other words, how much increase (or decrease) occurs in the number of hours of television watched for every change of 1 year in the respondents' education. To get the line of best fit, then, we could simply draw a line on the scatterplot that seems to reflect best the trend in the data and then determine the values of a and b from the graph. Of course, there are many lines that we could draw—a and b can take on an infinite number of values; so, how do we know when we have obtained the best fit?

Regression analysis uses the method of least squares as the criterion for selecting the line that best describes the data. According to this method, the best-fitting line minimizes the sum of the squared vertical distances from the data points to the line. We have drawn the *regression line*, also called the *least squares line*, on the scatterplot. We also have drawn a dashed line that shows the vertical distance, as measured in number of television hours, between a specific data point and the regression line. The regression line represents the equation for predicting Y from X; the vertical distances between data points and this line represent prediction errors (also called *residuals*). Thus, by finding the line that minimizes the sum of the squared distances from it we are, in effect, finding the best linear predictor of television viewing from a knowledge of the respondents' education. The precise equation generated by the method of least squares can be found via a mathematical formula with the aid of a computer. When we applied this formula to the data in Figure 14.3, we got the following equation:

$$\text{Number of TV hours} = 5.47 - .18 \text{ (years of education)}$$

In other words, someone with 0 years of education would be predicted to watch 5.47 hours of television on an average day; and, for every increase of 1 year in education, a *decrease* of .18 is expected in hours of television watched.

The regression equation gives the best linear prediction of the dependent variable based on the data at hand. By itself, however, it does not tell us whether the predictions are any good. It does not tell us how strong the linear association is or whether the relationship is likely to exist in the population.

The strength of the association between two variables measured at the interval/ratio level is usually measured by the *correlation coefficient* (symbolized as r), which may vary between -1 and $+1$. The sign of the coefficient, which is always the same as the sign of the regression coefficient, indicates the direction of the relationship. The magnitude of its value depends on two factors: (1) the steepness of the regression line and (2) the variation or scatter of the data points around this line. If the line is not very steep, so that it is nearly parallel to the X-axis, then we might as well predict the same value of Y for every unit change in X, as there is very little change in our prediction (as indicated by b in the equation) for every unit change in the independent variable. By the same token, the greater the spread of values about the regression line, regardless of the steepness of the slope, the less accurate are predictions based on the linear regression. The scatterplot for the regression of television hours on years of schooling shows that the line is not very steep in relation to the horizontal axis and that there is considerable variation around the line. Not surprisingly, therefore, the correlation coefficient indicates a weak negative association of $-.23$.

To illustrate a larger effect, we produced a linear regression for two other 1985 GSS variables, as shown in Figure 14.4. Respondents were asked to give the first names or initials of people with whom they had discussed important matters over the last 6 months. We chose as our dependent variable the age of the first person so named, excluding parents and children. The independent variable is the age of the respondent. Once again, we took a sample of 100 to make the figure easier to read. The regression equation drawn on the figure is

Age of confidant $= 10.26 + .77$ (age of respondent)

We cannot compare this slope coefficient with the one in the previous example, because slope values depend on the unit of measurement. For example, the slope here would be twelve times greater if we measured the age of the confidant in months instead of years. Notice, however, that there is much less scatter of points about the regression line in this figure than in the previous figure. Accordingly, the correlation coefficient of $+.75$ shows a substantially stronger association.

Statistics also exist for testing whether the correlation coefficient and the regression coefficient are significantly different from zero. These may be found in most statistics textbooks. Both of these coefficients are significant for the data in Figures 14.3 and 14.4.[14]

As we noted earlier, we can apply regression analysis to nominal/ordinal scale variables such as gender by the use of dummy-coding. We could, for example, code

FIGURE 14.4. Scatterplot of confidant's age by respondent's age, 1985 GSS.

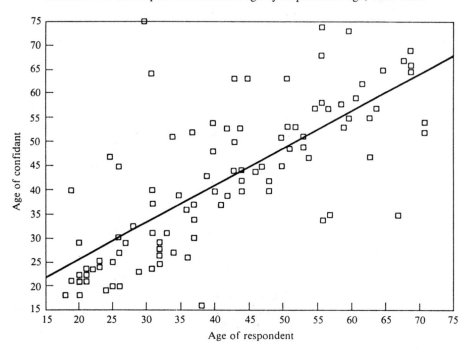

females as 1 and males as 0 and proceed to regress an interval/ratio level variable, such as number of television hours watched, on gender. The horizontal axis would have only two values, 0 and 1, and the regression coefficient would indicate the difference between men and women in the mean number of television hours watched. Performing this analysis for the 1985 GSS data, we find a regression coefficient of .41; hence, women (mean = 3.17 hours) watch .41 more hours of television per day than men (mean = 2.76 hours).[15] This coefficient as well as the correlation of .09 are both significantly different from zero. The value of regression analyses involving dummy variables will become more apparent in the next chapter when we consider the regression of one dependent variable on several independent variables.

Summary

Data analysis involves an iterative comparison of theory and data. Data analysis begins and ends with the researcher's hypotheses or theoretical model. Such models guide the collection and analysis of data, indicating what variables should be measured and statistically controlled. And the analyses, in turn, suggest new theoretical formulations and new directions for research.

Prior to quantitative analysis, the researcher must process the data by putting the information in computer-readable form. In survey research, this entails five steps:

coding, editing, data entry, cleaning, and data modification. Coding consists of assigning numbers to the categories of each variable. Most coding in survey research is done prior to data collection, as answers are precoded directly on the questionnaire or interview schedule. Codes for open-ended questions are developed after the data are collected and usually edge-coded on the form. The researcher usually prepares a codebook, which gives the answers that correspond to each numerical code, the location of each variable in the data file, as well as coding and decision rules.

Editing is designed to ensure that the data to be read into the computer are as complete, error-free, and readable as possible. It begins immediately after data collection, as the interviewer carefully checks over completed interviewer forms, and it continues as the forms are processed by an editor in a central research office. After editing is complete, the data are entered into the computer and stored in a data file. The format of the file consists of a specified number of lines, or records, per case, with data on each variable located in specified columns of each record.

After entry into a data file, the data are cleaned for errors in coding and transmitting the data to the computer. This is a multistep process, often beginning with a verification procedure whereby all data are entered into the computer a second time and each dual entry is checked for noncomparable codes. Wild-code checking consists of checking for "illegal" codes among the values recorded for each variable. Consistency checking consists of checking for unreasonable patterns of responses, such as whether contingency questions are answered only by those for whom the questions are intended. Once cleaned, some of the data may be modified prior to or as part of the analysis (e.g., by collapsing the categories of a variable).

With the data cleaned, the researcher is ready to instruct the computer to carry out various statistical analyses. The primary functions of statistics are descriptive and inferential. Descriptive statistics are designed to summarize the data at hand; inferential statistics indicate the extent to which one may generalize beyond the data at hand. In relation to the modeling of relationships, which we consider further in the next chapter, statistics can generate estimates of various effects hypothesized in a model and can evaluate how well the data fit a given model.

Statistical analysis usually begins with the inspection of each variable singly (univariate analysis). The categories or values of each variable first are organized into frequency and percentage distributions. If the data constitute interval-level measurement, then the researcher will also compute statistics that define various properties of the distribution. Statistical measures of central tendency reveal various points of concentration: the most typical value (mode), the middle value (median), and the average (mean). Common measures of dispersion are the difference between the lowest and highest values (range) and an index of the spread of the values around the mean (standard deviation). Distributions also may be described in terms of their shape, such as their skewness.

Bivariate analysis examines the nature of the relationship between two variables. For relationships involving exclusively nominal- or ordinal-scale variables, such analysis begins with the construction of cross-tabulations, with table cells containing the bivariate distribution. The rule for percentaging cross-tabulations is to percentage in the direction of the independent variable; the rule for reading such tables is to make comparisons in the opposite direction from the way the percentages are run.

For relationships involving interval- or ratio-scale variables, the data are plotted in a scatterplot and characterized in terms of a mathematical function. Linear regression analysis identifies the straight-line function that provides the best fit with the data by virtue of minimizing the sum of the squared deviations from the line. The slope of the line reveals the predicted change in the dependent variable per unit change in the independent variable. Nominal/ordinal scale variables may be included in regression analyses as independent variables by dummy-coding categories 0 and 1, in which case the slope indicates the mean difference between categories on the dependent variable.

Regardless of measurement level, bivariate analysis assesses both the likelihood that the observed relationship is the product of random error, and the strength of the association between the variables. The first task usually is accomplished for cross-tabulations by means of the chi-square test for independence. Statistical measures of association generally vary from -1 to $+1$, with the sign indicating the direction of the relationship and the magnitude indicating the strength of the association.

Key Terms

data processing	percentage distribution
coding	mean
precoding	median
edge coding	mode
codebook	range
editing	standard deviation
computer file	frequency/percentage polygon
data file	bivariate analysis
record	marginal frequencies
format	cell frequencies
fixed-column format	chi-square test of independence
data cleaning	measures of association
wild-code checking	dummy variable
consistency checking	regression analysis
data modification	scatterplot
descriptive statistics	Y-intercept
inferential statistics	slope/regression coefficient
univariate analysis	regression line
frequency distribution	correlation coefficient

Review Questions and Problems

1. Carefully state Gerbner and Gross's hypothesis regarding television viewing and fear of violence. How might the variables of age and gender each create a spurious association between television viewing and fear of violence?

2. When and how is coding generally carried out in survey research?

3. Why is it a good idea to include as much information as practical when coding data for analysis?

4. What is edge coding? When is it used? How is it similar to precoding?

5. What information generally is contained in a codebook?

6. What is the purpose of editing?

7. Describe the general structure of a data file with a fixed-column format.

8. Assuming eighty-column records, what is the minimum number of records per case required to store the following information: four-digit respondent identification number; thirty variables with one-column codes; twenty variables with two-column codes; five variables with three-column codes; four variables with four-column codes; and one variable with a six-column code?

9. Imagine that you have collected data from 100 students using a four-page questionnaire containing about thirty-five questions. Describe how you would go about cleaning your data once you have entered them into the computer.

10. What is the difference between wild-code checking and consistency checking?

11. Give an example of data transformation other than one mentioned in this chapter.

12. What are the functions of descriptive and of inferential statistics? Are these the same as the scientific goals of description and explanation? Briefly explain.

13. How may univariate analyses of variables aid multivariate analyses?

14. Why do data analysts compute percentage distributions? What do they tell you that frequency distributions do not?

15. Why is it sometimes necessary to collapse or combine categories when presenting the frequency distribution of an interval/ratio scale variable?

16. What are the three statistical properties of frequency distributions of interval/ratio scale variables?

17. Identify the three measures of central tendency. What does each tell you about the distribution?

18. What does the standard deviation describe about a distribution?

19. What was the general shape of the distribution of the hours of television watched for the 1985 GSS?

20. How can an examination of the frequency distribution inform researcher decisions about collapsing variable categories?

21. What do bivariate analyses in general tell you about the relationships between two variables?

22. What is the rule for percentaging bivariate tables? What is the rule for comparing percentages in such tables?

23. What does the chi-square test for independence tell you about the association between variables?

24. Consider the following values of Yule's Q for three different sets of variables: (a) $-.82$; (b) $+.04$; (c) $+.35$. Which association is strongest? Which association is negligible?

25. Describe the recommended statistical procedure for determining the relationship between an interval/ratio scale variable and a nominal/ordinal scale variable. How else may such a relationship be estimated statistically?

26. Dummy code the following variables: gender; attitude toward capital punishment (favor/oppose); race (white/black, treating "other" as missing). What does the mean value of a dummy variable indicate?

27. Why do data analysts examine the form of the relationship before doing a regression analysis?

28. Consider the following equation based on 1985 GSS data.

Respondent's years of education = 9.39 + .342 (father's years of education)

Describe the predicted relationship in this equation. How much change in respondent's education is associated with each increase of 1 year in father's education? What is the predicted years of education of a respondent whose father has completed 16 years of education? (This will require some calculation.)

29. Describe the difference between a regression coefficient and a correlation coefficient.

30. What does the regression coefficient indicate when an interval/ratio variable is regressed on a dummy variable?

NOTES

1. Samples for each survey were drawn independently. Block quota sampling was used in the 1972, 1973, and 1974 surveys, a transitional, one-half block quota and one-half probability sampling design was used in 1975 and 1976, and full probability (multistage cluster) sampling was employed in the remaining surveys. The interviews, lasting about 1 hour, were conducted with "English-speaking persons 18 years of age or over, living in non-institutional arrangements within the continental United States."

2. There are other options for data coding and entry. Before interactive computer terminals became popular and data were entered on disk or tape, punched cards were the most common means of input. Researchers also may use an optical scanner. This device reads pencil marks on special code sheets, such as the answer forms to the Scholastic Aptitude Test (*SAT*), and then enters this information into a computer file. Another more recently developed option is a form of direct data entry found in telephone interviewing. In this process, the interviewer types the respondent's answers directly into the computer terminal.

3. Other arrangements are used for managing complex data sets, such as records for students that are linked to informational records for their teachers and their schools (see Sonquist and Dunkelberg, 1977:17–40; Karweit and Meyers, 1983:398–404).

4. The alternative method is called *freefield format*. Required by some microcomputer packages, this method places one or more blanks between adjacent values, thereby relying on the sequence in which information is entered rather than on fixed column locations.

5. Social scientists today seldom write their own programs of instructions to the computer. Instead, they rely on "canned" or "packaged" programs stored in the computer and specially written to perform statistical analyses of social science data. To use these programs, you must (1) give the computer a command that accesses the particular package, (2) using the rules for that package, describe the format and location of the data file, and (3) indicate the specific analyses you want done. Thorough discussions of these procedures can be found in the manuals for SPSS, SAS, BMDP, or for any other packages available for your computer.

6. The distinction between descriptive and inferential statistics should not be confused

with the scientific goals of description and explanation. Both forms of statistical analysis may be used to accomplish both goals. The first purpose of inferential statistics identified here is description, and the second purpose is explanation. Similarly, descriptive statistics may provide a summary measure of some characteristic of the sample data (description) or may indicate the strength of a hypothesized association between two variables (explanation).

7. Chance may enter into theoretical explanations, which has important implications for popular statistical techniques (Berk, 1983).

8. "Don't know" responses sometimes are meaningful and should be treated as "non-missing" and included in the percentage distribution. For example, the "don't know" responses may represent those who take a middle position between two extreme response categories. A 1984 GSS question asks, "Would you say that most of the time people try to be helpful, or that they are mostly just looking out for themselves?" Since a sizable number of respondents answered "don't know" or "it depends," it is best not to treat these answers as missing, but as middle responses in a three-category ordinal scale, with "try to be helpful" and "just look out for themselves" as the two "extreme" categories.

9. Sometimes these rules are broken for descriptive reasons (e.g., to ascertain the educational background of different income groups), or because the data are unrepresentative of the population with respect to the dependent variable (see Zeisel, 1968:30–36).

10. For Table 14.5, Pearson's chi-square statistic $= 7.17$ (p $< .01$); for Table 14.6, chi-square $= 190.46$ (p $< .001$).

11. For an explanation of Yule's Q and other popular measures of association, see chapter 9 in Bohrnstedt and Knoke (1982).

12. See Bohrnstedt and Knoke (1982:291–296) for a discussion of gamma.

13. For Table 14.10A, chi-square $= 6.25$ ($p < .05$); Table 14.10B, $t = 1.69$ ($p < .05$, one-tailed); and Table 14.10C, $F = 3.13$, ($p < .05$).

14. For Figure 14.3, $t = 2.32$ ($p < .05$); Figure 14.4, $t = 11.11$ ($p < .001$).

15. The general form of the regression equation would be: TV hours $= a + b$(gender). The equation for men is $2.76 + .41(0) = 2.76$; for women, $2.76 + .41(1) = 3.17$.

15

Multivariate Analysis

In the last chapter we examined bivariate relationships; statistically, this amounted to calculating the degree of association or correlation between variables. Bivariate analysis provides a basis, as exemplified by regression slope coefficients, for predicting the values of one variable from values of another. However, if our goal goes beyond prediction to testing causal hypotheses, then calculating bivariate associations is never sufficient. As we have emphasized repeatedly, causal inferences are based not only on association but also on theoretical assumptions and empirical evidence about direction of influence and nonspuriousness.

In a cross-sectional survey, for example, a correlation between X and Y may imply that X causes Y, that Y causes X, that X and Y mutually cause each other, or that X and Y are causally unrelated (spurious association). The statistical techniques introduced in this chapter help the researcher to choose among such possible interpretations. But it is important to realize that statistical analyses by themselves do not provide a basis for inferring causal relationships. Instead, a researcher starts with a theory of the causal process linking X and Y, and then determines if the data are consistent with the theory.

Direction of influence, in particular, is usually based on formal theory or practical knowledge. In experiments, of course, the direction is set by the manipulation of the independent variable, which always precedes measurement of the dependent variable. Similarly, direction is determined by the natural time order of many nonexperimental variables. In relating high school students' occupational aspirations to their parents' education, for example, the latter occurs earlier in time and may be a cause but not an effect of students' occupational aspirations. When time order is indeterminate, causal direction often is determined on the basis that one variable is more fixed, permanent, or less alterable than the other (M. Rosenberg, 1968:11–12). Gender, a fixed variable, may influence fear of walking alone at night, but not vice versa. Religious affiliation may influence happiness if we theorize that the former is relatively unchangeable compared to the latter.

Theoretical knowledge sometimes dictates treating direction of influence as mutual (*reciprocal causation*). Reviewing explanations of the inverse correlation between American women's employment and childbearing, Waite and Stolzenberg (1976) found strong arguments for mutual causation. Young women may be having fewer children because they want to work more outside the home (career aspirations influence fertility). And women may be working more because they want fewer children (fertility plans influence employment). Using a statistical method appropriate for studying mutual causation, Waite and Stolzenberg concluded that employment plans dominate fertility expectations. (For related studies, see Smith-Lovin and Tickamyer, 1978; Cramer 1980.)

Theory also guides tests for spuriousness. Through theory, for example, we identify extraneous variables that might produce spurious statistical associations. Utilizing such theoretical knowledge, we can apply statistical techniques that go a long way toward demonstrating nonspuriousness. In principle, these techniques have the same effect as randomization in experiments. The main difference is that whereas randomization is assumed to control for *all* extraneous variables, statistical control in nonexperimental studies can be applied only to measured variables. Obviously, this places a premium on identifying and measuring relevant variables and on specifying their causal relations. Thus it is easy to see why modeling has become so important, because modeling is a way of specifying various possible causal relations among a set of variables. It is now time to take a closer look at the data analyst's conception of a model.

Modeling Relationships

Most generally, a model is a simplified picture of reality; models for data analysis depict the hypothesized, or theoretical, relations among two or more variables. The translation of a theory into a statistical model ordinarily takes the form of one or more mathematical equations. However, to convey the logic of modeling and analysis, we will use easily understood arrow diagrams, which often serve as an aid to statistical modeling.

Arrow diagrams represent the causal ordering of a set of variables. Each arrow indicates causal direction. Thus, the arrow pointing from X to Y in Figure 15.1A means that X is hypothesized to be a cause of Y. Two arrows pointing in opposite directions (Figure 15.1B) indicate reciprocal causation—that X and Y are thought to influence each other. A single line (often curved) with arrows on both ends (Figure 15.1C) indicates that there may be a statistical association between the variables, but that a causal explanation of the association is not part of the model. Finally, the absence of an arrow connecting two variables means that no causal relationship is hypothesized.

Besides causal order, arrow diagrams can indicate the direction of a relationship. This is generally signified with a sign, + or −, above the arrow. A + sign indicates a positive relationship: as X increases in value, Y increases. A − sign indicates a negative relationship: as X increases in value, Y decreases.[1] To clarify the use of these conventions, let us examine their application to the studies of Gerbner et al. of the effects of television viewing on fear of violence (see chapter 14).

FIGURE 15.1. Arrow diagrams for different causal relationships.

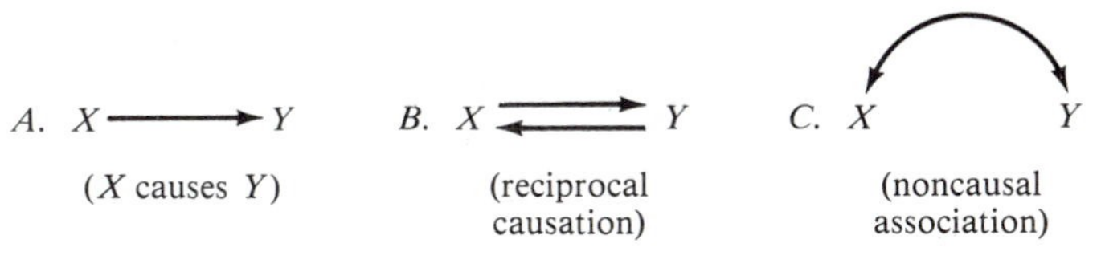

A. $X \longrightarrow Y$ B. $X \rightleftarrows Y$ C. $X \quad\quad Y$

(X causes Y)   (reciprocal causation)   (noncausal association)

FIGURE 15.2. Alternative models of relationships among three variables.

A. Television viewing $\xrightarrow{+}$ Fear of violence

(Television viewing affects fear of violence)

B. Education $\begin{array}{c}\xrightarrow{-}\ \text{Fear of violence}\\ \searrow^{-}\\ \text{Television viewing}\end{array}$

(Spurious relationship between television viewing and fear of violence produced by education)

C. Education $\xrightarrow{\quad-\quad}$ Television viewing $\xrightarrow{\quad+\quad}$ Fear of violence

(Education indirectly affects fear of violence via television viewing)

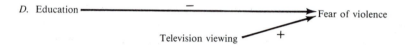

D. Education $\xrightarrow{\qquad\qquad-\qquad\qquad}$ Fear of violence

Television viewing $\nearrow^{+}$

(Education and television viewing independently affect fear of violence)

E. Education $\begin{array}{c}\xrightarrow{\qquad-\qquad}\ \text{Fear of violence}\\ \searrow^{-}\ \text{Television viewing}\ \nearrow^{+}\end{array}$

(Education has both direct and indirect effects on fear of violence)

Figure 15.2A shows a diagram of the original hypothesis: the more hours of television watched per day, the more likely that one will harbor fears of encountering violence. Recall, however, that Gerbner and associates included other variables in their analysis. One of these variables was the respondent's level of education. Adding this variable to the picture creates several other possible models: that education affects both television viewing and fear of violence, creating a spurious relationship (Figure 15.2B); that education has an *indirect* effect on fear of violence— that is, education affects television viewing which, in turn, affects fear of violence (Figure 15.2C); that both education and television viewing have *direct* effects on fear of violence (Figure 15.2D); and that education has both direct and indirect effects on fear of violence (Figure 15.2E).

These alternative models have different implications for Gerbner and Gross's hypothesis: models A and D support it; model B does not support it; and models C and E, in addition to supporting the basic hypothesis, provide a more thorough understanding of the causal sequence. And these models do not exhaust the possibilities. For example, education and television viewing may interact in promoting fear of violence, with television influencing fear among the less educated but having no influence among the better educated.

In the last chapter we did a bivariate analysis of television's effect on fear of violence (model A), finding a weak association (gamma = +.08). But as you can see, to draw conclusions from this analysis alone could be very misleading. The question now is, how do we analyze the data to estimate effects represented by these other, three-variable models? Or, more generally, how do we find out which models fit the data?

Multivariate analysis of nonexperimental data is basically a matter of statistical control. Statistical control is analogous to randomization in experiments; both procedures are designed to eliminate the possibility that prior variables (e.g., in model B, the variable education in relation to television viewing and fear of violence) have created a spurious association. Randomization does this by creating random variation across experimental conditions in all extraneous variables; statistical control does it by examining the relationship between an independent and a dependent variable with specified extraneous variables held constant. As we have noted, statistical controls cannot be applied to unmeasured extraneous variables. Despite this limitation, however, this form of analysis does have one major advantage over experimental randomization: it enables us to test for indirect as well as direct effects and to analyze much more complex models than are possible with experimental designs. For example, experimentally testing the relationship between hours of television watched and fear of violence eliminates the possible effect of education by virtue of random assignment. Such a test would therefore rule out model B as a plausible rival interpretation. But the experimental manipulation of television viewing alone would not enable us to estimate the effects of education represented in models C, D, or E.

Among the several strategies for multivariate analysis, we introduce three: elaboration, multiple regression, and log-linear analysis.

Elaboration

Throughout the 1950s and 1960s multivariate analysis with contingency tables usually involved a simple technique known as *elaboration* (Lazarsfeld, 1955). This technique, which is still popular, introduces a third (and sometimes additional) variable into the analysis in order to enhance or "elaborate" our understanding of a two-variable relationship. Thus, we begin with the cross-tabulation between television viewing and fear of violence, and we speculate that the observed association is a result of the third variable of education; then, we introduce education into the analysis by holding it constant.

In elaboration analysis, third variables are held constant by means of subgroup classification. Each category of the third variable constitutes a distinct subgroup, and the original two-variable relationship is recomputed separately for each subgroup. Table 15.1 does this for the variables of fear of violence, television viewing, and education. The table gives the actual marginal frequencies for the 1985 GSS with hypothetical percentages. Notice that we now have three tables, one for each category of the variable of education. These are called *partial tables*, because each

TABLE 15.1. Percentage Afraid of Walking Alone at Night, by Television Viewing and Education (Hypothetical Data)

	Low education			Medium education			High education		
	Light	Medium	Heavy	Light	Medium	Heavy	Light	Medium	Heavy
Afraid	50.0	50.0	49.7	38.2	38.6	38.2	36.6	36.4	37.2
	(154)	(78)	(179)	(217)	(114)	(170)	(366)	(118)	(113)

table shows the association between television viewing and fear of violence for part of the total number of observations. Education is held constant, because in each partial table all respondents are alike with respect to their level of education. Look over the partial tables carefully. What do they reveal about the relationship between television viewing and fear of violence when education is controlled?

Reading across each partial table we find virtually no association between television viewing and fear of violence. In other words, the original relationship (shown in Table 14.10A) has disappeared when education is controlled. These hypothetical data, therefore, support model B in Figure 15.2: the relationship is spurious, produced by a common association with education. We draw this inference not only on the basis of the data, however, but also on the basis of prior theoretical assumptions about the causal ordering of these variables. These same data might just as well have been generated by the following model:

Television viewing → education → fear of violence

Here education is an *intervening variable* between television viewing and fear of violence, whereas in model B education is *antecedent* with respect to these variables. We prefer model B as an interpretation because it is unreasonable to believe that the daily number of hours that adults watched television in 1985 determined the years of education that they had completed. But it is crucial to realize that this interpretation rests on theory; the data in Table 15.1 are consistent with either model.

Several other outcomes are possible when we control for a third variable: the original association may remain unchanged in the partial tables (which would be consistent with model D); it may be reduced in the partials but not disappear (which would be consistent with model E); it may disappear or be reduced in some partials but not in others; or it might even increase in the partials. Remember that the data presented in Table 15.1 are hypothetical; we did not use the real data at the outset so that we could illustrate the ideal case in which the original relationship turns out to be completely spurious. The outcomes of elaboration analysis are seldom this tidy; indeed, the actual data for the 1985 GSS reveal a much more complex relationship among these three variables. As Table 15.2 shows, the relationship between television viewing and fear of violence reduces to near zero for respondents with low and medium education, but remains essentially the same for those with high education. (Compare the latter partial relationship with Table 14.10A.) This particular outcome, an interaction effect, is known as *specification*: the control variable has *specified* the conditions under which the original relationship holds.

TABLE 15.2. Percentage Afraid of Walking Alone at Night, by Television Viewing and Education (Actual Data)

	Low education			Medium education			High education		
	Light	*Medium*	*Heavy*	*Light*	*Medium*	*Heavy*	*Light*	*Medium*	*Heavy*
Afraid	48.1	51.3	50.8	39.2	33.3	40.6	35.8	32.2	44.2
	(154)	(78)	(179)	(217)	(114)	(170)	(366)	(118)	(113)

In their analysis of the 1977 GSS data, Gerbner and associates (1978) found a similar pattern of specification when education was controlled. However, they emphasized the tendency for heavy viewers to be more fearful than light viewers when separate controls for age, gender, and education were introduced. This conclusion opened them to two criticisms that pertain to much elaboration analysis: (1) they failed to control for several other variables (e.g., race, income, hours worked per week) that might produce a spurious association between television viewing and fear of violence; and (2) they controlled for extraneous variables separately rather than simultaneously. We can never be absolutely certain that television viewing causes fear of violence. But our confidence in this causal relationship depends on our holding constant all extraneous variables that might reasonably be expected to produce a spurious relationship. Moreover, we should not introduce controls one at a time, since spuriousness may be created by the simultaneous action of two or more extraneous variables. (See Box 15.1 for a summary of other research on television viewing and fear of violence.)

Multiple regression, a technique described below, is generally better when we want to analyze the simultaneous effects of several independent variables on a dependent variable. Still, because of its simplicity and clarity, elaboration analysis will continue to be used when there are a limited number of control variables and the variables have relatively few categories.

Multiple-Regression Analysis

Multiple regression is simply an extension of bivariate regression (chapter 14) to include two or more independent variables. Like the partial tables of elaboration analysis, it provides information on the impact of an independent variable on the dependent variable while simultaneously controlling for the effects of other independent variables. Unlike partial tables, control is not limited to a few variables nor is information lost from collapsing variables into fewer categories. Here we present a cursory exposition of this very powerful and popular linear-modeling technique.[2] Our main purpose is to make it easier for you to read and understand research employing multiple regression analysis.

A Three-Variable Example

Let us start with an early application of multiple regression in sociology—Robert Angell's 1951 study of "The Moral Integration of American Cities." Angell was

BOX 15.1

Television Viewing and Fear of Violence: The "Final" Verdict

Throughout the past two chapters we have replicated analyses originally carried out by Gerbner and associates (1978) with 1977 GSS data. Whereas we have restricted ourselves to GSS data and to the relationship between television viewing and fear of being victimized, the studies of Gerbner et al. involved many other data sets and a more general hypothesis about the effects of watching television. Their general hypothesis, called cultivation theory, was that heavy television viewing cultivates perceptions of reality that are consistent with television content. Because of the excessive violence on television, heavy viewers will tend to see the world as more violent than it really is. They also will tend to overestimate the number of violent crimes and the number of people employed in law enforcement, and are more likely than light viewers to be alienated and distrustful of others. In short, heavy viewers are likely to have an exaggerated "mean world" conception of reality.

To test this hypothesis, Gerbner and associates used several different data sources, including data on children as well as adults, and analyzed several effects other than a fear of being the victim of violence. Despite their impressive array of supportive evidence, however, reanalyses of their data as well as other research calls into question the viability of their hypothesis. These additional studies provide important lessons in data analysis.

It is important to consider carefully all extraneous variables that reasonably might be expected to produce a spurious relationship. One variable that Gerbner and associates ignored in their early studies was the amount of violence in the neighborhoods where people live. Doob and Macdonald (1979) hypothesized that this might account for the association between viewing and fear of violence: People who live in more violent neighborhoods tend to watch a lot of television and, quite naturally, tend to be more fearful of being the victim of a violent crime. To test this hypothesis, they interviewed adults in Toronto, Ontario, Canada, dividing their sample into those living in high-crime versus low-crime areas. Sure enough, when they controlled for the incidence of crime in the neighborhood, the effect of television on fear of violence "reduced to almost nothing."

Reanalyzing the 1977 GSS data, M. Hughes (1980) sought to rectify the failure of Gerbner et al. to control for extraneous variables simultaneously. Hughes used several dependent-variable measures besides the item on fear of walking alone at night. And in addition to age, gender, and education, he controlled for race, income, hours worked (per week), church attendance, number of voluntary associations one belongs to, and the population size of the place where one lives. All of these variables arguably might produce a spurious relationship between television viewing and a "mean world" view.

First analyzing the effects of his extraneous variables on television watching, Hughes found that all variables except gender and population size were significantly related to television watching after simultaneous controlling. Population size showed no relationship before or after controls, whereas the relationship between gender and television watching was fairly strong before controls, but disappeared when controls were introduced. This disappearance was accounted for by the variable hours worked; women watch more television than men because they work fewer hours outside the home. The relationship between television watching and age was quite different before and after controls. Before controls, younger and older people watched television the most, but afterward, age and television watching were inversely related. Apparently, "older persons watch more television than others for reasons associated with socioeconomic, social, and employment variables" (p. 293).

When Hughes controlled for all extraneous variables simultaneously, he found that only one of nine different dependent variables was related to television viewing in the manner hypothesized by Gerbner et al. Although the relationship was nonsignificant, the key variable, fear of walking alone at night, reversed direction after controls, with the heaviest viewers least likely to be afraid.

Although his analyses fail to support cultivation theory, Hughes points out that the theory might be supported if researchers measured precisely what people watch rather than total exposure to television. Gerbner and associates (1980b) further contend that Hughes's finding of "no overall relationship" does not necessarily imply "no relationship." The absence of an overall effect may obscure important specifications—meaningful relationships within particular subgroups. They point out, for example, that in Doob and Macdonald's study, the relationship between television viewing and fear of crime did hold up for city residents in high-crime areas (Gerbner et al., 1980a). And in a refinement of their theory, Gerbner et al. (1980a) argue that cultivation may be most pronounced among people whose attitudes diverge from the "mainstream." Television cultivates homogeneous outlooks throughout American culture, but the amount of television watched has its greatest impact among those less in tune with the dominant cultural outlook.

interested in understanding why the populations of various cities differ in their conformity to certain social mores ("moral integration"). As an operational definition of moral integration, he constructed an elaborate index combining information on crime rates (negative integration) with local contributions to community charity funds (positive integration) for forty-three cities with a population over 100,000. Angell theorized that moral integration is more easily maintained in homogeneous populations and in those with a low turnover of members. Two measures were constructed to test these hypotheses: a heterogeneity index based on the relative number of nonwhites and foreign-born whites in each city, and a mobility index based on the relative number of persons moving into and out of each city.

An arrow diagram representing Angell's model is shown in Figure 15.3. The arrows pointing from mobility and from heterogeneity to moral integration indicate the hypothesized negative relationships. The curved arrow indicates that mobility and heterogeneity may be correlated, which is taken as given and not to be explained in the model. An incorrect approach to testing Angell's theory would be to test each hypothesis separately using bivariate regression. The results from such an approach show that each of these variables is significantly related to moral integration in the predicted direction; for ethnic heterogeneity, $b = -.1027$, and for residential mobility, $b = -.1789$.

Thus, on the basis of bivariate regressions, Angell appears to be right: moral integration decreases with increasing heterogeneity and with increasing mobility. Unfortunately, this is not a proper test of his model. Study Figure 15.3 again. First, since the theory signifies that both independent variables *simultaneously* influence

FIGURE 15.3. Angell's moral integration model.

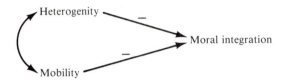

moral integration, they should be analyzed accordingly. Second, since hetero-geneity and mobility may be strongly correlated (curved arrow), some or all of the apparent contribution of one to a bivariate prediction of moral integration actually may be due to the other. Suppose, for example, that heterogeneity but not mobility is causally related to moral integration and that mobility and heterogeneity are strongly correlated. Then a bivariate regression of moral integration on mobility could produce a significant regression coefficient, which would be entirely a conse-quence of the correlation between mobility and heterogeneity. Leaving out impor-tant variables from a model, which may produce misleading results, is called a *specification error*. Clearly, therefore, bivariate regressions represent misspecifica-tion of Angell's theory.

Now that we are convinced that a multivariate test is in order, how do we proceed? The general formula for a multiple-regression equation is

$$Y = a + b_1X_1 + b_2X_2 + b_3X_3 + \ldots + e$$

where Y is the dependent variable, each X represents an independent variable, the b values are *partial-regression coefficients* or *partial slopes*, the value a is the Y-inter-cept (the predicted value of Y when all of the X values are equal to zero), and the value of e represents the prediction error or residual. This, of course, is the linear equation for bivariate regression (chapter 14), augmented to include additional independent variables. For Angell's data, the equation reduces to:

$$\text{Moral integration} = a + b_1 \text{ heterogeneity} + b_2 \text{ mobility} + e$$

Estimation of the coefficients in a multiple-regression equation follows the same logic as bivariate regression. In the case of two independent variables, the approach is easy to visualize geometrically. Imagine constructing a three-dimensional scat-terplot of Angell's data within a large room. The forty-three cities will appear as a "swarm" of points within the room, with the location of each point determined by that city's score for moral integration (using the room height as the axis of measure-ment), heterogeneity (room length), and mobility (room width). The multiple-regression solution appears as a (two-dimensional) plane in this three-dimensional space. (The bivariate-regression solution was also a geometric figure, a line, in a two-dimensional space.) Now, if we mentally position the regression plane in the room so as to minimize the sum of the squared residuals (vertical distances from the city points to the regression plane), we have found the multiple-regression solution.

A computer program, of course, is a more practical approach to multiple-regression estimation. Computing estimated coefficients for Angell's data gives the following prediction equation:

$$\text{Moral integration} = 19.993 - .108(\text{heterogeneity}) - .193(\text{mobility})$$

These results are consistent with Angell's model and are statistically significant. The multiple-regression or partial coefficients reveal the amount by which the dependent variable is expected to change with a one-unit change in the independent variable *when* the other independent variables are held constant (controlled). Thus, the moral integration index for a city is expected to fall by .193 units for every unit increase in the residential mobility index. What is predicted when ethnic heterogeneity decreases by 10 units?

The partial coefficients address questions like the following: If several cities have the same degree of residential mobility, but differ on ethnic heterogeneity, how will these differences in heterogeneity affect moral integration? A geometric interpretation of partial coefficients for the case of two independent variables is provided in Figure 15.4. As discussed above, this regression equation represents a plane positioned to minimize the sum of the squared vertical distances (Y axis) of the observations (not shown) from the plane. Now if we construct a plane perpendicular to the X_1 axis, we are in effect holding X_1 constant, since any observation lying on this plane has the same X_1 value. This plane intersects the regression plane in a straight line (heavy line in the figure), the slope of which is the partial coefficient for independent variable X_2. That is, this partial slope indicates the amount by which the dependent variable (Y) is expected to change with each unit change in X_2 when the other independent variables (only X_1 in this case) are controlled.

The basic principle underlying partial coefficients, and partial tables, is the same expounded for good experimental design (chapter 8): "doing only one thing at a time"—that is, allowing only one independent variable to vary while controlling all other variables. Sometimes this is difficult to achieve in regression analysis

FIGURE 15.4. The multiple regression plane.

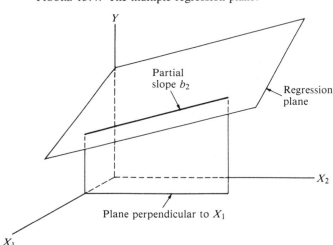

because of high correlations among the independent variables. Consider the extreme case of a *collinear* or perfect association between two independent variables. Suppose that we inadvertently included two collinear predictors in a regression equation: age and year of birth. Then it would be impossible to estimate the regression equation, since age could not be varied while holding constant year of birth. Perfect collinearity is easily handled by dropping one of the collinear variables from the regression equation. A far more difficult problem is high *multicollinearity*, which arises when combinations of two or more independent variables are highly correlated with each other. The presence of high multicollinearity requires great care in interpreting the regression results, since estimates of the coefficients will be quite unstable (varying greatly from sample to sample) and it will be difficult to distinguish significant from nonsignificant independent variables.

Use of Dummy Variables

To illustrate how nominal-scale independent variables may be included in multiple regression, let us return to modeling the television-viewing habits of the 1985 GSS respondents. A series of models will be presented that are intended to give you a feel for the modeling enterprise and to show you how to interpret regression results as usually presented in research articles.

In the last chapter, television viewing was regressed on educational attainment for a subsample of 100 GSS respondents. Using the full 1985 sample (which consists of 1523 respondents after removing those with missing information on either variable) produces similar results:

$$\text{TVHOURS} = 4.72 - .14(\text{EDUC}) \qquad \text{[Model 1]}$$

The bivariate slope coefficient indicates a negative relationship: for every increase of 1 year of education, television viewing is predicted to decrease by .14 hours. Did you notice our use of nicknames for the variables? Most statistical computer packages allow short names for identifying variables, and researchers often find it convenient to use the same names in equations and tables.

The full 1985 GSS sample includes a few extreme outliers for reported television viewing (discussed in Box 14.2). That ordinary least-squares (*OLS*) regression is very sensitive to outliers is quite evident if we reestimate the bivariate regression equation after removing the four respondents who claimed they watched television 20 hours a day.

$$\text{TVHOURS} = 4.88 - .16(\text{EDUC}) \qquad \text{[Model 2]}$$

In other words, just four outliers among 1523 respondents are enough to lower the absolute value of the regression coefficient for education from .16 to .14. Let us drop these four outliers in subsequent models.

Our modeling results are summarized in Table 15.3, which is typical of the format used in research articles. Model 2 coefficient estimates for the *Y*-intercept (4.88) and education (−.16) are listed in column three. The next column displays

TABLE 15.3. Average Daily Television Viewing Regressed on Selected Independent Variables, 1985 GSS

Variable	Model 1 (N = 1523)		Model 2 (N = 1519)		Model 3 (N = 1519)		Model 4 (N = 1519)		Model 5 (N = 1519)	
	Coefficient	t-value	Coefficient	t-value	Coefficient	t-value	Coefficient	t-value	Coefficient	t-value
INTERCEPT	4.72	20.88*	4.88	23.65*	4.64	21.31*	4.07	14.20*	3.21	10.72*
EDUC	−0.14	−7.92*	−0.16	−9.71*	−0.15	−9.47*	−0.11	−4.94*	−0.06	−2.85*
FEMALE					0.35	3.43*	1.55	3.76*	1.17	2.83*
EDUCF							−0.10	−3.00*	−0.08	−2.60*
PARTTIME									0.11	0.66
TEMPOFF									0.27	0.85
UNEMPLOY									1.63	5.46*
RETIRED									1.02	6.41*
INSCHOOL									0.00+	0.00+
HOMEMAKE									1.08	7.04*
OTHER									1.69	3.37*
Adjusted R^2	0.04		0.06		0.06		0.07		0.12	

*Statistically significant at $p < .01$ for two-tail test.

t-values from *t-tests*, which indicate whether a regression coefficient is significantly different from zero when the other independent variables are taken into account. *t*-values have the same sign as the regression coefficients, and those large enough to be significant at some predetermined probability level are flagged by a marker (an asterisk * in Table 15.3) or otherwise noted.[3] Consequently, for model 2 the likelihood is less than 1 in 100 that the observed coefficient for education could have occurred by chance.[4] Table 15.3 also lists for each model a popular but flawed measure of fit, *adjusted* R^2, which indicates approximately the proportion of the variance in the dependent variable (spread of observations around the mean) predicted or "explained" by the independent variable(s). Adjusted R^2 is not a particularly useful measure in causal modeling because it mechanically focuses on prediction instead of the theory under investigation and because it is subject to other weaknesses (Berk, 1983:526–527).

Now suppose that, in addition to the effect of education, we hypothesize that women will report more television viewing than men. The hypothesized gender effect is easily incorporated into a multiple-regression equation by adding a dummy variable named FEMALE, which is coded 1 for females and 0 for those who are not (males). The selection of the gender category to code as 1 is an arbitrary decision. Adding the gender variable to our model yields a new regression estimate.

$$\text{TVHOURS} = 4.64 - .15(\text{EDUC}) + .35(\text{FEMALE}) \qquad [\text{Model 3}]$$

The gender effect is in the direction hypothesized and statistically significant (Table 15.3). Since the value of the FEMALE dummy variable is zero for males, it drops out of the prediction equation for men.

$$\text{TVHOURS} = 4.64 - .15(\text{EDUC}) \qquad [\text{Males, model 3}]$$

For females, on the other hand, the FEMALE dummy variable may be viewed as an adjustment to the *Y*-intercept to take into account heavier female television viewing:

$$\text{TVHOURS} = (4.64 + .35) - .15(\text{EDUC}) \qquad [\text{Females, model 3}]$$

In effect, then, there are separate regression lines for males and females, as shown in Figure 15.5. Both lines have the same partial slope for education, but the line for females is slightly higher by .35 hours. Consequently, the *Y*-intercept value represents the omitted or zero category of the dummy variable (i.e., males), and the FEMALE dummy adjusts the intercept height of the regression line for female-male differences while controlling on education.

Instead of parallel slopes on education, we might have hypothesized that gender and education would interact in determining television-viewing habits. You should recall from chapter 8 that two independent variables are said to interact if the effect of one on the dependent variable varies according to the value of the other. Suppose we hypothesized that education will have a greater impact (negative relationship) on the television viewing behavior of women than of men. The hypothesized interac-

FIGURE 15.5. Television viewing regressed on education, gender.

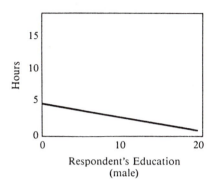

Respondent's Education
(male)

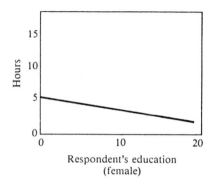

Respondent's education
(female)

tion is easily tested by including a new variable in the regression, EDUCF, which is constructed by multiplying the values of EDUC and FEMALE for each respondent. Thus, EDUCF represents years of schooling if the respondent is female and the value zero if the respondent is male. Adding EDUCF to our model produces a new regression estimate:

$$\text{TVHOURS} = 4.07 + 1.55(\text{FEMALE}) - .11(\text{EDUC}) - .10(\text{EDUCF}) \qquad [\text{Model 4}]$$

Again, our hypothesis is confirmed and all of the regression coefficients are statistically significant (Table 15.3).

Figure 15.6 shows that the model 4 regression equation produced different *Y*-intercepts and partial slopes for males and females. In the case of males, dropping the zero terms (FEMALE and EDUCF) from the regression equation gives the following estimate:

$$\text{TVHOURS} = 4.07 - .11(\text{EDUC}) \qquad [\text{Males, model 4}]$$

FIGURE 15.6. Television viewing, gender-education interaction, gender.

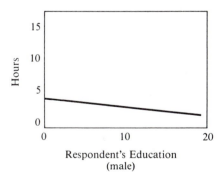

Respondent's Education
(male)

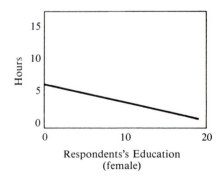

Respondents's Education
(female)

For females, the coefficients FEMALE and EDUCF serve to adjust the male Y-intercept and partial slope values, respectively, for female differences:

$$\text{TVHOURS} = (4.07 + 1.55) - (.11 + .10)(\text{EDUC}) \qquad \text{[Females, model 4]}$$

Consequently, the regression line for females (Figure 15.6B) has an intercept of 5.62 and a slope of $-.21$. The results of model 4 suggest that, compared to females, males watch less television when the effects of education are controlled; and education has a lesser impact on male than female viewing.

One possible interpretation of the gender-education differences in model 4 is that the respondents' current work situation may be an intervening variable. That is, education and gender are determinants of labor force status, which in turn may influence television-viewing habits. Modeling labor force status seems, at first, a difficult task, since it is an eight-category variable in the 1985 GSS. However, the complete information on current labor force status is easily represented by seven dummy variables:

> PARTTIME = 1 if the respondent is working part time; 0 if not
> TEMPOFF = 1 if the respondent has a job but not at work because of temporary illness, vacation, strike; 0 if not
> UNEMPLOY = 1 if the respondent is unemployed; 0 if not
> RETIRED = 1 if the respondent is retired; 0 if not
> INSCHOOL = 1 if the respondent is going to school; 0 if not
> HOMEMAKE = 1 if the respondent is keeping house; 0 if not
> OTHER = 1 if the respondent gave some other response to the labor force question; 0 if not

The key to the use of dummy variables is that one category of the original variable must be omitted from the dummy variable set. We represented gender, for example, by the dummy FEMALE and left out the male category. The excluded labor force category consists of full-time workers. What to exclude is an arbitrary decision. We could have just as easily included a dummy variable for full-time workers and excluded some other category.

Coefficient estimates for our final model (5), which includes the information on current labor force status, are listed in Table 15.3. Although the partial coefficients for education (EDUC and EDUCF) are still statistically significant, they are somewhat smaller. This would be expected if part of the effect of education on television viewing is indirect through the intervening variable of labor force status.

One has to be careful in interpreting the coefficients of model 5 because the Y-intercept refers to the omitted categories (male full-time workers) instead of the omitted category (males) of model 4. For the omitted or baseline group, model 5 reduces to simply

$$\text{TVHOURS} = 3.21 - .06(\text{EDUC}) \qquad \text{[Male full-time workers]}$$

Adding the estimated coefficient for the UNEMPLOY dummy variable adjusts the prediction equation for the heavier television viewing of the unemployed.

$$\text{TVHOURS} = (3.21 + 1.63) - .06(\text{EDUC}) \qquad \text{[Unemployed males]}$$

For retired men, the equation becomes

$$\text{TVHOURS} = (3.21 + 1.02) - .06(\text{EDUC}) \qquad \text{[Retired males]}$$

And finally, for retired women, adjustments are also made for gender differences.

$$\text{TVHOURS} = (3.21 + 1.02 + 1.17) - (.06 + .08)(\text{EDUC}) \qquad \text{[Retired females]}$$

Four of the labor force dummy variables are statistically significant: the unemployed, retired, those keeping house, and the "others" watch more television than male full-time workers. The television habits of the remaining groups—part-time workers, those temporarily away from work, and those in school—are not significantly different from male full-time workers.

Our exploratory modeling excursion was for the purpose of exposition, and not to demonstrate the typical approach a researcher would take. In an actual application, a model of television-viewing habits would include many other explanatory variables such as age, hours worked, and income. Otherwise, coefficient estimates may be off because of model misspecification. The importance of proper specification is evident in Table 15.3, in which estimated values of the EDUC coefficient bounce around as different model specifications are tried.

Other Linear Techniques

This discussion has just scratched the surface of linear modeling. There are special techniques for modeling dichotomous dependent variables, for straightening or transforming nonlinear relationships into a form suitable for linear modeling, for modeling mutual causation and other complex relationships, and for modeling processes over time (longitudinal analysis). Of special importance is *path analysis*, a form of causal modeling that provides, among other things, quantitative estimates of the total direct and indirect effects of one variable on another. For example, model E of Figure 15.2 postulated that education has both direct and indirect effects on fear of violence. To do path analysis it is necessary to put the various partial-regression coefficients on common footing by standardizing them. A *standardized regression coefficient* may be computed by multiplying the unstandardized coefficients (which we have been using) by the ratio of the standard deviation of the independent variable to the standard deviation of the dependent variable (Pindyck and Rubinfeld, 1981:90). Standardized regression coefficients are easily interpreted as slopes in standard deviation units; a standardized coefficient of +.50, for example, indicates that the dependent variable increases by a unit of one-half standard deviation for every standard deviation increase in the independent variable.

Again, we must warn that our exposition of linear modeling is quite superficial and cannot be substituted for formal coursework in statistics. Our emphasis has been on descriptive statistics to the neglect of important inferential issues. It is like a 5-minute introduction to the cockpit instruments of a Boeing 707: one would have a better understanding of flying the Boeing, but one would not have a license to fly it.

Log-Linear Modeling

Log-linear modeling is rapidly becoming the method of choice for analyzing categorical data. The older analytical techniques, such as elaboration with descriptive percentages and measures of association, are inefficient, inflexible, and incapable of addressing important theoretical issues (e.g., complex interaction effects). Log-linear analysis may be used to test the significance and measure the magnitude of two-variable and higher-order (three or more variable) interaction effects in multidimensional tables, to study dichotomous or polytomous dependent variables, to test the appropriateness of collapsing variable categories, to compare tables from different samples, to study mobility tables or panel data, to measure social change from survey replications, and to measure the various effects of a set of independent variables on a set of dependent variables.[5]

Despite its formidable name, the log-linear technique is essentially an extension of the material we have covered in this chapter. Like multiple regression (linear modeling), models are estimated with an equation containing coefficients that serve to adjust the predicted results for various hypothesized effects. We will start with a simple bivariate table to introduce the log-linear approach.

Using Odds to Describe Relationships

Instead of percentages and summary measures of association, log-linear analysis relies exclusively on the wagering concept of *odds* to describe relationships. Let us reconsider Table 14.4—the cross-classification of 1985 GSS respondents' attitudes toward the death penalty by their gender. The observed frequencies and marginals (in parentheses) for the table are displayed in the upper panel of Table 15.4. The odds that a GSS respondent will favor the death penalty is 1154 to 297 (column marginals) or $1154/297 = 3.886$ (almost 4 to 1). The ratio of the number favoring to the number opposing capital punishment among men is $547/115 = 4.757$, and the corresponding *conditional odds* for women is $607/182 = 3.335$. Thus the odds that a GSS respondent favors capital punishment is greater than 3 to 1 for females and almost 5 to 1 for males.

The association between attitude toward capital punishment and gender may be summarized with an *odds ratio*, computed by dividing the conditional odds for males by the conditional odds for females: $4.757/3.335 = 1.426$. This odds ratio means that the observed odds of favoring the death penalty is about 1.4 times greater among men than among women.[6] An odds or odds ratio of 1.0 indicates the absence of a relationship. If the GSS sample had included an equal number of males and females, then the odds of being female would equal 1.0. Similarly, if females were as likely to favor the death penalty as males, the odds ratio of 1.0 would indicate the absence of a gender difference in attitude.

Modeling Cell Frequencies

The odds computed above describe the *observed* frequencies in the GSS sample. To test models of how these data might have been generated, we must (1) translate our

TABLE 15.4. Attitude toward Capital Punishment by Gender, 1985 GSS

	Attitude (A)			Favor/oppose odds	Odds ratio
Gender (G)	Favor	Oppose			
	Observed frequency				
Male	547	115	(662)	4.757	
Female	607	182	(789)	3.335	1.426
	(1154)	(297)	(1451)		
	Model 1: Sample size fitted				
Male	362.75	362.75	(725.5)	1.000	
Female	362.75	362.75	(725.5)	1.000	1.000
	(725.5)	(725.5)	(1451)		
	Model 2: {G} fitted				
Male	331	331	(662)	1.000	
Female	394.5	394.5	(789)	1.000	1.000
	(725.5)	(725.5)	(1451)		
	Model 3: {G} {A} fitted				
Male	526.5	135.5	(662)	3.886	
Female	627.5	161.5	(789)	3.886	1.000
	(1154)	(297)	(1451)		
	Model 4: {GA} fitted				
Male	547	115	(662)	4.757	
Female	607	182	(789)	3.335	1.426
	(1154)	(297)	(1451)		

theory into a log-linear model, (2) use the model to estimate *expected* or *fitted* frequencies, and (3) evaluate how well the model fits the observed frequencies. For example, our model might be based on the hypothesis that attitudes toward capital punishment are *not* influenced by gender; that is, the gender differences observed in the sample (odds ratio of 1.426) are merely due to chance processes.

To illustrate log-linear modeling, let us estimate some models of the observed gender-death penalty frequencies (upper panel of Table 15.4). In the simplest (model 1), all of the cells have the same frequency (second panel of Table 15.4), which is equivalent to hypothesizing that all odds and odds ratios are 1.0 (i.e., no effects). One restriction was placed on the estimating procedure: the four fitted frequencies must add up to the observed sample size (1451 respondents). That is, the sample size is taken as given and not part of the theory to be tested. Although the table has four cells, only three need to be estimated because the value of the fourth may be determined by subtracting the sum of the first three from the fixed sample size. Since the model is based on three estimates, it is said to have 3 *degrees of freedom* (abbreviated *df*). In general, degrees of freedom will be equal to the number of cells less the number of restrictions or constraints placed on the model.

Since the row marginals (gender) were also a consequence of the GSS sampling plan, let us likewise take them as given and constrain model 2 to fit the gender marginals. The third panel of Table 15.4 confirms that the model 2 fitted frequencies do indeed sum to the same row marginals and total sample size as the observed frequencies. In exchange for the improved fit, an additional degree of freedom associated with the row marginals is lost in model 2.[7] Thus, model 2 has 2 df because it estimates four cells with two restrictions (fitted sample size and row marginals). Although model 2 appears as theoretically vacuous as the first model, it could have theoretical underpinnings. For example, one might hypothesize that people are indifferent about capital punishment and are just as likely to favor as to oppose the death penalty (hypothesized odds of 1.0).

If the column marginals (attitude toward capital punishment) are not pertinent to our theory, the expected frequencies could be constrained to sum to the column as well as to the row marginals (model 3 of Table 15.4). The three restrictions on model 3 (sample total, row and column marginals) leave 1 df. You can confirm that model 3 requires only one cell estimate by crossing out any three of the cell estimates and then recalculating them from the constraints (rows must add up to row totals, etc.). Model 3 is equivalent to the common chi-square test for independence (chapter 14). It posits that attitudes toward the death penalty are the same for men and women (equal conditional odds or, equivalently, an odds ratio of 1.0).

Log-linear models are often represented by a shorthand notation using capital letters to represent variables and enclosing related variables within parentheses or braces. Let us use *A* and *G* to denote attitude toward capital punishment and gender, respectively. Then model 3 may be represented as {*G*} {*A*}. The model implies that variables *G* and *A* are unrelated to each other, but that it is necessary to fit both one-way marginals (row and column totals). Our last model (4) is called a *saturated model* because it fits all possible marginals, including the two-way association between attitude and gender, which obviously provides a perfect fit to the sample data (last panel of Table 15.4). Model 4 may be represented, in shorthand notation, as {*GA*}. It is not necessary to list the one-way marginals, {*G*} and {*A*}, since fitting two-way {*GA*} implies that all subsets of the variables in {*GA*} will also be fitted. Model 4 has 0 df because it uses four restrictions (fit sample size, both one-way, and two-way marginals) to estimate four cells.[8]

Model Testing

To assess the fit of a model to the data, we use the likelihood-ratio chi-square test.[9] If the observed and fitted cell frequencies are not significantly different on the chi-square test, the model is said to fit the data. The poorer the fit between model and data, the larger will be the chi-square value for the given degrees of freedom. Results from testing our previous models are summarized in Table 15.5. Our first model provides a terrible fit as evidenced by the huge chi-square value of 559.06. Since chi-square values vary according to the degrees of freedom, a "*p*-value" or

TABLE 15.5. Tests of the Models Listed in Table 15.4

Model or comparison[a]	Degrees of freedom	Likelihood-ratio chi-square	p
Models			
1: {fitted sample size}	3	559.06	<.001
2: {G}	2	547.92	<.001
3: {G} {A}	1	7.24	.007
4: {GA}	0	0.0	
Stepwise comparisons			
1 vs. 2: {G} marginals	1	11.14	<.001
2 vs. 3: {A} marginals	1	540.68	<.001
3 vs. 4: {GA} marginals	1	7.24	.007

[a] Abbreviations: A, death penalty attitude (favor/oppose); G, gender.

significance level (last column of Table 15.5) is used to interpret them. For example, model 2 has a chi-square value of 547.92 that for 2 df has a probability value too small ($p < .001$) to attribute the poor fit to a chance occurrence. Since model 3 is also a poor fit, we reject it in favor of the saturated model (4), which, of course, fits the data perfectly.

To simplify our exposition, we picked a series of models that are not substantively profound. In typical research situations, on the other hand, a choice of the "best" model may not be clear-cut. That is, by the criterion of the chi-square test, a number of models may fit and may be indistinguishable from each other at some predetermined level of significance. For example, six different models might have p-values greater than .20. In such a situation, criteria of simplicity and ease of interpretation may also guide model selection.

Log-linear modeling often proceeds by stepwise testing of models of increasing or decreasing complexity. The bottom panel of Table 15.5 illustrates the former or forward-selection procedure. A model may be tested against a more complex model by subtracting the degrees of freedom and chi-square value of the latter from the former, and then determining the p-value for the two differences. For example, adding the {G} marginals to model 1 significantly improves fit (chi-square reduction of $559.06 - 547.92 = 11.14$, df reduction of $3 - 2 = 1$, $p < .001$). Similarly, in exchange for giving up 1 df in fitting the {GA} marginals, the chi-square value is reduced by 7.24, which is a significant improvement in fit ($p = .007$). For a discussion of how log-linear models are estimated, see the Appendix to this chapter.

"Logit" Modeling

The number of possible models rapidly increases with the number of variables included in a cross-tabulation. For example, several thousand models may be formulated for a five-variable table. As a step toward simplification, researchers often limit themselves to *hierarchical* and to "*logit*" models. To illustrate these strategies, suppose we have a four-way classification of attitude toward the death penalty (A), education (E), gender (G), and race (R). In hierarchical modeling, fitting higher order marginals (e.g., {AEG}) also implies that all subsets of the variables in the higher order marginals will also be fitted (in this example, {A}, {E}, {G}, {AE}, {AG}, and {EG}). Nonhierarchical models present problems of interpretation. It is difficult to explain how the effect of education on attitude toward the death penalty varies by race (three-way interaction {AER}), if there is no association between the attitude and education ({AE}).

A "logit" model takes for granted all possible marginal combinations of the independent variables and the one-way marginals for the dependent variable.[10] The starting or baseline model for a hierarchical "logit" analysis of the above four-way classification would be {EGR} {A}. It hypothesizes that the four-way classification may be adequately modeled by constraining the expected cell frequencies to fit the marginal distribution of the dependent variable ({A}), and all possible marginal combinations of the independent variables ({EGR}). This baseline model is similar to a multiple-regression equation in which all of the partial slopes are equal to zero. The possible relationships among the independent variables ({EG}, {ER}, {GR}, and {EGR}) are viewed as extraneous to the theory under investigation and are neither tested nor interpreted. "Logit" modeling proceeds by adding marginals comprising the dependent and independent variables. For example, the model, {EGR} {AE} {AG}, implies that education and gender each exert independent effects (analogous to partial-regression coefficients) on attitude toward capital punishment.

As an illustration of the "logit" procedure, let us analyze the results of an experiment employing a 2×2 factorial design. Straits et al. (1982) were interested in understanding why subjects sometimes lie to experimenters. Previous studies had shown that subjects are typically dishonest in postexperimental interviews by refusing to admit prior knowledge of the experiment imparted to them by a confederate. Using a similar confederate tip-off design, Straits and associates hypothesized that high evaluation apprehension (anxiety about being judged by the experimenter) and high commitment to (involvement in) the experiment would lead to more subjects' lying. Table 15.6 shows the percentage of honest subjects in each experimental condition. The results are in the hypothesized direction for the commitment manipulation but in the opposite direction for the evaluation apprehension manipulation (for discussion, see Straits, Wuebben, and Cowle, 1982).

TABLE 15.6. Percentage Honest by Evaluation
Apprehension and Commitment

Commitment	Evaluation apprehension (%)		Total (%)
	High	Low	
High	59 (22)[a]	50 (22)	55 (44)
Low	91 (22)	62 (21)	77 (43)
Total	75 (44)	56 (43)	66 (87)

[a]Number of subjects in parentheses.
Source: Page 238 of Straits, Wuebben, and Crowley (1982). Used by permission of the authors and Academic Press.

TABLE 15.7. Log-Linear Models of the Results Shown
in Table 15.6

Model or comparison[a]	Degrees of freedom	Likelihood-ratio chi-square	p
Models			
1: {EC} {L}	3	10.51	.014
2: {EC} {LE}	2	6.93	.031
3: {EC} {LC}	2	5.70	.058
4: {EC} {LC} {LE}	1	2.01	.156
5: {ECL}	0	0.0	
Stepwise comparisons			
1 vs. 3: C main effect	1	4.81	.028
3 vs. 4: E main effect	1	3.69	.055
4 vs. 5: E–C interaction	1	2.01	.156

[a]Abbreviations: *L*, confession (honest/dishonest); *E*, evaluation apprehension (high/low);
C, commitment (high/low).
Source: Page 239 of Straits, Wuebben, and Crowley (1982). Used by permission of the
authors and Academic Press.

Inspection of the percentages in Table 15.6 for the four conditions suggests a possible interaction between commitment and evaluation apprehension. To test for this possibility and for the main effects of the experimental variables, the series of "logit" models displayed in Table 15.7 were fitted. Since the marginal association between the experimental variables, {EC}, is fixed by design, these models represent various dependent-experimental variable relationships. For example, model 4 assumes main but not interaction effects for the two experimental factors. This model fits the data quite well, and the excluded interaction term is nonsignificant (model 4 compared to model 5). Comparisons of other adjacent models reveal that both main effects are significant at approximately the .05 level ($p = .028$ for commitment and .055 for evaluation apprehension). Thus, the probability is small that these findings occurred by chance.

As a final example, please study Table 15.8, which is taken from Sedgely and Lund's 1979 analysis of 1975 GSS data. They set out to test the hypothesis that personal exposure to violence increases tolerance for violence. An index of tolerance for hitting others was formed from four GSS questions concerning hypothetical situations (e.g., "Would you approve of a man punching a stranger who had hit the man's child after the child accidentally damaged the stranger's car?"). Scores on the tolerance index were then trichotomized and cross-tabulated with self-reported beatings as a child and/or adult ("Have you ever been punched or beaten by another person?"). What do you conclude from studying Table 15.8? Is tolerance for violence related to being child or adult victims of violence? Do the childhood and adult beatings independently affect tolerance, or do they interact? The last question, in particular, is difficult to assess informally from comparing percentages. Let us turn to log-linear analysis.

The results of the log-linear testing is displayed in Table 15.9. The information

TABLE 15.8. Tolerance for Hitting Others by Self-reported Beatings

Tolerance for hitting others	Percentage of self-reported beatings			
	Never been beaten	Beaten only as a child	Beaten only as an adult	Beaten both as a child and adult
Low	31.8	17.6	23.4	11.1
Moderate	36.2	31.0	29.8	29.4
High	32.0	51.4	46.8	59.5
Total %	100.0	100.0	100.0	100.0
Total N	(1010)	(210)	(154)	(99)

Source: Page 35 of Sedgely and Lund (1979). Used by permission of Elsevier Science Publishing Company, Inc.

on beatings was rearranged as two dichotomous variables to facilitate testing for an interaction effect. Comparison of models 5 (saturated) and 4 reveal that the interaction effect, $\{CAT\}$, is not significant. The two-way associations, $\{TA\}$ and $\{TC\}$, contribute significantly to the fit of model 4. Therefore, we conclude that childhood and adult beatings independently affect tolerance for hitting others. Inspection of the fitted frequencies for model 4 reveals that the odds of being in the "high" tolerance category is about 1.7 times greater among adult beating victims than nonvictims, and 2.1 times greater among childhood victims than nonvictims.

TABLE 15.9. Log-Linear Models of the Results Shown in Table 15.8

Model or comparison[a]	Degrees of freedom	Likelihood-ratio chi-square	p
Models			
1: $\{CA\}$ $\{T\}$	6	64.32	<.001
2: $\{CA\}$ $\{TC\}$	4	15.57	.004
3: $\{CA\}$ $\{TA\}$	4	38.84	.000
4: $\{CA\}$ $\{TA\}$ $\{TC\}$	2	1.18	.554
5: $\{CAT\}$	0	0.0	
Stepwise comparisons			
1 vs. 2: $\{TC\}$	2	48.75	<.001
1 vs. 3: $\{TA\}$	2	25.48	<.001
2 vs. 4: $\{TA\}$	2	14.39	<.001
4 vs. 5: $\{CAT\}$	2	1.18	.554

[a]Abbreviations: T, tolerance for hitting others (low/moderate/high); C, beaten as child (yes/no); A, beaten as adult (yes/no).

Summary

Causal understanding—the goal of much social research—ultimately rests upon a comparison of theory and data. Data alone cannot establish causal relationships. Rather, researchers construct theory-based models of relationships and then determine statistically the fit between data and model. Researchers base assumptions about direction of influence, which are built into their models, on theoretical knowledge. Likewise, theory guides statistical tests for nonspuriousness by suggesting potential causes of spurious relationships. Leaving out important variables from a model is called a specification error.

The models for data analysis often are represented by arrow diagrams. Arrows indicate causal order; the signs above the arrows indicate the direction of the relationship—positive or negative. Very often alternative models are analyzed to determine which ones fit the data. Model testing occurs through multivariate analysis, which enables one to examine the effects of an independent variable on a dependent variable while controlling for all other variables, and to examine interactions among variables.

A traditional technique for the multivariate analysis of contingency tables is elaboration. This approach begins with a two-variable relationship, and then systematically reassesses this relationship when controls are introduced for third (and sometimes additional) variables. Variables are controlled, or held constant, by computing partial tables—that is, computing the original two-variable relationship separately for each category of the control variable. If the model specifies the control variable as causally antecedent to the other two variables, and the original relationship disappears in each partial table, then the original relationship is spurious. If the control variable is modeled as intervening, and the original relationship disappears in the partials, then the original relationship is not spurious and the independent variable has an indirect effect on the dependent variable. Among other possible outcomes is specification, an interaction effect involving the increase, reduction, or disappearance of the original relationship in some partials but not in others.

A better technique for analyzing the simultaneous effects of several independent variables on a dependent variable is multiple regression. The partial-regression coefficients in a multiple-regression equation show the effects of each independent variable on the dependent variable when all other variables in the equation are held constant. Holding variables constant may prove difficult and result in unstable coefficients when some of the independent variables are highly correlated with each other, a problem known as multicollinearity. Nominal- and ordinal-scale variables may be incorporated into multiple regressions by means of dummy-coding, which also may be used to model interaction effects.

Log-linear analysis, a newer and more powerful technique for analyzing contingency tables, describes relationships in terms of odds and odds ratios. Odds and odds ratios of 1 indicate the absence of a relationship. Log-linear modeling utilizes different marginal frequencies to estimate expected or fitted cell frequencies, and then checks the latter against the actual data. Models are represented notationally by enclosing the letters for variables in braces, as in $\{G\}$ $\{A\}$, which signifies that variables G and A are unrelated to each other. A saturated model fits all possible marginal frequencies, providing a perfect fit to the data.

Models are tested by means of the chi-square statistic, with significant differences between observed and fitted cell frequencies indicating a lack of fit. Degrees of freedom (df) equal the number of estimated cells minus the number of restrictions in the model. In stepwise model testing, models of increasing or decreasing complexity are compared; chi-square values and degrees of freedom are subtracted, and the resulting chi-square difference provides a test of whether the increased or decreased complexity marks a significant improvement in fit.

The number of possible models increases rapidly as the number of variables increases. Consequently, model testing is usually limited to hierarchical models, in which the fitting of higher-order marginals implies that all subsets of variables in the higher-order marginals are also fitted. Modeling is also simplified by employing "logit" models, in which the possible relationships among the independent variables are taken for granted and are neither tested nor interpreted.

Key Terms

modeling/causal modeling	*dummy-variable coding*
antecedent variable	*t-tests/t-values*
intervening variable	*adjusted* R²
reciprocal causation	*path analysis*
noncausal association	*standardized regression coefficient*
direct effects	*log-linear modeling*
indirect effects	*odds*
specification error	*conditional odds*
multivariate analysis	*odds ratio*
elaboration	*observed frequencies*
partial tables	*expected/fitted frequencies*
specification	*degrees of freedom*
multiple regression	*saturated model*
partial-regression coefficients/slopes	*likelihood-ratio chi-square test*
collinear association	*"logit" models*
multicollinearity	*hierarchical models*

Review Questions and Problems

1. For each of the following pairs of variables, state a "theory" of the causal process linking the two variables and indicate the likely direction of influence: (a) marital adjustment and length of the engagement period; (b) educational attainment and occupational achievement; (c) place of residence (rural, urban) and happiness; and (d) amount of interaction with and liking of others.

2. Draw an arrow diagram representing a causal ordering of the following variables: respondent's occupational prestige; family income when respondent was a teenager; respondent's educational attainment.

3. What is the difference between antecedent and intervening variables in causal modeling?

4. Surveys typically report that residents of large cities are more tolerant of deviant behavior than are residents of smaller cities and rural areas. Suppose that data are available for three variables: (1) respondent's tolerance of deviant behavior, (2) size of current place of residence, and (3) the size of place in which the

respondent was living at age 16. For each of the following hypotheses, draw arrow diagrams to specify a causal model incorporating the hypothesis: (a) the social environment of the current residence renders people more or less tolerant; (b) tolerance is learned as an adolescent and remains relatively constant thereafter; (c) both age–16 and current residential environments affect tolerance of deviant behavior.

5. What is a specification error? Is it likely to occur in a true experimental design? Why or why not?

6. Explain the difference between the regression coefficient in bivariate regression and the partial-regression coefficients in multiple regression. Why are they called "slopes"?

7. In a multiple regression analysis of grade-point average (range 0–4.0) for the college freshman year, the partial coefficients for gender (dummy variable = 1 for females, 0 for males), high-school grade-point average (range 0–4.0), and employment during the school year (range 0–50 hours) were, respectively, +0.30, +0.50, and −0.01. Given that the three partial coefficients were statistically significant, explain the meaning of each. Hint: explain as partial slopes.

8. Which of the following variables are collinear: (a) respondent's education; (b) annual family income; (c) respondent's age; (d) respondent's income; (e) weekly family income; (f) respondent's year of birth; (g) family size? Why?

9. What is meant by high multicollinearity? Why is it a problem in multiple regression?

10. Consider the following results of t-tests for three different regression coefficients: (a) t-value $= -1.77$, $p = .430$; (b) t-value $= 2.70$, $p = .007$; (c) t-value $= -.01$, $p = .746$. Which are statistically significant—that is, not likely to have occurred by chance?

11. What is adjusted R^2? Why is it called a measure of fit?

12. The General Social Survey (GSS) codes age–16 place of residence as a six-category variable: rural farm, rural nonfarm, small city, medium-size city, suburb near a large city, and large city. Show how this information could be represented by a set of dummy variables.

13. Interpret the following standardized regression coefficients: (a) +.40; (b) −1.5; (c) 0.0; and (d) −0.02.

14. Suppose that the conditional odds that a male will complete high school is 3.0 (3 to 1), and the corresponding conditional odds for females is 6.0. What percentage of males complete high school? What percentage of females? Compute an odds ratio from the two conditional odds. What does it mean?

15. Explain the difference between observed and fitted frequencies.

16. Compute the number of degrees of freedom for the following log-linear models: (a) four cells restricted to add up to the observed sample size; (b) a 2 × 2 table with three restrictions; and (c) a three-variable table with three rows, three columns, and two layers constrained to fit all one-way marginals.

17. What is a saturated model? When might it be useful to estimate one?

18. Suppose that data from the 1974–1985 GSSs are used to classify respondents' attitude toward the death penalty (A) by their education (E), gender (G), race

(R), and survey year (Y). Interpret the meaning of each of the following hierarchical log-linear models:

    a. $\{EGRY\}$ $\{A\}$
    b. $\{EGRY\}$ $\{AE\}$ $\{AR\}$ $\{AY\}$
    c. $\{EGRY\}$ $\{AER\}$ $\{AYR\}$
    d. $\{EGRYA\}$

19. Consider the following probability values for likelihood-ratio chi-square tests of four different log-linear models: (a) $p = .0001$; (b) $p = .765$; (c) $p = .0003$; and (d) $p = .835$. Which models provide a poor fit to the data?

APPENDIX 15.1

Log-Linear Model Estimation

How were the models in Table 15.4 estimated? Essentially, a log-linear model contains coefficients or parameters that raise or lower odds and odds ratios according to the modeler's hypotheses. The expected frequencies for saturated model 4 were estimated from the following equation:

$$F_{ij} = kgar$$

F_{ij} represents the estimated cell frequency for row i and column j. The term k is a norming factor that assures that the fitted cell frequencies sum to the observed sample size. The remaining parameters adjust the cell frequencies up or down to take into account gender marginals (g), attitude marginals (a), and the two-way association between attitude and gender (r). This representation is called a multiplicative equation, since the estimated frequency is a product of a series of parameters.

Nonsaturated models are formed by eliminating certain parameters. In the "no-effects" model 1, for example, all parameters except k (fixed sample size) are deleted. The parameters used to estimate each cell frequency for the four models are listed in Figure 15.7. A dummy-variable scoring system is used to introduce the gender parameter in model 2; that is, the g parameter is present for males but not for females (see Figure 15.7, model 2). Inclusion of the g coefficient has the effect of lowering the expected frequencies for the male cells (Table 15.4, model 2), and the presence of the k parameter assures a simultaneous adjustment of the female cells (to the fixed sample size).

The parameter scoring system is shown in the bottom panel of Figure 15.7. A 1 indicates the presence of a parameter and a 0 the absence. Adding attitude parameter a to the "favor death penalty" response in model 3 has the effect of raising the fitted "favor" cell frequencies (compare model 2 with model 3, Table 15.4). The scoring of parameter r (two-way association) is determined by multiplying the gender and attitude scores for each cell (e.g., 1 × 1 = 1 for the first cell). Adding this parameter increases the odds ratio (Table 15.4). If

FIGURE 15.7. Scoring system for Table 15.4 log-linear models.

GENDER	ATTITUDE	
	Favor	Oppose
Male	k	k
Female	k	k

Model 1:   fixed sample size

GENDER	ATTITUDE	
	Favor	Oppose
Male	kga	kg
Female	ka	k

Model 3: {G} {A}

GENDER	ATTITUDE	
	Favor	Oppose
Male	kg	kg
Female	k	k

Model 2: {G}

GENDER	ATTITUDE	
	Favor	Oppose
Male	kgar	kg
Female	ka	k

Model 4: {GA}

Cell		Fixed sample size (k)	Gender (g)	Death penalty attitude (a)	Attitude by gender association (r)
row	column				
1	1	1	1	1	1
1	2	1	1	0	0
2	1	1	0	1	0
2	2	1	0	0	0

gender and attitude had been unrelated, parameter r would have had an estimated value of 1.0, which would not have changed the cell frequencies in the multiplicative equation. Otherwise, r will either raise (estimated value > 1.0) or lower (value < 1.0) the expected frequency for the first cell relative to the other cells.

After mastering a conceptual understanding of multiple regression, you may be dismayed to discover that adjustments for hypothesized effects in log-linear modeling is done by multiplication instead of addition (linear form). Actually, log-linear estimates are computed from a linear form obtained by a logarithmic transformation of the multiplicative form. That is, if we take natural logarithms (symbolized by "ln") of the terms in our model 4 equation, we end up with an additive or linear form:

$$\ln(F_{ij}) = \ln(k) + \ln(g) + \ln(a) + \ln(r)$$

Although this "log-linear" form is amenable to computer estimation and is somewhat analogous to multiple regression, its coefficient estimates are difficult to interpret compared to regression coefficients. Consequently, relationships are usually described in the multiplicative form of odds and odds ratios.

Polytomous Variables

A major advantage of log-linear modeling is the ease with which polytomous (multicategory) dependent and independent variables may be handled. The key idea is an extension of the parameter scoring system introduced in Figure 15.7. Associated with each additional category in one-way marginals is an additional degree of freedom that can be modeled by an added parameter.[11]

The following is a parameter scoring system, based on dummy-variable coding, for representing all of the information (3 df) contained in a four-category measure of religious preference:

Religion	r1	r2	r3
Protestant	1	0	0
Catholic	0	1	0
Jewish	0	0	1
Other	0	0	0

In fitting one-way marginals, adjustments for the number of Protestant, Catholic, and Jewish respondents is performed by parameters $r1$, $r2$, and $r3$, respectively. The number giving an "other" response is automatically determined by the fixed sample size restriction. Multiplying these scores by those for other variables (e.g., attitude toward the death penalty) yields parameters for two-way and higher-order effects (in this case, attitudinal differences by religion).

Scoring systems other than dummy coding may be used (Taylor, 1983:595–601). Consider the parameter scoring shown below for a four-category attitudinal survey response:

Attitude	a1	a2	a3
Strongly agree	1	1	1
Agree	1	0	0
Disagree	0	0	0
Strongly disagree	0	1	0

The first parameter, $a1$, represents attitudinal direction. It adjusts the one-way marginals depending on whether the odds favor agreement or disagreement responses. The second parameter, $a2$, registers the intensity of the attitude. The third, $a3$, picks up any interaction between direction and intensity; that is, one direction may be more intense than the other.

Suppose that the above attitudinal response has been cross-classified by educational attainment (six categories). The association in this 4×6 table may be described by $(4 - 1) \times (6 - 1) = 15$ odds ratios (15 df). This two-way association may be represented by 15 two-way parameters formed by taking the products of the scores for the one-way effects. Then interesting questions may be explored through log-linear modelng. How does educational attainment relate to attitudinal direction and intensity? If there is a direction-intensity interaction, does it vary by education? Is it reasonable to dichotomize attitude into agree and disagree categories in this table? An affirmative answer to the last question requires a satisfactory fit for a model that excludes all attitude-education association parameters formed from the $a2$ and $a3$ scoring. Clearly, the log-linear approach is more powerful and amenable to theoretical notions than standard measures of association. Indeed, it provides in this example up to fifteen pieces of information, compared to the single value obtained by computing gamma or a similar bivariate measure.

NOTES

1. See J. A. Davis (1985) for a discussion of arrow diagrams as these apply to the logical rules for causal ordering among a set of variables.

2. Berk (1983) provides an excellent overview of linear modeling. Elementary introductions may be found in Tufte (1974) and Cohen and Cohen (1983). More advanced treatments are available in the texts by Fox (1984) and Pindyck and Rubinfeld (1981).

3. These *t*-values are computed by dividing each regression coefficient by its estimated standard error. Researchers sometimes list standard error estimates in lieu of *t*-values.

4. Strictly speaking, the probability level is a crude approximation, since it depends on the extent to which the assumptions underlying the regression model are met and proper specification of the process being modeled.

5. An excellent elementary introduction to log-linear analysis may be found in Appendix A of Duncan and Duncan (1978). Other introductory treatments include Knoke and Burke (1980) and Fienberg (1977). More advanced treatments are available in Bishop, Fienberg, and Holland (1975) and Goodman (1984).

6. The popular measure of association, Yule's Q, is easily computed from this odds ratio:

$$\text{Yule's Q} = \frac{\text{odds ratio} - 1}{\text{odds ratio} + 1} = \frac{1.426 - 1}{1.426 + 1} = 0.18$$

7. One degree of freedom is associated with the row marginals, since it consists of two cells (male and female totals) with the restriction that the two must sum to the fixed sample size.

8. One degree of freedom is associated with the two-way marginals since it consists of four cells with three restrictions that the cells must sum to row, column, and sample size totals.

9. Pearson's chi-square statistic may also be used (with generally similar results), but it lacks an important partitioning property of the likelihood-ratio statistic (Bishop, Fienberg, and Holland, 1975:125–130).

10. Although the "logit" approach is named after a regression technique for analyzing a dichotomous dependent variable, it is more flexible in that the dependent variable may have more than two categories.

11. If R, C, and L represent the number of rows, columns, and layers in a three-way table, then the $\{R\}$ marginals have $(R - 1)$ df, the $\{CL\}$ marginals have $[(C - 1) \times (L - 1)]$ df, the $\{RCL\}$ marginals have $[(R - 1) \times (C - 1) \times (L - 1)]$ df, and so forth.

16

Research Ethics

Thus far we have dealt with the technical side of social research—with issues of logic and research design, data collection and analysis. Besides these technical aspects, there is another dimension to social science that must be considered—the moral dimension. When we think about how to conduct research, we must think not only of using the *right* techniques but also of *rightly* using the techniques we have learned. We must think about research ethics.

Ethics is a branch of philosophy and theology. Both theological ethicists, who define the field in terms of religious tradition and sacred texts, and philosophical ethicists, who define it strictly on the basis of reasoning independent of religious faith, are concerned with the same fundamental question: What ought to be done? Ethics is the study of "right behavior." For the social scientist, ethics poses questions concerning how to proceed in moral and responsible ways.

This chapter discusses ethical considerations that underlie many decisions about research methods. Just as practical considerations can prevent researchers from implementing the ideal research design or obtaining as large or diverse a sample as desired, so too can ethical considerations constrain scientific inquiry. Ethics may prohibit researchers from using experimental treatments that could harm research participants, from asking questions that would prove extremely embarrassing or threatening, from making observations that would deceive or place subjects under duress, and from reporting information that would constitute an invasion of privacy. In addition, researchers are expected to be completely honest in observing, analyzing, and reporting findings, and to be responsible about the limits and application of scientific knowledge.

There are three broad areas of ethical concern in scientific research: the ethics of data collection and analysis, the ethics of responsibility to society, and the ethics of treatment of participants (Reese and Fremouw, 1984). Let us briefly examine each of these areas of *research ethics*.

The norms of science tacitly require scientists to be "unremittingly honest" in their observations and analyses, to be tolerant, questioning, willing to admit error, and to place the pursuit of knowledge and understanding above personal gain or the promotion of a particular philosophy or ideology (Cournand, 1977). Being ethical in this sense is synonymous with being a good research scientist. Unfortunately, there are instances of dishonesty in social research, ranging from the selective presentation of data by not mentioning negative or ambiguous findings to deliberately falsifying or altering the data. In chapter 2, for example, we mentioned the case of Cyril Burt, whose fabricated data on twins reared apart provided major support for the view that heredity largely determines intelligence. The scientific community uniformly condemns violations of this sort. Because scientific progress rests upon the trustworthiness of findings from the work of many investigators, dishonesty and inaccuracy in reporting and conducting research undermine science itself. We cannot overemphasize the importance of accurately carrying out research and honestly reporting findings. For the scientist, this is the most fundamental ethical dictum, and it requires no further elaboration here.

The second area of ethical concern involves the relationship between science and society, especially regarding the uses of scientific knowledge. Many social scientists believe that the researcher has a responsibility to assess the possible uses of scientific findings, to promote their beneficial application, and to speak out against their destructive application. Later in the chapter we examine the delicate relationship between science and society.

This chapter deals mainly with the third area of ethical concern regarding the treatment of human subjects. Basic ethical principles accepted in our cultural and legal tradition demand that research participants be treated with respect and protected from harm. Historically, however, these principles sometimes have clashed with scientific practice, generating a great deal of controversy. The ethical codes developed by professional societies such as the American Anthropological Association, the American Sociological Association, and the American Psychological Association all address the welfare of research participants. Furthermore, the novice researcher is most likely to encounter ethical problems with respect to this issue, not because people are naturally unethical, but because ethical issues are not always apparent, especially to the inexperienced. Even experienced researchers sometimes have trouble sorting out the ethical implications of their actions. Although in our society it is generally considered wrong to lie, deception is common in experimental research. Not until recently, however, has there been much concern about its widespread use by social psychologists.

Treatment of Human Subjects

Four problem areas have been identified most often regarding the ethical treatment of human subjects: potential harm, lack of informed consent, deception, and privacy invasion (Diener and Crandall, 1978). Each of these problems arises when research practices violate basic human rights. It is considered a violation of basic rights to harm others, to force people to perform actions against their will, to lie or mislead them, and to invade their privacy. While most social research poses no threat to these individual rights, there have been some ethically questionable studies in the social sciences. A review of these four issues will sensitize the reader to research situations that are potentially unethical as well as to strategies and guidelines that help to ensure subjects' rights.

Harm

All new physicians take an oath of ethical, professional behavior attributed to the Greek physician Hippocrates (460–377 B.C.). One of the first provisions of the Hippocratic Oath is that the doctor "abstain from whatever is deleterious. . . ." These words of Hippocrates, advising that the physician do no harm, would appear to be sound ethical advice for research scientists as well. The first right of any participant in a research project is the right to personal safety. Ethical researchers recognize this right and are careful to respect it. Research that would endanger the life or physical health of a human subject is simply not acceptable in the social science community. Even research that harms animals, although it might directly benefit humans, has been the focus of contemporary ethical concern (Tannenbaum and Rowan, 1985).

The issue of harm is not quite so simple and straightforward as it may appear, however. For one thing, harm is sometimes difficult to define and predict. Given the nature of social science research projects, physical harm to subjects is highly unlikely. Yet, not all harm is of a physical nature. People can be harmed personally (by being humiliated or embarrassed), psychologically (by losing their self-esteem), and socially (by losing their trust in others) through their participation in research which might never threaten their physical well-being (Diener and Crandall, 1978:17f). Moreover, it is often difficult to predict whether, or the extent to which, one's investigative procedures will be harmful to research participants. The prison simulation study of Zimbardo et al. (1973) is a good example. These investigators created a mock prison in the basement of a Stanford University building in which subjects role-played prisoners and guards. The study was scheduled to run 2 weeks but had to be terminated after only 6 days because of its unanticipated adverse effects on subjects. Guards physically and psychologically abused prisoners, and prisoners broke down, rebelled, or became servile and apathetic. The subjects got so caught up in the situation, became so absorbed in their roles, that they began to confuse role-playing and self-identity. While Zimbardo and colleagues intended to study how the roles of "guard" and "prisoner" influenced subjects' reactions, they never anticipated such extreme effects.

Besides the difficulty of predicting harm, most scientists would not adhere to the dictum that no harm whatsoever should ever come to research participants. Some researchers take the position that potential harm should be weighed against the benefits that might be derived from the research. This stance is implied by the statement of ethical principles by the American Psychological Association (1981:638): "Research procedures likely to cause serious or lasting harm to a participant are not used unless the failure to use these procedures might expose the participant to risk of greater harm or *unless the research has great potential benefit.* . . ." (our emphasis). If there is little or no scientific value from a study that knowingly exposes subjects to harm, then the study should not be done, no matter how small the harm. But if a study has considerable scientific merit, then some degree of potential harm may be justified. For example, although some research on hypothermia requires subjecting informed volunteers to physical harm, such as by immersing them in cold water, this is justified by the potential scientific benefit of such an investigation.

A major difficulty with this approach lies in being able to assess the full extent of costs and benefits. Costs and benefits may be impossible to predict or to measure; and a *cost-benefit analysis* ignores individual rights, or at least makes them subservient to societal benefits and to pragmatic considerations. Research seems most justifiable when the person exposed to the risks will also receive the benefits of potentially harmful procedures. However, the benefits of much scientific research accrue not to the individual research participant but to the investigator, to science, or to the general public, and it is more questionable to justify costs to an individual solely on these grounds (Diener and Crandall, 1978).

In spite of these problems, a cost-benefit analysis can be a helpful first step in examining the ethics of a proposed study. One should also be sensitive to areas of study and to research procedures that pose the greatest risk of harm. The potential for doing harm to subjects may be highest in social research that investigates negative aspects of human behavior (e.g., aggression, obedience to malevolent authority, cheating). The principal arena for such research is in laboratory and field experiments. Through experimental manipulation, subjects may suffer a temporary loss of self-esteem or experience a high degree of stress, and as a result they may be embarrassed or may become angry about their involvement in research.

Consider, for example, the work of Stanley Milgram (1974) on obedience to authority. Under the guise of a teacher-learner experiment, Milgram asked subjects playing the role of teacher to deliver to learners what the subjects thought were dangerously high levels of electric shock. It goes without saying that the learner, a confederate of the experimenter, was not actually being shocked. But to the subjects this was a highly stressful conflict situation: should they obey the experimenter in administering the shocks or should they refuse to continue in the experiment? The subjects showed many obvious signs of stress; indeed, one subject had a convulsive seizure that made it necessary to terminate his participation. Milgram, in turn, was severely criticized for not protecting his subjects from potential harm. For example, he made no effort to determine prior to their participation whether subjects should be excluded from the experiment for physical or psychological reasons. Some researchers also questioned the long-term effects that the experiment might have had on subjects' self-concepts. What would subjects think of themselves knowing that they were capable of inflicting pain on another person?

Field experiments present even greater problems. In these settings the researcher may find it virtually impossible to intervene when subjects are about to experience harm. The laboratory setting guarantees a certain amount of control over subjects' behavior, allowing for intervention if necessary, but that control may be altogether absent in a field setting. Latané and Darley (1970), for example, staged a crime (looting of a liquor store) in order to explore the conditions under which bystanders intervene to help. One bystander in their field experiment telephoned the police, who showed up with guns drawn to arrest the researchers. This was a situation in which considerable harm could have come to both subjects and researchers.

The ethical issue of harm is much less a problem for survey researchers and participant observers than it is for experimentalists, but even they must be alert to the potential for doing harm. Survey researchers can harm people by asking threatening questions. Participant observers can harm people by their own active involvement as participants. William Foote Whyte (1981:313), for example, reports that during the course of his study of Cornerville, he voted four different times in the fall 1937 congressional election. Whatever damage might have been done to the opposition candidate by Whyte's illegal actions, while probably insignificant, is not irrelevant.

Aside from assessing the risk of harm to research participants and designing one's research to minimize such risks, there are several widely adopted ethical principles that are designed to protect research participants from harm (see Diener and Crandall, 1978).

1. Researchers should inform subjects of any reasonable or foreseeable risks or discomforts before the study begins and should give subjects sufficient opportunity to consider whether or not to participate. Indeed, federal regulations mandate such "informed consent," discussed below, for all federally funded research. A major criticism of Milgram's experiment, which predates the latter regulation, is that he did not obtain prior permission from subjects to allow him to place them in a highly stressful conflict situation.

2. Where appropriate, researchers should screen out research participants who might be harmed by the research procedures. In their prison simulation study, Zimbardo and associates (Zimbardo, 1973) gave several personality tests to volunteers in order to select subjects with "normal" personality profiles and thereby minimize the possibility of destructive effects. Another criticism of Milgram's experiment is that he failed to administer examinations prior to the experiment in order to determine whether subjects suffered from psychological or physical problems that might have excluded their participation.

3. If stress or potential harm is possible, then measures should be taken to assess harm after the study, and research participants should be informed of procedures for contacting the investigator. The debriefing session in experiments can help to assess as well as ameliorate negative reactions. But if long-lasting effects are possible, then the researcher has a special obligation to conduct follow-up interviews and possibly to provide counseling. Zimbardo (1973) held an encounter session after his study to allow subjects to express their feelings. He also conducted follow-up interviews to assess the impact of the experience and found no evidence of long-lasting negative effects. Indeed, most subjects regarded the experiment as a valuable learning experience. Milgram (1974) also carefully questioned his subjects, interviewing all of them immediately after the experiment, and sending them reports of the study and follow-up questionnaires asking for their reactions to their participation in his research. His ultimate ethical justification for this research was that it was judged acceptable by those who took part in it.

Informed Consent

The second ethical issue arises from the value placed on freedom of choice in Western societies. For moral and legal reasons, subjects should not be coerced into participating in social research. Not only must subjects understand that their participation is voluntary; they must also be given enough information about the research to make an informed decision about whether to participate. In other words, researchers should obtain the explicit or implicit *informed consent* of their subjects to take part in an investigation.

Just how much information about the research must be conveyed to subjects for them to exercise their *informed* consent is not always clear and depends largely on the nature of the research. Full disclosure of the research purpose and procedures is usually not necessary, although subjects generally should be given some explanation of the general purpose of the research and who is sponsoring it. Minimally, they should be told that their participation is voluntary and that they are free to withdraw from the study at any time; moreover, they must be given a clear description of the risk of harm involved and of personal rights that might be jeopardized by their participation. Milgram's subjects, for example, should have been told that they would feel stress and that this stress conceivably could have harmful effects.

Ethical regulations for federally funded research dictate that a written consent form, signed by the subject or the subject's legal guardian, must be used when more than "minimal risk" of harm is anticipated. Minimal risks refer to risks that are no greater than those ordinarily encountered in one's daily life (Code of Federal Regulations, 1981). In such cases, informed consent protects both subjects and researchers. Subjects are protected from harm by being able to make up their own minds about the risks of participation; researchers are legally protected by subjects' explicit voluntary agreement. However, while written informed consent is accepted practice in biomedical research, it has several limitations as an ethical safeguard and is not always desirable in social research.

As Diener and Crandall (1978) point out, it is often difficult, even in biomedical research, truly to inform subjects about all the risks of research, since these are not always known. Moreover, the subject's consent to participate does not remove the researcher's reponsibility to minimize danger to the subject, and it should never be used to justify other unethical practices. Finally, the use of informed-consent procedures presents methodological problems for several kinds of studies. Research by Singer (1978) has shown that requiring a signature on a consent form reduces the response rate and elicits more socially desirable responses in surveys. And in laboratory experiments, the provision of full information about the study can completely undermine its validity. As the concept of demand characteristics implies, subjects who are told the true purpose of the study may not behave naturally. It is not surprising, then, that studies that convey hypothesis-related information in their informed-consent procedures have failed to replicate findings of studies not containing such information (Adair, Dushenko, and Lindsay, 1985).

While it is clear that documentation of consent and full disclosure of research purposes and procedures can present methodological problems, there are ways of circumventing these problems while following the doctrine of informed consent. In survey research, obtaining a signature to document consent "seems unnecessarily burdensome," as Singer (1978:159) notes, given that the "same protection is afforded respondents by the right to refuse the interview, or to refuse to answer particular questions within the interview." In fact, federal regulations do not require written consent as long as the information collected is not about sensitive topics (e.g., sexual behavior, drug abuse, illegal conduct) and the subject population has the ability to give informed consent (e.g., adults rather than children). Federal regulations also provide for a waiver of documentation or an alteration of some of the elements of informed consent when these would adversely affect the study. However, the waiver of documentation can only be made when the research involves minimal risk to subjects. Finally, it is common in medical and experimental research today to forewarn subjects that a full disclosure of the purposes of the research is not possible until after their participation. They might be told, in addition, that they may be in one of several treatment conditions, but that the study results would be invalid if they knew their assigned condition prior to the conclusion of the research.

Field experiments and disguised or covert participant observation present the greatest ethical risk from the standpoint of informed consent. In both types of studies, the researcher's desire to observe subjects' spontaneous and natural behavior is incompatible with the acquisition of consent: to obtain informed consent destroys subjects' naivete and defeats the purpose of the study. Whether such research is regarded as unethical depends, for some people, on other ethical considerations, such as invasion of privacy, risk of harm, and the costs incurred in terms of time and money. If the research does not the invade subjects' privacy, is harmless, and not costly to the subjects, then informed consent may be ethically unnecessary. In this sense, testing the effects of different appeals when soliciting donations for a charitable organization, such as Cialdini and Schroeder (1976) did in a field experiment, would not be considered ethically questionable, since subjects were not at risk and their rights were not violated. However, Latané and Darley's 1970 field experiment involving the staging of a crime would be ethically questionable because subjects were exposed to considerable stress and risk of harm.

One of the most controversial studies involving covert participant observation was Laud Humphreys's study (1975), mentioned in chapter 11, of sexual encounters in public restrooms. Humphreys posed as a voyeur and "watchqueen," whose job was to warn homosexuals of intruders as they engaged in fellatio. He also recorded the license numbers of these men, traced their identities through the Department of Motor Vehicles by misrepresenting himself as a market researcher, and later interviewed them in their homes after changing his appearance so that he would not be recognized. Despite the fact that Humphreys carefully guarded the confidentiality of his subjects, this study now is considered ethically indefensible by many social scientists. Among several other problems, Humphreys failed to obtain his subjects' informed consent and risked doing serious damage to their psyches and reputation.

Disguised participant observation studies such as the one by Humphreys are relatively rare and do not always pose such dangers. No matter what the apparent risk of harm, however, this kind of research is invariably controversial. In contrast to the relativist ethical judgments about field experiments, some social scientists take the absolutist position that research simply should not be done where investigators deliberately misrepresent their identity in order to enter an otherwise inaccessible social situation. Sociologist Kai Erikson (1967:368), for example, argues that this kind of research "can injure people in ways we can neither anticipate in advance nor compensate for afterward"; that it "may be painful to the people who are . . . misled; and even if that were not the case, there are countless ways in which a stranger who pretends to be something else can disturb others by failing to understand the conditions of intimacy that prevail in the groups he has tried to invade." In regard to this kind of research, Erikson also reiterates one of the most basic assumptions of informed consent:

> If we happen to harm people who have agreed to act as subjects, we can at least argue that they knew something of the risks involved and were willing to contribute to that vague program called the "advance of knowledge." But when we do so with people who have expressed no readiness to participate in our researches (indeed, people who presumably would have refused if asked directly), we are in very much the same ethical position as a physician who carries out medical experiments on human subjects without their consent (p. 368).

Deception

Deception—the third area of ethical concern—in some ways is the most controversial. On the one hand, deception is a widely used and accepted practice in social research, especially in experiments; one study found that, in 1983, 58 percent of the empirical studies reported in three major social psychology journals used some form of deception (Adair, Dushenko, and Lindsay, 1985). The most common deception involves misleading subjects or respondents about the purpose of the study. A cover letter for a survey, for example, might indicate that the study's objective is to examine general beliefs about health when, in fact, the investigators are interested specifically in their respondents' knowledge of and beliefs about the relationship between smoking and lung cancer.

In their epileptic seizure experiment, described in chapter 7, Darley and Latané (1968) told subjects that they were interested in the kinds of personal problems faced by college students when in reality they were testing subjects' willingness to intervene in an emergency. They also deceived subjects about the reasons for the experimental setup, explaining that it was necessary to separate subjects to avoid the embarrassment of face-to-face interaction and that the experimenter would not be present lest they feel inhibited by his presence. The actual reasons for these conditions were to allow the experimenters to simulate the discussion of other subjects and to remove the experimenter from the scene of the emergency. Other frequent forms of deception in experiments are using confederates to mislead subjects about research purposes and tasks, and providing false feedback about subjects' own behavior as a way of manipulating their feelings and thoughts.

The basic rationale for deception is that it is necessary in order to place research participants in a mental state where they will behave naturally. If subjects know the true purpose of a study, then the results are meaningless. As we have seen, subjects typically will act so as to present the most favorable impression of themselves or to help out the researcher by confirming the hypothesis. Deceiving subjects about the true purpose of a study diverts their attention from the hypothesis and enhances experimental realism by giving subjects a believable and engrossing explanation for what they are doing. Defenders of deception also maintain that without it one simply could not effectively study behavior that people normally find objectionable, such as aggression, conformity, cheating, or failing to aid others in an emergency.

On the other hand, there are strong and vocal opponents of deception. Perhaps the most vocal is psychologist Diana Baumrind (1985), who argues that "intentional deception in the research setting is unethical, imprudent, and unwarranted scientifically" (p. 165). Deception is unethical, according to Baumrind, because it violates a subject's right to informed consent (i.e., consent obtained by deceit, by definition, cannot be informed), and violates the trust implicit in the investigator-subject relationship. It is imprudent because it ultimately damages the credibility of behavioral scientists as well as trust in other expert authorities. And it is unwarranted scientifically because deceptive practices do not accomplish the scientific objectives that justify their use. Baumrind claims that the almost routine use of deception in experiments is common knowledge among some groups of subjects (presumably college students), which makes them suspicious and unlikely to accept the experimenter's cover story. Because of this, deception may not produce the naive and spontaneous behavior that it is designed to elicit, thereby making experimental results inherently ambiguous.

Despite these objections, the prevailing sentiment among social scientists is not to rule out deception entirely. The code of ethics of the American Psychological Association (1981:638) specifically allows for deception when it states: "Methodological requirements of a study may make the use of concealment or deception necessary." Since describing the whole purpose of the study beforehand invalidates most social research, omitting such information is considered a mild and acceptable form of deception as long as none of the omitted information concerns serious risks. However, because of the legitimate concerns expressed by Baumrind and others, deceptions of greater magnitude, such as telling direct lies to subjects, using confederates, or deliberating misrepresenting oneself, warrant special attention. The APA code also states that the investigator using deception

> has a special responsibility to (i) determine whether the use of such techniques is justified by the study's prospective scientific, educational, or applied value; (ii) determine whether alternative procedures are available that do not use concealment or deception; and (iii) ensure that the participants are provided with sufficient explanation as soon as possible (American Psychological Association, 1981:638).

Regarding the first two of these three instructions, Adair and colleagues (1985) point out that the negative consequences in deception research are usually minimal and that there is a lack of viable alternative methodologies. Therefore, the deception dilemma is probably best rectified by the APA's third instruction—adequate debriefing.

Debriefing. Debriefing serves methodological and educational as well as ethical purposes; ideally, it should occur in all studies with human participants, not just those studies involving deception. By interviewing subjects after their participation, researchers may gain valuable information about subjects' interpretations of research procedures; furthermore, by understanding the nature of the study, subjects can gain a greater appreciation for their research experience. If subjects are deceived, however, then the debriefing session becomes critically important. Not only must the researcher explain the true purpose of the study and the reasons for the deception; he or she must do so with great care and sensitivity.

Researchers must be alert to the fact that, when exposed to the truth, subjects may feel embarrassed or angered about having been "fooled" and may harbor resentment toward the investigator and toward social research in general. To obviate such feelings, investigators have developed elaborate debriefing techniques (see Carlsmith, Ellsworth, and Aronson, 1976; Mills, 1976). While we will not describe these techniques in detail, certain common aspects deserve mention. First, it is best to debrief subjects as soon after their participation as possible, especially if the deception or its revelation is likely to cause discomfort. Second, the debriefing should be carried out slowly and deliberately, first eliciting subjects' reactions and then gradually explaining the nature of the experiment until subjects fully understand every point. Third, since negative feelings about being deceived are worsened when the deceiver is smug about it, researchers can relieve some of their subjects' discomfort by expressing their own discomfort about the necessity of using deception in order to arrive at the "truth." Fourth, researchers should point out to subjects that if the experiment works well—if the cover story is convincing—then virtually *everyone* gets fooled. Finally, above all, researchers should follow Herbert Kelman's guideline "that a subject ought not to leave the laboratory with greater anxiety or lower self-esteem than he came in with" (1968:222).

Research on the effects of deception and debriefing indicates that, in general, carefully administered debriefing is effective. Smith and Richardson (1983) found that subjects who were deceived and subsequently debriefed reported more positive experiences—for example, greater enjoyment and greater educational benefit— from their research participation than subjects who were not deceived and, as a consequence, received less adequate debriefing. Indeed, the final word on deception may be the finding of another study of subjects' reactions: "[i]t appears that subjects are willing to accept or tolerate certain discomfitures or unpleasantries if they are viewed as necessary elements of a scientific enterprise. Thus, learning that they had been deceived . . . *enhanced* the subject's assessment of the experiment's scientific value; elaborate deceptions are apparently viewed as good social science methodology!" (Straits, Wuebben, and Majka, 1972:515).

Privacy

The idea of the right to privacy goes back to antiquity. For example, Hippocrates' oath promises: "Whatever. . . I see or hear, in the life of men, which ought not to be spoken of abroad, I will not divulge as reckoning that all such should be kept secret." Despite its ancient origins, however, the moral claim to privacy was not widely respected as a fundamental right until the last few centuries. The Industrial Revolution made physical privacy possible, and political democracies granted and increasingly protected the privacy of individual belief and opinion (Ruebhausen and

Brim, 1966). Today, invasion of privacy remains a public concern as a result of widely publicized accounts of government wiretapping, police entrapment, and corporate drug testing.

The right to privacy is the individual's right to decide when, where, to whom, and to what extent his or her attitudes, beliefs, and behavior will be revealed. Social research presents many possibilities for invading the privacy of research participants, and it is essential that researchers be sensitive to the ways in which their actions can violate this basic right.

The dramatic case of the Wichita Jury Study in 1954 shows how social research can come into direct conflict with the value of privacy (Vaughan, 1967). In an effort to understand and perhaps even improve the operations of juries, researchers secured the permission of judges to record six actual jury deliberations in Wichita, Kansas without the knowledge of the jurors. When news of the study became known, it was roundly criticized by columnists and commentators across the country, investigated by a Senate subcommittee, and led ultimately to the passage of a law prohibiting the recording of jury deliberations. The argument against this study was that jury deliberations must be sacrosanct to protect the inalienable right to trial by impartial jury. Surveillance "threatens impartiality to the extent that it introduces any question of possible embarrassment, coercion, or other such considerations into the minds of actual jurors" (Vaughan, 1967:72).

As this study shows, one way in which subjects' privacy can be invaded is through the use of concealed devices such as one-way mirrors, microphones, and cameras. If such devices are used with subjects' knowledge and consent, then they pose no problem. If they are used without subject's knowledge to record behavior in public places (e.g., restaurants and waiting rooms), then they also are acceptable to many researchers so long as subjects remain anonymous and are not at risk. But when hidden recording devices are used to observe behavior in private settings to which the research participant would not ordinarily allow the researcher access, an invasion of privacy occurs. Besides juries, other settings that are considered private are homes, personal offices, closed meetings, and physicians' examining rooms (Diener and Crandall, 1978).

Closely related to the use of concealed recording devices is the use of a false cover to gain information that subjects would not reveal if their informed consent were obtained. This became a major problem in the second phase of Laud Humphreys's study, mentioned above, when he got the names of men he had observed performing homosexual acts and interviewed them in their homes. When Humphreys observed these men in public restrooms, he did not know their names or other details of their private lives. But the identifying information he subsequently obtained intruded on his subjects' privacy and, in the worst of circumstances, could have led to legal difficulties or even blackmail. (Unlike physicians, lawyers, and the clergy, social scientists are subject to subpoena and cannot promise their respondents legal immunity.)

Whether we define access to information as an invasion of privacy will depend on how private that information is. Humphreys's research drew attention not just because he used questionable means to procure information, but also because he was investigating a sensitive area—sexual behavior. Clearly, some information is considered more private or sensitive than others. Among the most sensitive and threatening areas are sexual behavior and illegal activities. Researchers investigating these areas have a special obligation to protect the privacy of their informants.

Anonymity and confidentiality. No matter how sensitive the information, however, ethical investigators protect the right to privacy by guaranteeing anonymity or confidentiality. Obviously, information given anonymously secures the privacy of individuals, but this safeguard is usually possible only in surveys using self-administered questionnaires without names attached or in some available data studies. Most often the investigator can identify each individual's responses; therefore, the principal means of protecting research participants' privacy is to ensure confidentiality. The researcher can do this in a variety of ways: by removing names and other identifying information from the data as soon as possible, by not disclosing individuals' identities in any reports of the study, and by not divulging the information to persons or organizations requesting it without the research participant's permission.

Laud Humphreys defended his research partly in terms of the steps he took to assure confidentiality, such as destroying all data containing personally identifying information after the completion of his study. Likewise, the researchers in the Wichita Jury Study acted to protect privacy by destroying the original recording of each jury deliberation after transcribing the recording and editing the transcript so as to avoid the identification of any of the persons involved. The Census Bureau protects confidentiality in a variety of ways, for example, by not releasing individual responses to the census of population and housing for 72 years—a person's average lifetime—and, when releasing the Public Use Microdata Sample, suppressing identifying information (Kaplan and Van Valey, 1980).

Field research usually requires more ingenuity to safeguard anonymity and confidentiality. The traditional approach is to use fictitious names for individuals, groups, and locations, although this alone may not be sufficient to prevent people from recognizing themselves and others. For example, in a study of the community of "Springdale," a small town in upstate New York, the researchers promised their informants that no individuals would be identified in printed reports. However, when Arthur Vidich and Joseph Bensman (1958) published their research in a book, the people of the town could clearly identify each character in spite of their pseudonyms. The townspeople were so outraged by the transparency of their characterizations and the consequent invasion of their privacy that they featured a float in the annual Fourth of July parade with a large-scale copy of the jacket of the book, *Small Town in Mass Society.* This was followed first by residents "riding masked in cars labeled with the fictitious names given them in the book" and then by a manure spreader, with an effigy of the author Vidich bending over the manure (Whyte, 1958).

Because Vidich and Bensman reported private material without protecting the anonymity or obtaining the consent of their informants, they were severely criticized by other social scientists. To remove the possibility of recognition, the authors might have altered some of the information about people, such as their family background, occupation, or other intimate details of their lives, or they might have developed composite characters based on more than one informant. Perhaps the best solution, however, is to ask the subjects themselves if the material considered for presentation or publication is acceptable to them. This is the strategy adopted by Bettylou Valentine in her study of a community called "Blackston."

Valentine (1978:166) believed that some intimate details of people's lives involving family size, family structure, and interrelationships were relevant to important points she wanted to make. She "did not see how it would be possible to disguise the people enough to make them unrecognizable even to themselves and at the same time accurately illustrative of the Blackston community." Therefore, after she had completed a draft of her manuscript, she sent copies to all the major characters. She explained that her story might be published in the future, and she asked each person (1) whether her account was accurate and fair; (2) whether any material would be embarrassing to anyone; and (3) whether they had any comments, corrections, or other reactions. Finally, she subsequently returned to Blackston to talk to several of the persons involved. As a result of these contacts, Valentine not only worked out additional disguises that protected the privacy of her informants but also gained valuable insights and suggestions for her book.

Making Ethical Decisions

Ethical issues arise in social research when conflicts occur between societal values such as freedom and privacy and scientific methods aimed at obtaining the highest quality data. In the preceding sections we have identified some areas of potential conflict—when research involves harm to participants, involuntary participation, intentional deception, and an invasion of privacy. We also have examined some current resolutions of these ethical issues. It should be clear from our discussion that there are no easy answers; indeed, frequently there is considerable disagreement among reviewers about the ethicality of research proposals that raise ethical issues (Ceci, Peters, and Plotkin, 1985). With this in mind, how does the researcher decide what to do?

Some social scientists, such as Diana Baumrind (1971:890), take the position that "scientific ends, however laudable they may be," should never justify the use of means, such as lying to subjects, which violate fundamental moral principles or sacrifice the welfare of research participants. In philosophy, this ethical position is known as *deontology*: basic moral principles should allow no exceptions, no matter what the consequences. By contrast, the operating ethical philosophy of most social scientists today—the philosophy behind professional ethical codes and federal ethical guidelines for research—is basically *teleological*: the morality of acts should be judged in relation to the ends they serve. The overall guiding principle is that "the potential benefits of the research (e.g., advancement of scientific knowledge, beneficial technological applications, advantages to subjects) must be weighed against the potential costs (e.g., harm to subjects, detrimental technological applications)" (Schlenker and Forsyth, 1977:371–372). As we saw in our discussion of harm, cost-benefit analyses do not always help to resolve ethical dilemmas. Nonetheless, as Schlenker and Forsyth (1977:371) note, it is from this guiding cost-benefit principle that other rules for the conduct of social research have been derived.

> These include obtaining informed consent; remaining open and honest with the participants; respecting the participants' freedom to decline participation; insuring

the confidentiality of the participants' data; protecting the participants from physical and mental discomfort, harm, and danger; completely debriefing the participants; and removing any undesirable effects of the research.

Although exceptions sometimes are made to these rules, these exceptions must be based on a careful analysis of the possible benefits and costs of the study.

Initially, the individual researcher is responsible for examining the ethics of a study and its prospective benefits and costs. And, of course, when attempting to make difficult ethical decisions, it is always a good idea to solicit others' opinions. However, increasingly the ultimate decision about whether a given study will be conducted rests not with the researcher, but with a committee responsible for reviewing research proposals involving the use of human (and animal) subjects. The Department of Health and Human Services (DHHS), as well as most other federal agencies, institutes, and foundations, requires the approval of all research proposals by a human subjects committee (called an *institutional review board*, or IRB) as a precondition for the release of its funds. Virtually every college and university in the United States and most tax-exempt private research foundations have IRBs. And, in recent years, over 90 percent of these IRBs have "mandated the routine review of *all* proposals, not just those that are, or hope to be, funded" (Ceci, Peters, and Plotkin, 1985) (our emphasis).

According to federal regulations (Code of Federal Regulations, 1981), each IRB has at least five members, with varying backgrounds that assure the adequate review of research proposals. To provide a diversity of expertise, the members must include at least one nonscientist (such as a lawyer, ethicist, or member of the clergy), at least one member not affiliated with the research institution, as well as persons competent to review specific research activities (such as a sociologist in the case of social research). Investigators submit written documents to the IRB that describe the proposed research and specifically outline how research participants' rights are to be protected, such as provisions for informed consent and measures to ensure confidentiality. IRBs then approve, modify, or disapprove the research according to their interpretation of federal regulations outlined by DHHS.

Besides federal regulations, social scientists are guided by ethical codes for the treatment of research participants developed by professional societies. Box 16.1 provides excerpts from the ethical codes of three such societies: the American Anthropological Association (1983), the American Psychological Association (1981), and the American Sociological Association (1984). These codes cover ethical responsibilities not only to those studied, but also to the profession, the public, and students. In the next section, we examine ethical responsibilities to society.

The Uses of Research: Science and Society

Social scientists have become increasingly sensitive not only to the ethical implications of their work for research participants but also to its moral and ideological

BOX 16.1

Codes of Professional Ethics

The following statements are excerpts from the professional codes of ethics of three national organizations: the American Anthropological Association (AAA), the American Psychological Association (APA), and the American Sociological Association (ASA). You can acquire the complete codes of ethics by writing directly to these associations.

Professional Practice in the Conduct of Research

Anthropologists should attempt to maintain such a level of integrity and rapport in the field that, by their behavior and example, they will not jeopardize future research there. The responsibility is not to analyze and report so as to offend no one, but to conduct research in a way consistent with a commitment to honesty, open inquiry, clear communication of sponsorship and research aims, and concern for the welfare and privacy of informants. (AAA)

As scientists, psychologists accept responsibility for the selection of their research topics and the methods used in investigation, analysis, and reporting. They plan their research in ways to minimize the possibility that their findings will be misleading. They provide thorough discussion of the limitations of their data, especially where their work touches on social policy or might be construed to the detriment of persons in specific age, sex, ethnic, socioeconomic, or other social groups. In publishing reports of their work, they never suppress disconfirming data, and they acknowledge the existence of alternative hypotheses and explanations of their findings. Psychologists take credit only for work they have actually done. (APA)

[S]ociologists are obligated to report findings fully and without omission of significant data. Sociologists should also disclose details of their theories, methods and research designs that might bear upon interpretation of research findings. (ASA)

Treatment of Research Participants

In research, anthropologists' paramount responsibility is to those they study. When there is a conflict of interest, these individuals must come first. Anthropologists must do everything in their power to protect the physical, social, and psychological welfare and to honor the dignity and privacy of those studied. . . .

The aims of the investigation should be communicated as well as possible to the informant.

Informants have a right to remain anonymous. . . .

There is an obligation to reflect on the foreseeable repercussions of research and publication on the general population being studied.

The anticipated consequences of research should be communicated as fully as possible to the individuals and groups likely to be affected. (AAA)

In planning a study, the investigator has the responsibility to make a careful evaluation of its ethical acceptability. To the extent that the weighing of scientific and human values suggests a compromise of any principle, the investigator incurs a correspondingly serious obligation to seek ethical advice and to observe stringent safeguards to protect the rights of human participants.

Considering whether a participant in a planned study will be a "subject at risk" or a "subject at minimal risk," according to recognized standards, is of primary ethical concern to the investigator. (APA)

Individuals, families, households, kin and friendship groups that are subjects of research are entitled to rights of biographical anonymity. . . .

The process of conducting sociological research must not expose subjects to substantial risk of personal harm. Where modest risk or harm is anticipated, informed consent must be obtained.

To the extent possible in a given study, researchers should anticipate potential threats to confidentiality. Such means as the removal of identifiers, the use of randomized responses, and other statistical solutions to problems of privacy should be used where appropriate.

Confidential information provided by research participants must be treated as such by sociologists, even when this information enjoys no legal protection or privilege and legal force is applied. (ASA)

Responsibility to the Public

Anthropologists should not communicate findings secretly to some and withhold them from others. . . .

[A]nthropologists bear a positive responsibility to speak out publicly, both individually and collectively, on what they know and what they believe as a result of their professional expertise gained in the study of human beings. (AAA)

Psychologists clarify in advance with all appropriate persons and agencies the expectations for sharing and utilizing data. They avoid relationships that may limit their objectivity or create a conflict of interest. Interference with the milieu in which data are collected is kept to a minimum.

Psychologists have the responsibility to attempt to prevent distortion, misuse, or suppression of psychological findings by the institution or agency of which they are employees. (APA)

When it is likely that research findings will bear on public policy or debate, sociologists should take particular care to state all significant qualifications on the findings and interpretations of their research. . . .

[With regard to cross-national research] because research and/or findings may have important political repercussions, sociologists must weigh carefully the political effects of conducting research or disclosure of findings on international tensions or domestic conflicts. . . . ordinarily research should not be undertaken or findings released when they can be expected to exacerbate international tensions or domestic conflicts. (ASA)

Source: American Anthropological Association (1983), American Psychological Association (1981), copyright 1981 by the American Psychological Association, and American Sociological Association (1984). Reproduced by permission. Not for further reproduction.

implications for the larger society. In the interest of promoting the scientific side of social research, some people once held that social scientists should be "value-free." According to this position (Lundberg, 1961), we can and should make a sharp distinction between the roles of scientist and citizen. Science is nonmoral. The methods of science are designed to eliminate personal preferences and values; and "there is nothing in scientific work, as such, which dictates to what ends the products of science shall be used" (Lundberg, 1961:32). Scientists' only imperative is "to say what they know"—to present relevant findings and theoretical interpretations. In their capacity as citizens, scientists may take moral positions, campaigning, for example, against nuclear weapons, acid rain, or racial oppression. But if social scientists are to be taken seriously as scientists, then they should not confuse this role with that of citizen and should not let their personal values affect their research.

This value-free ideology is no longer tenable for two main reasons. First, it is now clear that values have a substantial influence on the research process. Personal values and political beliefs inevitably affect how scientists select and conceptualize problems and how they interpret their findings. As we noted in chapter 4, many nonscientific factors affect problem selection: personal interests and ideologies, the availability of funding, the climate of opinion in society, research fads and fashions. Similar factors affect the perspective that researchers take and the kinds of questions they ask, which in turn determine the kinds of answers they will find. When IQ tests were first administered on a large scale during World War I, the prevailing belief in both scientific and nonscientific circles was that ethnic groups migrating from southern and eastern Europe were inferior to earlier immigrant groups. Consequently, when the former groups scored consistently lower than Americans of northern and western European ancestry, this was seen not only as proof of existing beliefs about ethnic differences but also as a validation of the tests as measures of innate intelligence. Of course, neither of these interpretations is acceptable today because social scientists, whose perspective led them to focus on the social environment, have demonstrated conclusively the effects of language, culture, and socioeconomic factors on test scores.

The value-free ideology alleges that as scientists, social researchers can remain neutral in accumulating facts about social life that are of equal utility to Democrats and Republicans, liberals and conservatives. The second problem with this position is that while claiming to be value-neutral seemingly protects the scientist's self-interest and autonomy, in effect it places researchers in the service of others' values, such as those of research sponsors or anyone else who chooses to use one's findings. Those who advocated complete value neutrality took physical scientists as their model, claiming that these "real" scientists could serve equally well under fascistic or democratic political regimes (Lundberg, 1961). But the moral bankruptcy of this position comes into sharpest focus when we consider such "real" scientists under the Nazi regime. German physicians, apparently operating out of a value-free model of science, "systematically froze human beings in tubs of ice and, in the conduct of sterilization experiments, sent electrical charges through female ovaries" (Gray, 1968). This example is extreme; no one today would argue that value neutrality justifies harming others. More to the point, scientists have come to realize that they bear some responsibility for applications of their research. Physicists who worked on the atomic bomb did not do so out of a value-free ideology, but out of patriotism and a belief that Japan and Germany had to be stopped. However, many of them had second thoughts about helping to build the bomb, especially after they saw its destructive effects.

Both of these problems of maintaining value neutrality are exacerbated for social scientists, who typically study problems that have immediate relevance to people's lives. Indeed, more often than the astronomer or chemist or physicist, the social researcher is drawn to the study of particular phenomena for their social as well as their scientific significance. The nature of the problems selected and the motivation to study them are inherently value-laden in social research. Social scientists, therefore, must be aware not only of the influence of personal values and political preferences on their own work, but also of the implications of their findings for constructive or destructive use by others.

Among social scientists, anthropologists probably have been most keenly aware of the impact of values on the research process. They developed the sensitizing concept of "cultural relativity" to guard against the tendency to judge other cultures in relation to one's own cultural world view. *Cultural relativity* is the idea that cultural values—standards of truth, morality, beauty, correct behavior, and so forth—vary widely and must be judged in relation to a given society. In addition, anthropologists also have pointed out the importance of language—that Western scientific language may not be appropriate for "translating" the behavior of another culture and that it is therefore necessary to understand how subjects perceive the world in their own terms.

In a similar vein, sociologist Howard Becker (1967) pointed out that research is always contaminated by personal and political sympathies, but that the way to deal with this is not to forsake the standards of good scientific work and take sides, but rather to consider carefully "whose side we are on." Becker had in mind field researchers, who often study the "underdog"—the deviant, oppressed, or subordinate. In trying to understand reality from the subjects' perspective, field researchers may become sympathetic with that point of view, which usually is contrary to the accepted view of the conventional, economically well-off, or superordinate. However, this does not mean that one should always present all sides or should avoid taking sides. These options are seldom, if ever, possible. What we should do, according to Becker, is admit to whose side we are on, use our theories and techniques impartially—taking precautionary measures designed to guard against bias—and make "clear the limits of what we have studied, marking the boundaries beyond which our findings cannot be safely applied" (Becker, 1967:247). Part of this "sociological disclaimer," Becker (1967:247) believes, should be a statement

> in which we say, for instance, that we have studied the prison through the eyes of the inmates and not through the eyes of the guards or other involved parties. We warn people, thus, that our study tells us only how things look from that vantage point—what kinds of objects guards are in the prisoners' world—and does not

attempt to explain why guards do what they do or to absolve the guards of what
may seem, from the prisoners' side, morally unacceptable behavior.

Becker does not argue that social scientists should stand pat with their "one-
sided" views of reality. In fact, he sees the long-term solution to an enlarged
understanding of institutions as the accumulation of many one-sided but different
views of reality. This position is analogous to the methodological principle of
triangulation introduced in chapter 13. However, whereas before we suggested
various triangulation techniques as ways of eliminating methodological biases and
errors, here we suggest that these techniques also might be used to shed light on
personal values that may be embedded in a particular methodological approach or
view of reality.

For many social scientists, guarding against the intrusion of values in research
and carefully noting the limitations of conclusions are not the extent of one's ethical
responsibility to society. We also must be aware of and, some believe, provide
direction to how others use social science findings. There is little question that the
products of social science will be used by others. They already have had and will
continue to have a major impact on social policy. To cite one prominent example,
the Supreme Court decision of 1954 (Brown v. Board of Education of Topeka),
which declared that separate educational facilities for blacks and whites were inherently unequal, was based in large part on social science findings. The unanimous
opinion cited several studies showing that segregation had a detrimental psychological effect on black children.

Since this decision, social scientists have continued to be among the staunchest
and most vocal supporters of integration and civil rights, with many testifying in
cases involving school desegregation, busing, and affirmative action. These
scholars have taken the initiative in offering their expert advice in areas of social
policy. For the most part, they have attempted to show how social science findings
supported positions that most of their colleagues favored, and their political
involvement is noncontroversial. The hard ethical debate concerns how much
responsibility researchers bear for applications that are destructive or contrary to
prevailing scientific and public sentiment. That is the question that physicists
debated after the bomb. Should one try to foresee possible misuses and abuses of
scientific findings? If one can foresee misuse or abuse, should the research be
conducted at all? And if such research is conducted, how active a role should the
researcher play in the dissemination of the findings? Is the researcher responsible
for the way information is presented and for assessing the public's reaction?

The most controversial studies in the annals of social science raise just these
issues. For example, Project Camelot, a multimillion-dollar research study funded
by the U.S. Army, was designed to measure and forecast the causes of revolution
and insurgency in underdeveloped areas of the world (Horowitz, 1967). Because of
its huge scope, the project drew a large team of respected social scientists. Some
saw the project as an unprecedented opportunity to do fundamental research on a
grand scale and may not have inquired too deeply into the ultimate purpose of the
project. Others believed for various reasons that they were, in no sense, "selling

out" to the military. They believed that they would have great freedom in handling the project, that there was a possibility of improving conditions in underdeveloped nations, and that they could have an enlightening influence on the military (Horowitz, 1967). What they failed to envision was the "uses to which the United States Army or Central Intelligence Agency could have put the information, such as fostering revolutions against regimes hostile to the United States. They failed to recognize the grave concern those in other countries would have over such potential uses" (Diener and Crandall, 1978:108). Indeed, in July of 1965, 7 months after the project began, after its revelation made it a *cause celebre* in Chile, Project Camelot was canceled by the Defense Department.

It is precisely this potential (and actual) abuse of findings that led many social scientists to condemn the research of educational psychologist Arthur Jensen. In 1969, Jensen (1969) published an article in the *Harvard Educational Review* entitled "How Can We Boost IQ and Scholastic Achievement?" In arguing that IQ was determined largely by heredity, Jensen concluded that genetic differences accounted for the higher scores of whites than blacks on IQ tests, and that no amount of compensatory education could undo this difference. Such a view had not been propounded in respectable academic circles for many years prior to Jensen's article, and as a result, it created a furor. Many scholars severely criticized Jensen's conclusions on methodological grounds. But the point here is that Jensen apparently failed to consider the uses to which his article might be put. Although he himself was opposed to segregation and argued that his research suggested the need for educational programs tailored to individual differences (Edson, 1970), others seized upon Jensen's research to oppose integration. Less than a week after a report of his article made headlines in Virginia newspapers, defense attorneys quoted heavily from Jensen's article in a suit in federal district court to integrate schools in two Virginia counties (Brazziel, 1969). Their main argument was that differences in intelligence between whites and blacks were innate; that white teachers could not understand blacks; and that black children should be admitted to white schools strictly on the basis of standardized tests.

What are the ethical implications of such controversies? First, social scientists have an obligation to consider how their findings will be used. Research that is clearly intended to be exploitative, such as management-sponsored research intended to quiet labor unions, should not be done (Diener and Crandall, 1978). Second, given that eventual applications usually are unknown, scientists should disseminate knowledge to the widest possible audience, to increase public knowledge and encourage debate, so that no one group can exploit the knowledge for its own welfare (Diener and Crandall, 1978). Third, when research has obvious and immediate applications, as in applied and evaluation research, scientists have a special obligation to promote actively appropriate uses and prevent misuses of their findings. Finally, scientists can assume responsibility collectively for the application of research through organizations that communicate on their behalf and provide a forum for the discussion of policy-related issues (Diener and Crandall, 1978). One such organization is the Society for the Psychological Study of Social Issues (SPSSI); another is the Society for the Scientific Study of Social Problems (SSSP).

Summary

Ethics is not something one simply accedes to or ignores. Research ethics are a set of moral principles against which the actions of scientists are judged. They are not hard and fast do's and don'ts; rather, they pose dilemmas for researchers, offering choices and opportunities to weigh the costs and benefits of actions and decisions. Each stage in the research process presents its own problems for the investigator who would do the "right" thing. This interaction of ethics and science repeated throughout the research process should be a part of every social scientist's consciousness.

The three major areas of ethical concern are the ethics of data collection and analysis, the ethics of the treatment of human subjects, and the ethics of responsibility to society. The first set of ethics prescribes that scientists carry out their research and report their findings honestly and accurately; violations of these principles undermine science as a body of knowledge. The second area of ethics consists of a set of rules that are designed to protect the rights of research participants. The third area, which deals with the relationship between societal values and the dissemination and use of scientific findings, generally advises scientists to promote the general welfare.

Ethical considerations regarding the effects of research on participants are a major part of any research design. Presently, it is common practice for IRBs to pass judgment on the ethics of proposed research. Before and after institutional approval, researchers are guided in their decisions by federal regulations and professional ethical codes. While the various codes in use differ in language and specificity, and while some social scientists take issue with current practice, certain rules of conduct are fairly standard.

    1. Foremost, the researcher should not expose participants to substantial risk of physical or psychological harm—unless the benefits of participation exceed the risks and subjects knowingly choose to participate.

    2. Participants should be informed that their participation is voluntary and should be informed of any aspects of the research that might influence their willingness to participate.

    3. If deception is deemed necessary, then the researcher must gently and fully inform subjects of the deception as soon after their participation as possible.

    4. Researchers should use all possible means to protect the confidentiality of information provided by research participants. The overall guiding principle is that the potential benefits of research must be weighed against the potential costs.

Researchers also must consider the ethical implications of their research for the larger society. It is now widely recognized that values—personal and societal—are implicated throughout the research process. With this in mind, researchers should be conscious of the ways in which their decisions constitute ethical judgments. They should be aware of the potential uses and abuses of the knowledge they seek, guard against the intrusion of personal values in the conduct of research, and carefully point out the limitations of their research; finally, where appropriate, they should promote the beneficial application and fight against the harmful application of research findings.

Key Terms

ethics
research ethics
cost-benefit analysis
informed consent
deception

debriefing
anonymity
confidentiality
institutional review board (IRB)
cultural relativity

Review Questions and Problems

1. Why is it so important for scientists to be completely honest and accurate in conducting and reporting their research?

2. In what ways can research participants in social research be harmed?

3. Is it ever considered ethical to use procedures that might expose research participants to physical or mental discomfort, harm, or danger? Explain.

4. What are the limitations of a cost-benefit analysis of proposed research?

5. What safeguards do social scientists use to protect research participants from harm?

6. What are the basic ingredients of informed consent? How did Stanley Milgram violate this principle in his research on obedience to authority?

7. Which research approaches present the most serious problems from the standpoint of informed consent?

8. Why do researchers use deception? What are the arguments against its use in social research?

9. What is the most basic safeguard against the potentially harmful effects of deception? Is it effective? Explain.

10. When is social research likely to invade people's privacy?

11. How is research participants' right to privacy typically secured in (a) surveys, and (b) field research?

12. What are institutional review boards (IRBs)? What part do they play in evaluating the ethics of research?

13. What is meant by "value-free" sociology? Identify the major challenges to this position.

14. Explain Howard Becker's position that social scientists should declare "whose side they are on." What purposes does this declaration serve?

15. What obligations do social scientists have regarding the use of the knowledge they generate?

16. Discuss the ethical problems raised by the following research examples.

   a. (Hypothetical) A criminologist meets a professional fence through an ex-convict he knows. As part of a study, the researcher convinces the fence to talk about his work—why he sticks with this kind of work, what kind of people he deals with, how he meets them, and so forth. To gain the fence's cooperation, the researcher promises not to disclose any personal details that would get the fence in trouble. However, when subpoenaed, he agrees to reveal his informant rather than go to jail. Has the researcher violated an ethical principle in agreeing to talk?

b. (Hypothetical) A researcher gains access to a clinic serving AIDS patients by responding to a call for volunteers. While working at the clinic, she makes a record of patients' names, and later approaches them, identifies herself as a social scientist, fully explains the nature of her research, and asks for their cooperation in her in-depth survey of AIDS victims. Most patients agree, although some react negatively to the request. What aspects of the researcher's strategy are ethically problematic?

c. West, Gunn, and Chernicky (1975) tested a proposition from attribution theory in social psychology regarding the way that people perceive reprehensible acts. To do this they tempted subjects to participate in a burglary and then tested whether those agreeing to participate differed from those refusing and from subjects not approached with regard to their perceptions (attributions) about this illegal act. One of the experimenters, posing as a local private detective, contacted students and presented an elaborate plan for burglarizing a local advertising firm. In two of the conditions, subjects were told that the burglary was to be committed for a government agency; in another condition, subjects were promised $2000 for their participation. The subject's agreement or refusal to take part in the burglary and his or her reasons for the decision were the major dependent variables, and the researchers did not, of course, carry out the crime. What ethical problems does this study pose? Describe how you would debrief subjects in this study.

17

Writing Research Reports

Scientific research is a social activity, even when done by a solitary researcher. Without communication with others, one cannot participate in or contribute to the shared, cumulative body of knowledge that defines each scientific discipline. Much scientific communication takes place verbally, but the advancement of science is not based on the oral tradition; it ultimately depends on writing. Through written research reports, books, and articles, researchers communicate with others, who learn about, apply, replicate, and extend their work. The purpose of this chapter is to enhance the development of research writing skills. We will consider not only how to write about research, but also how to locate materials that can inform your research and writing.

The audience and forms of research reports vary. For the professional researcher the audience is most often peers in his or her field; the vehicle is generally an article in a scholarly journal. For the student researcher, the audience may be a class listening to a seminar presentation or a professor reading a term paper; the vehicle is the oral presentation or the paper. In all cases, however, the task is to communicate precisely and accurately what questions framed the research, what literature informed it, what the researcher did, what was found, and what conclusions might be drawn. When this is done well, the researcher clearly conveys what he or she learned, and others are able to make an informed evaluation of the study.

Virtually all research is grounded in an existing literature, and research reports should document the relationship of the present work to this literature. However, many students come to the tasks of doing social research and of writing a research paper with no notion of where to begin. Before discussing the mechanics of research writing, therefore, we will address ourselves to this issue. Where do research ideas come from? How are topics narrowed and informed by previous research? Where does research actually begin? The library is almost always the answer to these questions.

Using the Library for Research

Before going to the library you should have at least a general idea of what you want to study. You need not and probably should not have your topic "narrowed down" at the outset—although eventually it will be essential that you do so. At the beginning it is enough to know the broad area you are interested in, for example, "sex roles" or "altruism" or "white-collar crime."

There are many places in the library where you can begin your research. Many students are in the habit of going first to the card catalogue. Others go to indexes such as the *Reader's Guide to Periodical Literature* or abstracting services such as *Sociological Abstracts*. Although these are not necessarily bad ways to begin, books in the card catalogue rarely represent the most current thinking or the most recently published sources of literature on a given topic; the *Reader's Guide* usually provides information only from popular (e.g., *Time*, *Newsweek*) as opposed to scholarly publications; and *Sociological Abstracts*, though the best of these options, contains many references to unpublished papers and theses that may prove difficult to obtain.

We recommend instead that you refer first to a periodical called the *Social Sciences Index* (SSI). This was known as the *Social Sciences and Humanities Index* until 1974 when the social sciences and humanities parted company. The SSI is published four times each year and contains a detailed list of articles that have appeared recently in scholarly social and behavioral science journals. One of its advantages is that the indexing is done by a human being who figures out what the subject of the article really is, in contrast to computer-generated indexes based only on words appearing in titles.

Suppose that you are interested in "sex roles," but have yet to narrow your topic for research purposes. If you were to look in the most recent SSI available at the time of this writing (Vol. 12, No. 4, March 1986) under "sex roles," you would find thirty-three articles listed (all published during 1985). Figure 17.1 reproduces this page from the SSI. Notice first, following 'See also," the references to other related headings such as "Masculinity (Psychology)." If you were to refer to "Masculinity" in the same issue of the SSI you would find still other suggested topics as well as reference to five additional articles (Figure 17.2). All articles represent the most recent work on this topic available in major scholarly journals. Looking at earlier editions of the SSI would provide you with somewhat older but still very useful additional references.

Another valuable though less widely accessible reference source is the *Social Sciences Citation Index* (SSCI). The SSCI, published three times a year, is divided into three separate parts: the Permuterm Subject Index (which lists topics based on key words in the titles of articles), the Corporate and Source Index (which contains complete reference listings from recent articles), and the Citation Index (which lists organizations or authors who have been cited as well as the sources of the citations). A computerized version of the SSCI available in many college libraries makes possible quick, inexpensive, and comprehensive literature searches done by computer. When this is not available, students might start with the printed version of the SSCI Subject Index.

Looking up the topic "sex roles" in the most recently available Subject Index (January–April 1986), you would find a number of key-word references (see Figure 17.3A). Suppose that as a result of your reading, you decide to narrow your topic to deal only with male sex roles. Under "sex roles" the SSCI Subject Index lists one article with the key word "male." According to the index, it was written by "Taubman, S." Clearly, this is a reference you should look at.

FIGURE 17.1. Index listings for "sex role" from the *Social Sciences Index* (SSI) (Vol. 12, No. 4, March 1986).

Sex role—See also—*cont.*
   Masculinity (Psychology)
   Sex of children, Parental preferences for
   Sexism
   Success, Fear of
Attributes and roles assigned to characters in children's writing: sex differences and sex-role perceptions. M. L. Trepanier and J. A. Romatowski. *Sex Roles* 13:263-72 S '85
Beyond the reinforcement principle: another step toward understanding sex role development. B. I. Fagot. bibl *Dev Psychol* 21:1097-104 N '85
Boundaries, negotiation, consciousness: reconceptualizing gender relations. J. M. Gerson and K. Peiss. bibl *Soc Probl* 32:317-31 Ap '85
Comparison of the gender-linked language effect and sex role stereotypes. A. Mulac and others. bibl *J Pers Soc Psychol* 49:1098-109 O '85
Coping with a handicapped child: differences between mothers and fathers. R. F. Schilling, II and others. *Soc Sci Med* 21 no8:857-63 '85
The epistemology of gender identity: implications for social policy. M. Ayim and B. Houston. *Soc Theory Pract* 11:25-59 Spr '85
Evaluation of sex-typed tasks by black men and women. P. G. Carr and others. bibl *Sex Roles* 13:311-16 S '85
Gender differences in leisure-need activity patterns. J. W. White and K. J. Gruber. bibl *Sex Roles* 12:1173-86 Je '85
Gender, sex role, and career decision making of certified management accountants. D. E. Keys. bibl *Sex Roles* 13:33-46 Jl '85
Jurors' responses to victims' behavior and legal issues in sexual assault trials. G. D. LaFree and others. bibl *Soc Probl* 32:389-407 Ap '85
An officer and a lady: organizational barriers to women working as correctional officers in men's prisons. N. C. Jurik. bibl *Soc Probl* 32:375-88 Ap '85
Power, oppression and gender. J. Andre. *Soc Theory Pract* 11:107-22 Spr '85
Predicting math anxiety and course performance in college women and men. M. M. Llabre and E. Suarez. bibl *J Couns Psychol* 32:283-7 Ap '85
Predicting young women's role preference for parenting and work. L. C. Jensen and others. bibl *Sex Roles* 13:507-14 N '85
Preschool children's selective imitation of adults: implication for sex role development. K. B. Nicholas and H. McGinley. *J Genet Psychol* 146:143-4 Mr '85
Race class stereotypes of women. H. Landrine. bibl *Sex Roles* 13:65-75 Jl '85
Relationship of nontraditional sex-role attitudes to severity of women's criminal behavior. J. Lasley and others. *Psychol Rep* 56:155-8 F '85
Research on wife/mother role strain in dual career families: its present state has laid an adequate basis for representative empirical studies. J. B. Stanfield. *Am J Econ Sociol* 44:355-63 Jl '85
Risk in a parent's eyes: effects of gender and parenting experience. S. Kronsberg and others. bibl *Sex Roles* 13:329-41 S '85
Ritual hierarchy and secular equality in a Sepik River village. S. J. Harrison. bibl *Am Ethnol* 12:413-26 Ag '85
Sex and position differences among predictors of perceived work-related competence. N. S. Bruning and R. A. Snyder. bibl *Sex Roles* 13:485-98 N '85
Sex differences in career self-efficacy, consideration, and interests of eighth and ninth graders. P. Post-Kammer and P. L. Smith. bibl *J Couns Psychol* 32:551-9 O '85
Sex effects in evaluating leaders: a replication study. D. N. Izraeli and D. Izraeli. bibl *J Appl Psychol* 70:540-6 Ag '85
Sex of authority role models and achievement by men and women: leadership performance and recognition. F. L. Geis and others. bibl *J Pers Soc Psychol* 49:636-53 S '85
Sex-related errors in job evaluation: a "real-world" test. D. P. Schwab and R. Grams. bibl *J Appl Psychol* 70:533-9 Ag '85
Sex-role attitudes and perceptual learning. J. I. Gackenbach and S. M. Auerbach. bibl *J Soc Psychol* 125:233-43 Ap '85
Sex role development as a function of parent models and oedipal fixation. S. Juni and others. bibl *J Genet Psychol* 146:89-99 Mr '85
What will he think? men's impressions who initiate dates and achieve academically. C. L. Muehlenhard and T. J. Scardino. bibl *J Couns Psychol* 32:560-9 O '85

Women and agricultural change in Latin America: some concepts guiding research. F. Wilson. bibl *World Dev* 13:1017-35 S '85
Women, girls, and computers [symposium]; ed. by M. E. Lockheed. *Sex Roles* 13:115-251 Ag '85
Women in popular music: a quantitative analysis of feminine images over time. V. W. Cooper. bibl *Sex Roles* 13:499-506 N '85
Women returning to school: the consequences of multiple roles. J. M. Gerson. bibl *Sex Roles* 13:77-92 Jl '85
Women who return to orthodox Judaism: a feminist analysis. D. R. Kaufman. bibl *J Marriage Fam* 47:543-51 Ag '85
Sex shops See Sex oriented businesses
Sex symbolism
A projective assessment of the effects of Freudian sexual symbolism in liquor advertisements. W. J. Ruth and H. S. Mosatche. bibl *Psychol Rep* 56:183-8 F '85
Sex typing See Sex role
Sexism
The aye of the beholder: susceptibility to sexism and beautyism in the evaluation of managerial applicants. T. F. Cash and R. N. Kilcullen. bibl *J Appl Soc Psychol* 15 no7:591-605 '85
A comparison between strategies used on prisoners of war and battered wives. M. Romero. bibl *Sex Roles* 13:537-47 N '85
Embarrassing age spots or just plain ugly? physical attractiveness stereotyping as an instrument of sexism on American television commercials. A. C. Downs and S. K. Harrison. bibl *Sex Roles* 13:9-19 Jl '85
Perpetuation of gender inequality: a content analysis of comic strips. D. Chavez. bibl *Sex Roles* 13:93-102 Jl '85
The sexual mountain and black women writers. C. Hernton. *Black Sch* 16:2-11 Jl/Ag '85
Sexism in language
Redefining the situation: negotiations on the meaning of "woman". D. R. Margolis. bibl *Soc Probl* 32:332-47 Ap '85
Use of nonsexist pronouns as a function of one's feminist orientation. M. B. Jacobson and W. R. Insko, Jr. bibl *Sex Roles* 13:1-7 Jl '85
Sexual arousal
   See also
   Penile tumescence
Pavlovian conditioning of sexual arousal: first- and second-order effects. E. Zamble and others. bibl *J Exp Psychol Anim Behav Processes* 11:598-610 O '85
Sexual attitudes
Conservatism as a factor of sexual responding to a word-association test. V. C. Joe and others. *J Soc Psychol* 125:275-6 Ap '85
Evaluation of a church-based sexuality education program for adolescents. L. H. Powell and S. Jorgensen. bibl *Fam Relat* 34:475-82 O '85
Sexual behavior See Sex behavior
Sexual dimorphism (Man)
Accuracy and direction of error in the sexing of the skeleton: implications for paleodemography. R. S. Meindl and others. bibl *Am J Phys Anthropol* 68:79-85 S '85
Dental wear in the Libben population: its functional pattern and role in the determination of adult skeletal age at death. C. O. Lovejoy. bibl il *Am J Phys Anthropol* 68:47-56 S '85
The supraorbital torus: "a most remarkable peculiarity". M. D. Russell. bibl il *Curr Anthropol* 26:337-50 Je '85; Discussion. 26:350-60 Je '85; 26:522 Ag/O '85
The "unisex phantom," sexual dimorphism, and proportional growth assessment. R. J. Shephard and others. bibl *Am J Phys Anthropol* 67:403-12 Ag '85
Sexual disorders
   See also
   Anorgasmy
EEG hemispheric asymmetry during sexual arousal: psychophysiological patterns in responsive, unresponsive, and dysfunctional men. A. S. Cohen and others. bibl *J Abnorm Psychol* 94:580-90 N '85
Sexual ethics
   See also
   Dating (Social customs)
   Incest
   Sex and religion
   Sexual harassment
Sexual harassment
Administrative risk and sexual harassment: legal and ethical responsibilities on campus. C. F. Cnudde and B. A. Nesvold. *PS* 18:780-9 Fall '85

FIGURE 17.2. Index listings for "masculinity (psychology)" from the *Social Sciences Index* (SSI) (Vol. 12, No. 4, March 1986).

Marxism—*cont.*
A link between the social and natural sciences: the case of scientific psychology. C. M. J. Braun and J. M. C. Baribeau. *Sci Soc* 49:131-58 Summ '85
Marx and Keynes? Marx or Keynes? R. Brandis. bibl *J Econ Issues* 19:643-59 S '85
Marxism and development sociology: interpreting the impasse. D. Booth. bibl *World Dev* 13:761-87 Jl '85
Marxism and secular faith. R. J. Arneson. bibl *Am Polit Sci Rev* 79:627-40 S '85
Method, analysis, and politics in Max Weber: disentangling Marxian affinities and differences. J. W. Russell. bibl *Hist Polit Econ* 17:575-90 Wint '85
An ontological model of class consciousness confirmatory maximum likelihood factor analysis. A. Ben-Porat. *Int J Comp Sociol* 26:60-74 Mr/Je '85
Primitive accumulation, agrarian reform and socialist transitions: an argument. A. Saith. bibl *J Dev Stud* 22:1-48 O '85
Reproduction and the development: a case for a 'Darwinian' mechanism in Marx's theory of history. J. Torrance. *Polit Stud* 33:382-98 S '85
The social origins of environmental determinism. R. Peet. bibl *Ann Assoc Am Geogr* 75:309-33 S '85
Sociology and knowledge in the middle of nowhere: Constantin Dobrogeanu-Gherea. M. Shafir. *East Eur Q* 19:321-36 Fall '85
Mary, Blessed Virgin, Saint
Apparitions and miracles
Cork's 'miracle': did Mary's statue really move? P. Kellner. *New Statesman* 110:7 Ag 16 '85
Maryland
See also
Washington metropolitan area
Maschler, Michael
(jt. auth) See Aumann, Robert J., and Maschler, Michael
Masculinity (Psychology)
See also
Androgyny (Psychology)
Infertility, macho style. L. Miller. *Psychol Today* 19:78-9 N '85
Masculinity inhibits helping in emergencies: personality does predict the bystander effect. D. M. Tice and R. F. Baumeister. bibl *J Pers Soc Psychol* 49:420-8 Ag '85
Self-conceptions and gender role: the correspondence between gender-role categorization and open-ended self-descriptions. L. A. Jackson. bibl *Sex Roles* 13:549-66 N '85
Sex-role orientation and psychological adjustment: implications for the masculinity model. C. H. Adams and M. Sherer. bibl *Sex Roles* 12:1211-18 Je '85
Sexual identification and gender identity among father-absent males. S. A. Kagel and K. M. Schilling. bibl *Sex Roles* 13:357-70 S '85
Masculinity-femininity tests
See also
Bem sex role inventory
Mashona (African people)
Rites and ceremonies
Expressive space in the Zimbabwe culture. T. N. Huffman. bibl map *Man* 19:593-612 D '84; Discussion. 20:542-5 S '85
Social life and customs
When in Harare. K. Kellaway. *New Statesman* 110:34-5 S 6 '85
Mashona architecture See Architecture, Mashona
Masking, Visual See Figure background relation
Maslach, Christina, and others
Individuation: conceptual analysis and assessment. bibl *J Pers Soc Psychol* 49:729-38 S '85
Masochism
Uproar over violent images. A. Durell. *New Statesman* 109:16-17 Je 14 '85
Mason, David
Nationalism and the process of group mobilisation: the case of 'loyalism'in Northern Ireland reconsidered. *Ethn Racial Stud* 8:408-25 Jl '85
Mason, J. Russell, and others
Avfail in color avoidance learning by starlings (Sturnus vulgaris) and red-winged blackbirds (Agelaius phoeniceus). bibl *J Comp Psychol* 99:403-10 D '85
Mason, Robert L.
(jt. auth) See Keating, Jerome P., and Mason, Robert L.
Mason, Susan E., and others
Adult age differences in visual search. *Int J Aging Hum Dev* 21 no3:187-96 '85
Masoni, Vittorio
Nongovernmental organizations and development. *Finance Dev* 22:38-41 S '85

Mass communication See Mass media; Telecommunication
Mass demonstrations See Demonstrations
Mass media
See also
Cross-cultural studies—Mass media
Maps in mass media
Motion pictures
Newspapers
Periodicals
Radio broadcasting
Television broadcasting
Economic aspects
See also
Mass media ownership
The marketplace of ideas revisited [symposium] *J Commun* 35:80-165 Summ '85
Political aspects
See also
Mass media policy
Diversity of news: "marginalizing" the opposition. E. S. Herman. bibl *J Commun* 35:135-46 Summ '85
Two politicians in a realistic experiment: attraction, discrepancy, intensity of delivery, and attitude change. O. Wiegman. bibl *J Appl Soc Psychol* 15 no7:673-86 '85
Psychological aspects
See also
Violence in mass media
Loneliness and use of six mass media among college students. B. A. Austin. bibl *Psychol Rep* 56:323-7 F '85
Research
Here we go again—research phobia. A. Karpf. *New Statesman* 110:14 Jl 19 '85
Social aspects
See also
Violence in mass media
Affirmative action, the media, and the public: a look at a "look-away" issue. F. R. Lynch. bibl *Am Behav Sci* 28:807-27 Jl/Ag '85
Media: the watchdog press: howling at the moon. R. J. Trotter. *Psychol Today* 19:19 Ag '85
A prescription for a socially responsible press. D. S. M. Mohamad. *Far East Econ Rev* 130:26-8 O 10 '85
The role of mass media in alcohol and highway safety campaigns. J. B. Haskins. bibl *J Stud Alcohol* supp no10:184-91 Jl '85
The role of the press and the medical community in the epidemic of "mysterious gas poisoning" in the Jordan West Bank. A. Hefez. *Am J Psychiatry* 142:833-7 Jl '85
Pakistan
Press freedom debated by officials, Muslims, secularists. H. Haqqani. *Far East Econ Rev* 129:28-31 S 19 '85
Southeast Asia
The media's proper place. J. Clad. *Far East Econ Rev* 130:34-5 O 3 '85
Mass media and blacks
See also
Television and blacks
Mass media and children
See also
Television and children
Mass media and the aged
The mass media and the aged. L. A. Powell and J. B. Williamson. bibl *Soc Policy* 16:38-49 Summ '85
Mass media ownership
U.S. cultural productions: the impact of ownership. P. M. Hirsch. bibl *J Commun* 35:110-21 Summ '85
Mass media policy
See also
Government and television
Government and the press
Pakistan
Strict press laws remain in force, but are used less. H. Haqqani. *Far East Econ Rev* 129:32-3 S 19 '85
Mass political attitudes See Public opinion
Mass screening (Health programs) See Medical screening
Mass transportation See Local transit
Massachusetts
See also
Boston (Mass.)
Cambridge (Mass.)
Springfield (Mass.)
See also subhead Massachusetts under the following subjects
Community mental health services
Water pollution
Social conditions
See also
Crime and criminals—Massachusetts

Source: Social Sciences Index Copyright © 1986 by The H. W. Wilson Company. Material reproduced by permission of the publisher.

FIGURE 17.3. Various listings from the *Social Sciences Citation Index* (SSCI) (January–April 1986).

A. Permuterm® Subject Index B. Source Index C. Citation Index

A. Permuterm® Subject Index

SEX-ROLES

SEX-ROLES
ADOLESCENT — HEIMER C+
ADULTHOOD — SEDNEY MA
AGGRESSION — CAPLAN PJ
AMERICAN - - NOL E
ANDROGYNY - - CAPLAN PJ
CHANGES - - - KRONENFE JJ
CHILDREN - - GUNTER B+
CHILDRENS - - DAVIES D
CHOICES - - -
COMMUNITY — GRIFFIN PB+
CONCEPTIONS - SEDNEY MA
CONSUMER — DEBEVEC K
DEPRESSION — FLETT GL
EMOTIONAL — GANONG LH
EXPLOITIVE - — TAUBMAN S
EXPRESSIVE. - GANONG LH
FEAR - - - - DILLON KM
FEMINIST - - - KRONENFE JJ
GENDER - - - - DILLON KM
GROUPS - - - CAPLAN PJ
              — KERR NL
INVESTIGAT — TESCH SA
JOB-SATISF — SELNOW GW
MALE - - - - - TAUBMAN S
MOTIVATION - KERR NL
MOVEMENTS - KRONENFE JJ
OYSTERCATC. - NOL E
PERCEPTIONS — DEBEVEC K
PRODUCTS -
PROMOTIONS -
PSYCHOPATH. — KIRSHNER LA+
              — STEINER BW+
PUBLIC-REL. - SELNOW GW
SCHOOL - - - - DAVIES D
SELF - - - - - DEBEVEC K
SEX - - - - - GANONG LH
SEX-DIFFER. - CAPLAN PJ
SOCIAL-CHA. - HEIMER C+
STUDIES - - - TESCH SA
SUBJECTS - - - DAVIES D
TASK - - - - - KERR NL
TELEVISION - GUNTER B+
TURKEY - - - - GRIFFIN PB+
VALIDATION - TESCH SA
VIEWS - - - - DAVIES D
VOCATIONAL -
WOMEN - - - - CAPLAN PJ

B. Source Index

TAUBMAN S
BEYOND THE BRAVADO - SEX-ROLES AND THE EXPLOITIVE
MALE
SOCIAL WORK 31(1):12-18   86   33R
ALAMEDA CTY MENTAL HLTH SERV,OUTPATIENT SERV, OAKLAND,
CA, USA

CHODOROW N	78 REPRODUCTION MOTHERL		
DAILEY DM	63 SOC WORK RES ABSTR	19	20
DAVIDSON I	78 CONJUGAL CRIME		
DOBASH RE	79 VIOLENCE WIVES CASE		
ERIKSON E	50 CHILDHOOD SOC		253
FESHBACH S	80 CHILD ABUSE AGENDA A		48
FROMM E	56 ART LOVING		16
GANDHI M	69 GANDHI NONVIOLENCE		9
GIL D	70 VIOLENCE CHILDREN		
GILLIGAN C	82 AM J ORTHOPSYCHIAT	52	199
GOLDBERG H	76 HAZARDS BEING MALE S		
HERMAN J	81 FATHER DAUGHTER INCE		
JUSTICE B	79 BROKEN TABOO SEX FAM		
KRAVETZ D	81 AM J ORTHOPSYCHIAT	51	502
KROTH J	78 EVALUATION CHILD SEX		
LAING RD	67 POLITICS EXPERIENCE		58
LYND HM	58 SHAME SEARCH IDENTIT		68
LYNN DB	79 DAUGHTERS PARENTS PA		
LYSTAD MH	75 AM J ORTHOPSYCHIAT	45	298
MAY ET	78 J SOCIAL HIST	12	190
MAY R	72 POWER INNOCENCE SEAR		23
MORRISON M	82 AEGIS	36	20
PLECK E	80 AM MAN		
PLECK JH	81 MYTH MASCULINITY		
ROTH L	83 INTIMATE STRANGERS M		
RUSSELL D	80 RAPE MARRIAGE		
SHENGOLD LL	79 J AM PSYCHOANAL ASS	27	536
STEVENS D	83 J SOCIAL WORK HUMAN	1	35
STRAUSS M	81 CLOSED DOORS VIOLENC		
TAUBMAN S	84 SOC WORK	29	35
ULLIAN DZ	81 AM J ORTHOPSYCHIAT	51	493
WALKER LE	79 BATTERED WOMAN		
YANKELOVICH D	74 WORKER JOB		

THOMPSON EH
PALLIATIVE AND CURATIVE CARE NURSES ATTITUDES
TOWARD DYING AND DEATH IN THE HOSPITAL SETTING
OMEGA-J D 16(3):233-242   85   11R
HOLY CROSS COLL,DEPT SOCIOL, WORCESTER, MA 01610, USA

FOLTA JR	65 NURS RES	14	232
GLASER BG	65 AWARENESS DYING		
	68 TIME DYING		
GOLUB S	71 NURS RES	20	503
GOW CM	77 SOCIAL SCI MED	11	191
HOPPING BL	77 NURS RES	26	443
POPOFF D	75 NURSING	5	39
QUINT JC	66 NURSING OUTLOOK	12	16
	67 NURSE DYING PATIENT		
STOLLER EP	80 NURS RES		
TEMPLER DI	70 J GEN PSYCHOL	82	165

GRISANTI C PLECK JH—ATTITUDES TOWARD THE MALE-
ROLE AND THEIR CORRELATES
SEX ROLES 13(7-8):413-427   85   45R
HOLY CROSS COLL,DEPT SOCIOL, WORCESTER, MA 01610, USA

ALLEN DA	54 AM SOCIOL REV	19	591
BELL RR	81 PSYCHOL WOMEN QUART	5	402
BRANNON R	76 49 PERCENT MAJORITY		1
	78 PSYCHOL WOMEN FUTURE		647
	84 PSYCHOL DOCUMENTS	14	6
BROVERMAN IK	72 J SOC ISSUES	28	59
CAPLAN RD	75 JOB DEMANDS WORKER H		
CICONE MV	78 J SOC ISSUES	34	5
COZBY P	73 PSYCHOL BULL	84	73
DAVIS JA	80 GENERAL SOCIAL SURVE		
DERLEGA VJ	76 J CONSULT CLIN PSYCH	44	376
DOYLE JA	78 JSAS CATALOG SELECTE	8	35
FALBO T	82 PSYCHOL WOMEN QUART	6	399
FIEBERT MS	83 PERCEPT MOTOR SKILL	56	83
FISCHER JL	81 PSYCHOL WOMEN Q	5	444
FRIEDMAN M	74 TYPE A BEHAVIOR YOUR		
GRAMICK J	83 SOC WORK	28	137
GROSS AE	78 J SOC ISSUES	34	87
HACKER HM	81 PSYCHOL WOMEN QUART	5	385
HARRISON J	78 J SOC ISSUES	34	65
HENLEY NM	73 DOING OTHERS JOINING		
JOURARD SM	58 J ABNORMAL SOCIAL PS	56	91
	71 TRANSPARENT SELF		
KOMAROVSKY M	76 DILEMMAS MASCULINITY		
KRULEWITZ JE	80 J PERS SOC PSYCHOL	38	67
LEHNE GK	76 49 PERCENT MAJORITY		66
LEWIS RA	78 J SOC ISSUES	34	108
MATTHEWS KA	82 PSYCHOL BULL	91	293
MINNINGERODE FA	76 SEX ROLES	2	3
MOORE D	81 PERSONALITY SOCIAL P	7	320
MORELAND J	78 UNPUB ATTITUDES MASC		
MORIN SF	78 J SOC ISSUES	34	29
NUTT RL	74 J COLLEGE STUDENT PE	15	346
PEPLAU LA	78 WOMEN FEMINIST PERSP		
PLECK JH	78 PSYCHOL WOMEN FUTURE		647
	81 MYTH MASCULINITY		
PLOG S	65 J SOC PSYCHOL	65	193
SALES SM	69 DISS ABSTR INT B	30	2407
SATTEL JW	76 SOC PROBL	23	469
SAWYER J	70 LIBERATION	15	32
SMITH KT	71 PSYCHOL REP	29	1091
TURNER R	70 FAMILY INTERACTION		
VILLEMEZ WJ	77 PSYCHOL REP	41	411
WEINBERGER LE	79 J HOMOSEXUALITY	4	237
YANKELOVICH D	74 NEW MORALITY PROFILE		

C. Citation Index

PLECK E				
78 AM FAMILY SOCIAL HIS				
ROSE SO	HIST WORKSH		113	86
80 AM MAN				
TAUBMAN S	SOCIAL WORK		31	12 86
83 SIGNS	8 451			
HANMER J	INT J S LAW		13	357 85
PLECK J				
75 MEN MASCULINITY				
THOMPSON DC	EDUC LEADER		43	53 86
81 MYTH MASCULINITY				
BREINES W	SOCIOL INQ		56	69 86
	WOMEN ST IN		8	601 85
HILLER DV	SOC PSYCH Q	N	48	373 85
THOMPSON DC	EDUC LEADER		43	53 86
81 WIVES EMPLOYMENT ROL				
TILLY LA	J HIST BEH	B	22	81 86
PLECK JH				
** WORKING WIVES WORKIN				
MARKHAM WT	SOCIOL Q		27	121 86
75 SEX ROLES	1 161			
COWAN G	SEX ROLES		14	211 86
76 J SOC ISSUES	32 155			
DAVIS SK	HISPAN J B		7	317 85
77 SOC PROBL	24 417			
KING AC	BEHAV THER	N	17	57 86
SORENSEN G	J HEALTH SO		26	379 85
SPITZE G	SOCIAL FORC		64	689 86
STAINES GL	J OCCUP BEH	N	7	147 86
78 PSYCHOL WOMEN FUTURE			619	
THOMPSON EH	SEX ROLES		13	413 85
79 FAMILY COORDINATOR	28 481			
PEARSON JM	J AM DIET A		86	339 86
81 MYTH MASCULINITY				
TAUBMAN S	SOCIAL WORK		31	12 86
THOMPSON EH	SEX ROLES		13	413 85
82 MYTH MASCULINITY				
FOREMAN MD	NURS CLIN N		21	65 86
MCNEILL S	ACAD PSYCH		7	299 85
83 RES INTERWEAVE SOCIA		251		
SHAMIR B	J MARRIAGE		48	195 86
	SOCIAL PROB		33	67 85
83 RES INTERWEAVE SOCIA	3			
SAGI A	CHILD CARE		14	273 85
83 RES INTERWEAVE SOCIA	3 251			
ROSS CE	J HEALTH SO		26	312 85

Going, therefore, to the SSCI Source Index for January–April 1986 (Figure 17.3B), you would find under S. Taubman's name a full reference to this article, "Beyond the Bravado: Sex-roles and the Exploitive Male," published in 1986 in the journal, *Social Work* (Vol. 31, No. 1, pp. 12–18). You can also see that Taubman cites thirty-three references in the bibliography, such as Pleck, E 80 Am Man, and Pleck, JH 81 Myth Masculinity. (The absence of other numbers, denoting volume and beginning page, to the right of these references, indicates that these are books rather than journal articles.) In order to get a more complete reference to these citations, you could read the Taubman article. Doing so would reveal that the full reference to JH Pleck's book is *The Myth of Masculinity*, published in 1981 in Cambridge, Massachusetts by MIT Press.

Alternatively, you could refer first to the SSCI Citation Index (January–April 1986), which catalogues citations of articles known to you. There you can see if Pleck's book has been cited recently by other scholars in the field (see Figure 17.3C). You also would see that several other items by Pleck have been cited. The 1981 book in which you are interested was cited by S. Taubman—something you already knew—and by EH Thompson in the journal *Sex Roles* (Vol. 13, p. 413f). Turning back to the Source Index you can look up EH Thompson's article to get the complete set of references from it (Figure 17.3B). There you will see two articles by EH Thompson, the second of which is the one you are looking for—an article coauthored by Thompson, Grisanti, and Pleck entitled "Attitudes toward the Male-Role and Their Correlates." This article contains a bibliography with some forty-five references, many of which might be of interest as you continue to narrow your research on the topic "male sex roles."

Using this system of cross-checking articles through the various parts of the SSCI often can yield a current and quite comprehensive set of references. Before you spend hours perusing subject indexes, however, we recommend that you find and read one or more of the most recent references. As you read these references, you can better decide which of the works discussed and/or cited should be read next. Then you can examine these additional articles and books for further references, and so on, as you "reference-hop" your way through the literature. This will enable you quickly to get a hold on the literature and to think of how to narrow the topic appropriately. As you identify each source, it is a good idea to fill out index cards containing complete bibliographic information, as well as Library of Congress (or Dewey Decimal) numbers found in the library card catalogue. The notes you take on books or articles also should be cross-referenced to the index cards, so that when it comes time to write the research report you will have no trouble connecting ideas to references.

Outlining and Preparing to Write

Before you begin to write, you should have a conception of the overall organization of the research report. We recommend writing an outline that organizes the paper in terms of the following sections typically found in articles reporting empirical research.

—An *introduction* that includes a statement of the problem under investigation
—A *literature review* that summarizes and places the problem in the context of related theory and research
—A description of the *design and execution of the study* that indicates how the research was done in sufficient detail to allow a reasonable replication of it
—A presentation of the *data analysis and findings* that identifies the method of analysis and the specific results of the study
—A *discussion* of the findings that offers a broad interpretation of the results

Within each of these major headings, you should list subtopics and important points. As you may discover, outlining frequently brings out the recognition of new ideas and the necessity for transition topics that lead from one point to the next. You should ask continually as the outline becomes detailed: "How can I move logically from this point to that point?" "Does the organization make sense?" "Have I left out anything essential?" A report-length paper of 15–20 pages requires an outline of at least one and possibly two or more single-spaced pages.

When the outline is complete, the writer is ready to begin the actual report. At this point, it is critical to have a clear grasp of the audience's level of knowledge and sources of interest. This does not mean that you should "talk down" or "write down" to the consumers of your work. But you should keep in mind who is going to read it. For the social science reader familiar with the area of study, the report may include technical language, an abbreviated presentation of previous research, and a detailed presentation of methods and findings; for lay readers, it should omit technical terms and should provide a more detailed presentation of the background of the research and a more general presentation of methods and findings. Since it seems more common to err in providing too little information about research methods and using too many technical terms, we recommend that students write for intelligent and educated peers.

Of course, only you the researcher are fully aware of why the study was done, how it is related to previous research, what decisions in design, operations, and measurement were made, and why. And the overriding concern should be to communicate these points as accurately and clearly as possible. As in all good writing, this requires proper grammar, punctuation, and style. The principles of being concise and direct, of avoiding unnecessary jargon, of providing examples to clarify points, and so forth, apply just as strongly to technical as to any other form of writing. (Several excellent references that provide helpful hints on writing are provided in Box 17.1.)

With these points in mind, let us consider in some detail the topical outline suggested above. It is important to note that this is only one of many possible outlines. It probably applies best to explanatory studies involving experimentation and survey research and least to exploratory and descriptive studies, especially field research. Moreover, considerations of length, subject matter, purpose, and audience may influence the organization and elaboration of this outline in the actual paper. A paper may emphasize measurement, or sampling, or something else depending on the study. No perfect outline exists ready to be adopted for every

---

BOX 17.1

References for Improving Your Research Writing

Writing style is just as essential to good report writing as proper format and organization. Although style is not an altogether proper consideration for this volume, we stress its importance and refer the interested reader to some of the excellent references that are available:

American Psychological Association. 1983. *Publication Manual of the American Psychological Association*. 3d ed. Washington, D.C.: Author.

Bart, Pauline, and Linda Frankel. 1986. *The Student Sociologist's Handbook*. 4th ed. New York: Random House.

Becker, Howard S. 1986. *Writing for Social Scientists*. Chicago: University of Chicago Press.

Crews, Frederick. 1984. *The Random House Handbook*. 4th ed. New York: Random House.

Selvin, Hanan C., and Everett K. Wilson. 1984. On sharpening sociologists' prose. *Sociological Quarterly* 25:205–22.

Selvin, Hanan C., and Everett K. Wilson. 1984. Cases in point: A limited glossary of stumblebum usage. *Sociological Quarterly* 25:417–27.

The Sociology Writing Group. 1986. *A Guide to Writing Sociology Papers*. New York: St. Martin's.

Strunk, William, Jr., and E. B. White. 1979. *The Elements of Style*. 3d ed. New York: MacMillan.

---

research paper. The important point is to develop a functional outline that facilitates the writing.

Major Headings

The social sciences publish numerous professional journals reporting current research. The journals encountered in the development of a literature review provide models for the research report. These models vary according to the field, but in general, you can expect to find components similar to those suggested here.

The Abstract

Generally the first portion of a scientific paper is the abstract, a capsule version of the full report written after the report is completed. Abstracts do not describe what takes place in the report (e.g., "after a review of the literature, a hypothesis is formulated and tested. . . ."), but rather summarize the content. They act as a prose table of contents. They typically use the same words as the report and, in fact, may be pieced together by "abstracting" phrases from the finished report.

Abstracts rarely exceed half a page and frequently are limited to 150–200 words. The purpose of the abstract is to help potential readers decide if they are sufficiently interested in the topic to read the full report. Keeping this in mind will help in the formulation of a concise abstract. Authors should include only the essential information that they would want to know if they were unfamiliar with the study and wanted to assess its utility for them. In many ways the title of a report serves the same purpose and may be seen as an abstract of the abstract.

Introduction

This section sets up the rest of the paper. It should contain a clear statement of the problem and why it is of general interest and importance. This may be demonstrated by relating the problem briefly to the theoretical context of the study or by pointing to its social and practical significance. For example, Bruce Straits (1985) opens his article in the *Journal of Marriage and the Family* (see chapter 7) by briefly describing current *theoretical* explanations for low U.S. birthrates, each of which emphasizes a different set of factors influencing childbearing plans. The point of his research, he then explains, is to disentangle and determine the relative importance of these factors among a sample of young college women. Paul Burstein's (1979) introduction to his article in *Public Opinion Quarterly* (see chapter 12) emphasizes both the social and theoretical significance of the problem. Burstein begins by noting that prior to 1957 "Congress had not passed any laws protecting the civil rights of minorities since adopting the Civil Rights Act of 1875 . . . over 80 years before." He then notes the remarkable and rapid legislative changes in this area after 1957, and concludes his introduction as follows:

> Under what circumstances did Congress act against discrimination? This paper describes the relationship between public opinion, civil rights demonstrations, and the passage of antidiscrimination legislation. The aim is to examine the link between what the public wants and what legislation it gets—a critical issue in democratic politics (Burstein, 1979:158).

Literature Review

The literature review must make clear the theoretical context of the problem under investigation and how it has been studied by others. The idea is to cite relevant literature in the process of presenting the underlying theoretical and methodological rationale for the research. This means citing key studies and emphasizing major findings rather than trying to report every study ever done on the problem or providing unnecessary detail.

In studies designed to test specific hypotheses, the aim of this section should be to show, if possible, how the hypotheses derive from theory or previous research. When this is not possible—for example, because the hypothesis was based on everyday observations and experiences—one should still show the relevance of the study to previous research and theory, if only to show how it contradicts existing evidence or fills a gap in scientific knowledge. Indeed, even when there are no clearly formulated hypotheses or the research is basically descriptive or exploratory, it is still appropriate to place the research in some theoretical context.

Finally, it is a good idea, especially for lengthy literature reviews, to end this section with (1) a concise restatement of hypotheses, (2) a presentation of the theoretical model in a figure, such as an arrow diagram, or (3) a brief overview of the study.

Methods

This section should state clearly and accurately how the study was done, providing enough information to permit replication by others. The following subtopics may help to accomplish this objective.

Design. First you must tell what type of study this is: experiment, survey, field research, or available data analysis. The particular approach determines the primary design and procedural issues that must be addressed: (1) in the case of experiments, the key issues will include the type of experimental design and the procedures of its implementation; (2) in surveys, the type of survey instrument, its length, and the sampling design; (3) in field research, the nature of the setting(s) and the researcher's relationship to informants; (4) in research using available data, the sources of data and their completeness.

Subjects. This section should make clear who participated in the study, how many cases were sampled, how they were selected, and whom or what they represent. It is necessary to discuss sampling procedures as well as the generalizability of the data.

Measurement. Here operational definitions are described. No matter what approach was used, the researcher should clarify the way in which observations were translated into variables and concepts. In an experiment, this means specifying the procedures for manipulating the independent variable and measuring the dependent variable. In surveys, this should include the specific questions that were asked as measures of each variable in the theoretical model. In field research, this means noting the kinds of observations that were made and, if relevant, other sources of information such as documents and in-depth interviewing. Longer reports may contain appendixes with some of these materials, such as copies of the complete questionnaire or transcripts of selected interviews.

Procedures. This section, which may be a part of the description of sampling and measurement, presents a summary of the various steps in the conduct of the research. This is especially important in experiments and field research. Experiments should include a step-by-step account of the study from the subject's point of view. Field researchers should give a chronological account of the research, telling how they selected and gained entry into the setting, how they met and developed relationships with informants, and how long they were in the setting. In fact, the research reports of field researchers often follow a narrative, either from the researcher's or informant's point of view, which begins with a discussion of these methodological issues.

Findings

The heart of the research paper is the findings section, toward which the entire report should be aimed. This is where the problems, questions, or hypotheses that framed the research are answered. Before presenting the main results, however, the researcher should first provide any evidence on reliability and validity that was not presented in the methods section. For example, it is at the beginning of the results section that one ordinarily finds the outcome of manipulation checks, survey response rates, and tests for measurement reliability and validity. Once this is done, then the researcher presenting a quantitative analysis should describe what sort of statistical analyses were performed on the data. This description should be very specific with regard to the kind of analysis (e.g., "three-way analysis of variance," "paired *t*-tests," "ordinary least-squares regression") and may include (which we recommend for the student researcher) references to descriptions of the statistical techniques or to the computer software package used to carry out the analysis.

In quantitative analyses, the researcher often constructs tables, charts, and graphs to facilitate the presentation of findings. Here we have several recommendations. First, use tables and figures sparingly, to summarize large amounts of information. During the course of research, investigators usually generate many more tables than they can possibly present in the research report. These interim tables guide the researcher in determining the course of the analysis, but more often than not they contain single facts that can be reported in the text of the report. Second, organize this section around the major hypotheses or theoretical questions and/or major findings. If there is a single main hypothesis, then a single table may suffice to summarize the findings. Third, discuss the data in terms of what they show about the research problem or hypothesis; do not let the data speak for themselves, and do not discuss the data merely in terms of the variables or the numbers in a table. In other words, subordinate the data to your argument and use the data and tables to help tell a story.

This last point also applies to "qualitative" research. The data in such studies are usually not numbers but quotations, concrete observations, and historical events. Still, the data should be used in the same way: organized around the thesis of the report, and presented to support arguments.

Discussion

This section may begin or end with a brief summary. The summary serves as a sort of "caboose abstract," reviewing the highlights of the report. This is particularly useful in cases in which the paper is long or necessarily complex. One should try not to be too repetitious here; in other words, do not lift passages from earlier parts of the paper, but rather restate the basic problem and basic findings.

The discussion section, however, generally has more lofty goals. First, it provides a place to point out the shortcomings of the research. For example, the data may be drawn from populations or under conditions that limit the generalizability of the findings. Honesty regarding such limitations is important in preventing readers from making more from the research than is warranted. Second, it provides a chance to point out inconsistencies, account for anomalies, and suggest improvements in the research design. Finally, the discussion section allows the writer an opportunity to place the whole project into broader perspective, to mention the theoretical and practical implications of the study, and to discuss possible future work.

References

Finally, some sort of bibliography must be included. Although the usual practice is to list only works cited in the body of the report, uncited works that were important in the development of the study may also be included. The format of the references varies slightly from one discipline to another. This book uses the University of Chicago *Style Manual*.

Other Considerations

The Writing-Reading Interface

All good writers are careful to structure their material in accordance with readership patterns, and research writing is no different. Thus the "tell them what you are going to say—say it—tell them what you said" structure is a good outline for readers who may be interested in skimming an article quickly in order to assess its relevance to their interests. Writing done for other purposes may be structured differently. For example, newspaper readers normally peruse articles in a top-downward fashion (headline, first paragraph, etc.) and often do not complete every article they start because of limitations of interest or time. Journalists, therefore, like to pack as much information as possible into the headline. They often like to tell the whole story in the first paragraph (Who? What? Where? When? Why?); then they can elaborate and provide details in subsequent paragraphs. Perhaps if you think about the way you read newspaper articles, you will recognize this pattern in your own reading. This kind of reading has a purpose, but the purpose differs from that of research reading and, as a consequence, so does the writing.

Many busy readers of research reports follow a different pattern, which the structure of the writing ought to anticipate. These readers generally do not read in a top-downward fashion. They may begin at the title; then, if they are interested, they will study the abstract. Only if the abstract is relevant is the busy reader likely to go on. You may also recognize this pattern of reading from your own experiences developing research bibliographies. If the abstract is deemed immediately relevant, the reader may hurry through the "introduction," skim through the "methods" for keys to the author's perspective, then dwell on the "findings" and their implications. It should be noted, however, that while such skimming and racing may be useful when you are trying to assess the relevance of an article for your research interests, it is not the best practice when you really are trying to digest a piece of research.

Revisions

Many students believe that the first draft is the only draft. Most professional writers, on the other hand, assume that the first draft will be one in a series of drafts designed to sharpen and improve the final product. The advent of word processing computers has greatly facilitated the opportunity to produce subsequent drafts. The purpose of a first draft is to transfer ideas, thoughts, and facts from the mind of the writer into some material form that can be reflected on by the author. We cannot put a number on how many subsequent drafts should be written; however, it is hard to imagine a polished report that is not the product of numerous drafts. Good writing requires attention to detail; it means writing as if every word and sentence should be taken seriously. And that requires extensive rewriting.

For many people the best time to revise a paper is after taking some time away from the work. Writers who wait until the last few hours or days to write a paper will not produce a good paper. Authors' judgments about the quality of their work may vary directly with the recency of the effort. The passage of time tends to bring perspective and also a renewed energy to tackle a job that perhaps did not seem necessary earlier. Much revision, of course, can be of the "cut and paste" variety. This job usually involves the revision of what is unclear, the deletion of what is extraneous, and the addition of what had been omitted. Again, word-processing technology makes this sort of revision relatively painless.

Finally, at some point in the successive drafting of a report, a "working" draft should be shown to others who can provide critical feedback. We realize that much of the writing students do, with its rigid time constraints, does not allow for this. But there is no better way of judging the clarity of your writing than asking others if they understand what you are saying. Professionals know this and often develop a circle of friends who will read their work. We encourage students to do the same.

Length

Probably the most frequently asked question regarding student papers is "How long should they be?" The most appropriate but usually unsatisfying answer is "As long as they need to be." Many students make the mistake of underestimating the length that thoroughness demands, often through one or more serious omissions. On the other hand, some students make the mistake of thinking that the longer a report is, the better it is. The techniques of "padding" a paper through overuse of citations, excessive use of full quotations when paraphrasing would be preferable, and reliance on vocabulary and jargon intended to impress the audience are mistakes that experienced readers usually see through. Katzer, Cook, and Crouch (1978) refer to these smokescreens as "paraphernalia of pedantry" and conclude that they are more likely to be distracting than to facilitate communication. And it is communication that is the essence of the research process.

Summary

Doing social research demands that one not only be a careful producer of research but also clearly and accurately communicate the products of the research to others. Useful models for such communication can be found in professional social science journals; indeed, library searches of the professional literature are where most research ideas come from and where research writing essentially begins. Two indexing references that we highly recommend for library searches are the *Social Sciences Index* and the *Social Sciences Citation Index*.

Writing the research report is facilitated greatly by preparing an outline, keeping in mind the intended audience and how they will read the report, and writing several drafts as well as soliciting others' critical comments on early drafts.

Most research reports contain the following components: (1) an abstract or short summary placed at the beginning of the paper; (2) an introduction to the problem pointing out its theoretical, practical, and/or social significance; (3) a literature review relating the research problem to previous theory and research; (4) a methods section outlining precisely how the research was done, including the overall approach and design, and methods of sampling and measurement; (5) a findings section; (6) a discussion of the limitations and anomalies as well as the broader theoretical and practical implications of the research; and (7) a list of references cited in the report.

Review Questions and Problems

1. Locate the *Social Sciences Index* in your library and, using the most recent issues of these sources, find one reference held by the library for each of the following topics: (a) juvenile delinquency; (b) aged or aging; and (c) race relations. Locate each reference in the library and write down the library call number of the article or book as well as complete bibliographic information.

2. Repeat exercise 1 using the *Social Sciences Citation Index*.

3. Write down the major topical headings from one of the articles found in exercise 1. How do these headings differ from those outlined in this chapter?

GLOSSARY

acquiescence response set a response bias whereby respondents tend to answer in the direction of agreement, regardless of item content (chapter 10).

adjusted R² a measure of fit in multiple regression that indicates approximately the proportion of the variance in the dependent variable (spread of observations about the mean) predicted or "explained" by the independent variables (chapter 15).

affirming the antecedent a valid argument of the form: (a) If p, then q; (b) p; (c) therefore, q (chapter 3).

age effect changes in behavior or attitudes associated with growing older (life-course changes); *see* cohort analysis (chapter 12).

aggregate data information about one set of units that is statistically combined to describe a larger social unit; for example, information about students (gender, race, college board scores, etc.) might be aggregated to describe characteristics of their colleges (sex ratio, ethnic composition, average college board score, etc.) (chapter 4).

anonymity an ethical safeguard against invasion of privacy; the condition wherein researchers are unable to identify data with particular research participants (chapter 16).

antecedent the first part of a conditional proposition (chapter 3).

antecedent variable a variable causally antecedent to others in a theoretical model; two variables may be spuriously associated because both are affected by an antecedent variable (chapter 15).

argument in logic, a set of two or more propositions of which one is claimed to follow either necessarily or probably from the others (chapter 3).

association the strength of the observed relationship between two variables (chapter 4).

bivariate analysis statistical analysis of the relationship between two variables (chapter 14).

causal relationship a theoretical notion that change in one variable forces, produces, or brings about a change in another; although the concept of "cause" is unobservable and philosophically controversial, causal theorizing is commonly and productively used in scientific investigations (chapters 2 and 4).

cell frequencies the number of cases in a cell of a cross-tabulation table (chapter 14).

chain argument a valid argument of the form: (a) If p, then q; (b) if q, then r; (c) therefore, if p, then r; also called "hypothetical syllogism" (chapter 3).

chi-square test of independence a test of statistical significance used to assess the likelihood that an observed bivariate relationship differs significantly from that which easily could have occurred by chance (chapter 14).

closed questions survey questions that require respondents to choose responses from those provided; also called fixed-choice questions (chapter 10).

cluster sampling a probability-sampling procedure in which the population is broken down into natural groupings or areas, called clusters, and a random sample of clusters is drawn. Cluster sampling may occur in a series of stages, moving from larger to smaller clusters, with individual cases sampled at the last stage (chapter 6).

codebook a "dictionary" for a survey study, which lists the answers or categories that correspond to each numerical code, the location of each variable in the data file, as well as coding and decision rules (chapter 14).

coding the categorizing and sorting of raw data into groups, such as responses to open-ended questions or field data (chapters 11 and 14).

cohort analysis a longitudinal research technique that attempts to assess the relative effects of age (life-course changes), period (current history), and cohort ("generations" who share the same past history) on attitudes and behavior (chapter 12).

cohort effect differences in behavior or attitudes due to the effects of membership in particular cohorts (individuals or other units who share a common past history); *see* cohort analysis (chapter 12).

collinear association a perfect linear relationship between two variables (chapter 15).

computer file a collection of information stored together on a computer disk, tape, or other device; also called a "data file" when the information is limited to data (chapter 14).

concept abstractions communicated by words or other signs that refer to common properties among phenomena (e.g., the concept "extroversion" represents a broad range of specific behaviors); concepts developed for scientific purposes are sometimes called "constructs" (chapters 2 and 5).

conceptualization the development and clarification of concepts (chapters 2 and 5).

conclusion the statement or proposition that is claimed to follow from the others in an argument (chapter 3).

concurrent validity a criterion-related approach to assessing measurement validity in which the criterion variable represents an individual's *present* situation or standing; for example, scores on a test of motor coordination (the measure under consideration) might be compared with performance on an airplane simulator (the criterion) (chapter 5).

conditional odds the odds on one variable for a category of another; for example, the odds of completing high school among men (chapter 15).

conditional proposition a statement (the antecedent) introduced by an "if" followed by a second statement (the consequent) preceded by a "then"; for example, "If this is a conditional proposition, then it should have an antecedent and a consequent" (chapter 3).

confidence interval a range (interval) within which a population value is estimated to lie at a specific level of confidence; used to qualify sample estimates to take into account sampling error; for example, a researcher might report that she is 99 percent confident (confidence level) that the mean personal income for a population lies within plus or minus \$359 of the sample mean of \$18,325 (i.e., confidence interval of \$18,684-\$17,966) (chapter 6).

confidentiality an ethical safeguard against invasion of privacy; the assumption that all data on research participants is given to the researcher in strict confidence, not to be divulged to anyone without the participants' permission (chapter 16).

consequent the second part of a conditional proposition (chapter 3).

consistency checking a data-cleaning procedure involving checking for unreasonable patterns of responses, such as a 12 year-old who voted in the last presidential election (chapter 14).

construct validation measurement validation based on an accumulation of research evidence, which may include evidence that the measure in question (1) relates to other variables in a theoretically-expected manner, (2) correlates highly with other measures of the same concept (convergent validity), (3) correlates not too highly with measures of other concepts (discriminant validity), and (4) varies among groups known to differ on the characteristic being measured (chapter 5).

content analysis a set of methods for analyzing the symbolic content of communications, which typically entails (1) defining a set of content categories, (2) sampling elements of the communication that are described by the categories, (3) quantifying the categories such as by counting their frequency of occurrence, and (4) relating category frequencies to one another or to other variables (chapter 12).

content validity a subjective judgment of whether a measure adequately represents all facets (the domain) of a concept (chapter 5).

contextual design a survey design in which information about respondents and their social environments (contexts) is collected for the purpose of studying the separate and joint effects on individuals of personal characteristics and of social contexts (chapter 9).

context units larger units in which the recording units of content analysis are embedded and which provide the "context" necessary to classify the recording units; for example, the meaning of words (recording units) might be determined from the sentences (context units) in which they appear (chapter 12).

contingency question a survey question intended for a subset of the respondents, it addresses only those persons for whom the question is relevant; *see also* filter question (chapter 10).

control/control variable Controls are procedures that eliminate, as far as possible, unwanted variation, such as sources of bias and error that may distort study results; a common approach is to control potentially confounding variables by holding them constant, or by preventing them from varying, during the course of observation or statistical analysis (chapters 2 and 4).

convenience sampling a form of nonprobability sampling in which the researcher simply selects cases that are conveniently available; also called "haphazard," "fortuitous," and "accidental" sampling (chapter 6).

convergent validity the extent to which independent measures of the same concept correlate with each other; the higher the correlation, the greater the convergent validity (chapter 5).

correlation coefficient Pearson's correlation coefficient (symbolized as r) is a measure of association that describes the direction and strength of a linear relationship between two variables measured at the interval or ratio level; the square of Pearson's r represents the proportion of variance in one variable that may be predicted from the other using linear regression (chapters 4 and 14).

cost-benefit analysis an examination of the potential costs (e.g., harm to subjects) and benefits (e.g., knowledge gained, beneficial applications) of a study as a way of assessing the ethics of the study (chapter 16).

cover letter in a survey, a letter designed to obtain cooperation from persons in the sample; the cover letter is sent prior to an interviewer's call on the respondent, or, in mail surveys, it accompanies the questionnaire (chapter 9).

cover story an introduction provided to experimental subjects to obtain their cooperation while disguising the research hypothesis (chapter 7).

criterion-related validation assesses the validity of a measure in terms of the degree to which it correlates with an objective criterion; *see* concurrent validity and predictive validity (chapter 5).

cross-cultural surveys studies in which equivalent sample surveys are conducted in different countries; also called comparative studies (chapter 9).

cross-sectional design the most common survey design, in which data on a cross section of respondents chosen to represent a larger population of interest are gathered at essentially one point in time; *see also* longitudinal design (chapter 9).

cultural relativity the principle that the cultural standards of a given society must be examined on their own terms and that researchers should be nonjudgmental regarding the society or group that is being studied (chapter 16).

data archives repositories of precollected survey or ethnographic data collected by various agencies and researchers that are accessible to the public (chapter 12).

data cleaning the detection and correction of errors that occur during data collection, coding, and data entry (chapter 14).

data file a collection of data stored together on a computer disk, tape, or other device (chapter 14).

data processing the preparation of data for analysis, which, in survey research, entails five steps: coding, editing, entry, cleaning, and modification (chapter 14).

debriefing a session at the end of an experiment in which the experimenter discusses with the subject what has taken place, the real purpose of the study, the need for confidentiality, the subject's responses and feelings, and so on (chapters 7 and 16).

deduction a reasoning process such that the conclusion necessarily follows if the premises are true (chapter 3).

degrees of freedom in log-linear analysis the number of estimated table cells less the number of restrictions (constraints) placed on the model (chapter 15).

demand characteristics cues in an experiment that convey to subjects the experimenter's hypothesis or what is expected of them (chapter 7).

denying the consequent a valid argument of the form: (a) If p, then q; (b) not q; (c) therefore, not p (chapter 3).

dependent variable a variable that the researcher tries to explain or predict; the presumed effect of one or more independent variables (chapter 4).

descriptive research studies undertaken to collect facts about a specified population or sample; for example, a public opinion poll (chapters 4 and 9).

descriptive statistics procedures for organizing and summarizing data (chapter 14).

differential mortality a threat to internal validity; the existence of varying dropout rates among conditions of an experiment, which tends to make the conditions nonequivalent in composition (chapter 8).

dimensional sampling a strategy used by field researchers in which dimensions of units (time periods, places, roles, etc.) are sampled rather than the units (individuals, groups, etc.) under study (chapter 11).

direct effects one variable is hypothesized to affect another directly in a causal model; there may also be "indirect effects" in which the impact of one variable on another is transmitted through one or a series of causally intervening variables; the total impact of one variable on another is the sum of the direct and indirect effects (chapter 15).

direct questions survey questions in which there is a direct, clear link between what is asked and what the researcher wants to know; *see also* indirect questions (chapter 10).

direction of influence for a presumed asymmetric causal relationship, refers to the identification of which variable is the cause (independent) and which the effect (dependent) (chapter 4).

discriminant validity the extent to which a measure of a particular concept differentiates that concept from other concepts from which it is intended to differ; discriminant validity is lacking if measures of supposedly different concepts correlate too highly (chapter 5).

disproportionate stratified sampling sampling procedure in which strata are sampled disproportionately to population composition; for example, a study of religious leaders might sample female pastors at a much higher rate than male pastors to assure a sufficient number of the former for analysis purposes (chapter 6).

double-barreled question a survey question in which two separate ideas are erroneously presented together in one question (chapter 10).

double-blind technique both subjects and research personnel are prevented from knowing the subjects' treatment conditions during the running of the experiment (chapter 7).

dummy variable a data-modification procedure that involves recoding the categories of nominal or ordinal scale variables for the purpose of regression or other numerical analysis; for example, gender categories may be represented by a single dummy variable having a value of 1 if the respondent is female and a value of 0 if male (chapters 14 and 15).

ecological fallacy erroneously using information pertaining to an aggregate (e.g., organizations) to draw inferences about the units of analysis that comprise the aggregate (e.g., individual members of organizations) (chapter 4).

edge coding entering codes for open-ended questions, which are usually developed after the data have been collected, at the edge of the question on the questionnaire or interview form (chapter 14).

editing a quality control process designed to ensure that survey or other data to be read into the computer are as complete, error-free, and readable as possible (chapter 14).

elaboration a traditional technique for the multivariate analysis of contingency tables that "elaborates" the relationship between two variables by introducing a third (and sometimes additional) variables and testing the resultant causal models (chapter 15).

empirical generalization a generalization or hypothesis inductively derived from observations (chapter 2).

empirical/empiricism a way of knowing or understanding the world that relies directly or indirectly on what we experience thorough our senses—sight, hearing, taste, smell, and touch; admissible evidence in science is limited to empirical phenomena (chapters 1 and 2).

ethics guidelines or standards for moral conduct; in research, ethical codes prescribe principles for upholding the values of science and for resolving conflicts between scientific ideals and societal values (chapter 16).

evaluation apprehension subjects' anxiety about being evaluated by the experimenter, typically a psychologist, which may make them overly concerned with producing "normal" behavior (chapter 7).

evaluation research an area of social science research concerned with analyzing the extent to which social policies and social programs achieve particular effects; it takes the true experiment as its methodological model (chapter 8).

expected/fitted frequencies the cell frequencies estimated (predicted) by a log-linear model; a significant difference between observed and fitted cell frequencies indicates that the model does not fit the observed data (chapter 15).

experimental realism in an experiment, when subjects become involved in or are affected by the procedures rather than remain detached (chapter 7).

experimenter expectancy effect influences on subjects' behavior due to the experimenter's expectations about how the experiment will turn out (chapter 7).

explanatory research studies that investigate relationships between two or more variables, attempting to explain them in cause-and-effect terms (chapters 4 and 9).

explanatory variables those variables that are the focus of the research; *see also* extraneous variables (chapter 4).

exploratory research studies undertaken to explore a phenomenon or topic about which very little is known (chapter 4).

external validity the extent to which experimental findings are generalizable to other settings, subject populations, and time periods (chapter 7).

extraneous variables all variables that are not objects of the research; *see also* explanatory variables (chapter 4).

face validity a personal judgment that an operational definition appears, on the face of it, to measure the concept it is intended to measure (chapter 5).

factorial experimental designs an extension of the basic experimental design in which two or more independent variables (factors) are manipulated; information is provided about the separate (main) effects and joint (interaction) effects of the independent variables (chapter 8).

fallacy of affirming the consequent an invalid argument of the form: (a) If p, then q; (b) q; (c) therefore, p (chapter 3).

fallacy of denying the antecedent an invalid argument of the form: (a) If p, then q; (b) not p; (c) therefore, not q (chapter 3).

field experiment a "true" experimental design conducted in a natural setting (chapter 7).

filter question a type of survey question, the responses to which determine which subjects are to answer which of subsequent contingency questions (chapter 10).

fixed-column format a format for arranging data in a computer file in which the information for each variable is stored in the same column(s) for each respondent or case (chapter 14).

frequency distribution a tabulation of the number of cases falling into each category of a variable (chapter 14).

funnel sequence a sequence of survey questions that progress from a very general question to gradually more specific questions (chapter 10).

gatekeepers authorities whose permission is needed to conduct research in their setting (chapter 11).

grounded theory theory developed inductively from firsthand observations, in contrast to theories generated by other means (chapter 11).

Guttman scaling a scaling procedure that attempts to ensure a unidimensional scale by selecting a set of items that when *ordered* in terms of their "strength" will *order* individuals or other relevant units on the concept being measured (chapter 13).

heterogeneity the degree of dissimilarity among cases with respect to a particular characteristic; for example, the gender composition of groups might vary from 100 percent female (maximum homogeneity) to 50 percent female (maximum heterogeneity) (chapter 6).

hierarchical models a class of log-linear models in which the fitting of higher-order marginals implies that all subsets of variables in the higher order marginals also are fitted (chapter 15).

history a threat to internal validity; events in the subjects' environment, other than the intended experimental manipulation, that occur during the course of an experiment and that may affect the outcome (chapter 8).

hypothesis an expected but unconfirmed relationship among two or more variables (chapters 2 and 4).

hypothetico-deductive method a common form of inductive reasoning in science involving four steps: (1) formulation of a hypothesis, (2) deduction of testable consequences from the hypothesis, (3) checking through observation (or research) to see if the consequences are true, and (4) drawing conclusions about the hypothesis on the basis of one's observations (chapter 3).

independent variable a presumed cause of a dependent variable (chapter 4).

in-depth interview intensive interviews that in field research are much less structured than in survey research and much longer, often requiring several sessions (chapter 11).

index a composite measure of a concept constructed by adding or averaging the scores of separate indicators; differs from a scale, which uses less arbitrary procedures for combining indicators (chapters 5 and 13).

indicator an empirical manifestation of a concept; for example, the indicator "years of schooling" often represents the concept "education" (chapter 5).

indirect effects in a causal model, one variable is hypothesized to affect another indirectly through one or a series of intervening variables; *see also* direct effects (chapter 15).

indirect questions questions in which the relationship between the researcher's objectives and the questions asked is not obvious; a technique usually based on the psychological concept of projection; *see also* direct questions (chapter 10).

induction a reasoning process in which the conclusion goes beyond information contained in the premises; unlike in a deductive argument, the premises of an inductive argument may be true and the conclusion false (chapter 3).

inductive generalization a common reasoning process in science in which a statement is made about an entire class of objects or events on the basis of information on only part of the class (chapter 3).

inferential statistics procedures for determining the extent to which one may generalize beyond the data at hand (chapter 14).

informed consent an ethical practice of providing research participants with enough information about a study, especially its potential risks, to enable them to make an informed decision about whether to participate (chapter 16).

institutional review board (IRB) a committee formed at nearly all research institutions (e.g., universities), which is responsible for reviewing research proposals in order to assess provisions for the ethical treatment of human (and animal) subjects; IRB approval is required for federally funded research (chapter 16).

instrumentation a threat to internal validity; unwanted changes in characteristics of the measuring instrument or measurement procedure (chapter 8).

interaction effect an outcome in which the effect of one independent variable on the dependent variable varies according to the value or level of another independent variable; that is, the effects of the variables together differ from the effects of either alone (chapter 8).

intercoder reliability an "equivalence" method for assessing reliability that examines the extent to which different interviewers, observers, or coders get equivalent results using the same instrument or measure (chapter 5).

internal-consistency reliability an "equivalence" method of assessing reliability in which a statistical procedure is used to examine the consistency of "scores" across all the items constituting a measure (chapter 5).

internal validity sound evidence in an experiment that rules out the possibility that extraneous variables, rather than the manipulated independent variable, are responsible for the observed outcome (chapter 7).

interrupted time-series design a quasi-experimental design resembling the one-group pretest-posttest design but with a series of observations (measurements) before and after the treatment manipulation (chapter 8).

intersubjective testability condition wherein two or more scientists can agree on the results of observations (chapter 2).

interval scale a level of measurement that has the qualities of the ordinal level plus the requirement that equal distances (intervals) between assigned "numbers" represent equal distances in the variable being measured; consequently, it is possible to perform basic mathematical operations such as addition and subtraction (chapter 5).

intervening variable a variable that is intermediate between two other variables in a causal chain; for example, if the model specifies that X affects W, which in turn affects Y, then W is an intervening variable that interprets the causal process by which X affects Y (chapter 15).

interview schedule a survey form used by interviewers that consists of instructions, the questions to be asked, and, if they are used, response options (chapter 9).

inverted-funnel sequence a sequence of survey questions that begins with the most specific questions on a topic and ends with the most general (chapter 10).

key informant a contact who helps a field researcher gain entry to, acceptance within, and information about the research setting (chapter 11).

law scientific laws refer to propositions that have been repeatedly verified and are widely accepted (chapter 2).

leading question a survey question that suggests a possible answer or makes some responses seem more acceptable than others (chapter 10).

likelihood-ratio chi-square test a statistic used to test the fit of log-linear models; if the observed and fitted cell frequencies are not significantly different on this chi-square test, the model is said to fit the data (chapter 15).

Likert response scale a scaling approach commonly used to measure attitudes in which respondents choose from an ordered series of responses (e.g., ranging from "strongly approve" to "strongly disapprove") to indicate their reaction to a sequence of statements (chapter 10).

"logit" models a class of log-linear models that simplify the analysis by ignoring possible relationships among the independent variables, which are viewed as extraneous to the theory under investigation and are neither tested nor interpreted (chapter 15).

log-linear modeling a powerful statistical technique for analyzing multivariate categorical data (chapter 15).

longitudinal design survey designs in which data are collected over an extended period of time; *see* trend study, panel study, and cohort analysis (chapter 9).

main effect in a factorial experimental design, the effect of a single independent variable (factor) by itself (chapter 8).

manipulation check evidence collected in an experiment that the manipulation of the independent variable was experienced or interpreted by the subject in the way intended (chapter 7).

manuscript census the original schedules on which census enumerators record their data, which are released to the public after a period of 72 years (chapter 12).

marginal frequencies row and column totals in a contingency table (cross-tabulation) that represent the univariate frequency distributions for the row and column variables (chapter 14).

matching a technique for assigning subjects to experimental groups so that the composition of each group matches the others on one or more characteristics thought to be related to the dependent variable; should be used in conjunction with but not as a substitute for randomization (chapter 7).

maturation a threat to internal validity; any psychological or physiological changes taking place within subjects that occur over time, regardless of experimental manipulations (chapter 8).

mean a measure of central tendency that indicates the average value of a univariate distribution of interval or ratio scale data; the mean or arithmetic average is calculated by adding up the individual values and dividing by the total number of cases (chapter 14).

measures of association descriptive statistics used to measure the strength and direction of an observed bivariate relationship (chapter 14).

median a measure of central tendency indicating the midpoint in a univariate distribution of interval or ratio scale data; the median indicates the point below and above which 50 percent of the values fall (chapter 14).

methodological empathy a fundamental approach to field research that attempts to understand behavior as it is perceived and interpreted by those under study (chapter 11).

mode a measure of central tendency representing the value or category of a frequency distribution having the highest frequency; the most typical value (chapter 14).

modeling in statistical analysis, formal representations of hypothesized, or theoretical, relations among two or more variables; usually alternative models are compared to determine their fit to the observed data (chapter 15).

mortality the loss of subjects during the course of a study; *see also* differential mortality (chapter 8).

multicollinearity a problem that arises in multiple regression when combinations of two or more independent variables are highly correlated with each other, and which renders regression results (estimates of the coefficients) difficult to interpret (chapter 15).

multiple regression a statistical method for studying the simultaneous effects of several independent variables on a dependent variable (chapter 15).

multiple time-series design a quasi-experimental design in which a series of pretreatment and posttreatment observations (measurements) are made on a treatment group as well as on nonequivalent control groups (chapter 8).

multistage sampling occurs when sampling takes place at two or more steps or stages (e.g., a sample of school districts, then a sample of schools from the selected school districts, and then a sample of pupils from the selected schools) (chapter 6).

multivariate analysis statistical analysis of the simultaneous relationships among three or more variables (chapter 15).

mundane realism when the events in an experiment are similar to everyday experiences (chapter 7).

N an abbreviation representing the number of observations on which a statistic is based (e.g., $N = 279$) (chapter 14).

negative (inverse) relationship exists between two variables if an increase in the value of one variable is accompanied by a decrease in the value of the other; that is, changes in one variable are opposite in direction to changes in the other (chapter 4).

nominal scale the lowest level of measurement, in which numbers serve only to label category membership; categories are not ranked but should be exhaustive and mutually exclusive (chapter 5).

noncausal association two variables are allowed to be statistically associated in a model, although a causal explanation of the association is not part of the model (chapter 15).

nonequivalent control group design a quasi-experimental design that resembles a true experiment (the pretest-posttest control group design), except that random assignment of subjects to treatment and control groups is lacking (chapter 8).

nonparticipant observation an approach to field research in which the researcher attempts to observe people without interacting with them and, typically, without their knowing that they are being observed (chapter 11).

nonprobability sampling processes of case selection other than random selection (chapter 6).

nonreactive measurement any process of measurement that by itself does not bring about changes in what is being measured; in contrast, reactive measures may produce changes in behavior because of people's awareness that they are being studied or observed (chapter 12).

nonresponse bias in survey sampling, when nonrespondents (sampled individuals who do not respond or who cannot be contacted) differ in important ways from the respondents (chapter 6).

nonspuriousness a criterion for inferring causality that requires that an association or correlation between two variables cannot be explained away by the action of extraneous variables (chapter 4).

observed frequencies the actual cell frequencies in the study data; *see also* expected frequencies (chapter 15).

odds a ratio of two numbers, such as the ratio of "yes" to "no" answers, that is used as a descriptive statistic in log-linear analysis; *see also* conditional odds and odds ratio (chapter 15).

odds ratio a descriptive measure of association in log-linear analysis, which is obtained by computing the ratio of two conditional odds; for example, if the conditional odds of high-school graduation is 5.67 for males and 9.00 for females, an odds ratio of $9.00/5.67 = 1.59$ means that the odds of completing high school is about 1.6 times greater among women than among men; an odds or odds ratio of 1.0 indicates the absence of a relationship (chapter 15).

one-group pretest-posttest design a preexperimental design in which a group of subjects is observed or measured (the pretest), a treatment is introduced, and the subjects are measured again (the posttest); threats to internal validity include maturation, history, testing, instrumentation, and sometimes statistical regression (chapter 8).

one-shot case study a preexperimental design in which a treatment is administered to a group, after which the group is observed or tested to determine the treatment effects; threats to internal validity include mortality, maturation, and history (chapter 8).

open questions survey questions that require respondents to answer in their own words; also called "free-response" questions (chapter 10).

operationalization the detailed description of the research operations or procedures necessary to assign units of analysis to the categories of a variable in order to represent conceptual properties (chapter 5).

ordinal scale a level of measurement in which different "numbers" indicate the rank order of cases on some variable (chapter 5).

outliers unusual or suspicious values that are far removed from the preponderance of observations for a variable (chapters 14 and 15)

panel study a longitudinal design in which the same individuals are surveyed more than once, permitting the study of individual and group change (chapter 9).

parallel-forms reliability an "equivalence" method for assessing reliability, which involves calculating the correlation between the "scores" on different but equivalent forms of the measure (chapter 5).

partial tables a control procedure used in elaboration that involves recomputing the original two-variable relationship separately for each category of the control variable; each partial table displays the association between the two original variables when the control variable is held constant (chapter 15).

partially structured interview a type of interview that, while having specific objectives, permits the interviewer some freedom in meeting them; *see also* structured interview and unstructured interview (chapter 9).

partial-regression coefficients/partial slopes coefficients in a multiple-regression equation that estimate the effects of each independent variable on the dependent variable when all other variables in the equation are held constant (chapter 15).

participant observation an approach to field research in which the researcher actively participates, for an extended period of time, in the daily lives of the people and situations under study (chapter 11).

path analysis a form of causal modeling utilizing standardized regression coefficients that provides, among other things, quantitative estimates of the total direct and indirect effects of one variable on another (chapter 15).

percentage distribution a norming operation that facilitates interpreting and comparing frequency distributions by transforming each to a common yardstick of 100 units (percentage points) in length; the number of cases in each category is divided by the total and multiplied by 100 (chapter 14).

period effect longitudinal changes in behavior or attitudes due to the effects of specific time periods (current history), such as the impact of depressions or prosperity on birth rates; *see* cohort analysis (chapter 12).

population the total membership of a defined class of people, objects, or events; also called "universe" (chapter 6).

position response set a tendency of some respondents to mark options located in a certain position, such as the first choice in a series (chapter 10).

positive (direct) relationship exists between two variables if an increase in the value of one is accompanied by an increase in the value of the other, or a decrease in one is accompanied by a decrease in the other; that is, the two variables consistently change in the same direction (chapter 4).

posttest-only control group design the simplest of the true experimental designs, it incorporates these features: random assignment to treatment and control groups, introduction of the independent variable to the treatment group, and a posttreatment measure of both groups (chapter 8).

precoding the printed codes for classifying responses as well as other data-processing instructions on questionnaires or interview schedules prior to data collection (chapter 14).

predictive validity a criterion-related approach to assessing measurement validity in which the criterion variable represents the individual's *future* situation or standing; for example, scores on a college entrance examination (the measure under consideration) might be compared with subsequent college grades (the criterion) (chapter 5).

preexperimental designs designs that lack one or more features of true experiments, such as a comparison group or random assignment (chapter 8).

premises in logical analysis, propositions that supply evidence for accepting the conclusion of an argument (chapter 3).

pretesting a trial run of an experiment or survey instrument with a small number of preliminary subjects or respondents to evaluate and rehearse the study procedures and personnel (chapters 7, 9, 10).

pretest-posttest control group design a true experimental design in which subjects are randomly assigned to (1) a treatment group measured before (the pretest) and after (the posttest) the experimental treatment and (2) a no-treatment control group measured at the same times (chapter 8).

primary sampling unit the sampling units in the first stage of a multistage sample (chapter 6).

probability sampling sampling based on a process of random selection, which gives each case in the population an equal chance of being included in the sample; when random selection is applied to stratified or multistage sampling, each case will have a known but not necessarily equal chance of selection (chapter 6).

proposition in logical analysis, an expression of a judgment about some term or terms; in the grammatical sense, it is a declarative sentence (chapter 3).

Public Use Microdata Sample a computer-based sample of individual census returns with certain information excluded to ensure confidentiality (chapter 12).

purposive sampling a form of nonprobability sampling that involves the careful selection of typical cases or of cases that represent relevant dimensions of the population (chapter 6).

qualitative variable has discrete categories, usually designated by words or labels, and nonnumerical differences between categories (i.e., nominal level of measurement); *see also* quantitative variable (chapter 4).

quantitative variable has categories that express numerical distinctions (ratio, interval, and ordinal levels of measurement); *see also* qualitative variable (chapter 4).

quasi-experimental designs lack some features (usually randomization) of true experiments, but permit stronger inferences about cause and effect than do preexperimental designs by means of special design features and supplementary data testing (chapter 8).

quota sampling a form of nonprobability sampling that involves the allocation of quotas of cases for various strata (usually proportionate to representation in the population) and the nonrandom selection of cases to fill the quotas (chapter 6).

random assignment the assignment of subjects to experimental conditions by means of a random device, such as a coin toss or use of a table of random numbers, thus assuring that each subject has an equal chance of being in any of the treatment and control conditions (chapter 7).

random-digit dialing a sampling-frame technique for resolving the problem in telephone surveys of missing those with unlisted numbers: dialable telephone numbers are generated (sampled) from a table of random numbers or from a computer random-number program (chapter 9).

random measurement error error unrelated to the concept being measured that is the result of temporary, chance factors; random errors are inconsistent across measurements (unpredictably varying in extent and direction) and affect reliability; *see also* systematic measurement error (chapter 5).

random selection a process that gives each case in the population an equal chance of being included in the sample (chapter 6).

range a univariate measure of variability or dispersion indicating the difference between the lowest and highest values, which is usually reported by identifying these two extreme values (chapter 14).

ratio scale the highest level of measurement, which has the features of the other levels plus an absolute (nonarbitrary) zero point; consequently, it is possible to form ratios of the numbers assigned to categories (chapter 5).

reactive measurement effect an effect whereby the process of measurement itself, due to people's awareness of being studied, produces changes in what is being measured (chapters 5 and 7).

reciprocal causation two variables are hypothesized to be causally linked in terms of their mutual influence on each other; also called "mutual causation" (chapter 15).

record a "row" of information in a computer data file that describes an individual respondent, household, or other unit; since record length is usually restricted to eighty columns, more than one record may be needed to store the data for each respondent or unit (chapter 14).

recording units units of analysis in content analysis, such as words, sentences, paragraphs, or plots (chapter 12).

regression analysis a statistical method for studying bivariate (simple regression) and multivariate (multiple regression) relationships among interval or ratio scale variables (chapters 14 and 15).

regression line a geometric representation of a bivariate regression equation that provides the best linear fit to the observed data by virtue of minimizing the sum of the squared deviations from the line; also called the "least squares line" (chapter 14).

reliability the stability or consistency of an operational definition (chapter 5).

replication a repetition of a previous study, using a different sample of cases and often different settings and methods, for the purpose of exploring the possibility that the original findings were an artifact of particular research conditions and procedures (chapter 13).

research ethics *see* ethics.

residuals the difference between observed values of the dependent variable and those predicted by a regression equation (chapters 14 and 15).

response bias tendency a tendency of a respondent to answer in a certain biased direction (such as in the direction of social desirability) as a function of the content or form of survey questions (chapter 10).

response effect in survey research, a general term for systematic errors due to such factors as biased or confusing questions, response bias tendencies (e.g., social desirability effects), the effects of interviewer's physical characteristics, and so on (chapter 9).

response rate in a survey, the proportion of people in the sample from whom completed interviews or questionnaires are obtained (chapter 9).

sample a subset of cases selected from a population (chapter 6).

sample bias systematic error or bias in sample results due to problems in executing the sampling plan, such as incomplete sampling frames and incomplete data collection (not-at-home respondents, refusals, etc.) (chapter 6).

sampling distribution a theoretical distribution of sample results (means, proportions, etc.) that would result from drawing all possible samples of a fixed size from a particular population (chapter 6).

sampling error the difference between an actual population value (e.g., a mean) and the population value estimated from a sample (chapter 6).

sampling fraction the proportion of the population included in the sample (chapter 6).

sampling frame an operational definition of the population that provides the basis for drawing a sample; a sampling frame is constructed by either (1) listing all cases from which a sample may be selected, or (2) defining population membership by a rule that provides a basis for case selection (chapter 6).

sampling interval the ratio of the number of cases in the population to the desired sample size, which is used to select every Kth (the interval) case in systematic sampling (chapter 6).

saturated model a log-linear model that fits all possible marginal frequencies, thus providing a perfect fit to the data (chapter 15).

scale a composite measure of a concept constructed by combining separate indicators according to procedures designed to ensure unidimensionality or other desirable qualities (chapters 5 and 13).

scatterplot a graph plotting the values of two variables for each observation (chapter 14).

secondary analysis analysis of survey or other data originally collected by another researcher ordinarily for a different purpose (chapter 12).

selection a threat to internal validity; systematic differences in the composition of the control and experimental groups (chapter 8).

selective deposit systematic biases in the content of available historical data due to actions such as selective destruction or editing of written records (chapter 12).

selective survival incompleteness of available historical data due to the fact that some objects survive longer than others (chapter 12).

self-administered questionnaire a survey form filled out by respondents; when an interviewer records survey responses, the form is called an "interview schedule" (chapter 9).

separate-sample pretest-posttest design a quasi-experimental design having two groups that receive the treatment, one group randomly selected for pretreatment measurement and the other randomly selected for posttreatment measurement (chapter 8).

serendipity pattern unanticipated findings that cannot be interpreted meaningfully in terms of prevailing theories and that give rise to new theories (chapter 2).

simple random sampling a probability sampling procedure in which every possible combination of cases has an equal chance of being included in the sample (chapter 6).

slope/regression coefficient a bivariate regression statistic indicating how much the dependent variable increases (or decreases) for every unit change in the independent variable; the slope of a regression line (chapter 14).

snowballing technique a field research technique for sampling informants, whereby each contact is used to arrange additional introductions to others (chapter 11).

social desirability bias/effect a tendency of some respondents to bias their answers in the direction of socially desirable traits or attitudes, thereby endeavoring to enhance self-esteem or make a favorable impression on the interviewer or researcher (chapters 5 and 10).

social indicators broad measures of important social conditions, such as measures of crime, family life, health, schools, or job satisfaction (chapter 9).

sociometric design a survey design in which all individuals in a group are interviewed in order to delineate networks of personal relationships (chapter 9).

Solomon four-group design an experimental design requiring four groups: a treatment and a control group that are pretested as well as a treatment and control group that are not pretested; this design provides information regarding the effect of the treatment, the effect of pretesting alone, the possible interaction of pretesting and treatment, and the effectiveness of the randomization procedure (chapter 8).

specification (1) an outcome in elaboration analysis involving the increase, reduction, or disappearance of the original relationship in some partial tables but not in others (i.e., an interaction effect); (2) the formulation of a formal theoretical model (chapter 15).

specification error fitting a false model to the data, such as omission of an important variable, which may produce misleading results (chapter 15).

spurious relationship a statistical association between two variables produced by extraneous variables rather than by a causal link between the original variables (chapter 4).

standard deviation a univariate measure of variability or dispersion that indicates the average "spread" of observations about the mean; it is the square root of the variance, which is calculated by subtracting each value from the mean and squaring the result, and taking the arithmetic average of the squared differences (chapters 6 and 14).

standard error a statistical measure of the "average" sampling error for a particular sampling distribution; it is the standard deviation of a sampling distribution and thus a measure of how much sample results will vary from sample to sample (chapter 6).

standardized regression coefficients obtained from a norming operation that puts the various partial-regression coefficients on common footing by standardizing them to the same metric of standard deviation units; consequently, a standardized coefficient indicates the number of standard deviation units the dependent variable changes for every unit change of one standard deviation in an independent variable (chapter 15).

static-group comparison a preexperimental design in which a treatment group and a no-treatment group are both measured following the treatment; threats to internal validity include selection, differential mortality, and sometimes maturation (chapter 8).

statistical regression a threat to internal validity; the tendency for extreme scorers on one measurement to move (regress) closer to the mean score on a later measurement; also known as "regression toward the mean" (chapter 8).

statistical significance *see* test of statistical significance.

stratified random sampling a probability sampling procedure in which the population is divided into strata and independent random samples are drawn from each stratum (chapter 6).

structural equation modeling a statistical technique for testing different theorized models, including "structures" of relationships among *observed* indicators and their underlying *unobserved* concepts (chapter 13).

structured interview a type of standardized interview in which the objectives are highly specific, all questions are written beforehand and asked in the same order for all respondents, and the interviewer's remarks are standardized; the preferred interviewing approach when the research purpose is to test hypotheses; *see also* unstructured interview (chapter 9).

subjective validation validity assessment based on the researcher's judgments; *see* face validity and content validity (chapter 5).

syllogism the basic unit of logical analysis, which consists of three propositions: two premises and the conclusion that the premises logically imply (chapter 3).

systematic measurement error error from factors that systematically influence (bias) either the process of measurement or the concept being measured; systematic errors are consistent across measurements taken at different times or are systematically related to characteristics of the cases being measured (e.g., the cultural bias of IQ tests) and thereby affect validity; *see also* random measurement error (chapter 5).

systematic sampling a probability sampling procedure in which cases are selected from an available list at a fixed interval after a random start (chapter 6).

***t*-tests/*t*-values** a *t*-value is the outcome (statistic) computed from a *t*-test of significance, which in multiple regression tests the hypothesis that a regression coefficient is significantly different from zero when the other independent variables are taken into account (chapter 15).

target population in sampling, the population to which the researcher would like to generalize his or her results (chapter 6).

term the simplest element of logical analysis; a term is whatever is meant by a word or phrase (chapter 3).

test of statistical significance a statistical procedure used to assess the likelihood that the results of an experiment or other study could have occurred by chance (chapters 7, 14, and 15).

test-retest reliability a "stability" method for assessing reliability that involves calculating the correlation between repeated applications of a measure (chapter 5).

testing a threat to internal validity; changes in what is being measured that are brought about by reactions to the process of measurement; the effects of being measured once on being measured a second time (chapter 8).

treatment the manipulated conditions comprising an independent variable in an experiment (chapter 7).

trend study a longitudinal design in which a research question is investigated by repeated surveys of independently selected samples of the same population (chapter 9).

triangulation addressing a social research question with multiple methods or measures that do not share the same methodological weaknesses; if different approaches produce similar findings, our confidence in the results increases (chapter 13).

unidimensionality evidence that a scale or index is measuring only a single dimension of a concept (chapter 13).

unit of analysis the entity about whom or which the researcher gathers information; these may be people, social roles and relationships, groups, organizations, communities, nations, and social artifacts (chapter 4).

univariate analysis statistical analysis of one variable at a time; *see also* bivariate and multivariate analysis (chapter 14).

unstructured interview a type of nonstandardized interview in which the objectives may be very general and the questions developed as the interview proceeds; preferred when the purpose is to acquire preliminary data or understandings; *see also* structured interview (chapter 9).

validity (1) the congruence or "goodness of fit" between an operational definition and the concept it is purported to measure; (2) in logical analysis, the adequacy of the reasoning (premises must be properly related to the conclusion so that the argument is logically correct) as opposed to the truth of the premises (chapters 5 and 3).

variance *see* standard deviation.

vital statistics demographic data collected from the registration of "vital" life events, such as births, deaths, marriages, and divorces (chapter 12).

wild-code checking a data cleaning procedure involving checking for out-of-range and other "illegal" codes among the values recorded for each variable (chapter 14).

Y-intercept the predicted value of the dependent variable in bivariate regression when the independent variable has a value of zero; graphically, the point at which the regression line crosses the Y-axis (chapter 14).

REFERENCES

Adair, J. G., T. W. Dushenko, and R. C. L. Lindsay. 1985. Ethical regulations and their impact on research practice. *American Psychologist* 40:59–72.

Alexander, C. S., and H. J. Becker. 1978. The use of vignettes in survey research. *Public Opinion Quarterly* 42:93–104.

Allon, N. 1979. The interrelationship of process and content in field work. *Symbolic Interaction* 2:63–78.

American Anthropological Association. 1983. *Professional Ethics*. Washington, D.C.: Author.

American Psychological Association. 1981. Ethical principles of psychologists. *American Psychologist* 36:633–638.

American Sociological Association. 1984. *Code of Ethics*. Washington, D.C.: Author.

Andrews, F. M., and S. B. Withey. 1976. *Social Indicators of Well-Being*. New York: Plenum.

Angell, R. C. 1951. The moral integration of American cities. *American Journal of Sociology* 57(Pt. 2):1–140.

Archer, D., B. Iritani, D. D. Kimes, and M. Barrios. 1983. Face-ism: Five studies of sex differences in facial prominence. *Journal of Personality and Social Psychology* 45:725–735.

Argyris, C. 1968. Some unintended consequences of rigorous research. *Psychological Bulletin* 70:185–197.

Armer, M., and A. Schnaiberg. 1972. Measuring individual modernity: A near myth. *American Sociological Review* 37:301–316.

Arnold, D. O. 1970. Dimensional sampling: An approach for studying a small number of cases. *American Sociologist* 5:147–150.

Aronson, E., and J. M. Carlsmith. 1968. Experimentation in social psychology. In *The Handbook of Social Psychology*, 2nd Edition, Vol. 2 (eds. G. Lindzey and E. Aronson), pp. 1–79. Reading, Mass.: Addison-Wesley.

Asimov, I. 1980. Science must be understood and understanding. *The Evening Gazette* (Worcester, Mass.), 19 August, 19.

Babbie, E. 1983. *The Practice of Social Research*, 3rd Edition. Belmont, Calif.: Wadsworth.

Bagby, J. M. 1957. A cross-cultural study of perceptual predominance in binocular rivalry. *Journal of Abnormal and Social Psychology* 54:331–334.

Bailey, K. D. 1982. *Methods of Social Research*, 2nd Edition. New York: Free Press.

Bainbridge, W. S. 1982. Shaker demographics 1840–1900: An example of the use of U.S. Census enumeration schedules. *Journal for the Scientific Study of Religion* 21:352–365.

Ball, S., and G. A. Bogatz. 1970. *The First Year of Sesame Street: An Evaluation*. Princeton, N. J.: Educational Testing Service.

Barker, S. F. 1974. *The Elements of Logic*, 2nd Edition. New York: McGraw-Hill.

Barry, V. E. 1976. *Practical Logic*. New York: Holt, Rinehart and Winston.

Bass, B. M. 1955. Authoritarianism or acquiescence. *Journal of Abnormal and Social Psychology* 51:616–623.

Batten, T. F. 1971. *Reasoning and Research: A Guide for Social Science Methods*. Boston: Little, Brown.

Baumrind, D. 1971. Principles of ethical conduct in the treatment of subjects: Reaction to the draft report of the Committee on Ethical Standards in Psychological Research. *American Psychologist* 26:887–896.

Baumrind, D. 1985. Research using intentional deception: Ethical issues revisited. *American Psychologist* 40:165–174.

Becker, H. S. 1967. Whose side are we on? *Social Problems* 14:239–247.

Becker, H. S., and B. Geer. 1957. Participant observation and interviewing: A comparison. *Human Organization* 16:28–32.

Becker, H. S., B. Geer, E. C. Hughes, and A. Strauss. 1961. *Boys in White: Student Culture in Medical School*. Chicago: University of Chicago.

Beckner, M. 1967. Aspects of explanation in biological theory. In *Philosophy of Science Today* (ed. S. Morgenbesser), pp. 148–159. New York: Basic Books.

Berelson, B., and R. Freedman. 1964. A study in fertility control. *Scientific American* 210(5):29–37.

Berglund, E., D. A. Bernstein, R. A. Eisinger, G. M. Hochbaum, E. Lichtenstein, J. L. Schwartz, and B. C. Straits. 1974. *Guideline for Research on the Effectiveness of Smoking Cessation Programs: A Committee Report*. National Interagency Council on Smoking and Health. Chicago: American Dental Association.

Berk, R. A. 1983. Applications of the general linear model to survey data. In *Handbook of Survey Research* (eds. P. H. Rossi, J. D. Wright, and A. B. Anderson), pp. 495–546. New York: Academic Press.

Bernstein, I. N., G. W. Bohrnstedt, and E. F. Borgatta. 1975. External validity and evaluation research: A codification of problems. *Sociological Methods and Research* 4:101–128.

Bernstein, I. N., and H. E. Freeman. 1975. *Academic and Entrepreneurial Research: The Consequences of Diversity in Federal Evaluation Studies*. New York: Russell Sage.

Beveridge, W. I. B. 1957. *The Art of Scientific Investigation*, 3rd Edition. London: William Heinemann.

Bielby, W. T., and R. M. Hauser. 1977. Structural equation models. *Annual Review of Sociology* 3:137–161.

Bigus, O. E. 1978. The milkman and his customer: A cultivated relationship. In *Interaction in Everyday Life* (ed. J. Lofland), pp. 85–119. Beverly Hills, Calif.: Sage.

Bishop, Y. M. N., S. E. Fienberg, and P. W. Holland. 1975. *Discrete Multivariate Analysis: Theory and Practice*. Cambridge, Mass.: MIT Press.

Blalock, H. M., Jr. 1964. *Causal Inferences in Nonexperimental Research*. Chapel Hill, N. C.: University of North Carolina.

Blalock, H. M., Jr. 1979. *Social Statistics*, Revised 2nd Edition. New York: McGraw-Hill.

Blau, P. M. 1955. Determining the dependent variable in certain correlations. *Public Opinion Quarterly* 19:100–105.

Blumberg, A. E. 1976. *Logic: A First Course*. New York: Alfred A.Knopf.

Bogdan, R. 1980. Interviewing people labeled retarded. In *Fieldwork Experience: Qualita-*

tive Approaches to Social Research (eds. W. B. Shaffir, R. A. Stebbins, and A. Turowetz), pp. 235–243. New York: St. Martin's.

Bogdan, R., and S. J. Taylor. 1975. *Introduction to Qualitative Research Methods: A Phenomenological Approach to the Social Sciences*. New York: Wiley.

Bohrnstedt, G. W., and D. Knoke. 1982. *Statistics for Social Data Analysis*. Itasca, Ill.: F. E. Peacock.

Boydstun, J. E., M. E. Sherry, and N. P. Moelter. 1978. Patrol staffing in San Diego: One- or two-officer units. In *Evaluation Studies Review Annual 3* (eds. T. D. Cook, M. L. Del Rosario, K. M. Hennigan, M. M. Mark, and W. M. K. Trochim), pp. 455–472. Beverly Hills, Calif.: Sage.

Boyer, P., and S. Nissenbaum. 1974. *Salem Possessed: The Social Origins of Witchcraft*. Cambridge, Mass.: Harvard University.

Brazziel, W. F. 1969. A letter from the South. *Harvard Educational Review* 39:348–356.

Bromley, D. G., and A. D. Shupe, Jr. 1979. *Moonies in America: Cult, Church and Crusade*. Beverly Hills, Calif.: Sage.

Browne, J. 1976a. Personal journal: Fieldwork for fun and profit. In *The Research Experience* (ed. M. P. Golden), pp. 71–84. Itasca, Ill.: F. E. Peacock.

Browne, J. 1976b. The used car game. In *The Research Experience* (ed. M. P. Golden), pp. 60–71. Itasca, Ill.: F. E. Peacock.

Brownlee, K. A. 1965. A review of "smoking and health." *Journal of the American Statistical Association* 60:722–740.

Bruner, E. M., and J. P. Kelso. 1980. Gender differences in graffiti: A semiotic perspective. *Women's Studies International Quarterly* 3:239–252.

Bruyn, S. T. 1966. *The Human Perspective in Sociology: The Methodology of Participant Observation*. Englewood Cliffs, N. J.: Prentice-Hall.

Bryan, J. H., and M. A. Test. 1967. Models and helping: Naturalistic studies in aiding behavior. *Journal of Personality and Social Psychology* 6:400–407.

Bryson, M. C. 1976. The Literary Digest poll: Making of a statistical myth. *The American Statistician* 30:184–185.

Burstein, P. 1979. Public opinion, demonstrations, and the passage of antidiscrimination legislation. *Public Opinion Quarterly* 43:157–172.

Bushman, R. L. 1967. *From Puritan to Yankee: Character and the Social Order in Connecticut, 1690–1765*. Cambridge, Mass.: Harvard University.

Byrne, D. 1971. *The Attraction Paradigm*. New York: Academic Press.

Campbell, D. T. 1969. Reforms as experiments. *American Psychologist* 24:409–429.

Campbell, D. T., and J. C. Stanley. 1963. *Experimental and Quasi-experimental Designs for Research*. Chicago: Rand McNally.

Campbell, D. T., and H. L. Ross. 1968. The Connecticut crackdown on speeding: Time series data in quasi-experimental analysis. *Law and Society Review* 3:33–53.

Cannell, C. F., and R. L. Kahn. 1968. Interviewing. In *The Handbook of Social Psychology*, 2nd Edition, Vol. 2 (eds. G. Lindzey and E. Aronson), pp. 526–571. Reading, Mass.: Addison-Wesley.

Cannell, C. F., K. H. Marquis, and A. Laurent. 1977. *A Summary of Studies of Interviewing Methodology. Vital and Health Statistics*. Series 2, Data evaluation and methods research. No. 69. DHEW Publ. No. (HRA) 77–1343. Health Resources Administration, National Center for Health Statistics, U. S. Department of Health, Education and Welfare. Washington, D.C.: U. S. Government Printing Office.

Card, J. J., and L. L. Wise. 1978. Teenage mothers and teenage fathers: The impact of early childbearing on the parents' personal and professional lives. *Family Planning Perspectives* 10:199–205.

Carlsmith, J. M., P. C. Ellsworth, and E. Aronson. 1976. *Methods of Research in Social Psychology*. Reading, Mass.: Addison-Wesley.

Carnap, R. 1966. *Philosophical Foundations of Physics*. New York: Basic Books.

Carter, R. E., Jr., V. C. Troldahl, and R. S. Schuneman. 1963. Interviewer bias in selecting households. *Journal of Marketing* 27:27–34.

Caspi, A. 1984. Contact hypothesis and inter-age attitudes: A field study of cross-age contact. *Social Psychology Quarterly* 47:74–80.

Cavan, S. 1966. *Liquor License: An Ethnography of Bar Behavior*. Chicago: Aldine.

Ceci, S. J., D. Peters, and J. Plotkin. 1985. Human subjects review, personal values, and regulation of social science research. *American Psychologist* 40:994–1002.

Chambliss, W. J. 1976. Functional and conflict theories of crime: The heritage of Emile Durkheim and Karl Marx. In *Whose Law? What Order? A Conflict Approach to Criminology* (eds. W. J. Chambliss and M. Mankoff), pp. 1–28. New York: Wiley.

Charmaz, K. 1983. The grounded theory method: An explication and interpretation. In *Contemporary Field Research: A Collection of Readings* (ed. R. M. Emerson), pp. 109–126. Boston: Little, Brown.

Chein, I. 1981. An introduction to sampling. In *Research Methods in Social Relations*, 4th Edition (L. H. Kidder), pp. 418–444. New York: Holt, Rinehart and Winston.

Cialdini, R. B. 1980. Full-cycle social psychology. In *Applied Social Psychology Annual*, Vol. 1 (ed. L. Bickman), pp. 21–47. Beverly Hills, Calif.: Sage.

Cialdini, R. B., and D. A. Schroeder. 1976. Increasing compliance by legitimizing paltry contributions: When even a penny helps. *Journal of Personality and Social Psychology* 34:599–604.

Cleveland, W. S. 1985. *The Elements of Graphing Data*. Monterey, Calif.: Wadsworth.

Clogg, C. C., and D. O. Sawyer. 1981. A comparison of alternative models for analyzing the scalability of response patterns. In *Sociological Methodology 1981* (ed. S. Leinhardt), pp. 240–280. San Francisco: Jossey-Bass.

Clore, G. L., R. M. Bray, S. M. Itkin, and P. Murphy. 1978. Interracial attitudes and behavior at a summer camp. *Journal of Personality and Social Psychology* 35:107–116.

Code of Federal Regulations. 1981. Title 45—Public Welfare. Office of the Federal Register. Washington, D.C.: U.S. Government Printing Office.

Cohen, J., and P. Cohen. 1983. *Applied Multiple Regression/Correlation Analysis for the Behavioral Sciences*. Hillsdale, N. J.: Lawrence Earlbaum.

Coleman, J. S. 1961. *The Adolescent Society: The Social Life of the Teenager and Its Impact on Education*. New York: Free Press.

Coleman, J. S. 1964. Research chronicle: *The Adolescent Society*. In *Sociologists at Work* (ed. P. E. Hammond), pp. 184–211. New York: Basic Books.

Coleman, J. S., E. Katz, and H. Menzel. 1966. *Medical Innovation: A Diffusion Study*. Indianapolis: Bobbs-Merrill.

Cook, T. D., and D. T. Campbell. 1976. The design and conduct of quasi-experiments and true experiments in field settings. In *Handbook of Industrial and Organizational Psychology* (ed. M. D. Dunnette), pp. 223–326. Chicago: Rand McNally.

Cook, T. D., and D. T. Campbell. 1979. *Quasi-experimentation: Design and Analysis Issues for Field Settings*. Chicago: Rand McNally.

Cook, T. D., and R. F. Conner. 1976. The educational impact. *Journal of Communication* 26(2):155–164.

Cook, T. D., F. L. Cook, and M. M. Mark. 1977. Randomized and quasi-experimental designs in evaluation research: An introduction. In *Evaluation Research Methods: A Basic Guide* (ed. L. Rutman), pp. 103–139. Beverly Hills, Calif.: Sage.

Copi, I. M. 1973. *Symbolic Logic*, 4th Edition. New York: Macmillan.

Cottrell, N. B. 1972. Social facilitation. In *Experimental Social Psychology* (ed. C. G. McClintock), pp. 185–236. New York: Holt, Rinehart and Winston.

Cournand, A. 1977. The code of the scientist and its relationship to ethics. *Science* 198:699–705.

Crain, R. L., E. Katz, and D. B. Rosenthal. 1969. *The Politics of Community Conflict.* Indianapolis: Bobbs-Merrill.

Cramer, J. C. 1980. Fertility and female employment: Problems of causal direction. *American Sociological Review* 45:167–190.

Crosby, F., S. Bromley, and L. Saxe. 1980. Recent unobtrusive studies of black and white discrimination and prejudice: A literature review. *Psychological Bulletin* 87:546–563.

Dane, F. C. 1981. *Student Workbook for Selltiz, Wrightsman, and Cook's Research Methods in Social Relations.* New York: Holt, Rinehart and Winston.

Danziger, S. K. 1979. On doctor watching: Fieldwork in medical settings. *Urban Life* 7:513–532.

Darley, J. M., and B. Latané. 1968. Bystander intervention in emergencies: Diffusion of responsibility. *Journal of Personality and Social Psychology* 8:377–383.

Davis, F. 1959. The cabdriver and his fare: Facets of a fleeting relationship. *American Journal of Sociology* 65:158–165.

Davis, J. A. 1964a. *Great Aspirations*. Chicago: Aldine.

Davis, J. A. 1964b. Great books and small groups: An informal history of a national survey. In *Sociologists at Work* (ed. P. E. Hammond), pp. 212–234. New York: Basic Books.

Davis, J. A. 1966. The campus as a frog pond: An application of the theory of relative deprivation to career decisions of college men. *American Journal of Sociology* 72:17–31.

Davis, J. A. 1971. *Elementary Survey Analysis*. Englewood Cliffs, N. J.: Prentice-Hall.

Davis, J. A. 1980. Conservative weather in a liberalizing climate: Change in selected NORC General Social Survey items, 1972–1978. *Social Forces* 58:1129–1156.

Davis, J. A. 1985. *The Logic of Causal Order*. Beverly Hills, Calif.: Sage.

Davis, J. A., and T. W. Smith. 1985. *General Social Surveys, 1972–1985*. [machine-readable data file]. Principal Investigator, J. A. Davis; Senior Study Director, T. W. Smith. NORC Editior. Chicago: National Opinion Research Center, producer; Storrs, Conn.: Roper Public Opinion Research Center, University of Connecticut, distributor.

Dawes, R. M., and T. W. Smith. 1985. Attitude and opinion measurement. In *Handbook of Social Psychology*, 3rd Edition, Vol. 1 (eds. G. Lindzey and E. Aronson), pp. 509–566. New York: Random House.

DeMaio, T. J. 1984. Social desirability and survey measurement: A review. In *Surveying Subjective Phenomena*, Vol. 2 (eds. C. F. Turner and E. Martin), pp. 257–282. New York: Russell Sage Foundation.

Deutsch, M., and M. E. Collins. 1951. *Interracial Housing: A Psychological Evaluation of a Social Experiment.* Minneapolis: University of Minnesota.

Diener, E., and R. Crandall. 1978. *Ethics in Social and Behavioral Research*. Chicago: University of Chicago.

Dillman, D. A. 1978. *Mail and Telephone Surveys: The Total Design Method*. New York: Wiley.

Doherty, M. E., and K. M. Shemberg. 1978. *Asking Questions about Behavior: An Introduction to What Psychologists Do*, 2nd Edition. Glenview, Ill.: Scott, Foresman.

Domhoff, W. G. 1974. *The Bohemian Grove and Other Retreats: A Study of Ruling-Class Cohesiveness*. New York: Harper and Row.

Doob, A. N., and A. E. Gross. 1968. Status of frustrator as an inhibitor of horn-honking responses. *Journal of Social Psychology* 76:213–218.

Doob, A. N., and G. E. Macdonald. 1979. Television viewing and fear of victimization: Is the relationship causal? *Journal of Personality and Social Psychology* 37:170–179.

Dorfman, D. D. 1978. The Cyril Burt question: New findings. *Science* 201:1177–1186.

Dornbusch, S. M., and L. C. Hickman. 1959. Other-directedness in consumer-goods advertising: A test of Riesman's historical theory. *Social Forces* 38:99–102.

Duncan, B., and O. D. Duncan. 1978. *Sex Typing and Social Roles: A Research Report*. New York: Academic Press.

Duncan, O. D. 1975. *Introduction to Structural Equation Models*. New York: Academic Press.

Durkheim, E. 1951. *Suicide: A Study in Sociology* (trans. J. A. Spaulding and G. Simpson). Glencoe, Ill.: Free Press.

Edson, L. 1970. Jensenism, *n.*—the theory that IQ is largely determined by the genes. In *Prejudice and Race Relations* (ed. R. W. Mack), pp. 35–55. Chicago: Quadrangle.

Emerson, R. M. 1981. Observational field work. *Annual Review of Sociology* 7:351–378.

Emerson, R. M., ed. 1983. *Contemporary Field Research: A Collection of Readings*. Boston: Little, Brown.

Erikson, K. T. 1966. *Wayward Puritans: A Study in the Sociology of Deviance*. New York: Wiley.

Erikson, K. T. 1967. A comment on disguised observation in sociology. *Social Problems* 14:366–373.

Erikson, K. T. 1976. *Everything in Its Path: Destruction of Community in the Buffalo Creek Flood*. New York: Simon and Schuster.

Etkowitz, H. 1984. Solar versus nuclear energy: Autonomous or dependent technology? *Social Problems* 31:417–434.

Evans, R. I. 1976. *The Making of Psychology: Discussions with Creative Contributors*. New York: Alfred A. Knopf.

Farley, R. 1984. *Black and Whites: Narrowing the Gap?* Cambridge, Mass.: Harvard University.

Farley, R., H. Schuman, S. Bianchi, D. Colasanto, and S. Hatchett. 1978. 'Chocolate city, vanilla suburbs': Will the trend toward racially separate communities continue? *Social Science Research* 7:319–344.

Felson, M. 1983. Unobtrusive indicators of cultural change: Neckties, girdles, marijuana, garbage, magazines, and urban sprawl. *American Behavioral Scientist* 26:534–542.

Feshbach S., and N. Feshbach. 1963. Influence of the stimulus object upon the complementary and supplementary projection of fear. *Journal of Abnormal and Social Psychology* 66:498–502.

Festinger, L. 1954. A theory of social comparison processes. *Human Relations* 7:117–140.

Festinger, L. 1959. Sampling and related problems in research methodology. *American Journal of Mental Deficiency* 64:358–366.

Fienberg, S. E. 1971. Randomization and social affairs: The 1970 draft lottery. *Science* 171:255–261.

Fienberg, S. E. 1977. *The Analysis of Cross-Classified Data*. Cambridge, Mass.: MIT Press.

Fienberg, S. E., and W. M. Mason. 1979. Identification and estimation of age-period-cohort models in the analysis of discrete archival data. In *Sociological Methodology 1979* (ed. K. F. Schuessler), pp. 1–67. San Francisco: Jossey-Bass.

Filstead, W. J., ed. 1970. *Qualitative Methodology: Firsthand Involvement with the Social World*. Chicago: Markham.

Fine, G. A. 1979. Small groups and culture creation: The idioculture of Little League baseball teams. *American Sociological Review* 44:733–745.

Fine, G. A., and B. Glassner. 1979. Participant observation with children: Promise and problems. *Urban Life* 8:153–174.

Fox, J. 1984. *Linear Statistical Models and Related Methods*. New York: Wiley.

Freedman, J. L., S. A. Wallington, and E. Bless. 1967. Compliance without pressure: The effect of guilt. *Journal of Personality and Social Psychology* 7:117–124.

Galle, O. R., W. R. Gove, and J. M. McPherson. 1972. Population density and pathology: What are the relations for man? *Science* 176:23–30.

Gans, H. 1967. *Levittowners: Ways of Life and Politics in a New Suburban Community*. New York: Pantheon Books.

Geer, B. 1964. First days in the field. In *Sociologists at Work* (ed. P. E. Hammond), pp. 322–344. New York: Basic Books.

Gerbner, G., and L. Gross. 1976a. Living with television: The violence profile. *Journal of Communication* 26(2):173–199.

Gerbner, G., and L. Gross. 1976b. The scary world of TV's heavy viewer. *Psychology Today* April:41–45,89.

Gerbner, G., L. Gross, M. F. Eleey, M. Jackson-Beeck, S. Jeffries-Fox, and N. Signorielli. 1977. TV violence profile no. 8: The highlights. *Journal of Communication* 27(2):171–180.

Gerbner, G., L. Gross, M. Jackson-Beeck, S. Jeffries-Fox, and N. Signorielli. 1978. Cultural indicators: Violence profile no. 9. *Journal of Communication* 28(3):176–207.

Gerbner, G., L. Gross, M. Morgan, and N. Signorielli. 1980a. The "mainstreaming" of America: Violence profile no. 11. *Journal of Communication* 30(2):10–29

Gerbner, G., L. Gross, M. Morgan, and N. Signorielli. 1980b. Some additional comments on cultivation analysis. *Public Opinion Quarterly* 44:408–410.

Gerbner, G., L. Gross, M. Morgan, and N. Signorielli. 1981. A curious journey into the scary world of Paul Hirsch. *Communication Research* 8:39–72.

Glaser, B. G., and A. L. Strauss. 1967. *The Discovery of Grounded Theory: Strategies for Qualitative Research*. Chicago: Aldine.

Glazer, M. 1972. *The Research Adventure: Promise and Problems of Field Work*. New York: Random House.

Glenn, N. D. 1977. *Cohort Analysis*. Beverly Hills, Calif.: Sage.

Glenn, N. D. 1978. The General Social Surveys: Editorial introduction to a symposium. *Contemporary Sociology* 7:532–534.

Glenn, N. D. 1981. Age, birth cohorts, and drinking: An illustration of the hazards of inferring effects from cohort data. *Journal of Gerontology* 36:362–369.

Glenn, N. D., and W. P. Frisbie. 1977. Trend studies with survey sample and census data. *Annual Review of Sociology* 3:79–104.

Glock, C. Y., and R. Stark. 1966. *Christian Beliefs and Anti-Semitism*. New York: Harper and Row.

Goffman, E. 1979. *Gender Advertisements*. Cambridge, Mass.: Harvard University.

Gold, D. 1969. Statistical tests and substantive significance. *The American Sociologist* 4:42–46.

Gold, R. L. 1958. Roles in sociological field observations. *Social Forces* 36:217–223.

Goldberger, A. S., and O. D. Duncan, eds. 1973. *Structural Equation Models in the Social Sciences*. New York: Seminar Press.

Golden, M. P., ed. 1976. *The Research Experience*. Itasca, Ill.: F. E. Peacock.

Goodman, L. A. 1984. *The Analysis of Cross-Classified Data Having Ordered Categories*. Cambridge, Mass.: Harvard University.

Gorden, R. L. 1975. *Interviewing: Strategy, Techniques, and Tactics*, Revised Edition. Homewood, Ill.: Dorsey.

Gordon, R. A., J. F. Short, Jr., D. S. Cartwright, and F. L. Strodtbeck. 1963. Values and gang delinquency: A study of street-corner groups. *American Journal of Sociology* 69:109–128.

Gottschalk, L. 1969. *Understanding History: A Primer of Historical Method*, 2nd Edition. New York: Alfred A. Knopf.

Gray, D. J. 1968. Value-free sociology: A doctrine of hypocrisy and irresponsibility. *Sociological Quarterly* 9:176–185.

Griswold, W. 1981. American character and the American novel: An expansion of reflection theory in the sociology of literature. *American Journal of Sociology* 86:740–765.

Groves, R. M. 1979. Actors and questions in telephone and personal interview surveys. *Public Opinion Quarterly* 43:190–205.

Groves, R. M. and R. L. Kahn. 1979. *Surveys by Telephone: A National Comparison with Personal Interviews*. New York: Academic Press.

Gurwitsch, A. 1974. *Phenomenology and the Theory of Science* (ed. L. Embree). Evanston, Ill: Northwestern University.

Guttman, L. 1950. The basis for scalogram analysis. In *Measurement and Prediction* (eds. S. A. Stouffer, L. Guttman, E. A. Suchman, P. F. Lazarsfeld, S. A. Star, and J. A. Clausen), pp. 60–90. Princeton: Princeton University.

Haire, M. 1950. Projective techniques in marketing research. *Journal of Marketing* 14:649–656.

Hakim, C. 1982. *Secondary Analysis in Social Research: A Guide to Data Sources and Methods with Examples*. London: George Allen and Unwin.

Hall, C. S., and G. Lindzey. 1970. *Theories of Personality*, 2nd Edition. New York: Wiley.

Hallinan, M. T., and A. B. Sorenson. 1983. The formation and stability of instructional groups. *American Sociological Review* 48:838–851.

Hansen, C. 1969. *Witchcraft at Salem*. New York: George Braziller.

Heberlein, T. A., and R. Baumgartner. 1978. Factors affecting response rates to mailed questionnaires: A quantitative analysis of the published literature. *American Sociological Review* 43:447–462.

Heer, D. M. 1979. What is the annual net flow of undocumented Mexican immigrants to the U.S.? *Demography* 16:417–423.

Heilman, S. C. 1976. *Synagogue Life: A Study in Symbolic Interaction*. Chicago: University of Chicago.

Hempel, C. G. 1965. *Aspects of Scientific Explanation and Other Essays in the Philosophy of Science*. New York: Free Press.

Hempel, C. G. 1966. *Philosophy of Natural Science*. Englewood Cliffs, N.J.: Prentice-Hall.

Hempel, C. G. 1967. Scientific explanation. In *Philosophy of Science Today* (ed. S. Morgenbesser), pp. 78–88. New York: Basic Books.

Hempel, C. G., and P. Oppenheim. 1948. The logic of explanation. *Philosophy of Science* 15:135–175.

Henderson, M. R. 1975. Acquiring privacy in public life. *Urban Life and Culture* 3:446–455.

Henretta, J. A. 1965. Economic development and social structure in colonial Boston. *William and Mary Quarterly* 22:75–92.

Higbee, K. L., and M. G. Wells. 1972. Some research trends in social psychology during the 1960's. *American Psychologist* 27:963–966.

Hirsch, P. M. 1980. The "scary world" of the nonviewer and other anomalies: A reanalysis of Gerbner et al.'s findings on cultivation analysis. *Communication Research* 7:403–456.

Hirschi, T., and H. C. Selvin. 1967. *Delinquency Research: An Appraisal of Analytic Methods*. New York: Free Press.

Hollingshead, A. B. 1971. Commentary on "the indiscriminate state of social class measurement." *Social Forces* 49:563–567.

Holloway, M. 1966. Shaker societies. In *Heavens on Earth: Utopian Communities in America, 1680–1880*, 2nd Edition (ed. M. Holloway), pp. 64–79. New York: Dover.

Holsti, O. R. 1969. *Content Analysis for the Social Sciences and Humanities*. Reading, Mass.: Addison-Wesley.

Horowitz, I. L., ed. 1967. *The Rise and Fall of Project Camelot: Studies in the Relationship between Social Science and Practical Politics*. Cambridge: MIT Press.

Howell, J. T. 1973. *Hard Living on Clay Street: Portraits of Blue Collar Families*. Garden City, N.Y.: Anchor/Doubleday.

Huck, S. W. and H. M. Sandler. 1979. *Rival Hypotheses: Alternative Interpretations of Data Based Conclusions*. New York: Harper and Row.

Hughes, E. C. 1960. Introduction: The place of field work in social science. In *Field Work: An Introduction to the Social Sciences* (B. H. Junker), pp. iii–xiii. Chicago: University of Chicago.

Hughes, M. 1980. The fruits of cultivation analysis: A reexamination of some effects of television watching. *Public Opinion Quarterly* 44:287–302.

Hume, D. 1748 (1951). An inquiry concerning human understanding. In *Theory of Knowledge* (ed. D. C. Yalden-Thomson). Edinburgh: Nelson.

Hummon, D. H. 1986. Urban views: Popular perspectives on city life. *Urban Life* 15:3–36.

Humphreys, L. 1975. *Tearoom Trade: Impersonal Sex in Public Places*, Enlarged Edition. Chicago: Aldine.

Hyman, H. H. 1955. *Survey Design and Analysis*. Glencoe, Ill.: The Free Press.

Hyman, H. H. 1972. *Secondary Analysis of Sample Surveys: Principles, Procedures, and Potentialities*. New York: Wiley.

Hyman, H. H., C. R. Wright, and J. S. Reed. 1975. *The Enduring Effects of Education*. Chicago: University of Chicago.

Inkeles, A., and D. H. Smith. 1974. *Becoming Modern: Individual Change in Six Developing Countries*. Cambridge, Mass.: Harvard University.

ISR Newsletter. 1977. Refined survey techniques greatly improve quality of data: required increased effort for researchers. Institute for Social Research, University of Michigan.

Isen, A. M., and P. F. Levin. 1972. Effect of feeling good on helping: Cookies and kindness. *Journal of Personality and Social Psychology* 21:384–388.

Jacob, H. 1984. *Using Published Data: Errors and Remedies*. Beverly Hills, Calif.: Sage.

Jacobs, J. 1967. A phenomenological study of suicide notes. *Social Problems* 15:60–72.

Jacobson, A. L., and N. M. Lalu. 1974. An empirical and algebraic analysis of alternative techniques for measuring unobserved variables. In *Measurement in the Social Sciences* (ed. H. M. Blalock, Jr.), pp. 215–242. Chicago: Aldine.

Jensen, A. R. 1969. How much can we boost IQ and scholastic achievement? *Harvard Educational Review* 39:1–123.

Johnson, R. C. 1978. A procedure for sampling the manuscript census schedules. *Journal of Interdisciplinary History* 8:515–530.

Jöreskog, K. G., and D. Sorbom. 1979. *Advances in Factor Analysis and Structural Equation Models*. Cambridge, Mass.: Abt Books.

Junker, B. H. 1960. *Fieldwork: An Introduction to the Social Sciences*. Chicago: University of Chicago.

Kahn, R. L., and C. F. Cannell. 1957. *The Dynamics of Interviewing: Theory, Technique, and Cases*. New York: Wiley.

Kanter, R. M. 1977. *Men and Women of the Corporation*. New York: Basic Books.

Kaplan, C. P., and T. L. Van Valey. 1980. *Census '80: Continuing the Factfinder Tradition*. Washington, D.C.: U.S. Bureau of the Census.

Karp, D. A. 1973. Hiding in pornographic bookstores: A reconsideration of the nature of urban anonymity. *Urban Life* 1:427–452.

Karweit, N., and E. D. Meyers, Jr. 1983. Computers in social research. In *Handbook of Survey Research* (eds. P. H. Rossi, J. D. Wright, and A. B. Anderson), pp. 379–414. New York: Academic Press.

Kasarda, J. D. 1976. The use of census data in secondary analysis: The context of ecological discovery. In *The Research Experience* (ed. M. P. Golden), pp. 424–431. Itasca, Ill.: F. E. Peacock.

Katz, D. 1949. An analysis of the 1948 polling predictions. *Journal of Applied Psychology* 33:15–28.

Katz, E., and P. F. Lazarsfeld. 1955. *Personal Influence: The Part Played by People in the Flow of Mass Communication*. Glencoe, Ill.: Free Press.

Katzer, J., K. H. Cook, and W. W. Crouch. 1978. *Evaluating Information: A Guide for Users of Social Science Research*. Reading, Mass.: Addison-Wesley.

Kelman, H. C. 1968. *A Time to Speak: On Human Values and Social Research*. San Francisco: Jossey-Bass.

Kemeny, J. G. 1959. *A Philosopher Looks at Science*. Princeton, N. J.: D. Van Nostrand.

Kenny, D. A. 1985. Quantitative methods for social psychology. In *Handbook of Social Psychology*, 3rd Edition, Vol. 1 (eds. G. Lindzey and E. Aronson), pp. 487–508. New York: Random House.

Kephart, W. M. 1982. *Extraordinary Groups: The Sociology of Unconventional Life-Styles*, 2nd Edition. New York: St. Martin's.

Kerlinger, F. N. 1973. *Foundations of Behavioral Research*, 2nd Edition. New York: Holt, Rinehart and Winston.

Keyfitz, N. 1976. World resources and the world middle class. *Scientific American* 235:28–35.

Kidder, L. H., and D. T. Campbell. 1970. The indirect testing of social attitudes. In *Attitude Measurement* (ed. G. F. Summers), pp. 333–385. Chicago: Rand McNally.

Kiecolt, J. 1978. *Instructor's Manual to Accompany Methods of Social Research*. New York: Free Press.

Kiecolt, K. J., and L. E. Nathan. 1985. *Secondary Analysis of Survey Data*. Beverly Hills, Calif.: Sage.

Kiesler, C. A., in collaboration with R. P. Lowman. 1980. Hutchinson versus Proxmire. *American Psychologist* 35:689–690.

Kirkpatrick, C. 1936. The construction of a belief-pattern scale for measuring attitudes toward feminism. *Journal of Social Psychology* 7:421–437.

Kish, L. 1959. Some statistical problems in research design. *American Sociological Review* 24:328–338.

Kish, L. 1965. *Survey Sampling*. New York: Wiley.

Knoke, D., and P. J. Burke. 1980. *Log-Linear Models*. Beverly Hills, Calif.: Sage.

Komarovsky, M. 1976. *Dilemmas of Masculinity: A Study of College Youth*. New York: W. W. Norton.

Kotarba, J. A. 1977. The chronic pain experience. In *Existential Sociology* (eds. J. D. Douglas and J. M. Johnson), pp. 257–272. New York: Cambridge University.

Kotarba, J. A. 1980. Discovering amorphous social experience: The case of chronic pain. In *Fieldwork Experience: Qualitative Approaches to Social Research* (ed. W. B. Shaffir, R. A. Stebbins, and A. Turowetz), pp. 57–67. New York: St. Martin's.

Kuhn, T. S. 1962. *The Structure of Scientific Revolutions*. Chicago: University of Chicago.

Labov, W. 1973. The linguistic consequences of being a lame. *Language in Society* 2:81–115.

Labovitz, S., and R. Hagedorn. 1976. *Introduction to Social Research*, 2nd Edition. New York: McGraw-Hill.

Latané, B., and J. M. Darley. 1970. *The Unresponsive Bystander: Why Doesn't He Help?* Englewood Cliffs, N. J.: Prentice-Hall.

Latané, B., and S. Nida. 1981. Ten years of research on group size and helping. *Psychological Bulletin* 89:308–324.

Lazarsfeld, P. F. 1955. Interpretation of statistical relations as a research operation. In *Language of Social Research* (eds. P. F. Lazarsfeld and M. Rosenberg), pp. 115–125. Glencoe, Ill.: Free Press.

Lazarsfeld, P. F., B. Berelson, and H. Gaudet. 1948. *The People's Choice*. New York: Columbia University.

Lazarsfeld, P. F., B. Berelson, and H. Gaudet. 1968. *The People's Choice: How the Voter Makes Up His Mind in a Presidential Campaign*, 2nd Edition. New York: Columbia University.

Lee, G. R. 1984. The utility of cross-cultural data: Potentials and limitations for family sociology. *Journal of Family Issues* 5:519–541.

Leik, R. K. 1972. *Methods, Logic, and Research of Sociology*. Indianapolis: Bobbs-Merrill.

Lever, J. 1978. Sex differences in the complexity of children's play and games. *American Sociological Review* 43:471–483.

Liebert, R. M. 1976. Evaluating the evaluators. *Journal of Communication* 26(2):165–171.

Lincoln, J. R., and G. Zeitz. 1980. Organizational properties from aggregate data: Separating individual and structural effects. *American Sociological Review* 45:391–408.

Lipset, S. M., M. Trow, and J. Coleman. 1956. *Union Democracy*. Garden City, N.Y.: Doubleday.

Lofland, J. 1976. *Doing Social Life: The Qualitative Study of Human Interaction in Natural Settings*. New York: Wiley.

Lofland, J., and L. H. Lofland. 1984. *Analyzing Social Settings: A Guide to Qualitative Observation and Analysis*, 2nd Edition. Belmont, Calif.: Wadsworth.

Lofland, L. H. 1971. *A World of Strangers: Order and Action in Urban Public Space*. Unpublished doctoral dissertation, University of California, San Francisco.

Lofland, L. H. 1973. *A World of Strangers: Order and Action in Urban Public Space*. New York: Basic Books.

Loomis, W. F. 1970. Rickets. *Scientific American* 223:76–82.

Luker, K. 1975. *Abortion and the Decision Not to Contracept*. Berkeley: University of California.

Lundberg, G. A. 1961. *Can Science Save Us?* New York: Longmans, Green.

Manheim, H. L. 1977. *Sociological Research: Philosophy and Methods*. Homewood, Ill.: Dorsey.

Marcoux, M. 1982. *Cursillo: Anatomy of a Movement*. New York: Lambeth Press.

Mazur, A. 1968. The littlest science. *The American Sociologist* 3:195–200.

McCain, G., and E. M. Segal. 1977. *The Game of Science*, 3rd Edition. Belmont, Calif.: Brooks/Cole.

McCall, G. J. 1984. Systematic field observation. *Annual Review of Sociology* 10:263–282.

McCall, G. J., and J. L. Simmons, eds. 1969. *Issues in Participant Observation: A Text and Reader*. Reading, Mass.: Addison-Wesley.

McGuigan, F. J. 1978. *Experimental Psychology: A Methodological Approach*, 3rd Edition. Englewood Cliffs, N. J.: Prentice-Hall.

McGuire, M. B. 1982. *Pentecostal Catholics: Power, Charisma, and Order in a Religious Movement*. Philadelphia: Temple University.

McKinney, J. C. 1966. *Constructive Typology and Social Theory*. New York: Appleton-Century-Crofts.

Melbin, M. 1969. Behavior rhythms in mental hospitals. *American Journal of Sociology* 74:650–665.

Menzel, H., and E. Katz. 1955. Social relations and innovation in the medical profession: The epidemiology of a new drug. *Public Opinion Quarterly* 19:337–352.

Merton, R. K. 1957. *Social Theory and Social Structure*, Revised and Enlarged Edition. Glencoe, Ill.: The Free Press.

Midlarsky, E. 1968. Aiding responses: An analysis and review. *Merrill-Palmer Quarterly of Behavior and Development* 14:229–260.

Milgram, S. 1974. *Obedience to Authority: An Experimental View*. New York: Harper and Row.

Mills, J. 1976. A procedure for explaining experiments involving deception. *Personality and Social Psychology Bulletin* 2:3–13.

Morrison, D. E., and R. E. Henkel, eds. 1970. *The Significance Test Controversy*. Chicago: Aldine.

Mosteller, F., and D. L. Wallace. 1964. *Inference and Disputed Authorship: The Federalist*. Reading, Mass.: Addison-Wesley.

Murdock, G. P. 1967. Ethnographic atlas: A summary. *Ethnology* 6:109–236.

Murdock, G. P., and D. R. White. 1969. Standard cross-cultural sample. *Ethnology* 8:329–369.

Myers, D. G. 1983. *Social Psychology*. New York: McGraw-Hill.

Nagel, E. 1967. The nature and aim of science. In *Philosophy of Science Today* (ed. S. Morgenbesser), pp. 3–13. New York: Basic Books.

Namenwirth, J. Z. 1969. Marks of distinction: An analysis of British mass and prestige newspaper editorials. *American Journal of Sociology* 74:343–360.

Navazio, R. 1977. An experimental approach to bandwagon research. *Public Opinion Quarterly* 41:217–225.

Neale, J. M., and R. M. Liebert. 1973. *Science and Behavior: An Introduction to Methods of Research*. Englewood Cliffs, N. J.: Prentice-Hall.

Nettler, G. 1970. *Explanations*. New York: McGraw-Hill.

Nunn, C. Z., H. J. Crockett, and J. A. Williams, Jr. 1978. *Tolerance for Nonconformity: A National Survey of Americans' Changing Commitment to Civil Liberties*. San Francisco: Jossey-Bass.

Nunnally, J. C., Jr. 1970. *Introduction to Psychological Measurement*. New York: McGraw-Hill.

Oakes, W. 1972. External validity and the use of real people as subjects. *American Psychologist* 27:959–962.

Orne, M. T. 1962. On the social psychology of the psychological experiment: With particular reference to demand characteristics and their implications. *American Psychologist* 17:776–783.

Orne, M. T. 1969. Demand characteristics and the concept of quasi-controls. In *Artifact in Behavioral Research* (eds. R. Rosenthal and R. L. Rosnow), pp. 147–179. New York: Academic Press.

Orne, M. T., and F. J. Evans. 1965. Social control in the psychological experiment: Antisocial behavior and hypnosis. *Journal of Personality and Social Psychology* 1:189–200.

Osgood, C. E., C. J. Suci, and P. H. Tannebaum. 1957. *The Measurement of Meaning.* Urbana, Ill.: University of Illinois.

Padgett, V. R., and D. O. Jorgenson. 1982. Superstition and economic threat: Germany, 1918–1940. *Personality and Social Psychology Bulletin* 8:736–741.

Page, E. B. 1958. Teacher comments and student performance: A seventy-four classroom experiment in school motivation. *Journal of Educational Psychology* 49:173–181.

Pearson, W., Jr., and L. Hendrix. 1979. Divorce and the status of women. *Journal of Marriage and the Family* 41:375–385.

Phillips, D. L. 1971. *Knowledge from What?* Chicago: Rand McNally.

Phillips, D. P. 1974. The influence of suggestion on suicide: Substantive and theoretical implications of the Werther effect. *American Sociological Review* 39:340–354.

Phillips, D. P. 1980. The deterrent effect of capital punishment: New evidence on an old controversy. *American Journal of Sociology* 86:139–148.

Pierce, A. 1967. The economic cycle and the social suicide rate. *American Sociological Review* 32:457–462.

Piliavin, J. A., and I. M. Piliavin. 1972. Effect of blood on reactions to a victim. *Journal of Personality and Social Psychology* 23:353–361.

Piliavin, J. A., P. L. Callero, and D. E. Evans. 1982. Addiction to Altruism? Opponent-process theory and habitual blood donation. *Journal of Personality and Social Psychology* 43:1200–1213.

Pindyck, R. S., and D. L. Rubinfeld. 1981. *Econometric Models and Economic Forecasts.* New York: McGraw-Hill.

Preston, S. H. 1984. Children and the elderly in the U.S. *Scientific American* 251(6):44–49.

Reese, H. W., and W. J. Fremouw. 1984. Normal and normative ethics in behavioral science. *American Psychologist* 39:863–876.

Reiss, A. J., Jr. 1967. *Studies in Crime and Law Enforcement in Major Metropolitan Areas.* Field Studies III, Vol. 2, Section I. Washington, D.C.: U.S. Government Printing Office.

Reiss, A. J., Jr. 1968. Stuff and nonsense about social surveys and observation. In *Institutions and the Person* (eds. H. S. Becker, B. Geer, D. Riesman, and R. S. Weiss), pp. 351–367. Chicago: Aldine.

Reynolds, P. D. 1971. *A Primer in Theory Construction.* Indianapolis: Bobbs-Merrill.

Riesman, D., with N. Glazer, and R. Denney. 1950. *The Lonely Crowd.* New Haven, Conn.: Yale University.

Riley, M. W. 1963. *Sociological Research I. A Case Approach.* New York: Harcourt, Brace and World.

Robinson, J. P. 1976. Interpersonal influence in election campaigns: Two-step flow hypotheses. *Public Opinion Quarterly* 40:304–319.

Robinson, W. S. 1950. Ecological correlations and the behavior of individuals. *American Sociological Review* 15:351–357.

Roethlisberger, F. J., and W. J. Dickson. 1939. *Management and the Worker: An Account of a Research Program Conducted by the Western Electric Co. Hawthorne Works, Chicago.* Cambridge, Mass.: Harvard University.

Rokeach, M. 1960. *The Open and Closed Mind*. New York: Basic Books.

Rosenberg, M. J. 1965. When dissonance fails: On eliminating evaluation apprehension from attitude measurement. *Journal of Personality and Social Psychology* 1:28–42.

Rosenberg, M. J. 1969. The conditions and consequences of evaluation apprehension. In *Artifact in Behavioral Research* (eds. R. Rosenthal and R. L. Rosow), pp. 279–349. New York: Academic Press.

Rosenberg, M. 1965. *Society and the Adolescent Self-Image*. Princeton, N. J.: Princeton University.

Rosenberg, M. 1968. *The Logic of Survey Analysis*. New York: Basic Books.

Rosenthal, R. 1966. *Experimenter Effects in Behavioral Research*. New York: Appleton-Century-Crofts.

Rosenthal, R. 1967. Covert communication in the psychological experiment. *Psychological Bulletin* 67:356–367.

Rosenthal, R. 1969. Interpersonal expectations: Effects of the experimenter's hypothesis. In *Artifact in Behavioral Research* (eds. R. Rosenthal and R. L. Rosnow), pp. 187–227. New York: Academic Press.

Rosenthal, R., and K. L. Fode. 1963. Psychology of the scientist: V. Three experiments in experimentor bias. *Psychological Reports* 12:491–511.

Rosenthal, R., and R. L. Rosnow, eds. 1969. *Artifact in Behavioral Research*. New York: Academic Press.

Rossi, P. H. 1972. Testing for success and failure in social action. In *Evaluating Social Programs: Theory, Practice and Politics* (eds. P. H. Rossi and W. Williams), pp. 11–49. New York: Seminar Press.

Rossi, P. H., and S. R. Wright. 1977. Evaluation research: An assessment of theory, practice and politics. *Evaluation Quarterly* 1:5–52.

Roth, J. 1963. *Timetables: Structuring the Passage of Time in Hospital Treatment and Other Careers*. Indianapolis: Bobbs-Merrill.

Rubin, Z. 1970. Measurement of romantic love. *Journal of Personality and Social Psychology* 16:265–273.

Rubin, Z. 1976. On studying love: Notes on the researcher-subject relationship. In *The Research Experience* (ed. M. P. Golden), pp. 508–513. Itasca, Ill.: F. E. Peacock.

Ruebhausen, O. M., and O. G. Brim, Jr. 1966. Privacy and behavioral research. *American Psychologist* 21:423–437.

Runkle, G. 1978. *Good Thinking: An Introduction to Logic*. New York: Holt, Rinehart and Winston.

Sales, S. M. 1973. Threat as a factor in authoritarianism: An analysis of archival data. *Journal of Personality and Social Psychology* 28:44–57.

Sales, S. M., and K. E. Friend. 1973. Success and failure as determinants of level of authoritarianism. *Behavioral Science* 18:163–172.

Salmon, W. C. 1967. *The Foundation of Scientific Inference*. Pittsburgh: University of Pittsburgh.

Salmon, W. C. 1973. *Logic*, 2nd Edition. Englewood Cliffs, N.J.: Prentice-Hall.

Sanders, W. B., ed. 1976. *The Sociologist as Detective: An Introduction to Research Methods*, 2nd Edition. New York: Praeger.

Schlenker, B. R., and D. R. Forsyth. 1977. On the ethics of psychological research. *Journal of Experimental Social Psychology* 13:369–396.

Schuman, H., and G. Kalton. 1985. Survey methods. In *Handbook of Social Psychology*, 3rd Edition, Vol. 1 (eds. G. Lindzey and E. Aronson), pp. 635–697. New York: Random House.

Schuman, H., and S. Presser. 1977. Question wording as an independent variable in survey analysis. *Sociological Methods and Research* 6:151–170.

Schuman, H., and S. Presser. 1978. The assessment of "No Opinion" in attitude surveys. In *Sociological Methodology 1979* (ed. K. F. Schuessler), pp. 241–275. San Francisco: Jossey-Bass.

Schuman, H., and S. Presser. 1979. The open and closed question. *American Sociological Review* 44:692–712.

Schwartz, H., and J. Jacobs. 1979. *Qualitative Methodology: A Method to the Madness.* New York: Free Press.

Schwartz, R. D., and J. C. Miller. 1964. Legal evolution and societal complexity. *American Journal of Sociology* 70:159–169.

Sedgely, J., and D. Lund. 1979. Self reported beatings and subsequent tolerance for violence. *Review of Public Data Use* 7:30–38.

Seider, M. S. 1974. American big business ideology: A content analysis of executive speeches. *American Sociological Review* 39:802–815.

Selltiz, C., L. S. Wrightsman, and S. W. Cook. 1976. *Research Methods in Social Relations*, 3rd Edition. New York: Holt, Rinehart and Winston.

Shaffir, W. B., R. A. Stebbins, and A. Turowetz, eds. 1980. *Fieldwork Experience: Qualitative Approaches to Social Research.* New York: St. Martin's.

Shapiro, A. K. 1960. A contribution to a history of the placebo effect. *Behavioral Science* 5:109–135.

Shosteck, H., and W. R. Fairweather. 1979. Physician response rates to mail and personal interview surveys. *Public Opinion Quarterly* 43:206–217.

Shotland, R. L., and C. A. Stebbins. 1983. Emergency and cost as determinants of helping behavior and the slow accumulation of social psychological knowledge. *Social Psychology Quarterly* 46:36–46.

Shryock, H., J. S. Siegel, and Associates. 1976. *The Methods and Materials of Demography*, Condensed Edition (ed. E. G. Stockwell). New York: Academic Press.

Sigall, H., E. Aronson, and T. Van Hoose. 1970. The cooperative subject: Myth or reality. *Journal of Personality and Social Psychology* 6:1–10.

Sigall, H., and N. Ostrove. 1975. Beautiful but dangerous: Effects of offender attractiveness and nature of the crime on juridic judgment. *Journal of Personality and Social Psychology* 31:410–414.

Silverman, I. 1968. Role-related behavior of subjects in laboratory studies of attitude change. *Journal of Personality and Social Psychology* 4:343–348.

Simon, J. L. 1978. *Basic Research Methods in Social Science: The Art of Empirical Investigation*, 2nd Edition. New York: Random House.

Singer, E. 1978. Informed consent: Consequences for response rate and response quality in social surveys. *American Sociological Review* 43:144–162.

Singleton, R., Jr., and J. B. Christiansen. 1977. The construct validation of a short-form attitudes towards feminism scale. *Sociology and Social Research* 61:294–303.

Skinner, B. F. 1953. *Science and Human Behavior.* Toronto: Macmillan.

Slonim, M. J. 1957. Sampling in a nutshell. *Journal of the American Statistical Association* 152:143–161.

Slonim, M. J. 1960. *Sampling in a Nutshell.* New York: Simon and Schuster.

Smith, E. R., M. M. Ferree, and F. D. Miller. 1975. A short scale of attitudes toward feminism. *Representative Research in Social Psychology* 6:51–56.

Smith, H. W. 1975. *Strategies of Social Research: The Methodological Imagination.* Englewood Cliffs, N. J.: Prentice-Hall.

Smith, S. S., and D. Richardson. 1983. Amelioration of deception and harm in psychological research: The important role of debriefing. *Journal of Personality and Social Psychology* 44:1075–1082.

Smith-Lovin, L., and A. R. Tickamyer. 1978. Nonrecursive models of labor force participation, fertility behavior, and sex role attitudes. *American Sociological Review* 43:541–557.

Sonquist, J. A., and W. C. Dunkelberg. 1977. *Survey and Opinion Research: Procedures for Processing and Analysis.* Englewood Cliffs, N. J.: Prentice-Hall.

Sorokin, P. A. 1950. *Altruistic Love: A Study of American "Good Neighbors" and Christian Saints.* Boston: Beacon Press.

Spradley, J. P., and B. J. Mann. 1975. *The Cocktail Waitress: Woman's Work in a Man's World.* New York: Wiley.

Stannard, D. E. 1977. *The Puritan Way of Death: A Study in Religion, Culture, and Social Change.* New York: Oxford University.

Stephan, F., Jr., and P. J. McCarthy. 1958. *Sampling Opinions: An Analysis of Survey Procedure.* New York: Wiley.

Stevens, S. S. 1951. Mathematics, measurement, and psychophysics. In *Handbook of Experimental Psychology* (ed. S. S. Stevens), pp. 1–49. New York: Wiley.

Stinchcombe, A. L. 1968. *Constructing Social Theories.* New York: Harcourt, Brace and World.

Stouffer, S. 1966. *Communism, Conformity, and Civil Liberties.* New York: Wiley.

Straits, B. C. 1967. Resume of the Chicago study of smoking behavior. In *Studies and Issues in Smoking Behavior* (ed. S. V. Zagona), pp. 73–78. Tuscon, Ariz.: University of Arizona.

Straits, B. C. 1985. Factors influencing college women's responses to fertility decision-making vignettes. *Journal of Marriage and the Family* 47:585–596.

Straits, B. C., and P. L. Wuebben. 1973. College students' reactions to social scientific experimentation. *Sociological Methods and Research* 1:355–386.

Straits, B. C., P. L. Wuebben, and A. J. Crowle. 1982. Confession of prior knowledge about experimental procedures as a function of evaluation apprehension and commitment. *Social Science Research* 11:227–244.

Straits, B. C., P. L. Wuebben, and T. J. Majka. 1972. Influences on subjects' perceptions of experimental research situations. *Sociometry* 35:499–518.

Sudman, S. 1976. *Applied Sampling.* New York: Academic Press.

Sudman, S., and N. S. Bradburn. 1974. *Response Effects in Surveys: A Review and Synthesis.* Chicago: Aldine.

Sudman, S., and N. S. Bradburn. 1982. *Asking Questions: A Practical Guide to Questionnaire Design.* San Francisco: Jossey-Bass.

Survey Research Center. 1976. *Interviewer's Manual*, Revised Edition. Ann Arbor, Mich.: Institute for Social Research.

Swigert, V. L.; and R. A. Farrell. 1977. Normal homicides and the law. *American Sociological Review* 42:16–32.

Taeuber, R. C., and R. C. Rockwell. 1982. National social data series: A compendium of brief descriptions. *Review of Public Data Use* 10:23–111.

Tannenbaum, J., and A. N. Rowan. 1985. Rethinking the morality of animal research. *Hastings Center Reports* 15(October):32–43.

Taylor, D. G. 1983. Analyzing qualitative data. In *Handbook of Survey Research* (eds. P. H. Rossi, J. D. Wright, and A. B. Anderson), pp. 547–612. New York: Academic Press.

Taylor, D. G., P. B. Sheatsley, and A. Greeley. 1978. Attitudes toward racial integration. *Scientific American* 238:42–49.

Taylor, S. J., and R. Bogdan. 1984. *Introduction to Qualitative Research Methods: The Search for Meanings*, 2nd Edition. New York: Wiley.

Thomas, W. I., and F. Znaniecki. 1918. *The Polish Peasant in Europe and America*. Boston: Gorham Press.

Timberlake, M., and K. R. Williams. 1984. Dependence, political exclusion, and government repression: Some cross-national evidence. *American Sociological Review* 49:141–146.

Titmuss, R. M. 1971. *The Gift Relationship: From Human Blood to Social Policy*. New York: Random House.

Tittle, C. R. 1980. *Sanctions and Social Deviance: The Question of Deterrence*. New York: Praeger.

Tufte, E. R. 1974. *Data Analysis for Politics and Policy*. Englewood Cliffs, N. J.: Prentice-Hall.

Tukey, J. W. 1977. *Exploratory Data Analysis*. Reading, Mass.: Addison-Wesley.

United States Department of Health, Education and Welfare (USDHEW). 1973. *Plan and Operation of the Health and Nutrition Examination Survey, United States, 1971–73*. *Vital and Health Statistics*. Series 1, Nos. 10a and 10b. DHEW Publ. No. (HSM) 73-1310. Washington, D.C.: U. S. Government Printing Office.

United States Department of Labor. 1978. *Years for Decision Volume 4*. Manpower Administration, R and D Monograph 24. Washington, D.C.: U. S. Government Printing Office.

Useem, B. 1980. Solidarity model, breakdown model, and the Boston anti-busing movement. *American Sociological Review* 45:357–369.

Vaughan, T. R. 1967. Governmental intervention in social research: Political and ethical dimensions in the Wichita jury recordings. In *Ethics, Politics, and Social Research* (ed. G. Sjoberg), pp. 50–77. Cambridge, Mass.: Schenkman.

Valentine, B. 1978. *Hustling and Other Hard Work: Life Styles in the Ghetto*. New York: Free Press.

Van Dusen, R. A., and N. Zill, eds. 1975. *Basic Background Items for U.S. Household Surveys*. Washington, D.C.: Social Science Research Council.

Vidich, A. J., and J. Bensman. 1958. *Small Town in Mass Society*. Princeton, N.J.: Princeton University.

Wade, N. 1976. IQ and heredity: Suspicion of fraud beclouds classic experiment. *Science* 194:916–919.

Waite, L. J., and R. M. Stolzenberg. 1976. Intended childbearing and labor force participation of young women: Insights from nonrecursive models. *American Sociological Review* 41:235–252.

Wallace, W. L. 1971. *The Logic of Science in Sociology*. Chicago: Aldine-Atherton.

Wallis, W. A., and H. V. Roberts. 1956. *Statistics: A New Approach*. New York: Free Press.

Warden, G. B. 1976. Inequality and instability in eighteenth-century Boston: A reappraisal. *Journal of Interdisciplinary History* 6:585–620.

Warwick, D. P., and C. A. Lininger. 1975. *The Sample Survey: Theory and Practice*. New York: McGraw-Hill.

Wasserman, I. M. 1984. Imitation and suicide: A reexamination of the Werther effect. *American Sociological Review* 49:427–436.

Wax, R. H. 1971. *Doing Fieldwork: Warnings and Advice*. Chicago: University of Chicago.

Webb, E. J., D. T. Campbell, R. D. Schwartz, and L. Sechrest. 1966. *Unobtrusive Measures: Nonreactive Research in the Social Sciences*. Chicago: Rand McNally.

Webb, E. J., D. T. Campbell, R. D. Schwartz, L. Sechrest, and J. B. Grove. 1981. *Nonreactive Measures in the Social Sciences*, 2nd Edition. Boston: Houghton-Mifflin.

Weber, R. P. 1985. *Basic Content Analysis*. Beverly Hills, Calif.: Sage.

Weber, S. J., and T. D. Cook. 1972. Subject effects in laboratory research: An examination of subject roles, demand characteristics, and valid inference. *Psychological Bulletin* 77:273–295.

Webster, F. E., Jr., and F. von Pechmann. 1970. A replication of the "shopping list" study. *Journal of Marketing* 34:61–63.

Weick, K. E. 1968. Systematic observational methods. In *The Handbook of Social Psychology*, 2nd Edition, Vol. 2 (eds. G. Lindzey and E. Aronson), pp. 357–451. Reading, Mass.: Addison-Wesley.

Weimann, G. 1982. On the importance of marginality: One more step into the two-step flow of communication. *American Sociological Review* 47:764–773.

Weinberg, M., and C. J. Williams. 1972. Fieldwork among deviants: Social relations with subjects and others. In *Research on Deviance* (ed. J. D. Douglas), pp. 165–186. New York: Random House.

Weiss, R. S. 1966. Alternative approaches in the study of complex situations. *Human Organization* 25:198–206.

West, S. G., S. P. Gunn, and P. Chernicky. 1975. Ubiquitous Watergate: An attributional analysis. *Journal of Personality and Social Psychology* 32:55–65.

Westoff, C. F., and N. B. Ryder. 1977. *The Contraceptive Revolution*. Princeton, N. J.: Princeton University.

Wheelwright, P. 1962. *Valid Thinking: An Introduction to Logic*. New York: Odyssey.

Whyte, W. F. 1958. Editorial. Freedom and responsibility in research: The "Springdale" case. *Human Organization* 17(Summer):1–2.

Whyte, W. F. 1981. *Street Corner Society: The Social Structure of an Italian Slum*, 3rd Edition, Revised and Enlarged. Chicago: University of Chicago.

Winston, S. 1932. Birth control and the sex-ratio at birth. *American Journal of Sociology* 38:225–231.

Wiseman, J. P. 1979. Close encounters of the quasi-primary kind: Sociability in urban second-hand clothing stores. *Urban Life* 8:23–51.

Wiseman, J. P., and M. S. Aron. 1970. *Field Projects for Sociology Students*. Cambridge, Mass.: Schenkman.

Zanes, A., and E. Matsoukas. 1979. Different settings, different results? A comparison of school and home responses. *Public Opinion Quarterly* 43:550–557.

Zeisel, H. 1968. *Say It with Figures*. New York: Harper and Row.

Zelditch, M., Jr. 1962. Some methodological problems of field studies. *American Journal of Sociology* 67:566–576.

Zeller, R. A., and E. G. Carmines. 1980. *Measurement in the Social Sciences: The Link between Theory and Data*. Cambridge/New York: Cambridge University.

Zelnick, M., and J. F. Kantner. 1978. Contraceptive patterns and premarital pregnancy among women aged 15–19 in 1976. *Family Planning Perspectives* 10:135–142.

Zimbardo, P. G. 1973. On the ethics of intervention in human psychological research: With special reference to the Stanford prison study. *Cognition* 2:243–256.

Zimbardo, P. G., C. Haney, W. C. Banks, and D. Jaffe. 1973. The mind is a formidable jailer: A pirandellian prison. *New York Times Magazine* 122(April 8):38–60.

Zito, G. V. 1975. *Methodology and Meanings: Varieties of Sociological Inquiry*. New York: Praeger.

Zoble, E. J., and R. S. Lehman. 1969. Interaction of subject-experimenter expectancy effects in a tone length discrimination task. *Behavioral Science* 14:357–363.

Zurcher, L. A. 1968. Social psychological functions of ephemeral roles: A disaster work crew. *Human Organization* 27:281–297.

Name Index

a = appendix
b = box
f = figure
n = note
t = table

Adair, J. G., 449, 451, 452
Alexander, C. S., 195
Allon, N., 297
American Heritage Dictionary of the English Language, The, 8
American Anthropological Association, 458–59b
American Psychological Association, 446, 452, 458–59b
American Sociological Association, 458–59b
Andrews, F. M., 237, 283b
Angell, R. C., 419–23
Archer, D., 333, 336, 337, 347, 349
Argyris, C., 188, 242
Armer, M., 128
Arnold, D. O., 305
Aron, M. S., 302
Aronson, E., 181, 182, 184, 185, 188, 190, 453
Asimov, I., 20b

Babbie, E., 148, 150
Bagby, J. M., 32
Bailey, K. D., 134, 340
Bainbridge, W. S., 330–31b
Ball, S., 193, 225
Banks, W. C., 446, 448
Barker, S. F., 53
Barrios, M. 333, 336, 337, 349
Barry, V. E., 51b
Bass, B. M., 287
Batten, T. F., 74
Baumgartner, R., 248, 260

Baumrind, D., 452, 456
Becker, H. J., 195
Becker, H. S., 297, 302, 461
Becker, S., 332–33
Beckner, M., 23
Benedict, R., 308b
Bensman, J., 455
Berelson, B., 196, 238, 372
Berglund, E., 219
Berk, R. A., 413n, 426, 443n
Bernstein, D. A., 219
Bernstein, I. N., 227
Beveridge, W. I. B., 30b
Bianchi, S., 102
Bielby, W. T., 375n
Bigus, O. E., 297
Bishop, Y. M. N., 443n
Blalock, H. M., Jr., 79, 151
Blau, P. M., 237
Bless, E., 191, 369, 371
Blumberg, A. E., 51b
Boas, F., 308b
Bogatz, G. A., 193, 225
Bogdan, R., 296, 302, 307, 309, 311, 312–13, 316, 320
Bohrnstedt, G. W., 227, 413n
Borgatta, E. F., 227
Boydstun, J. E., 196, 225
Boyer, P., 346
Bradburn, N. S., 129n, 254, 266, 274, 275, 278, 280, 285, 286, 295n
Bray, R. M., 219–21
Brazziel, W. F., 463
Brim, O. G., Jr., 453–54
Bromley, S., 113
Bromley, D. G., 297
Browne, J., 297, 314, 315, 316
Brownlee, K. A., 82
Bruner, E. M., 351–52b
Bruyn, S. T., 296
Bryan, J. H., 192

Bryson, M. C., 133*b*
Burke, P. J., 443*n*
Burstein, P., 334–35, 336, 353, 475
Burt, C., 33, 189, 445
Bushman, R. L., 333–34
Byrne, D., 102

Callero, P. L., 193
Campbell, D. T., 112, 113, 154, 191, 217,
    221–25*b*, 225, 226, 231*n*, 232*n*, 271, 338,
    339, 340, 361–62
Cannell, C. F., 259, 266, 276, 282, 285, 286
Card, J. J., 239
Carlsmith, J. M., 181, 182, 184, 185, 190,
    453
Carmines, E. G., 122
Carnap, R., 32
Carter, R. E., Jr., 155
Cartwright, D. S., 273
Caspi, A., 86
Cavan, S., 316
Ceci, S. J., 456, 457
Chambliss, W. J., 346, 347
Charmaz, K., 318
Chein, I., 153, 155, 168*n*
Chernicky, P., 466
Christiansen, J. B., 122–23*b*
Cialdini, R. B., 193, 194–95*b*, 450
Cleveland, W. S., 395*b*
Clogg, C. C., 366, 367
Clore, G. L., 219–21
Code of Federal Regulations, 449
Cohen, J., 443*n*
Cohen, P, 443*n*
Colasanto, D., 102
Coleman, J. S., 85, 239, 283*b*, 373
Collins, M. E., 231
Conner, R. F., 193
Cook, F. L., 218, 226, 228
Cook, K. H., 31, 479
Cook, S. W., 31
Cook, T. D., 154, 189, 191, 193, 218, 226,
    228, 232
Copi, I. M., 42, 46
Cottrell, N. B., 49
Cournand, A., 444
Crain, R. L., 234, 235
Cramer, J. C., 415
Crandall, R., 445, 446, 447, 448, 449, 454,
    463
Crockett, H. J., 238
Crosby, F., 113
Crouch, W. W., 31, 479
Crowle, A. J., 434–35

Dane, F. C., 230
Danziger, S. K., 297
Darley, J. M., 178–79, 180–81*b*, 181–85,
    194*b*, 447, 450, 451
Davis, F., 297, 307
Davis, J. A., 99, 111, 124, 235, 242, 249–
    50*b*, 251, 271, 272, 274, 363, 379, 401,
    443*n*
Dawes, R. M., 367
DeMaio, T. J., 286
Denney, R., 69
Deutsch, M., 231
Dickson, W. J., 30*b*
Diener, E., 445, 446, 447, 448, 449, 454, 463
Dillman, D. A., 244, 246, 247, 255*b*, 259
Doherty, M. E., 20, 32
Domhoff, W. G., 297
Doob, A. N., 100–101, 104, 200, 420
Dorfman, D. D., 33
Dornbusch, S. M., 70, 105, 116
Duncan, B., 443*n*
Duncan, O. D., 375*n*, 443*n*
Dunkelberg, W. C., 385, 387, 412*n*
Durkheim, E., 55–58, 64*n*, 68, 71, 84, 106,
    327–28
Dushenko, T. W., 449, 451, 452

Edson, L., 463
Eisinger, R. A., 219
Eleey, M. F., 380–81, 388, 403, 416, 420–
    21*b*
Ellsworth, P. C., 453
Emerson, R. M., 296, 317
Erikson, K. T., 311, 317, 328, 335, 338, 343,
    345–47, 358*n*, 450–51
Etkowitz, H., 86
Evans, D. E., 193
Evans, F. J., 186, 187
Evans, R. I., 85

Fairweather, W. R., 244, 263*n*
Farley, R., 102, 329, 336
Farrell, R. A., 332, 337, 338
Felson, M., 331, 336, 338
Ferree, M. M., 103–4*b*, 122*b*, 123*b*
Feshbach, N., 32
Feshbach S., 32
Festinger, L., 62, 176
Fienberg, S. E., 167*n*, 355, 443*n*
Filstead, W. J., 296
Fine, G. A., 297, 313
Fode, K. L., 189

Forsyth, D. R., 456–57
Fox, J., 443n
Freedman, J. L., 191, 369, 371
Freedman, R., 196
Freeman, H. E., 227
Fremouw, W. J., 444
Friend, K. E., 342
Frisbie, W. P., 336

Galle, O. R., 95
Gans, H., 297
Gaudet, H., 238, 372
Geer, B., 297, 302, 307
Gerbner, G., 380–81, 388–90, 397, 399, 403, 416, 418, 420–21b
Glaser, B. G., 306, 317–18
Glassner, B., 313
Glazer, M., 312
Glazer, N., 69
Glenn, N. D., 334, 336, 353–55
Glock, C. Y., 121
Goffman, E., 333, 347
Gold, D., 226, 389
Gold, R. L., 300, 311, 312
Goldberg, P. A., 200
Goldberger, A. S., 375n
Golden, M. P., 200
Goodman, L. A., 443n
Gorden, R. L., 313
Gordon, R. A., 273
Gottschalk, L., 343
Gove, W. R., 95
Gray, D. J., 460
Greeley, A., 364, 365
Griswold, W., 348, 349, 350
Gross, A. E., 100–101, 104, 200
Gross, L., 380–81, 388–90, 397, 399, 403, 416, 418, 420–21b
Grove, J. B., 338, 339, 340, 361–62
Groves, R. M., 245, 246, 247
Gunn, S. P., 466
Gurwitsch, A., 37
Guttman, L., 366

Hochbaum, G. M., 219
Hagedorn, R. 82
Haire, M., 271
Hakim, C., 358n
Hall, C. S., 26
Hallinan, M. T., 86
Haney, C., 446, 448
Hansen, C., 347

Hatchett, S., 102
Hauser, R. M., 375n
Heberlein, T. A., 248, 260
Heer, D. M., 344–45
Heilman, S. C., 307
Hempel, C. G., 23, 25, 59b, 62, 86
Henderson, M. R., 297
Hendrix, L., 335, 336, 339
Henkel, R. E., 226, 389
Henretta, J. A., 343
Hickman, L. C., 70, 105, 116
Higbee, K. L., 176
Hirsch, P. M., 397
Hirschi, T., 84
Holland, P. W., 443n
Hollingshead, A. B., 364
Holloway, M., 330b
Holsti, O. R., 348, 349, 350
Horowitz, I. L., 462, 463
Howell, J. T., 313–14
Huck, S. W., 82–83b
Hughes, E. C., 297, 308b
Hughes, M., 403, 420–21b
Hume, D., 79
Hummon, D. H., 153
Humphreys, L., 312, 450, 454
Hyman, H. H., 84, 234, 335, 336, 337, 355

Inkeles, A., 234
Iritani, B., 333, 336, 337, 349
ISR Newsletter, 252
Isen, A. M., 10, 192
Itkin, S.M., 219–21

Jackson-Beeck, M., 380–81, 388, 397, 403, 416, 418, 420–21b
Jacob, H., 344
Jacobs, J., 296, 320, 332, 339, 340
Jacobson, A. L., 369
Jaffe, D., 446, 448
Jeffries-Fox, S., 380–81, 388, 397, 403, 416, 418, 420–21b
Jensen, A. R., 463
Johnson, R. C., 330b
Jöreskog, K. G., 375n
Jorgenson, D. O., 337
Junker, B. H., 311, 312

Kahn, R. L., 245, 246, 266, 276, 282, 285, 286
Kalton, G., 247, 254
Kanter, R. M., 297

Kaplan, C. P., 329, 358n, 455
Karp, D. A., 297
Karweit, N., 412n
Kasarda, J. D., 339
Katz, D., 133b
Katz, E., 234, 235, 372, 373
Katzer, J., 31, 479
Kelman, H. C., 453
Kelso, J. P., 351–52b
Kemeny, J. G., 28, 50, 63n, 64n
Kenny, D. A., 389
Kephart, W. M., 330b
Kerlinger, F. N., 79, 85, 86, 129n
Keyfitz, N., 364
Kidder, L. H., 271
Kiecolt, J., 166
Kiecolt, K. J., 339
Kiesler, C. A., 19n
Kimes, D. D., 333, 336, 337, 349
Kirkpatrick, C., 103b
Kish, L., 72, 73, 137, 147, 159
Knoke, D., 413n, 443n
Komarovsky, M., 236
Kotarba, J. A., 297, 313
Kroeber, A., 308b
Kuhn, T. S., 36

Labov, W., 310
Labovitz, S., 82
Lalu, N. M., 369
Latané, B., 178–79, 180–81b, 181–85, 194b, 447, 450, 451
Laurent, A., 259
Lazarsfeld, P. F., 238, 372, 417
Lee, G. R., 339
Lehman, R. S., 189
Leik, R. K., 75
Lever, J., 305
Levin, P. F., 10, 192
Lichtenstein, E., 219
Liebert, R. M., 81, 193
Likert, R., 104b
Lincoln, J. R., 135
Lindsay, R. C. L., 449, 451, 452
Lindzey, G., 26
Lininger, C. A., 254
Lipset, S. M., 239, 283b
Lofland, J., 296, 303, 307, 311, 313
Lofland, L. H., 300–301, 303, 307, 311, 313, 314, 315, 317
Loomis, W. F., 27
Luker, K., 236, 242

Lund, D., 341, 435–36
Lundberg, G. A., 460

Macdonald, G. E., 420
Majka, T. J., 453
Malinowski, B., 308b
Manheim, H. L., 48
Mann, B. J., 319–20
Marcoux, M., 302
Mark, M. M., 218, 226, 228
Marquis, K. H., 259
Mason, W. M., 355
Matsoukas, E., 256
Mazur, A., 17
McCain, G., 24, 28
McCall, G. J., 296, 299, 300, 302, 311
McCarthy, P. J., 130, 154
McGuigan, F. J., 87, 231
McGuire, M. B., 297, 321–22
McKinney, J. C., 314
McPherson, J. M., 95
Mead, M., 308b
Melbin, M., 306
Menzel, H., 373
Merton, R. K., 30b
Meyers, E. D., Jr., 412n
Midlarsky, E., 8
Milgram, S., 447, 448
Miller, F. D., 103–4b, 122b, 123b
Miller, J. C., 375
Mills, J., 453
Moelter, N. P., 196, 225
Morgan, M., 397, 416, 420–21b
Morris, J. N., 82–83b
Morrison, D. E., 226, 389
Mosteller, F., 359b
Murdock, G. P., 335
Murphy, P., 219–21
Myers, D. G., 194b

Nagel, E., 33, 34
Namenwirth, J. Z., 348, 349, 350
Nathan, L. E., 339
Navazio, R., 196
Neale, J. M., 81
Nettler, G., 22
Newcomb, T., 68
Nida, S. 181b
Nissenbaum, S., 346
Nunn, C. Z., 238
Nunnally, J. C., Jr., 119

Oakes, W., 176
Oppenheim, P., 86
Orne, M. T., 186, 187, 190
Osgood, C. E., 294*n*
Ostrove, N., 216*b*, 230

Padgett, V. R., 337
Page, E. B., 172–73, 175–76, 183, 185, 191, 209
Park, R., 68, 308*b*, 314, 325*n*
Pearson, W., Jr., 335, 336, 339
Pechmann, F. von, 271
Peters, D., 456, 457
Phillips, D. L., 254, 286–87
Phillips, D. P., 5, 94
Pierce, A., 106
Piliavin, I. M., 192
Piliavin, J. A., 192, 193
Pindyck, R. S., 429, 443*n*
Plotkin, J., 456, 457
Presser, S., 268–70*b*, 294*n*
Preston, S. H., 68
Proxmire, W., 19–20*b*

RAND Corporation, 140
Reed, J. S., 234
Reese, H. W., 444
Reiss, A. J., Jr., 301–2, 304
Reynolds, P. D., 22, 24, 26
Ribicoff, A., 221*b*
Richardson, D., 453
Riesman, D., 69
Riley, M. W., 342
Riverside California *Press-Enterprise*, 4
Roberts, H. V., 81, 152
Robinson, J. P., 374
Robinson, W. S., 71
Rockwell, R. C., 339
Roethlisberger, F. J., 30*b*
Rokeach, M., 122
Rosenberg, M. J., 187–88, 190–91
Rosenberg, M., 120, 121, 414
Rosenthal, D. B., 234, 235
Rosenthal, R., 176, 189, 190
Rosnow, R. L., 176
Ross, H. L., 216*b*, 221–25*b*, 225, 231
Rossi, P. H., 225, 227
Roth, J., 307
Rowan, A. N., 446
Rubin, Z., 68, 104, 121–22, 128
Rubinfeld, D. L., 429, 443*n*
Ruebhausen, O. M., 453–54

Runkle, G., 55, 63
Ryder, N. B., 134, 234

Sales, S. M., 328–29, 332, 336, 337, 342, 347, 348, 349
Salmon, W. C., 40, 44, 45, 46, 47, 53, 59, 64*n*
Sanders, W. B., 299
Sandler, H. M., 82–83*b*
Sawyer, D. O., 366, 367
Saxe, L., 113
Schlenker, B. R., 456–57
Schnaiberg, A, 128
Schroeder, D. A., 193, 195*b*, 450
Schuman, H., 102, 247, 254, 268–70*b*, 294*n*
Schuneman, R. S., 155
Schwartz, H., 296, 320
Schwartz, J. L., 219
Schwartz, R. D., 112, 113, 338, 339, 340, 361–62, 375
Sechrest, L., 112, 113, 338, 339, 340, 361–62
Sedgely, J., 341, 435–36
Segal, E. M., 24, 28
Seider, M. S., 348
Selltiz, C., 31
Selvin, H. C., 84
Shaffir, W. B., 296, 303
Shapiro, A. K., 33
Sheatsley, P. B., 364, 365
Shemberg, K. M., 20, 32
Sherry, M. E., 196, 225
Short, J. F., Jr., 273
Shosteck, H., 244, 263*n*
Shotland, R. L., 192
Shryock, H., 341, 358*n*
Shupe, A. D., Jr., 297
Siegel, J. S., 341, 358*n*
Sigall, H., 188, 216*b*, 230
Signorielli, N., 380–81, 388, 397, 403, 416, 418, 420–21*b*
Silverman, I., 187
Simmons, J. L., 296, 302, 311
Simon, J. L., 108
Singer, E., 449
Singleton, R., Jr., 122–23*b*
Skinner, B. F., 27
Slonim, M. J., 168*n*
Smith, D. H., 234
Smith, E. R., 103–4*b*, 122*b*, 123*b*
Smith, H. W., 74
Smith, S. S., 453
Smith, T. W., 245, 271, 272, 274, 363, 367, 379, 387

Smith-Lovin, L., 415
Sonquist, J. A., 385, 387, 412n
Sorbom, D., 375n
Sorenson, A. B., 86
Sorokin, P. A., 13
Spradley, J. P., 319–20
Stanley, J. C., 217, 231n, 232n
Stannard, D. E., 334
Stark, R., 121
Stebbins, C. A., 192
Stebbins, R. A., 296, 303
Stephan, F., Jr., 130, 154
Stevens, S. S., 108
Stinchcombe, A. L., 56, 57
Stolzenberg, R. M., 414–15
Stouffer, S., 238
Straits, B. C., 188, 195–96, 219, 295n, 382–83b, 434–35, 453, 475
Strauss, A. L., 297, 306, 317–318
Strodtbeck, F. L., 273
Suci, C. J., 294n
Sudman, S., 129n, 132, 134, 151, 155, 156, 160, 161, 254, 266, 274, 275, 278, 280, 285, 286, 295n
Survey Research Center, 148–49b, 256
Swigert, V. L., 332, 337, 338

Taeuber, R. C., 339
Tannenbaum, J., 446
Tannebaum, P. H., 294n
Taylor, D. G., 364, 365, 442a
Taylor, S. J., 296, 302, 307, 309, 311, 312–13, 320
Test, M. A., 192
Thomas, W. I., 308b, 325n, 331–32, 339
Tickamyer, A. R., 415
Timberlake, M., 86
Titmuss, R. M., 11
Tittle, C. R., 156
Treiman, D. J., 364, 365
Troldahl, V. C., 155
Trow, M., 239, 283b
Tufte, E. R., 443n
Tukey, J. W., 395b
Turowetz, A., 296, 303

United States Department of Health, Education and Welfare, 234
United States Department of Labor, 288b
Useem, B., 134, 135

Valentine, B., 298, 456
Van Valey, T. L., 329, 358n, 455

Van Hoose, T., 188
Vaughan, T. R., 454
Van Dusen, R. A., 275
Vidich, A. J., 455

Wade, N., 33
Waite, L. J., 414–15
Wallace, D. L., 359n
Wallace, W. L., 36
Wallington, S. A., 191, 369, 371
Wallis, W. A., 81, 152
Warden, G. B., 343, 344
Warwick, D. P., 254
Washington, B. T., 325n
Wasserman, I. M., 85
Wax, R. H., 308b
Webb, E. J., 112, 113, 338, 339, 340, 361–62
Weber, R. P., 348, 349, 350, 352, 359n
Weber, S. J., 189, 191
Webster, F. E., Jr., 271
Weick, K. E., 298, 300
Weimann, G., 374
Weinberg, M., 310
Weiss, R. S., 298
Wells, M. G., 176
West, S. G., 466
Westoff, C. F., 134, 234
Wheelwright, P., 41, 43
White, D. R., 335
Whyte, W. F., 309–10, 448, 455
Williams, C. J., 310
Williams, J. A., Jr., 238
Williams, K. R., 86
Winston, S., 328, 336, 338
Wise, L. L., 239
Wiseman, J. P., 297, 302
Withey, S. B., 237, 283b
Wright, C. R., 234
Wright, S. R., 227
Wrightsman, L. S., 31
Wuebben, P. L., 188, 434–35, 453

Zanes, A., 256
Zeisel, H., 284–85, 295n, 413n
Zeitz, G. 135
Zelditch, M., Jr., 317
Zeller, R. A., 122
Zill, N., 275
Zimbardo, P. G., 446, 448
Zimmerman, D. H., 304
Zito, G. V., 21
Znaniecki, F., 308b, 331–32, 339
Zoble, E. J., 189
Zurcher, L. A., 12, 298

Subject Index

Abortion, measurement of attitudes toward, 363, 366–67

Abridged Compendium of American Genealogy, 328

Abstract, of research report, 474–75, 478

Acceptable incompetent, researcher as, 313

Accidental sampling, 153

Accounting schemes, 284–85, 295*n*

Acquiescence response set, 113, 287

Adjusted R², 426

Affirming the antecedent, 46–47, 49

Affirming the consequent, 47, 56

Age effect, 353–55

Aggregate data
defined, 70
ecological fallacy and, 71
use of, 70

Aggregation. *See* Aggregate data

Alcoholic beverages, cohort analysis of, 353–55, 354*t*

Alternate-forms procedure for assessing reliability, 115

Alternative hypotheses, elimination of, 56–57, 218–21, 221–25*b*, 374, 417

Altruism research, 8–13
available data, 13
experiment, 10
field research, 12
survey, 11
Titmuss's survey of motives for, 11

American Anthropological Association (AAA), 458–59*b*

American Demographics, 339

American novels, Griswold's study of, 348, 349, 350–52

American Psychological Association (APA), 452, 458–59*b*

American Sociological Association (ASA), 458–59*b*

Anonymity, of respondents and subjects, 455–56

Antecedent, definition of, 42

Antecedent variable, 418

Antibusing movement, Useem's study of, 134, 135

"Anxious subject," 187–88, 434–35

Archival records, 105, 326–35

Argument, 42–48
chain argument, 47
definition, 42
invalid forms of, 47–48
justification of, 44
premise of, 42
syllogism, 42–43
valid forms of, 46–47

Arrow diagrams. *See* Causal ordering

Artifacts and nonverbal evidence as data sources, 333–34

Association, statistical, 75–80, 397–408

Attitude measurement, 101–2, 270–71, 272–74, 363–67

Attribute. *See* Categories

Available data analysis and interpretation, 345–55
cohort analysis, 353–55
content analysis, 347–53
historical interpretation, 345–47
indirect measures, 342
limited or inadequate data, 340–41
measurement issues, 340–45
reliability and validity, 342–45
research advantages, 335–38

Available data sources, 12–13, 326–35
access, 338–40
data archives, 334–35
mass media, 332–33
physical, nonverbal evidence, 333–34
private documents, 331–32
public documents and official records, 326–31
sampling, 339–40

"Bad subject," 188–89
Barometer states in election forecasts, 154
Basic unit of logical analysis. *See* Syllogism
Bell-shaped curve, 394
Bias. *See also* Experimenter effects; Response
  bias tendencies; Social nature of experiments; Systematic measurement error
  controlling for, 287–88
  emotionally loaded words, 280
  in face-to-face interviews, 245
  introduced by interviewer, 245
  leading questions, 280
  response bias, 286–88
  response effect, 254
Bias in sampling, 130, 162–63
  cases omitted from sampling frame, 136,
    162
  in draft lotteries, 167–68*n*
  interviewer, in quota sampling, 155
  investigator, 137, 152, 154, 155
  in nonprobability sampling, 152–55
  nonresponse, 133*b*, 162–63
  sample bias from selective deposit, 339
  in systematic sampling, 151–52
  in telephone surveys, 246
Bivariate analysis, 397–408
  bivariate percentage distribution, 398–99
  purpose of, 397
  regression, 406–8
  relationship between interval/ratio scale
    variables, 405–8
  relationship between nominal/ordinal and
    interval/ratio variables, 403–4
  relationship between nominal variables,
    397–401
  relationship between two ordinal variables,
    401–3
Box-and-whisker plot, 395–96*b*
Box-plot, 395–96*b*
Boyle's law, 22–26
Brady's Bar, Spradley and Mann's study of,
  319–20
Breakdown in random assignment of subjects,
  226
Brown *v.* Board of Education of Topeka, 462
b-values. *See* Partial regression coefficients
Bystander intervention in emergencies, Latané
  and Darley's study of, 178–79, 180–81*b*,
  447, 450, 451

Capital punishment as deterrent, Phillips's
  study of, 5
Career choices of college men, Davis's study
  of, 235, 242

Cases. *See* Units of analysis
Categorical proposition, 41–42
Categories, 72–74
  collapsing categories, 381, 382–83*b*, 384,
    390, 403
  number of and sample size, 161–62
Causal hypotheses, testing of, 79–85, 172–74,
  240, 414–17
Causal inference, requirements of. *See*
  Causality, evidence for
Causal ordering, 415–17
  noncausal association, 415
  reciprocal causation, 414–15
Causal relationships, 26–27. *See also* Variables, dependent; Variables, independent
  criteria to establish, 79–81
  direction of influence, 80–81
  Hume's analysis of cause, 79
  implied by "if-then" statement, 86
  intervening mechanisms and theory develop-
    ment, 84–85
  nature of, 79–81
  nonspuriousness, 81–84, 82–83*b*
  spurious relationship, defined, 81
  statistical association, 75–76, 79–80
Causality, evidence for, 172–74
  association, 173
  direction of influence, 173
  elimination of rival explanations, 173
CBS-*New York Times* Poll, 275
Cell frequencies, 398, 400, 430–32
Cell size in factorial experimental design, 213
Census data
  collection and uses of, 329–31
  confidentiality, 329
  manuscript census, 329, 330–31*b*
  Public Use Microdata Sample, 329
Census of Manufacturers, 331, 336
Central tendency, measures of, 392
  mean, 392
  median, 392
  mode, 392
Chain argument, 47
Chance processes, 211, 389. *See also statisti-
  cal tests of significance*
Chicago School, 308*b*
Chi-square test
  for independence, 400–401
  in log-linear modeling, 432–33, 443*n*
Cigarette papers and marijuana use, Felson's
  study of, 338
Civil rights and legislation, Farley's study of,
  329
Cleaning data, 386–388
  consistency checking, 387

contingency questions, 387
  defined, 386
  editing and cleaning of the General Social
    Survey, 387–88
  techniques for, 386–87, 390
  wild-code checking, 387
Closed-ended question
  advantages and disadvantages of, 266
  choice of, considerations in, 266–68
  coding of, 381
  defined, 265
  developing from pretests and open ques-
    tions, 266
  examples of, 265, 268*b*
  in mail surveys, 248
  respondents and, 266
Cluster sampling, 147–50
  cost efficiency of, 147–48, 161
  compared to other random methods, 150
  less precision of, 150, 161
  limited population lists and, 148
  multistage cluster sampling, 147, 148–49*b*,
    150
  sampling error and, 150
Codebook, 385
Codes, numerical, 381
Coding, 381–85
  categories, development of, 382–83*b*
  closed-ended questions, 381
  codebook, 385
  coding schemes, 384
  combining code categories, 381, 384
  in content analysis, 350
  defined, 381
  edge coding, 384
  in field research, 318–19
  numerical codes in, 381
  open-ended questions, 266, 381
  precoded forms, example of, 384
  precodes, 384
Coding categories, development of, 382–83*b*
Cohort analysis, 353–55
  defined, 353
  problems, 355
  three influences associated with time, 353
Cohort effect, 353, 354
Collinearity, 423–24
Column marginals, 398
Combining code categories, 381, 384
Comic strips as available data, 347–48
Comparative studies, 234
Complete observer, 311
Complete participant, 311
Compliance and guilt, Freedman et al.'s study
  of, 369–71

Composite measures, 99, 363–67
Computer file, 386
Computer terminal, 385–86
  interactive, 412*n*
Concepts, 98–100
  definition of, 8, 21
  empirical manifestations of, 98
  language and, 21–22
  measurement of, 98–100. *See also* Indica-
    tors; Operational definition; Variables
  operationalizing, 8–9
Conceptualization, 98
Concurrent validity, 119
Conditional proposition, 42
Confidence interval, 96*n*, 144
  related to standard error, 159
Confidentiality, research findings and, 455–56
Confirming hypotheses, logic of 56–57
Congressional Record, 339
Conjunctive proposition, 63*n*
Connecticut crackdown on speeding, Campbell
  and Ross's study of, 221–25*b*
Consequent, defined, 42
Consistency checking, 387
Constant, defined, 73
Construct validation, 120–22, 122–23*b*
  convergent validity, 121, 123*b*, 361
  correlations with theoretically related vari-
    ables, 121, 123*b*
  difference from criterion-related validation,
    120–21
  difference from subjective evaluation, 120
  discriminant validity, 121–22; 123*b*
  known groups validity, 122, 123*b*
Consumer attitudes, Haire's study of, 271
Consumer finances, University of Michigan
  survey of, 276–77
Content analysis, 347–53, 381
  applications, 348, 351–52*b*
  assignment of units to clearly defined
    categories, 348
  defining the recording units, 349
  procedures, 350–52
  quantification, 349–50
  as systematic observation, 348
Content validity, 118
Context units, 349
Contextual design in survey research, 239
Contingency question, 288, 288–89*b*, 387
Contingency table. *See* Cross-tabulation
Continuous statement, 87
Contraception decisions, Luker's study of,
  236, 242–43
Control
  control group, 34, 172

Control (*continued*)
  double-blind studies, 34–35
  for extraneous factors, 81, 82–83*b*, 418–19
  principle of, 33–35
  and randomization, 84
Control group, 34, 172
Control variable, 73
Convenience sampling, 153
Convergent validity, 121, 123*b*, 361
Correlation coefficient, Pearson product-
  moment, 78, 407
Cost-benefit analysis in research ethics, 447
Costs, and available data research, 337
Cottrell's evaluation apprehension theory of
  audience effect, logical statement of, 49–
  50
Cover letter, in interview surveys, 253–54,
  255*b*
Cover story, 181, 451
Covert participant observation, 454
  incompatibility with informed consent, 450–51
Covert research, 311–12
Crime statistics
  differing operational definitions of crime,
  344
  measurement error in, 344
  sources of, 344
Criminal-stereotype effect on adjudication,
  Swigert and Farrell's study of, 332, 338
Criterion-related validation, 119–120
  concurrent validity, 119
  difference from construct validation, 120–21
  predictive validity, 119
Cross-classification. *See* Cross-tabulation
Cross-cultural studies and existing data, 336
Cross-cultural surveys, 234
Cross-sectional survey, 237–38, 414
Cross-tabulation, 397–403
  defined, 397
  limitations of, 402–403
  reading percentage tables, 399
Cultivation theory, 420–21*b*
Cultural relativity, 461
Cumulative Book Index, 329
Current Population Survey (CPS), 132, 160,
  331
Curvilinear relationship, 78, 406

Data analysis, quantitative, 379–80
  anticipating alternative explanations, 380
  beginning of, 380
  defined, 379
Data analysis and theory formulation in field
  research, 317–20
  coding, 318–19
  data requirements, 317–18
  interplay of data collection and analysis,
  318–19
  theory development, 317–18, 320
Data archives, 275
  as resource for research, 334–35
  source listings, 275, 339
Data collection methods, 9–13
Data entry, 385–386
  computer file, 386
  computer terminal, 385–86
  data format, 386
  data record, 386
  fixed column format, 386
Data file, 386
Data format, 386
Data modification, reasons for, 388
Data processing, 381–88
  cleaning, 386–88
  coding, 381–85
  data entry, 385–86
  data modification, 388
  editing, 385
  essential steps in, 381
Data record, 386
Debriefing, 183–84, 448, 452–53
  caution against discussing experiment, 184
  explaining deception, 183
  relieving subjects' feelings, 183
Deception, 451–53. *See also* Cover story;
  Debriefing
  code of ethics and, 452
  debriefing after, 452–53
  experiments and, 451
  forms of, 451
  opposition to, 452
  rationale for, 451–52
Decision making, Katz and Lazarsfeld's study
  of, 372
Decision process, accounting schemes and,
  284–85
Deductive argument, validity of, 45–48
Deductive reasoning, 44–48
Demand characteristics, 186–87, 190–91
  consequences of, 187
  defined, 186–87
  detection of, 187
  and the "good subject," 187
  methods for minimizing the effects of, 190–
  91
Denying the antecedent, 47–48
Denying the consequent, 47
Department of Health and Human Services
  (DHHS), 457

Dependent variable, 72
  influenced by causal factor, 80
Descriptive statistics, definition of, 389
Descriptive studies, 90
Descriptive surveys, 236–37, 239
Deviance, societal and altruism, 13
Deviance in puritan New England, Erickson's
  study of, 328, 338–39, 345–46, 347
Difference statement, 87
Differential mortality, 205
Dimensional analyses of concepts, 98
Dimensional sampling, 305–6
Direct effects, 415–17
Direction of influence, 80–81, 414
  and permanance of variable, 414
  and time ordering, 173, 414
Directionality of relationships, 76–78
Direct observation, 104–5, 300–301
Direct question, 270
Direct relationship, 76–77
Disaster and work roles, Zurcher's field study
  of, 12
Disclosure of research purposes, 453
  and bias of subsequent results, 449–50
  and informed consent, 449
Disconfirming hypotheses, logic of, 57–58
Discovering hypotheses, 64*n*
Discriminability of scale items, assessment of,
  103–4*b*
Discriminatory attitudes and civil rights legis-
  lation, Burstein's study of, 334–35, 353
Discussion section of research reports, 477–78
Disjunctive proposition, 63*n*
Dispersion, measures of, 392–93
  range, 392
  standard deviation, 392–93
Disproportionate stratified sampling, 147
Divorce and women's status, Pearson and
  Hendrix's study of, 335, 336, 339
"Don't know" responses, 413*n*
Double-barreled question, 280
Double-blind technique, 34–35, 191
Draft lotteries, bias in, 167–68*n*
Dummy-coding. *See* Dummy variable
Dummy variable, 403–4, 407–8, 424–29,
  440*a*
Durkheim's theory of suicide, 55–58, 71, 84,
  327–28
  Pierce's test of, 106

Ecological fallacy
  and aggregate election data, 71
  defined, 71

Economic inequality and social structure in
  Boston, Henretta's study of, 343
Edge coding, 384
Editing data, 385
  editor, responsibilities of, 385
Editorials in British newspapers, Namenwirth's
  analysis of, 348, 349
Educational effects, Hyman, et al.'s study of,
  234
Effect of television viewing
  on fear of violence, 380–81, 397, 403–4,
    416, 420–21*b*
  on perceptions of reality, 420–21*b*
Einstein's theory of relativity, 25, 28, 87
Elaboration, 417–19
  antecedent variables, 418
  control variables, 418
  defined, 417
  intervening variables, 418
  partial tables, 417–18
  specification, 418
Empirical generalization, 24, 28. *See also*
  Empirical rules
Empirical rules, 22
Empiricism, 31–32
  measurable observation and, 31
  sophisticated vs. naive, 32
Equation for a straight line, 406
Equivalence of measurement, 115–16
Error, 363. *See also* Random measurement
  error; Systematic measurement error
Ethical issues in research, 444. *See also*
  Human subjects, treatment of; Research
  ethics
  American Psychological Association's prin-
    ciples, 446, 452
  in experiments, 181, 211, 446–48, 450
  to minimize subjects' harm, 448
  use of indirect questions, 271
Ethnographic Atlas, 335
Ethnography, 308*b*
Evaluation apprehension, 187–88, 434–35
Evaluation research, 225–228
  goals of, 225
  obstacles to use of true experimental
    designs, 225
  statistical vs. substantive significance in,
    226
  threats to external validity in, 227–28
  threats to internal validity in, 225–26
Evidence, quality of, 58–59
Expected frequencies, 431–32
Experimental design, 9–10, 171–77, 201,
  211–12. *See also* Factorial experimental
  designs; Quasi-experimental designs

Experimental design (*continued*)
  basic features of, 171–77
  basic principle of, 201
  ethical considerations in, 181, 211
  variations in, 211
Experimental realism, 184–85
  defined, 184
  and multiple meanings, 185
  live vs. audio presentation of instructions,
    185
Experimenter effects, 189–91
  experimenter expectancy effects, 189
  experimenter traits, 189
  methods for minimizing effects of, 190–91
  strength of, 190
Experimenter expectations. *See* Experimenter
    effects
Experiments, stages of, 177–84
  cover story, 181
  debriefing, 183–184
  introduction to experiment, 179, 181
  manipulation checks, 182
  manipulation of independent variable, 181–
    82
  measurement of dependent variable, 183
  pretesting, 184
Explanation vs. prediction, 25–27
Explanatory surveys, 237, 239
Explanatory variable, 72, 90
Exploratory data analysis, 395–96*b*
Exploratory studies, 90
External validity, 175–77, 180–81*b*
  defined, 175
  in evaluation research, 227–28
  limitations on, 176–77
  replication as a means of increasing, 177,
    180–81*b*
External validity, threats to, 209–12
  history-treatment interaction, 212
  maturation-treatment interaction, 212
  sample selection-treatment interaction, 211–
    12
  testing-treatment interaction, 209–10
Extraneous variable, 72–73
  spuriousness and, 81

Fabricated data, 33, 444–45
Face validity, 117–18
Facial prominence, different gender presenta-
    tions of, Archer et al.'s study of, 333,
    336, 347, 349
Factorial experimental designs, 212–17
  advantages of, 215, 217
  cell size, 213

  defined, 212
  factors, 212
  interaction effects, 214–15, 216*b*
  levels, 213
  main effects, 213–14
Factors, 212
  levels of, 213
Fallacies, 47–48
  affirming the consequent, 47, 56
  denying the antecedent, 47–48
  identification of, 48
False cover identity, 454
Field experiments, 192–93, 195
  advantages of, 192–93
  defined, 192
  disadvantages of, 193
  ethical and legal issues in, 195
Field observation, 299–300. *See also* Field
    research
  vs. casual observation, 299
  vs. generic scientific observation, 299–300
Field research, 11–12, 296–99, 304–20. *See
    also* Field observation
  and the cumulative nature of science, 320–
    21
  ethical issues in, 298, 450
  exploratory and descriptive purposes of,
    296–99
  flexibility of, 297–98
  origins of, 308*b*
  qualitative and quantitative aspects of, 296
  reasons for employing, 297–99
  relative cost of, 298
  research design in, 304–5
  role of observation in, 296
  sampling in, 305–6
  stages of, 306–19
  and "studying down," 297
  substantive focus of, 296–97
Field research, stages of, 306–7, 309–19
  access, 309–11
  data analysis and theory formulation, 317–19
  information gathering, 314–17
  researcher's presentation of self, 311–14
  selecting research site, 307, 309
Field studies
  approaches to research design for, 304–5
  incompatibility with obtaining informed con-
    sent, 450
  intrusion of values, 461–62
  and potential harm, 447–48, 450
  safeguards for anonymity and confiden-
    tiality, 455
Fieldwork administration in survey research,
    251–60

coordination, 245
follow-up on nonresponses, 259–60
gaining entry to field, 253–54
interviewers, 251–52
interviewing, 254–58
pretesting, 253
staff supervision and quality control, 245, 258–59
Figures, use of in research reports, 477
Filter question, 288, 288–89*b*
Findings, section of research report, 477
Fitted frequencies, 431–32
Fixed-choice question. *See* Closed-ended question
Fixed-column format, 386
Fluoridation decisions, Crain, Katz, and Rosenthal's study of, 234
Format design, 288–90
Fortuitous sampling, 153
Frame of reference, controlling for, 281–82
probes, 281
question arrangement, 282
Freefield format, 412*n*
Free-response question. *See* Open-ended question
Frequency distribution, 390–91
Frequency measures in content analysis, 349–50
Frequency polygon, 394
Freudian psychology, 26
Frustration and agression, Doob and Gross's study of, 100–101
Fund for Adult Education, 249–50*b*
Funnel and inverted-funnel sequence, 282, 283*b*

Gaining access to research sites, 309–11
access problems, 309–10
gatekeepers, 309
marginal informants, 310
public settings, 309
research in formal organizations, 309
snowballing technique for locating infor-mants, 310–11
use of key informants for, 310
Galileo's law, 25
Gallup presidential polls, 132–33*b*
Gamma, 402
Gatekeepers, 309
Gathering information in the field, 314–17, 319
description vs. analysis, 314
field interviews, 316
other data sources, 316–17

and researcher role, 314, 319
use of memory for, 316
use of note taking for, 315–16
use of tape recording for, 315
Gender differences in graffiti, Bruner & Kelso's study of, 351–52*b*
Gender displays in advertisements, Goffman's study of, 333, 347
Generalization of experimental results. *See* External validity
General law, inference from, 48–50
guidelines for reconstructing, 51–52*b*
logical form of, 45–48
validity of, 46–48
General Social Survey (GSS), 245, 334, 336, 341, 379–80, 420–21*b*
editing and cleaning of, 387–88
Glock and Stark's Index of Anti-Semitic Beliefs, 121
"Good subject," 187
Graphic procedures for data analysis, 394, 395–96*b*, 405
Great Books and Small Groups, Davis's study of, 249–50*b*
Great Books Foundation, 249*b*
Grounded theory, 317–18
Guttman scaling technique, 366–67
criteria for, 366
and nonscale types, 366
and respondent's response pattern, 366–67
sample dependent character of, 366–67
and scale scores, 366–67

Haphazard sampling, 153
Harm, potential, to research subjects, 445–48
Hawthorne effect, 30*b. See also* Subject awareness of participation in an experiment
Health and Nutrition Examination Survey (HANES), 234, 237
Heterogeneity, 158–59
Hierarchical models, 433–34
Hippocratic Oath, 446, 453
Historical studies and available data, 335–36, 345–47
History, threat to internal validity, 202, 223*b*
Hollingshead's Index of Social Position, 364
Holmes, Sherlock, 40, 44
Human Relations Area Files (HRAF), 335
Human subjects, treatment of, 445–457. *See also* Ethical issues in research; Research ethics
cost-benefit analysis of harm vs. benefit, 447

Human subjects (*continued*)
  deception, 451–53
  disclosure of research purposes, 449
  ethical principles to protect from harm, 448
  field studies and potential harm, 447–48, 450
  informed consent, 200*n*
  issues in experiments, 181, 211
  laboratory studies and, 447–48, 449
  lack of informed consent, 448–51
  making ethical decisions, 456–57
  "minimal risk" concept, 449
  potential harm, 446–48
  privacy invasion, 453–56
  stress, anger, and loss of self-esteem, 447
  voluntary nature of participation, 449
  written consent forms, 449
Hustling and Other Hard Work: Life Styles in the Ghetto, Valentine's study of, 456
Hypotheses, 23, 86–89
  continuous statement, 87
  defined, 86
  difference statement, 87
  implication, 86
  inference from, 48–49
  mathematical statement, 87
  in research report, 475–76
  rival, 81
  testable, 86
  writing, 88*b*
Hypothetico-deductive method, 54–60
  defined, 54–55
  and discovering hypotheses, 64*n*
  and elimination of alternative hypotheses, 56–57
  example of, 59–60*b*
  and logic of confirming hypotheses, 56–57
  and logic of disconfirming hypotheses, 57–58
  and multiple confirmation of hypotheses, 56–57
  and predictive ability of hypotheses, 55–56
  and search for disconfirming evidence, 59

"If-then" statements, 86–87
Illegal activities research, and privacy, 455
Impersonal sex in public places, Humphrey's study of, 311–12, 450, 454, 455
Implication, 86
Independence, test for, 400–401
Independent variable, 72
  as causal factor, 80
In-depth interviews, 316
Index. *See* Composite measures

Index of hetereogeneity. *See* Standard deviation
Index vs. scale, 365
Indicators, 98–99, 364
Indirect effects, 416–17
Indirect questions, 270–71
  attitude and motivation research and, 271
  clinical diagnoses and, 270
  ethical considerations, 271
  market research example of, 271
  validity, 271
Induction, 50, 52–54
  defined, 50, 52
  inductive generalization, 52–54
  and observation, 50
  and probability, 52
Inductive generalization, 52–54, 168*n*
  defined, 52
  and diversity of cases, 53
  evaluation of, 54
  and number of cases, 53–54, 177
  relationship to statistical techniques, 54
  and relevance to prior knowledge, 54
  scope, 53
Inductive reasoning, 44, 50–54
Inferential statistics, definition of, 389
Informants, 316. *See also* Key informants
Informed consent, doctrine of, 200*n*, 448–451, 452. *See also* Human subjects, treatment of
  disguised or covert participant observation and, 450–51
  federal requirements, 449, 450
  field studies and, 450
  limitations of, 449
  methodological problems resulting from, 449
  waiver of documentation, 450
Institutional review board (IRB), 457
Instrumentation as a threat to internal validity, 203, 224*b*
Intelligence and genetics, Burt's research, 33, 445
Intelligence (IQ) tests
  and heredity, Jensen's article on, 463
  misinterpretation of, 460
Intensive interviews, 316
Interaction effects, 214–15, 216*b. See also* Specification
Intercoder reliability, 116
Internal consistency reliability procedure, 115–16
Internal states, measurement of. *See* Direct observation; Verbal reports
Internal validity, 175

Internal validity, threats to, 201–5, 211
  chance, 211, 226
  differential mortality, 205, 226
  history, 202, 223*b*
  instrumentation, 203, 224*b*
  interaction between two or more threats, 205
  maturation, 202–3, 224*b*
  mortality, 204–5
  selection, 204
  statistical regression, 203–4, 224–25*b*
  testing, 203, 224*b*
Interpersonal influence among medical doctors, Menzel and Katz's study of, 372–73
Interpersonal Judgement Scale, 101–4
Interracial attitudes and behavior at a summer camp, Clore et al.'s study of, 219–21
Interrupted time-series design, 222*b*
Intersubjective testability, 32
Interval measurement, 109
Intervening mechanisms and theory development, 84
Intervening variable, 418
Interviewer. *See also* Interviewing; Interviews
  desirable qualities of, 251
  effect of physical characteristics, 254
  instructions for, 256–58
  morale problems of, 259
  selection, 251–52
  supervision of, 258–59
  training, 252–53
Interviewing, 254–58. *See also* Interviewer; Interviews
  procedures for, 256–58
  rules of, 256
Interviews, 243–47. *See also* Interviewing; Interviewers; Questionnaires; Survey instrument design
  advantages of, 243–44
  bias, 245
  closed-ended questions, 243
  confidentiality in, 256
  costs of, 244–45
  cover letters for, 253–54, 255*b*
  disadvantages of, 244–48
  face-to-face, 244–245
  field staff coordination, 245
  gaining access to, 253–54
  as interaction, 254
  and interviewer rapport, 243
  open-ended questions in, 243, 275
  opening questions in, 275–76
  partially structured, 236
  probing questions in, 244, 281
  rapport in, 243–44, 247, 253, 257, 275, 276, 287

and response rate, 244, 246, 247–48
  schedule of, 243
  sensitive questions in, 276
  setting of and response to, 254–58
  structured, 235–36, 242
  telephone, 245–47
  unstructured, 235, 242
  and visual aids, 274
Introduction, of research report, 475
Introduction stage of an experiment, 179, 181, 190
  cover story, reasons for, 181, 190
  deception, purposes of, 181
  explanation of purpose, 179
  instructions to subject, 179
Invalid arguments. *See* Fallacies
Inverse relationship, 77

Jury deliberations, the Wichita Jury Study of, 454, 455

Kepler's law, 25
Key informants, 310
Kitty Genovese murder, 194*b*

Laws, 24–25
Leading question, 280
Least-squares line, 406–8
Levels of measurement, 106–10
  and information provided, 110
  interval, 109
  nominal, 107–8
  ordinal, 108–9
  ratio, 109–10
  and statistical techniques, 110
Library references, 467–72, 478
Life course effect, 353–55
Likelihood-ratio chi-square test, 432–33, 443*n*
Likert response format, 103–4*b*, 272, 287
Linear regression, 406–8
Linear relationship, 77–78
Lists
  of population elements, 136, 148, 151–52
  as sampling frame, disadvantages of, 243, 246
Literary Digest poll of 1936, 132–33*b*
Literature review
  in research reports, 475–76
  searches, 338–39
Loaded words, avoidance of, 280
Logical analysis, 40–43
  elements of, 41–43
  vs. reasoning, 40–41

Logical terms, definition of, 41
"Logit" models, 433–34
Log-linear modeling, 430–36, 440–42a
  conditional odds, 430
  criteria for model selection, 432–33
  degrees of freedom, 431–32, 441–42a
  expected frequencies, 430–31
  hierarchical models, 433–34
  likelihood-ratio chi-square test, 432–33,
    443n
  "logit" models, 433–34
  odds, 430, 440–42a
  odds ratio, 430–31, 440–42a
  saturated model, 432
  testing the model, 432–33
  uses of, 430
Longitudinal research design, 238
  panel study, 238
  trend study, 238

Mail surveys. See Self-administered
  questionnaire
Main effects, 213–14
Manipulation of the independent variable,
  100–101, 172, 181–82. See also
  Experiments
  multiple meanings, problem of, 181–182
Manuscript census, 329, 330–331b
Marginals, 398
Marketing research, 271
Marlowe-Crowne Social Desirability Scale,
  122
Mass media as data source, 332–33
Matching, 174–75
  in conjunction with random assignment, 174
  purpose of, 174
Mathematical statement, 87
Maturation, as threat to internal validity, 202–
  3, 224b
Mean, 392
Measurement, types of, 101–5
  archival records, 105
  observation, 104–5
  verbal reports, 101–4
Measurement error, 204, 362, 368, 386, 389,
  396b. See also Random measurement
  error; Systematic measurement error
Measurement process, 97–105
  and conceptualization, 98
  defined, 97–98
  direct vs. indirect measures, 183
  everyday examples of, 97
  and formulating hypotheses, 97
  and level of abstraction, 99

operationalization, 105–6
  and specification of variables and indicators,
    98–99
  verbal vs. observational measures, 183
Measures of association. See Bivariate analysis
Measures of central tendency, 392
Measures of dispersion, 392–93
Median, 392
Memory, as an information-gathering device,
  316
Methodological approaches to social science
  inquiry, 7–13
  available data, 12–13
  experiments, 9–10
  field research, 11–12
  surveys, 10–11
Methodological empathy, 297
Methodology section, in research reports, 476
Metric, 109
Misspecification of model, 422, 429
Mode, 392
Model, statistical, definition of, 415
Mood's influence on altruism, Isen and
  Levin's study of, 10
Mortality, as threat to internal validity, 204–5
Multicategory variables. See Polytomous
  variables
Multicollinearity, 424
Multiple confirmation of hypotheses, 56–57
Multiple-group pretest-posttest design, 220
Multiple-group time-series design, 222b
Multiple methods. See Triangulation
Multiple regression (OLS), 419–29
  adjusted R^2, 426
  collinearity, 423–24
  defined, 419
  dummy variables, 424–29
  multicollinearity, 424
  partial-regression coefficients, 422–24
  residuals, 422
  specification error, 422, 429
  t-values, 426
  t-tests, 426
Multiplicative equations, 440a
Multistage sampling, 147–48, 148–49b, 150
  primary sampling units, 147
  and sampling error, 150, 161
Multistep communication flow, 373
Multivariate analysis. See Elaboration; Log-linear modeling; Multiple regression
Mundane realism, 185

National Center for Health Statistics, 327
National Crime Survey, 344

National Fertility Study (1970), 233–34, 235
National Opinion Research Center (NORC), 245, 249*b*, 275
Negative (inverse) relationship, 77
Net flow of migration, 358*n*
New York Times Index, 275, 327
Newton's theory of motion and gravitation, 25
Nominal measurement, 107–8
  equivalence classes, 107
  exhaustive classification, 107
  mutually exclusive classification, 107–8
Nonequivalent control group designs, 218, 222–23
  alternative to randomized control group, 218
  defined, 218
  example of, 222–23
Nonparticipant observation, 300–302
Nonprobability sampling, 152–55
  accidental sampling, 153
  advantages and weaknesses of, 152–53
  convenience sampling, 153
  defined, 152
  fortuitous, 153
  haphazard, 153
  purposive sampling, 153–54
  quota sampling, 154–55
Nonreactive measurement, 337–38
Nonrespondents, and follow up in surveys, 259–60
Nonresponse bias, 133*b*, 162–63
Nonspuriousness, 81–84. *See also* Causal hypotheses, testing of
Note taking in the field, 315–16
Number vs. numeral, 128*n*

Obedience to authority, Milgram's experiment on, 447, 448
Objectivity, 32–33
Observables, 31
Observation in scientific process, 31–32
Observer as participant, 312
Odds, 430, 440–42*a*
Odds ratio, 430–31, 440–42*a*
OLS. *See* Multiple regression
Omitted categories in dummy variable regression, 428
One-group pretest-posttest design. 206–7
  defined, 206
  improvement over one-shot case study, 207
  remaining threats to internal validity, 207
One-shot case study, 205–6
  critical flaw in, 206
  defined, 205–6

Open-ended question, 265–68, 268–70*b*
  advantages and disadvantages of, 265–66
  avoidance of in self-administered question-naires, 266
  to begin an interview, 275
  coding, 266, 381, 382–83*b*
  considerations in choosing, 266–67
  defined, 265
  examples of, 265, 268*b*, 275–76
Operational definition, 8–9, 100–106
  arbitrary nature of, 100
  describing in reports, 476
  evaluation of, 111
  selection, 105–6
  and theory, 106
  types of, 100–106
Ordinal measurement, 108–9
Ordinary least-squares regression (OLS). *See* Multiple regression
Other-directedness, Riesman's theory of, 69, 105
Outliers, 396*b*
Overt behavior, measurement of. *See* Direct observation

Packaged computer programs, 412*n*
Panel study, 238
Parallel forms reliability procedure, 115
Parameter scoring system, 440–42*a*
Partial regression coefficients, 422–24
Partial slopes, 422–24
Partial tables, 417–18
Participant as observer, 312
Participant observation, 296, 302–4
  advantages of, 302–3
  and balancing participant and observer roles, 304
  defined, 302
  and going native, 304
  and insider knowledge, 302–3
  vs. nonparticipant observation, 302
  risks of, 303–4
Party platforms, Weber's content analysis of, 348, 349–50, 352
Pasteur's discovery of immunization, 30*b*
Path analysis, 429
Pearson product-moment correlation coefficient (*r*), 78, 407
Pearson's chi-square statistic, 400–401, 413*n*, 443*n*
People's Choice, The, Lazarsfeld et al.'s 1948 study of voter behavior, 238
Percentage distribution, 391–92, 399–400
Percentage polygon, 394

Percentage table. *See* Cross-tabulation
Percentaging cross-tabulations, rules for, 399
Perfect association, 76, 80, 401
Performance domain, 118
Period effect, 353, 354
Phenomenology, 37
Placebo, 34
Place ideology, Hummon's study of, 153
Police patrol staffing study, 196
Polish immigrants, Thomas and Znaniecki's study of, 331–32, 339
Polytomous variables, 428, 430, 441–42*a*
Population, 131, 132. *See also* Target population
  defined, 134–136
  sampling frame as operational definition of, 135
Positive (direct) relationship, 76–77
Posttest-only control group design, 210
  advantages of, 210
  defined, 210
Precision and sample size, 159–60
Precodes, 384
Prediction, 23, 28–29
Prediction errors, 406, 422
Predictive ability of hypotheses, 55–56
Predictive validity, 119
Preexperimental designs, 205–8
  one-group pretest-postest design, 206–7
  one-shot case study, 205–6
  static group comparison, 207–8
Premises, truth of, 44
Pretesting
  in experiments, 184–85
  in measurement, 116
  in surveys, 253, 290–91
Pretest-posttest control group design, 208–10
  control of threats to internal validity of, 209
  defined, 208
  threats to external validity of, 209–10
Primary sources. *See* Sources
Primary sampling unit (PSU), 147
Prison simulation study, Zimbardo et al.'s 446, 448
Privacy, right to, 453–56
Private documents, as research data source, 331–32
Probability sampling, 137–52
  advantages over nonprobability sampling, 137, 144
  of available data, 338–39
  cluster sampling, 147–50
  defined, 137
  in field research, 305–6
  and random selection, 137–40

simple random sampling, 140–44
stratified random sampling, 145–47
in survey research, 233–34
systematic sampling, 151–52
theory, principles of, 140–44
value in experiments, 176–77
Probability theory, 389
Procedures, describing in reports, 476
Products of field research, 320–22
Project Camelot, 462–63
Project TALENT, 238–39
Projective techniques, 270–71
Propositions, 22–23, 41–42
  based on regularity, dangers of, 28
  categorical, 42
  conditional, 42
  conjunctive, 63*n*
  defined, 41
  disjunctive, 63*n*
  explanation and, 22–23
  truth of, 43–44
Proxmire's "Golden Fleece of the Month Awards," 19–20*b*
Public attitudes toward racial integration, Treiman's index of, 364–65
Public documents and official records, 326–31
  examples of research, 327–31
  sources and types of, 327
Public Opinion Quarterly, 275
Public Use Microdata Sample, 329, 455
Puritan attitudes toward death, Stannard's study of, 334
Purposive sampling, 153–54
  barometer states, 154
  defined, 153
  in field research, 306
  probability sampling vs., 154
Push-pull scheme in migration studies, 285
p-value, 432–33. *See also* Significance level

Qualitative variables
  association and, 75–76
  categorical character of, 73–74
  difference statements and, 87
Quantitative variables
  in content analysis, 349–50
  continuous statements and, 87
  positive and negative relationships, 76–78
Quasi-experimental designs, 217–25
  defined, 217
  example of, 219–21
  interrupted time-series design, 222*b*
  legal, ethical, and practical reasons for, 217
  multiple-group pretest-posttest design, 220

multiple time-series design, 222–23*b*
nonequivalent control group designs, 218
reducing threats to internal validity in, 217–21
relationship to preexperimental and true experimental designs, 217
separate-sample pretest-posttest design, 217–18
usefulness of, 218
Questionnaires. *See also* Question-writing; Survey instrument design; Survey questions
actual writing of, 278–90
opening questions, 275–76
pretesting, 253, 290–91
ranking questions, 273–74
response formats, 271–74
response option: "don't know," 267, 271
response option: need for exhaustive responses, 266
self-administered, 244, 247–48
sensitive and routine questions, placement of, 276
structured vs. unstructured approaches, 241–42
topic flow, 276–77
writing guidelines, 278–90
Question-writing, as a means of eliciting reasons for behavior, 282–85
Quota sampling, 154–55
biased case selection in, 154–55
vs. proportionate stratified random sampling, 154
reducing hazards in, 155

RAND Corporation, *A Million Random Digits with 100,000 Normal Deviates*, 139–40*t*
Random assignment of subjects, 173–75
compared with random sampling, 175
defined, 173
and matching, 174–75
purpose of, 173
Random digit dialing, 135, 246–47
Randomization
breakdown in, 225–26
vs. statistical control, 415, 417
Random measurement error, 112–13
Random numbers, table of, 139–40*t*
Random selection, 137–40. *See also* Probability sampling
Random start, 138
and possible bias in systematic sampling, 151–52
Range, 392

Ranking. *See* Ordinal measurement
Ranking questions, 273–74
Rapport, 307, 313–14
Ratio measurement, 109–10
Reactive measurement effect, 30*b*, 112, 337–38
and order of questions, 277
Reader's Guide to Periodical Literature, 327, 329, 468
Reason analysis, 282–85
Reasoning, types of. *See* Deductive reasoning; Inductive reasoning
Recall, stimulating accuracy in, 286
Recording units, 349
Reducing threats to internal validity in quasi-experimental designs, 217–21
use of additional data, 220–21
pretests and nonequivalent control groups, 218–19
rejecting alternative explanations on reasonable grounds, 221
repeated administration of measurement instruments, 220
use of multiple dependent measures, 220
use of multiple quasi-experimental designs, 220
References for research writing, 474*b*
Regression analysis, simple linear, 405–8. *See also* Multiple regression
Regression coefficient, 406, 422–23, 429
Regression line, 406–8
Regression toward the mean. *See* Statistical regression
Relationship between variables, 74–85, 397–408. *See also* Causal relationships
between qualitative and quantitative variables, 78–79, 403–4
between qualitative variables, 75–76, 397–401
between quantitative variables, 76–78, 401–3, 405–8
curvilinear relationship, 77–78
form of, 77–78, 87
linear relationship, 77–78
negative (inverse) relationship, 77
positive (direct) relationship, 76–77
statistical significance, 96*n*, 400
strength of, 76, 78. *See also* Bivariate analysis
Reliability, 110–11
improvement of 116–17
vs. validity, 111
Reliability, measurement of, 114–17
intercoder reliability, 116
internal consistency procedure, 115–16

Reliability (*continued*)
parallel forms procedure, 115
split-half procedure, 115
test-retest procedure, 114–15
Reliability and validity of available data, 342–45
authentication of documents, 343
reconstructing original data-gathering process, 342–43
using several data sources, 344
Replication, 56–57, 177, 362, 369–74
and available data, 337
and external validity, 177
and multiple tests of hypotheses, 362, 369–74
and triangulation, 362
using different research strategies, 371–74
using same research strategy, 369–71
Research, stages of, 91–93
Research design, 67–94
describing for reports, 476
Researchers
ethics of. *See* Research ethics
personal values and problem selection, 68, 460–62
and potential application of findings, 462–63
Researchers, in field research, 311–14, 319
and available roles in setting, 313, 319
disclosure of research interests, 312–13
ethical issues in, 311–12
and interpersonal skills, 313–14
types of researcher roles, 311–12, 319
Research ethics, 444–465. *See also* Human subjects, treatment of
abusive exploitation of findings, 463
codes of, 452, 458–59*b*
cost-benefit principle, 456
data collection and analysis and, 444–45
deontological position, 456
dilemmas, 456–57
disclaimers, 461–62
intrusion of values, 460–62
institutional review board, 457
principles to protect participants, 448
research knowledge, proper use of, 444–45, 457–63
teleological position, 456
treatment of participants, 445–57
Research findings, 4–6
consumer use and production of, 4–6
misleading use of, 4
uses of, 457–63
Research ideas, origins of, 194–95*b*
Research purposes, 89–91

description, 90
explanation, 90–91
exploration, 90
Research reports, writing, 467–79
length, 479
library research for references, 467–72
major headings, 474–78
organization and outline, 472–74
revisions, 479
working drafts, 479
writing-reading interface, 478–79
writing style for audience, 473
Research topic selection, 6–7, 67–69
criteria for, 6–7
factors affecting, 67–69
justifying, 69
practical considerations and cost, 68
prestige and, 68
social problems as historical source, 67–68
support funding and, 68–69
Research using available data, 326–55
Residuals, 406, 422
Respondents
bias, sampling and response, 133*b*, 162–63, 245
clarifying questions to, 244
eliciting reasons for decisions, 282–85
existing opinions and knowledge of topic, 267
frame of reference, 281–82
hidden motivation and indirect measurement, 270–71
lack of recall, 285
and memory distortion, 285–86
motivation of, 243, 267, 275
point of view, 276, 277
researcher's knowledge of, 267
self esteem of, 286–87
stimulating accurate recall, 286
type of question and reaction, 265–68
Response bias tendencies, 286
acquiescence response set, 113, 287
position response set, 288
social desirability bias, 113, 286–87
Response effect, 254
Response formats, 271–74
Response rate, 162–63, 244, 246, 247–48
affected by consent forms, 449
decline in urban areas for face-to-face interviews, 244, 245
improving, 259–60
and response selectivity bias, 248
Responses, balanced alternatives in, 280–81
Rickets, discovery of cause and cure, 27
Rival hypotheses. *See* Alternative hypotheses,

elimination of; Hypothetico-deductive method

Rokeach Dogmatism Scale, 122

Romantic love, Berscheid and Walster's study of, 19*b*

Roper Center, 275

Rosenberg's self-esteem scale, validation of, 120

Row marginals, 398

Rubin's Love Scale, 121–22

Safety and well-being of research subjects. *See* Human subjects, treatment of

Saints and good neighbors, Sorokin's altruism analysis of, 13

Salem witchcraft hysteria
  Boyer and Nissenbaum's interpretation of, 346, 347
  Chambliss's study of, 346, 347
  contrasting historical interpretations of, 345–47
  Erikson's study of, 345–46, 347

Sample bias
  avoidance of, 162–63
  in evaluation research, 227
  response rates and, 163
  sampling frame and, 133*b*, 136
  selectivity and, 130, 133*b*
  sources of, 162
  systematic sampling and, 151–52

Sample size
  factors in determining, 158–62
  number of subcategories and, 161–62
  population heterogeneity and, 158–59
  precision desired and, 144, 159–60
  resources, 161
  type of sample design and, 160–61

Sampling, 130–64
  and precision, 143–46, 150, 159–61
  reasons for, 131–32

Sampling design, 136–37. *See also* Cluster sampling; Convenience sampling; Quota sampling; Simple random sampling; Stratified random sampling; Systematic sampling
  combined probability and nonprobability, 155–56
  defined, 137
  factors affecting choice of, 156–58
  nonprobability, 152–55
  probability, 137–52
  representativeness and, 136–37

Sampling distribution, 142, 145
  examples, 142*f*, 143*t*, 146*t*

Sampling error, 143–44
  and sampling across clusters, 150

Sampling fraction, 159

Sampling frame, 135–36
  bias, 133*b*, 136
  defined, 135
  as distinguished from sample, 135
  as operational definition of population, 135
  lists and directories, 136
  omitted cases and bias, 136
  two ways to construct, 135

Sampling in experiments, 176–77

Sampling in field research, 305–6
  determining sampling frame, 305
  dimensional sampling, 305–6
  purposive nonprobability sampling, 306
  sampling problems, 305

Sampling in survey research
  combining, 234
  large scale, 233–34

Sampling issues in available data research, 339–40
  in content analysis, 350

Scales, 99
  construction, 363–67
  Guttman, 366–67
  Likert, 103–4*b*, 272
  numerical ratings, 272
  ordinal, 272
  stimulus words and, 273
  summated ratings, 103–4*b*

Scatterplot, 405–6

Scholastic Aptitude Test (SAT), 412*n*

Science, 18–35, 45–60
  cyclical process of, 28–29, 45, 397
  deductive reasoning in, 45–50
  goals of, 18–28
  hypothetico-deductive method in, 54–60
  inductive reasoning in, 50–54
  nature of, 17–18
  principles underlying, 29
  as process, 28–35
  as product, 18–28

Scientific explanation, deductive pattern of, 48–50

Scientific knowledge, 18–28
  description, 21–22
  explanation and prediction, 22–25
  steps to, 21–22
  tentative nature of, 27–28
  understanding, 25–27
  verifiability, 18, 20–21

Scientific language. *See* Concepts

Scientific merit vs. potential harm, issue of, 446–47

Scientific objectives, 22–25
Scientific process, 28–35, 45, 379
Scientific vs. nonscientific questions, 18–21
Secondary analysis
  of societies, 335
  of survey data, 234, 334–35
Secondary sources. *See* Sources
Selecting field research sites, 307–9, 319
  criteria for, 307
  "starting where you are" principle, 307, 309
Selection, threat to internal validity of, 204. *See also* Sample bias
Selective deposit, 339
Selective survival, 339
Self-administered questionnaire, 247–48
  follow-up, 259–60
  response rate, 247–48
  sample bias, 247–48
Self-images of the elderly, Blau's study of, 237
Semantic-differential scaling technique, 294n
Semmelweis's study of childbed fever, 59–60b
Sensitive questions
  placement of, 276
  tactful wording of, 281
Separate-sample pretest-posttest design, 217–18
Serendipity pattern, 30b
Sex ratios at birth, Winston's study of, 328, 336, 338
Sexual behavior research, and privacy, 454–55
Shaker populations, Bainbridge's research on, 330–31b
Shape, 394
  bell-shaped curve, 394
  frequency polygon, 394
  skewed distributions, 394
Sigma (σ), 158–59
Significance level, 173–74, 226, 389, 400, 424–26, 432–33
Simple random sampling, 140–44
  defining property of, 140
Skewed distribution, 394
Slope coefficient, 406, 422–23
Small Town in Mass Society, Vidich and Bensman's study of, 455
Smith, et al.'s FEM Scale, 103–4b, 122–23b
Smoking, Straits's study of, 295n, 382–83b
Smoking and cancer, relationship between, 82
Snowballing technique for locating key informants, 310–11. *See also* Key informants
Social desirability effect, 113, 286–87
Social facilitation effect, 22–23
Social indicators research, 237

Social integration effect, 84
Social nature of experiments, 185–91
  demand characteristics, 186–87
  effects of subjects' movtives, 186–89
  evaluation apprehension, 187–88
  experimenter effects, 189–90
  minimizing bias deriving from, 190–91
Social Science Citation Index (SSCI), 468,471f
Social Science Research Council's *Basic Background Items,* 275
Social Sciences Index, 468, 469f, 470f
Social scientific research, definition of, 6–7
Society for the Psychological Study of Social Issues (SPSSI), 463
Society for the Scientific Study of Social Problems (SSSP), 463
Sociological Abstracts, 468
Sociometric measures, 239, 372–73
Solomon four-group design, 210–13
  advantages of, 211
  defined, 210
  disadvantages of, 211
  as a 2 × 2 factorial experimental design, 212–13
Sources
  primary, 344, 358n
  secondary, 344, 358n
Specification, 418
Specification error, 422, 429
Split-half reliability procedure, 115
Spontaneous remission, 202–3, 205
Spurious association, 81–84, 414, 416–17, 418–19
Stability of measurement over time. *See* Test-retest reliability procedure
Standard Cross-Cultural Sample (SCCS), 335
Standard deviation, 158–59, 392–93
Standard error, 144
  formula, 158–59, 160
  and precision, 159
Standard measurement unit. *See* Metric
Standardized regression coefficient, 429
Static-group comparison, 207–8
  defined, 207
  threats to internal validity, 208
Statistic, definition of, 389
Statistical analysis in social research, 388–90
Statistical association, 75–79. *See also* Bivariate analysis
  vs. causality, 79–85, 414
  indices of, 76
  perfect, 76
Statistical control vs. randomization, 417
Statistical regression, threat to internal validity of, 203–4, 224–25b

Statistical significance. *See* Significance level
Strata. *See* Stratified Random sampling
Stratified random sampling, 145–47
 efficiency compared to simple random sampling, 145, 151
 in multistage sampling, 150
 proportionate vs. disproportionate, 146–47
 and sample precision, 145, 146, 161
Structural equation modeling, 367–69
Structured observation, 301–2
Subject awareness of participation in an experiment, 185–86. *See also,* Demand characteristics; Evaluation apprehension; Reactive measurement effect; Social nature of experiments
Subjective validation, 118–19
 content validity, 118–19
 face validity, 118
Subjects, research. *See* Human subjects, treatment of; Respondents
Subjects' emotions. *See* Debriefing
Suicide, Durkheim's study of, 55–58, 71, 84, 327–28
Suicide notes, Jacobs's study of, 332, 339, 340
Summated ratings, 103–4b
Survey instrument design, 264–92. *See also* Interviews; Questionnaires; Survey questions
 direct and indirect questions, 270–71
 existing questions, 274–75
 format design, 288–90
 funnel sequences, 282, 283b
 open vs. closed questions, 265–68, 268–70b
 organizing questions, 275–78
 pretesting, 290–91
 question types, 265–71
 reason analysis, 282–85
 response formats, 271–74
 visual aids, 274
 writing questions, 278–90
Survey questions
 appropriate vocabulary level, 279–80
 avoidance of words causing bias, 280
 balanced and exhaustive response options, 280–81
 establishing common frame of reference, 281–82
 precision and readability, 279
 sources of, 274–75
 tact and face-saving in sensitive questions, 281
 wording guidelines, 278–81
Survey research, 10–11, 233–60. *See also* Survey instrument design

 advantages and disadvantages of, 239–40
 data analysis techniques, 236–37
 design, types of, 237–39
 fieldwork administration, 251–60
 general features of, 233–37
 interviews, 243–47
 large-scale sampling, 233–34
 planning, data collection, 240–43
 sampling plan, 243
 structured vs. unstructured approaches, 242
 systematic procedures in, 235–36
 testing causal hypotheses, 240
 uses for, 239, 240
Survey research, experimental designs in, 195–96
 use of different questionnaires, 196
 variation in wording of questions, 195, 268–70b
 vignettes, 195–96
Survey Research Center (SRC), 148–49b
Syllogism, 42–43
 defined, 42–43
 validity of, 43
Systematic measurement error, 112–13
 acquiescence response set, 113, 287
 position biases, 288
 reactive measurement effect, 112
 social desirability effect, 113, 286–87
Systematic observation, 301–2
Systematic sampling, 151–52
 advantages and dangers of, 151–52
 biased sample and, 151–52
 and stratification effect, 151

Table of random numbers, 139–40t
 use of, 138–40
Tables, use of in research reports, 477
Tape recording in the field, 315
Target population
 defined, 134
 geographic and time referents, 135
 objective criteria for inclusion in, 135
Tax assessments in Boston, Warden's reanalysis of, 343–45
Teacher comments and student performance, Page's study of 172–76
 and basic features of experimental design 172–75
 and external validity, 175–76
Telephone interviews, 245–47
 advantages, 245–46
 disadvantages, 246–47
 high response rates of, 246
 sampling quality in, 246

Telescoping, 285

Testable propositions, 50

Testing, threat to internal validity, 203, 224b. *See also* Demand characteristics; Evaluation apprehension; Reactive measurement effect

Testing statistical models, key issues in, 389–90

Testing-treatment interaction, 209–10

Testing-X. *See* Testing-treatment interaction

Test-retest reliability procedure, 114–15

Tests of statistical significance 173–74, 226, 389, 424–26, 432–33

Theory
  defined, 24
  degree of accuracy, 35
  and guiding tests for spuriousness, 415–17
  and inferring causal relationships, 414
  logical form of, 50
  in science, 22–25, 28–29, 84–85
  translation into a statistical model, 415
  usefulness of, 35

Threat and authoritarianism, Sales's study of, 328–29, 332–33, 337, 342, 347, 348, 349

Tolerance and opinions on civil liberties, Stouffer's study of, 238

Tolerance for violence, Sedgely and Lund's study of, 435–36

Topic arrangement in survey instruments, 276–77, 282

Treatment. *See* Manipulation of independent variable

Treatment group, 172

Treatment-related mortality, 226

Trend study, 238
  and available data, 336

Triangulation, 360–62
  conventional meaning of, 360–61
  and convergent validity assessment, 121, 123b, 361
  multiple indicators of single concepts, 361–62
  multiple tests of hypotheses, 56–57, 362
  in social research, 361–62
  techniques, to reveal embedded values, 462

True experiment, minimum requirements for, 175. *See also* Causality, evidence for

True experimental designs, 208–12
  factorial designs, 212–17
  posttest-only control group design, 210
  pretest-posttest control group design, 208–10
  Solomon four-group design, 210–11

t-tests, 424, 426

t-values, 424, 426

Two-step flow of communication, Katz and Lazarsfeld's hypothesis of, 372

Undocumented entry into U.S., Heer's demographics of, 344–45

Unidimensionality, 365–66
  of indices, 365–66
  and patterns of response to Guttman scale items, 366–67
  of scales, 366–67
  and validity, 366

Uniform Crime Reports for the United States, 329, 344

Unintended events within treatment group, 232n

United States Catalog, 329

Units of analysis, 69–72
  choice of type, 131–32, 134
  in content analysis, 349
  defined, 69
  and ecological fallacy, 71
  in experimental design, 196–97
  identifying, 88–89b
  importance of identification, 70
  mixed units and false conclusions, 71
  selection of, 69
  in surveys, 234

Univariate analysis, 390–97
  assessing amount of variation in data, 392–93
  and collapsing categories of data, 390
  frequency distributions, 390–91
  measures of central tendency, 392
  measures of dispersion, 392–93
  percentage distributions, 391–92
  shape, 394
  use in describing data, 390

Unstructured observation, 300–301

U.S. Bureau of the Census, 132, 233, 235, 327, 329, 330–31b
  confidentiality, 455

Valid arguments, 45–48
  affirming the antecedent, 46, 49
  chain argument, 47
  denying the consequent, 47

Validity, 110–11
  assessment of, 117–24
  vs. reliability, 111

Validity and truth, independence of, 43–44, 46

Value neutrality
  notion of value-free research, 460
  untenability of, 460–61

Variability and information, 367
Variables, 72–74, 98–99
  changing categories of, 72
  control variable, 73
  defined, 72
  dependent variable, 72, 80
  derived. *See* Composite measures
  explanatory variable, 72
  extraneous variable, 72–73, 81
  identifying, 88–89*b*
  independent variable, 72, 80
  qualitative variable, 73, 75–76, 110
  quantitative variable, 73, 76–78, 110
  X and *Y* as symbols for, 73
Verbal reports, 101–4
  and attitude measurement, 101–2
  and background variables, 101
  and response formats, 102–4
Visual aids, 274
Vital statistics, 327–28

Voting decisions, Lazarsfeld et al.'s study of, 372

Weighting indicators, 364
Why subjects lie to experimenters, Straits et al.'s study of, 434–35
Wild-code checking, 387
Word counts in content analyses, 358–59*n*
Writing reports. *See* Research reports

X and *Y* as symbols, 73

Y-intercept, 406
Yule's Q, 401, 443*n*

Zeisel's system of reason analysis, 284–85
Zero point. *See* Ratio measurement